· THE DEATH PENALTY IN AMERICA ·

The Death Penalty in America

CURRENT CONTROVERSIES

Edited by **Hugo Adam Bedau**

Oxford University Press
New York · Oxford

22.50

Oxford University Press

Oxford New York
Athens Auckland Bangkok Bogotá Buenos Aires
Calcutta Cape Town Dar es Salaam Delhi
Florence Hong Kong Istanbul Karachi
Kuala Lumpur Madras Madrid Melbourne
Mexico City Nairobi Paris Singapore
Taipei Tokyo Toronto Warsaw

and associated companies in
Berlin Ibadan

Published by Oxford University Press, Inc.
198 Madison Avenue, New York, New York 10016

First published by Oxford University Press, Inc., 1997
First issued as an Oxford University Press paperback, 1998

Oxford is a registered trademark of Oxford University Press, Inc.

Library of Congress Cataloging-in-Publication Data
The death penalty in America—current controversies / edited by Hugo Adam Bedau.
p. cm.
Includes bibliographical references and index.
ISBN 0–19–510438–2
ISBN 0–19–512286–0 (Pbk.)
1. Capital punishment—United States. I. Bedau, Hugo Adam.
HV8699.U5D37 1996
364.6'6'0973—dc20 96–7028

9 10 8

Printed in the United States of America
on acid-free paper

PREFACE

The death penalty continues to make headlines across the nation, perhaps more than at any time in this century. Just consider two of the high-profile cases during 1995, the brisk trial of Susan Smith in South Carolina for murdering her two children and the seemingly endless trial of O. J. Simpson in Los Angeles for the murder of his ex-wife and her male friend. The national news media gave the nation a day-by-day account of each case from the courtrooms. For Simpson the prosecutors ruled out the death penalty before the defendant ever entered the courtroom. Smith, however, faced from the start a prosecutor openly seeking her death; fortunately for her, the jury thought otherwise.

Or consider the extensive media campaign during 1995 waged on behalf of Mumia Abu-Jamal, former Black Panther and radical journalist, under a death sentence for murdering a policeman in Philadelphia in 1981. Is he really innocent, as his friends and champions insist? Innocent or guilty, did he get a fair trial and review by the appellate courts? Each year for two decades, beginning with the death sentence and execution in Utah of Gary Gilmore in 1977, we have been bombarded from coast to coast with details about the latest gruesome murder or serial killings (Ted Bundy in Florida, John Wayne Gacy in Illinois) and the culminating events in such cases—trial, conviction, sentencing, and execution.

If one wants to probe more deeply, however, getting behind television sound bites, the often sensationalist reports in the print media, and the posturing of politicians, one will discover that there is a vast array of material in our libraries to help answer more accurately the familiar questions: Is the death penalty an effective deterrent? Why does it take so long from sentencing to execution? How do prosecutors and juries decide which murderers to sentence to death and which to life in prison? Are the innocent ever wrongly arrested, tried, convicted, sentenced to death—and executed? Is the death penalty administered in a racially biased manner? If so, can such bias be avoided? Why did the Supreme Court rule that the death penalty is not an unconstitutional "cruel and unusual punishment"? These and a host of other questions arise whenever the death penalty is discussed or seriously debated. Fortunately, good answers to most of them lie waiting in print for those who know where to look.

Unfortunately, even those who do cannot get these answers without access to a major university library. Most of the relevant information appears in law reviews, scholarly journals, government documents, local news stories, and unpublished memoranda of various sorts, almost none of which can be found on the shelves of the local public or college library. The purpose of this book is to remedy that problem, as much as a single volume can, by reprinting the essential material and providing a guide to locating the bulk of the rest.

By the mid-1990s, the wealth of relevant literature is little short of overwhelming. Consequently, no one volume can do full justice to all the important research, challenging arguments, vivid narratives, and cold statistics that are needed to tell the story in all its details. What can be done, and what I have attempted to do in editing this volume, is to review the bulk of the literature published during the past decade or so (references to events and research prior to 1985 are rare) and select from it representative items for reprinting here. Regrettably, for reasons of economy of space, I have had to cut inessential footnote references in many of the articles chosen for reprinting, as well as some text to avoid redundancies and digressions where possible. (Such deletions have been indicated in the usual manner.) The reader who demands all the details as they appeared in the originals will thus need to hunt them up.

A far more regrettable omission from the book as originally designed is the material I had planned to reprint on the Robert Alton Harris case in California. Perhaps better than any other recent case, the struggle culminating in his death in the gas chamber in April 1992 brought federal judges and the lawyers on both sides to a fever pitch. Their often bitter and angry exchanges, including the unprecedented peremptory behavior by the Supreme Court, make extraordinary reading. The curious reader can get the flavor of the controversy in the following items (fully cited in the bibliography): Kroll 1990, Lungren and Krotoski 1992, Noonan 1992, Reinhardt 1992, Caminker and Chemerinsky 1992, Calabresi and Lawson 1992, and Bork 1992.

The book consists of thirty-three chapters, including seven essays that appear here for the first time and excerpts from five important U.S. Supreme Court decisions, organized into seven parts. The introduction (chapter 1) sketches the main features of the death penalty today as it emerged during the past three centuries of our history. Part I digests information on the nation's capital punishment laws, the volume and rate of criminal homicide in recent years, the distribution of death row prisoners across the nation, the annual number of executions, and other similar data that can be presented in tabular form. The part concludes by placing the current American death penalty scene in an international context. Part II is devoted to reporting and examining public opinion on the death penalty and alternative punishments. Part III examines the debate over deterrence and incapacitation in light of the most recent research. Part IV reviews the Supreme Court's decisions and opinions on the issue of the death penalty as a "cruel and unusual punishment," followed by two commentaries on the constitutional debate and a brief examination of the death penalty in this country as seen from a perspective of international human rights law. Part IV also reviews other important Supreme Court decisions relevant to the death penalty, focusing on the decade-long controversy over federal habeas corpus. Part V considers two of the main charges brought against the death penalty as applied: that it is racist, and suffered only by the poor. Part VI focuses exclusively on the death penalty as applied and tracks the flow of capital cases from the prosecutor's office to the execution chamber. It opens with a study of a Pennsylvania prosecutor's decision making in murder cases, then looks at new research on juror decision making in the sentencing phase of capital trials. This is followed by a discussion of wrongful convictions in capital cases, a case study of a campaign to obtain clemency for a death row prisoner in Nebraska, a debate over whether executions ought to be shown on television, and an account from an eyewitness of an execution in Texas. The final chapter of this part closes by considering the economic costs of our current death penalty system. Part VII completes the book with two debates over the death penalty between Christian theologians and secular philosophers. Readers who have studied all the material preceding these debates should be in a reasonably good position to evaluate them on their merits.

In 1964, in my preface to *The Death Penalty in America: An Anthology* (the grandparent of this book), I warned the reader that it was not a volume conceived in scholarly neutrality. I was then and still am opposed to the death penalty in all its forms, no matter how awful the crime or how savage the criminal. Readers who do not share that conviction may well wonder whether I have been reasonably fair in presenting both sides of the many controversies that figure in the debate over the death penalty. I can only plead that I have tried, within the constraints of space and the relative importance of some material over other, and that the reader dissatisfied with my judgment should follow up the references I have made to the writings of those who disagree with me. By doing so one will easily trace out what is to be found in print presenting all shades of opinion. I do confess to having given the opponent of the death penalty the last word in several of these controversies—notably, on deterrence, on whether the death penalty is a "cruel and unusual punishment," on whether the death penalty is functionally racist, on the costs of our current death penalty systems, and on miscarriages of justice in capital cases. I have done this because I sincerely believe the critics of the death penalty have the better of the evidence and the argument on each of these topics.

It should be added that proponents of the death penalty have done little or no research on most aspects of the policy they favor. With few exceptions, they have confined themselves to poking holes in the empirical research that favors abolition and to making armchair rebuttals of abolitionist arguments; this is most evident in the controversies discussed in parts III, V, and VI. As a result, it is simply impossible to present both sides at comparable length and in comparable detail. The weight of the overall argument is reflected, and properly so in my judgment, by the greater bulk of the book being given over to the abolitionist side.

The table of cases mentions only cases I have cited in my introductions and essays; the references cited by the various authors whose work is reprinted here have not been reproduced in the bibliography. For these additional references one must consult the works cited (if any) at the end of each article. The reader should not suppose that I have tried to cite all the relevant publications in the bibliography; far from it. Nor is omission of an author's work from this list to be taken as evidence of my low estimate of its worth. No attempt has been made to edit the reprinted materials to achieve uniformity of citation style.

Readers familar with the third edition of *The Death Penalty in America* (1982) may well wonder to what extent the present volume overlaps and goes beyond that one. Although several of the topics, subtopics, and their sequence in the two books are the same, the content of this book is entirely new, except for excerpts in part

IV from four of the Supreme Court's death penalty cases. Similarly, the 1982 edition consisted entirely of new material with respect to the first (1964) edition. (The second edition of 1967 is only a slightly revised version of the first edition and for most purposes is indistinguishable from it.) Indeed, I have not called this book the fourth edition of *The Death Penalty in America* because it would be far more accurate to think of it as the third volume in a series that includes both the 1964 and the 1982 editions, since the overlapping contents among the three books is so slight. Taken together, these three volumes—nearly fifteen hundred pages—preserve and make available a large fraction of all of the most important material on the death penalty in this country covering the past forty years.

Carmel-by-the-Sea, California H. A. B.
October, 1996

ACKNOWLEDGMENTS

A book such as this could not be completed without the help and advice of a number of others actively involved in studying (and resisting) the death penalty. During 1994 the law faculty of the University of Westminster in London generously provided me with a scholarly home away from home, in which I could do the spadework undisturbed, leading to the first draft of this book. Twenty years of frequent conversation with Henry Schwarzschild have had a pronounced impact on my thinking, and many of his ideas have no doubt crept into this book and appear here as though they were originally my own. My colleague on the major research project described in the introduction to Part VI, Michael L. Radelet, has given me the benefit of his wide knowledge and has helped me avoid many errors and omissions. I am especially indebted to Joseph L. Hoffman, Larry Myers, and to William C. Bailey and Ruth D. Peterson for contributing essays that appear for the first time in this book. Without their willingness to drop everything in order to meet my deadline, the book would be less complete and up-to-date than it is. I am also indebted to Vivian Berger, William J. Bowers, Richard C. Dieter, Leigh Dingerson, Rick Halperin, David Hoose, Kika Matos, Michael Mello, Richard Moran, Diann Rust-Tierney, William Schabas, and Robert Spangenberg for their prompt responses to various specific requests for help. Jeff Silver's sharp eye saved me from several errors and Anne Belinsky contributed some last-minute typing. My editors, Cynthia Read and Kim Torre-Tasso, have been supportive from the start and a pleasure to work with. Above all I am indebted, and delighted to acknowledge that debt, to Constance E. Putnam. She alone has read all the manuscript, often putting her own work aside to do so, thereby saving me from countless errors, and making other sacrifices so that I could complete this manuscript. For the errors, omissions, and infelicities that remain I have only myself to blame.

CONTENTS

TABLES

FIGURES

· THE DEATH PENALTY IN AMERICA ·

1

Background and Developments

As of April 1996, more than three thousand persons were under death sentence in the United States. In 1995, 56 convicts were executed and more than two hundred were sentenced to death; on the average, thirty have been executed so far each year in this decade. In the past twenty years, thirty-eight of the fifty states have meted out at least one death sentence; twenty-four have carried out at least one execution. Over the whole course of this century more than seven thousand men and women have been lawfully executed; several thousand more were sentenced to death but spared for various reasons. Since George Kendall had the no-doubt-unsought distinction of being the first person of European extraction to be sentenced to death and hanged on these shores, in 1608 in the Jamestown Colony, Virginia,[1] perhaps as many as twenty thousand men and women have been lawfully punished by death. To be sure, some jurisdictions today—during 1995 there were thirteen[2]—administer a penal code devoid of capital statutes, mete out no death sentences, and execute no one. But these jurisdictions are and always have been the exception in this country, even if their abolition of the death penalty aligns them with all the nations of Western Europe—as chapter 6 will show.

The paragraphs that follow present, in capsule form, the salient facts about the death penalty in America today and their history.[3] At least a nodding acquaintance with the past is essential to an understanding of the present status of the death penalty and the prospects for its expansion or contraction in the years ahead.

The history of the death penalty in America can be usefully if roughly divided into six epochs of very uneven duration and importance: first, from the colonial period up to the adoption of the Constitution and the Bill of Rights; second, the seven decades leading up to the Civil War; then the five decades through the Progressive Era; third, from World War I through the post–World War II years; next, the two decades from the 1950s to the 1970s; and finally from the 1970s to the present.

Early 1600s to 1790s

Capital punishment was brought to these shores by the earliest colonial governments in the seventeenth century. The criminal law developed here was little more than a series of variations, colony by colony, on the law of England, the mother country. Although the capital laws of the thirteen colonies differed from each other in many interesting and important details concerning the death penalty, and various changes occurred during the century and a half of the colonial period, all the colonies authorized public execution by hanging as the mandatory punishment for various crimes against the state, the person, and property.

1790s to 1860s

The abolition movement in Western civilization is usually dated from 1763, the year Cesare Beccaria, a young Italian lawyer, published his short but provocative treatise *Dei delitti e delle pene* (On Crimes and Punishments). There he advocated penal servitude as the preferred substitute punishment for the death penalty; his argument elicited great interest and broad support among Enlightenment thinkers throughout Europe, and his book was widely read in the United States as well.[4]

Nevertheless, the founding of the United States and the adoption of the federal Bill of Rights in 1791 (with comparable constitutional developments in each of the thirteen original states) worked no significant changes on the practice of capital punishment in the colonial period. In particular, the adoption of the Eighth Amendment to the federal constitution, prohibiting "cruel and unusual punishments," was understood to be a prohibition only against inflicting the death penalty in its most aggravated forms, such as by crucifixion or burning at the stake. Nevertheless, during this period five significant developments reshaped the use of the death penalty in virtually the whole nation and set patterns that remain to this day.

Invention of Degrees of Murder

Whereas English law traditionally recognized only two kinds of criminal homicide—murder and voluntary manslaughter—American criminal law typically divides murder itself into two kinds, first-degree and second-degree, with the death penalty confined to persons convicted of the former offense. Pennsylvania in 1793 was the first jurisdiction to introduce this distinction;[5] it was clearly a product of compromise between those (mostly Quakers) who wanted to abolish the death penalty entirely and those who wished to keep it essentially unchanged. Indeed, in the distinction between first- and second-degree murder we see for the first time what would become the dominant (if often tacit) concern of the defenders of capital punishment: to shape the law and administration of the death penalty so as to winnow the worst offenders (for whom, they believe, death is appropriate) from the bad (those who are no doubt guilty of grave crimes but who for various reasons ought not to be executed),[6] and by this compromise to prevent the complete abolition of capital punishment.

In rapid order most states followed Pennsylvania's lead, so that today every American jurisdiction that authorizes the death penalty for murder does so by limiting it to those convicted of murder in the first-degree (or, in some jurisdictions, of "capital murder"; see Chapter 2).

Ending Public Executions

English history is replete with narratives by witnesses at public hangings, attesting that such spectacles did little to teach the folly of crime or vindicate the majesty of public justice. The general unruliness of the crowds that gathered to watch public executions constituted a growing threat to the legitimacy of the death penalty itself.[7] In this country as early as 1787 Dr. Benjamin Rush, a Philadelphian like his friend Benjamin Franklin, lectured and wrote against public executions. Not until 1835 in New York, however, were laws enacted to bring the hangman indoors—or, more precisely, behind a wall or fence and into the prison yard. Only official witnesses (variously defined) were henceforth permitted to view the event, thereby keeping the crowd at arm's length and ensuring that unwanted mishaps (decapitation of the offender and a slow death by strangulation were the worst) would not be seen by the mob and incite turmoil, marring the solemnity of the occasion.

A full century was to pass before every state followed New York's lead. Hanging in public occurred as late as 1936 in Kentucky and 1937 in Missouri. Today, strict control over who may witness an execution is characteristic of every death penalty jurisdiction.[8] In recent years, however, a proposal in the reverse direction has been much discussed and even litigated (but without success) in both Texas and California: filming executions and showing excerpts on prime-time television. This controversy will be explored in greater detail (see Chapter 27). Meanwhile, Texas has led the way in permitting members of the murder victim's family to attend the execution of the murderer.[9]

Giving the Trial Jury Sentencing Discretion

Under English law, conviction of a capital offense was tantamount to a death sentence, since the statutes empowered the trial judge to mete out no alternative. Occasionally juries would convict an offender of a capital crime and then recommend, even plead, that the court sentence the offender to banishment in the colonies or to prison in the hulks; the judges invariably ignored such unsought advice. American jurisdictions early in the nineteenth century, however, in keeping with populist attitudes and practices, began authorizing trial juries to make binding recommendations in capital cases, requiring the judge to sentence to death (as under the old law) or to grant "mercy" in the form of a life sentence in prison (defined variously by different state statutes).

The origins and growth of this practice, as well as its motivation, have yet to be traced and explained in satisfactory detail. We know, for instance, that in 1841 both Tennessee and Alabama gave the jury sentencing discretion in the punishment of murder, and in 1846 Louisiana extended this provision to all its capital crimes.

(Was it a device to allow all-white juries to sentence white offenders more leniently than others? We do not know.)

Jury sentencing discretion in capital cases slowly but steadily grew throughout the rest of the nineteenth century, although a mandatory death sentence for certain crimes remained lawful until fairly recently. For example, until 1951 Massachusetts provided a mandatory death penalty for anyone convicted of first-degree murder, and until 1975 felony-murder-rape was punishable by a mandatory death penalty.[10] Today, largely as a consequence of Supreme Court rulings in the 1970s, jury sentencing discretion in all capital cases is virtually universal across the land. (For further details, see Chapters 13 and 14.) In a few states, however, notably Florida, the jury's sentencing determination is only a recommendation, and so it can be—and often is—overridden by the trial judge.[11]

Reducing the Variety of Capital Statutes

In the early years of the nineteenth century, English criminal law imposed the death penalty for scores of crimes, ranging from the obvious (murder, treason) to the absurd (theft of linens from a bleaching ground). Hundreds of men, women, and children were sentenced to death each year, though many were spared and shipped off to the colonies instead. American criminal law never quite reached such excesses; during most of the same century American states rarely punished offenders with death except upon conviction for murder. To be sure, the details of progressive statutory abolition in our history still await the attention of legal historians. Nevertheless, the broad outlines of this reform are clear.

The story in the West and South, however, is somewhat different. Horse thievery, claim jumping, and cattle rustling in western states were often punished by hanging. In the South, in the aftermath of the Civil War, rape and other crimes against the person were capital offenses, especially if the victim was white and the offender black. Of all the nonhomicidal crimes punishable by death, rape was by far the most important—some 10 percent of all executions between 1930 and 1977 (when the death penalty for rape was abolished by the Supreme Court) were carried out for this crime. On occasion, public agitation over "the crime of the hour"—kidnapping for ransom in the 1930s is a good example; so is large-scale drug trafficking in the 1990s—could erupt in a rash of new capital statutes. As recently as three decades ago (1965) a wide variety of crimes were still punishable by death (indeed, even by a mandatory death penalty in a few cases); execution of offenders guilty of some of these nonhomicidal crimes was not unknown in modern times (see Table 1-1).

Today, the only crime clearly punishable by death under American law—the only crime for which anyone has been executed since 1977 and the only crime punishable by death whose constitutionality has been upheld by the Supreme Court—is some form of criminal homicide. This functional limitation of the death penalty to criminal homicide is a consequence of Supreme Court rulings in the 1970s (see part IV). Yet as we shall also see (in Chapter 3), legislators in many states never seem to tire of introducing bills that would authorize the death penalty for various crimes not involv-

Table 1-1.
Capital Crimes in the United States, by Executions and Numbers of Jurisdictions, 1965

Type of offense	Number of jurisdictions[a]	Execution(s) carried out between 1930 and 1965
Capitally punishable homicide	44	Yes
Murder	40	Yes
Other homicide	20	Yes
Kidnapping	34	Yes
Treason	21	No
Rape	19	Yes
Carnal knowledge	15	No
Armed robbery	10	Yes
Perjury in a capital case	10	No
Bombing	7	No
Assault by a life-term prisoner	5	Yes
Burglary	4	Yes
Arson	4	No
Train wrecking	2	No
Train robbery	2	No
Espionage	2	Yes
Bank robbery	2	Yes
Sabotage	1	Yes
Desertion in wartime	1	Yes
Other	14	No

[a]Fifty-five jurisdictions: fifty states, District of Columbia, Puerto Rico, Virgin Islands, federal civil and military.
Source: Bedau 1982:9, Table 1-1; National Prisoner Statistics, ''Capital Punishment,'' no. 42 (June 1968), Table 3; Savitz 1955.

ing homicide. Congress, in the summer of 1994, moved decisively in this direction when it enacted the Violent Crime Control and Law Enforcement Act, including the Federal Death Penalty Act, authorizing a federal death penalty for half a hundred crimes, a few of which do not involve homicide.

All these developments initiated early in the nineteenth century—inventing degrees of murder, empowering juries to extend mercy in sentencing, ending public executions, reducing the variety of crimes punishable by death—were responses to a growing movement to abolish the death penalty, especially active by the 1840s in Massachusetts, Ohio, New York, New Jersey, Pennsylvania, and Rhode Island.[12] The movement was led variously by secular reformers and Quakers, Unitarians, and other liberal Christians.

Abolitionists often supported these developments as painful compromises, the best that could be achieved in the face of strong opposition, and undeniably improvements in the right direction. Retentionists could view these revisions as relatively inexpensive concessions that left their main principle intact: Retributive justice and protection of the innocent required the death penalty in appropriate cases. Whether these reforms helped the cause of abolition in the long run or only entrenched what remained of the death penalty more securely is a nice question not easily answered.

Complete Abolition of the Death Penalty

The fifth and final important development during the years 1790 to 1865 was the first great triumph of the abolition movement: repeal of the death penalty for murder in Michigan in 1847, followed by Rhode Island in 1852 and Wisconsin a year later.[13] Abolition in Ohio and Pennsylvania almost succeeded in that period as well.[14] With these states setting the pace, a checkered pattern of abolition by state legislative action began across the nation. (The effort to abolish by legislative reform must be kept distinct from efforts in the period 1965–1976 to achieve abolition by judicial decree; see part IV.) During the past century, abolition in a given state by vote of the legislature was followed, more often than not, by legislative restoration of the death penalty a few years later, as Table 1-2 shows. The struggle—especially in Massachusetts and New York—between those who would reinstate and even expand the death penalty and those who would keep it abolished continues to this day.

1860s to 1910s

The third of the six periods in our history, roughly from the Civil War to the early years of the twentieth century, witnessed no important changes or new trends affecting the death penalty. The search for a method of execution more efficient than hanging led to the development in New York in 1888 of the electric chair, and this method of execution (despite its many drawbacks) eventually was adopted by more than three dozen states. But the abolition movement languished after the Civil War, and during the Gaslight Era few states significantly revised the death penalty provisions of their criminal codes.

1910s to the Early 1950s

This lassitude was abruptly ended during the Progressive Era. Within a few years outright repeal of all death penalties was accomplished in nine states (Arizona, Kansas, Minnesota, Missouri, North Dakota, Oregon, South Dakota, Tennessee, Washington). But the abolition tide rapidly receded, often within only a few years, in all but two of these jurisdictions.[15] The movement to abolish the death penalty by state legislative reform never regained momentum. Not only that: Within a few

Table 1-2.
Abolition, Partial Abolition, and Restoration of the Death Penalty, by Jurisdiction, 1846–1995

Jurisdiction	Year of partial abolition	Year of complete abolition	Year of restoration	Year of reabolition
Alaska		1957		
Arizona	1916[a]		1918	
Colorado		1897	1901	
Delaware		1958	1961	
D.C.		1973		
Hawaii		1957		
Iowa		1872	1878	1965
Kansas		1907, 1973	1935, 1994	
Maine		1876	1883	1887
Massachusetts		1984		
Michigan	1847[a]	1963		
Minnesota		1911		
Missouri		1917	1919	
New Mexico	1969[b,c]			
New York	1969[b,d]		1995	
North Dakota		1915		
Oregon		1914, 1964	1920, 1984	
Rhode Island	1852[d]			
South Dakota		1915, 1977	1939, 1979	
Tennessee	1915[e]		1919	
Vermont	1965[b,c]			
Washington		1913	1919	
West Virginia		1965		
Wisconsin		1853		

[a]Death retained for treason.

[b]Death retained for killing a law officer on duty.

[c]Death retained for a second offense of murder.

[d]Death retained for murder of a guard by a life-term prisoner.

[e]Death retained for rape.

Source: Bureau of Justice Statistics, "Capital Punishment, 1982," pp. 10–11; "Capital Punishment 1984," p. 4; NCADP "Lifelines," Jan.–Mar. 1994, p. 3; *New York Times,* 8 March 1995, p. 1.

years, during the 1930s and 1940s, executions reached their highest levels in this century (see Figure 1-1 and Table 1-3), most likely as a consequence of public anxiety over the "crime wave" generated by the Great Depression (1929–40) and Prohibition (1916–32). Nevertheless, two less radical changes inspired in part by the abolition movement also occurred during this period; each represents a trend still manifest today.

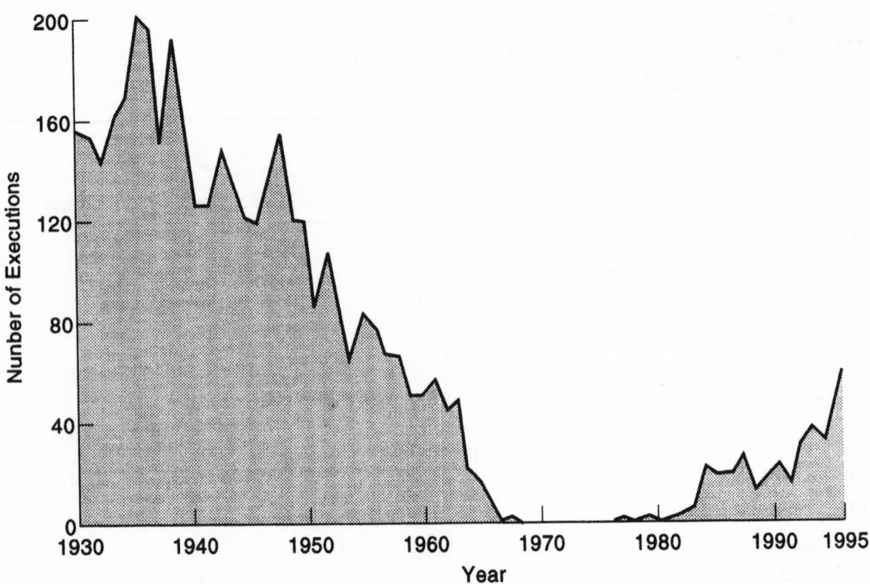

Figure 1–1. Persons executed under civil authority, annually, 1930–95.
Source: Bureau of Justice Statistics, "Capital Punishment 1993," Figure 2, p. 2; NAACP Legal Defense and Educational Fund, "Death Row, U.S.A." (winter 1995), p. 3.

Humanizing the Method of Execution

The electric chair, widely adopted early in this century, may have been an improvement over hanging in some respects.[16] But death in the electric chair was and remains one of the most barbaric ways to kill a person. Why it remains authorized by statute in a dozen states even today is unclear. The other widely adopted method of execution invented in this country during this period—lethal gas, first authorized and used in Nevada in 1923—was introduced precisely because it was viewed, with some plausibility, as a humane improvement on both hanging and the electric chair. Its days, however, seem to be numbered; in 1994 a federal judge in California ruled that death by cyanide gas violated the eighth amendment ban on "cruel and unusual punishments."[17]

What was true of attitudes toward the gas chamber in the 1930s is even truer today regarding lethal injection, first authorized by law in Oklahoma in 1977, first used in Texas in 1982, and now the law in some two dozen jurisdictions (see Table 1-4). Without doubt, humanizing executions so that they are as quick, painless, reliable, and as little disfiguring as possible is an essential aspect of preserving capital punishment in any society today that regards itself as civilized. Abolitionists and retentionists alike agree that the more barbaric the mode of execution, the less willing society will be to permit its use.[18] Objections on such humanitarian grounds to death by firing squad in Utah—still the method of lawful execution most fre-

Table 1-3.
Persons Executed Under Civil Authority, Annually, 1930–95

All years	4,175				
1995	56				
1994	31				
1993	38				
1992	31				
1991	14				
1990	23				
1989	16	1969	—	1949	119
1988	11	1968	—	1948	119
1987	25	1967	2	1947	153
1986	18	1966	1	1946	131
1985	18	1965	7	1945	117
1984	21	1964	15	1944	120
1983	5	1963	21	1943	131
1982	2	1962	47	1942	147
1981	1	1961	42	1941	123
1980	—	1960	56	1940	124
1979	2	1959	49	1939	160
1978	—	1958	49	1938	190
1977	1	1957	65	1937	147
1976	—	1956	65	1936	195
1975	—	1955	76	1935	199
1974	—	1954	81	1934	168
1973	—	1953	62	1933	160
1972	—	1952	83	1932	140
1971	—	1951	105	1931	153
1970	—	1950	82	1930	155

Source: Bureau of Justice Statistics, "Capital Punishment 1978," p. 16, Table 1 (for years 1930–79); NAACP Legal Defense and Educational Fund, "Death Row, U.S.A.," winter 1995, p. 3 (for years 1980–95).

quently used there (although death by lethal injection is also permitted)—were aired and argued in the state legislature in January 1996, just days prior to the execution of John Albert Taylor (Brooke 1996). Nor has death by hanging disappeared; this method was used in Delaware as recently as January 1996.

Expanding the Role of Federal Appellate Courts

Early in this century it was rare, though not unknown, for a capital offender to receive no review of his death sentence or of the underlying criminal conviction by any appellate court, state or federal. Bit by bit, however, at least perfunctory review by state appellate courts became almost routine, although very few states went so far as to enact statutes requiring their appellate courts to review convictions and sentences in every death penalty case.

Table 1-4.
Methods of Lawful Execution, by Jurisdiction, 1994

Lethal Injection	Electrocution	Lethal gas	Hanging	Firing squad
Arizona[a,b]	Alabama	Arizona[a]	Delaware[a,c]	Utah[a]
Arkansas[a,d]	Arkansas[a,d]	California[a]	Montana[a]	
California[a]	Connecticut	Maryland[a,e]	New Hampshire[a,f]	
Colorado	Florida	Mississippi[a,g]	Washington[a]	
Delaware[a,c]	Georgia	Missouri[a]		
Idaho	Indiana	North Carolina[a]		
Illinois	Kentucky	Wyoming[a,h]		
Kansas	Nebraska			
Louisiana	Ohio[a]			
Maryland[a,e]	South Carolina			
Mississippi[a,g]	Tennessee			
Missouri[a]	Virginia			
Montana[a]				
Nevada				
New Hampshire[a,f]				
New Jersey				
New Mexico				
North Carolina[a]				
Ohio[a]				
Oklahoma				
Oregon				
Pennsylvania				
South Dakota				
Texas				
Utah[a]				
Washington[a]				
Wyoming[a]				

Note: The method of execution of Federal prisoners is lethal injection, pursuant to 28 CFR, Part 26. For offenses under the Violent Crime Control and Law Enforcement Act of 1994, the method is that of the State in which the conviction took place, pursuant to 18 USC 3596.

[a]Authorizes 2 methods of execution.

[b]Arizona authorizes lethal injection for persons whose capital sentence was received after 11/15/92; for those sentenced before that date, the condemned may select lethal injection or lethal gas.

[c]Delaware authorizes lethal injection for those whose capital offense occurred after 6/13/86; for those whose offense occurred before that date, the condemned may select lethal injection or hanging.

[d]Arkansas authorizes lethal injection for those whose capital offense occurred after 7/4/83; for those whose offense occurred before that date, the condemned may select lethal injection or electrocution.

[e]Maryland authorizes lethal injection for those whose capital offense occurred after 3/25/94 and also for those whose offense occurred before that date, unless within 60 days from that date, the condemned selected lethal gas.

[f]New Hampshire authorizes hanging only if lethal injection cannot be given.

[g]Mississippi authorizes lethal injection for those convicted after 7/14/84 and lethal gas for those convicted prior to that date.

[h]Wyoming authorizes lethal gas if lethal injection is ever held to be unconstitutional.

Source: Bureau of Justice Statistics, ''Capital Punishment, 1994,'' p. 5, Table 2.

Major change occurred only when state prisoners on death row sought and found relief in the federal courts. In this connection it needs to be remembered, first, that the protections of the *federal* Bill of Rights have been used to review convictions and sentences in *state* criminal courts with some frequency only since the 1960s; and, second, that the vast proportion of all capital trials in this country occur in state, not federal, courts. Late in 1994, for example, of the roughly three thousand persons on death row in the United States, only six—fewer than 0.2 percent—had been convicted in a federal court under a federal death penalty statute. Landmark cases, notably those that grew out of the Elaine, Arkansas, race riot (*Moore v. Dempsey,* 1923)[19] and the Scottsboro Boys rape case (*Powell v. Alabama,* 1932),[20] paved the way for the federal courts to consider claims that the nation's Bill of Rights had been violated by state criminal proceedings in capital cases. At best, however, such litigation attacked the death penalty only case by case, and the litigation—aimed solely at protecting the rights of a given defendant—was intermittent and uncoordinated as well. Few, if any, jurists or legal scholars supposed that appeals to "due process of law" or to "equal protection of the law" could persuade the courts to reject the death penalty itself.

1950s to 1970s

During these two decades the abolition movement was significantly revived and achieved some of its greatest successes. Repeal of the death penalty by the Delaware legislature in 1958 proved to be the inspiring event,[21] galvanizing opponents of the death penalty in many states to organize and seek repeal of the capital statutes in their own backyard. Abolition by public referendum in Oregon in 1964[22] and by the legislatures in Iowa and West Virginia a year later were the chief accomplishments during this period. In addition, three new factors came into play, two of which remain important in understanding the current scene.

Decline in Executions

As Table 1-3 shows, executions dropped steadily in the 1950s to an annual average of seventy-two, a reduction by half of the annual average for the 1930s and 1940s. No single factor explains this precipitous drop, though increasing sensitivity of the federal courts to postconviction appellate litigation on behalf of capital defendants no doubt was one important cause. The decline in executions that began in the 1950s accelerated in the early 1960s, prefacing the complete cessation of executions from 1968 to 1976 while the constitutionality of the death penalty was being tested in the courts.

The judicial moratorium on executions ended in 1977; since then, despite the growing numbers under death sentence each year (see Figure 1-2), the number of those executed annually is still quite small, although it may be increasing slightly. In the short term it seems very likely that the rate of execution will increase,

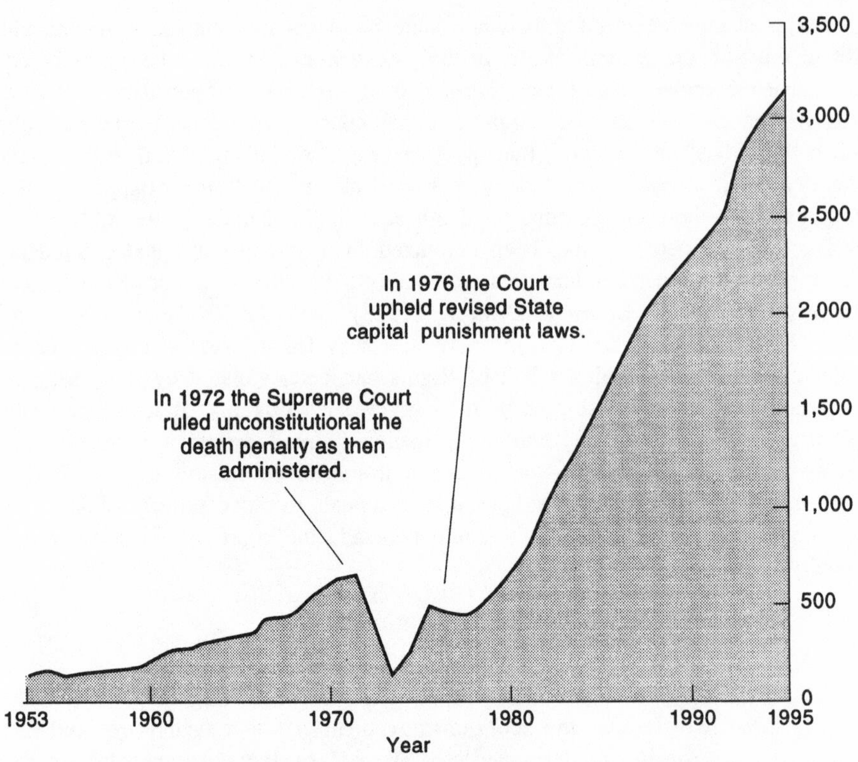

Figure 1–2. Persons under death sentence, annually, 1930–95.

Source: Bureau of Justice Statistics, "Capital Punishment 1993," Figure 3, p. 12; and NAACP Legal Defense and Educational Fund, "Death Row, U.S.A." Winter 1995, p. 1 (as of 31 January 1996).

perhaps even double the rate of the early 1990s (for reasons to be explained shortly and in greater detail in Chapters 7 and 22–24).

Increase in Time Served Under Death Sentence

Concomitant with the decline in executions in the 1950s, there has been a steady growth in the average time served on death row from imposition of the death sentence to the final disposition of the case. Already in the early 1960s voices were raised in alarm over this development. As Table 1-5 shows, the average time served under death sentence in the years since executions resumed (1977–92) has slowly grown to about ten years. Perhaps no other feature of the current administration of capital punishment so agitates those who favor executions as does (what they regard as) this flagrant example of the law's inordinate delay. Yet nothing short of a breathtaking rate of executions—two or three every day—or radical changes in the laws affecting postconviction appeals (or, even more radically, a sharp drop in the

Table 1-5.
Average Time Served Under Death Sentence, 1977–94

Year of execution	Number executed	Average elapsed time, in months, from sentence to execution for:
Total	226	94
1977–83	11	51
1984	21	74
1985	18	71
1986	18	87
1987	25	86
1988	11	80
1989	16	95
1990	23	95
1991	14	116
1992	31	114
1993	38	113
1994	31	122

Note: Average time was calculated from the most recent sentencing date.
Source: Bureau of Justice Statistics, "Capital Punishment, 1994," p. 10, Table 11.

number of death sentences issued by trial courts) could both dispose of the steadily increasing backlog of capital cases slowly wending its way through the appellate courts and prevent their replacement by as many or more in the future.

Challenges to the Constitutionality of the Death Penalty

Until fairly recently, opposition to executing a given capital prisoner usually took one or both of two forms: using the appellate courts to challenge the procedures whereby the defendant was tried and sentenced, and pleading for a commutation of the death sentence at a clemency hearing. Not until the mid-1960s was any serious attempt made to challenge the very constitutionality of the death penalty itself.[23]

This campaign caused an abrupt and complete suspension of all executions for nearly a decade and reached its climax in June 1972 with the ruling of the Supreme Court in *Furman v. Georgia.* For the brief period of a few months in the summer of 1972 (and apart from a few state mandatory death penalties, most of them in desuetude) the entire nation experienced for the first time virtually complete abolition of the death penalty.

The Supreme Court's decision in *Furman* also required the state courts to resentence all the more than six hundred prisoners then on death row because their death sentences (though not their convictions) had been nullified indirectly by this ruling. Other decisions by the Court in the aftermath of *Furman* further narrowed the scope and shaped the subsequent administration of capital punishment in many respects, three of which are paramount: no more mandatory death penalties, no more death penalties except for some form of criminal homicide, and no more executions without review of the death sentence and the underlying criminal conviction by a state appellate court. These decisions consolidated trends already evident and in some states incorporated by statute into their criminal codes. (Further details will be found in part IV.)

Yet the campaign to abolish the death penalty permanently and nationally by federal constitutional interpretation and court decree failed to achieve its principal aim. Within months after the decision in *Furman,* legislatures in many states enacted new death penalty statutes designed to repair the flaws identified by the Court. Four years later, in *Gregg v. Georgia* (1976) and allied cases from Florida and Texas, the Court itself sustained the constitutionality of capital punishment. Whether at some future date the Supreme Court will once again prove receptive to abolition, as it was in the 1970s, is impossible to predict.[24]

1970s to the Present

The current death penalty scene in the United States begins in 1976 when the Supreme Court held that the death penalty as such is not unconstitutional—or, to be more precise, that the prohibition against "cruel and unusual punishments" in the Eighth Amendment of the federal Bill of Rights does not bar the death penalty per se. Those decisions of the mid-1970s, in conjunction with an important ruling a decade later (*McCleskey v. Kemp,* 1987), have more or less settled the constitutionality of the death penalty for the foreseeable future.

Meanwhile, at least half a dozen factors now characteristic of the national posture toward the death penalty began to manifest themselves. Each is likely to continue at least into the immediate future.

Increasing Public Support for the Death Penalty

In his important concurring opinion in *Furman* in 1972, Justice William J. Brennan Jr. cited public opinion polls that showed the American people to be slightly inclined in favor of abolition. Four years later, in his plurality opinion for the Court in *Gregg,* Justice Potter Stewart cited subsequent polls to the opposite effect. Even the Supreme Court in interpreting the Bill of Rights apparently cannot ignore public opinion.

As Figure 1-3 shows, except for a brief period in the early 1960s, the American public has given lip service in support of the death penalty, and this support has been very large and stable for a generation. Beginning in the mid-1970s, probably no other factor regarding the death penalty in America has been so prominent, important, and enduring as the popular support for capital punishment. To be sure, it is far from clear whether this mile-wide support is more than an inch deep; recent research suggests it may not be (see part II). Here it suffices to identify and emphasize this factor because it is so closely connected with two others that deserve mention.

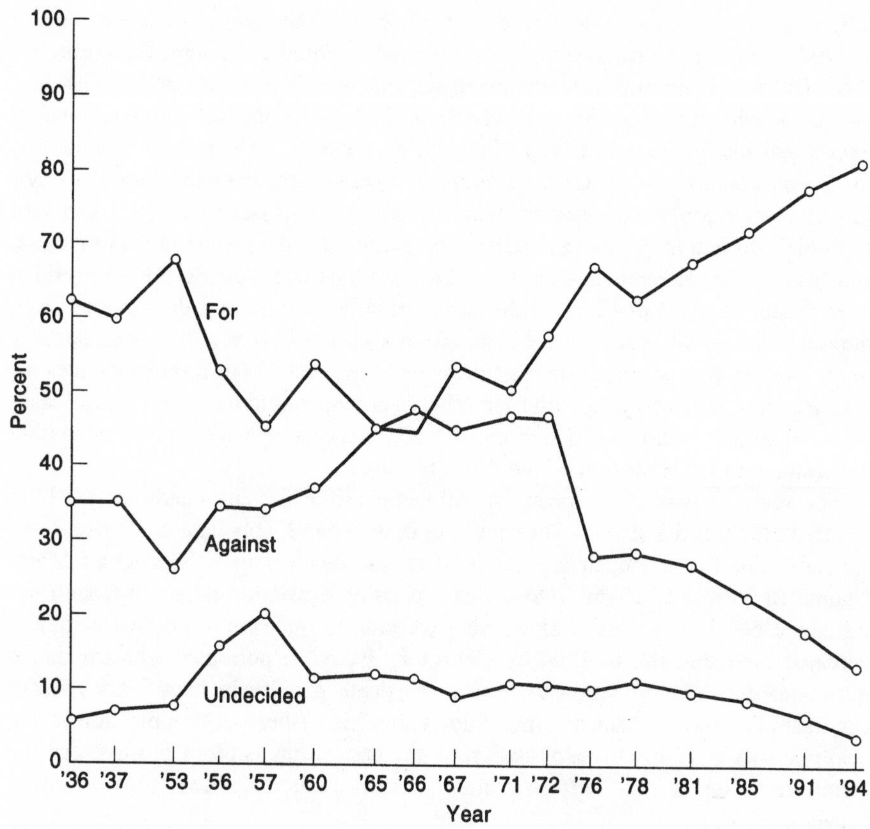

Figure 1–3. Public opinion on the death penalty, 1936–94.
Source: Erskine 1970:291; Gallup Poll 1994:5.

Politicization of the Death Penalty

Until recent decades, the death penalty played little or no visible role in American electoral politics. Neither major political party took any interest in the issue in national or state electoral contests or in deciding who should be elected or appointed to the judiciary. This indifference came to a noticeable end with two major Republican Party political campaigns, Richard Nixon's in 1968 (which put him in the White House) and Ronald Reagan's in 1972 (which gained him the governor's mansion in California). In each of these campaigns, the death penalty card was put into play with considerable effect against Democrats who were seeking reelection. Ironically, it was in the year 1968 that the Supreme Court, writing in *Witherspoon v. Illinois,* observed in passing that death penalty supporters were a "distinct and dwindling minority." Perhaps that had been true briefly in the early 1960s, but it would soon prove to be otherwise.

In recent years, notably in California, Florida, and Texas, campaigns for state offices have been fought out in part over which candidate would sentence to death and execute the most offenders. In the 1988 presidential campaign, Governor Michael Dukakis's opposition to the death penalty was effectively used against him by Vice President George Bush. In March of 1992, Governor Bill Clinton pointedly interrupted his campaign in New Hampshire seeking the Democratic nomination for the presidency so that he could return to Arkansas for the execution of Rickey Ray Rector, a convicted murderer whose brain was half destroyed by a gun-shot from his own hand.[25] Unlike his fellow competitors for the Democratic nomination and his eventual Republican opponent, Clinton alone could claim to have presided over executions (three)—and so the death penalty card quietly disappeared from the deck during the rest of the campaign, though not before it had been adroitly used. The off-year elections in 1994 presented the spectacle of rival candidates for various public offices vying with each other over who would prosecute capital cases more vigorously, who would sign more death warrants, and who would champion the restoration or expansion of the death penalty.

For several years it has been virtually impossible for any candidate for high elective office in the states—governor, attorney general, appellate court judge—to appear hesitant over (much less opposed to) the death penalty. (Governor Mario Cuomo in New York, who vetoed death penalty legislation annually from 1983 through 1994, is the most conspicuous exception to this rule—and he was finally defeated for reelection in 1994 by George E. Pataki, a politician who trumpeted his unqualified determination to restore the death penalty in New York.) Every candidate for higher elective office knows that his or her public objection to the death penalty risks instant exploitation by the opposition as proof positive that the candidate is hopelessly "soft on crime." (The issue is examined more closely in Chapters 23 and 29.)

Declining Use of Executive Clemency

Although English criminal law two hundred years ago punished thousands with death sentences, most of these sentences were never carried out. Instead, exercise of the royal clemency power intervened, and death sentences were reduced to transportion to the colonies or, less frequently, a lifetime of imprisonment. In this country the power of the chief executive (governor, president) to grant reprieves and commutations of otherwise lawful punishments has always been a feature, despite its royalist overtones, of American constitutional law. Two centuries ago, when the death sentence was mandatory upon conviction of a capital crime, many nonhomicidal crimes punishable by death, and less-than-adequate review afforded by the appellate courts, executive clemency played an important role in achieving rough justice by keeping many lesser offenders off the scaffold.

However, various developments in the law discussed here—notably, the distinction between degrees of murder, the power of capital juries to decide between a life and a death sentence, regular appellate review of death sentences, and reduction in the variety of capital laws—plus the enduring populist elements in

American life have combined to reduce the role for executive clemency. As Table 1-6 shows, this decline has been nothing if not spectacular in the period since the Supreme Court upheld the constitutionality of the death penalty in 1976.[26] What counted as good reasons for commutations in the past—reform by the criminal while on death row, unresolved doubts about guilt, a split verdict by the appellate courts reviewing the case, inequitable sentencing of codefendants—have virtually ceased to influence governors or pardon boards. A rare exception to the prevailing practice occurred in Illinois in January 1996. Human rights activists, led by celebrity Bianca Jaggar, succeeded in persuading Governor Jim Edgar to commute the death sentence of Guinevere Garcia, herself a victim of "incest, rape, battering, alcoholism, and depression." Governor Edgar commented, "this is not the kind of case I had in mind when I voted as a legislator to restore the death penalty" (Terry 1996). (For details about a recent case, see chapter 26.)

Increasing Complexity and Cost of Capital Punishment

A century ago—when hanging was quick and cheap, trials brief, and appeals infrequent—capital punishment as a system was relatively inexpensive and probably much cheaper than the alternative of long-term imprisonment. (No research on the comparative costs in those days has been conducted.) In the past three decades all this has changed. Numerous studies have been undertaken to carry out comparative cost accounting for a capital punishment system where everyone arrested for criminal homicide is a potential capital case versus the costs in a system in which no one is (as was true in 1994 of Massachusetts, New York, Wisconsin, and a dozen other jurisdictions). All these studies agree that the dollar costs of a capital punishment system—with taxpayers funding both the defense and the prosecution from trial through several rounds of appeals in state and federal courts—is greater than for a system where imprisonment is the norm. (A fuller discussion of these costs is presented in chapter 29.)

But the dollar costs are only part of the story. The administrative complexity of the present system of capital punishment in America can hardly be exaggerated. It is an unavoidable outgrowth of the Supreme Court's rulings in the 1970s. Those decisions rejected outright abolition on constitutional grounds but did force the states that wanted to keep the death penalty to control its use by introducing several administrative constraints, notably, provision of legal counsel for indigent defendants at trial and for appeals; a two-stage or bifurcated trial (first, a trial on the issue of guilt, followed by a second trial for the guilty on the issue of sentence); statutory guidelines to assist the jury in choosing between a death and a prison sentence; automatic review in state appellate courts; and discretionary review in the federal courts. In theory these protections were to provide greater fairness, if not the maximum possible fairness, in capital cases. What they provide in practice, in the judgment of all those who actually work within such systems, is neither fair nor efficient. The controversy is of central importance and is discussed in greater detail in parts V and VI.

Table 1-6.
Executive Clemency in Capital Cases, Annually, 1961–94

Year	BJS	R&Z
1961	17	*
1962	27	*
1963	15	*
1964	9	*
1965	19	*
1966	17	*
1967	13	*
1968	16	*
1969	20	*
1970	29	*
1971	*	*
1972	*	0
1973	9	0
1974	22	0
1975	21	0
1976	15	5
1977	7	1
1978	8	0
1979	6	2
1980	6	3
1981	4	13
1982	6	11
1983	4	8
1984	6	2
1985	3	0
1986	4	5
1987	1	3
1988	1	2
1989	3	2
1990	0	1
1991	0	10
1992	1	2
1993	0	*
1994	1	*

Source: Bedau 1990–91, Table 1, p. 263 (using Bureau of Justice Statistics for the years 1961–71, as revised) and Bureau of Justice Statistics, ''Capital Punishment 1994,'' p. 12, appendix Table 1; Radelet and Zsembik 1993, p. 297, Table 1.

Declining Importance of Deterrence and Incapacitation

In a day when horse thievery, counterfeiting, and other crimes against property and the state were punishable by death (as they have been in more than one jurisdiction in our history), defense of the death penalty had to rest at least in part on its deterrent effect. "We execute criminals not to punish them but to prevent future crimes" expresses the attitude of countless supporters of the death penalty in an earlier day. (Prevention, deterrence, and incapacitation are discussed in greater detail in part III.)

Once the death penalty is confined solely to criminal homicide, however, as is substantially true today, it can be more readily defended solely on grounds of just deserts or retribution. What does it matter whether the death penalty is a deterrent at all, much less a better deterrent than the alternative punishment? What does it matter if all (and not merely most) convicted murderers can be kept in prison without significant risk to the safety of other prisoners, guards, and visitors? What matters is that murderers deserve to die. Survey research in recent years (presented and discussed in detail in part II) has shown to all investigators that a large fraction of those who support the death penalty would do so regardless of whether it was shown to be an effective and superior deterrent.

This shift in the basic rationale for capital punishment has helped to immunize it from attack on empirical grounds. If murderers deserve to die, then it doesn't matter whether the evidence shows that society could be protected just as well by a policy of long-term imprisonment, or that it would be cheaper to get rid of the costly current death penalty system in favor of a system that sentences to prison terms, or that those who murder whites are being disproportionately and unfairly prosecuted, convicted, sentenced, and executed for capital crimes.

Regionalization of the Death Penalty

A glance at the data presented in Table 1-7 reveals that, so far as the death penalty is concerned, the nation can be divided roughly into three regions running from east to west.[27] First, there is a northern tier from Maine to Alaska; here the death penalty either is abolished or plays a very minor role (few, if any, prisoners on death row, infrequent executions, moderate public support). The second, middle tier, runs from Pennsylvania to California; here the death penalty has a more prominent role, but opposition to its use is quite vigorous, and executions since 1977 have been few and slow in coming despite large numbers on death row. Finally, there is the lower tier running from Virginia and the Carolinas west through Texas to Arizona. Here the death penalty thrives—many executions amidst clamor for more, hundreds on death row and more on the way. As of May 1996, two thirds of all executions since *Furman* have been carried out in just five southern states: Texas, Florida, Virginia, Louisiana, and Georgia.

Describe the South however one wishes—the erstwhile slavocracy, the Old Confederacy, the Bible Belt—in this region the death penalty is as firmly entrenched as grits for breakfast. Why the death penalty should be so deeply rooted in southern

Table 1-7.
Prisoners Executed by Jurisdiction in Rank Order, 1930–95 and 1977–95

Jurisdiction	Number executed 1930–95	Jurisdiction	Number executed 1977–95
U.S. total	4,172	U.S. total	313
Texas	401	Texas	104
Georgia	386	Florida	36
New York	329	Virginia	29
California	294	Louisiana	22
North Carolina	271	Georgia	20
Florida	206	Missouri	17
Ohio	172	Alabama	12
South Carolina	167	Arkansas	11
Mississippi	158	North Carolina	8
Louisiana	155	West Virginia	7
Pennsylvania	154	Illinois	7
Alabama	147	Oklahoma	6
Arkansas	129	Nevada	5
Virginia	121	Delaware	5
Kentucky	103	South Carolina	5
Illinois	97	Mississippi	4
Tennessee	93	Utah	4
Missouri	78	Arizona	4
New Jersey	74	Indiana	3
Maryland	69	California	2
Oklahoma	66	Washington	2
Arizona	51	Pennsylvania	2
Washington	49	Nebraska	1
Colorado	47	Idaho	1
Indiana	46	Montana	1
West Virginia	40	Maryland	1
District of Columbia	40	Wyoming	1
Nevada	34		
U.S. federal	33		
Massachusetts	27		
Connecticut	21		
Oregon	19		
Iowa	18		
Utah	17		
Delaware	17		
Kansas	15		
New Mexico	8		
Wyoming	8		

(*continued*)

Table 1-7. (*continued*)

Jurisdiction	Number executed 1930–95	Jurisdiction	Number executed 1977–95
Montana	7		
Nebraska	5		
Vermont	4		
Idaho	4		
South Dakota	1		
New Hampshire	1		

Source: Bureau of Justice Statistics, ''Capital Punishment 1994,'' p. 11, Table 10; and NAACP Legal Defense and Educational Fund, ''Death Row, U.S.A.,'' winter 1995, pp. 9–10.

culture is not entirely clear; conventional explanations (unsupported by any unambiguous empirical evidence) point to the relatively rural, religious, and racist attitudes of the native white residents in the region, attitudes whose roots go back to the days of slavery when the threat of violent repression of the resident African-American labor force was an essential instrument of social, political, and legal control. The death penalty today, so this explanation goes, is nothing but the survival in a socially acceptable form of the old Black Codes and the lynch law enforced by the Ku Klux Klan.

The truth, no doubt, is far more complex than this crude stereotype would allow. Still, whatever the explanation, it remains true that the death penalty in the United States has its strongest grip in the South. Indeed, Georgia's Chattahoochee Judicial District, which includes the city of Columbus and Fort Benning, has been labeled ''the Buckle of the Death Belt'' because of the way death sentences for African-Americans are routinely meted out.[28] Nothing in the foreseeable future internal to the politics of the Death Belt is likely to reduce the role of capital punishment, much less lead to its abolition.

Symbolic Role of Capital Punishment

There was a time when capital punishment could reasonably be believed to be an effective means of fighting crime—at least, a necessary form of incapacitation, since there was no adequate alternative prior to the development of prisons with trained correctional staff. That time has long passed, as a century and a half without the death penalty in Michigan and Wisconsin proves to anyone who cares to examine the record. Today, the death penalty plays a completely different role in American life. What good it does, apart from providing incapacitation of executed offenders, steady jobs for prison guards, frantic midnight labors for attorneys, stories for the media, and some vague sense of righteousness for those who believe murderers deserve to die, is difficult to say. Advocacy of the death penalty, however, performs a clearer function.[29]

No doubt some governors, legislators, prosecutors, and judges who answer to the electorate and publicly endorse the death penalty seriously believe that it is a better deterrent than imprisonment, that it is not seriously racist in its administration, that it violates no one's human rights, and that it is a legitimate retribution too infrequently practiced. But the invocation of these beliefs in political debate has become essentially ritualistic. They are symbolic affirmations intended mainly to respond to the public's fear of criminal victimization, smoldering indignation at youthful violent offenders, and frustration over the apparent failure of government to do anything about either. In today's electoral politics, a candidate's support for the death penalty amounts to saying: "Believe me, I care about you and I hear your anger and frustration. That's why I support the death penalty, whether or not it would do any good in removing the objective causes of your distress. Knowing where I stand ought to make you feel better—and more willing to put government into my hands than in the hands of liberals who disagree with us over the death penalty. They care more about the vicious criminals than they do about the victims and law-abiding citizens like you and me." Thus, we confront a corollary of Gresham's law, in which a debased political rhetoric drives out any reliance on the facts and norms relevant to developing a sound public policy on punishment.

Conclusion

At the risk of oversimplifying, the controversy over the death penalty in the United States today can be summarized as follows. Defenders of the death penalty believe that despite needless expense and avoidable delay, capital punishment as actually administered does a reasonable (not perfect) job of winnowing out the worst and most dangerous offenders from among the bad—and that an even better job would be done if the laws were changed to abolish frivolous appeals and to reduce costs and the pileup on the nation's death rows. Opponents of the death penalty disagree; they argue that the present system is but the latest version of death penalty practices that cannot be justified, that no significant improvements are likely, and that moral and practical objections to the death penalty ought therefore to prevail. The rest of this book is given over to spelling out the facts and factors that must be taken into account in deciding who has the better of this argument and why.

Notes

1. Clines 1992, reporting the research of Watt Espy, the nation's leading death penalty archivist.
2. Alaska, District of Columbia, Hawaii, Iowa, Maine, Massachusetts, Michigan, Minnesota, New York, North Dakota, Rhode Island, Vermont, West Virginia, and Wisconsin. In March 1995, New York reintroduced the death penalty; Kansas restored the death penalty in April 1994.
3. For a sampling of anti–death penalty sentiment in this country from 1797 to 1975, see Mackey ed. 1976.
4. In general for the period 1776–1865, see Masur 1989.
5. See Keedy 1949

6. See Acker and Lanier 1993a.

7. For marvelously detailed discussions of the death penalty in England between 1600 and 1900, see Linebaugh 1992; Gattrell 1994.

8. For a critical discussion of public executions, see Blum 1992.

9. *N.Y. Times,* 10 Feb. 1996, p. 9, and *Dallas-Morning News,* 10 Feb. 1996, p. 1A.

10. See Bedau 1976.

11. For further discussion, see Mello 1991 and Mello and Robson 1985.

12. For particular states, see Mackey 1975, 1982 (New York); Rogers 1993 (Massachusetts); Acton 1991 (Iowa); Blaine 1986 (New Hampshire).

13. See Mackey 1974 (Rhode Island); Lincoln 1987 (Michigan).

14. See Post 1944 and Savitz 1958 (both on Pennsylvania); Post 1945 (Ohio).

15. See Galliher, Ray, and Cook 1992. For particular states, see Hayner and Cranor 1952 (Washington); Guillot 1952 (Missouri); Dann 1952 (Oregon). See also Dressner and Altschuler 1975 (New York). Galliher et al. 1995 have attempted to explain why abolition efforts failed in many states.

16. For a full discussion, see Denno 1994a.

17. See San Francisco Examiner, 14 Jan. 1996, and N.Y. Times, 25 Oct. 1993, p. A15.

18. For a full discussion of current methods of execution in the United States, see Trombley 1992.

19. See Cortner 1988.

20. See Carter 1979,

21. See Bennett 1958; Cobin 1964; Samuelson 1969.

22. See Bedau 1980.

23. The campaign is fully discussed in Meltsner 1973; see also Wolfe 1973; Bedau 1977.

24. For the abolition movement since 1972, see Haines 1996.

25. The story is told in some detail in Frady 1993.

26. Although there is disagreement over the annual number of death penalty commutations for the years 1973 through 1992, the total commutations for this period as reported by the Bureau of Justice Statistics and by Radelet and Zsembik 1993 are virtually identical (71 versus 70, respectively). It should also be noted that the reports of commutations by the Bureau of Justice Statistics are extremely unstable, as virtually every issue of its ''Capital Punishment'' bulletin revises the reported commutation total of the previous year. For further information on these discrepancies and on the decline of executive clemency in capital cases, see Bedau 1990–91; Radelet and Zsembic 1993.

27. For more detail and a rather different account, see Zimring and Hawkins 1986: 126–47.

28. Death Penalty Information Center 1991.

29. For a discussion of the symbolic significance of recent death penalty debates, see Stolz 1983 (Congress); Koch and Galliher 1993 (Michigan).

PART I

The Laws, the Crimes, and the Executions

Useful discussion of the death penalty needs reliable and up-to-date information about several aspects of the criminal justice system and its current administration. What, exactly, are the crimes now punishable by death? What kinds of modifications are currently under review in the legislatures? How many capital crimes are committed each year, and how are they distributed around the nation, state by state? Who is on death row, and what are the demographics of this population? How many prisoners have been executed? And apart from execution, how else do prisoners leave death row? Finally, how does the use of the death penalty in America compare with the rest of the world? All these questions and more are addressed in this part.

The statistical data presented here (with one exception to be noted shortly) are supplied to the Department of Justice by state and local authorities for publication annually in two different series: "Crime in the United States," also known as the *Uniform Crime Reports* (UCR), is published by the Federal Bureau of Investigation (FBI); "Capital Punishment" is published by the Bureau of Justice Statistics (BJS). Both the FBI and the BJS are agencies of the U.S. Department of Justice. These data are also republished annually in the *Sourcebook of Criminal Justice Statistics.* The nongovernmental source relied on here for demographic information on prisoners under death sentence is available only from the series "Death Row, U.S.A.," published by the NAACP Legal Defense and Educational Fund (LDF).[1]

Capital Statutes

Chapter 2 presents a digest of capital offenses nationwide for the thirty-nine jurisdictions (thirty-seven states, plus the federal civil and military jurisdictions) that punish one or more crimes with death (see Tables 2-1 and 2-2).[2] The death penalty for all these crimes is discretionary; in sentencing a defendant convicted of a capital crime, the jury must weigh any "aggravating" circumstances against any "mitigating" circumstances, and must find one or more of the former to have been present if the defendant is to be sentenced to death. Table 2-3 shows the wide divergence among the states over the statutes governing the age at which a defendant can be tried as an adult on a capital charge.[3]

Three things should be noted about the list of capital crimes. First, the crime of murder, insofar as it is a capital offense, receives various definitions. The FBI uses the concept of "murder and nonnegligent manslaughter," and defines it as the "willful (nonnegligent) killing of one human being by another," thus including second-degree murder and some forms of manslaughter. In Arizona, and in most other states, the crime in question is described as "first-degree murder." In Kentucky, however, it is "aggravated murder"; in Washington it is "aggravated first-degree premeditated murder"; and in Arkansas it is called "capital murder." This last phrase is sometimes used (and will be used here) to refer to the crime of murder, however defined by statute, insofar as it is eligible for punishment by death. Only by careful study of the exact statutory language and the relevant case law in each jurisdiction can one tell just how much difference there really is among these various conceptions of murder and exactly what kinds of criminal homicide are subject to the death penalty.[4]

Second, since the "new" (post-1972) death penalty laws were enacted, no one has been executed for any crime except some form of criminal homicide. The death penalty for rape and for kidnapping was held by the Court in 1977 to be unconstitutional (see part IV for a fuller discussion). The Supreme Court has not yet had occasion to pass on the constitutionality of any of the nonhomicidal capital statutes enacted since 1972 by the states or by Congress. These nonhomicidal crimes include treason (California, Georgia), aircraft hijacking (Georgia, Mississippi), aggravated kidnapping (Idaho, South Dakota), and large-scale trafficking in drugs as well as conspiring or attempting to kill witnesses, jurors, prosecutors, or others involved in prosecuting defendants charged with engaging in a "continuing criminal conspiracy" (federal jurisdiction).[5] Whether a death sentence for any of these crimes would survive the inevitable constitutional challenge is arguable.

Third, during the 1990s the most explosive growth in death penalty statutes has occurred on the federal level. The 1996 revisions of federal habeas corpus enacted by Congress sharply limit the availability of that writ to state death row prisoners (see below, Chapter 18), just as the crime bill enacted by Congress the year before increased the number of federal capital offenses by several dozen. True, these statutes largely overlap with death penalty provisions already incorporated in the laws of the states. The chief effect of these new statutes is twofold: They permit the federal prosecutor in a state to preempt jurisdiction from the state prosecutor; and if the federal prosecutor secures a conviction under one of these statutes, it does not matter whether the state law provides a death penalty for the crime in question. Congress has thus effectively nationalized the death penalty. It remains to be seen whether there will be any or many federal prosecutions for crimes in states where the crime in question is not capitally punishable under state law.

Expanding and Modifying the Death Penalty

Chapter 3 presents extracts from a recent (1994) annual survey of state death penalty legislation prepared and distributed by the National Coalition to abolish the Death

Penalty (NCADP). The survey shows that in all but fourteen of the fifty states, one or more bills were filed during 1994 to reinstate, expand, revise, or repeal the death penalty. Most such bills failed to come to a vote, much less win enactment. Among the few bills of some importance that did become law are these: reenactment of the death penalty in Kansas; authorizing the state supreme court to review all death sentences and scrutinize the grounds for the sentence—"proportionality review" (Arizona and Idaho); permitt the jury to hear victim-impact evidence during the penalty phase (Louisiana); and authorizing the death penalty for the reckless killing of a child whom the defendant had previously abused (Tennessee). Perhaps the most extreme (serious?) proposal was offered by the Speaker of the House, Newt Gingrich, who urged Congress to enact a mandatory death penalty for the importation of large quantities of illegal drugs—and then carry out mass executions of those convicted of this crime. In a speech late in August, Gingrich said: "The first time we execute 27 or 30 or 35 people at one time, and they go around Colombia and France and Thailand and Mexico, and they say, 'Hi, would you like to carry some drugs into the U.S.?' the price of carrying drugs will have gone up dramatically."[6]

Capital Crimes

Chapter 4 is devoted to information regarding criminal homicide—the offenders and the victims.[7] Table 4-1 shows that, during the two-decade period of 1974 through 1993, cases of murder and nonnegligent manslaughter have fluctuated from a low in 1984 of 18,690 to a high in 1993 of 24,530. Numerous as these crimes are, in 1993 they constituted less than 0.2 percent of all the violent crimes reported to the FBI.[8] If we shift from the volume to the rate of criminal homicide (Table 4-2), we see that it has fluctuated from a low in 1984–85 of 7.9 victims per 100,000 population to a high in 1980 of 10.2. In 1993, the national criminal homicide rate was slightly lower than what it had been twenty years earlier (9.5 versus 9.8). If we look at the nation's ten leading causes of death (Table 4-3), we see that in 1992 homicide ranked tenth, just behind suicide and AIDS, and well behind the great killers: heart disease, cancer, and stroke. At the same time, for reasons not fully understood, the nation's homicide rate dropped in 1994 for the third year in a row.[9] Finally, if we look at the murder rates for abolition states in the 1990s and compare them with the rates in death penalty states (Table 4-4), we see that the rates are generally lower in the abolition states, although in both kinds of jurisdictions these rates wax and wane.

If we shift from these aggregate numbers to look at the *age, race,* and *gender* of arrested murderers (and assume that the demographic characteristics of those arrested hold true of the offenders not arrested), the following picture emerges: First, criminal homicide is by and large a crime committed by men. In 1993, of the total volume of this crime reported in this category (19,400), almost 90 percent (17,600) of these crimes were committed by men.[10] Likewise, the victims of criminal homicide are predominantly men. A decade ago, the BJS reported that more than three times as many men are murdered as are women;[11] Table 4-5 confirms this pattern. Second, criminal homicide is substantially a crime of the young.[12] In 1993, as the numbers in Table 4-6 show, 60 percent of all arrested offenders were between the ages of fifteen and twenty-four. Elsewhere we learn that in the 1990s so far, the homicide rate is slowly dropping among adults at the same time it is increasing sharply among the young: Between 1985 and 1991, the number of 17-year-old homicide arrestees more than doubled[13] and in the decade 1986–1996 the number of youths ages 14 to 17 arrested for homicide more than tripled.[13]

Finally, criminal homicide is disproportionately a crime committed by nonwhites. In 1993, according to the FBI,[15] out of 20,243 persons reported arrested in this category, all but 41 percent were nonwhite. At a time when African-Americans constituted about 12 percent of the nation's total population, 58 percent of all those arrested for criminal homicide were African-Americans. African-American males are also chiefly the victims of murder; a black man in America has roughly one chance in twenty-eight of being murdered during his lifetime, five times the likelihood a white male has.[16] Given the data reported here on the age, sex, and race of arrested murderers, it would appear that a considerable proportion of all criminal homicide in the United States today is committed by a minority of young black males.

Since data reported elsewhere in this part show that, as of the end of 1994, the nation's death row population was 40 percent African-American and 49 percent white, it may come as a surprise to those who believe the death penalty is blatantly racist in character to learn that black murderers are slightly *less* likely to end up on death row than are their white counterparts. Table 5-9 shows that killers of whites are far more likely to be sentenced to death than are killers of blacks, and the asymmetry in the distribution of racial crossover killings fits this pattern. Killers of blacks (whether white or black) rarely get sentenced to death, much less executed, whereas killers of whites (whether white or black) are far more at risk. As the numbers reported in Table 4-7 show, 90 percent of black murder victims were killed by black offenders and 83 percent of white victims were murdered by white offenders: Murder does not often cross racial lines.[17] This table also shows that at present black murder victims outnumber white murder victims, despite the fact that whites constitute about 80 percent of the nation's population. Murder, in short, is a social problem that plagues African-American communities to a far greater extent than it does the white population. (For more about race and the death penalty, see part V.)

Although murder rarely crosses racial lines, it does cross gender differences: the FBI reports that "9 out of every 10 female victims were murdered by males."[18]

As for the *weapons* used to commit murder, Table 4-8 shows that in the five-year period 1989 to 1993, guns were used in approximately seven of every ten murders—and the weapon of choice is a handgun. Whether effective gun control would result in fewer murders or only in fewer murders caused by handguns is an empirical question not yet answered to everyone's satisfaction. Evidently, long guns (rifles and shotguns)—since they cannot be easily concealed—play a minor role in the murderer's armory.

Table 4-9 shows us that circumstances in which murder is committed are quite varied; verbal disputes of various sorts apparently are the salient provocation. By contrast, brawls arising from the influence of alcohol or narcotics that result in murder are infrequent. So are several types of felony murder (homicide committed in the course of rape, burglary, arson, kidnapping, or other felony). Felony-murder-robbery, typically a crime between strangers, constitutes only 10 percent of all murders; it is the kind of crime most likely to lead to a death sentence. Juvenile gang killings show explosive growth—a 100 percent increase—between 1989 and 1993. Narcotics traffic murders are also a significant fraction of the whole. Whether the death penalty could be expected to serve as an effective deterrent for all or even any of these different types of murder is obviously an important question (it is discussed in some detail in part III).

Death Row Prisoners

Chapter 5 is devoted to statistical data concerning death row prisoners. Table 5-1 presents the racial breakdown (Asian, black, Latino, Native American, white, and unknown) of all persons on the nation's death rows as of the end of 1995. Tables 5-2 and 5-3, covering the two decades 1973–95, report the race and jurisdiction of juveniles (i.e., youths under the age of eighteen) and women sentenced to death, respectively.[19] Table 5-4 reports, state by state, year by year (1974 through 1994), the steady growth of the numbers of persons under death sentence. The next two tables show the final disposition of all death row prisoners (including cases still pending) during the years 1973–94; these data are reported annually (Table 5-5) and by jurisdiction (Table 5-6). (Readers interested in the prior criminal history of those currently on death row should turn to Table 11-1 in chapter 11.)[20]

Prisoners Executed

Table 5-7 shows the number of persons executed since 1977 by each of the five lawful methods of execution. Table 5-8 reports the names, jurisdictions, race, and age (at the time of the crime and at the time of execution) of each of the juveniles executed since 1977. Table 5-9 shows the sensitivity of execution to the race of the victim. It does show that execution of a white for killing a black is not entirely unknown, but it is rare—only two cases since 1977; only thirty have been identified in the nation's history.[21] Table 5-10 shows the number and percentage of all those sentenced to death who were executed in each jurisdiction during years 1973–94. The number ranges from a low of zero (no executions in sixteen death penalty jurisdictions, one of which had imposed no death sentences) to a high of 22 percent in Virginia, followed by Utah with about 17 percent and Texas with about 13 percent. This table also shows that three of the five states with the most death row prisoners were among the states with the least frequent executions.

What does not appear in these tables is the number of executions in which the prisoner ceases to pursue appeals or clemency and accepts death, as Gary Gilmore did in Utah in 1977 when he inaugurated the current era of executions in the United

States. The LDF reports that as of April 1996, 43, or 13 percent, of the 328 executions since 1977 have been consensual.[22] BJS also does not report the number of botched executions, where something goes wrong with the apparatus or the procedure, e.g., the electric chair malfunctions and the prisoner burns before he dies, or the lethal drugs are administered in an incorrect dosage causing the prisoner to die gasping and choking.[23]

Risk of Execution

A clearer picture of the death penalty's role in the nation's current criminal justice system can be obtained by the simple expedient of examining a handful of numbers (rounded off for ease of discussion):

22,000
15,000
13,500
10,000
2–4,000
250
22

The first and largest number—22,000—is the average annual number of criminal homicides reported by the FBI under its rubric of "murder and nonnegligent manslaughter" for the decade 1984–93 (recall Table 4-1). The second number—15,000—is an estimate of the annual average total of arrests for criminal homicide during the same years, based on a nationwide "clearance" (arrest) rate of 66 percent.[24] The third number—13,500—represents the volume of criminal homicide cases actually prosecuted; according to the FBI, this is about 90 percent of those arrested on a charge of criminal homicide.[25] The fourth number—10,000—is an estimate of the total annual average over the same years of convictions for some form of criminal homicide, roughly two-thirds of those arrested[26] and nearly three-fourths of all those prosecuted. If 1988 may be taken as typical, more than half (56 percent) of these convictions were obtained by a guilty plea, more than a third (36 percent) only after a jury trial, and the small remainder (8 percent) by the judge sitting alone.[27]

If we are to use the first four numbers in this list to shed light on the risk of execution, each needs to be recalculated downward so as to exclude all murders, arrests, prosecutions, and convictions in the jurisdictions that do not authorize the death penalty; a murderer in a noncapital jurisdiction runs no risk of execution. (At a guess, such recalculation would result in a reduction of up to 20 percent in each of the four numbers so far discussed.)

The fifth number represents all and only the convicted murderers who are at risk for a death sentence in capital jurisdictions. Only a fraction of murder, defendants are subject to a possible death sentence; homicide convictions for second-degree murder or voluntary manslaughter are not "death-eligible." Neither are all first-degree murders. Those that remain are the murders in which the "aggravating circumstances" are so grave or numerous and the "mitigating circumstances" so slight or few that the jury is receptive to the prosecution's argument for a conviction of capital murder followed by a death sentence.[28] (For a typical list of these two kinds of circumstances as specified by statute, see pp. 203–205.)

The sixth number—250—is the annual average over the same decade of the number of persons sentenced to death (recall Table 5-5). The enormous attrition here between more than two to four thousand death-eligible convictions annually and only 250 or so actual death sentences is largely a result of either the prosecutor's decision not to seek the death penalty in the first place (perhaps as a plea bargain in exchange for the defendant's guilty plea and testimony against codefendants) or the jury's sentencing decision (finding one or more mitigating circumstances that outweigh the aggravating circumstances). The seventh and final number in this set—22—is the average annual number of persons actually executed during the past decade (recall Table 1-3). This number seems to be on the increase. So far during the 1990s the average is more than thirty, and during 1995, fifty-six prisoners were executed—nearly double the number in 1994 and more than in any year since 1957.[29]

Reduced to ratios, what these figures tell us is roughly this:

- One person is executed each year for every 1,000 criminal homicides.
- One person is executed each year for every 700 arrested for criminal homicide.
- One person is executed each year for every 450 convicted of criminal homicide.
- One person is executed each year for every 100 on death row.
- One person exits death row each year by execution for every 10 who are admitted to death row.

There is much that these figures do not tell us, for example, the plea bargaining role played by the death penalty in securing confessions and thus solving crimes that otherwise would be dismissed for want of adequate evidence for a prosecution. Even so, the attrition reflected in these numbers is little short of astounding. One can hardly avoid the inference that, in the recent past, the death penalty—whether measured by the ratio of executions to death sentences, or to homicide convictions, or to the homicides themselves—plays a very small role in the overall "war on crime" endlessly waged by the police, the courts, and the politicians. (Twenty years ago criminologists Norval Morris and Gordon Hawkins put the point even more firmly: The death penalty, they wrote, is of "marginal significance [and] singular inconsequence" to the problem of "effective prevention of crime and the treatment of offenders" (79, 82). The data conveyed in Tables 5-5 and 5-6 (showing the final disposition of all those sentenced to death between 1973 and 1993) and in Table 5-10 (showing the percentage, state by state, of death row prisoners executed in these two decades) reinforce the conviction that actual executions are still something of a rarity and can be averted in many ways, including suicide.

(Suicide while awaiting execution of a death sentence is not identified as such in these BJS tables; it is buried in the columns entitled "Other death" and "Died." For the record, between 1973 and early 1996, forty-five death row prisoners died by their own hands.)[30]

Such subtleties aside, the chief question raised by this set of numbers is what accounts for the extraordinary attrition. Both friends and enemies of capital punishment must wonder how a death penalty system of criminal justice can be taken seriously when in a given year more than twenty thousand murders result in only two dozen or so executions. Some defenders of the death penalty will reply that this attrition represents a reasonably effective winnowing of the very worst offenders from among the bad, which is precisely what we would want a death penalty system to do in a civilized society. Others who favor the death penalty will insist that the death penalty system in today's America must be made more effective (used with greater certainty and frequency) and that the chief obstacles to this end are the seemingly endless, frivolous appeals in state and federal courts. In later chapters we will have an opportunity to consider such complaints in light of more evidence.

Worldwide Status of the Death Penalty

The final chapter in this part presents a brief tabular report on the status of the death penalty around the world, based on the most recent survey by Amnesty International (AI). From its international headquarters in London, AI conducts a vigorous international campaign against torture, detention without charge or trial, summary executions, and the death penalty. As this report shows, our immediate neighbors, Canada (by law) and Mexico (by practice), have abolished the death penalty for all crimes. So have most of the countries of Central and South America, though the British possessions and former colonies in the West Indies retain it. In Western Europe most countries have abolished the death penalty for all crimes; those few that retain it do so only for crimes committed in wartime or under military law. A few other countries are (like Mexico) de facto abolitionist, having carried out no executions in recent decades. In Eastern Europe, however, most of the nations that have emerged out of the erstwhile Soviet Union and Yugoslavia still retain the death penalty; so does Turkey. However, in March 1996, Amnesty International reported that Russia had agreed to an immediate moratorium on executions, as a condition for joining the Council of Europe. Two months later, German news sources reported that Russian President Boris Yeltsin had signed an order to abolish the death penalty; the report did not indicate when the new decree would become effective. Elsewhere in the world, save for Israel, the death penalty is used with some frequency, whether more or less than in earlier decades it is difficult to say. Late in June 1996, a Reuters dispatch reported that "China was believed to have executed hundreds of drug traffickers" after having sentenced nearly 800 to death (Macartney 1996).

No doubt the most remarkable abolitionist step taken in recent years occurred early in June 1995, when the new supreme court of South Africa ruled that the death penalty was unconstitutional because it violated the prohibition against "cruel, inhuman or degrading treatment or punishment." The eleven-member court, ethnically and racially diverse, was unanimous.[31] Only a few years ago South Africa was among the leaders in issuing death sentences and carrying out executions by hanging. At that time, Oxford criminologist Roger Hood voiced the opinion of many observers when he noted: "The situation in South Africa provides little hope for any move toward abolition" (1989:20; for a brief account of the practice of death sentencing and executions in South Africa in the late 1980s, see Amnesty International 1989:204–207).

Is there a worldwide trend toward abolition? There certainly is such a trend in international law, under the leadership of the United Nations and the Council of Europe, which have all but outlawed the death penalty through several human rights declarations, covenants, and treaties, as has been explained in thorough detail by Canadian law professor William Schabas in his book *The Abolition of the Death Penalty in International Law* (1993). The United States, however, has consistently kept itself aloof from all such commitments; an awkward legal situation is rapidly developing for our government as a consequence. (I have provided a brief discussion of its origin in chapter 19.)

Notes

1. Another nongovernmental source of great value is the annual review of death penalty developments in the U.S.A., as well as other reports, published by Amnesty International in London; see Amnesty International 1987, 1992, 1993, 1994, 1995b, 1996a, 1996b.

2. For information regarding capital statutes earlier in this century, see Savitz 1955; Deets 1948; Bye 1919.

3. For more information on the death penalty and juveniles, see Streib 1987, 1988; Merlo 1995. In 1994 the Florida Supreme Court ruled that no one under age sixteen at the time of the crime could be sentenced to death; see *Ft. Lauderdale Sun-Sentinel,* 25 March 1994.

4. Since the Supreme Court's rulings in *Gregg* and allied cases in 1976, the legal definition of capital murder has undergone various changes, tending to make it less a crime of malicious intention (the traditional conception) and more "objective," so that lethal results—whatever the intention—constitute murder. For discussion, see Acker and Lanier 1993a; Givelber 1994.

5. For a discussion of the bills introduced in 1990, see Dingerson 1990–91.

6. *New York Times,* 27 August 1995, p. 14.

7. For recent discursive accounts of homicide in the United States, see, e.g., Danto, Bruhns, and Kutscher 1982; Reidel, Zahn, and Mock 1985; Daly and Wilson 1988; Holmes and Holmes 1994.

8. *UCR 1993,* p. 8.

9. *N.Y. Times,* 24 Oct. 1995, p. A19.

10. *UCR 1993,* p. 226, Table 37.

11. BJS, "The Risk of Violent Crime," 1985, p. 2.

12. See Fox 1995. A graph published in the *Boston Globe* for 27 July 1995, p. 34, shows that the homicide rate among those over age twenty-five is slowly declining (from about 8

per 100,000 population in 1976 to about 5 in 1993), whereas it was twice this rate in 1976 for those (mostly men) between age eighteen and twenty-four, and as of 1993 was five times the rate for those over twenty-five.

13. *N.Y. Times,* 19 Oct. 1992, p. A8.

14. *N.Y. Times,* 12 May 1996, p. 1.

15. *UCR 1993,* p. 235, Table 43.

16. See Colburn 1990; Mydans 1990.

17. This generalization is sharply criticized in Wilbanks 1986. Surprisingly, racial crossover murder receives no discussion in the sources cited in note 7.

18. BJS, "The Risk of Violent Crime," 1985, p. 2.

19. For further information on death sentences and executions for women, see Streib 1990, 1992; Streib and Sametz 1989. See also Rapaport 1990, 1991.

20. For case histories of many death row prisoners, see the annual series *Death Row,* published beginning in 1989 by Glen Hare Publications.

21. See Radelet and Mello 1986; Radelet 1989b; Brown 1995.

22. LDF, "Death Row, U.S.A.," Spring 1996, pp. 1, 10. For discussions of consensual executions, see Urofsky 1984; White 1987.

23. For a discussion of some recent botched executions, see Weinstein and Bessent 1996: 101–106.

24. *UCR 1993,* p. 207. However, elsewhere in this volume (p. 217) the "total arrests" for 1993 is "estimated" at 95 percent of all the criminal homicide reported. As this extremely high percentage is unsupported by any other facts, the lower percentage is used in the text.

25. See the following BJS reports: "Felony Sentences in State Courts 1992," p. 2; "Tracking Offenders, 1984," p. 2; "Tracking Offenders, 1987," p. 2; and "Felony Sentences in State Courts, 1988," p. 4.

26. See *UCR 1993,* p. 287; cf. BJS, "Felony Sentences in State Courts, 1992," p. 5, estimating the prosecution/conviction rate at 65 percent.

27. *Sourcebook of Criminal Justice Statistics 1990,* p. 517, Table 5.34.

28. Baldus, Pulaski and Woodworth, 1990:235.

29. See "56 Executions This Year Are Most Since 1957," *New York Times,* 30 Dec. 1995, p. 28.

30. NAACP, "Death Row, U.S.A.," Spring 1996, p. 1.

31. See *New York Times,* 7 June 1995, pp. A3, A29. The full text of the decision and opinion appears in 16 Human Rights L. J. (30 Sept. 1995):154–208; for a full discussion see Schabas 1995b. For further information on the worldwide status of the death penalty, see Hood 1989, 1996; Hodgkinson and Rutherford 1996.

In addition to the influential global abolitionist agenda of AI, nominally initiated with the founding of AI in 1961 and active since its Stockholm Conference of December 1977, the Transnational Radical Party (created by the Italian Partito Radicale) has recently founded a wholly independent international abolitionist group, Hands Off Cain. The organization held its first congress in Brussels, Belgium, in December 1993. See the 1994 publication by Citizens and Parliamentarians Campaign for the Abolition of the Death Penalty Worldwide by 2000.

It is interesting to note the way in which this organization and the Vatican have (simultaneously but presumably quite independently) seized on the biblical story of Cain and Abel to focus reflection on what is morally wrong with the death penalty. See note 16 in the introduction to part VII.

2

Offenses Punishable by Death

Table 2-1.
Offenses Punishable by Death: State Jurisdictions, 1993

Alabama. Murder during kidnaping, robbery, rape, sodomy, burglary, sexual assault, or arson; murder of a peace officer, correctional officer, or public official; murder while under a life sentence; murder for pecuniary gain or contract; aircraft piracy; murder by a defendant with a previous murder conviction; murder of a witness of a crime; murder when a victim is subpoenaed in a criminal proceeding, when the murder is related to the role of the victim as a witness; murder when a victim is less than 14 years old; murder in which a victim is killed while in a dwelling by a deadly weapon fired from outside the dwelling; murder in which a victim is killed while in a motor vehicle by a deadly weapon fired from outside that vehicle; murder in which a victim is killed by a deadly weapon fired from a motor vehicle (13A-5-40).

Arizona. First-degree murder accompanied by at least 1 of 10 aggravating factors.

Arkansas. Capital murder as defined by Arkansas statute (5-10-101). Felony murder; arson causing death; intentional murder of a law enforcement officer, teacher or school employee; murder of prison, jail, court, or correctional personnel or of military personnel acting in line of duty; multiple murders; intentional murder of a public officeholder or candidate; intentional murder while under life sentence; contract murder.

California. Treason; homicide by a prisoner serving a life term; first-degree murder with special circumstances; train wrecking; perjury causing execution.

Colorado. First-degree murder; kidnaping with death of victim; felony murder. Capital sentencing excludes persons determined to be mentally retarded.

Connecticut. Murder of a public safety or correctional officer; murder for pecuniary gain; murder in the course of a felony; murder by a defendant with a previous conviction for intentional murder; murder while under a life sentence; murder during a kidnaping; illegal sale of cocaine, methadone, or heroin to a person who dies from using these drugs; murder during first-degree sexual assault; multiple murders; the defendant committed the offense(s) with an assault weapon.

Delaware. First-degree murder with aggravating circumstances.

Florida. First-degree murder; capital felonies (FS 921.141); capital drug trafficking felonies (FS 921.142).

Georgia. Murder; kidnaping with bodily injury when the victim dies; aircraft hijacking; treason; kidnaping for ransom when the victim dies.

Idaho. First-degree murder; aggravated kidnaping.

Illinois. First-degree murder accompanied by at least 1 of 12 aggravating factors.

(*continued*)

Table 2-1 (*continued*)

Indiana. Murder with 13 aggravating circumstances.

Kentucky. Aggravated murder; kidnaping when victim is killed.

Louisiana. First-degree murder; treason (La. R.S. 14:30 and 14:113).

Maryland. First-degree murder, either premeditated or during the commission of a felony.

Mississippi. Capital murder includes murder of a peace officer or correctional officer, murder while under a life sentence, murder by bomb or explosive, contract murder, murder committed during specific felonies (rape, burglary, kidnaping, arson, robbery, sexual battery, unnatural intercourse with a child, nonconsensual unnatural intercourse), and murder of an elected official. Capital rape is the forcible rape of a child under 14 years old by a person 18 years or older. Aircraft piracy.

Missouri. First-degree murder (565.020 RSMO).

Montana. Deliberate homicide; aggravated kidnaping when victim or rescuer dies; attempted deliberate homicide, aggravated assault, or aggravated kidnaping by a State prison inmate who has a prior conviction for deliberate homicide or who has been previously declared a persistent felony offender (46-18-303, MCA).

Nebraska. First-degree murder.

Nevada. First-degree murder with 9 aggravating circumstances.

New Hampshire. Contract murder; murder of a law enforcement officer; murder of a kidnaping victim; killing another after being sentenced to life imprisonment without parole.

New Jersey. Purposeful or knowing murder; contract murder.

New Mexico. First-degree murder; felony murder with aggravating circumstances.

North Carolina. First-degree murder (N.C.G.S. 14-17).

Ohio. Assassination; contract murder; murder during escape; murder while in a correctional facility; murder after conviction for a prior purposeful killing or prior attempted murder; murder of a peace officer; murder arising from specified felonies (rape, kidnaping, arson, robbery, burglary); murder of a witness to prevent testimony in a criminal proceeding or in retaliation (O.R.C. secs. 2929.02, 2903.01, 2929.04).

Oklahoma. Murder with malice aforethought; murder arising from specified felonies (forcible rape, robbery with a dangerous weapon, kidnaping, escape from lawful custody, first-degree burglary, arson); murder when the victim is a child who has been injured, tortured, or maimed.

Oregon. Aggravated murder.

Pennsylvania. First-degree murder.

South Carolina. Murder with statutory aggravating circumstances.

South Dakota. First-degree murder; kidnaping with gross permanent physical injury inflicted on the victim; felony murder.

Tennessee. First-degree murder.

Texas. Murder of a public safety officer, fireman, or correctional employee; murder during the commission of specified felonies (kidnaping, burglary, robbery, aggravated rape, arson); murder for remuneration; multiple murders; murder during prison escape; murder by a State prison inmate; murder of an individual under 6 years of age.

(*continued*)

Table 2-1
Offenses Punishable by Death: State Jurisdictions, 1993 (*continued*)

Utah. Aggravated murder (76-5-202, Utah Code annotated).

Virginia. Murder during the commission or attempts to commit specified felonies (abduction, armed robbery, rape, sodomy); contract murder; murder by a prisoner while in custody; murder of a law enforcement officer; multiple murders; murder of a child under 12 years during an abduction; murder arising from drug violations (18.2-31, Virginia Code as amended).

Washington. Aggravated first-degree premeditated murder.

Wyoming. First-degree murder, including both premeditated and felony murder.

Source: BJS, "Capital Punishment, 1993," p. 5, Table 1.

Table 2-2.
Federal Death Penalty, 1994

Newly created (1994) federal crimes punishable by death include:

- Drive-by shootings which result in death (18 U.S.C. § 36);
- Drug trafficking in large quantities, even where no death results (18 U.S.C. § 3591(b)(1));
- Attempting, authorizing or advising the killing of any public officer, juror or witness in a case involving a continuing criminal enterprise—regardless of whether such a killing actually occurs (18 U.S.C. § 3591(b)(2));
- Murder at a United States international airport (18 U.S.C. § 36);
- Murder by an escaped federal prisoner (18 U.S.C. § 1120);
- Murder by a federal life-term prisoner (18 U.S.C. § 1120);
- Murder by gun during federal crimes of violence and drug trafficking offenses (18 U.S.C. § 924(i));
- Murder involving firearm or other dangerous weapon during attack on federal facilities (18 U.S.C. § 930(c));
- Murder of federal jurors and court officers (18 U.S.C. § 1503(b));
- Murder of a federal witness, victim or informant (18 U.S.C. § 1513(a));
- Murder of a state correctional officer by a federal prisoner (18 U.S.C. § 1121);
- Murder of state or local officials engaged in assisting federal law enforcement officials (18 U.S.C. § 1121);
- Murder of a United States national abroad (18 U.S.C. § 1118);
- Murder of United States national abroad by terrorism (18 U.S.C. § 2332);
- Murder within the special maritime and territorial jurisdiction of the United States (18 U.S.C. §§ 2280, 2281);
- Smuggling aliens where death results (8 U.S.C. § 1324(a)(B)(iv));
- Torture resulting in death outside the United States (18 U.S.C. § 2340(A));
- Using weapons of mass destruction (for example, biological weapons or poison gas) which result in death (18 U.S.C. § 2332a).

Existing federal crimes to which a death penalty was added (1994) include:

- Carjacking which results in death (18 U.S.C. § 2119);
- Child molestation committed within federal territorial jurisdiction which results in death (18 U.S.C. § 2245);
- Genocide (18 U.S.C. § 1091);
- Hostage taking which results in death (18 U.S.C. § 1203);
- Murder for hire involving interstate travel or the use of interstate facilities (18 U.S.C. § 1958);
- Murder for the purpose of aiding racketeering activity (18 U.S.C. § 1959);
- Sexual abuse committed within federal territorial jurisdiction resulting in death (18 U.S.C. § 2245);
- Violating a person's federally-protected rights based on race, religion or national origin, where death results (18 U.S.C. §§ 241, 242, 245, 247).

So-called zombie federal statutes (enacted prior to *Furman* but never revised in accordance with the Supreme Court's rulings in *Gregg, Jurek,* and *Profitt*) recently revived (1994) include:

- Aircraft hijacking which results in death (49 U.S.C. § 1473);
- Assassination of the President or Vice-President (18 U.S.C. § 1751(a));
- Assassination of Members of Congress, Cabinet Members, Supreme Court Justices, and major presidential or vice presidential candidates (18 U.S.C. § 351);
- Destroying aircraft, motor vehicles or their facilities where death results (18 U.S.C. § 34);
- Destroying federal property with explosives or by arson where death results (18 U.S.C. § 844(f));
- Destroying property used in interstate commerce with explosives or by arson in a manner resulting in death (18 U.S.C. § 844(i));
- Espionage (18 U.S.C. § 794);
- First degree murder on federal land or federal property (18 U.S.C. § 1111);

(*continued*)

Table 2-2.
Federal Death Penalty, 1994 (*continued*)

- Kidnapping which results in death (18 U.S.C. § 1201);
- Killing or attempted killing by a drug kingpin of a public officer or juror for the purpose of obstructing justice (18 U.S.C. § 3591(b)(2));
- Mailing harmful articles (for example, explosives) where death results (18 U.S.C. § 1716);
- Murder of federal law enforcement officials or employees (18 U.S.C. § 1114);
- Murder of foreign officials or internationally-protected people on United States soil (18 U.S.C. § 1116);
- Robbery of a federally-insured bank where death results (18 U.S.C. § 2113(e));
- Train sabotage which results in death (18 U.S.C. § 1992);
- Transporting or receiving explosives with the intent to kill in a manner resulting in death (18 U.S.C. § 844(d));
- Treason (18 U.S.C. § 2381).

Source: Randall Coyne and Lyn Entzeroth, *Capital Punishment and the Judicial Process,* 1995 Supplement, pp. 79–83.

Table 2-3.
Minimum Age Authorized for Capital Punishment, by Jurisdiction, 1994

Age less than 18	Age 18	None specified
Alabama (16)	California	Arizona
Arkansas (14)[a]	Colorado	Idaho
Delaware (16)	Connecticut[d]	Montana
Georgia (17)	Federal system	Louisiana
Indiana (16)	Illinois	Pennsylvania
Kentucky (16)	Kansas	South Carolina
Mississippi (16)[b]	Maryland	South Dakota[e]
Missouri (16)	Nebraska	Utah
Nevada (16)	New Jersey	
New Hampshire (17)	New Mexico	
North Carolina (17)[c]	Ohio	
Oklahoma (16)	Oregon	
Texas (17)	Tennessee	
Virginia (15)	Washington	
Wyoming (16)		
Florida (16)		

Note: Reporting by States reflects interpretations by State attorney general offices and may differ from previously reported ages.

[a]See Arkansas Code Ann.9-27-318(b)(1)(Repl. 1991).

[b]Minimum age defined by status is 13, but effective age is 16 based on an interpretation of U.S. Supreme Court decisions by the State attorney general's office.

[c]Age required is 17 unless the murderer was incarcerated for murder when a subsequent murder occurred; the age then may be 14.

[d]See Conn. Gen. Stat. 53a-46a(g)(1).

[e]Juveniles may be transferred to adult court. Age may be a mitigating circumstance. No one under age 10 can commit a crime.

Source: Bureau of Justice Statistics, "Capital Punishment, 1994," p. 5, Table 3.

3

Proposed State Death Penalty Legislation, 1994

Table 3-1.
Proposed State Death Penalty Legislation, 1994

Alabama	
Bills Filed	*Status*
SB 23, making capitally punishable any killing of one or more persons during a continuous criminal enterprise.	Died on Senate calendar
SB 269, making capitally punishable three kinds of homicide.	Died on Senate calendar
HB 269, same as SB 269.	Died in House committee
HB 273, same as HB 269.	Enacted
HB 936, making capitally punishable killing a person by a deadly weapon fired into a crowd.	Died in House committee
Alaska	
Bills Filed	*Status*
SB 127, reinstating the death penalty for first-degree murder.	Died in Senate committee
HB 162, same as SB 127.	Died in House committee
Arizona	
Bills Filed	*Status*
SB 1001, making capitally punishable death resulting from child molestation.	Died in Senate committee
SB 1002, authorizing state supreme court review of all capital cases.	Enacted
SB 1047, prohibiting the death penalty where the defendant is able to prove insanity.	Died in Senate committee
HB 2307, prohibiting the death penalty for persons under 18 at the time of the crime, persons mentally retarded, and authorizing life without possibility of parole as the alternative sentence to death.	Died in House committee

(*continued*)

Table 3-1 (*continued*)

Bills Filed	*Status*
Arkansas	
No legislative session in 1994.	
California	
SB 207, revising rules on the use of a defendant's record in appeals.	Assembly committee
AB 177, revising the law governing county jurisdiction authority to try a capital case involving multiple felonies in several counties.	Died in Assembly committee
AB 961, authorizing state reimbursement to Marin County for certain costs in capital cases.	Senate committee
AB 1159, imposing the death penalty on anyone guilty of a violent offense who has been found guilty of two or more prior violent offenses.	Died in Assembly committee
AB 1415, permitting anyone 16 or 17 charged with murder to be tried as a capital defendant.	Died in Assembly committee
AB 1455, prohibiting anyone mentally retarded from being sentenced to death.	Died in Assembly committee
AB 1507, authorizing a death sentence to be carried out without further proceedings after expiry of a stay.	Died in Assembly committee
AB 2403, authorizing the court to ignore a petition for stay of execution unless signed by the defendant.	In Senate committee
AB 2443, imposing the death penalty on anyone convicted of first-degree murder with conviction of three or more prior violent felonies.	In Assembly committee
Initiative 631, imposing a mandatory death penalty on anyone guilty of first-degree murder, and reducing the minimum age for capital punishment from 18 to 16.	Failed
Colorado	
SB 136, creating additional aggravating circumstances.	Enacted
Connecticut	
HB 5708, requiring imposition of a death sentence if aggravating factors outweigh mitigating factors.	Vetoed
HB 5709, relieving state supreme court of duty to give proportionate review in capital cases.	Died on Senate calendar

(*continued*)

Table 3-1.
Proposed State Death Penalty Legislation, 1994 (*continued*)

Bills Filed	*Status*
Delaware	
SB 57, establishing the time of day for executions.	Enacted
SB 92, authorizing five new aggravating circumstances.	Enacted
SB 212, requiring automatic review of a death sentence by higher court, unless waived by defendant.	Died on Senate calendar
HB 222, repealing the death penalty.	Died in House committee
Florida	
SB 294, authorizing continuation of exemption of publicity identifying public executioner(s).	Passed in Senate, died in House
SB 1214, providing for continued effect of execution warrants and related matters.	Died in Senate committee
SB 1984, authorizing a death penalty for anyone convicted for the third time of certain sexual batteries.	Died in Senate committee
HB 125, identical with SB 1214.	Died in House committee
HB 353, prohibiting repeal of exemption requiring publicly identifying public executioner.	Enacted
Georgia	
SB 440, revising law governing detention of a juvenile accused of a capital offense.	Enacted
SB 441, imposing death or life without possibility of parole for a defendant convicted of a serious violent felony after having been convicted of a prior violent felony but not sentenced to death.	Enacted
SB 483, overlaps with SB 441, and restricts the activities of such a convict while in prison.	Died in Senate committee
SR 395, to amend the state constitution to prohibit pardon of anyone whose death sentence was commuted to life imprisonment unless at least 25 years of that sentence had been served.	Passed in Senate for inclusion on 1994 ballot
SR 405, to amend the state constitution to require a life sentence without possibility of parole for anyone convicted of a serious violent felony who has two such prior convictions.	Died in Senate committee
HB 1198, imposing the death penalty for a drive-by homicide.	Enacted

(*continued*)

Table 3-1 (*continued*)

Hawaii	
Bills Filed	*Status*
SB 2740, to restore the death penalty for first-degree murder.	Died in Senate committee
Idaho	
Bills Filed	*Status*
SB 1302, authorizing state supreme court to conduct proportionality review of all death sentences.	Enacted
Illinois	
Bills Filed	*Status*
SB 243, enacting additional aggravating circumstances.	In Senate committee
SB 244, enacting additional aggravating circumstances.	In Senate committee
HB 2167, essentially identical to SB 244.	Under study
HB 3089, expanding the list of felonies in which any homicide is felony murder.	On House calendar
Indiana	
Bills Filed	*Status*
HB 1002, prohibiting execution of the mentally retarded.	Died in House committee
HB 1063, enacting additional aggravating circumstances and authorizing a sentence of life in prison without possibility of parole for anyone not sentenced to death when one or more aggravating circumstances is present.	Enacted
Iowa	
Bills Filed	*Status*
No bills filed for 1994.	
Kansas	
Bills Filed	*Status*
SB 473, restoring the death penalty for first-degree murder.	Enacted
HB 2578, authorizing the death penalty for certain crimes.	Passed in House
Kentucky	
Bills Filed	*Status*
SB 155, providing life imprisonment without possibility of parole as the alternative to a death sentence.	Died in Senate committee
SB 265, authorizing use of statistical evidence to show racial bias in death sentencing.	Died in Senate Committee
HB 22, authorizing death by lethal injection and related regulations.	Died in House committee

(*continued*)

Table 3-1.
Proposed State Death Penalty Legislation, 1994 (*continued*)

HB 138, authorizing life without possibility of parole or life with possibility of parole after 20 years as alternatives to a death sentence, and requiring the trial judge in a capital case to conduct a sentencing hearing.	Died in House committee
HB 197, increasing the length of prison term for a defendant not sentenced to death.	Died in House committee
HB 375, transferring any juvenile 14 or older charged with a capital crime to trial as an adult.	Died in House committee
HB 412, equivalent to SB 155.	Died in House committee
HB 601, augmenting the list of aggravating circumstances.	Died in Senate committee
Louisiana	
Bills Filed	*Status*
HB 1, requiring jury in a capital case to hear victim-impact evidence.	Enacted
HB 85, prohibiting death or life sentence prisoner from applying for pardon prior to serving 10 years.	Vetoed
HB 191, abolishing the death penalty.	Died in committee
HB 208, authorizing the death penalty for aggravated rape when victim is under 12.	Died in committee
HB 326, identical with HB 85	Died in committee
HB 331, identical with HB 1.	Died in committee
HB 384, requiring a death sentence to be carried out within 5 years of its imposition.	Died in Committee
Maine	
Bills Filed	*Status*
No bills filed for 1994.	
Maryland	
Bills Filed	*Status*
SB 74, expanding the list of aggravating circumstances.	Died in House committee
SB 80, allowing a death-sentenced prisoner to waive an automatic stay of execution.	Died in Senate committee
SB 251, altering deadline for filing postconviction petition and shortening the period of automatic stay of execution.	Died in Senate committee
SB 303, altering various procedural requirements in death penalty cases.	Died in Senate committee
SB 304, changing the method of execution to lethal injection.	Died in Senate committee
SB 305, providing a referendum to modify change of venue conditions in capital trials.	Died in House committee

(*continued*)

Table 3-1 *(continued)*

SB 440, authorizing use of statistics to establish influence of race in capital sentencing.	Died in Senate committee
HB 137, substantially identical to SB 304.	Died in House committee
HB 485, companion bill to SB 304.	Died in House committee
HB 498, substantially equivalent to SB 304.	Enacted
HB 499, companion bill to SB 303.	Died on Senate floor
HB 791, companion bill to SB 440.	Died in House committee
HB 806, proposing various changes in substantive and procedural laws concerning the death penalty.	Died in House committee
HB 1006, overlaps with SB 80, and expands waiver by capital defendants of certain rights.	Died in House committee
HB 1149, includes provisions of SB 304 and HB 498, and redefines the numbers and kinds of persons eligible to observe an execution.	Died in House committee
Massachusetts	
Bills Filed	*Status*
HB 1625, restoring the death penalty for first-degree murder.	Died in Joint committee
HB 2197, identical to HB 1625.	Died in Joint committee
HB 4285, restoring the death penalty for several different kinds of murder.	Died in Joint committee
SB 147, enacting the death penalty for large-scale drug trafficking.	Died in Joint committee
Michigan	
Bills Filed	*Status*
SJR F, would amend the state constitution to permit reinstatement of the death penalty.	In Senate committee
Minnesota	
Bills Filed	*Status*
No bills filed for 1994.	
Mississippi	
Bills Filed	*Status*
SB 2441, abolishing requirement that physician attend execution.	Died in Senate committee
SB 2626, prohibiting a death penalty for anyone mentally retarded.	Died on Senate calendar
SB 2701, imposing requirements on jury sentencing to death a defendant for carnal knowledge of a child under 14.	Died in Senate committee

(continued)

Table 3-1.
Proposed State Death Penalth Legislation, 1994 (*continued*)

SB 2875, authorizing trial judge to sentence defendant to life in prison without possibility of parole.	Died in Senate committee
SB 2881, regulating trial jurisdiction in capital cases when multiple offenses are involved.	Died in Senate committee
SB 2928, authorizing replacement of trial judge unable to conduct presentencing hearing.	Died in Senate committee
SB 3097, requiring state supreme court to review all death sentences.	Died on Senate calendar
HB 114, authorizing trial jury to sentence defendant to life without possibility of parole as alternative to a death sentence.	Enacted
HB 390, identical to SB 2875	Died in House committee
HB 1002, requiring medical authority to witness and certify death of an executed prisoner.	Enacted
HB 1005, authorizing death by lethal injection in case of failure of gas chamber.	Died in House committee
HB 1130, prohibiting a death penalty for anyone mentally retarded.	Died in House committee
HB 1160, prohibiting a death penalty for anyone under 18 at the time of the crime.	Died in House committee
HB 1378, providing for reweighing and harmless error review.	Died in House committee
HB 1479, overlaps with SB 2928; requires trial judge to impose sentence in capital cases, and changes aggravating and mitigating circumstances.	Died in House committee
Missouri	
Bills Filed	*Status*
SB 447, prohibits a death penalty for anyone under 16 at the time of the crime.	Died on Senate calendar
HB 1122, authorizes the death penalty for anyone who kidnaps a person under 14.	Died in House committee
Montana	
Bills Filed	*Status*
No session in 1994.	
North Carolina	
Bills Filed	*Status*
SB 63, providing that a death sentence may be inflicted in public either by electrocution, hanging, lethal gas, or lethal injection in county seat where crime occurred.	Died in Senate committee
HB 2, authorizing life without possibility of parole as another alternative sentence to death.	Enacted

(*continued*)

Table 3-1 (*continued*)

HB 39, requires a life sentence without possibility of parole, unless a death sentence is imposed, for anyone convicted for the third time as a violent habitual felon.	Enacted
HB 47, substantially equivalent to HB 39.	Died in House committee
HB 1062, prohibiting the death penalty for anyone mentally retarded.	Died in conference committee
HB 5112, making killing of a law officer a capital offense.	Died in House committee
North Dakota	
Bills Filed	*Status*
No session in 1994.	
Nevada	
Bills Filed	*Status*
No session in 1994.	
New Hampshire	
Bills Filed	*Status*
No bills filed for 1994.	
New Jersey	
Bills Filed	*Status*
SB 263, providing life without possibility of parole for any prisoner whose death sentence is overturned on appeal.	In Senate committee
SB 579, imposing a mandatory death penalty for murder of a law officer while on duty.	In Senate committee
AB 1053, substantially equivalent to SB 263.	In Assembly committee
AB 1238, revising aggravating circumstances.	In Assembly committee
AB 1703, substantially equivalent to SB 263.	In Assembly committee
New Mexico	
Bills Filed	*Status*
No bills filed for 1994.	
New York	
Bills Filed	*Status*
SB 3139, reinstating the death penalty for first-degree murder.	In Senate committee
SB 3254, enacting the death penalty for felonious bombing.	In Senate committee
SB 6350, reinstating the death penalty for first-degree murder, and increasing the scope of capitally punishable murder.	Vetoed

(*continued*)

Table 3-1.
Proposed State Death Penalty Legislation, 1994 (*continued*)

SB 6406, revising criminal procedures to provide for administering the death penalty.	In Senate committee
SB 6658, imposing the death penalty for anyone convicted of a violent felony after having two prior violent felony convictions.	In Senate committee
SB 6712, introducing procedures for imposing the death penalty, and an alternative sentence of life in prison without possibility of parole.	In Senate committee
AB 5208, companion bill to SB 3139	In Assembly committee
AB 9237, providing a constitutional amendment to allow reinstatement of the death penalty without regard to executive approval.	Died in Assembly committee
AB 9666, substantially equivalent to SB 6712.	Died in Assembly committee
AB 10039, imposing the death penalty for murder.	Died in Assembly committee
Ohio	
Bills Filed	*Status*
SB 92, expanding the list of aggravating circumstances.	In Senate committee
SB 183, limiting number of postconviction appeals by a death row prisoner.	In Senate committee
SB 195, permitting victim-impact testimony during sentencing phase of a capital trial.	In Senate committee
SB 253, expanding the list of aggravating circumstances.	In Senate committee
HB 161, providing a life sentence without possibility of parole for certain persons not sentenced to death.	Passed in House; in Senate committee
HB 253, prohibiting imposing the death penalty on anyone mentally retarded.	In House committee
HB 610, expands the list of aggravating circumstances.	In House committee
HB 689, providing life in prison without possibility of parole as the only alternative to a death sentence.	In House committee
HJR 15, placing on the ballot a requirement that the state supreme court consider all appeals in capital cases but have discretion to refuse review in all other postconviction reviews.	Passed Senate committee, filed with secretary of state
Oklahoma	
Bills Filed	*Status*
SB 416, abolishing the death penalty for rape.	Died in Senate committee
SB 468, identical to SB 416.	Died in Senate committee
HB 1249, substantially revising procedural law in capital cases.	In Conference committee

(*continued*)

Table 3-1 (*continued*)

HB 1517, revising time between death sentencing and execution and authorizing due notice of execution date.	Died in House committee
HB 1888, denying bail to anyone under indictment for a capital offense.	Died in Senate committee
Oregon	
Bills Filed	*Status*
No session in 1994.	
Pennsylvania	
Bills Filed	*Status*
SB 174, prohibiting a death sentence for the mentally retarded.	In Senate committee
SB 175, prohibiting a death sentence for anyone 17 or younger at the time of the crime.	In Senate committee
SB 802, requiring governor to sign a death warrant within 6 months after the date a death sentence is upheld by state supreme court.	In Senate committee
HB 313, substantially equivalent to SB 174.	In House committee
HB 660, prohibiting a death sentence for anyone 18 or younger at the time of the crime, and for anyone mentally retarded.	In House committee
HB 2050, requiring the state supreme court to notify the governor within 60 days of upholding a death sentence.	In House committee
HB 2198, incorporating HB 2050 and also providing for the secretary of corrections to issue a death warrant upon failure of the governor to do so within the prescribed time period.	Vetoed; on Senate floor
Rhode Island	
Bills Filed	*Status*
SB 2033, submitting to voters a nonbinding referendum on reinstating the death penalty.	Died in Senate committee
SB 2035, establishing lethal gas as the method of execution.	Died in Senate committee
SB 3111, submitting to voters a proposition amending the state constitution to permit the death penalty.	Died in Senate committee
HB 7848, enacting a death penalty for terrorist activity and accompanying procedures.	Died in House committee
HB 8405, introducing the death penalty for first-degree murder.	Died in House committee
HB 8406, substantially equivalent to SB 3111.	Died in House committee
HB 9030, enacting a death penalty for murder of a police officer or firefighter and accompanying procedures.	Died in House committee

(*continued*)

Table 3-1.
Proposed State Death Penalty Legislation, 1994 (*continued*)

HB 9128, providing a mandatory death penalty for killing a law enforcement officer on duty.	Died in House committee
South Carolina	
Bills Filed	*Status*
SB 72, permitting a death sentence to be issued if only 10 of 12 jurors favor imposing it.	Died in Senate committee
SB 415, repealing the death sentence for murder and substituting life in prison without possibility of parole.	Died in Senate committee
HB 4465, identical to SB 415.	Died in House committee
HB 4675, identical to SB 72.	Died in House committee
HB 5013, revising a variety of procedures in capital cases.	Died in House committee
South Dakota	
Bills Filed	*Status*
SB 112, abolishing the death penalty.	Died in Senate committee
Tennessee	
Bills Filed	*Status*
SB 43, enacting the death penalty for reckless killing of a child owing to aggravated child abuse.	Enacted
SB 411, companion to HB 213.	Died in Senate committee
SB 632, abolishing the electric chair and mandating death by lethal injection if the condemned prisoner refuses to choose among hanging, the firing squad, and lethal injection.	Died in Senate committee
SB 1314, authorizing life in prison without possibility of parole as another alternative to the death penalty.	Died in Senate committee
SB 1384, identical with SB 1314.	Died in Senate committee
SB 2200, expanding the death penalty to the crime of soliciting to commit first-degree murder.	Died in Senate committee
HJR 48, amending the state constitution to impose mandatory death penalty for first-degree murder.	Died in Senate committee
HB 1089, barring postconviction appeals filed more than 5 years after initial state court review.	Died in House committee
HB 213, identical to SB 43.	Enacted
HB 598, barring postconviction review of a death sentence filed more than 5 years after initial state supreme court review.	Died in House committee
HB 764, companion to SB 632.	Died in Senate committee
HB 1088, barring postconviction appeal of a death sentence if filed more than 3 years after the trial court's judgment becomes final.	Died in House committee

(*continued*)

Table 3-1 (*continued*)

HB 1089, companion to SB 1314.	Died in House committee
HB 1533, companion to SB 1384.	Died in House committee
Texas	
Bills Filed	*Status*
No session in 1994.	
Utah	
Bills Filed	*Status*
No bills filed for 1994.	
Vermont	
Bills Filed	*Status*
No bills filed for 1994.	
Virginia	
Bills Filed	*Status*
SB 142, requiring the trial court in a capital case to complete a capital murder sentencing verdict form.	Died in Senate committee
SB 245, expanding the definition of capital murder.	Died in Senate committee
SB 246, expanding the definition of capital murder.	Carried over to 1995 session
SB 364, expanding the definition of capital murder.	Carried over to 1995 session
HJR 402, establishing a joint committee to study procedures in capital cases.	Approved; committee in process of formation
HB 212, authorizing court appointment of an investigator and expert witnesses to assist counsel for indigent capital defendant.	Vetoed
HB 213, permitting a death row prisoner to file at any time with the trial court a claim of innocence, and the court to reopen the case if the claim is probably true.	Died in House committee
HB 274, expanding the definition of capital murder.	Carried over to 1995 session
HB 431, limiting the number of victim's family members who may witness the execution of their loved one's murderer.	Died on Senate floor
HB 862, allowing death row prisoner to choose between the electric chair and lethal injection.	Enacted
Washington	
Bills Filed	*Status*
HB 2269, lowering the age of death eligibility to 16 at the time of the crime.	Died in House committee
West Virginia	
Bills Filed	*Status*
HB 4060, reinstating the death penalty for first-degree murder.	Died in House committee

(*continued*)

Table 3-1
Proposed State Death Penalty Legislation, 1994 (*continued*)

Wisconsin	
Bills Filed	*Status*
SB 30, reinstating the death penalty for first-degree murder.	Died in Senate committee
SJR 42, authorizing an advisory referendum on whether to reenact the death penalty for the murder of a child during first-degree sexual assault of a child.	Died in Senate committee
SJR 43, authorizing an advisory referendum on whether the legislature should reenact the death penalty for certain kinds of first-degree murder.	Died in Senate committee
SJR 96, identical with SJR 42.	Died in Senate committee
AB 123, reinstating the death penalty or life imprisonment without possibility of parole for first-degree murder by anyone 16 or older at the time of the crime.	Died in Assembly committee
AB 170, reintroducing the death penalty or life in prison without possible parole for first-degree murder (expanded) by anyone 16 or older at the time of the crime.	Died in Assembly committee
AB 358, identical with AB 170.	Died in Assembly committee
AB 835, reintroducing the death penalty for first-degree murder and revising parole eligibility.	Died in Assembly committee
Wyoming	
Bills Filed	*Status*
No bills filed for 1994.	

Source: NCADP, *1994 Survey of State Legislation* [1995]; status reported as of 25 July 1994.

4

Criminal Homicide

Table 4-1.
Volume of Crimes Against the Person, Annually, 1974–93

Population[1]	Crime Index total[2]	Violent crime[3]	Property crime	Murder and non-negligent man-slaughter	Forcible rape	Robbery	Aggra-vated assault
Population by year:							
1974-211,392,000	10,253,400	974,720	9,278,700	20,710	55,400	442,400	456,210
1975-213,124,000	11,292,400	1,039,710	10,252,700	20,510	56,090	470,500	492,620
1976-214,659,000	11,349,700	1,004,210	10,345,500	18,780	57,080	427,810	500,530
1977-216,332,000	10,984,500	1,029,580	9,955,000	19,120	63,500	412,610	534,350
1978-218,059,000	11,209,000	1,085,550	10,123,400	19,560	67,610	426,930	571,460
1979-220,099,000	12,249,500	1,208,030	11,041,500	21,460	76,390	480,700	629,480
1980-225,349,264	13,408,300	1,344,520	12,063,700	23,040	82,990	565,840	672,650
1981-229,146,000	13,423,800	1,361,820	12,061,900	22,520	82,500	592,910	663,900
1982-231,534,000	12,974,400	1,322,390	11,652,000	21,010	78,770	553,130	669,480
1983-233,981,000	12,108,600	1,258,090	10,850,500	19,310	78,920	506,570	653,290
1984-236,158,000	11,881,800	1,273,280	10,608,500	18,690	84,230	485,010	685,350
1985-238,740,000	12,431,400	1,328,800	11,102,600	18,980	88,670	497,870	723,250
1986-241,077,000	13,211,900	1,489,170	11,722,700	20,610	91,460	542,780	834,320
1987-243,400,000	13,508,700	1,484,000	12,024,700	20,100	91,110	517,700	855,090
1988-245,807,000	13,923,100	1,566,220	12,356,900	20,680	92,490	542,970	910,090
1989-248,239,000	14,251,400	1,646,040	12,605,400	21,500	94,500	578,330	951,710
1990-248,709,873	14,475,600	1,820,130	12,655,500	23,440	102,560	639,270	1,054,860
1991-252,177,000	14,872,900	1,911,770	12,961,100	24,700	106,590	687,730	1,092,740
1992-255,082,000	14,438,200	1,932,270	12,505,900	23,760	109,060	672,480	1,126,970
1993-257,908,000	14,141,000	1,924,190	12,216,800	24,530	104,810	659,760	1,135,100
Percent change: number of offenses:							
1993/1992	−2.1	−.4	−2.3	+3.2	−3.9	−1.9	+.7
1993/1989	−.8	+16.9	−3.1	+14.1	+10.9	+14.1	+19.3
1993/1984	+19.0	+51.1	+15.2	+31.2	+24.4	+36.0	+65.6

(*continued*)

Table 4-1.

Volume of Crimes Against the Person, Annually, 1974–93 (*continued*)

[1]Populations are Bureau of the Census provisional estimates as of July 1, except 1980 and 1990 which are the decennial census counts.

[2]Because of rounding, the offenses may not add to totals.

[3]Violent crimes are offenses of murder, forcible rape, robbery, and aggravated assault. Property crimes are offenses of burglary, larceny-theft, and motor vehicle theft. Data are not included for the property crime of arson.

Complete data for 1993 were not available for the states of Illinois and Kansas; therefore, it was necessary that their crime counts be estimated.

Source: Crime in the United States 1993, p. 58, Table 1.

Table 4-2.
Rate of Crimes Against the Person, Annually, 1974–93

	Crime Index Total[2]	Violent crime[3]	Murder and non-negligent man-slaughter	Forcible rape	Rob-bery	Aggra-vated assault
Year:						
1974	4,850.4	461.1	9.8	26.2	209.3	215.8
1975	5,298.5	487.8	9.6	26.3	220.8	231.1
1976	5,287.3	467.8	8.8	26.6	199.3	233.2
1977	5,077.6	475.9	8.8	29.4	190.7	247.0
1978	5,140.3	497.8	9.0	31.0	195.8	262.1
1979	5,565.5	548.9	9.7	34.7	218.4	286.0
1980	5,950.0	596.6	10.2	36.8	251.1	298.5
1981	5,858.2	594.3	9.8	36.0	258.7	289.7
1982	5,603.6	571.1	9.1	34.0	238.9	289.2
1983	5,175.0	537.7	8.3	33.7	216.5	279.2
1984	5,031.3	539.2	7.9	35.7	205.4	290.2
1985	5,207.1	556.6	7.9	37.1	208.5	302.9
1986	5,480.4	617.7	8.6	37.9	225.1	346.1
1987	5,550.0	609.7	8.3	37.4	212.7	351.3
1988	5,664.2	637.2	8.4	37.6	220.9	370.2
1989	5,741.0	663.1	8.7	38.1	233.0	383.4
1990	5,820.3	731.8	9.4	41.2	257.0	424.1
1991	5,897.8	758.1	9.8	42.3	272.7	433.3
1992	5,660.2	757.5	9.3	42.8	263.6	441.8
1993	5,482.9	746.1	9.5	40.6	255.8	440.1
Percent change: rate per 100,000 inhabitants:[1]						
1993/1992	−3.1	−1.5	+2.2	−5.1	−3.0	−.4
1993/1989	−4.5	+12.5	+9.2	+6.6	+9.8	+14.8
1993/1984	+9.0	+38.4	+20.3	+13.7	+24.5	+51.7

[1]Populations are Bureau of the Census provisional estimates as of July 1, except 1980 and 1990 which are the decennial census counts.

[2]Because of rounding, the offenses may not add to totals.

[3]Violent crimes are offenses of murder, forcible rape, robbery, and aggravated assault. Property crimes are offenses of burglary, larceny-theft, and motor vehicle theft. Data are not included for the property crime of arson.

Complete data for 1993 were not available for the states of Illinois and Kansas; therefore, it was necessary that their crime counts be estimated. See "Offense Estimation," page 376 for details.

All rates were calculated on the offenses before rounding.

Source: Crime in the United States 1993, p. 58, Table 1.

Table 4-3.
Ten Leading Causes of Death, 1992

Rank	Cause of death	Number[1]	Death rate[2]	Percent of total deaths
	All causes	2,177,000	853.3	100.0
1.	Heart disease	720,480	282.5	33.1
2.	Cancer	521,090	204.3	23.9
3.	Stroke	143,640	56.3	6.6
4.	Chronic obstructive lung diseases and allied conditions	91,440	35.8	4.2
5.	Accidents and adverse effects	86,310	33.8	4.0
	Motor vehicle accidents	41,710	16.4	1.9
	All other accidents and adverse effects	44,600	17.5	2.0
6.	Pneumonia and influenza	76,120	29.8	3.5
7.	Diabetes mellitus	50,180	19.7	2.3
8.	Human immunodeficiency virus (HIV) infection[3]	33,590	13.2	1.5
9.	Suicide	29,760	11.7	1.4
10.	Homicide and legal intervention	26,570	10.4	1.2

(1) Data are provisional, estimated from a 10 percent sample of deaths. Figures may not add to totals due to rounding. Rates have been recomputed based on revised population estimates. (2) Per 100,000 population. (3) HIV is the virus that causes AIDS.

Source: National Center for Health Statistics, U.S. Department of Health and Human Services, reprinted in *The World Almanac and Book of Facts 1994,* p. 956

Table 4-4.
Rates of Criminal Homicide, 1990–94, per Hundred Thousand Population, by Type of Punishment and Jurisdiction

1990				1991			
Jurisdiction	Prison Sentence	Death	Rate	Jurisdiction	Prison Sentence	Death	Rate
Alaska	7.5	Ala.	11.6	Alaska	7.4	Ala.	11.5
D.C.	77.8	Ariz.	7.7	D.C.	80.6	Ariz.	7.8
Hawaii	4.0	Ark.	10.3	Hawaii	4.9	Ark.	11.1
Iowa	1.9	Cal.	11.9	Iowa	2.0	Cal.	12.7
Kan.	4.0	Col.	4.2	Kan.	6.1	Col.	5.9
Maine	2.4	Conn.	5.1	Maine	1.2	Conn.	5.7
Mass.	4.0	Del.	5.0	Mass.	4.2	Del.	5.4
Mich.	10.4	Fla.	10.7	Mich.	10.8	Fla.	9.4
Minn.	2.7	Geo.	11.8	Minn.	3.0	Geo.	12.8
N.Y.	14.5	Idaho	2.7	N.Y.	14.2	Idaho	1.8
N.D.	0.8	Ill.	10.3	N.D.	1.1	Ill.	11.3
R.I.	4.8	Ind.	6.2	R.I.	3.7	Ind.	7.5
Vt.	2.3	Ky.	7.2	Vt.	2.1	Ky.	6.8
W. Va.	5.7	La.	17.2	W. Va.	6.2	La.	16.9
Wisc.	4.6	Md.	11.5	Wisc.	4.8	Md.	11.7
		Miss.	12.2			Miss.	12.8
		Mo.	8.8			Mo.	10.5
		Mont.	4.9			Mont.	2.6
		Neb.	2.7			Neb.	3.3
		Nev.	9.7			Nev.	11.8
		N.H.	1.9			N.H.	3.6
		N.J.	5.6			N.J.	5.2
		N.M.	9.2			N.M.	10.5
		N.C.	10.7			N.C.	11.4
		Ohio	6.1			Ohio	7.2
		Ok.	8.0			Ok.	7.2
		Ore.	3.8			Ore.	4.6
		Penn.	6.7			Penn.	6.3
		S.C.	11.2			S.C.	11.3
		S.D.	2.0			S.D.	1.7
		Tenn.	10.5			Tenn.	11.0
		Texas	14.1			Texas	15.3
		Utah	3.0			Utah	2.9
		Va.	8.8			Va.	9.3
		Wash.	4.9			Wash.	4.2
		Wy.	4.9			Wy.	3.3

Source: FBI, *Uniform Crime Reports,* 1991, pp. 60–66, Table 4; *Uniform Crime Reports,* 1993, pp. 60–66, Table 4.

Table 4-4.
Rates of Criminal Homicide, 1990–1994, per Hundred Thousand Population, by Type of Punishment and Jurisdiction (*continued*)

1992				1993			
Jursidiction	Prison Sentence	Death	Rate	Jurisdiction	Prison Sentence	Death	Rate
Alaska	7.5	Ala.	11.0	Alaska	9.0	Ala.	11.6
D.C.	75.2	Ariz.	8.1	D.C.	78.5	Ariz.	8.6
Hawaii	3.6	Ark.	10.8	Hawaii	3.8	Ark.	10.2
Iowa	1.6	Cal.	12.7	Iowa	2.3	Cal.	13.1
Kan.	6.0	Col.	6.2	Kan.	6.4	Col.	5.8
Maine	1.7	Conn.	5.1	Maine	1.6	Conn.	6.3
Mass.	3.6	Del.	4.6	Mass.	3.9	Del.	5.0
Mich.	9.9	Fla.	9.0	Mich.	9.8	Fla.	8.9
Minn.	3.3	Geo.	11.0	Minn.	3.4	Geo.	11.4
N.Y.	13.2	Idaho	3.5	N.Y.	13.3	Idaho	2.9
N.D.	1.9	Ill.	11.4	N.D.	1.7	Ill.	11.4
R.I.	3.6	Ind.	8.2	R.I.	3.9	Ind.	7.5
Vt.	2.1	Ky.	5.8	Vt.	3.6	Ky.	6.6
W. Va.	6.3	La.	17.4	W. Va.	6.9	La.	20.3
Wisc.	4.4	Md.	12.1	Wisc.	4.4	Md.	12.7
		Miss.	12.2			Miss.	13.5
		Mo.	10.5			Mo.	11.3
		Mont.	2.9			Mont.	3.0
		Neb.	4.2			Neb.	3.9
		Nev.	10.9			Nev.	10.4
		N.H.	1.6			N.H.	2.0
		N.J.	5.1			N.J.	5.3
		N.M.	8.9			N.M.	8.0
		N.C.	10.6			N.C.	11.3
		Ohio	6.6			Ohio	6.0
		Ok.	6.5			Ok.	8.4
		Ore.	4.7			Ore.	4.6
		Penn.	6.2			Penn.	6.8
		S.C.	10.4			S.C.	10.3
		S.D.	0.6			S.D.	3.4
		Tenn.	10.4			Tenn.	10.2
		Texas	12.7			Texas	11.9
		Utah	3.0			Utah	3.1
		Va.	8.8			Va.	8.3
		Wash.	5.0			Wash.	5.2
		Wy.	3.6			Wy.	3.4

Table 4-5.
Murder Victims, by Race and Sex, 1993

Race of victims	Total	Sex of victims: Male	Female	Unknown
Total white victims	10,709	7,764	2,945	
Total black victims	11,795	9,642	2,151	2
Total other race victims	563	417	146	
Total unknown race	204	126	36	42
Total victims[1]	23,271	17,949	5,278	44

[1]Total murder victims for whom supplemental data were received.
Source: Crime in the United States 1993, p. 14, Table 2.4.

Table 4-6.
Distribution of Arrests for Criminal Homicide, by Age, 1993

Age	Number of arrested offenders
Under 15	339
15 to 19	5,941
20 to 24	5,991
25 to 29	2,874
30 to 34	2,000
35 to 39	1,445
40 to 44	892
45 to 49	553
50 to 54	364
55 to 59	203
60 to 64	122
65 and over	180
Total	20,285

Source: Crime in the United States 1993, pp. 227–28, Table 38.

Table 4-7.

Victim/Offender Relationship in Criminal Homicide, by Race and Sex, 1993 [Single Victim/Single Offender]

	Race of offender				Sex of offender		
Race of victim	White	Black	Other	Unknown	Male	Female	Unknown
Total white victims	4,686	849	58	55	5,057	536	55
Total black victims	304	5,393	18	67	4,985	730	67
Total other race victims	61	40	137	2	210	28	2
Total unknown race	11	17	1	22	27	2	22

	Race of offender				Sex of offender		
Sex of victim	White	Black	Other	Unknown	Male	Female	Unknown
Total male victims	3,469	4,869	153	93	7,487	1,004	93
Total female victims	1,582	1,413	60	31	2,765	290	31
Total unknown sex	11	17	1	22	27	2	22

[1]Data based on 11,721 victims.

Source: Crime in the United States 1993, p. 17, Table 2.8.

Table 4-8.
Murder Victims, by Type of Weapon Used, 1989–93

Weapons	1989	1990	1991	1992	1993
Total	18,954	20,273	21,676	22,716	23,271
Total firearms	11,832	13,035	14,373	15,489	16,189
Handguns	9,013	10,099	11,497	12,580	13,252
Rifles	865	746	745	706	754
Shotguns	1,173	1,245	1,124	1,111	1,059
Other guns	34	25	30	42	38
Firearms—not stated	747	920	977	1,050	1,086
Knives or cutting instruments	3,458	3,526	3,430	3,296	2,957
Blunt objects (clubs, hammers, etc.)	1,128	1,085	1,099	1,040	1,024
Personal weapons (hands, fists, feet, etc.)[1]	1,050	1,119	1,202	1,131	1,164
Poison	11	11	12	13	9
Explosives	16	13	16	19	26
Fire	234	288	195	203	217
Narcotics	17	29	22	24	22
Drowning	60	36	40	29	23
Strangulation	366	312	327	314	329
Asphyxiation	101	96	113	115	113
Other weapons or weapons not stated	681	723	847	1,043	1,198

[1]Pushed is included in personal weapons.

Source: Crime in the United States 1993, p. 18, Table 2.10.

Table 4-9.
Murder Victims, by Type of Murder Circumstances, 1989–93

	1989	1990	1991	1992	1993
Total[1]	18,954	20,273	21,676	22,716	23,271
Felony type total:	4,049	4,209	4,636	4,917	4,451
Rape	131	152	132	138	116
Robbery	1,728	1,871	2,226	2,266	2,301
Burglary	212	202	197	212	179
Larceny-theft	18	28	32	41	32
Motor vehicle theft	37	55	53	66	61
Arson	165	152	138	148	151
Prostitution and commercialized vice	12	27	20	32	17
Other sex offenses	58	50	47	34	25
Narcotic drug laws	1,402	1,367	1,353	1,302	1,287
Gambling	23	11	33	20	10
Other—not specified	263	294	405	658	272
Suspected felony type	150	148	210	280	144
Other than felony type total	10,270	10,889	11,220	11,244	12,235
Romantic triangle	385	407	314	334	439
Child killed by babysitter	24	34	32	36	33
Brawl due to influence of alcohol	432	533	500	429	381
Brawl due to influence of narcotics	306	242	254	253	262
Argument over money or property	551	514	520	483	445
Other arguments	5,736	6,044	6,108	6,066	6,292
Gangland killings	56	104	206	137	147
Juvenile gang killings	542	679	840	813	1,147
Institutional killings	22	16	19	18	15
Sniper attack	49	41	12	33	7
Other—not specified	2,167	2,275	2,415	2,642	3,067
Unknown	4,485	5,027	5,610	6,275	6,441

[1]Total number of murder victims for whom supplemental homicide information was received.

Source: Crime in the United States 1993, p. 21, Table 2.14.

5

Death Row Prisoners

Table 5-1.
Prisoners Under Death Sentence, by Jurisdiction, Race, and Sex, 1995

Jurisdiction	Total under death sentence[a]	Race[b] A	B	L	N	W	U
Alabama	135 (4)	1	4	2	0	78	0
Arizona	119 (1)	0	15	20	4	79	1
Arkansas	36 (1)	0	14	1	1	20	0
California	438 (8)	7	158	62	13	179	19
Colorado	4	0	1	1	0	2	0
Connecticut	5	0	2	0	0	3	0
Delaware	12	0	6	0	0	6	0
Florida	346 (6)	1	122	36	1	186	0
Georgia	103	0	44	0	0	59	0
Idaho	20	0	0	1	0	19	0
Illinois	164 (4)	0	104	5	0	54	1
Indiana	51 (1)	0	17	1	0	33	0
Kentucky	28 (1)	0	6	0	0	21	1
Louisiana	53	0	33	3	0	13	4
Maryland	15	0	13	0	0	2	0
Mississippi	54 (1)	0	32	0	0	21	1
Missouri	93 (2)	1	38	1	1	48	4
Montana	6	0	0	0	1	5	0
Nebraska	10	0	2	0	1	7	0
Nevada	80 (1)	1	29	9	0	41	0
New Jersey	11	0	6	1	0	4	0
New Mexico	3	0	0	2	0	1	0
North Carolina	154 (4)	0	74	1	4	73	2
Ohio	150	0	74	3	2	70	1
Oklahoma	120 (4)	3	34	1	13	69	0
Oregon	14	0	0	1	1	12	0
Pennsylvania	196 (4)	2	122	10	0	62	0
South Carolina	58	0	29	0	1	28	0
South Dakota	2	0	0	0	0	2	0
Tennessee	102 (1)	1	32	1	2	66	0

(*continued*)

Table 5-1.
Prisoners Under Death Sentence, by Jurisdiction, Race, and Sex, 1995 (*continued*)

Texas	394 (6)	3	147	68	5	165	6
Utah	10	0	2	1	0	7	0
Virginia	54	0	27	1	0	26	0
Washington	13	1	2	0	0	10	0
U.S. military	8	1	6	0	0	1	0
U.S. civil	8	0	5	1	0	2	0
Total	3,061 (49)	22	1,246	233	50	1,470	40
Percent	100.0	0.7	40.7	7.6	1.6	48.0	1.3

[a]Numbers in parentheses are women

[b]Key to abbreviations: A = Asian, B = Black, L = Latino/Latina, N = Native American, U = Unknown, W = White

Source: NAACP Legal Defense and Educational Fund, "Death Row, U.S.A.," winter 1995 (31 January 1996).

Table 5-2.
Juvenile Offenders Sentenced to Death, by Jurisdiction, 1973–95

State	Race of offender			Sex of offender		Age at crime			Total juvenile sentences	Total juvenile offenders
	B	L	W	M	F	15	16	17		
Texas	15	9	7	31	0	0	0	31	31	30
Florida	8	0	14	22	0	3	6	13	22	18
Alabama	6	0	5	10	1	1	6	4	11	10
Georgia	4	0	6	9	1	1	0	9	10	7
Mississippi	6	0	4	9	1	0	4	6	10	9
Louisiana	7	0	0	7	0	2	2	3	7	7
Ohio	5	0	1	6	0	0	1	5	6	6
North Carolina	3	0	2	5	0	1	0	4	5	4
Pennsylvania	4	0	1	5	0	1	1	3	5	5
Oklahoma	0	0	5	5	0	1	2	2	5	5
Arizona	0	3	1	4	0	0	2	2	4	4
Missouri	2	0	2	4	0	0	2	2	4	4
South Carolina	2	0	2	4	0	0	1	3	4	4
Indiana	2	0	1	2	1	1	0	2	3	3
Kentucky	1	0	1	2	0	1	0	1	2	2
Maryland	2	0	1	3	0	0	0	3	3	2
Nevada	1	1	0	2	0	0	2	0	2	2
Virginia	1	0	1	2	0	0	0	2	2	2
Arkansas	1	0	0	1	0	1	0	0	1	1
Nebraska	1	0	0	1	0	0	1	0	1	1
New Jersey	1	0	0	1	0	0	0	1	1	1
Washington	0	0	1	1	0	0	0	1	1	1
Totals	71	13	56	136	4	13	30	27	40	128

Source: Streib, "The Juvenile Death Penalty Today," Sept. 19, 1995, p. 8, Table 4.

Table 5-3.
Women Sentenced to Death, by Jurisdiction and Race, 1973–95

Sentencing state	Race of offender				Total female sentences
	White	Black	Latino	American Indian	
Florida	11	2	1	0	14
North Carolina	8	3	0	1	12
Ohio	3	6	0	0	9
Texas	7	2	0	0	9
California	4	3	1	0	8
Alabama	5	2	0	0	7
Mississippi	4	2	0	0	6
Oklahoma	6	1	0	0	7
Georgia	4	1	0	0	5
Illinois	1	3	1	0	5
Missouri	4	0	1	0	5
Indiana	2	2	0	0	4
Maryland	1	0	0	2	3
Pennsylvania	1	3	0	0	4
Kentucky	2	0	0	0	2
Nevada	1	1	0	0	2
Arizona	1	0	0	0	1
Arkansas	1	0	0	0	1
Idaho	2	0	0	0	2
Louisiana	1	1	0	0	2
New Jersey	1	0	0	0	1
South Carolina	1	0	0	0	1
Tennessee	1	0	0	0	1
Totals	72	32	4	3	111

Source: Streib, "Capital Punishment of Female Offenders," Sept. 21, 1995, p. 4, Table 2.

Table 5-4.
Length of Time of Death Row, by Jurisdiction and Year of Entry, 1974–94

State	Year of sentence for prisoners sentenced to and remaining on death row, 12/31/94												Under sentence of death 12/31/94	Average number of years under sentence of death as of 12/31/94
	1974–79	1980–81	1982–83	1984–85	1986–87	1988	1989	1990	1991	1992	1993	1994		
Florida	26	15	29	35	34	26	17	20	41	27	33	39	342	6.6
Texas	19	18	26	40	63	30	31	25	28	39	32	43	394	6.4
California	11	21	54	39	47	30	30	32	24	38	33	22	381	6.8
Georgia	10	3	8	7	18	5	8	10	6	7	8	6	96	7.4
Arizona	7	10	12	11	7	10	5	10	14	11	14	10	121	6.6
Tennessee	6	9	10	16	19	6	3	7	10	8	2	4	100	8.0
Illinois	3	18	17	16	18	11	8	17	7	15	14	11	155	6.9
Nebraska	3	2		2	1	1						1	10	11.2
Oklahoma	3	3	9	18	24	16	11	8	12	5	8	12	129	6.5
Arkansas	2	1	1		5	1	4	3	1	3	7	8	36	4.7
Nevada[a]	2	4	10	9	5	5	9	7	4	1	2	8	66	7.1
South Carolina	2	4	7	7	7	2	4	2	8	2	7	7	59	6.7
Alabama	1	6	21	14	17	7	13	9	4	11	8	24	135	6.3
Indiana	1	5	6	10	6	6		3	2	4	2	2	47	7.9
Kentucky	1	2	8	2	4	1			2	3	2	4	29	7.5
Montana	1		1		1	2	1			2			8	*
North Carolina	1	4	6	5	1	1		6	10	18	32	27	111	3.3
Pennsylvania		5	17	20	27	20	16	6	18	16	16	21	182	5.8
Mississippi		4	4	2	4	3		7	5	4	12	5	50	5.1
Missouri		4	4	14	16	12	2	4	11	6	6	9	88	5.1

(continued)

Table 5-4.
Length of TIme of Death Row, by Jurisdiction and Year of Entry, 1974–94 (*continued*)

State	Year of sentence for prisoners sentenced to and remaining on death row, 12/31/94												Under sentence of death 12/31/94	Average number of years under sentence of death as of 12/31/94
	1974–79	1980–81	1982–83	1984–85	1986–87	1988	1989	1990	1991	1992	1993	1994		
Delaware		2	1			1				4	6		14	4.7
Idaho		1	3	4	1	3	2	1	1	1	2		19	7.6
Maryland		1	1	2	1	1	3	1	1	1	1		13	7.0
Virginia		1	1	1	13	2	3	6	6	6	6	10	55	4.4
Ohio			11	30	21	9	9	9	13	16	10	12	140	6.0
Louisiana			4	10	8	1		1	4	6	7	6	47	5.5
Utah			1	2	1	2	2		1		1		10	6.6
Washington			1	1	1			1	1	1	2	2	10	4.3
Colorado					2				1				3	*
New Jersey					1			2			3	3	9	*
New Mexico					1							1	2	*
Connecticut							1		2		1		4	*
Oregon							1		2	4	4	6	17	1.9
South Dakota										1	1		2	*
Federal									1		5		6	*
Total	99	143	273	317	374	214	183	197	240	260	287	303	2,890	6.3

*Averages not calculated for fewer than 10 inmates.

[a]Preliminary numbers, subject to revision.

Source: Bureau of Justice Statistics, ''Capital Punishment 1994,'' p. 13, Appendix Table 2.

Table 5-5. Prisoners on Death Row, by Type of Removal, Annually, 1973–94

	Number of prisoners removed from under sentence of death								
				Appeal or higher courts overturned					
Year of sentence	Number sentenced to death	Execution	Other death	Death penalty statute	Conviction	Sentence	Sentence commuted	Other or unknown reasons	Under sentence of death, 12/31/94
1973	42	2	0	14	9	8	9	0	0
1974	149	9	4	65	15	29	22	1	4
1975	298	5	4	171	24	66	21	2	5
1976	234	11	5	137	16	43	15	0	7
1977	138	16	2	40	26	33	7	0	14
1978	187	29	3	21	35	60	8	0	31
1979	156	15	8	2	28	58	6	1	38
1980	182	20	11	3	31	47	6	0	64
1981	233	31	10	0	40	68	4	1	79
1982	272	33	12	0	28	63	6	0	130
1983	253	26	10	1	19	48	4	2	143
1984	287	21	10	2	33	55	6	8	152
1985	277	7	3	2	31	63	3	3	165
1986	306	9	12	0	40	49	4	5	187
1987	290	3	7	2	32	52	1	6	187
1988	295	8	6	0	24	42	1	0	214
1989	264	3	6	0	21	48	3	0	183
1990	256	3	3	0	25	28	0	0	197
1991	277	1	4	0	16	16	0	0	240
1992	285	4	1	0	11	8	1	0	260
1993	295	1	4	0	1	2	0	0	287
1994	304	0	0	0	0	0	1	0	303
Total, 1973–94	5,280	257	125	460	505	886	128	29	2,890

Note: Table based upon most recent death sentence received.

Source: Bureau of Justice Statistics, ''Capital Punishment 1994,'' p. 12, Appendix Table 1.

Table 5-6.
Prisoners on Death Row, by Jurisdiction and Type of Removal, 1973–94

State	Total sentenced to death, 1973–94	Number of removals, 1973–94: Executed	Died	Sentence or conviction overturned	Sentence commuted	Other removals	Under sentence of death, 12/31/94
U.S. total	5,280	257	125	1,851	128	29	2,890
Federal	7	0	0	1	0	0	6
Alabama	227	10	4	77	1	0	135
Arizona	191	3	5	60	1	1	121
Arkansas	73	9	1	27	0	0	36
California	534	2	21	114	15	1	381
Colorado	14	0	1	9	1	0	3
Connecticut	5	0	0	1	0	0	4
Delaware	31	4	0	13	0	0	14
Florida	702	33	18	289	18	2	342
Georgia	246	18	7	119	5	1	96
Idaho	32	1	1	11	0	0	19
Illinois	223	2	6	53	0	7	155
Indiana	80	3	1	27	0	2	47
Kentucky	58	0	1	27	1	0	29
Louisiana	142	21	3	64	6	1	47
Maryland	37	1	1	20	2	0	13
Massachusetts	4	0	0	2	2	0	0
Mississippi	132	4	1	74	0	3	50
Missouri	117	11	4	13	1	0	88
Montana	13	0	0	4	1	0	8
Nebraska	21	1	2	6	2	0	10
Nevada	95	5	3	18	3	0	66
New Jersey	38	0	1	20	0	8	9
New Mexico	23	0	0	16	5	0	2
New York	3	0	0	3	0	0	0
North Carolina	364	6	4	239	4	0	111
Ohio	280	0	5	126	9	0	140
Oklahoma	236	3	4	100	0	0	129
Oregon	35	0	0	18	0	0	17
Pennsylvania	244	0	7	54	1	0	182
Rhode Island	2	0	0	2	0	0	0
South Carolina	129	4	3	63	0	0	59
South Dakota	2	0	0	0	0	0	2
Tennessee	163	0	4	57	0	2	100
Texas	624	85	12	90	43	0	394
Utah	23	4	0	8	1	0	10
Virginia	96	24	3	7	6	1	55

(*continued*)

Table 5-6 (*continued*)

State	Total sentenced to death, 1973–94	Number of removals, 1973–94: Executed	Died	Sentence or conviction overturned	Sentence commuted	Other removals	Under sentence of death, 12/31/94
Washington	25	2	1	12	0	0	10
Wyoming	9	1	1	7	0	0	0
Percent	100%	4.9	2.4	35.1	2.4	0.5	54.7

Note: For those persons sentenced to death more than once, the numbers are based on the most recent sentence to death.

Source: Bureau of Justice Statistics, ''Capital Punishment 1994,'' p. 14, Appendix Table 3.

Table 5-7.
Prisoners Executed, by Jurisdiction and Method, 1977–94

State	Number executed	Lethal injection	Electro-cution	Lethal gas	Firing squad	Hanging
Total	257	131	114	9	1	2
Texas	85	85				
Florida	33		33			
Virginia	24		24			
Louisiana	21	1	20			
Georgia	18		18			
Missouri	11	11				
Alabama	10		10			
Arkansas	9	8	1			
North Carolina	6	5		1		
Nevada	5	4		1		
Delaware	4	4				
Mississippi	4			4		
South Carolina	4		4			
Utah	4	3			1	
Arizona	3	2		1		
Indiana	3		3			
Oklahoma	3	3				
California	2			2		
Illinois	2	2				
Washington	2					2
Idaho	1	1				
Maryland	1	1				
Nebraska	1		1			
Wyoming	1	1				

Source: Bureau of Justice Statistics, "Capital Punishment 1994," p. 15, Appendix Table 4.

Table 5-8.
Juvenile Offenders Executed, 1976–94

Year of execution	Place	Race	Age at crime	Age at execution	Name
1985	Texas	White	17	28	Charles Rumbaugh
1986	So. Car.	White	17	25	J. Terry Roach
1986	Texas	White	17	24	Jay Pinkerton
1990	Louisiana	Black	17	30	Dalton Prejean
1992	Texas	White	17	28	Johnny Garrett
1993	Texas	Black	17	31	Curtis Harris
1993	Missouri	Black	17	29	Frederick Lashley
1993	Texas	Latino	17	26	Ruben Cantu
1993	Georgia	White	17	33	Chris Burger

Source: Streib, "The Juvenile Death Penalty Today," 1995, p. 3, Table 1.

Table 5-9.
Victim/Executed Offender Relationship, by Race and Gender, 1977–95[a]

Gender of Defendants Executed total number 318		Gender of Victims total number 426	
Female	1 (.37%)	Female	186 (43.66%)
Male	317 (99.68%)	Male	240 (56.34%)
race of defendants executed		race of victims	
White	175 (55.03%)	White	350 (82.16%)
Black	124 (38.99%)	Black	55 (12.91%)
Latino	17 (5.34%)	Latino	14 (3.29%)
Native American	1 (.31%)	Asian	7 (1.64%)
Asian	1 (.31%)		

[a]Includes 5 executions in January 1996.

Source: NAACP Legal Defense and Educational Fund, "Death Row, U.S.A.," winter 1995, p. 3.

Table 5-10.
Number and Percent of Death Sentences Carried out in Death Penalty Jurisdictions, by Rank Order of Death Sentences, 1973–94

Jurisdiction	Death sentences	Executions	Percent executed
Florida	702	33	4.7
Texas	624	85	13.6
California	534	2	0.4
North Carolina	364	6	1.6
Ohio	280	0	0.0
Georgia	246	18	7.3
Pennsylvania	244	0	0.0
Oklahoma	236	3	1.3
Alabama	227	10	4.4
Illinois	223	2	0.9
Arizona	191	3	1.6
Tennessee	163	0	0.0
Louisiana	142	21	1.4
Mississippi	132	4	3.0
South Carolina	129	4	3.1
Missouri	117	11	9.4
Virginia	96	24	22.2
Nevada	95	5	5.3
Indiana	80	3	3.8
Arkansas	73	9	12.3
Kentucky	58	0	0.0
New Jersey	38	0	0.0
Maryland	37	1	2.7
Oregon	35	0	0.0
Idaho	32	1	3.1
Delaware	31	4	12.9
Washington	25	2	8.0
Utah	23	4	17.4
New Mexico	23	0	0.0
Nebraska	21	1	4.8
Colorado	14	0	0.0
Montana	13	0	0.0
Wyoming	9	1	11.1
Connecticut	5	0	0.0
Massachusetts	4	0	0.0
New York	3	0	0.0
Rhode Island	2	0	0.0
South Dakota	2	0	0.0

(*continued*)

Table 5-10 (*continued*)

Jurisdiction	Death sentences	Executions	Percent executed
New Hampshire	0	0	0.0
Federal	7	0	0.0

Note: Subsequent to the publication of this report, two states—Montana and Pennsylvania—have carried out their first executions.

Source: Bureau of Justice Statistics, "Capital Punishment 1994," p. 14, Appendix Table 3.

6

The Status of the Death Penalty Worldwide

Table 6-1.
Abolitionist for All Crimes *(Countries and territories whose laws do not provide for the death penalty for any crime)*

Country	Date of abolition	Date of abolition for ordinary crimes	Date of last execution
ANDORRA	1990		1943
ANGOLA	1992		
AUSTRALIA	1985	1984	1967
AUSTRIA	1968	1950	1950
CAMBODIA	1989		
CAPE VERDE	1981		1835
COLOMBIA	1910		1909
COSTA RICA	1877		
CROATIA	1990		
CZECH REPUBLIC	1990*		
DENMARK	1978	1933	1950
DOMINICAN REPUBLIC	1966		
ECUADOR	1906		
FINLAND	1972	1949	1944
FRANCE	1981		1977
GERMANY	1949/1987**		1949**
GREECE	1993		1972
GUINEA-BISSAU	1993		1986***
HAITI	1987		1972***
HONDURAS	1956		1940
HONG KONG	1993		1966
HUNGARY	1990		1988
ICELAND	1928		1830
IRELAND	1990		1954
ITALY	1994	1947	1947
KIRIBATI			****
LIECHTENSTEIN	1987		1785

(continued)

Table 6-1 (*continued*)

Country	Date of abolition	Date of abolition for ordinary crimes	Date of last execution
LUXEMBOURG	1979		1949
MACEDONIA			
MARSHALL ISLANDS			****
MAURITIUS	1995		1987
MICRONESIA (Federated States)			****
MOLDOVA	1995		
MONACO	1962		1847
MOZAMBIQUE	1990		1986
NAMIBIA	1990		1988***
NETHERLANDS	1982	1870	1952
NEW ZEALAND	1989	1961	1957
NICARAGUA	1979		1930
NORWAY	1979	1905	1948
PALAU			
PANAMA			1903***
PORTUGAL	1976	1867	1849***
ROMANIA	1989		1989
SAN MARINO	1865	1848	1468***
SAO TOME AND PRINCIPE	1990		****
SLOVAK REPUBLIC	1990*		
SLOVENIA	1989		
SOLOMON ISLANDS		1966	****
SPAIN	1995	1978	1975
SWEDEN	1972	1921	1910
SWITZERLAND	1992	1942	1944
TUVALU			****
URUGUAY	1907		
VANUATU			****
VATICAN CITY STATE	1969		
VENEZUELA	1863		
TOTAL: 57 countries			

*The death penalty was abolished in the Czech and Slovak Federal Republic in 1990. On 1 January 1993 the Czech and Slovak Federal Republic divided into two states, the Czech Republic and the Slovak Republic. The last execution in the Czech and Slovak Federal Republic was in 1988.

**The death penalty was abolished in the Federal Republic of Germany (FRG) in 1949 and in the German Democratic Republic (GDR) in 1987. The last execution in the FRG was in 1949; the date of the last execution in the GDR is not known. The FRG and the GDR were unified in October 1990.

***Date of last known execution.

****No executions since independence.

Source: Amnesty International, ''The Death Penalty: List of Abolitionist and Retentionist Countries (March 1996).''

Table 6-2.
Abolitionist for Ordinary Crimes Only *(Countries whose laws provide for the death penalty only for exceptional crimes such as crimes under military law or crimes committed in exceptional circumstances such as wartime)*

Country	Date of abolition	Date of last execution
ARGENTINA	1984	
BRAZIL	1979	1855
CANADA	1976	1962
CYPRUS	1983	1962
EL SALVADOR	1983	1973*
FIJI	1979	1964
ISRAEL	1954	1962†
MALTA	1971	1943
MEXICO		1937
NEPAL	1990	1979
PARAGUAY	1992	1928
PERU	1979	1979
SEYCHELLES		**
SOUTH AFRICA	1995	1991
UNITED KINGDOM	1973	1964
TOTAL: 15 countries		

*Date of last known execution.

**No executions since independence.

†[Ed. note: Adolph Eichmann was executed in Israel in 1962 for ''crimes against humanity.'']

Source: Amnesty International, ''The Death Penalty: List of Abolitionist and Retentionist Countries (March 1996).''

Table 6-3.

Abolitionist De Facto *(Countries and territories which retain the death penalty for ordinary crimes but can be considered abolitionist in practice in that they have not executed anyone during the past 10 years or more, or in that they have made an international commitment not to carry out executions)*

Country	Date of last execution
ALBANIA*	
BELGIUM	1950
BERMUDA	1977
BHUTAN	1964**
BOLIVIA	1974
BRUNEI DARUSSALAM	1957
BURUNDI	1982
CENTRAL AFRICAN REPUBLIC	1981
CONGO	1982
COMOROS	***
COTE D'IVOIRE	
DJIBOUTI	***
GAMBIA	1981
MADAGASCAR	1958**
MALDIVES	1952**
MALI	1980
NAURU	***
NIGER	1976**
PAPUA NEW GUINEA	1950
PHILIPPINES	1976
RWANDA	1982
SENEGAL	1967
SRI LANKA	1976
SURINAME	1982
TOGO	
TONGA	1982
TURKEY	1984
WESTERN SAMOA	***
TOTAL: 28 countries and territories	

*Preparatory to Albania's joining the Council of Europe, in a declaration signed on 29 June, Pjeter Arbnori, President of the Albanian Parliament, said he was willing to commit his country "to put into place a moratorium on executions until [the] total abolition of capital punishment."

**Date of last known execution.

***No executions since independence.

Source: Amnesty International, "The Death Penalty: List of Abolitionist and Retentionist Countries (March 1996)."

Table 6-4.
Retentionist *(Countries which retain and use the death penalty for ordinary crimes)**

Country
AFGHANISTAN
ALGERIA
ANTIGUA AND BARBUDA
ARMENIA
AZERBAYDZHAN
BAHAMAS
BAHRAIN
BANGLADESH
BARBADOS
BELARUS
BELIZE
BENIN
BOSNIA-HERZEGOVINA
BOTSWANA
BULGARIA
BURKINA FASO
CAMEROON
CHAD
CHILE
CHINA (People's Republic)
CUBA
DOMINICA
EGYPT
EQUATORIAL GUINEA
ERITREA
ESTONIA
ETHIOPIA
GABON
GEORGIA
GHANA
GRENADA
GUATEMALA
GUINEA
GUYANA
INDIA
INDONESIA
IRAN
IRAQ
JAMAICA
JAPAN
JORDAN
KAZAKHSTAN
KENYA
KOREA (Democratic People's Republic) [North Korea]
KOREA (Republic) [South Korea]
KUWAIT
KYRGYZSTAN
LAOS
LATVIA
LEBANON
LESOTHO
LIBERIA
LIBYA
LITHUANIA
MALAWI
MALAYSIA
MAURITANIA
MONGOLIA
MOROCCO
MYANMAR
NIGERIA
OMAN
PAKISTAN
POLAND
QATAR
RUSSIA
SAINT CHRISTOPHER AND NEVIS
SAINT LUCIA
SAINT VINCENT AND THE GRENADINES
SAUDI ARABIA
SIERRA LEONE
SINGAPORE
SOMALIA
SUDAN
SWAZILAND
SYRIA
TADZHIKISTAN
TAIWAN (Republic of China)
TANZANIA
THAILAND
TRINIDAD AND TOBAGO
TUNISIA
TURKMENISTAN
UGANDA
UKRAINE
UNITED ARAB EMIRATES
UNITED STATES OF AMERICA
UZBEKISTAN
VIET NAM
YEMEN
YUGOSLAVIA (Federal Republic of)
ZAIRE
ZAMBIA
ZIMBABWE
TOTAL: 94 countries and territories

*Most of these countries and territories are known to have carried out executions during the past 10 years. On some countries Amnesty International has no record of executions but is unable to ascertain whether or not executions have in fact been carried out. Several countries have carried out executions in the past 10 years but have since instituted national moratoria on executions.

Source: Amnesty International, ''The Death Penalty: List of Abolitionist and Retentionist Countries (March 1996).''

Table 6-5.
List of Countries which have Abolished the Death Penalty Since 1976

1976:	*PORTUGAL* abolished the death penalty for all crimes. *CANADA* abolished the death penalty for ordinary crimes.
1978:	*DENMARK* abolished the death penalty for all crimes. *SPAIN* abolished the death penalty for ordinary crimes.
1979:	*LUXEMBOURG, NICARAGUA* and *NORWAY* abolished the death penalty for all crimes. *BRAZIL, FIJI* and *PERU* abolished the death penalty for ordinary crimes.
1981:	*FRANCE* and *CAPE VERDE* abolished the death penalty for all crimes.
1982:	The *NETHERLANDS* abolished the death penalty for all crimes.
1983:	*CYPRUS* and *EL SALVADOR* abolished the death penalty for ordinary crimes.
1984:	*ARGENTINA* abolished the death penalty for ordinary crimes.
1985:	*AUSTRALIA* abolished the death penalty for all crimes.
1987:	*HAITI, LIECHTENSTEIN* and the *GERMAN DEMOCRATIC REPUBLIC* abolished the death penalty for all crimes.[1]
1989:	*CAMBODIA, NEW ZEALAND, ROMANIA* and *SLOVENIA* abolished the death penalty for all crimes.[2]
1990:	*ANDORRA, CROATIA,* the *CZECH AND SLOVAK FEDERAL REPUBLIC, HUNGARY, IRELAND, MOZAMBIQUE, NAMIBIA* and *SÃO TOMÉ AND PRÍNCIPE* abolished the death penalty for all crimes.[2,3] *NEPAL* abolished the death penalty for ordinary crimes.
1992:	*ANGOLA* and *SWITZERLAND* abolished the death penalty for all crimes. *PARAGUAY* abolished the death penalty for ordinary crimes.
1993:	*GREECE, GUINEA-BISSAU* and *HONG KONG* abolished the death penalty for all crimes.
1994:	*ITALY* abolished the death penalty for all crimes.
1995:	*MAURITIUS, MOLDOVA* and *SPAIN* abolished the death penalty for all crimes. *SOUTH AFRICA* abolished the death penalty for ordinary crimes.

Notes: [1]In 1990 the German Democratic Republic became unified with the Federal Republic of Germany, where the death penalty had been abolished in 1949.

[2]Slovenia and Croatia abolished the death penalty while they were still republics of the Socialist Federal Republic of Yugoslavia. The two republics became independent in 1991.

[3]In 1993 the Czech and Slovak Federal Republic divided into two states, the Czech Republic and the Slovak Republic.

Source: Amnesty International, "The Death Penalty: List of Abolitionist and Retentionist Countries (March 1996)."

PART II

The Controversy over Public Support for the Death Penalty: The Death Penalty versus Life Imprisonment

Although the law in a constitutional democracy does not always march hand in hand with public attitudes, values, and preferences, too much distance between the two is a recipe for serious political tension. For years the American public has been convinced that it is being victimized by violent crime and that government at all levels has been unsuccessful in solving the problem. The result has been fear, anger, and frustration over the perennial "crime wave" threatening to engulf the body politic. One measure of how the public views the issue of violent crime is found in its attitude toward the death penalty.

There is little doubt that the American public gives vocal support—and has voted this support at the polls as well—for the death penalty. At least since the Supreme Court's *Furman* decision in 1972, a majority of the general public has given abstract support to the death penalty as a legitimate punishment for murder, if not in all cases then certainly in some. As a representative sample from a much larger body of evidence, consider these diverse reports of public opinion on the death penalty spanning the past few decades:

- In 1979 "The Playboy Report on American Men" reported that 68 percent of American men favored the death penalty, ranging from a high (nearly 75 percent) among men between 23 and 50, to a low (60 percent) among men aged 18 to 22.[1]
- The *Figgie Report on Fear of Crime,* published in 1981, reported that 92 percent of the "senior executives with *Fortune* 1,000 corporations" favor the death penalty for murder.[2]
- In New York City nearly half of the 1,329 city residents polled in 1985 reported that the death penalty would "help reduce crime a lot."[3]
- In South Carolina a 1985 newspaper survey reported that among those asked in the local population, the death penalty was supported by more than three

to two (68 percent versus 21 percent); only a small percentage (11 percent) was undecided.[4]

- A Media General/Associated Press survey in early 1985 reported that of the 1,476 adults asked nationwide, an "unprecedented 84% of Americans approve of the death penalty. . . . [Of these] 57 percent said the death penalty was appropriate in certain circumstances and 27 percent said it should be used in all murder cases." (One wonders whether these respondents knew or cared that, nine years earlier, the Supreme Court had ruled that a mandatory death penalty for murder was unconstitutional?) According to the same poll, "[H]alf of those [who support the death penalty also] believe the death sentence is not imposed fairly from case to case."[5]
- *Parade* magazine reported in 1987 that of the "nearly 40,000" persons from all over the country who volunteered their views on the death penalty, "nearly 80% believe there should be capital punishment in general," and "almost 55% think there should be no minimum age for the death penalty."[6]
- In Texas a sample of 1,008 persons polled by telephone in 1988 reported overwhelmingly (86 percent) that they thought "Texas should have capital punishment." This was an increase over 1985, when 75 percent favored the death penalty.[7]
- The annual survey of the attitudes of students entering college, *The American Freshman: National Norms,* reports a steady decline in support for abolition. In 1969, 54 percent of entering college freshmen favored abolition of the death penalty. That dropped to 27 percent in 1985, to 21 percent in 1989,[8] and to the all-time low of 20 percent in 1995.[9]

These reports are typical: Support for the death penalty appears to have steadily increased from around 65 percent in the early 1970s. According to a Gallup Poll in September 1994, public support for the death penalty is now at an all-time high of 80 percent. This poll also shows that a majority of the public now favors the death penalty for juveniles—an attitude in part fueled by an overestimate of the volume and rate of juvenile crime (though statistics reported in part I do show that teenage murder doubled in the period from 1989 to 1993). A prior Gallup Poll (June 1991) showed that retribution—"a life for a life"—was the main rationale invoked by death penalty supporters, thus demoting deterrence and incapacitation to lesser roles. However, that same poll also showed that support for the death penalty dropped from 76 percent to 53 percent if murderers were sentenced to life in prison without the possibility of parole (in the jargon, LWOP).[10] Will these attitudes hold steady, at least into the next century? Probably, unless changes in state and city law enforcement practices can significantly reduce violent crime and the anxieties it arouses in the public. Some recent good news in this direction from New York City and other major urban areas may indicate that new practices in law enforcement are having a beneficial effect.[11]

Yet this evidence of overwhelming support for the death penalty runs into a head-on collision with another indubitable fact: As data in part I show, this 80 percent support for the death penalty does not translate into anything remotely like an 80 percent death penalty sentencing rate in actual capital cases. On the contrary, juries in capital cases—all of whose members have been vetted to eliminate opponents of execution—do not vote for the death penalty in more than 10 percent of the actual cases. Thus it appears that when nominal supporters of the death penalty actually confront in the courtroom a living human being over whom they have the power of life and death in sentencing, enthusiasm for a death sentence evaporates more frequently than it hardens. There is no clearer evidence than this of the essentially *symbolic* role of the death penalty at present.

A striking illustration is provided in the Susan Smith case tried in the summer of 1995. According to a *Newsweek* poll at the end of Smith's trial in South Carolina, after she had been found guilty, 63 percent of the respondents wanted her sentenced to death.[12] Yet the jury that had just convicted her began its deliberations with a straw vote of eleven against and only one for the death sentence. Within less than three hours the jury voted unanimously to sentence Smith to prison for life.[13]

During the past decade several scholars have tried to shed further light on the real nature and strength of support for the death penalty. In 1986 criminologist Philip Harris showed that surveys relying on "questions of support for the death penalty which provide only a pro or con response" are likely "to lead to an inaccurate and greatly oversimplified view of public opinion" on this issue (453)—a conclusion that earlier investigators had also reached.[14] He also affirmed three substantive conclusions: (1) "[S]upport for the death penalty is largely a matter of emotion: revenge is a more powerful rationale than any of the utilitarian justifications"; (2) support for the death penalty might diminish "if life imprisonment without parole was an option"; and (3) "a just deserts response is unlikely to be seen as the main justification for the death penalty" by those who actually support it (453).

Criminologist James O. Finckenauer reviewed Harris's research as well as that of several other investigators, and supported Harris's first third conclusion; "revenge"—with all its unbridled retaliatory connotations—was in fact playing a larger role in public thinking about the death penalty than was "retribution," which differs from revenge in imposing constraints in the name of justice on the severity and quality of punishments.[15] He concluded that "the public's desire for revenge is dictating public policy regarding the death penalty" (1988:97).

A year later Hans Zeisel, well known for his statistical work on several aspects of the death penalty controversy,[16] published (with the assistance of Alec M. Gallup) a brief review of the polls, stretching back to 1966, when public opposition and support for the death penalty were about equally divided. Zeisel and Gallup reached a conclusion consistent with Harris's: "The present study . . . points up the relative weakness of utilitarian arguments" whether for or against abolition (1989: 295).

Criminologist Robert Bohm examined the extent to which demographic variables (notably age, gender, education, geographic region, political affiliation, income) correlated with support of or opposition to the death penalty in the twenty-one polls on the topic carried out by the Gallup organization in the years

1936 to 1986. He concluded: "[W]hites, wealthier people, males, Republicans, and Westerners have tended to support the death penalty more than blacks, poorer people, females, Democrats, and Southerners" (1991a:135). This description fits rather well the citizens of Washington, D.C., who resoundingly defeated a death penalty restoration referendum in 1992—the only such triumph for abolition in many years.[17] Bohm went on to add the characteristic caution expressed by all students of survey research on this subject: The ignorance of the public about the actual administration of the death penalty, the infrequency of executions in the 1970s and 1980s, and the nature of the questions asked by the pollsters—all were factors that cast doubt on just what to make of the apparently widespread support for the death penalty at that time. In the end, Bohm concluded, "[L]ittle is known about what the American public really thinks of capital punishment" (1991a:139).

Research by criminologists James Alan Fox and Julie L. Bonsteel and sociologist Michael L. Radelet (1990–91) took a different direction. They showed that public support for the death penalty depends a great deal on just what kind of murder is in question: Support for executing a serial murderer, such as the notorious Ted Bundy (electrocuted in Florida in 1989), is one thing; support for executing a battered wife who in desperation kills her abusive husband is another. They also confirmed the Gallup Poll of 1991 that showed a marked falloff in support for the death penalty if LWOP is the alternative. Finally, they urge (as have other investigators) that pollsters ask more carefully framed questions so that the answers will be more significant than a mere "Yes" or "No" to the question "Do you favor the death penalty?"

These conclusions, as well as other findings and recommendations, are supported in the most recent and sophisticated research and reflections on public opinion by social psychologist Phoebe C. Ellsworth and law professor Samuel R. Gross, reprinted here as chapter 7.

For those opposed to the death penalty, undoubtedly the most interesting and encouraging research discovery is that support for the death penalty falls off dramatically if its supporters are offered LWOP as an alternative (just as Harris conjectured a decade ago). This finding was first publicized in May 1990 in the *New York Times* by William J. Bowers, one of the nation's leading research investigators on all aspects of the death penalty. He reported that in California, for example, where 82 percent of the public professed support for the death penalty, a mere 26 percent continued to prefer it if offered the alternative of LWOP plus some form of restitution to surviving family members of the murder victim.[18] These findings have been supported by extensive further research, and Bowers now concludes that "as few as one in four people are staunch death penalty advocates who will accept no alternative, and that as many as two out of four people are reluctant supporters who *accept* the death penalty but would *prefer* an alternative" (Bowers, Vandiver, and Dugan 1992:81). Politicians, apparently, have much to learn about the real views of their constituents on the most favored way to punish murder.

A somewhat popularized account of these findings appears in an April 1993 report by the Death Penalty Information Center (DPIC) in Washington, D.C., written by its executive director, Richard C. Dieter. Excerpts from this report, "Sentencing for Life: Americans Embrace Alternatives to the Death Penalty,'' are reprinted here as chapter 8. As for why LWOP should be so attractive, a report in *USA Today* gave several plausible reasons: It is ''easier to win [in court] than the death penalty, and cheaper by one-third or one-half; raises no risk of wrongful execution; means killers can be required to live the rest of their lives working to compensate the victims's family; is indisputably constitutional; and may actually deter crime. . . .''[19]

Early in 1995, the DPIC reported that a new national survey showed the attitudes of police chiefs to be remarkably in line with those of the general public as revealed in the research Bowers published a year earlier. When Hart Research Associates polled randomly selected police chiefs, their principal finding was this: ''Although a majority of the police chiefs support the death penalty in the abstract, when given a choice between the sentence of life without parole plus restitution, versus the death penalty, barely half of the chiefs support capital punishment.''[20] The police chiefs were asked, ''If you had to choose one way to reduce crime, what would you choose?'' Only 1 percent chose the death penalty; 87 percent expressed no confidence in the doctrine that executions ''significantly reduce the number of homicides.'' Nevertheless, most of the chiefs professed to be in favor of the death penalty.[21]

What these research findings pass over in silence is that for many who oppose the death penalty, the alternative of life in prison without the possibility of parole is also unreasonably severe,[22] so much so that some opponents of executions lose heart when faced with supporting this alternative. And, indeed, even those death penalty opponents who embrace LWOP as a morally suitable (as distinct from politically necessary) alternative might change their minds if they studied the arguments by the Israeli criminologist Leon Sheleff in his book *Ultimate Penalties: Capital Punishment, Life Imprisonment, Physical Torture* (1987). Sheleff offers convincing reasons why none of these practices is really tolerable in a civilized society. The dilemma of the opponent of the death penalty, if current survey research is a reliable guide, is that at present the public is prepared to accept the abolition of capital punishment only if the alternative to it is itself a morally unacceptable deprivation of liberty.[23]

Can effective public education undermine support for the death penalty? Most opponents of the death penalty think it can, but the issue is rarely put to the test, mainly because resources for effective public education on this issue are so inadequate. Events in Washington, D.C., in the autumn of 1992 indicate what is possible. After a young aide to Senator Richard Shelby was murdered near Capitol Hill, Congress forced a death penalty referendum on the ballot for District voters at the regular November elections (Tolchin 1992). A citywide coalition to defeat the referendum put on a full-court press, mobilizing the media, the churches, and civic and community groups. When the votes were counted, the referendum was defeated 2 to 1.[24] However, many factors entered into this political struggle that would be absent elsewhere, notably the issue of District political autonomy vs. Congressional control. Nevertheless, the opponents of the death penalty can fairly point to that 1992 referendum as an example of what can be done when the attention of the electorate is sharply focused on the pros and cons of the death penalty.

Notes

1. *The Playboy Report on American Men* (1979), p. 46
2. *The Nation,* 4 July 1981, p. 8.
3. *New York Times,* 14 January 1985, p. B3.
4. *The State,* 31 January 1985, p. A1.
5. *Boston Globe,* 29 January 1985, p. 5. A *Newsweek* poll in late July 1995 reported that 31 percent of those asked favored a death penalty for "all those convicted of murder." *Newsweek,* 7 August 1995, p. 22.
6. *Parade Magazine,* 25 January 1987, p. 10.
7. *Dallas Morning News,* 15 November 1988, p. A17.
8. *Sourcebook of Criminal Justice Statistics—1992,* p. 228, Table 2.84.
9. *Boston Globe,* 9 January 1995, p. 3.
10. Gallup Poll 1991:40–42.
11. See *New York Times,* 8 July 1995, pp. 1, 22, reporting that the murder rate in the first half of 1995 had "fallen by nearly a third" from the previous year, and that a principal factor was "the aggressive efforts that [the police] have made in stopping all types of crimes; . . . shootings are down all across the city."
12. *Newsweek,* 7 August 1995, p. 20.
13. Morgenthau 1995:23.
14. See, e.g., Vidmar and Ellsworth 1974.
15. On the distinction between revenge and retribution, see Nozick 1981:366–70.
16. See Zeisel 1977, reprinted in Bedau 1982; also Zeisel 1968, 1981, and Zeisel & Gallup 1989.
17. For a thorough discussion of the referendum, see "D.C. Reinstatement Effort Blocked," NCADP *Lifelines,* no. 56 (April–June 1992), p. 1; and "Voters Defeat Death Penalty Referendum in D.C.," NCADP *Lifelines* No. 57/58 (July–December 1992), pp. 5, 10.
18. Bowers 1990. See also Bowers 1993 (criticizing the Supreme Court for its misuse of survey research on public attitudes toward the death penalty); and Bowers, Vandiver, and Dugan 1994 (recent survey research shows that the public prefers LWOP plus restitution to the death penalty).
19. *USA Today,* 8 April 1994, p. ?
20. See Dieter 1995a:2.
21. *USA Today,* 23 February 1995, p. 11A.
22. Elsewhere I have argued that this country, following what most Western European nations have done long ago, could adopt a general policy for the punishment of first-degree murder far less stringent (and less expensive) than LWOP: a mandatory minimum ten-year prison term, followed by indefinite further imprisonment contingent on annual review by the board of pardons and parole. See Bedau ed. 1982:100; Bedau ed. 1964:228–31. Variations on this general pattern are easily imagined; all would have the advantage of reducing the tendency of American prisons to become geriatric wards for aging convicts who are no longer dangerous.
23. I have discussed this dilemma in greater detail and in a larger context in Bedau 1990b.

7

Hardening of the Attitudes: Americans' Views on the Death Penalty

PHOEBE C. ELLSWORTH
SAMUEL R. GROSS

The best known fact about American attitudes toward capital punishment is that support for the death penalty is at a near record high. Figure 7-1 graphically displays this familiar fact in a familiar historical context; it is further documented in the Appendix [not reprinted here]. As measured by public opinion polls, support for capital punishment declined through the 1950s to a low of 47% in 1966; increased steadily from 1966 through about 1982; and has remained roughly stable since 1982, in the range of 70%–75%.[1]

Figure 7-2 shows two other well-known facts about American public opinion on the death penalty: Throughout the entire period for which poll data are available, men have favored the death penalty more than women, and Whites have favored it more than Blacks. Other smaller correlations have frequently been found: Republicans favor the death penalty more than Democrats, conservatives more than liberals, the middle class more than the poor, Westerners more than Easterners and Midwesterners, suburbanites more than city and country dwellers (Bohm, 1991; Erskine, 1970; Fox, Radelet, & Bonsteel, 1991; Smith, 1976; Zeisel & Gallup, 1989). These demographic variables, however, are weak predictors. For example, in a logistic regression model including all of these variables plus several others, Fox et al. (1991) were able to predict only 8% of the variance in general death penalty opinions on NORC surveys from 1972 through 1988.

Several writers have discussed the limitations of the single-question pro/con format typically used in general population surveys of death penalty attitudes (P. W. Harris, 1986; Vidmar & Ellsworth, 1974; Wallace, 1989). Answers to this kind of question tell us little about what people think or feel or notice—why they support or oppose capital punishment, what they know about it, how and to whom they believe it should be applied, how this attitude is related to their behavior or to other attitudes—the issues to which the bulk of this article is devoted.[2] Still, these soundings of general opinion are important.

From the *Journal of Social Issues* 50, no. 2 (1994): 19–52. Reprinted by permission of the publisher and the authors.

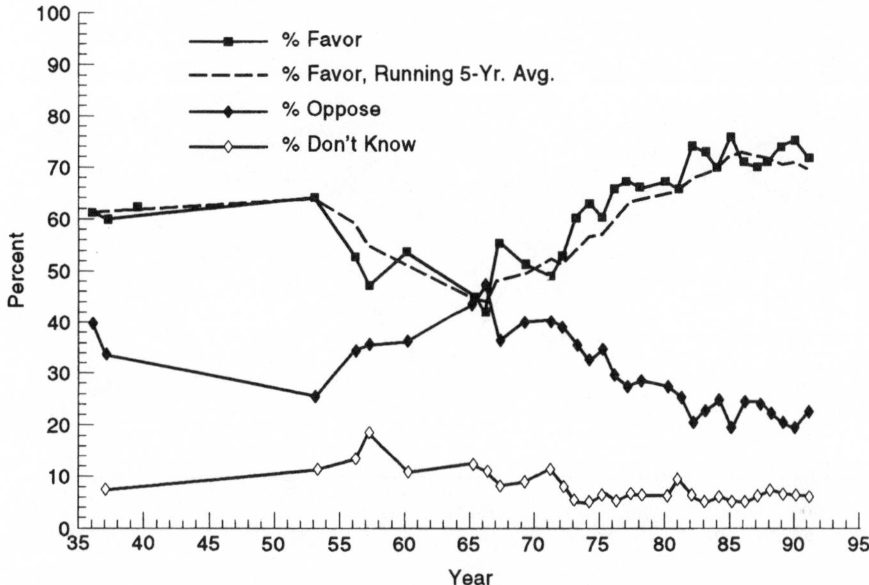

Figure 7–1. Attitudes toward the death penalty.

First, the legal status of the death penalty in the United States depends on popular support, actual and perceived. In 1972, when the Supreme Court first addressed the claim that the death penalty is a "cruel and unusual punishment" and therefore unconstitutional, all of the justices agreed that the legality of capital punishment depends on its acceptability under contemporary standards (*Furman v. Georgia,* 1972). The Court has maintained this position ever since, although various justices have disagreed about the value of opinion polls (as opposed to jury behavior and legislative enactments) as a source of information on "contemporary standards." In 1972—with public opinion on capital punishment fairly evenly split, but support on the rise—the Supreme Court's decision in *Furman* left the legal status of the death penalty in doubt. The Court held that all existing death sentences in the country were unconstitutional because they had been imposed under systems that permitted the "arbitrary" use of capital punishment, but it deferred a decision on the constitutionality of the death penalty as such. Four years later, when the Court revisited the issue and decided that capital punishment *is* constitutional (*Gregg v. Georgia,* 1976), the public was unmistakably pro–death penalty—as the polls revealed—and it has remained so ever since.

In the long run, popular support may not be *sufficient* to guarantee the retention of the death penalty. As Zimring and Hawkins (1986) have pointed out, in the past 30 years capital punishment has been abolished in West Germany, Great Britain, Canada, and France, despite majority support. The same could happen in the United States, although not likely soon. On the other hand, popular support may well be *necessary* to the continued use of the death penalty in this country. If a clear

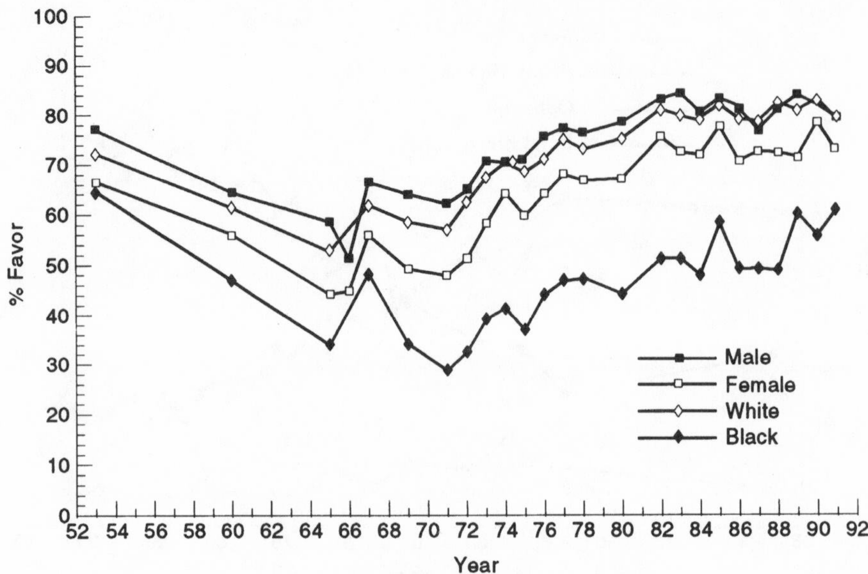

Figure 7–2. Attitudes toward the death penalty by gender and race.

majority comes to reject this form of punishment, we predict that the Supreme Court, if not Congress and the state legislatures, will soon follow suit.

Second, general opinions about the death penalty are subjectively important to many, perhaps most, people in this society. For example, in November 1986, 65% of the respondents in an Associated Press/Media General poll of the national adult population said that the death penalty is an issue they "feel very strongly about." This may not surprise anybody who watches TV news or reads newspapers in America. But it is surprising to learn that on an ABC News exit poll of 23,000 voters in the 1988 presidential election, 27% checked "the candidates' positions on the death penalty" as an issue that was "very important" to them in choosing between George Bush and Michael Dukakis. The only item that scored higher was abortion (33%); the presidential debates and the candidates' stands on illegal drugs were close behind (26% each); the candidates' political parties scored 23%; and their positions on matters such as education (22%), health care (21%), and social security (19%) all trailed.

Perhaps capital punishment is so important to people because it has become a point on which people do not so much form opinions as choose sides: *I* am for the death penalty, *George Bush* is for the death penalty, *Michael Dukakis* is against the death penalty. To the extent that this is true, the critical step is self-identification as a supporter or an opponent of capital punishment—and general opinion questions, however vague, may be perfectly suited to determine that identification. Indeed, the patterns of answers to these questions offer some slight evidence that death penalty attitudes are a matter of self-identification.

Inevitably, the precise distribution of responses to death penalty questions varies from survey to survey even within short periods of time. Most such differences are in the range from 1% to 5%, and are easily explained by random sampling error, and by the multitude of possible problems in the design and implementation of mass surveys. What is more striking, from our point of view, is the *absence of systematic differences* between the results of competing polls that phrase their questions about capital punishment differently. The usual question asked on the General Social Survey (GSS) is, "Do you favor or oppose the death penalty for persons convicted of murder?" Before 1981, the usual Gallup question was, "Are you in favor of the death penalty for persons convicted of murder?" Harris polls generally ask, "Do you believe in capital punishment (the death penalty) or are you opposed?" None of the differences between these formats, or among the half-dozen other questions that we have grouped together in Appendix 1 under the heading "Standard Question," has any noticeable impact on the answers. Consider, for example, the results of three polls conducted in 1976: GSS, 4/76—Favor 66%, Oppose 30%, Don't know 5%; Gallup, 4/76—Yes 66%, No 26%, No opinion 7%; Harris, 12/76—Favor 67%; Oppose 25%; Not sure 8%.

Experiments using different forms of survey questions have shown that some variations in wording are likely to matter much more than others. For example, formal balance ("favor or oppose" vs. "favor") usually makes little difference (Schuman & Presser, 1981, pp. 180–84). By contrast, providing a context for the opinion ("If [another] situation like Vietnam were to develop," should the United States "send troops" vs. should the United States "send troops *to stop a communist takeover*") often changes the results by a substantial margin (Schuman & Presser, 1981, pp. 275–96)—but on this issue it makes no difference. Indeed, the distribution of responses remains roughly unchanged even when aggravated categories of death-worthy crimes are mentioned. Compare, for example, the 12/82 Yankelovitch survey question ("Wider use of the death penalty *for such crimes as hijacking or killing a police officer*"—73% favor) to the standard question on the 4/83 GSS survey (73% favor). Nor does it seem to make much of a difference if a popular justification for the death penalty is spelled out. For example, the 6/84 AP/Media General survey asked, "Various proposals have been made *as possible solutions to the increased crime rate*. Please tell me whether you personally favor or oppose the following measures *to reduce the crime rate*. . . ." The death penalty alternative got about the same level of "Favor" responses (69%) as the death penalty questions on a 1/84 Roper survey, which referred to ". . . *serious crimes such as murder, kidnapping, etc.*" (68%), and the 4/84 GSS (70%), which asked the standard question.

The form of endorsement of the death penalty that is offered also appears to make little difference. It can be "Are there any crimes for which the death penalty *is justified?*" (CBS/NYT, 7/77, 7/88, 4/89), or "Do you favor or oppose . . . *bringing back* the death penalty?" (Yankelovitch, 9/83, 12/83, 9/84), and the levels of support are close to those obtained with general attitude questions. It does not matter if the respondents are asked whether they would *vote* for a proposition favoring the death penalty (Gallup, 10/74, 9/82); nor—despite large acquiescence response bias effects in other contexts (Schuman & Presser, 1981, pp. 203–30)—does it matter if they are required to state that they would vote to *oppose* "Amending the constitution to outlaw the death penalty" (NBC/*Wall Street Journal,* 12/91). The only changes in question format that seem to have predictable effects on levels of support are those that deal with the frequency of death sentences. On the one hand, questions that ask whether the respondents favor a *mandatory* death penalty produce substantially lower support; for example, compare the 12/81 Gallup survey (54% favor mandatory death penalty) to the 4/82 GSS (74% generally favor death penalty). On the other hand, some surveys ask whether, among "persons convicted of first degree murder," the death penalty should be given to "all," "no one," or whether it "should depend on the circumstances of the case and the character of the person." If we interpret the answer "no one" as opposition to capital punishment, and "all" and "depends" as support, these questions produce a sizable pro–death penalty shift; for example, compare the 4/73 Harris survey "All" + "Depends" = 81%) to the 4/73 GSS (60% general support for capital punishment).

It seems that most Americans know whether they "favor" or "oppose" the death penalty, and say so in response to any question that can reasonably be interpreted as addressing that issue. This conclusion is reinforced by evidence that the form of the response categories has little effect on overall levels of expressed support for capital punishment. Several surveys have allowed respondents to say that they favor or oppose the death penalty "strongly" or somewhat" (*L.A. Times,* 4/81, 7/86, 3/89), or "very strongly" and "not too strongly" (Gallup, 1/86). The total proportions on each side of the neutral point are consistent with roughly contemporaneous surveys that offered only two choices. In addition, three *Los Angeles Times* surveys (3/85, 7/86, 3/89) offered the choice "I haven't heard enough about that to say." Similar manipulations have been shown to have dramatic consequences in related contexts. For example, Schuman and Presser (1981, p. 120) describe an experiment on the 1974 GSS in which the following question was asked to a split sample in two forms, with and without the italicized portion: "In general, do you think the courts in this area deal too harshly or not harshly enough with criminals, *or don't you have enough information about the courts to say?*" In the first form 6.8% volunteered that they didn't know; in the second 29% chose "Not enough information to say." By comparison, only 4% of the respondents in the 1989 *Los Angeles Times* survey said that they "hadn't heard enough" to express an opinion on the death penalty (an additional 9% said they were not sure or refused to answer), and only 2% said so on the other two surveys that offered this option.

Expressed Reasons for Death Penalty Attitudes

Before 1970, almost no one thought to ask survey respondents *why* they favored or opposed the death penalty. Since then several researchers have attempted to do so; their general conclusion is that simply asking people about the reasons for their attitudes is not an effective means of discovering those reasons. Ellsworth and Ross (1983), for example, found that respondents tended to endorse *all* "reasons" that were consistent with their basic position. If they favored capital punishment, they agreed with almost all the reasons for support; if they opposed capital punishment, they agreed with almost all the reasons for opposition. Ellsworth and Ross concluded that most people's attitudes toward capital punishment are basically emotional. The "reasons" are determined by the attitude, not the reverse.

Even though it now seems naive to think we can discover the reasons for people's attitudes toward capital punishment simply by asking direct questions, an examination of people's expressed reasons can still be illuminating. Overall levels of support for the death penalty are far higher than they were in 1973, executions have resumed, thousands of people are now on death row, and there have been conspicuous cases of innocent people narrowly escaping execution. Do people give the same reasons for their attitudes as they did 20 years ago?

There are two basic methods for asking people about reasons for their death penalty attitudes. The first is to provide a list of possible reasons for supporting or opposing the death penalty and to ask respondents which ones they agree with. The second, less common, is simply to ask the open-ended question, "*Why* do you favor (or oppose) capital punishment?" The first method is susceptible to the problem discovered by Ellsworth and Ross (1983): Any reason on the list that supports one's basic attitude is likely to be endorsed, and the only way to differentiate among them is to look at relative strength of endorsement. The second method is potentially much more useful, as it does not suggest reasons to respondents that they had not previously entertained. However, people are often unaware of the bases for their attitudes, and if they have not thought much about why they favor or oppose the death penalty they may not be able to give valid answers (Nisbett & Wilson, 1977).

Deterrence and Retribution

Twenty years ago the reason most commonly given for supporting the death penalty was that it was a deterrent to crime (Thomas, 1977; Thomas & Foster, 1975; Vidmar, 1974; Vidmar & Ellsworth, 1974). At that time the deterrent effectiveness of the death penalty was a hotly debated issue, and surveys of death penalty attitudes began to include questions about belief in deterrence. Thus, unlike other rationales for the death penalty, we have two decades of comparable data on belief in deterrence. The top portion of Figure 7-3 shows the percent of people supporting the death penalty, and the percent of people agreeing that the death penalty is a deterrent to murder (or crime, the wording varies slightly from one poll to the next) in surveys of nationwide random samples of adults from 1972 to 1991. Only polls that offered two alternatives, rather than scales of belief strength, are presented, for the sake of comparability.

It is clear that the marked increase in support for the death penalty is not due to a growing belief that the death penalty is a deterrent to murder. Belief in the deterrent efficacy of the death penalty hovers around 60% for most of the 19-year period, while support for the death penalty rises from 58% to 75%. Indeed, a number of recent polls indicate that people believe other measures, such as job training and drug rehabilitation programs, are more effective than capital punishment in reducing crime (Bowers, 1993; Bowers & Vandiver, 1991a, 1991b).

Proponents of capital punishment, of course, are far more likely than opponents to agree that the death penalty is a more effective deterrent than life imprisonment. In their 1974 survey of California Bay Area residents, Ellsworth and Ross (1983) found that 93% of proponents agreed that "the death penalty is a more effective deterrent than life imprisonment," while 92% of opponents disagreed, and many other polls have found that belief in deterrence is highly correlated with support for the death penalty. However, in their attempt to find out whether people's belief in deterrence was a fundamental *reason* for people's death penalty attitudes, Ellsworth and Ross (1983) asked people whether their basic position on the death penalty would change if it could be proven that they were wrong about its deterrent efficacy. They found that most proponents would still favor the death penalty if life imprisonment were an equally effective deterrent, and most opponents would still oppose it even if it were a "much more effective" deterrent than life imprisonment. The same hypothetical question was added to the Gallup Poll in 1985, with very similar results. Proponents would still favor the death penalty if it "does not lower the murder rate" (72%, 73%, and 69% in 1985, 1986, and 1991, respectively), and opponents would still oppose it if it were a deterrent (67%, 71%, 65%; Gallup Poll News Service, 1991). Thus current public opinion poll data continue to support the conclusion that people's attitudes about the death penalty are not determined by their beliefs in its deterrent effectiveness.

The other major reason for favoring the death penalty is retribution. Commentators in the early 1970s (Thomas & Foster, 1975; Vidmar & Ellsworth, 1974) argued that an expressed belief in deterrence was a more socially acceptable, "legitimate" rationale for supporting the death penalty than the more emotional, possibly vengeful motive of retribution, and thus was more likely to be a reason people were willing to offer to pollsters. Several scholars have suggested that the norms of social desirability have changed, and that retribution is now an acceptable reason for favoring the death penalty (Fox et al., 1991; Haney, Hurtado, & Vega, 1993; P. W. Harris, 1986; Warr & Stafford, 1984). As support for the death penalty has increased, so has willingness to endorse retribution as a motive.

The measurement of people's belief in retribution is much more problematic than the measurement of their death penalty attitudes or their belief in deterrence. We have seen that changes in question wording have little effect on general levels of support for the death penalty, and the same is true for belief in deterrence. For example, the 1980 and 1981 polls reported in Figure 7-3 were conducted by two different organizations (Research & Forecasts, 5/80; Audits & Surveys, 10/81). The first asked, "Does the death penalty discourage murder?" The second asked, "Do you believe that capital punishment—the death penalty—is or is not a deterrent to crime?" In both cases 63% of the population expressed a belief in deterrence. Harris (4/73) found the same level of belief in the deterrent superiority of capital punishment over life imprisonment, regardless of whether "life imprisonment"

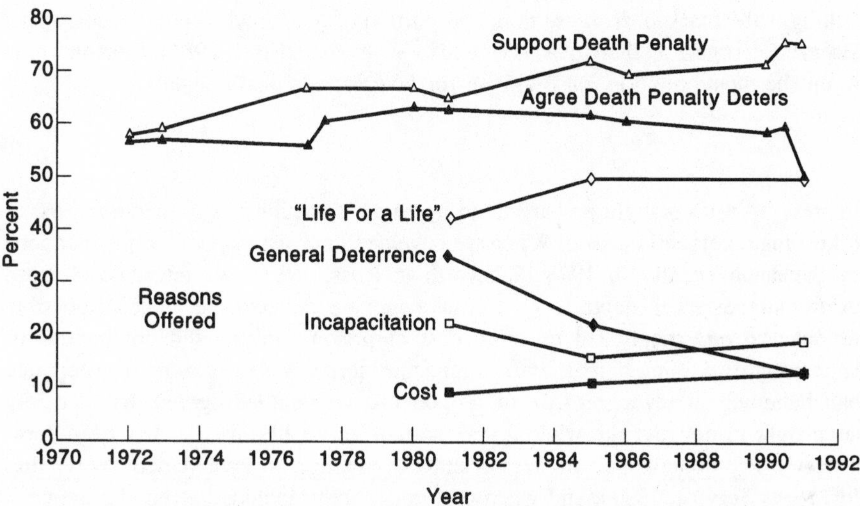

Figure 7–3. Reasons given for death penalty support.

The top two lines show the percentage of Americans supporting the death penalty and the percentage agreeing that the death penalty deters crime (yes-no questions). The deterrence questions are taken from the following national samples: Opinion Research Corp. 7/72; Harris 4/73; CBS/New York Times 1/77, 7/77, 3/90, 8/90; Research & Forecasts 5/80; Audits & Surveys 10/81; Gallup 1/85, 1/86, 6/91. For 1973, and all years from 1985 to 1991, the general support questions come from the same surveys; for the other years the data points are from the surveys reported in Figure 7–1.

The lower four lines show responses to open-ended questions asking, "Why do you favor the death penalty?" The data are from the following polls: ABC News/Washington Post 5/81; Gallup 1/85, 6/91.

included parole as an option. Retribution questions, on the other hand, can be phrased in terms of a principled belief in justice, a merciless passion of revenge, or anywhere in between. Very few researchers have used agree–disagree retribution questions comparable to the deterrence questions, and every survey phrases the question differently. Not surprisingly, endorsement of items designed to tap retributive sentiments ranges from quite low (when words like "revenge" are used) to quite high. The variation due to question wording makes it impossible to tell if there has been any long-term trend.

Since 1980 there have been three national random-sample polls that asked open-ended questions about respondents' reasons for supporting or opposing the death penalty (ABC News/*Washington Post,* 5/81; Gallup 1985 and 1991, reported in Gallup Poll News Service, July 26, 1991). The lower graph on Figure 7-3 presents these data. Retribution ("a life for a life") has been a more popular reason than belief in deterrence since 1981. It is possible that people were more reluctant to express retributive motives a decade earlier, but we have no comparable data. Support for the law of talion has increased over the past 10 years, but far more striking is the marked *decrease* in the proportion of people who spontaneously give general deterrence as their reason (see also Warr & Stafford, 1984). Retribution is by far the most common reason given for favoring the death penalty.

Cost

Figure 7-3 shows a slight upward trend in people's willingness to mention the cost of keeping a person in prison. When we developed our list of possible justifications for the death penalty in 1973 (Ellsworth & Ross, 1983), we interviewed death penalty supporters in depth to try to make sure we covered the range of possible reasons. *No one* mentioned the high cost of prison, and we did not include it. Apparently discussing human lives in monetary terms was even more unacceptable than believing in revenge (45% of proponents we sampled agreed that "society has a right to get revenge when a very serious crime like murder has been committed"). People have become less hesitant to mention cost spontaneously (Gallup Poll News Service, 1991), and when cost is explicitly included as an alternative, a substantial minority of proponents endorse it. In 1986 P. W. Harris found that 38% of those who favored a death penalty in all circumstances and 21% of those who favored it in some circumstances endorsed "the high cost of imprisonment" as one of their reasons. If this is a genuine basis for supporting the death penalty, it is a misguided one; the available evidence suggests that the death penalty is far more expensive than life imprisonment (Cook & Slawson, 1993; Costanzo & White, this issue; Dieter, 1992).

Incapacitation

Finally, Figure 7-3 indicates that only 20% or fewer respondents give incapacitation—keeping a particular killer from killing again—as a reason for favoring the death penalty, and there is no clear trend over the decade. However, a series of recent studies aimed at discovering whether there are any alternatives to capital punishment that would satisfy the public (Bowers, 1993; Bowers & Vandiver, 1991a, 1991b; Dieter, 1993) suggests that incapacitation may be more important to people than their responses have indicated.

We have argued, as have many others (Ellsworth & Ross, 1983; P. W. Harris, 1986; Tyler & Weber, 1982; Wallace, 1989), that death penalty attitudes are an aspect of people's ideological self-definition, and that they are strongly held. Bowers (1993) argues that the apparent strength of people's commitment to capital punishment may be due to the fact that survey questions rarely allow them to compare it with any alternative; either no alternative is given or "life imprisonment" is presented without further specification. Twenty years ago it made no difference whether "life imprisonment" or "life imprisonment without parole" was included as the alternative to the death penalty (Harris, 4/73), but there are reasons to believe times have changed. *First,* an increasing number of studies indicates that most people, including jurors in capital cases (Bowers, 1993; Dieter,

1993), do not believe "life imprisonment" means anything of the sort. In a recent study, only 4% of respondents believed murderers sentenced to life actually spend their whole lives in jail; the average estimate of a "life sentence" was 15.6 years (Costanzo & Costanzo, 1994; Dieter, 1993). In states where the only alternative to the death penalty is life without parole, few citizens realize that this is so (Dieter, 1993). (In California, the state does not leave these impressions to chance. The jury in a capital case is instructed by the judge that "a Governor may in the future commute or modify a sentence of life imprisonment without the possibility of parole to . . . include the possibility of parole." [*California v. Ramos,* 1982].) *Second,* Willie Horton and other high-publicity cases have made the image of the released prisoner who immediately commits new atrocities highly available to the public.

Bowers asks respondents, "If convicted murderers in this state could be sentenced to life in prison with absolutely no chance of ever being released on parole or returning to society, would you prefer this as an alternative to the death penalty?" In all five states (California, Florida, Georgia, Nebraska, New York) where this question has been asked, more people have preferred this form of life imprisonment (Bowers, 1993). Adding a requirement that the murderer "be required to work in prison industries for money that would go to the families of their victims" further diminishes support for the death penalty. Dieter (1993) replicated these results in a national poll.

Both incapacitation and retribution probably play a role in people's willingness to endorse these alternatives. People want to be absolutely sure that vicious murderers never ever have a chance to victimize anyone else (outside of prison), and they do not believe "life imprisonment" currently provides that sort of guarantee. But they also want to be sure the murderer never ever has a chance to live a normal life, because he does not deserve to. The addition of a commitment to contribute to the victim's family adds a further element of retribution—in the form of restitution—and undercuts the argument that death is the only punishment that could recompense the surviving victims.

There are problems with demand characteristics in Bowers' work. The question wording is very strong, and the alternatives to the death penalty are arranged in a sequence of severity from "parole after 25 years" to "parole after 40 years" to "absolutely no chance of parole" to "no chance of parole" plus restitution. Also, we must remember that (as on all contemporary surveys) strong majorities in each of these states do support the death penalty under the conditions that they believe actually prevail. In that context, it's hard to say what these results mean. Would anything short of death convince most Americans that there is really no chance that a prisoner will ever return to society? Is the popularity of *real* "life without parole" best understood as a qualification on popular support for the death penalty, or as an expression of cynicism about the prison system? Despite these problems, this is the first new approach to studying attitudes toward capital punishment in many years, and the first approach that has suggested that there might be substantial flexibility on the part of those who favor the death penalty.

Emotions

Many commentators have argued that death penalty attitudes are not based on rational considerations at all, but are fundamentally noninstrumental symbolic attitudes, based on emotions and ideological self-image (Ellsworth & Ross, 1983; Gorecki, 1983; P. W. Harris, 1986; Tyler & Weber, 1982; Wallace, 1989). Oddly enough, despite the popularity of this idea, hardly anyone has asked respondents questions that give them the opportunity to express their emotions directly, and some have intentionally confined their response alternatives to those that are rational (P. W. Harris, 1986). Perhaps researchers have feared that respondents might be reluctant to express emotional bases for their attitudes, but this fear may be groundless. Ellsworth and Ross (1983), for example, found that 79% of these who favored the death penalty said that they had sometimes "felt a sense of personal outrage when a convicted murderer was sentenced to a penalty less than death," and 34% said that the death of a murderer could give them "a sense of personal satisfaction." In any case, we will not find out unless we ask. Emotions are becoming a legitimate topic in the study of other political attitudes (Kinder, 1994), and we would hope to see the emotional correlates of death penalty attitudes studied directly, rather than being inferred from the failure of nonemotional beliefs to be very informative.

Reasons for Opposing Capital Punishment

Many fewer polls have asked why the opponents oppose capital punishment. This may be partly because by the time survey researchers started asking detailed questions about reasons, the proponents were a clear majority, so their views were more relevant to public policy. It may be because the clash between utilitarian reasons (deterrence, cost) and reasons based on values (retribution) is less salient.

Just as most proponents say they would still favor the death penalty if it had no deterrent effect, most opponents would still oppose it even if it were an effective deterrent (61%, 71%, and 65% in 1985, 1986, and 1991, respectively; Gallup Poll News Service, 1991). Thus, like the attitudes of the proponents, attitudes of most opponents are very strong, and not based on utilitarian considerations. They are willing to sacrifice lives to avoid having a death penalty. On the other hand, saying that they would be unmoved by evidence of superior deterrence does not reflect any inconsistency: When asked why they oppose the death penalty, opponents rarely refer to its failure as a deterrent. In response to open-ended questions in surveys over the last 10 years, only 5%–10% of opponents mentioned deterrence. Other "utilitarian" reasons, such as the unfair application of the penalty, the risk of executing innocent people, or the possibility of rehabilitation, are also very infrequently mentioned as reasons for opposition.

People oppose the death penalty because they think it is wrong. In 1981, 1985, and 1991 (ABC/*Washington Post,* 5/81; Gallup Poll News Service, 1991) the most commonly given "reason" has been that it is "wrong to take a life" (or the slightly more ambiguously coded "taking a life solves nothing"), and the proportion of opponents giving this opinion has held steady at about 40%. The next most popular reason is basically that same reason with an explicitly religious rationale, e.g., "punishment should be left to God."

People *favor* the death penalty because they think *killing* is wrong: "a life for a life" is the most popular reason spontaneously given for supporting it. For both proponents and opponents, their preferred rationale is moral and absolute; they are taking a stand that brooks no argument and suggests little differentiation. Such attitudes are unlikely to be swayed by arguments based on factual information.

Knowledge and Beliefs

In his concurring opinion in *Furman v. Georgia* (1972), Justice Thurgood Marshall argued that popular support for the death penalty was based on ignorance. There are two parts to this famous hypothesis: (1) The American public is generally unaware of several unhappy "facts" about capital punishment—that it does not deter homicide more than long terms of imprisonment, that its operation is inhumane, that its administration is discriminatory, that convicted murderers are rarely executed, and that they pose little future threat to society (pp. 364–65). (2) If these "facts" were well known, "the great mass of citizens . . . would conclude that the death penalty is immoral and therefore unconstitutional" (p. 363). Virtually all the published studies on the relationship between death penalty attitudes and factual knowledge were conducted in response to this Marshall Hypothesis; the two best, within three years after *Furman.*

Sarat and Vidmar (1976) interviewed 181 residents of Amherst, Massachusetts, in 1975. Most of their respondents knew that capital punishment is rarely imposed and that it is subject to discrimination by wealth (59% on each item), but few knew that "studies have shown" that it does not deter homicide (36% and 22%, depending on the form of the question). They conclude that the first step in the Marshall Hypothesis is supported in part: their respondents were reasonably well informed on the *use* of the death penalty, but ill informed on its *effects.* Ellsworth and Ross (1983) provide more detailed data on a survey of 500 northern Californians in 1974, which also revealed widespread ignorance. Most respondents, from 54% to 89%, did not know that most Western European countries had abolished capital punishment, that comparisons across time and jurisdiction fail to show that the death penalty deters, that it is more costly than life imprisonment, and so forth. In general, opponents of the death penalty were more likely to answer correctly, but, as the authors note, this does not necessarily mean that they were better informed. It is also possible that the two groups were equally ignorant, but each tended to agree with the items supporting their position. This would create a bias, since on most of the items the correct answer was consistent with the anti–death penalty position. In addition, supporters and opponents were in general agreement on several issues. Majorities in both camps (62% and 81%, respectively) agreed correctly on the discrimination item, and pluralities agreed incorrectly on relative cost and abolition in Europe. The only strong differences were on several items related to deterrence and on a related item concerning the average length of time served under a life sentence.[3]

Ellsworth and Ross also found a great deal of uncertainty about the operation and effects of the death penalty. Many respondents happily checked "I have no idea" in response to these questions. On a 5-point scale, this admission of ignorance drew from 25% to 49% of the respondents on seven of nine information items, and was the modal response on four. The exceptions were the cost item (16% said "I have no idea"—but only 11% answered correctly that capital punishment is *not* cheaper than life imprisonment) and an item on discrimination by wealth (9% had "no idea," and 68% correctly said that poor murderers were more likely to be sentenced to death). Both of these questions seem to call for common sense social-economic reasoning; in one case, common sense is probably accurate, in the other it is misleading. Equally striking is the tentativeness with which those respondents who did have an idea answered. On every item, those who said, "I think it's true," outnumbered those who said, "I'm sure it's true," and those who said, "I think it's false," outnumbered those who said, "I'm sure it's false." These comparisons hold for respondents who favor the death penalty, oppose it, or are undecided. In only 1 out of 36 possible comparisons did those who were sure (pro or con) outnumber those in the same group who had tentative thoughts in the same direction.

The second step in Justice Marshall's argument—that if the facts were known, capital punishment would be rejected—is an expression of democratic optimism: knowledge persuades. Unfortunately, the best study on the point is discouraging. Lord, Ross, and Lepper (1979) compared subjects who believed the death penalty deters homicide and subjects who believed it does not. Both groups were given a pair of fictitious studies, one providing data that clearly supported the deterrence hypothesis and the other strongly refuting it. In each group (and regardless of the methodologies of the studies) the subjects accepted the evidence that favored the position they already held, and rejected the contrary evidence. The net effect of reading two balanced but contradictory studies was that prior beliefs were strengthened and preexisting differences were polarized. Similarly, Roberts (1984) found that pro– and anti–death penalty subjects remembered those portions of stimulus literature that supported their positions.

The world, however, does not have the same structure as Lord et al.'s elegant study. Facts about the death penalty are not neatly balanced; as Justice Marshall wrote, on the important factual issues that have been in dispute (deterrence, cost, discrimination, consistency) the truth is on the side of anti–death penalty arguments. Moreover, some citizens (unlike the subjects in this study) have weak opinions on the death penalty, or are entirely undecided. Sarat and Vidmar (1976) examined the effect of information on attitudes by asking their respondents to read one or both of two 1500-word essays containing information about Utilitarian aspects of capital punishment (deterrence and recidivism) and Humanitarian aspects (discrimination and the process of executions); a control group was given an unrelated essay about other legal issues. A posttest of the respondents' death penalty attitudes seemed to support Justice Marshall. The informational essays did produce a shift in the direction of opposition to capital punishment; the Utilitarian essay produced a larger change than the Humanitarian, and the combination was more effective than either separately.

A close review of these findings shows them to be entirely consistent with Lord et al. Sarat and Vidmar measured death penalty attitudes on a 7-point scale, from "very strongly in favor" to "very strongly opposed." In the three experimental conditions, only 4% (1/24) of respondents who favored the death penalty "very strongly" changed their attitude in the expected direction, and only 21% (6/28) of those who favored it "strongly." By comparison, 57% (34/60) of respondents who were "uncertain" or who favored or opposed the death penalty "somewhat" moved in the direction of opposition. Moreover, only 2 of the 46 respondents whose attitudes changed to any extent (4%) moved from any position in support for the death penalty to any level of opposition. All other shifts were changes of intensity within groups (primarily among the less intense) and movement in and out of the undecided group. This suggests that general knowledge of the truths that Justice Marshall wanted to teach the public would have only a modest effect on public opinion. At most, it might increase opposition by about the proportion of people who are undecided—currently around 8%—and it would probably have little or no impact on those who support the death penalty most strongly.

Recent national poll data are consistent with this conclusion. We have already discussed the data on beliefs about deterrence. In addition, Gallup polls in 1985 and 1991 found that 39% and 45% of the respondents, respectively, agreed that Blacks are more likely to be sentenced to death than Whites. On the same polls, 64% and 60% agreed that poor defendants were more likely to be sentenced to death than rich defendants. Gallup (Gallup Poll News Service, 1991) also reports that Black respondents were considerably more likely than Whites to agree that these forms of discrimination take place, 73%–41% for race and 72%–59% for poverty. Similarly, on a 11/86 AP/Media General poll, 50% said that the death penalty "Is not carried out fairly," and only 32% said that it "Is carried out fairly." Given the overall levels of support for the death penalty since 1985, the inescapable conclusion is that a large proportion of the American public already believes the death penalty is unfair, but supports it nonetheless.

Who Should Be Sentenced to Death?

Mandatory vs. Discretionary Death Penalty

When the Supreme Court declared current capital punishment statutes unconstitutional in 1972, it did so on the ground that the discretion allowed to jurors in deciding who should live and who should die was so unlimited that the choice was ultimately arbitrary (*Furman v. Georgia,* 1972). Some states attempted to remedy this arbitrariness by instituting mandatory capital punishment: everyone convicted of specified categories of murder would automatically be sentenced to death. In 1976 the Supreme Court held that mandatory death penalties are unconstitutional

(*Woodson v. North Carolina,* 1976; *Roberts v. Louisiana,* 1976). The public apparently shares the view that not everyone who is eligible for the death penalty should get it. Support for a mandatory death penalty is consistently weaker than general support for the death penalty (see above, p. 94), although it too has grown in the recent past. When respondents are given a choice between a mandatory and a discretionary death penalty, they prefer the latter. The Harris poll included this question in 4/73, 12/76, 1/83, and Gallup in 7/85. Except for 1976, when there was only a slight preference for a discretionary death penalty, over 50% of those polled favored a discretionary death penalty, while fewer than 30% favored a mandatory death penalty.

Further, some of those who express support for a "mandatory" death penalty do not think that everyone convicted should be executed. Ellsworth and Ross (1983) found that the percentage of people who said that 100% of those convicted of a given crime should be executed was always lower than the percentage of people who endorsed a "mandatory" death penalty for that crime. In that same survey, some opponents of the death penalty felt the proportion of people who should be executed for a given crime should be greater than zero. It is clear that proponents of mandatory death penalties want the discretion to spare an occasional sympathetic killer, while some opponents of capital punishment want the discretion to execute a few especially villainous ones. Most people prefer a death penalty that allows the decision maker to make distinctions in every case.

Most capital sentencing statutes attempt to codify the important distinctions by providing juries with lists of aggravating factors that might justify a sentence of death, while reminding them that *any* factor may be considered as a justification for rejecting the death penalty. No national poll has examined people's views of the kinds of considerations that should distinguish between life and death for a given crime, although a few smaller scale surveys have done so (e.g., Haney et al., 1993; Harris, 1986). The national polls have focused primarily on the types of crimes that should be punishable by death, and occasionally on the type of criminal.

Which Crimes Should Be Punishable by Death?

Table 7-1 displays levels of support for the death penalty for selected crimes, based on nationwide surveys using questions of the general form, "Do you favor the death penalty for the crime of X?" Questions allowing the three options "death for all," "death for some," and "death for none" generally show higher levels of support when the "all" and "some" categories are combined. Open-ended questions ("What do you think should be the penalty for X?") generally show lower levels.

The most obvious conclusion to be drawn from the table is that the rise in general support for the death penalty has been accompanied by an across-the-board rise in support for capital punishment for the various specific crimes. These trends can also be seen in the percentage of people who favor death as the penalty for crimes not included in the table: arson, robbery, hijacking, or kidnapping in which someone is killed (Roper 3/74, 3/76, 4/80); and assassination of high public officials

Table 7-1.
Percent Favoring the Death Penalty for Specific Crimes

	Crime						
Year	Murder	Rape	Hijacking	Kill police/ guard	Paid killing	Terrorism	Child sex
1972	53		38	60			
1973	60						
1974	63			54	58		
1975	60						
1976	66			52	56		
1977	67					55	
1978	66	32	37				
1979							
1980	57			58	64		
1981	66	37	22				
1982	74						
1983	73						
1984	70						
1985	76	45	45				
1986	71	54		62 (Police) 56 (Guard)	74	79	35
1987	70						
1988	71	51	50				
1989	74						
1990	75						

Note. The data are from national polls asking yes-no questions of the format, "Do you favor the death penalty for the crime of X?" The sources are as follows: Hijacking—1972 Opinion Research Corp., all other years Gallup; Terrorism—Harris; Rape—1986 Associated Press/Media General, all other years Gallup; Paid killing—1986 Associated Press/Media General, all other years Roper; Child Sexual Molestation—Associated Press/Media General; Killing a policeman or prison guard—1972 Opinion Research Corp.; 1974, 1976, 1980 Roper; 1986 Associated Press/Media General. The sources of the data on Murder are described in footnote 1.

(Roper, 3/74, 3/76, 4/80; Gallup, 11/85, 9/88). In general death is favored more for the crimes involving killing, although a substantial number of people also favor death for rape, hijacking, and spying.

It also seems that particular crimes are singled out for death when they have attracted public attention. For example, public support for the death penalty for rape and for terrorism has increased much more during the past 15 years than support for the execution of people who kill police officers or prison guards. The feminist movement has clearly affected public consciousness about the seriousness of rape, and terrorism has become a much more salient issue. Salient crimes change with the times. In 1942, in wartime, 85% of a nationwide sample *spontaneously* named the death penalty as the appropriate punishment for spies (Gallup, 7/42); since then a majority has always opposed it. In 1986 the sexual molestation of a child became a survey item for the first time, and 35% of the population favored the death penalty for this crime (AP/Media General, 11/86); it would be wonderful to know what people would have said in 1970, or 1960, or 1950, before the crime was widely publicized.

Another media crime of the late 1980s and 1990s is drug dealing. In a 6/51 Gallup poll, in response to an open-ended question, 14% of Americans said they favored the death penalty for "selling drugs to teenagers." In 1969 only 2% mentioned the death penalty as a possible punishment for "dope peddling" (Gallup, 1/69); in both years, the plurality favored long prison sentences. Those are the only two national surveys before 1985 to ask about the death penalty for selling drugs. Since then eleven surveys have asked about it, but their questions are so different that support ranges from 1% (AP/Media General, 11/86) in which only the 40% who said they favored the death penalty for crimes other than murder were asked about specific crimes, to 73% (Times Mirror, 5/90), in which 42% of the population "strongly favored" and 31% "favored" the death penalty for "drug traffickers." The idea of death for drug dealing is new, and question wordings suggest everything from the little kid who sells cocaine on his block to major drug "kingpins," so it is impossible to say how the public feels on this issue. It is a new issue, a hot issue, the public is uncertain, and question wording makes a big difference. Not enough time has elapsed to observe trends on any particular question.

Which Criminals Should Be Punished with Death?

Three groups—women, young people, and people suffering from mental retardation—have been singled out by survey researchers as possible exceptions to statutes authorizing the death penalty. In 1937, 58% of the population favored the death penalty for women, about the same proportion as favored the death penalty in general (Gallup, 12/37). By 1953 the proportion had fallen to 51%: 75% of those who favored the death penalty in general (68%) also favored it for women (Gallup, 1953). Although women are hardly ever sentenced to death, it appears that there is no overwhelming public sentiment against it; more likely it is because women are much less likely than men to commit capital murder (Rapaport, 1991). Since 1953 the question has not been included on any national survey.

Support for the execution of young people ("under 21," "under 18," "teenager") has risen dramatically since 1936, when this question was first asked. In 1936, 28% of Americans were "in favor of the death penalty for persons under 21" (Gallup, 12/36). By 1953 this proportion had dropped to 19%, and by 1957 it had dropped still further to 11% (Gallup, 11/53, 9/57). In 1965 it had risen to 21% (Gallup, 1/65) even though general support for the death penalty was at its lowest. The question was not asked again until 1988 (Harris, 9/88) when 44% favored the death penalty for persons under 18, and in a 1989 poll (with a considerably smaller sample than the others) 57% favored the death penalty for 16- and 17-year-olds (Time/CNN/Yankelovich, 6/89). While this last figure may be exaggerated, clearly the former reluctance to execute adolescents has been muted, perhaps because people's current image of a violent killer *is* an adolescent.

That these two recent polls do not reflect a willingness to execute *all* murderers is indicated by people's views, on the same two polls, about the execution of "mentally retarded individuals." In 1988 only 21% of the population favored the death penalty for mentally retarded killers; in 1989 the figure was 27%. This lack of public support for the execution of mentally retarded offenders is particularly noteworthy because it has not been reflected either in practice—several retarded people have been executed and many more are awaiting execution—or in law. The Supreme Court held in 1989 that it does not offend public standards of morality to execute a person who was mentally retarded (*Penry v. Lynaugh,* 492 U.S. 302).

No nationwide survey has asked about aggravating factors other than the type of crime and the demographic characteristics of the criminal. A few more limited-sample surveys provide some data about the kinds of cases that provoke the strongest support for the death penalty, the criminals the public most wants to see executed. Two characteristics stand out: (1) the murder was especially brutal (Haney et al., 1993; Harris, 1986), and (2) more than one person was killed (Ellsworth & Ross, 1983; Haney et al., 1993; Harris, 1986). Although the data are sparse, it is plausible that these are the killers who come to mind when people are asked about the death penalty—the remorseless, brutal, uncontrollable killer. A few studies have found that people are far more likely to favor the death penalty in the abstract than they are to favor it in specific, concrete cases (Doob & Roberts, 1984; Ellsworth, 1978; Fein & Lord, 1987), and have raised the hypothesis that this is because most real murderers seem less deviant and horrible than the nightmare vision of a killer that comes to mind when we are asked about capital punishment.

Conclusion

Support for the death penalty is at an all-time high, both in the proportion of Americans who favor capital punishment and in the intensity of their feelings. Most people care a great deal about the death penalty but know little about it, and have no particular desire to know. This is not surprising, as their attitudes are not based on knowledge. Although all justifications consistent with one's position are typically endorsed, those that are offered spontaneously and endorsed most strongly are not the kind that could be easily changed by information. This characterization of death penalty attitudes is based on hypotheses that have been in the literature for nearly 20 years (Ellsworth & Ross, 1983; Sarat & Vidmar, 1976); indeed, much of the work of the past 20 years has simply provided empirical support for old hypotheses rather than generating new ideas. In particular, it does not explain why support for the death penalty has steadily increased beyond all previous levels.

In the 1930s and 1940s pollsters rarely asked about the death penalty, probably because it was an accepted and uncontroversial fact of life. (Interestingly, two of the earliest death penalty questions on national polls—Gallup 12/36 and Gallup 11/53—were asked on the heels of unusual and highly publicized executions: Bruno Hauptmann for the Lindbergh baby kidnap-murder in April 1936, and the Rosenbergs for espionage in June 1953.) In any event, no trend can be inferred from the sketchy data that are available before the 1950s. Since then, however, overall trends in support for the death penalty have been well documented and, at the aggregate level, they seem easy to explain by reference to crime and homicide rates (Page & Shapiro, 1992, pp. 92–94; Rankin, 1979). The initial period of declining support (1953–1966) occurred at a time when the reported violent crime rate and the homicide rate were both comparatively low; the rapid increase in support that followed (1966–1982) corresponded roughly to a period of rapid increase in both of these indices of criminal violence; and the current pattern of high but stable support (1982–1992) developed in a period of high and reasonably stable violent crime and homicide rates. Figure 7-4 shows these trends.

This is a simple commonsensical explanation: when crime goes up, people look for harsher punishments to bring it back down. Page and Shapiro report similar changes in the 1960s and 1970s for other sketchier attitudinal measures of punitiveness, such as the proportion of respondents who felt the courts are "not harsh enough" in their treatment of criminals (1992, pp. 90–93). The actual relationship between crime and death-penalty attitudes is bound to be more complicated. Public attitudes are not shaped by events themselves, but by public perception of those events. Thus it may be appropriate to assume a time lag between the reported crime rate and its impact on public opinion (Rankin, 1979), and it is likely that other factors—such as changes in media coverage—exaggerate or dampen the effects of the underlying phenomena.

Despite these qualifications, the first two stages we have described seem clear enough: support for capital punishment declined when crime was low, and increased when it rose. What has happened since, and what to expect in the future, are different matters. For example, Fox et al. point out that the homicide rate peaked in 1980 at 10.2 (per 100,000 people), and declined to 8.4 by 1988, while support, if anything, increased slightly (1991, p. 509, Fig. 3). This could mean that the decrease in homicide had not yet been noticed and absorbed; for example, Fox et al. cite data showing that, in 1989, 82% of a national sample believed, erroneously, that crime was on the increase (Strasser, 1989). It could also mean that the decrease in homicide (assuming it was known) was too small or short term to matter. (And indeed, as Figure 7-4 reveals, the homicide and crime rates have both increased again since 1987.) Finally, it is possible that this is not a symmetrical relationship, at least not in the short run. People who came to support the death penalty because of increasing crime may not change their minds back once the crime rate goes down. Under some circumstances, they might interpret the decrease as evidence that the death penalty, or other punitive measures, were successful.

Whatever the relationship between crime and support for the death penalty, it is not driven by personal experience. Many studies have shown that people who have been victimized themselves, or who fear for their personal safety, are no more likely to support the death penalty than those who have been more fortunate, or are less fearful (Fattah, 1979; Fox et al., 1991; Rankin, 1979; Smith, 1976; Stinchcombe et al., 1980; Taylor, Scheppele, & Stinchcombe, 1979; Tyler & Weber, 1982). On the other hand, a few studies have shown that concern about crime as a social issue *is* associated with support for capital punishment, if only weakly (Stinchcombe et al., 1980). If there is any one emotion that mediates between crime

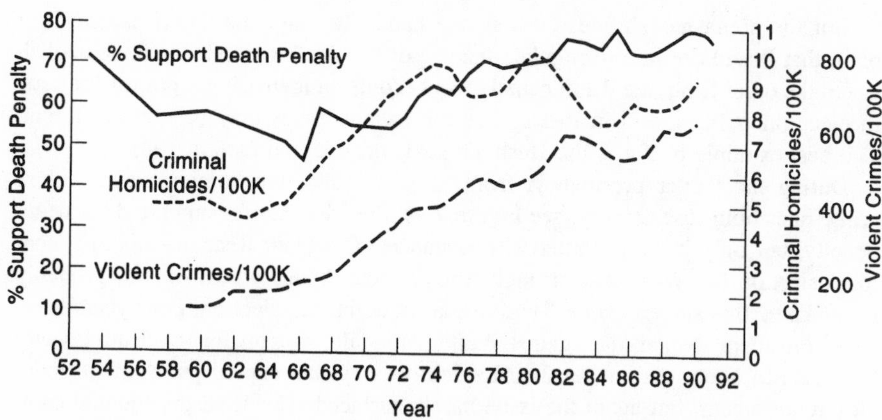

Figure 7–4. Support for the death penalty, and crime and homicide rates. Percentage of the population supporting the death penalty is represented in the scale on the left; see footnote 1 for data sources. The scale on the right axis represents the annual number of homicides per 100,000 inhabitants and the scale on the extreme right represents the annual number of violent crimes per 100,000 inhabitants; the data for the corresponding lines are from U.S. Department of Justice (1957–1990).

and support for the death penalty, it is probably frustration rather than fear. Year after year we live with high crime rates, we see graphic coverage of violence, we hear politicians promise to win the war against violence, against gangs, against drugs, against crime—but nothing changes. It is not hard to understand why many people support capital punishment even though they believe it does not deter crime and is not fair. The death penalty is concrete, it is forceful, and it is final (which nothing else seems to be); it is *something,* and being for it means that you insist that *something* be done.

In the 1970s and 1980s, most research on capital punishment in the United States was addressed to constitutional issues that were pending in the Supreme Court. This explains the interest in deterrence in the early 1970s: the constitutional significance of the deterrent effect of the death penalty was left open by the *Furman* decision in 1972. In 1976, however, in *Gregg v. Georgia,* the Court disposed of that issue by setting it aside, and interest in the topic diminished. Similarly, scholarly interest in death qualification was driven by the litigation leading up to the Supreme Court's definitive rejection of social science research in *Lockhart v. McCree* (1986), and interest in racial discrimination in capital punishment peaked in preparation for the Court's rejection of that claim in *McCleskey v. Kemp* (1987). To some extent, the same is true of research on attitudes toward capital punishment. Several of the best studies conducted in the 1970s were addressed to Justice Marshall's hypothesis in *Furman* that public support of the death penalty was caused by public ignorance, and several other studies since have also attempted to explain public attitudes in terms of the justifications for capital punishment that are described in *Furman* and *Gregg:* deterrence, retribution, incapacitation.

But the arena has shifted. On the one hand, the Supreme Court has made it plain that it will do little to regulate the use of the death penalty, let alone abolish it. On the other hand, the death penalty has become an increasingly prominent issue in electoral politics, and in that sphere the salient issues may be quite different. The best example by far is the Bush–Dukakis presidential race in 1988.

During the Carter presidency, from 1976 to 1980, the homicide and violent crime rates both rose sharply (see Figure 7-4). President Carter supported the death penalty, but only in very limited circumstances; Governor Reagan—his opponent for reelection in 1980—was strongly for it. Most Americans, however, probably never knew this since "crime" was not an issue in that election. Four years later, when President Reagan ran against Walter Mondale, support for the death penalty had risen to about current levels. Mondale was against capital punishment under all circumstances, but again the issue barely surfaced. The 1988 presidential campaign started out the same way. In a national poll in May, respondents were asked which candidate "comes closer to your way of thinking" on the death penalty; 18% chose Dukakis, 21% chose Bush, and 61% said there was no difference or had no opinion (Gallup, 5/88). We can only conclude that Dukakis's position was not yet well known. In July, 15% said Dukakis had "the best policy on the death penalty," 19% said Bush did, 14% were unsure, and nearly half—49%—had not heard enough to say (*L.A. Times,* 7/88). That did not last. In October, 71% of a national sample correctly chose Dukakis as the candidate who opposed the death penalty (12% chose Bush; Gallup, 10/88), and 63% of another national sample agreed that Dukakis "is too soft on law enforcement because he is against the death penalty and because he let a dangerous murderer go on furlough in Massachusetts, who then committed rape" (Harris, 10/88). By early November, respondents picked Bush over Dukakis as the candidate who would "do a better job of requiring the death penalty for crimes involving murder" by 61% to 24% (Yankelovitch, 11/88). After the election, 57% of Bush voters and 38% of Dukakis voters said the death penalty was "very important" to them in deciding who to vote for (Gallup, 11/88).

What happened between May and October is no secret. Starting in August, and accelerating in September after the national conventions were over, the Bush campaign drummed home the theme that is captured succinctly in the Harris poll question reproduced above: Dukakis is soft on crime because he is against the death penalty, and because he is responsible for the furlough of Willie Horton, the "dangerous murderer," who immediately committed a vicious rape. The attention this issue received seems to have created a short-term spike in general support for capital punishment. In April 1988, the GSS measured support at 71%. In the heat of the campaign, two Gallup polls, in September and in October of 1988, both found 79% support (an all-time record for "standard" death penalty questions), and a CBS/*N.Y. Times* poll in October registered 78% support. A second CBS/*N.Y. Times* poll taken two months after the election, in January 1989, was back at 71% support, and the 1989 GSS, in April of that year, found 74% in favor of capital punishment.

There are two major lessons to be learned from the Willie Horton campaign.

The first is that (for now at least) a candidate for president must support the death penalty. Governor Clinton made his support clear by presiding over two executions in Arkansas during the 1992 presidential campaign. As a result, the issue never surfaced in the presidential debates, in Republican campaign ads, or for that matter, in the national opinion polls—and Clinton won. Criminal justice in the United States is primarily a state and local function, and the federal death penalty in particular is a miniscule part of the nation's capital punishment system. Nonetheless, it may be a long time before anyone who opposes the death penalty is considered eligible for a major party nomination. The death penalty was not always so powerful a political issue. In 1978 Governor Jerry Brown, a life-long opponent of capital punishment, won reelection in California on the same ballot on which 72% of the electorate voted for a death penalty referendum, despite the fact that he had vetoed death penalty legislation just the year before (Poulos, 1990). By 1990, the California Democratic gubernatorial primary seemed to have become a contest over which candidate could be counted on to put more people to death (Gross, 1993).

The second lesson is that capital punishment, like violence and crime in general, is racially charged. It is no coincidence that Willie Horton is Black, or that the Bush campaign did everything humanly possible to make sure that every American voter got to see his picture.

Some Future Directions

Attitudes about capital punishment cannot be explained once and for all. Their meaning changes as the political climate changes, as the world changes, and as the media change people's perceptions of the world. New avenues of research are suggested.

The Willie Horton episode epitomizes the importance of studying racial factors. To what extent do attitudes toward the death penalty draw strength from the increasing association of race and crime in White people's minds? Not entirely, to be sure: the most horrifying criminals—Dahmer, Gacy, Bundy—are White, but these are the crazies, separate from people's perceptions of routine out-of-control violence in our cities. The relations between attitudes toward Blacks, crime, and the death penalty have not been explored in any depth. A second, equally interesting and even more neglected topic is Black Americans' attitudes toward capital punishment. Always more opposed than Whites, always more conscious of its discriminatory application, Blacks nonetheless are now more likely to favor the death penalty than to oppose it. It is very unlikely that the dynamics of Black attitudes are the same as those of the Whites, but there is no research on the topic.

Bowers' (1993) finding that people prefer guaranteed life imprisonment to the death penalty also raises new questions. In his research, the motives of incapacitation and retribution are inextricably confounded. If people were satisfied that a murderer could never commit another crime, would that be enough, or must he also suffer? What would people say if asked, "Would you rather Willie Horton was sentenced for life to a pleasant but utterly secure prison in Tahiti, with no possibility of ever returning to society, or would you rather he was sentenced to a vicious overcrowded maximum security prison for 30 years?'' We have not moved far in untangling utilitarian and emotional bases for death penalty attitudes.

People's feelings about the death penalty are intense, yet we still have done very little to explore the underlying emotions. Research suggests that fear is not the driving emotion. Future research should focus on other emotions, particularly frustration and anger. Anger is the most positive of the negative emotions, because it is the only one that confers a sense of power (Ellsworth & Smith, 1988; Roseman, 1984). When politicians argue, angrily, for the death penalty, they may communicate that they are in control, and at the same time arouse a satisfying sense of outrage and power in the voter. This is, of course speculation; the emotional dynamics of death penalty attitudes may be quite different. But there is no doubt that emotions play a role, and so far there has been little effort to understand that role.

Notes

1. The time line displayed in Figure 7-1 is based on data from polls by the Gallup organization for 1936–71 and for 1981, and on data from the NORC's General Social Surveys (GSS) for 1972–78, for 1980, and for 1982–91. These choices reflect competing considerations. The General Social Survey is the best periodic national opinion poll available, but Gallup has the longest history of conducting national surveys that include questions on capital punishment. Therefore, we have used GSS data when possible, and Gallup data otherwise. These are not, of course, the only national polls on general attitudes toward the death penalty. A computerized data base that is publicly available from the Roper Center for Public Opinion Research at the University of Connecticut included 90 such surveys as of July 1993. The Appendix includes a list of all these surveys, the text of the questions asked, and the proportions of respondents giving each coded answer. Unless otherwise attributed, the polls we refer to in the text are taken from the Roper data base, which can be accessed through LEXIS or WESTLAW, and will be referred to simply by survey organization and the month and year in which the survey was completed (e.g., ''Gallup, 10/74''). In general, we focus on national surveys, and refer to local and regional studies to the extent that they cover ground not covered by the national polls.

2. Two limitations on the scope of this article are appropriate at this point. We do not discuss the issue of death penalty attitudes and jury selection in capital cases, commonly known as ''death qualification'' (see Ellsworth, 1988), and we do not discuss the personality correlates of death penalty attitudes.

3. Ellsworth and Ross (1983) also included the item, ''In several cases people executed for murder in the United States were later proven innocent.'' Supporters of capital punishment were less likely than opponents to agree with this statement, 46% to 66%, and more likely to reject it, 23% to 10%. Ellsworth and Ross, in keeping with the accepted wisdom of the time, interpreted the claim as false, and agreement with it as error. More recent research, however, suggests that several people executed for murder in the United States were indeed later proven innocent by reliable means (e.g., a death bed confession of the true criminal) if not in formal judicial proceedings (Radelet, Bedau, & Putnam, 1992).

References

Bohm, R. M. (1991). American death penalty opinion, 1936–1986: A critical examination of the Gallup polls. In R. M. Bohm (Ed.), *The death penalty in America: Current research* (pp. 113–45). Highland Heights, KY, and Cincinnati, OH: ACJS/Anderson.

Bowers, W. J. (1993). Capital punishment and contemporary values: People's misgivings and the Court's misperception. *Law and Society Review, 27,* 157–75.

Bowers, W. J., & Vandiver, M. (1991a). *New Yorkers want an alternative to the death penalty: Executive summary of a New York State survey.* Boston: Criminal Justice Research Center, Northeastern University.

Bowers, W. J., & Vandiver, M. (1991b). *Nebraskans want an alternative to the death penalty: Executive summary of Nebraska State Survey.* Boston: Criminal Justice Research Center, Northeastern University.

California v. Ramos, 463 U.S. 992 (1982).

Cook, P. J., & Slawson, D. B. (1993). *The costs of processing murder cases in North Carolina.* Terry Sanford Institute of Public Policy, Duke University.

Costanzo, S., & Costanzo, M. (1994). Life or death decisions: An analysis of capital jury decision making under the special issues sentencing framework. *Law and Human Behavior, 18,* 151–70.

Dieter, R. C. (1992). *Millions misspent: What politicians don't say about the high costs of the death penalty.* Washington, DC: The Death Penalty Information Center.

Dieter, R. C. (1993). *Sentencing for life: Americans embrace alternatives to the death penalty.* Washington, DC: The Death Penalty Information Center.

Doob, A. N., & Roberts, J. (1984). Social psychology, social attitudes, and attitudes toward sentencing. *Canadian Journal of Behavioural Science, 16,* 269–80.

Ellsworth, P. C. (1978, November). *Attitudes toward capital punishment: From application to theory.* Paper presented at the Society of Experimental Social Psychology Symposium on Psychology and Law, Stanford, CA.

Ellsworth, P. C. (1988). Unpleasant facts: The Supreme Court's response to empirical research on the death penalty. In K. C. Haas & J. Inciardi (Eds.), *Challenging Capital Punishment: Legal and Social Science Approaches.* (pp. 177–221). Beverley Hills, CA: Sage.

Ellsworth, P. C., & Ross, L. (1983, January). Public opinion and capital punishment: A close examination of the views of abolitionists and retentionists. *Crime and Delinquency,* pp. 116–69.

Ellsworth, P. C., & Smith, C. (1988). From appraisal to emotion: Differences among unpleasant feelings. *Motivation and Emotion, 12,* 271–302.

Erskine, H. (1970). The polls: Capital punishment. *Public Opinion Quarterly, 34,* 290–307.

Fattah, E. A. (1979). Perceptions of violence, concern about crime, fear of victimization and attitudes to the death penalty. *Canadian Journal of Criminology, 21,* 22–38.

Fein, S., & Lord, C. G. (1987). *Concrete prototypes for abstract attitudes: The case of capital punishment.* Paper presented at the 59th annual meeting of the Midwestern Psychological Association, Chicago.

Fox, J. A., Radelet, M. L., & Bonsteel, J. L. (1991). Death penalty opinion in the post-*Furman* years. *New York University Review of Law and Social Change, 28,* 499–528.

Furman v. Georgia, 408 U.S. 238 (1972). Gallup Poll News Service. (1991). *56,* no. 8a.

Gorecki, J. (1983). *Capital punishment: Criminal law and social evolution.* New York: Columbia University Press.

Gregg v. Georgia, 428 U.S. 153 (1976).

Gross, S. R. (1993). The romance of revenge: Capital punishment in America. *Studies in Law, Politics and Society, 13,* 71–104.

Haney, C., Hurtado, A., & Vega, L. (1993). *Enlightened by a humane justice: Public opinion and the death penalty in California.* Unpublished manuscript, University of California, Santa Cruz.

Harris, P. W. (1986). Oversimplification and error in public opinion surveys on capital punishment. *Justice Quarterly, 3,* 429–55.

Kinder, D. R. (1994). Reason and emotion in American political life. In R. Schank & E. Langer (Eds.), *Beliefs, reasoning, and decision making* (pp. 277–314). Hillsdale, NJ: Erlbaum.

Lockhart v. McCree, 476 U.S. 162 (1986).

Lord, C. G., Ross, L., & Lepper, M. R. (1979). Biased assimilation and attitude polarization: The effects of prior theories on subsequently considered evidence. *Journal of Personality and Social Psychology, 37,* 2098–109.

McCleskey v. Kemp, 481 U.S. 279 (1987).

Nisbett, R. E., & Wilson, T. (1977). Telling more than we can know: Verbal reports on mental processes. *Psychological Review, 84,* 231–51.

Page, B. I., & Shapiro, R. Y. (1992). *The rational public.* Chicago: University of Chicago Press.

Penry v. Lynaugh, 492 U.S. 302 (1989).

Poulos, J. W. (1990). Capital punishment, the legal process, and the emergence of the Lucas Court in California. *University of California at Davis Law Review, 23,* 157–332.

Radelet, M. L., Bedau, H. A., & Putnam, C. E. (1992). *In spite of innocence.* Boston: Northeastern University Press.

Rankin, J. (1979). Changing attitudes towards capital punishment. *Social Forces, 58,* 194–211.

Rapaport, R.(1991). The death penalty and gender discrimination. *Law & Society Review, 25,* 367–83.

Roberts, J. V. (1984). Public opinion and capital punishment—The effects of attitudes upon memory. *Canadian Journal of Criminology, 26,* 283–91.

Roberts v. Louisiana, 428 U.S. 325 (1976).

Roseman, I. (1984). Cognitive determinants of emotions: A structural theory. In P. Shaver (Ed.), *Review of personality and social psychology: Vol. 5. Emotions, relationships, and health* (pp. 11–36). Beverly Hills, CA: Sage.

Sarat, A., & Vidmar, N. (1976). Public opinion, the death penalty, and the eighth amendment: Testing the Marshall hypothesis. *Wisconsin Law Review, 17,* 171–206.

Schuman, H., & Presser, S. (1981). *Questions and answers in attitude surveys.* San Diego, CA: Academic Press.

Smith, T. W. (1976). A trend analysis of attitudes towards capital punishment, 1936–1974. In J. E. Davis (Ed.), *Studies of social change since 1948* (Vol II). Chicago: NORC.

Stinchcombe, A., Adams, R., Heimer, C., Scheppele, K., Smith, T., & Taylor, D. (1980). *Crime and punishment: Changing attitudes in America.* San Francisco: Jossey-Bass.

Strasser, F. (1989). One nation, under seige. *National Law Journal,* S2–S15.

Taylor, D. G., Scheppele, K. L., & Stinchcombe, A. L. (1979). Salience of crime and support for harsher criminal sanctions. *Social Problems, 26,* 413–24.

Thomas, C. W. (1977). Eighth amendment challenges to the death penalty: The relevance of informed public opinion. *Vanderbilt Law Review, 30,* 1005–30.

Thomas, C. W., & Foster, S. C. (1975). A sociological perspective on public support for capital punishment. *American Journal of Orthopsychiatry, 45,* 641–57.

Tyler, T., & Weber, R. (1982). Support for the death penalty: Instrumental response to crime, or symbolic attitude? *Law and Society Review, 17,* 21–45.

U.S. Department of Justice. (1957–1990). *Crime in the United States, Uniform Crime Reports.* Washington, DC: Government Printing Office.

Vidmar, N. (1974). Retributive and utilitarian motives and other correlates of Canadian attitudes towards the death penalty. *The Canadian Psychologist, 15,* 337–56.

Vidmar, N., & Ellsworth, P. C. (1974). Public opinion and the death penalty. *Stanford Law Review, 26,* 1245–70.

Wallace, D. H. (1989). Bloodbath and brutalization: Public opinion and the death penalty. *Journal of Crime and Justice, 12,* 51–77.

Warr, M., & Stafford, M. (1984). Public goals of punishment and support for the death penalty. *Journal of Research in Crime and Delinquency, 21,* 95–111.

Woodson v. North Carolina, 428 U.S. 280 (1976).

Zeisel, H., & Gallup, A. M. (1989). Death penalty sentiment in the United States. *Journal of Quantitative Criminology, 5,* 285–96.

Zimring, F. E., & Hawkins, G. (1986). *Capital punishment and the American agenda.* Cambridge: Cambridge University Press.

8

Sentencing for Life: Americans Embrace Alternatives to the Death Penalty

RICHARD C. DIETER

Contrary to the conventional wisdom that Americans wholeheartedly support the death penalty, the latest national opinion poll released in conjunction with this report shows that more people in this country would prefer alternative sentences that guarantee both protection and punishment over the death penalty. Death penalty support becomes a minority opinion when the public is presented with a variety of alternative sentences. Most Americans, however, are unaware that the length of imprisonment embodied in these alternatives is now the norm almost everywhere in the country. . . .

Public Opinion and the Death Penalty

In 1966, more Americans opposed the death penalty than favored it.[1] Executions were halted in 1967 and did not resume for 10 years when support for the death penalty had grown. Today, a new phenomenon is emerging from the polls. Support for the death penalty drops precisely to the same low percentage as in 1966 when people are given the choice of stringent alternative sentences.

In March of this year, the polling firms of Greenberg/Lake and the Tarrance Group conducted a national survey of people's opinions about the death penalty. This poll revealed an increasing trend, first detected in a series of state polls on this issue, that Americans would favor certain alternative sentences over the death penalty. Although a majority of those interviewed said they favored capital punishment abstractly, that support is reversed when the sentence of life without parole,

From a report by the Death Penalty Information Center, Richard C. Dieter, executive director, Washington, D.C., April 1993. Some text, tables, figures, and references have been deleted, and the remaining references renumbered. Reprinted by permission of the author.

The latest poll results cited in this report are based on a nationwide telephone survey of 1,000 registered voters conducted between February 28 and March 1, 1993, by Greenberg/Lake and the Tarrance Group. The sample was distributed based upon voter turnout in the last three presidential elections. A sample of this type is likely to yield a margin of error of +/−3.1%.

coupled with a requirement of restitution, is offered as an alternative. Forty-four percent favor that alternative, while only 41% selected the death penalty. Even the choice of a sentence which guaranteed restitution and no release for at least 25 years caused death penalty support to drop by 33%.

These results indicate a strong desire on the part of the public for protection from those who have committed society's worst crimes. There is also a preference for connecting punishment with restitution to those who have been hurt by crime. Support for the death penalty drops below 50% with a range of alternative sentences, especially those including restitution. Compared to the 77% who favor the death penalty in the abstract, support drops by 21% when a sentence of life with no parole for 25 years is considered; if a requirement of restitution is added to that sentence, support drops by 33%. And the sentence of life without parole plus restitution causes a support drop of 36% and relegates capital punishment to a minority position. . . .

Doubts About the Death Penalty

Most people express doubts about the death penalty when presented with some of the problems which have plagued this ultimate punishment for years. Forty-eight percent responded that the issue of racism in the application of capital punishment raised some or serious doubts about the death penalty. The perception of racial injustice within the criminal justice system, symbolized by the image of Rodney King in Los Angeles, is reinforced by the fact that Blacks are represented on death row three and half times their proportion in the population as a whole. And defendants who kill a white person in America are many times more likely to get the death penalty than those who kill a black person.[2] It is not surprising that almost three-fourths of Blacks believe that a black person is more likely than a white person to receive the death penalty for the same crime.[3] As these facts about capital punishment become more widely known, the enthusiasm for the death penalty may continue to wane.

Americans also expressed doubts about the death penalty after hearing information about the costs of the death penalty and the absence of any unique deterrent effect. The strongest doubts, however, were raised by the prospect that innocent people could be executed. Fifty-eight percent of those polled said the question of innocence raised doubts in them about the death penalty. . . .

Results from State Polls

Although the results from this latest poll may be surprising to those who believe that capital punishment has wide and unwavering support, they are consistent with a series of state polls which have explored some of the same issues over the past five years. These polls repeatedly showed that when people were presented with alternatives to the death penalty, their support for the death penalty dropped dramatically. Polls conducted in recent years in California, Florida, Georgia, Kentucky, Minnesota, Nebraska, New York, Oklahoma, Virginia and West Virginia all concluded that people prefer various alternative sentences to the death penalty.[4]

Another interesting finding reported consistently in the state polls, and confirmed by the national poll, is that death penalty support drops more with an alternative sentence of no parole for 25 years than with a sentence mandating absolutely no parole, *provided* that the lesser sentence is combined with the requirement of restitution.[5] This result challenges the notion that people automatically favor the harshest of all possible sentences, such as the death penalty or life with no parole. Rather, people support reasonable alternatives which attempt to restore equilibrium and justice where it has been fractured in society. . . .

Moreover, the support for alternatives to the death penalty appears to be growing. In a national poll in 1986, Gallup reported a 19% drop in support for the death penalty when life without parole was offered as an alternative.[6] The same question produced a 23% drop in 1991.[7] Now, in 1993, support for the death penalty dropped 28% when this same alternative was offered in the Greenberg/Lake poll. Similarly, a state poll conducted in New York in 1989 revealed that 62% of the people would prefer a sentence of life without parole plus mandatory restitution rather than the death penalty. In 1991, the same question was asked and 73% supported this alternative.[8] . . . These and similar results from other states show the shallowness in the support for capital punishment. People are frustrated and frightened about violent crime. If they are offered no alternatives which reasonably meet their concerns for protection and punishment, then the death penalty seems attractive.

Jurors, too, look for alternatives. As many prosecutors who have brought "sure fire" death cases to juries know, there is often a reluctance by jurors to actually impose the death sentence on guilty murderers.[9] Jurors faced with making life and death decisions repeatedly inquire about the true meaning of a "life sentence," apparently hoping that this sentence will provide them with an acceptable alternative to sentencing someone to death.[10] When they are told that parole eligibility will not be explained, they incorrectly assume that the defendant will be out again in seven years. Faced with that alternative, jurors often choose death. . . .

The Trend Toward Longer Incarceration

The development of prison sentences in which parole is restricted either for a substantial number of years or forever is a growing trend among states today. As a response to violent murders, almost every state, as well as the federal government, now uses a lengthy guaranteed minimum sentence before parole can even be considered. (See Figure 8-1) The perception that a murderer convicted of a capital crime will be back on the streets in seven years if not given the death penalty is totally inaccurate. . . .

Effectiveness of Alternative Sentences

People are frightened by press accounts of parole consideration for such notorious criminals as Charles Manson and Sirhan Sirhan. No doubt, people believe that if

Alabama	Idaho	Missouri	Rhode Island*
Arkansas	Illinois	Montana	South Dakota
California	Iowa*	Nebraska	Utah
Colorado	Louisiana	Nevada	Vermont*
Connecticut	Maine*	New Hampshire	Washington
Delaware	Maryland	Oklahoma	West Virginia*
District of Col.*	Massachusetts*	Oregon	Wyoming
Hawaii*	Michigan*	Pennsylvania	
*States without the death penalty.			

Figure 8–1. Life without parole states.

these criminals are eligible for parole, anyone would be. But neither of these men was sentenced under a life *without* parole scheme, since that penalty had not been enacted when they had committed their crimes. The fact that these and similar cases receive consideration for parole, even though denied, tends to obscure the fact that today such offenders would not even be eligible for parole. In every state, the myth that if people are not given the death penalty they will be released in seven years is simply not true.

People are also disturbed by reports of prisoners who actually are released after a relatively short time, some of whom commit additional crimes. In Texas, for example, there is much confusion about sentencing. Prisoners, on the whole, are only serving 20% of their sentences and recidivism is a serious problem.[11] Typically, even those with a life sentence have been getting out in less than six years, partly due to the overcrowding in Texas' prisons.[12] What is not widely known, however, is that for those convicted of *capital murder,* the reality is now quite different: a life sentence for them means they would not even be *eligible for parole* for thirty-five years. (See Figure 8-2) However, Texas law forbids either side from informing the jury about the true meaning of a life sentence in a capital case, and so death sentences are being returned under a gross misperception. Jurors, and the public in general, mistakenly believe they must choose between releasing a violent murderer in six years or imposing the death penalty, even though the reality is quite different.

States that have used the sentence of life without parole say it works as promised. California has had a sentence of life without parole for over twenty-five years and not one person sentenced under this law has been released from prison.[13] In Alabama, U.S. Court of Appeals Judge Edward Carnes, who headed the state's capital punishment division as assistant attorney general for many years, said that "life without parole in Alabama means just that—no parole, no commutation, no way out until the day you die, period."[14] . . .

Most of the states without the death penalty now utilize a sentence of life without parole for their worst offenders. Michigan, for example, has had a mandatory life law for first degree murder at least since 1931. . . . For the past decade, the governor

Alaska* 33 yr	Minnesota* 30 yr	Ohio 20 yr
Arizona 25 yr	New Jersey 30 yr	S. Carolina 30 yr
Florida 25 yr	New Mexico 30 yr	Tennesee* 25 yr
Indiana* 30 yr	New York* 25 yr	Texas 35 yr
Kansas* 40 yr	N. Carolina 20 yr	Virginia* 21 yr
Kentucky 25 yr	N. Dakota* 30 yr	

*States without the death penalty.

Figure 8–2. Restricted parole: years before parole eligibility under available sentences for 1st degree murder convictions.

has averaged only one commutation per year of those sentenced to life for first degree murder. The time served for those few who were commuted between 1983 and 1990 averaged 27 years.[15] In the District of Columbia, the voters overwhelmingly rejected the death penalty shortly after the city council passed legislation allowing for a sentence of life without parole for first degree murder. . . .

Commutation of Sentence

For those who would opt for a sentence under which prisoners could never be released, the theoretical possibility of executive clemency may appear to be a problem. In most states, either the governor or an appropriate board has the power to commute sentences.[16] Unless restricted by law, such a process could result in the reduction of a life without parole sentence to a simple life sentence where parole is possible.

In reality, however, this is a very remote possibility. Governors have the same power to grant clemency in death sentences but rarely do. On the average, there has only been 1 such commutation in 20 years for each state with the death penalty.[17] Presumably, if the same defendants had been given life without parole sentences, governors would have had even less incentive to commute them since the possibility of a mistaken execution would no longer be a motivation. This is borne out in states like Michigan, California and South Dakota which have had a life without parole sentence for some time and where commutations of those convicted of first degree murder are exceedingly rare or nonexistent.[18]. . . .

Juror Awareness of Alternative Sentencing

In America, juries are the voice of the people. As with the public at large, those who have served as jurors often prefer alternative sentences to the death penalty. A 1992 survey of nearly 800 jurors revealed that only 41% supported the death penalty if alternatives like life without parole were offered.[19] But just as the public is unaware of the fundamental changes in U.S. sentencing laws which have led to longer sentences, so, too, those with the responsibility for considering death sentences are without the correct information. Jurors in capital cases are particularly troubled because they believe they must choose between sentencing someone to death or allowing them to be released in a relatively short time. As the late Georgia Supreme Court Judge Charles Weltner said, "Everybody believes that a person sentenced to life for murder will be walking the streets in seven years." He went on to predict that the option of 20 to 25 years parole ineligibility "would lower the number of death penalties that are given."[20]

The only problem with this prediction is that Georgia law (and the law of many other states) forbids the judge from explaining anything to the jury about parole possibilities, even if the judge receives a direct question from the panel while they are deliberating on a defendant's life or death sentence. In 23 of the 29 states which utilize sentencing by the jury in capital cases, there is an absolute prohibition against any evidence or argument on parole.[21] As a result, jurors are left to their own misperceptions. . . .

A study by the National Legal Research Group demonstrated the danger of uninformed jurors. The study found that prospective jurors in a sample Virginia county:

- Believed that a capital defendant sentenced to life imprisonment will likely serve only ten years in prison;
- Believed that the length of time a capital defendant will *actually* serve when sentenced to life imprisonment is important to the penalty determination;
- Would disregard a judge's instruction not to consider parole when sentencing a capital defendant; and
- Would be influenced significantly in their sentencing decisions by information about Virginia's mandatory minimum sentence of 25 years for capital defendants.[22]

From this and similar studies in other states,[23] it is clear that many jurors are sentencing people to death because they either lack adequate alternatives or because they are unaware that such alternatives exist. . . . Even when a state has incorporated a life without parole option into its choice of sentences, the jurors are likely to believe that the defendant will still be released and, therefore, are more likely to return a death verdict. In a survey of 250 potential jurors in Louisiana, an overwhelming 92% of those polled interpreted a "life sentence without the benefit of probation, parole or suspension of sentence" as meaning that the individual would still be eligible for release in a number of years.[24]

Politicians often add to these inaccurate perceptions when they use the death penalty to bolster their campaigns. For example, while running for governor of California as a pro–death penalty candidate, Dianne Feinstein claimed: "You can't expect somebody to be deterred from committing murder if they know they will only serve four to five years."[25] What she neglected to say is that for those who face the death penalty, the only alternative sentence in California is life imprisonment with *no possibility of parole.* It is not surprising, then, that 64% of Californians erroneously believe that those sentenced under life without parole would nevertheless be released.[26] Interestingly, politicians mistakenly believe that their constituents strongly prefer the death penalty over its alternatives. In New York, for example, 70% of the legislators polled thought their constituents would prefer the death penalty over a variety of alternatives. In fact, over 70% of the people would choose the alternative of life without parole plus restitution.[27]

This research implies that a sentence which eliminates parole for a substantial period, especially if coupled with a restitution requirement, is an appropriate alternative. It is appropriate because people prefer such an alternative to capital punishment and it protects society as well as the death penalty. Under the present system people are being sentenced to death under the erroneous assumption that, otherwise, the prisoner would be released early. To the extent that jurors have been choosing the death sentence in past cases based on this assumption, the executions which resulted are tragic mistakes.

The Effects of a Life Sentence

The existence of a stringent life sentence can either partially or completely eliminate the imagined need for the death penalty. In some states, a life without parole sentence is used as an option when the death penalty is not selected; in other states, like Michigan and Massachusetts, it exists as a complete replacement to capital punishment. In Maryland, for example, the state added the sentence of life without parole in 1987 as a choice for the jury in capital cases. Jurors are specifically instructed that they can choose a sentence of life without parole instead of the death penalty. In the five years since then, only eight new defendants have been added to the state's death row. A similar reduction in death sentences has resulted since Oklahoma introduced life without parole in 1988. That year, Oklahoma sentenced 18 people to death. Last year, there were only five death sentences.[28] In contrast, Florida, which does not have life without parole, added 45 people to its death row in 1991.[29]

Sentences with significant minimum terms can also provide the public with the protection from repeat offenders that they want. An inmate released at the age of 55 or 60 years old is statistically far less likely to engage in crime than someone in their late 20s. Violent crime arrest rates peak at age 18 and then gradually decline to almost zero at age 60 and over.[30] As Louisiana's district attorney, Harry Connick, Sr., said: "When a guy gets to be 60, he's not gonna rip and run a lot. Not like he used to."[31] In addition, convicted murderers are among the least likely offenders to repeat their crime, even if released. . . .[32]

Prisoners Serving Life

Inside prison, a number of wardens report that those serving life sentences are the best-behaved prisoners in their entire system. Leo Lalonde of the Michigan Department of Corrections says of those serving life without parole sentences: "After a few years, lifers become your better prisoners. They tend to adjust and just do their time. They tend to be a calming influence on the younger kids, and we have more problems with people serving short terms.''[33] Similarly, Alabama officials noted that their life without parole inmates commit 50% fewer disciplinary offenses per capita than all other types of inmates combined.[34]

Lifers can also make a significant contribution to society in the time given them. For example, Craig Datesman at Graterford Prison in Pennsylvania coordinates a Lifers project to help young people who have had some trouble with the law to go straight. ''We have taken a life and so we feel it's our responsibility to save a life now,'' said Datesman.[35] Executions, of course, cut off the possibility of any restitution to society or the family of the victim. . . .

Restitution

Requiring those who have committed murder to make some monetary restitution to the family of the victim is strongly supported by those choosing alternatives to the death penalty. However, this sanction has not yet been widely employed by states. Inmates generally receive little in the way of remuneration for work performed in prison, usually barely enough for cigarettes or candy. A requirement of restitution might mean raising the pay for prison work. Nevertheless, the various opinion polls discussed above show that a requirement of restitution is one of the most consistent demands by those preferring alternatives to the death penalty.

One measure of what might be a feasible form of restitution was included in a New York opinion poll. New Yorkers were about evenly split in saying that $150,000 in restitution to the family of the victim would be either ''about right'' or ''too little.'' The $150,000 restitution figure was derived from a requirement that the prisoner work 40 hours per week, 50 weeks per year, over 25 years at $3 per hour.[36] While the details of a restitution plan need to be worked out, polls show that the concept is extremely important to many people and could be incorporated further into the correctional system.

Many states are becoming more conscious of the needs of victims in their criminal justice systems.[37] Although funds for victim assistance are often provided directly from the state budget, some states are proposing restitution from the work of prisoners themselves. A bill before the 1993 Nebraska legislature would abolish the state's death penalty and instead impose a restitution requirement along with a sentence of life without parole. And in Arkansas, California, Wisconsin, Idaho, and Oregon, restitution to the victim's family can already be required of the offender in homicide cases.[38] . . .

The Politics of Death

In some states, politicians who favor the death penalty have resisted stiffer sentences which eliminate parole because they fear that with real alternatives in place there will be no more need for the death penalty. In New York, for example, the politicians who have succeeded in derailing Gov. Cuomo's alternative of life without parole are those who favor the death penalty. They do not hide their manipulation of the issue: they would rather have criminals get out sooner than give up the death penalty as a cheap symbol for being tough on crime. This is what Gov. Cuomo called "the politics of death":

> Life without parole is achievable immediately. The Legislature could enact it Monday. I would sign the measure Tuesday. It would apply to crimes committed the next day. In fact, the only thing preventing the next cop killer from spending every day of the rest of his life in jail is the politics of death. . . . [39]

In the end, . . . people will select politicians who conform to their opinions. For years, the myth that Americans love the death penalty has fueled an expansion of capital punishment and politicians' cry for more executions. But as the public's preference for alternative sentences becomes more widely known, and as those sentences become incorporated into law, the justifications for the death penalty will have finally disappeared. . . .

Notes

1. H. Zeisel & A. Gallup, *Death Penalty Sentiment in the United States,* 5 Journal of Quantitative Criminology 285, 287 (1989).

2. See, e.g., *Death Penalty Sentencing: Research Indicates Pattern of Racial Disparities,* U.S. General Accounting Office, at 5 (1990).

3. A. Gallup & F. Newport, *Death Penalty Support Remains Strong, But Most Feel Unfairly Applied,* The Gallup Poll News Service, June 26, 1991, at 4.

4. Information regarding the various polls is on file with the Death Penalty Information Center.

5. W. Bowers & M. Vandiver, *New Yorkers Want an Alternative to the Death Penalty,* Executive Summary, appendix summarizing other state polls (1991).

6. Zeisel & Gallup, note 1, at 290.

7. M. Leary, *Counter-Trend to Death Penalty Emerging in California,* Pacific News Service, April 20–24, 1992, at 6 (reporting on California and national polls); see also Gallup & Newport, note 3.

8. See Bowers & Vandiver, note 5, at 3, 13.

9. See, e.g., J. DeParle, *Abstract Death Penalty Meets Real Execution,* The New York Times, June 30, 1991 (only 36% of those in a Justice Department survey voted for the death penalty in simulated cases typical of those punishable by death).

10. See Lane, *"Is There Life Without Parole?": A Capital Defendant's Right to a Meaningful Alternative Sentence,* 26 Loyola of Los Angeles Law Review 325, 390 (1993).

11. See *Funding the Justice System: A Call to Action,* the American Bar Association, at 54 (1992).

12. B. Denson, *The Pros, Cons of Throwing Away Key,* The Houston Post, July 14, 1991, at A-1.

13. Editorial, *No Parole Means What It Says,* San Francisco Chronicle, April 13, 1990 (citing a governor's study covering 1965 to 1990).

14. A. Malcolm, *Capital Punishment Is Popular, But So Are Its Alternatives,* The New York Times, Sept. 10, 1989, at 4E.

15. See Michigan Department of Corrections Memoranda, Feb. 10, 1993 (Terry Murphy), and April 11, 1991.

16. For example, all 36 States that authorize capital punishment have provisions for clemency. Herrera v. Collins, No. 91-7328, slip opinion, at 23, n. 14 (Jan. 25, 1993).

17. M. Radelet, *Clemency in Post-Furman Cases,* manuscript (Nov. 29, 1991).

18. See note 15; also M. Cuomo, *New York State Shouldn't Kill People,* The New York Times, June 17, 1989, and J. Kerkhove, *Lifer?,* The Messenger, July–Sept. 1992, at 19.

19. *The View From the Jury Box,* The National Law Journal, Feb. 22, 1993, at S2.

20. Savannah News-Press, Mar. 23, 1986, at 7C (quoted in Paduano & Smith, *Deathly Errors: Juror Misperceptions Concerning Parole in the Imposition of the Death Penalty,* 18 Columbia Human Rights Law Review 211, 213, n. 4 (1987)).

21. See Paduano & Smith, *Deathly Errors: Juror Misperceptions Concerning Parole in the Imposition of the Death Penalty,* 18 Columbia Human Rights Law Review 211, 216 (1987).

22. See W. Hood, Note: *The Meaning of "Life" for Virginia Jurors and Its Effect on Reliability in Capital Sentencing,* 75 Virginia Law Review 1605, 1624–25 (1989).

23. See, e.g., Dayan, Mahler, & Widenhouse, *Searching for an Impartial Sentencer Through Jury Selection in Capital Trials,* 23 Loyola of Los Angeles Law Review 151, 164–176 (1989).

24. Cypress Research and Development Corporation, letter and report to the Loyola Death Penalty Resource Center, Aug. 31, 1990.

25. The Sunday Times (London), Mar. 18, 1990 (quoted in G. Pierce & M. Radelet, *The Role and Consequences of the Death Penalty in American Politics,* 18 N.Y.U. Review of Law & Social Change 711, 725 (1990–91)).

26. *Californians' Attitudes About the Death Penalty: Results of a Statewide Survey,* public opinion poll implemented by the Field Research Corporation in Dec., 1989.

27. See Bowers & Vandiver, note 5, at 3 & 9.

28. *Death Verdicts Slip as No-Parole Grows,* The Daily Oklahoman, Nov. 10, 1992.

29. Bureau of Justice Statistics, *Capital Punishment 1991,* at 8 (October, 1992).

30. See Bureau of Justice Statistics, *Report to the Nation on Crime and Justice,* Second Edition, at 41–42 (March, 1988).

31. B. Denson, see note 12.

32. See Marquart & Sorenson, *A National Study of the* Furman*—Commuted Inmates: Assessing the Threat to Society from Capital Offenders,* 23 Loyola of Los Angeles Law Review 5, 23 (1989). In 1972, all the existing death sentences were overturned by the Supreme Court's decision in *Furman v. Georgia.* In 1989, Marquart and Sorenson looked at the cases of the 558 inmates whose death sentences were commuted to life imprisonment by *Furman.* Of these, 243 of the inmates were released to the community. Only one of those released committed a new homicide. Id. at 22–24

33. Katz, *In Mich., Life Without Parole,* Newsday, June 20, 1989, at 5. Thomas Coughlin, (former) Commissioner of the New York State Department of Correctional Services, made similar statements about "true lifers" in New York. See Tabak & Lane, *The Execution of Injustice: A Cost and Lack-of-Benefit Analysis of the Death Penalty,* 23 Loyola of Los Angeles Law Review 59 (1989), at 124–25.

34. See J. Wright, *Life-Without-Parole: An Alternative to Death or Not Much of a Life at All?,* 43 Vanderbilt Law Review 529 (1990), at 549.

35. S. Eisele, *Lifers Help Youths Stay Out of Jail,* Philadelphia Inquirer, Mar. 20, 1991, at 1-B.

36. W. Bowers, M. Vandiver, and P. Dugan, *A New Look at Public Opinion on Capital*

Punishment: What Citizens and Legislators Prefer, 22 American Journal of Criminal Law 77 (1994).

37. See, e.g., B. Galaway, *Restitution as Innovation or Unfilled Promise?,* 52 Federal Probation 3 (1988).

38. See *Restitution: Eligibility/Types of Restitution Allowed* (draft), National Victim Center, Arlington, VA (1993).

39. M. Cuomo, *New York State Shouldn't Kill People,* The New York Times, June 17, 1989.

PART III

The Controversy over Deterrence and Incapacitation

Crimes can be prevented by many different tactics and strategies, ranging from the use of so-called target-hardening devices (double-locked doors, bullet-proof glass), to incapacitating known or likely offenders (sedating the violent, incarcerating the dangerous), to moral persuasion (convincing would-be offenders to respect the rights of others). The death penalty plays a double role in prevention, but only one of them involves deterrence—preventing crimes by making the would-be offender believe it's a bad bargain. Crime is a bad bargain whenever the costs risked by committing the crime exceed what one is willing to pay given the prospects of gain from the crime. Of course, the threatened punishment works as a deterrent only if the would-be offender believes the costs to him outweigh the benefits (discounted, of course, by the risks). As the typical offender probably sees it, the chief costs at risk are of two kinds: those that arise at or near the scene of the crime, in possible interference from the prospective victim or from the police (a shoot-out or an arrest); and those that arise subsequently, in court, jail, and prison. The latter are remote, however, as well as conditional on arrest, prosecution, and conviction. Without an arrest, no prosecution; without prosecution, no trial; without a trial (or a plea bargain), no conviction; without a conviction, no sentence; and without a sentence, no punishment—or at least nothing the law would recognize as punishment. Thus, reducing crime by a strategy of deterrence is no easy matter. Fraught with objective contingencies, it depends for its efficacy on communicating those contingencies to those who have the opportunity, means, and motive to commit crime.

But any strategy of crime reduction via deterrence is also fraught with subjective contingencies. Perhaps the offender-about-to-be is confident he won't get caught (no witnesses). Or he believes the crime won't be discovered or that—if caught—he will get off lightly. Or perhaps he is so absorbed in the criminal act or so preoccupied with avoiding arrest that he radically (and foolishly) discounts the future possibility of being severely punished. Or perhaps his criminal acts are impulsive or even the work of a madman. Counsels of rational deterrence can play little or no role in the actions of such offenders, because those actions are governed by false beliefs and misperceptions. No wonder that those who have most carefully studied the concept and contingencies of effective general deterrence virtually despair of controlling the bulk of society from the path of crime by such methods.

Where the death penalty is concerned, the issue of deterrence—quite apart from these contingencies—is controversial for several reasons of very different character. The first are *conceptual;* discussions of the deterrent effect of the death penalty are constantly subject to confusion on several different conceptual grounds. Two are illustrated in a recent newspaper editorial by Sharon Keller, a former assistant district attorney for Dallas County, Texas, and in 1994 elected to the Texas Court of Criminal Appeals. During her election campaign she defended her support for the death penalty as a deterrent by pointing to the way it incapacitates: "[I]t is indisputable that capital punishment prevents at least the executed from committing further crimes."[1] Defense of the deterrent benefits of the death penalty in similar language is constantly heard; unfortunately, it is doubly confused.

First, it fails to keep distinct *deterrence* and *incapacitation.* It is too rarely noticed that the death penalty is unique in being the only punishment whose infliction cannot have any deterrent effect on those who undergo it. The reason, of course, is that you cannot be deterred if you cannot weigh—as the dead cannot—the perceived risks you face in committing a crime. (Criminologists have inadvertantly added to this confusion by their distinction between "special" and "general" deterrence, the former referring to the deterrent effect on the offender of being punished and the latter referring to the deterrent effect of the offender's punishment on everyone else—a distinction of no relevance to the death penalty.)

Now this is not a mere quibble over how to use the term "deterrence." It is crucial to the entire debate over the role the death penalty can be expected to have in crime prevention. Its actual and possible deterrent effects must be kept distinct from its incapacitative effects; for one thing, the incapacitative effects are not in dispute, but the deterrent effects are. Whatever may be said for killing offenders in the name of crime prevention, the crimes (if any) these executions prevent, thanks to deterrence, are entirely distinct from the crimes they prevent thanks to incapacitation.

Another conceptual confusion is more subtle; it consists in the failure to keep distinct *incapacitation* from *prevention.* Incapacitating a person from further crime by death (or by life in prison, for that matter) does not necessarily prevent any crime by that person. While it is true that a person adequately incapacitated *cannot* commit further crimes, it does not follow that if he were not incapacitated, he *would* recidivate; but if he wouldn't recidivate, he hasn't been prevented from committing any crimes. Nor is his current punishment the only way to explain his failure to recidivate. At most, there is a very rough correlation between incapacitating a convicted offender and preventing further crimes from that source. Supporters of the death penalty too easily assume that every execution "prevents" a long list of felonies, when at most there is a high probability that it prevents some. Even if, as the BJS reports (see chapter 11), about one in ten of those admitted each year onto the nation's death rows had a prior conviction of criminal homicide, that tells us only that we could have prevented those crimes if we had incapacitated these offenders more effectively after their first homicide—a homicide that, for various reasons, might not have been punishable by death. But now that such offenders are again in custody and under death sentence, we cannot do more than guess how many further homicides—if any—will be prevented by executing them.

A third conceptual confusion surrounding the discussion of deterrence merges when we consider the empirical evidence for and against the death penalty as a deterrent. This confusion is, ironically enough, illustrated in the obituary published by the *New York Times* on the occasion of the death of Thorsten Sellin, one of this century's leading criminologists. The obituary reads in part: "Professor Sellin was outspoken in his opposition to the death penalty and contended that comparisons of statistical data from jurisdictions with and without the death penalty showed that it was no deterrent to crime."[2] This passage badly misrepresents Sellin's research; the only way the conclusion—the death penalty was "no deterrent to crime"—could be supported by the data would be if the jurisdictions without the death penalty had *no* penalty whatever for murder. But of course they did punish murder, not with death but with long-term imprisonment. The obituary writer failed (as Sellin did not) to keep distinct two questions: Does the death penalty deter at all? and Does the death penalty deter *better than the alternative* of imprisonment? Sellin's research was focused entirely on the latter question. As he well knew, these two issues are not of equal importance to the debate over the death penalty.

Most people believe that punishments deter and that the more severe the punishment, the better it deters. So abolitionists look like fools if they insist (as they often do) that "the death penalty is no deterrent to murder" since this flies in the face of what passes for common sense.[3] Clearly, since abolitionists and retentionists alike favor some sort of severe punishment for murderers, rapists, and other violent offenders, the dispute between them turns entirely on whether capital punishment is a better, more effective deterrent than some less severe alternative punishment. Thus, empirical evidence that the death penalty deters is of no interest; abolitionists might as well concede that, indeed, the death penalty probably does deter someone, sometime, somewhere—just as retentionists must concede that the thousands of criminal homicides each year in the 1990s in America's death penalty jurisdictions prove that the death penalty is at best a far cry from a perfect deterrent. The only empirical evidence that is relevant compares the deterrent (and, one should add, the brutalizing) effect of death with some suitable alternative punishment. Retentionists presumably believe that the death penalty deters better than the available alternatives, which is what abolitionists typically deny.

Notice, too, that the controversy has to be narrowed still further. The issue is not whether boiling in oil or crucifixion is a better deterrent than some form of incarceration, because these savage forms of execution are simply ruled out (as uncivilized and unconstitutional) from the start. Even if they were marvelously superior as a deterrent to twenty years in prison, they are not (and, barring social catastrophe, will not become) available under law; the relative deterrent efficacy of barbaric and hence clearly unconstitutional punishments is not at issue. Nor is the issue whether the death penalty might be a better deterrent if only it could be carried out more swiftly, with less delay between sentence and execution. For reasons discussed further in parts V and VI, considerable delay between arrest and execution is all but unavoidable. The *only* issue is whether currently permissible forms of execution of the sort now used in this country, with protection of the rights of the accused as afforded by law, are a better deterrent than any form of incarceration currently authorized by law.

The second major area of controversy raised by the issue of deterrence concerns exactly what the *empirical evidence* does show. Does it show that, on balance, the death penalty is a better deterrent than imprisonment? Or that it is no better? Do executions have a counterdeterrent or brutalizing effect that matches or even exceeds their deterrent effect? Or is the evidence too inconclusive to permit drawing any conclusions on these points, with the result that one either falls back on intuition (''punishments deter, and the more severe the better the deterrence'') or dismisses the whole issue as a snare and a delusion?

Since 1974 William C. Bailey, a sociologist at Cleveland State University, has been searching for statistically significant evidence of a deterrent effect of the death penalty in America. Working with various collaborators, most recently Ruth D. Peterson, a sociologist at Ohio State University, Bailey has published more than a dozen studies. In none have signs of a deterrent effect of death sentences or of actual executions been identified. Bailey and Peterson's most recent survey of the whole issue, specially prepared for this volume, is reprinted here as chapter 9.

Stephen K. Layson, an economist at the University of North Carolina–Greensboro, is one of the few investigators who believes that multiple regression analysis of aggregate national data does show a deterrent effect of the death penalty. His research, he claims, shows that each execution in the United States during the years 1933 to 1969 resulted in fifteen fewer homicides (1986:312). To his credit, Layson has not made exaggerated claims for the finality of his research. When giving testimony before the House Subcommittee on the Judiciary, he said: ''I don't regard my evidence on the deterrent effect of capital punishment as conclusive'' (1986: 313). He also conceded that ''among experts in this area I am not sure my views would be held by a majority. In fact, I doubt that they would'' (1986:315). And, indeed, Layson's testimony was followed by the sharply critical testimony of James Alan Fox, dean of the School of Criminal Justice at Northeastern University. (A revision of Fox's testimony, written in collaboration with sociologist Michael L. Radelet, was subsequently published; see Fox and Radelet 1989.) As their use of statistics shows, the issues in dispute are highly technical and do not admit of easy paraphrase or simplification. That has been reason enough for many opponents and defenders of the death penalty to shift their attention away from the deterrence controversy to other issues.

By way of summing up the state of the empirical evidence on the whole question of deterrence, one can say without fear of significant contradiction that the vast bulk of the research done on the allegedly superior deterrent effect of the death penalty so far in this century in the United States fails to reveal any such effect, and that the few research studies with results to the contrary are fraught with unresolved difficulties. Accordingly, it is difficult to see how a convincing defense of the death penalty in the United States today could rest solely or even primarily on deterrent grounds.

Fighting terrorism with the death penalty attracts support in part because of the belief in its superior deterrent effects. But such reasoning is put in doubt by most actual terrorist attacks, such as the one in Saudi Arabia in June 1996, in which 19 American military personnel were killed when a giant bomb exploded outside their quarters. As Philip Shenon of the *New York Times* reported, "the bombing was almost certainly tied to the explosion last November (1995), in which five Americans and two Indians were killed" in Riyadha. Four Saudi confessed to the crime. The American Embassy reported "it was warned that Americans would be harmed if the executions were carried out." The Saudi government executed the prisoners by beheading. Thus it appears that those executions in 1995 provided the incentive for the bombing attack six months later in which 19 were murdered.[4]

The final area of controversy raised by the deterrence issue is neither conceptual nor empirical but *normative:* Suppose the death penalty did deter, and that it deterred better than the available alternatives—what then? If executions (or the threat thereof) deter two or three homicides per year, is that sufficient to warrant its use, because even a small deterrent effect wipes out on balance whatever objections there may be to executions? Or must the death penalty be a much more effective deterrent than that if we are going to run the risk (as abolitionists believe we do) of executing the innocent, brutalizing society generally, imposing unequal risks on poor offenders, and spending vast sums on the whole jerry-built death penalty system? At one extreme are those retentionists who argue that if the death penalty prevents (via deterrence or incapacitation) even one homicide, it is worth it. At the other extreme are those retentionists who do not rest their case on grounds of superior deterrence at all; their support for the death penalty relies entirely on considerations of retribution and related principles. Most retentionists fall uneasily somewhere between these extremes.

But it is not only retentionists who must face uncomfortable choices posed by the evidence on deterrence. Most abolitionists today are convinced that there is no evidence to show that the death penalty in the United States, however it has been administered in this century, has had any measurable deterrent effect better than the alternative of imprisonment. But suppose it were demonstrated to the general satisfaction of social scientists that the death penalty really is a superior deterrent to imprisonment. Would abolitionists still favor the alternative of imprisonment? Suppose the differential deterrent effect in favor of executions was really quite considerable, as research by James A. Yunker (1976) purported to show. Would it be reasonable to insist that the other costs of a policy of executions outweigh the value of the many lives lost through choosing the less effective deterrent? When facing this question, many abolitionists are inclined to agree with Professor Charles L. Black Jr., of Yale Law School, who once observed that these questions are like asking what mathematics would be like if pi were a rational number—they are questions no rational person need answer because the questions make no sense. As a riposte this perhaps cannot be beat, but it leaves unanswered the question of just what role superior deterrence (or the lack thereof) ought to play in the overall decision whether to retain or abolish the death penalty. How many abolitionists would remain opposed to the death penalty even if they were convinced it was a superior deterrent is uncertain; whether they would be justified in their opposition is even more surely debatable.

If we shift our attention from the evidence on prevention by deterrence to the evidence on prevention by *incapacitation,* it appears at first that the death penalty has and always will have a clear edge over imprisonment so far as incapacitating offenders is concerned. But it is not so clear that this edge constitutes much of an advantage in crime prevention, since not every murderer executed constitutes one or more murders prevented: Most convicted murderers do not murder again. As explained a few paragraphs earlier, the distinction between total incapacitation (by death) and crime prevention ought to be kept as clear and incontrovertible as the distinction between deterrence and incapacitation.

A good example of confusion here can be found in the October 1994 issue of *Fortune* magazine, in which we are told that "the death penalty clearly does prevent *some* homicides" and that abolitionists refuse to acknowledge its superior "incapacitating" effects. As relevant evidence, the writer cites the fact that "since 1982 more than five federal prison guards have been killed by inmates." The implication is that if only the federal government had made murder of a prison guard a capital offense, some or all of these five killings would not have occurred. What we are not told is whether these "inmates" were convicted murderers who might have been sentenced to death and executed; if they were not, then these prison murders could not have been prevented by the incapacitating effects of a prior execution. We are also not told whether five murders by federal prison inmates in a thirteen-year span (1982–94) is a disproportionately high ratio of murders to prisoners and to prison personnel when measured against the prison murders in earlier years and against murders in state death penalty jurisdictions over the same span of years. Until we know that, we have no evidence at all for believing that the death penalty is a better deterrent for prison murder than a less severe punishment.

The issue of murder by prisoners is but a special case of a more fundamental empirical question concerning incapacitation and the death penalty: What is the likely volume and rate of *recidivist murder,* that is, murder committed by those convicted of but not executed for murder? It is useful to contrast the present state of our knowledge on this question with what we knew in earlier years. At the time of the 1964 edition of *The Death Penalty in America,* no information on the question of recidivist murder was available. Not so by 1982; that edition reported evidence of recidivism (based on data from the National Council on Crime and Delinquency for the period 1965–75) showing that 0.3 percent of offenders—three in a thousand—released after conviction for murder were later convicted of another "willful homicide" (Bedau ed. 1982:177). Other data from other sources for the years 1971 through 1975 (also reprinted in the 1982 edition) showed that 0.2 percent of persons convicted of "willful homicide" were convicted of another such crime within the first year of release (179).

Low though these figures are, it is not hard to find vivid and frightening examples of recidivist murder. Newspapers, all too frequently, it seems, tell us about violent crimes committed by released or escaped prisoners with a record of prior homicide:

- In New Hampshire, Ernest Therrien, aged thirty-eight, was charged with killing Helen Ring. He had been released ten months earlier from a mental hospital, to which he had been committed for life in 1976 after having been found insane during trial for the murder of his niece.[5]
- In New York, Arthur Shawcross, aged forty-four, had served nearly fifteen years of a twenty-five-year term for murdering two children. Released in 1987, he murdered ten women in the Rochester area within the next two years.[6]
- In Nebraska, Ronald Fort had served more than twelve years in prison after a murder conviction. A month after his parole in July 1991, he was arrested for another murder.[7]
- In New Jersey in May 1995, Robert Simon, aged forty-three, was charged with the murder of a police officer. He had served part of a ten- to twenty-year prison term in Pennsylvania for murder.[8]

Cases like these understandably give a bad name to releasing a murderer from prison—no matter what the reason for release. Hardly less infuriating and inflammatory is the occasional show of bravado and contempt by a man under sentence of death. Twenty years ago young Carl Isaacs, convicted in Georgia of murdering a family of six—and guilty by his own admission of having murdered nine others—announced from his death row prison cell, "I started killing when I was 14. . . . If they want to stop me, they'd better strap me in that chair, because my ambition is to kill 1,000 people. . . . As long as killers know all they'll get is life, they'll keep right on killing—and that includes me."[9] Whether we should believe Isaacs is, of course, another matter. In any case, as of January 1995 he was still on Georgia's death row awaiting execution.

These illustrative anecdotes to one side, what can we learn from systematic research into recidivism of convicted murderers in general and death row prisoners in particular? Thanks to the investigations by James W. Marquart and Jonathan R. Sorensen, sociologists at Sam Houston State University in Texas, we have the results of a natural experiment that bears directly on this subject. Marquart and Sorensen examined the postresentencing behavior of all the hundreds under death sentence in 1972 who were never executed, having been spared by the *Furman* decision of that year. Did they murder again while in prison or after release? In the research reprinted here as chapter 10, Marquart and Sorensen point out that if all of the more than five hundred prisoners whose post-*Furman* careers they were able to identify and trace had been executed, they would not have committed the nearly four hundred subsequent felonies—only seven of them homicides (all but one in prison)—of which they were convicted after 1972. But Marquart and Sorensen also show that if all these offenders had been executed, four who were later judged to be innocent would have been wrongfully executed, too. Thus, the trade-off between murders prevented and innocents executed in this group was roughly two to one. And if the results of this research are generalizable, they show that, yes, executing all convicted murderers would almost certainly prevent some murders and many other felonies—but only at a terrible cost. Which cost it is better for society to pay is not a question easily answered, and in any case it is only one facet of the whole death penalty controversy.

In an effort to shed a bit more light on the problems of criminal homicide in prison, recidivism among released murderers, and the alternative punishment to death now favored by many abolitionists—life in prison without the possibility of parole—I have provided a brief discussion on these topics in chapter 11.

Notes

1. *Dallas Morning News,* 25 September 1994, p. J6.
2. *New York Times,* 20 September 1994, p. D22.
3. This concession to common sense is not to be construed as a tacit acceptance of Michael Davis's "common sense" argument for the superior deterrent efficacy of the death penalty; see Davis 1981. His version of this argument claims that because persons would rationally prefer a less severe to a more severe punishment (hence would prefer prison to death), therefore such persons are more terrified by the death penalty and thus more deterred. But this inference is unwarranted: From the fact that Jones prefers cloudy weather to rain, it does not follow that he fears (or is more afraid of) rain. One's order of preferences is not the inverse of one's order of fears. Even more to the point, it does not follow that because one fears A more than one fears B, the fear of B is insufficient to deter one from whatever it is that fear of A would also deter one from doing.
4. Senator Arlen Spector has presented a detailed argument in favor of the death penalty for terrorism; see Spector 1991. The best critique of such a policy is still the article by Thomas Thornton; see Thornton 1976.
5. *Boston Globe,* 15 August 1985, p. 26.
6. *New York Times,* 6 January 1990, p. 1.
7. Ibid., 17 September 1991, p. B6.
8. Ibid., 1 June 1995, p. B4. Additional recent cases include Reginald McFadden, pardoned in Pennsylania in 1995 after a murder conviction and arrested in New York for rape and murder a few months later. See *N. Y. Times,* 28 September 1995, p. B6.
9. *National Enquirer,* 18 February 1975, p. 2.

9

Murder, Capital Punishment, and Deterrence: A Review of the Literature

WILLIAM C. BAILEY
RUTH D. PETERSON

Few, if any, issues have received more intense and long-term attention in criminology than the proper place, if any, of capital punishment in an enlightened criminal justice system. Concerns about the death penalty were at the forefront of attention of a number of the early founders of criminology (Beccaria in 1764; Bentham in 1843), and the debate continues today as the United States maintains the distinction of being the only Western nation to retain capital punishment for common murder.

Even a brief sampling of the relevant literature demonstrates the tremendous breadth of the death penalty debate. Many issues are of a moral or ethical nature, and are therefore beyond the scope of empirical inquiry. However, some core issues regarding the death penalty are factual in nature and have received considerable attention by social scientists. These include questions regarding the general deterrent effect of capital punishment, how legal and extralegal factors such as race and economic status influence judicial outcomes in murder cases, the nature of and correlates of public opinion about the death penalty, and errors of justice and wrongful convictions in capital cases. In these areas social scientists have made important contributions to a better understanding of capital punishment.

Of these topics, the deterrence issue has received the most systematic attention over the years. Here, the crucial question is whether capital punishment is more effective than alternative sanctions, namely, long terms of imprisonment, in preventing (deterring) murder. In other words, what is the marginal deterrent effect, if any, achieved by capital punishment? This is the appropriate question since the alternative sanctions for murder in the United States are death or imprisonment, not death or no sanction at all.

In this chapter we review and assess the empirical literature regarding the marginal deterrent effect of capital punishment for murder. In light of the large body of deterrence research, we note the following considerations in our review. First, since this volume is focused on the death penalty in America, our analysis is restricted to deterrence investigations conducted in the United States. (The reader should consult works by Archer and Gartner [1984], Bowers [1988], Chandler [1976], Fattah [1972] Jayewardene [1977], and Phillips [1980] for a sampling of deterrence research for Canada and selected other countries.)

Second, we are concerned solely with deterrence studies in which murder is the criterion variable. Historically, in the United States the death penalty has been authorized for a variety of crimes, including kidnapping, treason, espionage, rape, robbery, arson, and train wrecking (Bowers 1984). However, actual executions largely have been restricted to convicted murderers. For the period 1864–1982, Bowers (1984) reports that 96.5 percent of whites and 80.7 percent of nonwhites who were executed under state authority were put to death for committing murder. And, since the mid-1960s, no one in the United States has been executed for a crime other than murder. In light of these statistics, death penalty investigators have focused almost exclusively on the crime of murder. The exceptions are studies by Bailey (1977) and Boyes and McPheters (1977) of the relationship between states' execution practices and rates of forcible rape. These two analyses produced no indication that capital punishment is more effective than imprisonment in preventing rape.

Third, our review and assessment of the literature focuses on studies of capital punishment and "general" rather than "special" deterrence (Andenaes 1974). The concern is with how capital punishment practices influence would-be (potential) homicide offenders, rather than assessing the relative merits of long terms of imprisonment versus executions in preventing *convicted murderers* from killing again. Given the many costs associated with capital punishment, including wrongful convictions (Radelet, Bedau, and Putnam 1992) and the financial costs of capital trials and their judicial aftermath (Costanzo and White 1994), the question of how much more "cost-effective" the death penalty is than lengthy incarceration in preventing murderers from killing again is an interesting issue. However, this question has not received systematic empirical attention and therefore is not a concern here.

Fourth, although our specific focus is deterrence, we will also examine the findings of studies of the "brutalization" effect of the death penalty. Brutalization studies test the long-held hypothesis that capital punishment actually encourages rather than discourages murder by setting a "savage example" for society to follow (Beccaria 1963). As Bowers and Pierce (1980) point out, the brutalization argument poses an identification process that is the opposite of that assumed by the deterrence argument. The assumption underlying deterrence theory is that would-be-murderers identify with the executed person. In contrast, the brutalization thesis assumes that observers identify the person who is executed with someone who has offended them greatly. By so doing, he or she may identify with the state as executioner and thus justify and reinforce his or her desire for lethal vengeance (Bowers and Pierce 1980:456).

Most studies of brutalization are virtually identical to deterrence analyses in their methodology; they differ only in the direction of the expected relationship between capital punishment and murder. Consequently, the overlapping bodies of deterrence and brutalization literature can be reviewed and summarized as a single body of work.

Fifth, because of the large volume of work on deterrence and capital punishment, our review of the literature for the United States will be selective rather than exhaustive. In selecting studies to present and summarize, we will provide a sampling of the different methodological approaches and research designs that have been employed by investigators. Also, although the literature is overwhelmingly negative regarding the preventive effects of capital punishment, we are mindful that a few investigators have reported what they interpret to be a significant deterrent effect for capital punishment. Because of their contrasting findings, all but one of these studies will be given specific attention in our review. We will not examine in detail a study by Layson (1985) that purports to identify a significant deterrent effect for executions on the U.S. national murder rate.

Finally, we caution the reader that the present authors have been frequent contributors to the deterrence literature. Thus our own work is assessed along with that of our colleagues. We do our best to remain objective, pointing to the strengths and weaknesses of all the studies, including our own.

Organizing the Literature

Deterrence theory contends that to be effective in preventing crime, criminal sanctions must be severe enough to outweigh the pleasures (psychic and material gains) to be derived from crime, administered with great certainty, administered promptly so there is a clear cause-and-effect connection between crime and punishment in the minds of would-be offenders, and made known to the public (Andenaes 1974; Gibbs 1975; Zimring and Hawkins 1973). These properties of punishment interact in impacting would-be offenders. To illustrate, although the death penalty constitutes a very severe penalty, it cannot be expected to be an effective deterrent to murder if its level of certainty is zero or very slight. Similarly, even if administered with a high level of certainty, capital punishment will not be effective in discouraging crime if it is administered secretly. Rather, deterrence is a communication theory, and it is the *perceived* severity, certainty, and celerity of punishment that result from sanctioning practices that are predicted to influence offense rates (Gibbs 1975).

In the discussion that follows, we have organized deterrence and death penalty studies according to their focus on one or more of these four dimensions of punishment—severity, certainty, celerity, and publicity. In addition, we will address as separate topics deterrence investigations that have considered specific types of murder—capital homicides.

Comparative Studies and the Severity Hypothesis

From early in this century through the 1960s the comparative methodology provided the most common approach to testing for the possible deterrent effect of the death penalty. Investigators compared homicide rates for jurisdictions with (retentionist states) and without (abolitionist states) capital punishment (Bye 1919; Savitz

1958; Sellin 1955, 1959, 1961, 1967, 1980; Sutherland 1925), or examined rates for states before and after the abolition and/or reinstatement of the death penalty (Bedau 1967; Schuessler 1952; Sellin 1955, 1959, 1967). In the former case, the deterrence hypothesis is that murder rates should be higher in abolitionist states. In the case of longitudinal comparisons, the deterrence thesis predicts that abolition should be followed by an increase in murder rates, and reinstatement should result in a decrease in killings. In both types of investigations, the punishment measure of concern was the statutory provision or absence of the death penalty.

Over the decades, the findings from comparative studies were very consistent and quite contrary to the deterrence thesis. For example, studies of changes in murder rates before and after the abolition and/or reinstatement of capital punishment revealed that states that abolished the death penalty did not experience unusual increases in homicides. Rather, abolition and/or reintroduction of capital punishment was sometimes followed by an increase in murders and sometimes not. In addition, changes in the murder rates of states experiencing a change in the provision for the death penalty paralleled almost exactly changes in homicides in neighboring states where no statutory change had occurred. Also contrary to the deterrence thesis, simple comparisons of retentionist and abolitionist jurisdictions showed that the provision for the death penalty had no discernible effect on murder. Indeed, such studies often showed an opposite pattern of higher murder rates for death penalty states.

Sellin and others employing these methods recognized that abolitionist and retentionist jurisdictions may differ in other respects that might influence murder rates, for example, population composition, region, and socioeconomic conditions. To control for how such factors may differentiate abolitionist and retentionist jurisdictions, and thereby distort simple comparative analyses of homicide rates for the two types of states, researchers also compared murder rates for clusters of contiguous, and presumably more similar, abolitionist and retentionist jurisdictions. Findings for contiguous state comparisons for the first half of this century also showed that in general murder rates tended to be lower for neighboring death penalty jurisdictions.

This nondeterrence pattern holds for the contemporary period as well. To illustrate, Table 9-1 presents murder rates for six groupings of neighboring death penalty and abolition states for the period 1977 through 1993. The figures indicate the number of murders per 100,000 population for each jurisdiction. To illustrate, during 1977 rates ranged from a low of 1 murder per 100,000 population in Vermont to a high of 10 murders per 100,000 persons in Illinois. We selected the 1977–93 period because 1977 marks the year of the resumption of executions in the United States after a ten-year moratorium, and 1993 is the most recent year for which Federal Bureau of Investigation (FBI) figures for homicide (murder and nonnegligent manslaughter) are available.

The data in Table 9-1 allow us to address three basic questions: (1) Are murder rates significantly lower for neighboring states that provided for capital punishment during the period?[1] (2) Is there an indication of a significant increase in rates during the years when some ''retentionist'' states were without the provision for capital

Table 9-1.
Murder Rates for Neighboring Death Penalty and Abolitionist States, 1977–93

State	Abolition period	1977	1978	1979	1980	1981	1982	1983	1984	1985	1986	1987	1988	1989	1990	1991	1992	1993
Maine*	1977–93	2	3	3	3	3	2	2	2	2	2	3	3	3	2	1	2	2
Vermont*	1977–93	1	3	1	2	4	2	4	2	3	2	2	2	2	2	2	2	4
New Hampshire		3	1	2	3	3	2	2	1	2	2	3	2	3	2	4	2	2
Rhode Island*	1979–93	4	4	3	4	4	4	3	3	4	4	4	4	5	5	4	4	4
Massachusetts*	1977–78 1980–82 1984–93	3	4	4	4	4	4	4	4	4	4	3	4	4	4	4	4	4
Michigan*	1977–84	9	11	9	10	9	9	10	10	11	11	12	11	11	10	11	10	10
Ohio*	1978–80	8	7	8	8	7	6	6	5	5	6	6	5	6	6	7	7	6
Indiana		7	6	8	9	7	7	5	6	6	6	6	6	6	6	8	8	8
Wisconsin*	1977–93	3	3	3	3	3	3	3	3	3	3	4	3	4	5	5	4	4
Iowa*	1977–93	2	3	2	2	3	2	2	2	2	2	2	2	2	2	2	2	2
Illinois		10	10	11	11	11	9	10	9	8	9	8	9	8	8	11	11	11
North Dakota*	1977–93	1	1	2	1	2	1	2	1	1	1	2	2	1	1	1	2	2
South Dakota*	1977–78	2	2	2	1	2	3	2	2	2	4	2	3	1	2	2	1	3
Montana		5	5	4	4	3	4	2	4	6	3	4	3	3	5	3	3	3
Wyoming		5	7	9	6	6	9	6	3	4	5	2	3	4	5	3	4	3
West Virginia*	1977–93	6	7	7	7	6	5	5	4	4	6	5	5	7	6	6	6	7
Virginia		9	9	9	9	9	7	7	8	7	7	7	8	8	9	9	9	8
Oregon*	1977 1981–83	5	5	4	5	4	5	4	5	5	7	6	5	5	4	5	5	5
Washington		4	5	5	6	5	4	5	5	5	5	6	6	4	5	4	4	5
Idaho		6	5	5	3	4	3	4	3	2	3	3	4	3	3	2	4	3

*States without capital punishment for murder for the periods indicated. Death penalty status determined as of 31 December of the years indicated.

punishment (such as with Massachusetts, Ohio, South Dakota, and Oregon)? (3) Is there evidence of a significant decrease in rates for the years following a state's return to capital punishment? The answer to each of these questions appears to be no. Across the six groupings of states there is no clear pattern of murder rates being higher for death penalty jurisdictions. In some cases rates are higher for abolitionist jurisdictions (e.g., Michigan), and in some cases the opposite is true (e.g., Illinois). In addition, examining changes in homicide for individual states over time, there is no indication of either an increase in murder during abolition years or a decrease in rates following reinstatement of capital punishment. In brief, then, early comparative analyses and recent comparative data do not support the deterrence argument regarding capital punishment and homicide. The data leave unchallenged Sellin's (1967:138) early conclusion that "the presence of the death penalty in law and practice has no discernible effect as a deterrent to murder."

The Certainty Hypothesis

As noted previously, fundamental to deterrence theory is the notion that to be effective in preventing crime, sanctions must be administered with a high degree of certainty. Neither simple nor contiguous state comparisons of homicide rates for death penalty and abolitionist jurisdictions provide a means of addressing this question. Rather, exploring this issue necessitates examining the relationship between levels of actual execution and murder rates.

With the exception of a study by Schuessler (1952), the certainty hypothesis did not receive systematic attention until the 1970s. Schuessler correlated average execution rates (the rate of executions to criminal homicides) with homicide rates for the period 1937 to 1941 for forty-one U.S. death penalty states. Contrary to deterrence predictions, he observed only a slight negative relationship ($r = -.26$, $r^2 = .067$) between executions and homicides. As a check on the consistency of this pattern, Schuessler examined execution and homicide rates for four groupings of death penalty states divided according to the size of the homicide rate. This analysis also showed that homicide rates do not consistently fall as the risk of execution increases. These observations led Schuessler to conclude that "the death penalty has little if anything to do with the relative occurrence of murder" (1952: 61).

More than two decades later Bailey (1975) examined for forty-one U.S. states the relationship between the ratio of executions to homicides for five-year periods leading up to 1967 and 1968 and (1) rates of murder and nonnegligent manslaughter derived from the annual FBI Uniform Crime Reports, and (2) rates of prison admission for first-degree murder. The first-degree murder data were gathered from a survey of state bureaus of correction for prison admissions for 1967 and 1968. Like the Schuessler investigation, a correlation analysis provided no evidence of a significant deterrent effect for the certainty of execution. Bailey found only slight and nonsignificant negative relationships between executions and rates for total criminal homicides (1967, $r = -.166$; 1968, $r = -.039$) and for first-degree murder (1967, $r = -.137$; 1968 $r = -.194$).

The Ehrlich Analysis

Perhaps the most important work on the deterrent effect of the certainty of capital punishment on homicide came from studies by Isaac Ehrlich in the mid-1970s (Ehrlich 1973, 1975). Ehrlich challenged the common wisdom gained from comparative studies that the death penalty does not deter. He dismissed previous death penalty research as simplistic and inadequate because investigators largely ignored the certainty-of-execution hypothesis. Ehrlich also complained that previous studies did not include criminal justice and sociodemographic control variables to guard against spurious results for the death penalty factors. Ehrlich argued that previous deterrence studies were fatally flawed due to these problems and that previous investigators were simply *wrong* in concluding that capital punishment is not an effective deterrent to murder.

Ehrlich sought to address the shortcomings of earlier work by conducting a statistical analysis that did the following: explicitly recognized the fundamental importance of the certainty hypothesis; considered multiple measures of the certainty of capital punishment; recognized the possible importance of the severity and certainty of alternative sanctions (imprisonment) in deterring murder; and considered a variety of law enforcement and sociodemographic factors associated with murder rates as formal control variables in examining the U.S. homicide rates for various periods between 1933 and 1969.

Aggregating his data on a national and annual basis, Ehrlich found a significant decline in executions over this period, as well as a general rise in homicide rates. The observed trade-off between homicide rates and different measures of execution certainty varied somewhat, but the pattern was convincing for Ehrlich. Based on his analyses, Ehrlich reported that each execution that was performed during the period may have prevented, on average, seven to eight murders.

The Ehrlich analysis brought to the forefront the complexity of the deterrence and death penalty issue, and the need for a more sophisticated methodology than found in earlier studies. Indeed, the Ehrlich paper stimulated a new round of deterrence and death penalty research in the 1970s and 1980s that addressed a number of important but traditionally ignored questions about deterrence and capital punishment. As we detail in the following, we take very strong issue with the Ehrlich analysis. However, we regard his efforts as probably the single most important factor in the last twenty years in stimulating the research needed to provide a better understanding of this important question.

Reactions to Ehrlich's Study

The reaction to Ehrlich's study was a series of replications of his national time-series analysis (Bowers and Pierce 1975; Klein, Forst, and Filatov 1978; Layson 1985; Passell and Taylor 1977; Yunker 1976). With the exceptions of Layson (1985) and Yunker (1976), these efforts did not support Ehrlich's claims. Rather, scholars revealed a number of theoretical and technical problems with his analysis, some of the most important of which are noted here. First, critics noted that such time-series analyses are subject to very serious aggregation error/bias problems when the unit of analysis is the entire nation, and when an obvious factor such as dramatic changes in the percentage of the U.S. population that is subject to the death penalty for murder is ignored as either a deterrence or a control variable. The proportion of the U.S. population residing in retentionist/abolitionist jurisdictions was far from uniform during the 1933–69 period. Ignoring this fact renders extremely suspect national aggregate studies such as Ehrlich's. Problems of interpretation also stem from the fact that Ehrlich aggregated his homicide and control variables on a national level, thus also ignoring the tremendous variation in these factors from state to state.

Second, critics noted that Ehrlich failed to differentiate between death penalty and abolitionist jurisdictions in computing execution rates at the national level. Rather, he treated all jurisdictions as retentionist in comparing the ratio of executions to arrests for murder, and the like. This is extremely misleading since the probability of execution is zero in abolitionist jurisdictions.

Third, some took issue with Ehrlich for operationalizing his main independent variable as execution risk and ignoring the legal status of the death penalty (Baldus and Cole 1975). While measuring execution risk takes into account the use of the death penalty (in retentionist states), Ehrlich's analysis ignores the policy issue of deterrence and abolition (or reinstatement) of capital punishment on the state level.

Fourth, critics debated the relative merits of econometric modeling versus other means of controlling for important etiological factors in attempting to isolate the possible deterrent effect of capital punishment. With this approach there is the risk that important variables might be overlooked or specified improperly (Baldus and Cole 1975). If important predictor variables are excluded, or if irrelevant variables are included in the model, the apparent precision in estimating the impact of given variables (such as executions) on homicide rates will result in misleading conclusions (Baldus and Cole 1975).

Finally, Ehrlich's findings of deterrence are not robust (Ehrlich 1973, 1975). This is evident in two ways. On the one hand, some of the statistical models he specified suggested a possible deterrent effect but some did not. Ehrlich chose to emphasize certain models over others. However, there is no a priori theoretical reason for viewing as superior the models that suggest a possible deterrent effect compared with models that produced no indication of deterrence (Klein, Forst, and Filatov 1978). In addition, Ehrlich's findings of deterrence are dependent upon the time period being examined, 1933–69. When the annual time series ends in the early to mid-1960s, any possible evidence of deterrence disappears. This raises the obvious question: Why was the death penalty *not* a significant deterrent to murder from 1933 through the mid-1960s although capital punishment *was* a significant deterrent for the period 1933–69? What could have happened during the latter half of the 1960s to so radically change the truth of the matter? In brief, then, the noted difficulties render the results of the Ehrlich study highly suspect.

Building upon the Ehrlich Analysis

The Ehrlich study is a very important chapter in the history of deterrence and death penalty research. Most importantly, his work inspired a renewed interest in the subject that brought to an end what was essentially a moratorium on death penalty investigations. These new efforts were aimed at addressing the many difficulties associated with Ehrlich's studies. For example, to address aggregation problems associated with a nationwide analysis, researchers examined time-series data for individual states for various periods extending back to the turn of the century. Among the jurisdictions examined were California (Bailey 1979c), Illinois (Decker and Kohfeld 1984), New York (Bowers and Pierce 1980), North Carolina (Bailey 1979a), Ohio (Bailey 1979d), Oregon (Bailey 1979b), Utah (Bailey 1978), and Washington, D.C. (Bailey 1984b). None of these analyses produced consistent evidence of a deterrent effect for the certainty of capital punishment.

Also building upon Ehrlich, researchers (including Ehrlich himself) conducted state-level cross-sectional analyses of the relationship between executions and murder rates while controlling for various sociodemographic factors associated with homicide. In some of these analyses, measures of the certainty of imprisonment for murder and the length of prison sentences for murder were incorporated as additional deterrence variables (Bailey 1975, 1977, 1980b, 1983; Ehrlich 1977; Forst 1977; Passell 1975; Peterson and Bailey 1988). Ehrlich (1977) was the only researcher among these to find evidence of a deterrent effect for executions. Because no other investigations observed a deterrence pattern, Ehrlich's work was once again subject to scrutiny. And once again scholars found serious theoretical and methodological difficulties with his analysis, rendering Ehrlich's cross-sectional findings suspect as well (Barnett 1981; Beyleveld 1982; Brier and Feinberg 1980; Friedman 1979; McGahey 1980).

In sum, with the lonely exception of Ehrlich, whose work generally has been seriously questioned if not totally discredited, death penalty researchers have found virtually no support for the argument that the level of use of capital punishment (certainty) influences U.S. murder rates. Importantly, the periods examined extend back to the early part of this century, when rates of execution for murder were at much higher levels than in recent decades. This suggests that contrary to the complaints of some death penalty proponents (e.g., van den Haag and Conrad 1983), a return to the "good old days" when there were more executions is not likely to result in greater deterrence.

The Celerity of Capital Punishment

Proponents of deterrence have long argued that for legal sanctions to be effective they must be administered *swiftly* (celerity). For example, Beccaria noted:

> An *immediate punishment is more useful;* because the smaller the interval of time between the punishment and the crime, the stronger and more lasting will be the association of the two ideas of "crime" and punishment; so that they may be considered, one as the cause, and the other as the unavoidable and necessary effect. . . . *Delaying* the punishment serves only to separate these two ideas. . . . (1809:75–76, emphasis added)

In a more recent discussion, Jeffery emphasized the importance of the celerity (and certainty) of sanctions in accounting for the negative evidence for the death penalty:

> The *uncertainty* of capital punishment is one major factor in the system. Another factor is the *time* element. A consequence [the death penalty] must be applied immediately if it is to be effective. . . . The lesson to be learned from capital punishment is not that punishment does not deter, but that the improper and sloppy use of punishment does not deter or rehabilitate. (1965:299)

The celerity of executions is a generally neglected issue in the empirical literature on deterrence and capital punishment. Indeed, our search of the literature produced only a single study (Bailey 1980a) of the celerity question. This is unfortunate. If celerity is important, then ignoring this factor may have biased the findings for the severity (imprisonment versus execution) and certainty (execution rates) of the death penalty reported by previous investigators (Black and Orsagh 1978).

Bailey (1980a) conducted a cross-state analysis examining the relationship between death penalty states' homicide rates and (1) the certainty of execution for homicide, (2) the certainty and severity of imprisonment for homicide, and (3) the celerity of the death penalty—the elapsed time between the sentencing and execution of convicted murderers. The analysis was confined to death penalty states because the celerity of executions is not an issue in abolitionist jurisdictions. As in previous investigations, sociodemographic factors were controlled to avoid spurious results for the sanction variables. For each death penalty state, National Prisoners Statistics data were used to compute the average elapsed time between the sentence of death and execution between 1956 and 1960.[2]

Contrary to theoretical expectations, Bailey found no evidence that speedy executions discourage murder. At the bivariate level there was a near-zero relationship ($r = -.01$) between 1960 murder rates and the average elapsed time between sentencing and executions. This slight pattern persisted in the multivariate analysis. Thus, Bailey's study provided no indication that the failure to confirm the severity and certainty hypotheses for capital punishment was a result of failing to consider the celerity of executions.

Analyses of Execution Publicity

Another fundamental premise of deterrence theory is that to prevent crime, the threat and application of the law must be communicated to the public. Proponents of deterrence theory have long contended that the publicity surrounding punishment serves important educative, moralizing, normative validation, and coercive functions (Andenaes 1974; Gibbs 1975, 1986). Applying this premise to capital punishment, high levels of execution publicity should result in lower homicide rates.

Research examining the effects of execution publicity dates back to the 1930s. In the first such investigation, Dann (1935) examined the number of homicides for the sixty-day periods before and after five highly publicized Philadelphia executions in 1927, 1929, 1930, 1931, and 1932. He found an increase, not a decline, in killings following each execution. Also contrary to deterrence predictions, examining four highly publicized death sentences in Philadelphia in 1944, 1946 (two), and 1947, Savitz (1958) found no change in definite and possible capital homicides during the eight-week periods before and after each event. These early execution publicity studies are informative, but they are limited since they are confined to a single location and involve limited time periods—and because neither attempts to measure the amount of media attention devoted to executions/death sentences or to link media coverage with changes in homicide rates.

In a more systematic analysis, King (1978) examined the impact of newspaper coverage of executions on monthly homicides in South Carolina for the period 1951–62. (King's analysis was framed as a test of the brutalization rather than the deterrence thesis.) Executions were categorized as either receiving or not receiving coverage in the South Carolina *State* newspaper. This paper had the largest circulation of any South Carolina newspaper during the 1951–62 period. Over the twelve years, there were twenty months in which executions received coverage in the *State*.

To test for a possible brutalization effect, the number of homicides for a news coverage month was compared with the average number of homicides for the same month for the years directly preceding and succeeding the year and month under consideration. Contrary to the brutalization thesis, King did not find a significant increase in killings during months when there was media coverage of executions. Nor did he find a significant decline in killings during media coverage months. A comparison of observed versus expected homicides for the media coverage months showed an increase in killings in eleven instances, and a decline in killings in eight months. The number of expected and observed killings was the same for one story month.

Most research on execution publicity has focused on more recent periods. After a nearly ten-year moratorium on capital punishment (1968–76), executions resumed in the United States in January 1977. The first few executions after the moratorium received considerable print and electronic media coverage. For example, the execution of Gary Gilmore in Utah on January 17, 1977, was front-page news across the country and the lead story for the evening news for the three major television networks.

McFarland (1983) examined whether the tremendous amount of news coverage given the Gilmore execution and the three executions to follow (John Spinkelink in Florida, 1979; Jesse Bishop in Nevada, 1979; and Steven Judy in Indiana, 1981) produced a significant decline in U.S. homicides. He speculated that the "media frenzy" surrounding the Gilmore execution should have had a dramatic deterrent effect, while the three later executions should have had a declining effect because each successive execution received less and less media coverage.

Examining weekly health statistics for homicide for various periods leading up to and following each of the four "celebrated" executions, McFarland found no evidence of a significant downward (or upward) shift in weekly killings. The Gilmore execution was followed by a decline in the level of U.S. weekly homicides for two weeks following the execution, but homicides during the next few weeks seemed to be unaffected. The dip in killings immediately following Gilmore's execution suggests a possible short-term deterrent effect, but McFarland rejects this interpretation. Rather, via a disaggregated regional analysis, he demonstrates that the significant decline in killings following the Gilmore execution was confined to parts of the country that experienced abnormally severe winter conditions during that period. Of particular note, following the Gilmore execution (in Utah) weather conditions were normal for the western states. For these jurisdictions there was no notable decline in homicides.

Stack (1987) took a different approach in examining the deterrent effect of media coverage of executions. He conducted a time-series analysis for the 1950–80 period in which monthly rates of murder were regressed against measures indicating the *amount* of newspaper coverage devoted to executions (high, medium, or low), with statistical controls being introduced for two factors associated with murder rates—the level of unemployment and the percentage of the population aged sixteen to thirty-four years. Executions recorded in *Facts on File* (a comprehensive national index of major news stories) and appearing in the *New York Times* were classified as receiving high levels of publicity. Those appearing in the *New York Times* but not in *Facts* were classified as receiving moderate media attention. And executions not receiving coverage in either source were classified as low-publicity cases. Stack found a significant decline in homicide rates for months with highly publicized executions, but there was only a chance association for cases receiving moderate or low publicity. Over the three decades, he estimates that "16 [highly] publicized executions may have saved as many as 480 lives," for an average of thirty persons saved per execution (Stack 1987:538).

Stack's analysis showing deterrence did not generate the response in the literature that Ehrlich's did, but his analysis was also subject to detailed scrutiny. Specifically, Bailey and Peterson (1989) critiqued and replicated Stack's investigation for the years Stack considered (1950–80) and for a more extended period (1940–86). Their critique indicated the following major problems. First, the dependent variable in Stack's investigation was the number of monthly homicides per 100,000 persons *sixteen years of age and older.* Since the numerator of the homicide index includes *all homicides* (regardless of the age of victims), it would have been preferable to compute homicide rates per 100,000 total population. Using this more conventional measure avoids the problem of how changes in the age structure of the U.S. population may artificially influence the number of potential homicide victims.

Second, like Ehrlich (1975), Stack failed to control for changes in the proportion of the U.S. population legally subject to capital punishment. Consequently, Stack makes the unwarranted assumption that execution publicity deters killings in abolitionist states. Doing so would be of only minor consequence if the proportion of the population residing in abolitionist jurisdictions was roughly constant over 1950–80. This is not the case. During the period this proportion varied from approximately 10 to 45 percent.

Third, deterrence theory predicts an inverse relationship between homicide rates and the levels of execution. However, the frequency of monthly executions for murder (which ranged from zero to sixteen during the period) is ignored completely in Stack's investigation.

Fourth, Stack did not include controls for a number of structural variables found to be associated with homicide rates: poverty, income inequality, race, the divorce rate, urban population, and region; nor did he control for the availability of firearms or the homicide arrest clearance rate (Bailey 1976; Ehrlich 1975; Kleck 1979; Logan 1982). (Of note, FBI-reported arrest clearance rates for homicide ranged from 72 to 94 percent over the 1950–80 period.) Finally, for the 1950–80 period, Stack classified twenty-three executions (occurring during sixteen different months) as receiving high levels of publicity. However, using his classification scheme, Bailey and Peterson documented twenty-six high-publicity executions spread over nineteen months.

Bailey and Peterson's replication of Stack's analysis revealed that these problems had a devastating effect on his findings. For example, merely correcting the coding errors for the execution publicity variables resulted in a chance-only association between execution publicity and homicide rates. This nondeterrence pattern remained when the monthly analysis was extended from 1940 through 1986, and when the other concerns noted previously were addressed.

Television News Coverage of Executions

For the periods considered by Stack (1950–80) and by Bailey and Peterson (1940–86), newspapers provided an important source of news for the U.S. population. However, over the period, the percentage of homes with television sets grew dramatically, from less than 10 percent in 1950 to over 98 percent by the early 1980s. Also during the period television gained in importance as a source of news for the American public. To illustrate, between 1959 and 1982 Roper pollsters periodically asked respondents: "Where [do] you usually get most of your news about what's going on in the world today?" (Roper Organization 1983). Newspapers and television were the most frequent sources mentioned (multiple sources could be cited). Their respective percentages were 57 percent and 51 percent in 1959, 48 percent and 60 percent in 1971, and 44 percent and 65 percent in 1982. Not only has television news grown in popularity, but survey data show that the American public views television as providing the most "complete," "intelligent," and "unbiased" source of news (Bower 1985:17).

Because of the growing importance of television news, Bailey (1990) extended deterrence publicity research by examining for the 1976–87 period the relationship between monthly murder rates and evening television news coverage devoted to executions in the United States. He used monthly homicide (murder and nonnegligent manslaughter) data from the FBI and news coverage data from the Vanderbilt Television News Archives.[3] Bailey coded the amount of news coverage devoted to each execution during the period, as well as the type of coverage. He found only a chance association between homicide rates and the *amount* of television news coverage devoted to executions. Similarly, Bailey did not observe consistent evidence of deterrence when different *types* of coverage were aired, for example, very graphic versus matter-of-fact presentation of the execution, murderers presented as fully deserving of executions versus those who raised concerns about the fairness of the execution (as in cases where youth or retarded persons were executed).

In sum, researchers have given attention to the possible deterrent effect of execution publicity. However, this body of work has produced no creditable evidence that the level of print or electronic media attention devoted to executions significantly discourages (deterrence) or encourages (brutalization) murder.

Deterrence and Different Types of Murder

Although support for deterrence has been negligible with but a few exceptions (Ehrlich 1975, 1977; Stack 1987), researchers have examined an undifferentiated category of general homicides. Thus, some critics of the mass of negative evidence that has accumulated over the decades have complained that neither in theory nor in policy has the death penalty been aimed at deterring all types of homicide (van den Haag 1969, 1975, 1978; van den Haag and Conrad 1983). To the contrary, only certain types of homicide are capital crimes in retentionist jurisdictions, and it is these "capital" murders, not the overall rate of homicide, that should be examined in deterrence investigations.[4] (Most death penalty jurisdictions restrict capital punishment to planned, intentional killings [premediated murder, first-degree murder, or aggravated murder] and/or killings that result from the commission of another felony [felony murders]).

Due to data limitations, addressing this criticism has been a formidable task. Most researchers have made use of either police data for murder and nonnegligent manslaughter or public health figures for homicide derived from coroners and medical examiners and available in the vital statistics reports of the National Center for Health Statistics (NCHS). This data limitation is true for analyses reporting *and* not reporting evidence of deterrence. Unfortunately, neither police nor public health homicide figures allow one to differentiate capital from noncapital killings.[5] In deterrence investigations, the use of a broad category of homicides would be acceptable if it could be assumed for time-series analyses that the proportion of capital to total homicides remained constant over the study period so that the more inclusive homicide data provide a reasonable proxy for capital offenses; and in cross-sectional analyses that the ratio of capital to total homicides is a constant from state to state such that observed variation in police or public health homicide figures reflects comparable variation in capital murder. Most death penalty investigators have been willing to accept these assumptions, but the empirical basis for doing so is questionable. Sellin's (1967) early observation that no one has succeeded in accurately identifying and counting capital offenses hidden in the available aggregate homicide figures still holds.

Studies of Capital Murder

Despite the difficulty of identifying capital homicides, there have been a few attempts to examine directly the impact of capital punishment on death-eligible killings. Earlier we presented very briefly the results of Savitz's (1958) short-term impact study of the influence of four highly publicized death sentences in Philadelphia. From an analysis of police and judicial records, Savitz was able to tally what he termed "definite" and "possible" capital homicides that occurred during the eight-week periods before and after the death sentences. As indicated, Savitz's analysis failed to yield support for deterrence arguments. Figures for definite and possible capital murders showed no indication of a significant decrease or increase following the handing down of death sentences.

Bailey's 1975 study (summarized previously) examined *first-degree murder* rates for death penalty and abolitionist jurisdictions for 1967 and 1968, controlling for a variety of sociodemographic factors associated with homicide rates. Figures for first-degree murder (the number of prison admissions for first-degree murder) came from a survey of state correctional authorities. Consistent with studies of general homicides, his analysis provided no indication of deterrence. Average rates of first-degree murder were not higher for abolitionist (1967 = .18; 1968 = .21) than death penalty (1967 = .47; 1968 = .58) jurisdictions, and there was only a slight inverse correlation between executions and rates of first-degree murder (1967, $r = -.137$; 1968, $r = -.194$).

In a third investigation Bailey (1984a) conducted a monthly time-series analysis of executions and first-degree murders in Chicago, Illinois, for the period 1915–21. Multiple regression analyses were performed where various execution measures and time-lag structures were considered. For 1915 through 1921, monthly (n = 84) first-degree murder figures were taken from the annual statistical reports of the Chicago Police Department. Cook County execution data were drawn from the records of the Cook County Prison. For 1915–21 there were a total of twenty-six executions.

At the bivariate level, Bailey found a slight positive relationship ($r = .158$) between rates of first-degree murder and the number of monthly executions. A very slight and nonsignificant relationship for these two variables generally persisted when a variety of control variables were incorporated into multivariate analyses. In no instance was there evidence of a significant decline in killings resulting from executions. However, for some models there was a tendency for executions to be associated with a significantly higher level of first-degree murder. This pattern is consistent with the brutalization argument that executions promote murder. Because this analysis is so time- and place-bound, it is not clear how generalizable this possible brutalization effect might be.

A recent analysis by Peterson and Bailey (1991) calls into question the possibility of both brutalization and deterrence for the most common type of capital homicide—killings that result from the commission of certain felonies. Felony murders and suspected felony murders constitute a quarter to a third of homicides annually, and they also account for a large majority of death sentences and executions. For the period of concern for Peterson and Bailey (1976–87), there were ninety-three executions in the United States. Of these, sixty-seven (72 percent) were for murders associated with robbery, rape, burglary, and kidnapping. On the basis of these figures Peterson and Bailey argue that for recent years, a felony murder analysis provides the most direct test possible of the deterrent effect of capital punishment for *capital murder.*

Using felony murder data drawn from unpublished FBI Supplementary Homicide Reports (SHR),[6] Peterson and Bailey replicated Bailey's 1990 analysis of monthly homicide rates and television news coverage of executions but substituted as dependent variables overall felony murder rates and rates for particular types of felony murders. These included killings resulting from rapes, robbery, burglary, larceny, vehicle theft, and arson.

Rates for these types of felony murder were regressed against monthly executions, various measures of the amount and type of news coverage devoted to executions, and selected law enforcement and sociodemographic factors as control variables. Consistent with studies of general homicides, the Peterson and Bailey study produced negative findings regarding deterrence. With one minor exception, the overall rate and rates of different types of felony murder were not responsive to the levels of execution or television news coverage of executions over the 1976–87 period. Rates of narcotics-related murders were found to be significantly lower during months when there was television news coverage of what might be considered ''questionable'' executions—those where the person who was put to death was retarded or was very young at the time of the crime, and where there were appeals for mercy from prominent figures. Peterson and Bailey are not able to offer a plausible explanation for this unique observation.

Finally, Cochran, Chamlin, and Seth (1994) conducted an interrupted time-series analysis to examine the possible deterrent effect of Oklahoma's return to capital punishment after a twenty-five-year moratorium. On September 10, 1990, Charles Coleman was executed at the Oklahoma State Penitentiary. This execution generated a significant amount of media coverage in the state. Cochran and his associates reasoned that if the death penalty has a deterrent potential, it certainly should be evident in comparing weekly rates of felony murder for periods before and after the Coleman execution.

Examining the period January 1989 through December 1991 (n = 156 weeks), Cochran, Chamlin, and Seth did not find a statistically significant decline in total felony murder resulting from the Coleman execution. The average number of weekly felony murders was only slightly higher for the pre- versus postintervention period (.73 versus .65). The decline was not statistically significant, and the investigators concluded that it did not warrant a deterrence label. However, Cochran and associates observed what they termed a strong brutalization effect for the Coleman execution for killings involving strangers. For the preexecution period, the mean number of weekly killings involving persons not known to one other was .42, compared with an average of .76 for the postexecution period. This increase in stranger killings (+.34) is statistically significant ($p < .05$) and is not an artifact of a general upward trend in such killings over the study period; nor was it due to any other nonexecution factor that Cochran and his associates could detect.

Police Killings and Capital Punishment

The apprehension of criminals is dangerous business. Each year thousands of police officers are assaulted and some are killed in the performance of their duties (FBI 1994). Do the threat and application of the death penalty afford the police an added measure of protection against being slain in the line of duty? Some law enforcement spokespersons have provided a loud and clear affirmative response to this question, but not all police are so convinced (see, e.g., opinions expressed in the 1995 Death Penalty Information Center report).

Scholars have sought to assess whether capital punishment in fact affords the police an added measure of protection against lethal assaults. The format of these analyses parallels the evolution of deterrence studies of general homicides, moving from simple comparative studies to increasingly complex multivariate analyses. Sellin (1955) provided the first study. Based on a survey of police departments in U.S. cities with a population of at least ten thousand (in 1950) in seventeen death penalty and six abolitionist jurisdictions, he examined annual police killing rates per 100,000 population for the period 1919–54. Sellin did not find support for the deterrence hypothesis. Rather, he observed that the average police homicide rate for cities in death penalty (1.3) and abolitionist (1.2) states was virtually identical.

The length of the time period (1919–54) and the number of jurisdictions (265) examined by Sellin are impressive, but he used a very unorthodox measure of police killings: the total number of police homicides per 10,000 *general,* not police, population. Correcting for this problem, Bailey (1982) examined, for abolitionist and death penalty states (1961–71), annual police homicide rates computed on the basis of the number of police killings per 1,000 *police officers.* He also examined the relationship between the certainty of execution for murder and police killings. For each year (1961–67), police killing rates were regressed against the ratio of total executions to total criminal homicides, a dummy variable differentiating death penalty from abolitionist states, and four control variables—proportions urban and black population, and rates of poverty and unemployment. Bailey's results were consistent with Sellin's. Policing was not found to be less hazardous in death penalty states, nor where executions were at higher levels. An extension of this analysis for the 1973–84 period also produced chance-only associations between state-level police killing rates and capital punishment (Bailey and Peterson 1987).

In a recent investigation of deterrence and police killings, Bailey and Peterson (1994) attempted to address a number of important concerns about the earlier studies. First, they argue that previous studies may not have addressed properly the *certainty* hypothesis. Bailey (1982) and Bailey and Peterson (1987) operationalized certainty as the ratio of total executions (or death sentences) to the total number of homicides, rather than as the ratio of executions for police killings to police killings.

Second, Bailey and Peterson argued that the dependent variables considered in earlier analyses may be problematic. Sellin used the size of the general population as the denominator in computing rates, and the remaining studies used the *total* number of police killings as the numerator in constructing rates. However, it is possible that not all types of police killings are equally subject to deterrence. For example, it is possible that on-duty police, but not off-duty police, are afforded an added measure of protection by capital punishment. Off-duty police killings often take place in situations where an apparent *civilian* is being robbed or a home is being burglarized. Similarly, it is possible that general jurisdiction officers (e.g., city police, county sheriffs, and state patrol) may gain a measure of protection from capital punishment but that specialized officers (e.g., fish and game protectors, customs agents, immigration and naturalization authorities, public housing and transit security) may not. Finally, Bailey and Peterson note that previous police killing studies did not consider the *publicity* hypothesis.

To address these concerns, Bailey and Peterson conducted a national, time-series analysis of police killings. Certainty was operationalized as the ratio of police killings to the number of monthly executions of "cop killers." They considered a general police killing rate (the number of officers killed per 100,000 police personnel), *and* rates for killings involving (1) on-duty and (2) off-duty police, and killings of (3) general jurisdiction and (4) special-function police. The monthly time series spanned January 1976 through December 1989. Over this period, 1,204 law enforcement officers were killed feloniously (FBI 1987–89), and there were 120 executions in the United States, 12 of which involved the execution of a "cop killer." Because of their relatively small number ($n = 12$), Bailey and Peterson also considered a broader execution rate measure—the ratio of total executions to total criminal homicides.

Despite the added features of this study, the analysis did not challenge the findings of previous investigations. Bailey and Peterson found no evidence that overall and specific types of police killing rates were responsive to changes in the provision for capital punishment, to the certainty of execution, or to the amount and type of television news coverage devoted to executions.

Summary and Conclusions

Criminologists have devoted a great deal of research attention to the deterrence and death penalty question. This attention is warranted and should not come as a surprise for several reasons. First, the capital punishment question is an emotionally charged issue for laypersons and policy makers. For many the deterrence issue is at the heart of the debate (Zimring and Hawkins 1986). Second, the United States is the only Western nation that retains capital punishment for common murder. This fact underscores questions about the utility of this form of punishment within the United States. Third, despite the relatively uniform pattern of negative findings on capital punishment and deterrence, recent studies have raised questions that have been addressed by investigators. Improvements in data availability and analysis techniques also have permitted scholars to respond to many previously unanswered deterrence and capital punishment issues.

Our concern in this chapter has been to review and assess the empirical evidence regarding the deterrent effect of capital punishment. And because the literatures are so linked, we have also considered the brutalization thesis: Do executions actually promote, rather than discourage, murder? Due to the volume of research, our analysis has not included a detailed review of all the various studies. Rather, within the context of the work concerning different dimensions of punishment, we have presented an overview of types of deterrence studies primarily in terms of substantive questions and methodological approaches. Detailed discussion of a few individual studies was provided, but only when warranted due to the nature of the findings (e.g., the study finds support for deterrence) and/or the uniqueness of the question examined or the research approaches taken.

In general, we have observed a number of features of the deterrence literature that are noteworthy. First, the various dimensions of punishment emphasized by deterrence theory have not been given equal attention in the empirical literature. Investigators have seldom addressed the celerity issue. Thus, although the findings from existing work on celerity are consistent with those for other dimensions of punishment, the role of celerity is the least well understood.

Second, the approaches taken in deterrence research follow a progression from using a comparative methodology whereby homicide rates are compared for abolitionist versus retentionist jurisdictions, or before and after a change in capital punishment policy, or before and after highly publicized executions, to the use of more and more sophisticated multivariate techniques. In general, the type of methodological approach taken has not affected the pattern of findings regarding the deterrent effect of capital punishment. Results have been quite uniform whatever approach is taken.

Third, the evidence on how different dimensions of capital punishment influence homicides is overwhelmingly contrary to deterrence theory. The bulk of evidence does not support the brutalization thesis either. While some may be reluctant to regard the existing evidence as conclusive, the consistency of findings is quite impressive. Without exception studies of severity have failed to indicate support for deterrence. The findings of the early comparative studies are especially important because they demonstrate that even during a period when the death penalty was in greater use in the United States, and when the delay between capital offenses and executions was considerably shorter, the provision for capital punishment did not appear to discourage murder.

The evidence regarding the certainty of punishment and execution publicity is not totally uniform. In particular, during the mid-1970s, Ehrlich found evidence of deterrence from time-series analyses of the United States (Ehrlich 1973, 1975) and a cross-sectional analysis of states (Ehrlich 1977). Layson (1985) also found evidence of a significant deterrent effect for the certainty of execution for the United States over a multidecade period. And Stack (1987) found evidence of deterrence from a monthly analysis of homicides and print media attention devoted to executions. As detailed in this review, and as shown by Fox and Radelet (1989) for the Layson study, these investigations suffer from a variety of theoretical and methodological problems that are so serious that few scholars are willing to lend credence to these findings.

The few isolated studies which report that capital punishment may actually incite killings (Bowers and Pierce 1980; Bowers 1984; Cochran, Chamlin, and Seth 1994) have not been subjected to detailed scrutiny. As a result, it is difficult to know what to conclude from these analyses. It is possible that for some types of homicide, capital punishment may encourage citizens to kill. But which citizens and under what conditions? Does the list of eligible killers include most citizens, or only select persons/groups who experience certain environmental conditions? How do factors such as a person's gender, age, race, economic status, access to an attorney for redress, and the like influence one's likelihood of identifying with the state (as executioner) and killing those who have wronged him or her? The brutalization literature is generally silent on these basic issues (Bowers 1984; Bowers and Pierce 1980). These remain important questions for future research.

Of course, a very large body of accumulated findings that are contrary to a theory such as deterrence does not necessarily provide a basis for discarding the theory. Consistent negative findings could stem from tests that ignore important variables or crucial questions, or from studies that do not provide critical tests of the issues. For example, due to data limitations, most of the studies reviewed here were not able to examine the effects of various death penalty characteristics for *capital* homicides. Yet, regardless of the level of the certainty of execution or the amount and type of media attention devoted to executions, only capital homicides are likely to be subject to deterrence. Thus it could be claimed that nondeterrence findings are based on studies that do not provide critical tests of the issue. It is noteworthy, however, that investigators who have been able to examine death-eligible killings also have found no evidence of deterrence (e.g., Bailey 1975, 1976, 1983; Cochran, Chamlin, and Seth 1994) but possibly some evidence for brutalization (Cochran, Chamlin, and Seth 1994).

It has been posited that the findings and conclusions of deterrence studies may be affected by a priori discipline-based beliefs and biases regarding the basic causes of crime, including homicide (McManus 1985). The argument is that due to such beliefs, some researchers (notably sociologists) working in the capital punishment area have been unable to find a significant deterrent effect, while economists (who are more comfortable with the fundamental tenets of deterrence theory) have not had such a problem. We take strong issue with such a characterization of the deterrence and death penalty literature. It is true that Isaac Ehrlich, the first investigator to report evidence of deterrence, is an economist. However, analyses by a number of other economists have failed to confirm Ehrlich's findings and conclusions (e.g., Forst 1977; Passell and Taylor 1977; Hoenack and Weiler 1980; Klein, Forst, and Filatov 1978). At the same time, a sociologist (Stack 1987) is one of the only other recent scholars to produce a study suggesting a possible deterrent effect for capital punishment within the U.S. context.[6]

Thus, it appears that neither economists nor sociologists, nor persons from any other discipline (law, psychology, engineering, etc.) have produced credible evidence of a significant deterrent effect for capital punishment. And not a single investigation to date has produced any indication that capital punishment deters capital murders—the crime of direct theoretical and policy concern.

Roughly thirty years ago, Thorsten Sellin (1967) and Hugo Bedau (1967) conducted a survey and assessment of the then available deterrence and death penalty literature. Neither found evidence of deterrence. In the early 1980s and in the aftermath of Ehrlich's work and the nation's return to the use of capital punishment, Sellin (1980) and Bedau (1982) again assessed the evidence, with the same result. In 1986 Zimring and Hawkins surveyed the literature regarding capital punishment and deterrence. This effort also failed to produce evidence of a marginal deterrent effect for capital punishment. Rather, they report that the evidence is "clear and abundant" that the death penalty is not an effective deterrent to murder.

It has now been almost a decade since Zimring and Hawkins's review. Over this period there have been a number of important studies aimed at tying up various "loose ends" regarding deterrence and the death penalty. These research efforts do not challenge the assessments by Sellin, Bedau, and Zimring and Hawkins. Rather, they add weight to their conclusions. The available evidence remains "clear and abundant" that, as practiced in the United States, capital punishment is not more effective than imprisonment in deterring murder.

For at least some death penalty proponents the nondeterrence evidence may not be viewed as sufficiently clear and abundant. We urge these persons to undertake the exercise that we have followed here of thoroughly examining the literature. We also urge those who question the negative state of the evidence to conduct the types of empirical analyses necessary to demonstrate the deterrent effectiveness of capital punishment. We look forward to these studies but have our doubts about their likelihood. This is because over the years, the authors of this essay, along with many other scholars, have attempted to address successive concerns about the adequacy of previous death penalty research. This includes examining different types of capital homicide, expanding the number of important deterrence variables (certainty, celerity, publicity) under consideration in a given study, and examining various time periods and a variety of jurisdictions. Additional studies may add to our knowledge. However, short of conducting controlled experiments with capital punishment, which are not possible in this society, we are hard-pressed to point to any unaddressed death penalty questions where additional research might alter the current pattern of nondeterrence findings. In the meantime, based upon our assessment of the literature, we feel quite confident in concluding that in the United States a significant general deterrent effect for capital punishment has not been observed, and in all probability does not exist.

Notes

1. Examination of the second column of the table shows that some states were without the death penalty for the entire period, while others provided for the death penalty each year. In still other jurisdictions there were changes in provision for capital punishment because of judicial and/or legislative actions.

2. Of note, for the 1956–60 period the median elapsed time between death sentences and executions was 14.4 months, with the range extending from only 4.6 months (for Texas) to 46.1 months (for Connecticut). In contrast, for persons executed in 1993, the median elapsed time between sentencing and execution was 113 months (U.S. Department of Justice 1994).

3. The archives has been videotaping and abstracting ABC, CBS, and NBC evening news programs since 1968. Of ninety-three executions during the 1976–87 period, thirty-three (distributed over twenty-five months) received television news coverage by one or more of the networks.

4. While van den Haag has been highly critical of the negative findings of most deter-

rence analyses, he has only praise for Ehrlich's research, which also relied upon general rather than capital homicide data (van den Haag and Conrad 1983). Similarly, outspoken abolitionists are quite aware of the limitations of the available homicide data but nonetheless view studies that rely upon these data as providing clear and convincing evidence that the death penalty does not deter.

5. The FBI, which collects homicide incident figures from police departments and stage-level law enforcement coordinating agencies across the country, defines murder and non-negligent manslaughter as "the willful (nonnegligent) killing of one human being by another" (FBI 1992:7). Excluded from the FBI homicide counts, which appear in the annual *Uniform Crime Reports (UCR),* are negligent manslaughters and justifiable and accidental killings. Observing the World Health Organization's *International Classification of Diseases (ICD),* the U.S. National Center for Health Statistics defines homicide as "a death resulting from an injury purposely inflicted by another person" (NCHS 1967:9). Published NCHS figures allow one to exclude from total homicide counts killings resulting from legal interventions—most notably lawful executions and justifiable homicides. For a detailed examination of the various features of the FBI and NCHS systems for compiling homicide figures, see Riedel (1990).

6. Of note, Phillips (1980), who is also a sociologist, reports evidence of deterrence from an analysis of homicide patterns in London, England, surrounding the execution of twenty-two infamous murderers during the 1858–21 period. He found a 35 percent decline in average homicides during the two weeks immediately following each execution. However, Phillips also observed a "rebound effect" for the next few weeks to follow. This effect essentially canceled out the immediate decline in killings. See Bowers (1988) for a detailed analysis of the Phillips study.

References

Andenaes, Johannes
1974 *Punishment and Deterrence.* Ann Arbor: University of Michigan Press.

Archer, Dane, and Rosemary Gartner
1984 *Violence and Crime in Cross-National Perspective.* New Haven, Conn.: Yale University Press.

Bailey, William C.
1975 "Murder and Capital Punishment: Some Further Evidence." *American Journal of Orthopsychiatry* 45:669–88.

1976 "Certainty of Arrest and Crime Rates for Major Felonies." *Journal of Research in Crime and Delinquency* 13:145–54.

1977 "Imprisonment vs. the Death Penalty as a Deterrent to Murder." *Law and Human Behavior* 1:239–60.

1978 "Deterrence and the Death Penalty for Murder in Utah: A Time-Series Analysis." *Journal of Contemporary Law* 5:1–20.

1979a "An Analysis of the Deterrence Effect of the Death Penalty in North Carolina." *North Carolina Central Law Journal* 10:29–51.

1979b "Deterrence and the Death Penalty for Murder in Oregon." *Willamette Law Review* 16:67–85.

1979c "The Deterrent Effect of the Death Penalty for Murder in California." *Southern California Law Review* 52:743–64.

1979d "The Deterrent Effect of the Death Penalty for Murder in Ohio." *Cleveland State Law Review* 28:51–81.

1980a "Deterrence and the Celerity of the Death Penalty: A Neglected Question in Deterrence Research." *Social Forces* 58:1308–33.

1980b "A Multivariate Cross-sectional Analysis of the Deterrent Effect of the Death Penalty." *Sociology and Social Research* 64:183–207.

1982 "Capital Punishment and Lethal Assaults Against Police." *Criminology* 19: 608–25.

1983 "The Deterrent Effect of Capital Punishment During the 1950's." *Suicide* 13: 95–107.

1984a "Disaggregation in Deterrence and Death Penalty Research: The Case of Murder in Chicago." *Journal of Criminal Law and Criminology* 74:827–59.

1984b "Murder and Capital Punishment in the Nation's Capitol." *Justice Quarterly* 1:211–33.

1990 "Murder and Capital Punishment: An Analysis of Television Execution Publicity." *American Sociological Review* 55:628–33.

Bailey, William C., and Ruth D. Peterson

1987 "Police Killings and Capital Punishment: The Post-*Furman* Period." *Criminology* 25:1–25.

1989 "Murder and Capital Punishment: A Monthly Time-Series Analysis of Execution Publicity." *American Sociological Review* 54:722–43.

1994 "Murder, Capital Punishment and Deterrence: A Review of the Evidence and an Examination of Police Killings." *Journal of Social Issues* 50:53–74.

Baldus, David, and James Cole

1975 "A Comparison of the Work of Thorsten Sellin and Isaac Ehrlich on the Deterrent Effect of Capital Punishment." *Yale Law Journal* 18:170–86.

Barnett, Arnold

1981 "The Deterrent Effect of Capital Punishment: A Test of Some Recent Studies." *Operations Research* 29:346–70.

Beccaria, Cesare

1809 *Essays on Crimes and Punishment.* New York: Gould.

1963 *On Crimes and Punishment.* Trans. H. Paolucci. Indianapolis, Ind.: Bobbs-Merrill. [Original work published in 1764.]

Bechdolt, Burley V.

1977 "Capital Punishment and Homicide and Rape Rates in the United States: Time Series and Cross Sectional Regression Analyses." *Journal of Behavioral Economics* 6:33–66.

Bedau, Hugo A., ed.

1967 *The Death Penalty in America.* Rev. ed. New York: Doubleday.

1982 *The Death Penalty in America.* 3rd ed. New York: Oxford University Press.

Bentham, Jeremy

1962 "The Rationale of Punishment." In J. Browning, ed., *Works of Jeremy Bentham.* New York: Russell and Russell, pp. 385–525. [Original work published in 1843.]

Beyleveld, D.

1982 "Ehrlich's Analysis of Deterrence." *British Journal of Criminology* 22:101–23.

Black, Theodore, and Thomas Orsagh

1978 "New Evidence on the Efficacy of Sanctions as a Deterrent to Homicide." *Social Science Quarterly* 58:616–31.

Bower, Robert T.
1985 *The Changing Television Audience in America.* New York: Columbia University Press.
Bowers, William J.
1984 *Legal Homicide: Death as Punishment in America.* Boston: Northeastern University Press.
1988 "The Effect of Executions Is Brutalization, Not Deterrence." In K. C. Haas and J. A. Inciardi, eds., *Capital Punishment: Legal and Social Science Approaches.* Newbury Park, Calif.: Sage, pp. 49–89.
Bowers, William J., and Glenn Pierce
1975 "The Illusion of Deterrence in Isaac Ehrlich's Research on Capital Punishment." *Yale Law Journal* 85:187–208.
1980 "Deterrence or Brutalization: What Is the Effect of Executions?" *Crime and Delinquency* 26:453–84.
Boyes, William J., and Lee R. McPheters
1977 "Capital Punishment as a Deterrent to Violent Crime: Cross Section Evidence." *Journal of Behavioral Economics* 6:67–86.
Brier, Stephen, and Stephen Feinberg
1980 "Recent Econometric Modeling of Crime and Punishment: Support for the Deterrence Hypothesis?" *Evaluation Review* 4:147–91.
Bye, Raymond T.
1919 *Capital Punishment in the United States.* Philadelphia: The Committee on Philanthropic Labor of Philadelphia Yearly Meeting of Friends.
Chandler, David B.
1976 *Capital Punishment in Canada: A Sociological Study of Repressive Law.* Ottawa: McClelland and Stewart Limited in Association with the Institute of Canadian Studies, Carleton University.
Cochran, John K., Mitchell B. Chamlin, and Mark Seth
1994 "Deterrence or Brutalization? An Impact Assessment of Oklahoma's Return to Capital Punishment." *Criminology* 32:107–34.
Costanzo, Mark, and Lawrence T. White
1994 "An Overview of the Death Penalty and Capital Trials: History, Current Status, Legal Procedures, and Cost." *Journal of Social Issues* 50:1–18.
Dann, Robert
1935 *The Deterrent Effect of Capital Punishment.* Philadelphia: The Committee of Philanthropic Labor of Philadelphia Yearly Meeting of Friends.
Death Penalty Information Center
1995 *On the Front Line: Law Enforcement Views on the Death Penalty.* Washington, D.C.: DPIC.
Decker, Scott H., and Carol W. Kohfeld
1984 "A Deterrence Study of the Death Penalty in Illinois, 1933–1980." *Journal of Criminal Justice* 12:367.
Ehrlich, Isaac
1973 The Deterrent Effect of Capital Punishment. National Bureau of Economic Research. Working Paper Series no. 18.
1975 "The Deterrent Effect of Capital Punishment: A Question of Life or Death." *American Economic Review* 65:397–417.
1977 "Capital Punishment and Deterrence: Some Further Thoughts and Additional Evidence." *Journal of Political Economy* 85:741–88.

Facts on File
1940–89 *Facts on File: An Index to National News.* New York: Facts on File.

Fattah, Ezzat Abdel
1972 A Study of the Deterrent Effect of Capital Punishment with Special Reference to the Canadian Situation. Department of the Solicitor General, Canada. [Reprinted in 1973.]

Federal Bureau of Investigation
1967–95 *Crime in the United States: Uniform Crime Reports.* Washington, D.C.: U.S. Government Printing Office, annually.
1982 *Law Enforcement Officers Killed and Assaulted: Uniform Crime Reports.* Washington, D.C.: U.S. Government Printing Office.

Forst, Brian
1977 "The Deterrent Effect of Capital Punishment: A Cross-State Analysis of the 1960's." *Minnesota Law Review* 61:743–67.

Fox, James Alan, and Michael L. Radelet.
1989 "Persistent Flaws in Econometric Studies of the Deterrent Effect of the Death Penalty." *Loyola of Los Angeles Law Review* 23:29–44.

Friedman, Lee.
1979 "The Use of Multiple Regression Analysis to Test for a Deterrent Effect of Capital Punishment: Prospects and Problems." In S. Messinger and E. Bittner, eds., *Criminology Review Yearbook.* Beverly Hills, Calif.: Sage, pp. 61–87.

Gibbs, Jack P.
1975 *Crime, Punishment and Deterrence.* New York: Elsevier.
1986 "Deterrence Theory and Research." In G. B. Melton, ed., *Nebraska Symposium on Motivation—1985: The Law as a Behavioral Instrument.* Lincoln: University of Nebraska Press, pp. 87–130.

Hoenack, Stephen A., and William C. Weiler.
1980 "A Structural Model of Murder Behavior and the Criminal Justice System." *American Economic Review* 70:327–44.

Jayewardene C. H. S.
1977 *The Penalty of Death: The Canadian Experiment.* Toronto: University of Ottawa; Lexington, Mass.: D. C. Heath.

Jeffrey, C. Ray.
1965 "Criminal Behavior and Learning Theory." *Journal of Criminal Law, Criminology, and Police Science* 56:294–300.

King, David R.
1978 "The Brutalization Effect: Execution Publicity and the Incidence of Homicide in South Carolina." *Social Forces* 57:683–87.

Kleck, Gary.
1979 "Capital Punishment, Gun Ownership, and Homicide." *American Journal of Sociology* 84:882–910.

Klein, Lawrence, Brian Forst, and Victor Filatov.
1978 "The Deterrent Effect of Capital Punishment: An Assessment of the Estimates." In A. Blumstein, J. Cohen, and D. Nagin, eds., *Deterrence and Incapacitation: Estimating the Effects of Criminal Sanctions on Crime Rates.* National Academy of Sciences, pp. 336–60.

Layson, Stephen K.
1985 "Homicide and Deterrence: An Examination of the United States Time-Series Evidence." *Southern Economic Journal* 52:68–89.

Logan, Charles H.
1982 "Problems in Ratio Correlation: The Case of Deterrence Research." *Social Forces* 60:791–810.

McFarland, Sam G.
1983 "Is Capital Punishment a Short-Term Deterrent to Homicide? A Study of the Effects of Four Recent American Executions." *Journal of Criminal Law and Criminology* 74:1014–30.

McGahey, Richard M.
1980 "Dr. Ehrlich's Magic Bullet: Economic Theory, Econometrics, and the Death Penalty." *Crime and Delinquency* 26:485–502.

McManus, Walter S.
1985 "Estimates of the Deterrent Effect of Capital Punishment: The Importance of the Researchers' Prior Beliefs." *Journal of Political Economy* 93:414–25.

National Center for Health Statistics.
1967 "Homicide in the United States 1950–1964." *Vital Health and Statistics* 20:9.

New York Times Company.
1940–86 *The New York Times Index.* New York: New York Times Company.

Passell, Peter.
1975 "The Deterrent Effect of the Death Penalty: A Statistical Test." *Stanford Law Review* 28:61–80.

Passell, Peter, and John Taylor.
1977 "The Deterrent Effect of Capital Punishment." *American Economic Review* 67: 445–51.

Peterson, Ruth D., and William C. Bailey.
1988 "Murder and Capital Punishment in the Evolving Context of the Post-*Furman* Era." *Social Forces* 66:774–807.
1991 "Felony Murder and Capital Punishment: An Examination of the Deterrence Question." *Criminology* 29:367–95.

Phillips, David P.
1980 "The Deterrent Effect of Capital Punishment: New Evidence on an Old Controversy." *American Journal of Sociology* 86:139–48.

Radelet, Michael L., Hugo Adam Bedau, and Constance E. Putnam.
1992 *In Spite of Innocence: Erroneous Convictions in Capital Cases.* Boston: Northeastern University Press.

Riedel, Marc.
1990 "Nationwide Homicide Data Sets: An Evaluation of the Uniform Crime Reports and the National Center for Health Statistics." In McKenzie, Doris Layton, Phyllis Jo Baunach, and Roy R. Roberg, eds. *Measuring Crime: Large-Scale, Long-Range Efforts.* Albany: State University of New York Press.

The Roper Organization.
1983 *Trends in Attitudes Towards Television and Other Media: A Twenty-Year Review.* New York: Television Information Office.

Savitz, Leonard.
1958 "A Study of Capital Punishment." *Journal of Criminal Law, Criminology, and Police Science* 49:338–41.

Schuessler, Karl.
1952 "The Deterrent Effect of the Death Penalty." *Annals* 284:54–62.

Sellin, Thorsten.
1955 *The Royal Commission on Capital Punishment,* 1949–1953. *Report of the Great*

Britain Parliament (Papers by Command 8932, pp. 17–24). London: H. M. Stationary Office.
1959 *The Death Penalty.* Philadelphia: American Law Institute.
1961 "Capital Punishment." *Federal Probation* 25:3.
1967 *Capital Punishment.* New York: Harper and Row.
1980 *The Penalty of Death.* Beverly Hills, Calif.: Sage.

Stack, Steven.
1987 "Publicized Executions and Homicide, 1950–1980." *American Sociological Review* 52:532–40.

Sutherland, Edwin.
1925 "Murder and the Death Penalty." *Journal of the American Institute of Criminal Law and Criminology* 51:522–29.

U.S. Department of Justice, Office of Justice Programs.
1994 *Capital Punishment 1993.* Washington, D.C.: Bureau of Justice Statistics.

van den Haag, Ernest.
1969 "On Deterrence and the Death Penalty." *Journal of Criminal Law, Criminology, and Political Science* 60:141–147.
1975 *Punishing Criminals: Concerning a Very Old and Painful Question.* New York: Basic Books.
1978 "In Defense of the Death Penalty: A Legal-Practical-Moral Analysis." *Criminal Law Bulletin* 14:51–68.

van den Haag, Ernest, and John Conrad.
1983 *The Death Penalty: A Debate.* New York: Plenum.

Vanderbilt Television News Archive.
1978–90 *Vanderbilt Television and News Index and Abstracts.* 1978–90. Nashville, Tenn.: Vanderbilt Television News Archive.

Yunker, James A.
1976 "Is the Death Penalty a Deterrent to Homicide? Some Time Series Evidence." *Journal of Behavioral Economics* 5:1–32.

Zimring, Franklin E., and Gordon Hawkins.
1973 *Deterrence: The Legal Threat in Crime Control.* Chicago: University of Chicago Press.
1986 *Capital Punishment and the American Agenda.* New York: Cambridge University Press.

10

A National Study of the *Furman*-Commuted Inmates: Assessing the Threat to Society from Capital Offenders

JAMES W. MARQUART
JONATHAN R. SORENSEN

. . . This study examines the prison and release behavior of all capital offenders commuted by *Furman.* What happened to the former death row prisoners? How accurate were the long-term predictions of violence? If released, did these offenders repeat their crimes and return to prison? Providing answers to these and other questions bears directly on the justification for capital punishment in many states today—particularly those eight states whose current capital statutes have a "future-dangerousness" provision.[1] Such a provision reflects the premise that incapacitation of capital offenders protects society from future violence inflicted by those offenders.[2] This study is a descriptive analysis of the institutional and post-release behavior of 558 *Furman*-commuted inmates in thirty states and the District of Columbia. First, we examine the relevant literature on commuted offenders. Then, we present the background characteristics of these inmates with special emphasis on the race of offenders and victims. Next is an in-depth analysis of the institutional behavior of the *Furman*-commuted inmates that addresses whether these inmates were a special threat to the custodial staff, other prisoners, and institutional order. Finally, we examine the patterns of recidivism among these capital offenders. We conclude with a discussion of recidivism among capital murderers and the accuracy of long-term predictions of serious violence.

I. Previous Research on Commuted Capital Offenders

Little systematic research exists examining the behavior of commuted capital offenders. . . . Although the research literature on commuted offenders in prison is

Reprinted from *Loyola of Los Angeles Law Review,* vol. 23, no. 1, November 1989, pp. 5–28 and by permission of the authors. Some of the text and footnotes have been deleted and the remaining notes renumbered.

sparse, it does not suggest that these prisoners are more dangerous, violent or aggressive than other offenders. If anything, the prison behavior of commuted capital offenders paralleled that of murderers in general, the latter group being "settled" prisoners infrequently involved in homicidal or other violent types of behavior.[3]

B. *Recidivism of Commuted Capital Prisoners*

. . . Although systematic research is also lacking on the recidivism of commuted capital offenders, available research indicates that commuted prisoners, while on release, pose no significant threat to society when compared to other similar offenders. . . .[4]

II. Methodology

The first stage in this research was to obtain a list of inmates commuted by *Furman.* Douglas Lyons of the NAACP Legal Defense Fund prepared a "List of Persons on Death Row at Time of *Furman.*"[5] The list contained thirty states and 613 inmates whose capital sentences were set aside by the *Furman* ruling. We obtained a copy, telephoned each state department of corrections, developed a contact person, and explained our research goals. Next, a letter was forwarded to each contact person that identified the commutees and outlined the specific objectives and time frame for data collection. The necessary research agreement forms were then signed and our research plan was officially approved.

Once the research was formally approved we forwarded code sheets to the contact persons for data collection. These sheets covered six data categories:

1. current status (e.g., still in prison, paroled, deceased);
2. previous felony convictions;
3. total number of prior incarcerations;
4. prison disciplinary history;
5. victim information for the crime for which the defendant received the death penalty; and
6. whether the crime was committed in the commission of another felony. . . .

III. General Characteristics of the *Furman*-Commuted Offenders

A. *Region and State*

. . . Table 10-1 presents a state by state listing of how many capital offenders had their sentences commuted by *Furman.* We give both Lyons' and our figures.

Table 10-1.
Region and State Comparison by List

State	Lyons' list			Our study		
	Murder	Rape	Total#	Murder	Rape	Total#
TOTAL	527	82	613	474	80	558
NORTHEAST	59	0	59	61	0	61
Connecticut	4	0	4	4	0	4
Massachusetts	23	0	23	25	0	25
New Hampshire	2	0	2	2	0	2
New York	5	0	5	5	0	5
Pennsylvania	25	0	25	25	0	25
MIDWEST	123	0	123	88	0	88
Illinois	31	0	31	—	—	0*
Indiana	9	0	9	9	0	9
Kansas	2	0	2	2	0	2
Missouri	16	0	16	16	0	16
Nebraska	2	0	2	2	0	2
Ohio	63	0	63	59	0	59
WEST	25	0	25	25	0	25
Colorado	2	0	2	2	0	2
Nevada	8	0	8	8	0	8
Utah	5	0	5	5	0	5
Washington	10	0	10	10	0	10
SOUTH	320	82	406**	300	80	384**
Alabama	26	5	31	26	5	31
Arkansas	6	0	6	6	0	6
Delaware	3	0	3	3	0	3
District of Columbia	3	0	3	1	0	1
Florida	73	29	102	71	29	100
Georgia	29	12	43**	27	12	40**
Kentucky	21	0	21	21	0	21
Louisiana	36	12	48	29	10	39
Maryland	18	5	23	18	5	23
Mississippi	9	0	9	9	0	9
North Carolina	9	2	11	8	2	10
Oklahoma	15	0	15	15	0	15
South Carolina	10	1	11	10	1	11
Tennessee	11	5	16	11	5	16
Texas	42	8	52**	37	7	47**
Virginia	9	3	12	8	4	12

*Illinois did not complete the codesheets. However, an official stated that of the thirty-one Illinois offenders, nineteen have never been released from prison, ten have been discharged, and two have been paroled. No releases have returned to prison.

**Includes four robbers. The LDF listed two robbers from Georgia and two from Texas. In the current survey, however, one robber was from Georgia and three were from Texas.

Table 10-2.
Criminal History of the *Furman*-Commutees

	White (N = 240)	Nonwhite (N = 318)	Total (N = 558)
Prior record			
Convicted of UCR offense*	56.9%	52.7%	54.5%
Convicted of UCR property offense	46.3%	38.8%	42.1%
Convicted of UCR violent offense	24.5%	28.7%	26.8%
Prior adult prison incarceration	45.5%	33.1%**	38.6%
Prior jail term	31.7%	29.2%	30.3%
Prior juvenile incarceration	22.1%	24.7%	23.6%

*Offense documented by the Uniform Crime Reports.
**Chi square = 4.05; d.f. = 1; $p < .05$ level.

According to both lists, most of the death row population in 1972 resided in Southern prison systems. These data are consistent with previous research on region and capital punishment in America. In December 1988, 59% of those sentenced to death were confined on Southern death rows.[6] All *Furman*-commuted prisoners sentenced to death for rape and robbery were also from the South. . . .

B. Offender Characteristics

According to our data, there were 558 inmates (excluding Illinois) on death row awaiting execution in 1972 who were commuted as a result of *Furman.* Of these inmates, 474 (85%) were capital murderers, eighty-one (14%) were rapists, and four (1%) were sentenced to death for armed robbery. In terms of race and ethnicity, 309 (55%) prisoners were black, 240 (43%) were white, eight (1%) were hispanic, and one was an American Indian. As expected, the capital offenders were overwhelmingly male (only two were female), with a median age of thirty-two years in 1972.

We asked each state prison system to provide data on the prisoners' prior criminal history. According to our contact persons, these data were gleaned from initial classification interviews and cross-checked with FBI and local state police records. Table 10-2 presents this information.

These data reveal that the majority of commuted offenders had been convicted of a prior UCR [Uniform Crime Reports] offense. They were not first offenders. However, these conviction data also show that property crimes were their main criminal activity. Nearly three-quarters had no prior convictions for violent UCR offenses. Specifically, 97% had no previous conviction for murder, 96% for rape, 87% for armed robbery, and 85% for aggravated assault.[7] Additionally, 61% of these inmates had never been incarcerated in an adult correctional institution. In

Table 10-3.
Comparison of *Furman*-Murderers, Persons Arrested for Murder Only 1968–72, and the Current Death Row Population

	Furman (N = 474)	Arrestees* (N = 64,337)	Current** death row (N = 2,158)
Offender characteristics			
Sex			
Male	99.6%	84.3%	98.9%
Female	0.4%	15.7%	1.1%
Race			
White	47.5%	36.8%	51.8%
Nonwhite	52.5%	63.2%	48.2%
Victim characteristics			
Sex			
Male	67.4%	78.0%	56.0%
Female	32.6%	22.0%	44.0%
Race			
White	80.2%	44.4%	61.9%
Nonwhite	19.8%	55.6%	38.1%

*Source: FBI, UNIFORM CRIME REP., 1968–1972.
**Source: Tanya Coke and Karima Wicks of the NAACP Legal Defense and Education Fund.

short, the typical *Furman*-commutee was a southern male black murderer without a lengthy history of serious violence or repeated trips to prison.

IV. Offense Data

A. The Furman Murderers

. . . Table 10-3 compares the *Furman*-releases with persons arrested for murder during the preceding five years. While not offering conclusive evidence, these data provide support for the differential sentencing of capital offenders—in this case murderers. Clearly, capital juries consistently sentenced to death those defendants who killed whites. While a direct comparison between the groups is not possible, the differential treatment of male and female homicide offenders has been shown repeatedly and exists in pre-*Furman* and post-*Furman* periods. In the five years prior to 1972, 16% of those arrested for murder were women, yet less than 1% were on death row at the time of the *Furman* decision. During 1968–1972, an average of 22% of the victims of homicide were female. However, victims of death row inmates were female in 33% of the homicides.

Table 10-3 also presents data on those currently housed on death row. Today's death row population is somewhat dissimilar from the *Furman* prisoners. The majority of death row inmates are white males. Interestingly, 38% of today's victims were non-white, as compared to 20% in the *Furman* era. Perhaps prosecutors are more sensitive to minority victims of felony-murders than they were two or even three decades ago. Authorities may simply be more willing to prosecute these cases today.

To obtain a more focused picture of the capital murderer, we collected data on the victims of the *Furman* murderers. Table 10-4 presents data on these crimes.

These data indicate that white and non-white offenders were quite similar in terms of the number of victims, and the sex and age of the victim. By far the most striking difference between white and non-white murderers was the victim's race. White offenders killed whites in almost every circumstance. However, non-white offenders "crossed over" 65% of the time and were subsequently sentenced to death. This pattern of differential sentencing is also evident in Table 10-3. Less than half of the homicide victims during the five years prior to *Furman* were white. However, victims of offenders on death row were overwhelmingly (80%) white. Based on the victim's race, our data suggest bias and arbitrariness in the processing of capital murder cases.

If racial discrimination occurs through interaction with other variables, one would expect that non-white and white offenders on death row would have different background characteristics. Data would show that non-whites are less violent than whites, or that the circumstances of the crime were not as grave for non-whites to become death row inmates. However, data in this paper reveal that non-whites typically had more violence in their backgrounds and their capital offenses were more serious in that they occurred in the course of another felony.

B. The Furman Rapists

In the first several decades following the Civil War Reconstruction era, executions consisted mainly of lynchings of blacks convicted of crimes against whites. The penalty served to reassert social distance—and social control–between the racial groups and to primarily "protect" whites.[8] Early twentieth century trials appeared to be a continuation of the same process. Lawyers, social scientists, and other authors have noted discrimination occurring in these instances.[9] As a Southern student of law wrote:

> One has only to visit a Southern community at a time when some Negro is on trial for the rape or murder of a white person to obtain a vivid picture of the hate and passion and desire for vengeance which is often aroused in the hearts of the southern whites. . . . Under circumstances of this kind it is rather difficult for the jury or even the judge to escape being influenced by the feeling which permeates the throng.[10]

Statistics support the sentiment that the death penalty has been imposed in a discriminatory manner, especially in rape cases. The definitive work on racial discrimination and the imposition of capital punishment for rape prior to 1972 was conducted by Wolfgang and Riedel.[11] That study reported the following: of the 3,859 persons executed for all crimes since 1930, 54.6% have been black or mem-

Table 10-4.
Victim-Offender Relationship by Race of Offender

	White offenders (N = 225)	Nonwhite offenders (N = 249)	Total (N = 474)
Offense characteristics			
Multiple victims	20.3%	16.7%	18.4%
Sex of victim			
Male	64.7%	69.9%	67.4%
Female	35.3%	30.1%	32.6%
Median age of victim	38	34	37
Race of victim			
White	95.2%	65.5%*	80.5%
Nonwhite	4.8%	34.5%	19.5%
Victim-offender relationship			
Stranger	42.0%	60.8%**	52.3%
Law enforcer	13.0%	13.9%	13.5%
Acquaintance	29.0%	20.5%	24.3%
Family	15.9%	4.8%	9.9%
Committed during a felony	50.0%	64.4%***	58.0%

*Chi square = 45.6; d.f. = 1; $p < .00001$.
**Chi square = 13.18; d.f. = 1; $p < .0005$.
***Chi square = 7.07; d.f. = 1; $p < .01$.

bers of other minority groups. Of the 455 executed for rape alone, 89.5% have been non-white. . . .

Our data reveal a clear pattern of discrimination that parallels the findings of Wolfgang and Riedel. Of the eighty rapists on death row at the time of the *Furman* decision, all were incarcerated in southern prison systems. Furthermore, sixty-eight (85%) were non-white. The victims of these offenses were overwhelmingly white (91% of the instances). Most of these offenses (81%) involved a lone victim, who was unknown to the assailant (78% of the offenses). Most of the rapists lacked a prior record. Only 5% had a previous rape conviction, while 29% had been confined in an adult penitentiary for any crime. Nationwide, during 1968–1972, an average of 51% of persons arrested for rape were non-white.[12] Of the *Furman*-commuted offenders, 85% were non-white.

V. Institutional Behavior

Custodial officers, psychiatrists and prison administrators feared the release of the *Furman*-commuted inmates into the general prisoner population.[13] Many believed that these former death row prisoners were different from other inmates and represented a unique security risk.[14] In this section, we analyze the institutional disciplinary behavior of the *Furman* offenders from 1972–1987. . . .

A. *Serious Rule Violations*

The definition of serious rule violations and the classification of these offenses vary between states. To insure coder reliability, we designated three major generic categories of offenses: offenses against other prisoners such as murder and fighting with weapons; offenses against prison staff such as striking a guard; and offenses against institutional order such as inciting riots or work strikes. . . .

Table 10-5 presents the number of serious rule violations for *Furman*-commuted murderers and rapists and the percentage of each group involved in those violations.

The data in Table 10-5 indicate that over a fifteen-year period, slightly less than one-third of the former death row inmates committed serious prison rule violations. Over one-half (84 or 51.9%) of those inmates committing serious rule violations were involved in only one rule violation, and another quarter (38 or 23.5%) were involved in only two rule violations. These data demonstrate, at least among these violators, that most serious infractions were one-time events or situations. In short, most of the *Furman* inmates were not violent menaces to the institutional order. As a group, they were not a disproportionate threat to guards and other inmates.

B. *Chronic Rule Violators*

A small group of chronic offenders, forty inmates (7.4% of the total for whom disciplinary information was available) were involved in three or more serious rule violations, accounting for more than one-half of the total serious rule violations. Each of these forty inmates (thirty-six murderers and four rapists) committed an average of 5.1 serious rule violations over the fifteen-year period. This finding supports previous studies which have shown that within the prison community, as in the free world, a small group of offenders accounts for the majority of offenses.[15]

C. *Violent Rule Violators*

For the purposes of this study, violent rule violators were defined as those prisoners who committed murders and weapon-related aggravated assaults on prison staff or other inmates. Overall, the *Furman* offenders committed six killings in the institutional setting. The four prisoner homicides occurred in Alabama, Florida, Louisiana, and Pennsylvania. Both prison guard murders occurred in Ohio. Further, all six institutional killers were serving time for capital murder. Two of these murderers were again sentenced to death, one for the murder of an inmate in Florida, and the other for the murder of a correctional officer in Ohio. Of the other fifty-nine serious acts of violence, thirty-eight inmates (thirty-three murderers and five rapists) were involved. We investigated the differences between inmates committing serious violent acts and those who did not.

Table 10-5.
Number of Serious Rule Violations by Crime*

	Murderers (Valid N = 453)		Rapists (N = 80)	
Offense				
Prisoner-prisoner acts				
Homicide	4	(0.9%)	0	
Aggravated assault with a weapon	29	(4.4%)	6	(6.3%)
Aggravated assault without a weapon	113	(11.7%)	22	(17.5%)
Aggressive sexual attacks	20	(2.4%)	1	(1.3%)
Prisoner-staff acts				
Homicide	2	(0.4%)	0	
Aggravated assault with a weapon	17	(2.4%)	0	
Aggravated assault without a weapon	30	(4.6%)	4	(5.0%)
Acts against institutional order				
Escape	77	(12.6%)	7	(6.3%)
Rioting	30	(4.9%)	0	
Work strike	3	(0.7%)	1	(1.3%)
Total offenses	325	(30.2%)	41	(31.3%)

*Of the four armed robbers in the study, none committed any serious rule violations.

Neither offense characteristics (including whether the act was committed in the commission of another felony or the victim-offender relationship) nor the offender's race, age, or prior criminal history significantly differed between those who committed violent acts and those who did not. In short, no variable served as a predictor of these violent acts.

VI. Parole Behavior

Perhaps the greatest fear expressed after the *Furman* decision was that commuted inmates would someday be released to society and commit more heinous crimes. Enough of these inmates have been released to society so that predictions made in 1972 regarding their propensity toward violence on the community at large can be assessed. . . .

A. The Parolees

Of the 558 *Furman*-commuted inmates, 315 (56.5%) have not been released from prison. Of those, thirty-nine died, and three escaped and have not been recaptured.

Table 10-6.
Release from Prison by Region and Crime*

Region	Never released		Released	
SOUTH				
Murder	51.6%	(142)	48.4%	(133)
Rape	35.4%	(28)	64.6%	(51)
Armed robbery	0		100.0%	(4)
MIDWEST*	56.1%	(46)	43.9%	(36)
NORTHEAST*	81.5%	(44)	18.5%	(10)
WEST*	59.1%	(13)	40.1%	(9)
Total	52.9%	(273)	47.1%	(243)

**Furman* inmates in these three regions were all convicted of capital murder.

Two hundred forty-three (44%) of the capital offenders have been released to society. Of these, 191 (78.6%) have not been returned to prison: 147 are on their original parole, 19 discharged their sentences, 17 successfully completed their parole, 6 died in the community, and 2 were pardoned. Fifty-two (21%) of the releasees returned to prison for technical violations or new offenses. Of these, forty-two are currently incarcerated, eight have been re-paroled, and two have died in prison.

In the following analyses, those prisoners who have died or escaped will not be considered. Neither of the two females have been paroled. Very few of the chronic and violent prison rule violators have been paroled and those that were spent an average of nine and one-half years in the general prisoner population prior to release. Table 10-6 reports the number of parolees by region and crime.

As can be seen in Table 10-6, every armed robber and two-thirds of the rapists were released from confinement. Releases were most commonly granted in the southern states, and least often in the northeast. However, inmates have been released from confinement in all but three states.[16]

Unlike inmates in states with life-without-parole sentencing statutes, nearly all of the *Furman* inmates are eligible and will soon be reviewed for parole. Of those not yet released, almost every expected parole date for these inmates is set for the early 1990s.

How have the *Furman*-releasees fared on parole? Did these capital offenders present a great risk to society? Table 10-7 reports the percentages of the murderers and rapists who were released and returned to prison or recidivated (percent of offenders convicted of new crimes or returned to prison for technical violations).

The released *Furman*-commuted offenders have lived a combined total of 1,282 years in the community while committing twelve violent offenses—approximately two violent offenses per year for the released inmates or nine violent offenses per 1,000 releasees per year. Recidivism occurred an average of 3.4 years after release for murderers and 2.5 years for rapists. Of the 239 paroled offenders, one killed again. Two rapists raped again.

To determine if this level of recidivism is excessive for these criminals, we

Table 10-7.
Total Recidivism by Offense*

Release outcome	Murderers	Rapists
Total released	188 (43.4%)	51 (64.6%)
Mean time in community	5.3 years	5.6 years
Recidivated	38 (20.2%)	13 (25.5%)
Technical violations	15 (8.0%)	4 (7.8%)
Misdemeanor	3 (1.6%)	0
New felony offense	20 (10.6%)	9 (17.6%)
Murder	1	0
Rape	0	2
Robbery	4	2
Aggravated assault	1	2
Burglary	4	2
Larceny-theft	3	0
Possession of firearms	2	0
Drugs	4	1
Indecency with a child	1	0

*Of the four armed robbers released, one returned to prison in 1987 for commiting an armed robbery.

compared them to a like group of offenders, specifically other murderers. Bedau cites various data on the release behavior of paroled murderers.[17] The data show that, overall, only a small percentage (less than 1%) of released murderers were returned to prison for committing a subsequent homicide. For example, of 11,532 murderers released between 1971 and 1975, twenty-six committed new homicides in the first year after release from prison. However, our data reveal that after five years on parole, only one murderer committed a second murder while in the larger society. Though these data are not conclusive, they do suggest that the capital murderers on parole do not represent a disproportionate threat to the larger society.

The data in this study parallel other recidivism research on murderers in general.[18] While murderers on parole appear to rarely repeat their original crime, more research on these released offenders is needed. We agree with Bedau's conclusion on this point:

> While not complete, these data studies of murderers on parole are encouraging. Although they prove that the popular belief is true, that murderers do sometimes kill again even after years of imprisonment, the data also show that the number of such repeaters is very small. Both with regard to the commission of felonies generally and the crime of homicide, no other class of offender has such a low rate of recidivism. So we are left to choose among clear alternatives. If we cannot improve release and parole procedures so as to turn loose no one who will commit a further murder or other felony, we have three choices. Either we can undertake to execute every convicted murderer; or we can undertake to release none of them; or we can reconcile ourselves to the fact that release procedures, like all other human practices, are not infallible, and continue to improve rehabilitation and prediction during incarceration.[19]

Given the amount of time these parolees have spent in the free community (an average of five years), their overall post-release behavior takes on great significance when evaluating the incapacitation effect of the death penalty. Murder is the prime concern. Incapacitation advocates would insist that the execution of every *Furman*-offender would have prevented the one subsequent murder referred to above. Further, the executions would have prevented six prison murders (four inmates and two guards). This evidence supports permanent incapacitation as a means to prevent future capital crimes.[20] However, four inmates on death row at the time of *Furman* were innocent according to a study by Bedau and Radelet.[21] These four individuals could possibly have been executed had it not been for *Furman.*

At the same time, incapacitation advocates might argue that the death row experience itself was prophetic and acted as a deterrent that kept more of the *Furman*-releasees from killing again. That is, the *Furman* inmates were so close to death that they straightened up their act out of fear. Although this possibility seems far-fetched and self-serving, it is a viable explanation for the behavior of some prisoners. For example, a *Furman* inmate in Texas, a double murderer who has never been released from prison, wrote us and explained that his good prison conduct and overall positive outlook on life were the direct result of his time spent on death row. Moreover, this capital murderer has over the years completed more than a dozen furloughs successfully.

While execution would certainly have prevented seven additional murders, our data also show that 551 prisoners, or 98%, did not kill either in prison or in the free community. The vast majority served their time in prison with few challenges to the prison staff. Moreover, most of those released on parole were not menaces to the social order. The death row experience alone cannot account for deterring 551 inmates spread across thirty states. What can account for this fact?

In 1972, the average age of the *Furman* inmates was thirty-one years. These inmates were generally older than other "incoming" prisoners. Some had spent five, six, or even seven years on death row prior to commutation and this confinement eased their adjustment upon return to the general prisoner population. If anything, the death row experience was a learning experience. While confined on "the row," these prisoners learned how to survive in prison and how to "do time." When released to the general prisoner population in 1972, they were already "prisonized" and acclimated to institutional life. This minor adjustment translated into relatively few disciplinary infractions. The disciplinary data reported earlier support this point. The *Furman* prisoners represented an "older" cadre of convicts well-adapted to the penitentiary. . . .

VII. Conclusions

. . . While there is some ambiguity as to just how many death row prisoners were actually affected by *Furman,* the research reported here accounts for 558 inmates scattered across twenty-nine states and the District of Columbia. We tracked these 558 prisoners' institutional and release behavior for nearly fifteen years. In the prison setting, these prisoners committed six murders—killing four prisoners and two correctional officers. However, the majority of the former death row prisoners served out their sentences with few instances of serious institutional misconduct. A minority were responsible for the bulk of disciplinary infractions.

Over the course of fifteen years, 239 *Furman*-commuted prisoners were released to the free community. These parolees have spent an average of five years in society. Twenty-one percent recidivated and were returned to prison, 12% committing new felonies. Only one parolee from Texas committed a second homicide. On the other hand, nearly 80% of those released to the free society have not, at least officially, committed additional crimes.

H. L. A. Hart asked: "What is the weight and character of the evidence that the death penalty is required for the protection of society?"[22] This question, in our opinion, is the most salient one in any discussion of the utility of capital punishment. Seven (1.3%) *Furman*-commuted prisoners were responsible for seven additional murders. Certainly execution of all 558 prisoners would have prevented these killings. However, such a "preemptive strike" would not have greatly protected society. In addition, four innocent prisoners would have been put to death. The question then becomes whether saving the lives of the seven victims was worth the execution of four innocent inmates.

The data in this paper suggest that these prisoners did not represent a significant threat to society. Most have performed well in the prison; those few who have committed additional violent acts are indistinguishable from those who have not. Therefore, over-prediction of secondary violence is indicated.[23] More than two-thirds of the *Furman* inmates, using a very liberal definition of violence, were false positives—predicted to be violent but were not. We cannot conclude from these data that their execution would have protected or benefitted society. . . .

Notes

1. See Worrell, *Psychiatric Prediction of Dangerousness in Capital Sentencing: The Quest for Innocent Authority,* 5 BEHAV. SCI. 433, 433–36 (1987). For examples of future dangerousness provisions in capital punishment statutes see OKLA. STAT. ANN. tit. 21, § 701.12.7 (West 1983); VA. CODE ANN. § 19.2–264.2 (1983); WASH REV. CODE ANN. § 10.95.060(8) (Supp. 1989).

2. See generally P. Greenwood & A. Abrahamse, Selective Incapacitation (August 1982) (available at RAND Corp., Santa Monica, California, doc. no. R-2815-NIJ); von Hirsch & Gottfredson, *Selective Incapacitation: Some Queries About Research Design and Equity,* 12 N.Y.U. REV. L. & SOC. CHANGE 11 (1983–84).

3. See Flanagan, *Time Served and Institutional Misconduct: Patterns of Involvement in Disciplinary Infractions Among Long-term and Short-term Inmates,* 8 J. CRIM. JUST. 357 (1980).

4. Stanton, *Murderers on Parole,* 15 CRIME & DELINQ. 149, 150 (1969); Bedau, *Capital Punishment in Oregon, 1903–1964,* 45 OR. L. REV. 1 (1965); H. Bedau, *Recidivism, Parole, and Deterrence,* in THE DEATH PENALTY IN AMERICA 173, 174 (3d ed. 1982); Bedau, *Death Sentences in New Jersey, 1907–1960,* 19 RUTGERS L. REV 1 (1964).

5. Unpublished study from NAACP Legal Def. and Educ. Fund, Inc. (1982)

6. Unpublished study from NAACP Legal Def. and Educ. Fund, Inc. (1988).

7. In 1987, 88.8% of the prisoners on death row had never been convicted of a prior homicide. BUREAU JUST. STATISTICS BULL., U.S. DEP'T JUST., CAPITAL PUNISHMENT 1987 (July 1988).

8. Phillips, *Exploring Relations Among Forms of Social Control: The Lynching and Execution of Blacks in North Carolina, 1889–1918,* 21 LAW & SOC'Y REV. 361, 364 (1987).

9. See, e.g., C. Magnum, THE LEGAL STATUS OF THE NEGRO 274–370 (1940); G. Myrdal, AN AMERICAN DILEMMA 547–59 (1944).

10. C. Magnum, supra note 9 at 274.

11. Wolfgang and Riedel, *Race, Judicial Discretion, and the Death Penalty,* 407 ANNALS 119 (1973).

12. 1968 FBI UNIFORM CRIME REP. 13; 1969 FBI UNIFORM CRIME REP. 12–13; 1970 FBI UNIFORM CRIME REP. 14; 1971 FBI UNIFORM CRIME REP. 14; 1972 FBI UNIFORM CRIME REP. 14.

13. Interview with ex-warden of Texas prison system in Huntsville, Texas (September, 1987) (name withheld upon request).

14. For instance, one classification and records officer from Texas whom we interviewed predicted that the *Furman* inmates would commit serious acts of violence and generally be a disruptive element in the prison setting. Interview with Texas classification officer in Huntsville, Texas (September, 1987) (name withheld upon request).

15. See Fox, *Analysis of Prison Disciplinary Problems,* 49 J. CRIM L., CRIMINOLOGY, & POLICE SCI. 321, 324 (1958); Ramirez, *Race and Apprehension of Inmate Misconduct,* 11 J. CRIM. JUST. 413, 418 (1983); Wolf, Freinek & Shaffer, *Frequency and Severity of Rule Infractions as a Criteria of Prison Maladjustment,* 22 J. CLINICAL PSYCHOLOGY 244, 246 (1966).

16. Life terms in these three states in 1972 generally allowed parole after serving 10 to 20 years, including good time. Only Kansas, with two *Furman*-commuted inmates, indicated that those inmates were not eligible for parole without an executive pardon.

17. See H. Bedau, *Recidivism, Parole, and Deterrence,* in THE DEATH PENALTY IN AMERICA 175–80 (3d ed. 1982).

18. See Donnelly & Bala, *1977 Releases: Five Year Post Release Follow-Up,* ALBANY, N.Y., DEP'T OF CORRECTIONAL SERV. (1984); Auerbach, *Common Myths About Capital Criminals and Their Victims,* 3 GA J. CORRECTIONS 41 (1974); Wallerstedt, *Returning to Prison,* in BUREAU OF JUST. STATISTICS SPECIAL REP., U.S. DEP'T OF JUST. (1984).

19. H. Bedau, supra note 17, at 175–80.

20. See Gibbs, *Preventive Effects of Capital Punishment: Other Than Deterrence,* 14 CRIM. L. BULL. 34, 37–40 (1978).

21. See Bedau & Radelet, *Miscarriages of Justice in Potentially Capital Cases,* 40 STAN. L. REV. 21, app. B at 177 (1987).

22. H. Hart, PUNISHMENT AND RESPONSIBILITY 71 (1968).

23. See F. Dutile & C. Foust, THE PREDICTION OF CRIMINAL VIOLENCE (1987).

11

Prison Homicides, Recidivist Murder, and Life Imprisonment

H. A. BEDAU

Even if the death penalty's superiority as a general deterrent to murder cannot be reasonably argued—at least, on the basis of the evidence so far accumulated on that subject—it is nonetheless possible to argue in favor of the preventive efficacy of capital punishment on narrower grounds, especially two: First, the threat of execution is needed to reduce the likelihood of murderers in prison killing fellow prisoners, staff, or visitors; second, deterrence to one side, murderers are likely to repeat their crimes, and only the death penalty can guarantee adequate incapacitation. These sentiments were forcefully expressed during a Senate hearing by Norman A. Carlson, director of the federal Bureau of Prisons, when he said:

> In my opinion, the lack of a . . . death penalty makes a mockery of the . . . criminal justice system when we attempt to deal with multiple murderers who continue to prey on innocent victims, both staff and inmates. . . . Where assailants are already serving multiple consecutive life sentences, they can act with impunity [when] a life sentence is the most severe penalty that the . . . criminal justice system authorizes as punishment for murder. One more life sentence means absolutely nothing to such individuals. (1983:4, 5)

The argument sounds plausible, no doubt, but what is the empirical evidence in its support?

Prison Homicide

The most recent research on prison homicide and the death penalty was that conducted by Wendy Phillips Wolfson in 1981 and published in the 1982 edition of *The Death Penalty in America.* She argued that on the evidence of homicides in prison in death penalty states versus those in abolitionist states, "The threat of the death penalty in the retentionist jurisdiction does not even exert an *incremental* deterrent effect over the threat of a lesser punishment in the abolitionist state" (Wolfson 1982:167). But her data were confined to only three years several decades ago (1964, 1965, 1973), and one might reasonably wonder whether her conclusions were still valid for the 1990s.

Some more recent data suggest they are. In the six-year period 1984–89, a total of twenty-one prison staff members were killed by prisoners (how many of them were convicted murderers is not known). Two of these crimes occurred in an abolitionist jurisdiction (Michigan), but the rest occurred in ten jurisdictions that authorized the death penalty (California, Florida, Illinois, Kentucky, Maryland, Mississippi, New Mexico, Ohio, Texas, and the federal prisons).[1]

More recently, in a survey of prison homicides for the years 1992–93, we learn that in the thirty-eight death penalty jurisdictions of those years (six, including California, not supplying information), a total of sixty-five inmates were killed by other inmates. In the fourteen abolition jurisdictions (three, including Massachusetts and Michigan, not reporting), a total of thirteen inmates were killed. Thus, in the abolition jurisdictions, fewer than one prisoner per state was killed every two years by another inmate, whereas in the death penalty states an inmate was murdered by another inmate almost every year.[2]

These figures are hardly conclusive on the matter, but there seems to be no adequate research updating and testing Wolfson's results. And the data reported here surely are consistent with the claim that the death penalty is not necessary to protect prison inmates from their violent fellow inmates.

Recidivist Murder

The research by Marquart and Sorensen, reprinted here as chapter 10, gave interesting information about the recidivism of more than five hundred death row prisoners who were not executed. Several other recent studies shed some light on the recidivism of convicted murderers generally.

In Table 11-1 we learn that at the end of 1993, one in eleven (240 out of 2,643) of those then on death row were known to have a "prior homicide conviction." Of these, two out of three had a "prior felony conviction." This pattern of prior criminal history of death row convicts is more or less typical of recent years.[3] The vast majority of those under sentence of death are men (all but forty-nine, as of January 1996; recall Table 5-1) between the ages of twenty and forty-five—arguably mature offenders who are difficult, if not impossible, to house safely with other offenders in the general prison population, much less to reform and return to the streets better socialized than when they were convicted. Or so one is inclined to think if one believes the death penalty necessary and appropriate for at least some convicted murderers.

Turned around, however, these same figures suggest a rather different picture. The data reported in Table 11-1 also show that nearly one-third (822 out of 2,562) of those under death sentence had *no* prior criminal record. (To be sure, some may have had convictions as juveniles for crimes that would be felonies if committed by an adult, and others may have committed felonies without detection and arrest.)

Table 11-1.
Criminal History Profile of Persons Under Sentence of Death, by Type of Offense and Race, 1994

	Prisoners under sentence of death							
	Number				Percent[a]			
	All races[b]	White	Black	Hispanic	All races[b]	White	Black	Hispanic
U.S. total	2,890	1,441	1,185	224	100.0%	100.0%	100.0%	100.0%
Prior felony convictions								
Yes	1,810	878	791	124	67.1%	65.1%	71.5%	59.6%
No	889	471	315	84	32.9	34.9	28.5	40.4
Not reported	191	92	79	16				
Prior homicide convictions								
Yes	243	116	108	17	8.6%	8.2%	9.4%	7.8%
No	2,576	1,293	1,046	200	91.4	91.8	90.6	92.2
Not reported	71	32	31	7				
Legal status at time of capital offense								
Charges pending	175	95	64	13	6.8%	7.4%	6.1%	6.6%
Probation	251	124	104	20	9.8	9.6	10.0	10.2
Parole	518	216	245	53	20.2	16.9	23.4	26.9
Prison escapee	42	25	13	3	1.6	1.9	1.2	1.5
Prison inmate	61	31	27	3	2.4	2.4	2.6	1.5
Other status	31	51	14	1	1.2	1.2	1.3	0.5
None	1,487	779	580	104	58.0	60.6	55.4	52.8
Not reported	325	156	138	27				

[a]Percentages are based on those offenders for whom data were reported.

[b]Includes whites, blacks, Hispanics, and persons of other races.

Source: Bureau of Justice Statistics, ''Capital Punishment, 1994,'' p. 9, Table 8.

So it is far from obvious that this large fraction consists of hardened offenders who deserve to die if anyone does. Nor does the BJS report information about the mental condition—retardation or brain damage, for example—of those admitted to and imprisoned on death row. Most important, we have no basis for comparing the prior criminal history of those on death row with that of the thousands of other murderers convicted in death penalty states but sentenced to prison terms. As a result, it is impossible to paint in uniformly dark colors the three thousand men and women now under death sentence. For all we know, there are no important relevant demographic or criminogenic differences between the murderers sentenced to death and the murderers sentenced to prison.

Several other studies are worth at least brief notice. In one, covering seven states (four of them abolitionist), one out of five murderers released in the late 1970s was returned to prison for some cause or other (not necessarily criminal homicide). This was the lowest rate of return for any class of prisoner convicted for a violent felony and later released.[4] Another study showed that among all state-convicted murderers released in 1983, 6.6 percent were returned to prison within three years for another murder, 2.8 percent were returned on a rape conviction, 2.9 percent for robbery, and 17 percent for assault.[5] Another 1987 study covering "young parolees" showed that of those released after a conviction of murder, within six years after their release 70 percent had been rearrested, 25 percent reconvicted of a new crime, and 22 percent returned to prison.[6] (No information was reported on the kinds of crimes for which these offenders were arrested, convicted, and reincarcerated.)

The most recent research shows roughly the same pattern. Among released felons generally during the years 1986–89, 21 percent of all the released murderers were arrested in connection with subsequent felonies as follows: 5 percent were arrested for another murder, 2 percent for assault, and less than 1 percent each for rape or robbery.[7] (What percentage of these arrests led to convictions and prison or other sentences, we are not informed.)

Finally, we learn from the National Corrections Reporting Program, conducted by the BJS,[8] that in three recent years (1986, 1988, 1991) persons released after imprisonment for some form of criminal homicide, and the subset of those released after imprisonment for murder, were judged to have an "unsuccessful" release (a term not explained by the BJS but presumably including parole violations as well as rearrests for new felonies) in numbers as follows:

Year	*Released Homicide Offenders*	*Released Murder Offenders*
1986	244	98
1988	425	173
1991	362	113

All the data reviewed here agree on two things: Some offenders, returned to the general public after years served in prison for murder, do murder again. Perhaps it is more surprising that the great majority do not. Some would say that one released murderer who murders again is one too many. But whether the percentage who do murder again could be significantly reduced by a radically different regime behind bars in the first place, or by better supervision after release, is difficult to say. Parole and release authorities will make errors, releasing some who are dangerously violent (and failing to release others who have long since ceased to be dangerous); but so will trial courts err, convicting some charged with murder who are in fact innocent (and acquitting others who are guilty). It is very difficult to imagine how society could manage without either a policy of prison release or the institution of criminal trial courts, and so we seem to be condemned to run at least some kinds of terrible risks to some degree.

Life Imprisonment

If a jurisdiction abolishes the death penalty, what alternative punishment does it enforce? At present and for two centuries past, the only alternative worth considering has been deprivation of liberty through some form of imprisonment. Terms and conditions of imprisonment vary enormously, of course, and when opponents of the death penalty say they favor "life imprisonment," they often encounter the objection that "life imprisonment" rarely means *life* imprisonment. Indeed, today it rarely does.

In 1991 the median sentence for those in prison for a conviction of murder was natural life—but the mean sentence was less than fourteen years.[9] Unless those sentenced to death were rather elderly (and they were not), this meant that many would be released with some years of adult life ahead of them. In 1992, persons sentenced to prison for murder were sentenced to a minimum median term of twenty years, and to a maximum median term of fifty years.[10] (Life prison terms were factored into this figure.) Also in 1992 the estimated time that would actually be served by such prisoners was about nine years.[11] Both the maximum median sentence and the sentence actually served as estimated in 1992 show slight increases over comparable data reported for 1988.[12]

But what about the sentences *actually* served by such prisoners? In 1991 persons convicted of murder (excluding other kinds of criminal homicide) served a median of 78 months and a mean of 93 months—6.5 years and 8.7 years, respectively.[13] Elsewhere we learn that a person convicted on one charge of criminal homicide is likely to serve on the average 11.2 years in prison.[14] Yet another source[15] tells us that in 1991, more than six thousand persons convicted of some form of criminal homicide were released from prison, having actually served time as follows:

Months Served	*Percent Released*
1–6	4.6
7–12	7.4
13–24	16.2
25–36	13.2
37–48	10.5
49–60	8.5
61–84	12.9
85–119	12.0
120 or more	14.7

This distribution is roughly what was reported for immediately prior years. It shows that among those convicted of murder who serve time in prison and are released, many serve very little time at all: Roughly 10 percent serve no more than a year, another 40 percent serve no more than 4 years, and all but 15 percent serve no more than 10 years. (The source for all these data, the BJS, leaves us to speculate over the causes and reasons for these many early releases.) The most recent information (1995) informs us that persons released in 1992 from a prison sentence for murder served an average of 14 years, not quite half of the term to which they had been sentenced.[16]

Recent research shows that most Americans believe convicted murderers spend only about 7 years in prison—unless they are sentenced to death (Bowers and Steiner 1996:4, 17). Not surprisingly, the public views such a short period of punishment with considerable disapproval and as an unsatisfactory alternative to execution. But, as the data from BJS show, this *perceived* punishment in prison is just about *half* the *actual* average time served in the 1990s by convicted murderers in American prisons. Whether a majority of the public would regard life sentences averaging 14 years actually served as appropriate for those convicted of second-degree murder (perhaps as a result of plea bargaining) is not known.

But that gap between public misperception and the reality is of far less significance than a more fundamental confusion over the terms of imprisonment to which first-degree murderers are now typically sentenced. We must distinguish carefully between (a) the time served by first-degree murderers sentenced to life under laws that permit parole eligibility after 10 or 20 years, and (b) the time served by such offenders sentenced under the newer life-without-parole (LWOP) statutes. Increasingly, persons convicted of first degree murder but not sentenced to death are sentenced to LWOP. (Persons convicted of second degree murder may be given a life sentence without being denied parole eligibility.) The BJS statistics discussed in this chapter combine into one set of numbers the time served by these two classes of convicted murderers. Unfortunately, at present there is no information available to inform the public about the time being served by convicted murderers not sentenced to death but sentenced to LWOP. As a result, the myth remains that "they all get out and can murder again" and that talk of "life imprisonment" as an alternative to the death penalty lacks truth in advertising. As of 1994, twenty-six death penalty states both offer the jury LWOP as a sentencing option for a defendant convicted of capital murder and empower only the jury to decide on the sentence in capital cases. (In four states, sentencing is done by the trial judge or a panel of judges; in seven death penalty states there is no LWOP alternative available.)[17] How effectively is the LWOP alternative taken into account by capital trial juries? No information is available enabling us to compare the percentage of prison sentences to death sentences in these states that have the LWOP alternative with the other capital jurisdictions that do not have LWOP. (It seems plausible that the percentage would be higher in the LWOP states.) On the other hand, we know that prior to 1994, seventeen of the LWOP states permitted the jury to be informed of the fact that their state law provides for sentencing murder convicts to prison without any future eligibility for parole; three of these states require that the jury be so informed. In South Carolina, Pennsylvania, and Virginia, however, law expressly prohibits the judge or defense counsel from instructing capital juries on this point.[18] Where the future dangerousness of the defendant is an issue in the jury's decision whether to sentence to death or to life, information about parole eligibility and ineligibility for a defendant not sentenced to death might well make a crucial difference in the jury's choice of sentence. Accordingly, in 1994, in *Simmons v.*

South Carolina, the Supreme Court held that juries must be given this information (two justices, Antonin Scalia and Clarence Thomas, dissented).

Notes

1. *Sourcebook of Criminal Justice Statistics 1990,* p. 402.

2. *Sourcebook of Criminal Justice Statistics 1993,* p. 665, Table 6.106. Numbers significantly at variance with these (reporting a total of 151 prisoners for 1992–93) were discussed in Hallinan 1995, but no breakdown by state was provided.

3. See BJS reports, "Capital Punishment 1992," p. 8, Table 8; "Capital Punishment 1991," p. 11, Table 8; and "Capital Punishment 1990," p. 9, Table 8.

4. BJS, "Returning to Prison," 1984, p. 3, Table 5.

5. BJS, "Recidivism of Prisoners Released in 1983," p. 6, Table 9.

6. BJS, "Report to the Nation on Crime and Justice," 2d ed., 1988, p. 111.

7. BJS, "Recidivism of Felons on Probation, 1986–1989," p. 6, Table 4.

8. BJS, "National Corrections Reporting Program 1986," p. 45, Table 4-9; "National Corrections Reporting Program 1988," p. 46, Table 4-7, "National Corrections Reporting Program, 1991," p. 48, Table 4-9.

9. BJS, "Survey of State Prison Inmates, 1991," p. 7.

10. BJS, "National Corrections Reporting Program, 1992," p. 29, Table 1-21. However, the BJS report "Felony Sentences in State Courts, 1992," p. 3, Table 3, reports that twenty years was the *maximum* mean term for life sentence prisoners (an unspecified number of whom were convicted of crimes other than murder).

11. BJS, "Survey of State Prison Inmates, 1992," p. 4, Table 4.

12. BJS, "Felony Sentences in State Courts, 1988," p. 3, Table 3-4.

13. *Sourcebook of Criminal Justice Statistics 1993,* p. 650, Table 6.90. This is roughly the same length of sentence reported by the National Council on Crime and Delinquency; see Jones and Austin 1993:5, Table 3.

14. BJS, "Report to the Nation on Crime and Justice," 2d ed., 1988, p. 97.

15. BJS, "National Corrections Reporting Program 1991," p. 27, Table 2-4.

16. BJS, "Prison Sentences and Time Served," April 1995, p. 1.

17. *Simmons v. South Carolina* (1994), note 7, slip opinion for the Court of Justice Blackmun. For a general discussion of LWOP, see Wright 1990.

18. Ibid.

PART IV

The Controversy over Constitutionality

The broad outlines of the criminal justice system are initially defined by the legislatures—state and federal—and the statutes they enact to construct the criminal and penal code. But these statutory provisions are subject to review, revision, and repeal by litigation on the grounds that the statutes violate some constitutional provision protecting the rights of the accused, the arrested, the convicted, or the punished. Paramount among these rights are those specified in the Bill of Rights, adopted and incorporated into the nation's Constitution in 1791 and amplified in the subsequent two centuries by the Civil War amendments (1868) and thousands of decisions from the federal courts. Three of these constitutional rights in particular bear on the death penalty: the requirement of "due process of law" (Fifth Amendment), the requirement of "equal protection of the laws" (Fourteenth Amendment), and, above all, the prohibition of "cruel and unusual punishments" (Eighth Amendment).

Between the time these constitutional protections were adopted and the middle of this century—some 160 years—no serious effort was made to challenge the constitutionality of capital punishment as such. During these years challenges were made to every method of execution then in use (hanging, electrocution, firing squad, lethal gas) but to no avail.[1] The efforts were largely perfunctory, the arguments and evidence of the appellants meager, and the courts unsympathetic. Constitutional attacks had also been directed in particular capital cases against the procedures followed in securing a defendant's conviction. Such efforts occasionally were rewarded with a new trial for the defendant, sometimes followed by the prosecution's decision not to pursue the case any further.[2] But as of 1965 no constitutional challenge had been mounted directly against the death penalty itself; such a challenge would have had to argue that, inherently and unavoidably, a sentence of death violated "due process of law" or the "equal protection of the laws" or, most ominously, amounted to a "cruel and unusual punishment." Not until 1961 did any commentator seriously make such an argument in print; that pioneering effort was made by Los Angeles civil liberties attorney Gerald H. Gottlieb.[3]

The first hint that the Supreme Court might consider the momentous question of the constitutionality of the death penalty came two years later, in a dissent to a denial of certiorari in the case of *Rudolph v. Alabama* (1963).[4] Justice Arthur J. Goldberg, joined by Justices William O. Douglas and William J. Brennan Jr., questioned whether capital punishment was constitutionally permissible for the crime of rape—a not implausible question to raise during the height of the civil rights movement, given that most of those sentenced to death for rape were black men whose victims were white women. The Goldberg dissent caught the attention of many opponents of capital punishment. It was especially welcome to the lawyers for the LDF, some of whom had long believed that a full-scale attack on the death penalty for rape, rather than piecemeal, case-by-case litigation, was the best way to protect the interests of its African-American clientele—given that statutory repeal by racist state legislatures was wholly out of the question.[5]

In 1965 the LDF opened its attack on the constitutionality of the death penalty in the Arkansas rape case of *Maxwell v. Bishop.* Substantial empirical evidence was marshaled on behalf of petitioner William L. Maxwell, a black male convicted of raping a white woman, to show that black-on-white rape cases in Arkansas had a disturbing likelihood of resulting in a death sentence and execution, whereas this outcome was very unlikely in the other possible racial combinations of offender and victim—and completely unheard of in white-on-black rape cases. Maxwell's LDF attorneys argued that although the Arkansas capital statutes as *enacted* may have been color-blind, the law as *administered* was regularly and intentionally used to discriminate against black defendants and so violated their constitutional rights to "due process of law" and "equal protection of the laws." No qualified scholar who has examined this research has disputed its findings that racism deeply infected the administration of the death penalty for rape.[6]

The argument failed to persuade the Arkansas Supreme Court, the federal district court, and the federal circuit court of appeals, however. Writing for the latter, Judge Harry A. Blackmun (who would join the Supreme Court six years later) argued that a purely statistical argument showing racial disparities in sentencing was insufficient to establish *intentional* discrimination, and only intentional discrimination in criminal cases is properly condemned and remedied by the courts. This was the first dramatic indication of the differences between the reasoning of social scientists and of judges when confronted with evidence of racial bias in the criminal justice system.[7] The case was eventually pressed to the Supreme Court, but the Court agreed to consider only procedural issues (as it turned out, Maxwell's death sentence was nullified on grounds that made no important new constitutional law).[8]

Even before Maxwell's case was settled, the LDF had broadened its campaign by securing a court order in 1967 to suspend all executions in Florida, then in California, and eventually in all death penalty jurisdictions, on the grounds that the nation's death penalty system was effectively under fundamental constitutional review by the federal courts. The focus of the attack on the death penalty had also expanded to include not only those sentenced to death for rape but also the far greater number of those sentenced to death for murder. The initial challenges were wholly procedural and were marked by some successes (*Witherspoon v. Illinois,* 1968, and *Ralph v. Warden,* 1970) and some defeats (*McGautha v. California* and *Crampton v. Ohio,* both in 1971). Together, these cases set the stage for the momentous argument in 1971–72 over whether the death penalty was in violation of the "cruel and unusual punishments" prohibition of the Eighth Amendment.

As the Supreme Court was weighing its decision on this issue, the California Supreme Court struck down that state's death penalty as a "cruel or unusual punishment" in violation of the state constitution (*Aikens v. California,* 1972). Five months later, in a deeply divided five-to-four decision, the Supreme Court in *Furman v. Georgia* held that the death penalty throughout the nation, as then administered, violated the Eighth and Fourteenth Amendments. Reprinted here from the more than two hundred pages of opinions by the nine justices are excerpts from the text of only one of the concurring opinions, by Justice William Brennan Jr. (see chapter 12). Brennan's opinion is important for two reasons: It was at the time and has remained since the most original analytic argument offered by any member of the Supreme Court for construing the "cruel and unusual punishments" clause of the Eighth Amendment (and for judging the death penalty in violation of that prohibition as well). Also, Brennan's argument was aimed not only at the cases before the Court but at any possible future cases; if Brennan was right, the death penalty in our society was per se unconstitutional no matter how it was administered, no matter how or on whom it was inflicted, and no matter for what crime.[9]

Only Justice Thurgood Marshall concurred with Brennan's sweeping and comprehensive conclusion in *Furman;* Justice Douglas agreed with Brennan and Marshall that the Georgia statute and others like it were unconstitutional, but he reserved for another day the question whether the death penalty per se was unconstitutional. As a consequence, there would have been no majority of the Court against the death penalty in this case were it not for the more cautious reasoning of two other members, Justices Byron R. White and Potter Stewart. Their votes and voice were crucial. Stewart argued (much as did White) that since "death is different"—different from all other punishments in its deprivation and finality—the federal courts must be prepared to impose a higher standard on death sentencing practices under state and federal law (subsequently called "super due process")[10] so that the then-current arbitrariness of death sentences and executions would be brought to an end. While this argument sufficed to dispose of the cases before the Court, it did not indicate how Stewart (and White) would view future death penalty cases, if any, and whether in such cases they would join again with those who opposed the death penalty on constitutional grounds.

Four years later, in 1976, after the hundreds of pre-1972 death row prisoners had been resentenced to life imprisonment and most state legislatures had enacted new death penalty statutes in an effort to conform to the standards imposed by the *Furman* ruling, the Court faced the question whether these new statutes were constitutionally permissible. In the leading case of *Gregg v. Georgia,* the Court by a majority of seven to two declared they were. Only Justices Brennan and Marshall dissented, as they would for the rest of their careers on the Court in every case where the majority upheld the death penalty.[11] Justice Stewart not only defected to the other side, he wrote the plurality opinion for the Court in *Gregg;* excerpts from that opinion are reprinted here as chapter 13.[12] In two companion cases decided on the same day (*Proffitt v. Florida* and *Jurek v. Texas*), the Court gave its imprimatur to two other kinds of new capital statutes. In retrospect, one can see that the decisions in these three cases settled for the foreseeable future the constitutionality of capital punishment: It was not, per se, unconstitutional under the Eighth and Fourteenth Amendments.

As time would show, Georgia's new death penalty statute proved to be the model for most legislative reenactments of the death penalty. Three features were paramount in the new Georgia system: a two-phase trial system, the first phase to settle the issue of the defendant's guilt and the second to settle the question of sentence; a statutory list of "aggravating" circumstances and another list of "mitigating" circumstances on the basis of which the jury would make its sentencing decision (death or life in prison) in each case; and automatic review by the state supreme court of every death sentence and the underlying conviction.[13] The new Georgia law also required the state supreme court to evaluate each death sentence by reference to what other Georgia trial courts were doing in other death penalty cases—so-called proportionality review—a feature of Georgia law that many other states adopted. (Whether such review is in fact carried out in meaningful ways, and even what such ways might be, has received much scholarly attention. The courts, however, have proved relatively indifferent to this requirement.)[14]

At the same time that the Court upheld the constitutionality of death penalty statutes in Georgia, Florida, and Texas, it declared unconstitutional two other kinds of death penalty statutes, thereby effectively putting one boundary around the future of capital punishment. In *Woodson v. North Carolina,* announced on the same day as *Gregg,* the Court held that a mandatory death penalty on conviction of murder was unconstitutional. A year later the Court, reasoning in the same vein, held unconstitutional a mandatory death penalty for a defendant convicted of killing a police officer (*Roberts v. Louisiana,* 1976). A decade after that the Court went so far as to hold unconstitutional a mandatory death penalty for a defendant convicted of murder who committed that crime while serving a life sentence for a previous murder (*Sumner v. Shuman,* 1987).[15] *Woodson, Roberts,* and *Sumner* taken together seem to settle, once and for all, that if a jurisdiction is to have capital punishment it must give the sentencer—judge or jury—some form of guided discretion to help decide whether to sentence the offender to death or to imprisonment. The sentence may not be mandatory.[16]

Beginning just one year after the decisions in *Gregg* and *Woodson,* another boundary around the scope of the death penalty was imposed by the Supreme Court. Within a few months after the decision in *Furman,* several southern states reenacted discretionary death penalty laws for rape, kidnapping, and other nonhomicidal crimes, and a few defendants were soon sentenced to death under these laws. In 1977, five years in the wake of *Furman* and a year after the decisions in *Gregg* and *Woodson,* the Supreme Court ruled in *Coker v. Georgia* against the constitutionality of even a discretionary death penalty for rape.[17] Excerpts from Justice White's opinion for the Court are reprinted here as chapter 15. A few months later, in a little-known per curiam decision, the Court nullified the death penalty for kidnapping (*Eberheart v. Georgia,* 1977), citing its decision in *Coker.*

The line of cases stemming from *Coker,* against the death penalty for nonhomicidal crimes, is short and arguably not so strong as the line stemming from *Woodson* against the mandatory death penalty. Waiting to be decided at some future date is the constitutionality of the death penalty statutes enacted by the states and Congress in the 1990s for various nonhomicidal crimes. With a far less liberal Supreme Court than in the mid-1970s, it is unclear whether any or all of these statutes would fall before the Court's judgment, if and when the occasion arises to appeal a death sentence imposed under them.

Apart from the important ruling in *McCleskey v. Kemp* (1987), discussed in chapter 20, the Supreme Court has had little new to say since 1976 on whether the death penalty is a "cruel and unusual punishment." The matter seems to be settled, at least for the present and immediate future. However, it is not solely for the Court to say, even if its pronouncements have final authority so far as the law is concerned. Interestingly enough, the strongest and most detailed argument upholding the constitutional permissibility of the death penalty is to be found not in any of the Court's own opinions but in the book *Death Penalties: The Supreme Court's Obstacle Course* (1982), by legal scholar Raoul Berger. His thorough argument still serves as the definitive pronouncement on the subject for those who share his views about the proper limits on constitutional interpretation, the narrow role of the federal courts in regulating state criminal practices, and the silence of the Eighth Amendment on the issue of capital punishment. The argument of this book has not gone uncriticized,[18] however, and out of those criticisms many valuable insights emerged—whatever one may think about the ultimate merits of Berger's argument. One of the best of these critical reviews was written by New York University law professor David A. J. Richards; it is reprinted here as chapter 16. Richards's review essay is followed by a short essay of my own in chapter 17 (an abbreviated version of an argument that appears elsewhere),[19] in which I offer an interpretation of the "cruel and unusual punishments" clause that draws upon moral considerations rather different from those that dominate the thinking of legal scholars on this clause, thus sketching another route to the conclusion I share with Justices Brennan and Marshall and Professor Richards.

Throughout the period of our constitutional debate over the death penalty, the rest of the world—especially European nations and their governments—have been struggling to incorporate into their fundamental law recognition and protection of human rights. For these purposes they have used principally the declarations, covenants, and protocols issued by the United Nations and inspired by the Universal Declaration of Human Rights (1948). Although these international agreements have not been interpreted by our courts to have the force of constitutional law in the United States, it is nonetheless instructive to look at the legal status of the death penalty in this country from the vantage point that current international law provides. To that end I have supplied a note in Chapter 18 that briefly traces the growing tension between our law tolerating the death penalty and international law favoring its abolition.

Notes

1. For details on these cases, see Berkson 1975.

2. See especially *Moore v. Dempsey,* 261 U.S. 86 (1923); *Powell v. Alabama,* 287 U.S. 45 (1932).

3. See Gottlieb 1961

4. *Rudolph v. Alabama,* 375 U.S. 889 (1963); see Goldberg 1986; Marsel 1986; see also the discussion in Dershowitz 1982:305–10.

5. For a full account of this campaign, see Meltsner 1973; see also Wolfe 1973; Bedau 1977.

6. See Wolfgang and Riedel 1973, reprinted in Bedau 1982; Wolfgang 1974.

7. The topic has received extensive discussion by social scientists, beginning with Wolfgang 1974; for recent discussions see Ellsworth 1988; Acker 1993; Haney and Logan 1994.

8. See *Maxwell v. Bishop,* 398 U.S. 262 (1970).

9. I have discussed some features of Justice Brennan's argument in *Furman* in Bedau 1992b and 1996a.

10. See Radin 1980.

11. For the most recent remarks on the death penalty by Justice Brennan and Justice Marshall, apart from their dissents in capital cases reaching the Court, see Brennan 1986, 1987, 1994; T. Marshall 1986. For general discussion of the death penalty jurisprudence of Justices Brennan and Marshall, see Mello 1996, Bigel 1994, and Steiker 1993b.

12. I have criticized Justice Stewart's opinion in *Gregg* in Bedau 1985a.

13. Even today, not all states provide for automatic review of a death sentence conviction and sentence. "Arkansas ha[s] no specific provisions for automatic review, and the issue [i]s in litigation in South Carolina. . . . Idaho, Indiana, Montana, and Tennessee required review of the sentence only. In Idaho, review of the conviction had to be appealed or forfeited. In Indiana, a defendant could waive review of the conviction." BJS, "Capital Punishment 1993," p. 6.

14. As of 1984, "over thirty States were required either by statute or judicial decision [to afford] some form of comparative proportionality review before any death sentence may be carried out." *Pulley v. Harris,* 465 U.S. 37 (1984) at 71, citing Baldus, Pulaski, and Woodworth 1980:2–3. It is doubtful, however, whether state supreme courts take this requirement seriously, or even know what doing so would involve. The principal exception may be New Jersey; see Rodriguez, Perlin, and Apicella 1984; Bienen et al. 1988:78–81; Sullivan 1995.

15. For a discussion of this issue published prior to the ruling in *Sumner,* see Acker 1985.

16. See in general Poulos 1986.

17. See Goldberg 1978; Dorin 1981.

18. See also Bedau 1983; Gillers 1983; Kalis 1983; Radin 1983; Foley 1984; Cottrol 1985:380–86. For a more sympathetic review, see McDowell 1983.

19. See Bedau 1985b, 1990a, 1992b.

12

Furman v. Georgia, 1972: The Death Penalty as Administered Is Unconstitutional

Mr. Justice Brennan, concurring. . . . We have very little evidence of the Framers' intent in including the Cruel and Unusual Punishments Clause among those restraints upon the new Government enumerated in the Bill of Rights. . . .

[T]he Framers were well aware that the reach of the Clause was not limited to the proscription of unspeakable atrocities. Nor did they intend simply to forbid punishments considered "cruel and unusual" at the time. The "import" of the Clause is, indeed, "indefinite," and for good reason. A constitutional provision "is enacted, it is true, from an experience of evils, but its general language should not, therefore, be necessarily confined to the form that evil had theretofore taken. Time works changes, brings into existence new conditions and purposes. Therefore a principle to be vital must be capable of wider application than the mischief which gave it birth." *Weems* v. *United States,* 217 U.S., at 373. . . .

There are . . . four principles by which we may determine whether a particular punishment is "cruel and unusual." The primary principle, which I believe supplies the essential predicate for the application of the others, is that a punishment must not by its severity be degrading to human dignity. The paradigm violation of this principle would be the infliction of a torturous punishment of the type that the Clause has always prohibited. Yet "[i]t is unlikely that any State at this moment in history," *Robinson* v. *California,* 370 U.S., at 666, would pass a law providing for the infliction of such a punishment. Indeed, no such punishment has ever been before this Court. The same may be said of the other principles. It is unlikely that this Court will confront a severe punishment that is obviously inflicted in wholly arbitrary fashion; no State would engage in a reign of blind terror. Nor is it likely that this Court will be called upon to review a severe punishment that is clearly and totally rejected throughout society; no legislature would be able even to authorize the infliction of such a punishment. Nor, finally, it is likely that this Court will have to consider a severe punishment that is patently unnecessary; no State

Reprinted from the concurring opinion in *Furman v. Georgia,* 408 U.S. 238 (1972) by Justice William J. Brennan Jr. Substantial portions of the opinion have been omitted, and the remaining footnotes renumbered.

today would inflict a severe punishment knowing that there was no reason whatever for doing so. In short, we are unlikely to have occasion to determine that a punishment is fatally offensive under any one principle.

Since the Bill of Rights was adopted, this Court has adjudged only three punishments to be within the prohibition of the Clause. See *Weems* v. *United States,* 217 U.S. 349 (1910) (12 years in chains at hard and painful labor); *Trop* v. *Dulles,* 356 U.S. 86 (1958) (expatriation); *Robinson* v. *California,* 370 U.S. 660 (1962) (imprisonment for narcotics addiction). Each punishment, of course, was degrading to human dignity, but of none could it be said conclusively that it was fatally offensive under one or the other of the principles. Rather, these "cruel and unusual punishments" seriously implicated several of the principles, and it was the application of the principles in combination that supported the judgment. That, indeed, is not surprising. The function of these principles, after all, is simply to provide means by which a court can determine whether a challenged punishment comports with human dignity. They are, therefore, interrelated, and in most cases it will be their convergence that will justify the conclusion that a punishment is "cruel and unusual." The test, then, will ordinarily be a cumulative one: If a punishment is unusually severe, if there is a strong probability that it is inflicted arbitrarily, if it is substantially rejected by contemporary society, and if there is no reason to believe that it serves any penal purpose more effectively than some less severe punishment, then the continued infliction of that punishment violates the command of the Clause that the State may not inflict inhuman and uncivilized punishments upon those convicted of crimes.

. . . I will analyze the punishment of death in terms of the principles set out above and the cumulative test to which they lead: It is a denial of human dignity for the State arbitrarily to subject a person to an unusually severe punishment that society has indicated it does not regard as acceptable, and that cannot be shown to serve any penal purpose more effectively than a significantly less drastic punishment. Under these principles and this test, death is today a "cruel and unusual" punishment.

I. Death is a unique punishment in the United States. In a society that so strongly affirms the sanctity of life, not surprisingly the common view is that death is the ultimate sanction. This natural human feeling appears all about us. There has been no national debate about punishment, in general or by imprisonment, comparable to the debate about the punishment of death. No other punishment has been so continuously restricted. . . . And those States that still inflict death reserve it for the most heinous crimes. Juries, of course, have always treated death cases differently, as have governors exercising their commutation powers. Criminal defendants are of the same view. . . . This Court, too, almost always treats death cases as a class apart. And the unfortunate effect of this punishment upon the functioning of the judicial process is well known; no other punishment has a similar effect.

The only explanation for the uniqueness of death is its extreme severity. Death is today an unusually severe punishment, unusual in its pain, in its finality, and in its enormity. No other existing punishment is comparable to death in terms of physical and mental suffering. . . .

The unusual severity of death is manifested most clearly in its finality and enormity. Death, in these respects, is in a class by itself. Expatriation, for example, is a punishment that "destroys for the individual the political existence that was centuries in the development," that "strips the citizen of his status in the national and international political community," and that puts "[h]is very existence" in jeopardy. Expatriation thus inherently entails "the total destruction of the individual's status in organized society." [*Trop* v. *Dulles,* 356 U.S., at 101.] "In short, the expatriate has lost the right to have rights." Id., at 102. Yet, demonstrably, expatriation is not "a fate worse than death." Id., at 125. . . . Although death, like expatriation, destroys the individual's "political existence" and his "status in organized society," it does more, for, unlike expatriation, death also destroys "[h]is very existence." There is, too, at least the possibility that the expatriate will in the future regain "the right to have rights." Death forecloses even that possibility.

Death is truly an awesome punishment. The calculated killing of a human being by the State involves, by its very nature, a denial of the executed person's humanity. The contrast with the plight of a person punished by imprisonment is evident. An individual in prison does not lose "the right to have rights." A prisoner retains, for example, the constitutional rights to the free exercise of religion, to be free of cruel and unusual punishments, and to treatment as a "person" for purposes of due process of law and the equal protection of the laws. A prisoner remains a member of the human family. Moreover, he retains the right of access to the courts. His punishment is not irrevocable. Apart from the common charge, grounded upon the recognition of human fallibility, that the punishment of death must inevitably be inflicted upon innocent men, we know that death has been the lot of men whose convictions were unconstitutionally secured in view of later, retroactively applied, holdings of this Court. The punishment itself may have been unconstitutionally inflicted, see *Witherspoon* v. *Illinois,* 391 U.S. 510 (1968), yet the finality of death precludes relief. An executed person has indeed "lost the right to have rights." As one nineteenth century proponent of punishing criminals by death declared, "When a man is hung, there is an end of our relations with him. His execution is a way of saying, 'You are not fit for this world, take your chance elsewhere.' "[1]

In comparison to all other punishments today, then, the deliberate extinguishment of human life by the State is uniquely degrading to human dignity. I would not hesitate to hold, on that ground alone, that death is today a "cruel and unusual" punishment, were it not that death is a punishment of longstanding usage and acceptance in this country. I therefore turn to the second principle—that the State may not arbitrarily inflict an unusually severe punishment.

II. The outstanding characteristic of our present practice of punishing criminals by death is the infrequency with which we resort to it. The evidence is conclusive that death is not the ordinary punishment for any crime. . . .

When a country of over 200 million people inflicts an unusually severe punishment no more than 50 times a year, the inference is strong that the punishment is not being regularly and fairly applied. To dispel it would indeed require a clear showing of nonarbitrary infliction.

Although there are no exact figures available, we know that thousands of murders and rapes are committed annually in States where death is an authorized punishment for those crimes. However the rate of infliction is characterized—as "freakishly" or "spectacularly" rare, or simply as rare—it would take the purest sophistry to deny that death is inflicted in only a minute fraction of these cases. How much rarer, after all, could the infliction of death be?

When the punishment of death is inflicted in a trivial number of the cases in which it is legally available, the conclusion is virtually inescapable that it is being inflicted arbitrarily. Indeed, it smacks of little more than a lottery system. The States claim, however, that this rarity is evidence not of arbitrariness, but of informed selectivity: Death is inflicted, they say, only in "extreme" cases.

Informed selectivity, of course, is a value not to be denigrated. Yet presumably the States could make precisely the same claim if there were ten executions per year, or five, or even if there were but one. That there may be as many as 50 per year does not strengthen the claim. When the rate of infliction is at this low level, it is highly implausible that only the worse criminals or the criminals who commit the worst crimes are selected for this punishment. No one has yet suggested a rational basis that could differentiate in those terms the few who die from the many who go to prison. Crimes and criminals simply do not admit of a distinction that can be drawn so finely as to explain, on that ground, the execution of such a tiny sample of those eligible. Certainly the laws that provide for this punishment do not attempt to draw that distinction; all cases to which the laws apply are necessarily "extreme." Nor is the distinction credible in fact. . . .

Furthermore, our procedures in death cases, rather than resulting in the selection of "extreme" cases for this punishment, actually sanction an arbitrary selection. For this Court has held that juries may, as they do, make the decision whether to impose a death sentence wholly unguided by standards governing that decision. *McGautha* v. *California,* 402 U.S. 183, 196–208 (1971). In other words, our procedures are not constructed to guard against the totally capricious selection of criminals for the punishment of death.

III. . . . From the beginning of our Nation, the punishment of death has stirred acute public controversy. Although pragmatic arguments for and against the punishment have been frequently advanced, this longstanding and heated controversy cannot be explained solely as the result of differences over the practical wisdom of a particular government policy. At bottom, the battle has been waged on moral grounds. The country has debated whether a society for which the dignity of the individual is the supreme value can, without a fundamental inconsistency, follow the practice of deliberately putting some of its members to death. In the United States, as in other nations of the western world, "the struggle about this punishment has been one between ancient and deeply rooted beliefs in retribution, atonement or vengeance on the one hand, and, on the other, beliefs in the personal value and dignity of the common man that were born of the democratic movement of the eighteenth century, as well as beliefs in the scientific approach to an understanding of the motive forces of human conduct, which are the result of the growth of the sciences of behavior during the nineteenth and twentieth centuries.''[2] It is this essentially moral conflict that forms the backdrop for the past changes in and the present operation of our system of imposing death as a punishment for crime. . . .

The progressive decline in, and the current rarity of, the infliction of death demonstrate that our society seriously questions the appropriateness of this punishment today. The States point out that many legislatures authorize death as the punishment for certain crimes and that substantial segments of the public, as reflected in opinion polls and referendum votes, continue to support it. Yet the availability of this punishment through statutory authorization, as well as the polls and referenda, which amount simply to approval of that authorization, simply underscores the extent to which our society has in fact rejected this punishment. When an unusually severe punishment is authorized for wide-scale application but not, because of society's refusal, inflicted save in a few instances, the inference is compelling that there is a deepseated reluctance to inflict it. Indeed, the likelihood is great that the punishment is tolerated only because of its disuse. The objective indicator of society's view of an unusually severe punishment is what society does with it, and today society will inflict death upon only a small sample of the eligible criminals. Rejection could hardly be more complete without becoming absolute. At the very least, I must conclude that contemporary society views this punishment with substantial doubt.

IV. The final principle to be considered is that an unusually severe and degrading punishment may not be excessive in view of the purposes for which it is inflicted. This principle, too, is related to the others. When there is a strong probability that the State is arbitrarily inflicting an unusually severe punishment that is subject to grave societal doubts, it is likely also that the punishment cannot be shown to be serving any penal purpose that could not be served equally well by some less severe punishment.

The States' primary claim is that death is a necessary punishment because it prevents the commission of capital crimes more effectively than any less severe punishment. . . .

. . . We are not presented with the theoretical question whether under any imaginable circumstances the threat of death might be a greater deterrent to the commission of capital crimes than the threat of imprisonment. We are concerned with the practice of punishing criminals by death as it exists in the United States today. Proponents of this argument necessarily admit that its validity depends upon the existence of a system in which the punishment of death is invariably and swiftly imposed. Our system, of course, satisfies neither condition. A rational person contemplating a murder or rape is confronted, not with the certainty of a speedy death, but with the slightest possibility that he will be executed in the distant future. The risk of death is remote and improbable; in contrast, the risk of long-term imprisonment is near and great. In short, whatever the speculative validity of the assumption that the threat of death is a superior deterrent, there is no reason to believe that as currently administered the punishment of death is necessary to deter the commission of capital crimes. . . .

There is, however, another aspect to the argument that the punishment of death is necessary for the protection of society. The infliction of death, the States urge, serves to manifest the community's outrage at the commission of the crime. It is, they say, a concrete public expression of moral indignation that inculcates respect for the law and helps assure a more peaceful community. Moreover, we are told, not only does the punishment of death exert this widespread moralizing influence upon community values, it also satisfies the popular demand for grievous condemnation of abhorrent crimes and thus prevents disorder, lynching, and attempts by private citizens to take the law into their own hands.

The question, however, is not whether death serves these supposed purposes of punishment, but whether death serves them more effectively than imprisonment. There is no evidence whatever that utilization of imprisonment rather than death encourages private blood feuds and other disorders. Surely if there were such a danger, the execution of a handful of criminals each year would not prevent it. The assertion that death alone is a sufficiently emphatic denunciation for capital crimes suffers from the same defect. If capital crimes require the punishment of death in order to provide moral reinforcement for the basic values of the community, those values can only be undermined when death is so rarely inflicted upon the criminals who commit the crimes. Furthermore, it is certainly doubtful that the infliction of death by the State does in fact strengthen the community's moral code; if the deliberate extinguishment of human life has any effect at all, it more likely tends to lower our respect for life and brutalize our values. That, after all, is why we no longer carry out public executions. . . .

There is, then, no substantial reason to believe that the punishment of death, as currently administered, is necessary for the protection of society. The only other purpose suggested, one that is independent of protection for society, is retribution. . . .

Obviously, concepts of justice change; no immutable moral order requires death for murderers and rapists. The claim that death is a just punishment necessarily refers to the existence of certain public beliefs. The claim must be that for capital crimes death alone comports with society's notion of proper punishment. As administered today, however, the punishment of death cannot be justified as a necessary means of exacting retribution from criminals. When the overwhelming number of criminals who commit capital crimes go to prison, it cannot be concluded that death serves the purpose of retribution more effectively than imprisonment. The asserted public belief that murderers and rapists deserve to die is flatly inconsistent with the execution of a random few. As the history of the punishment of death in this country shows, our society wishes to prevent crime; we have no desire to kill criminals simply to get even with them.

In sum, the punishment of death is inconsistent with all four principles: Death is an unusually severe and degrading punishment; there is a strong probability that it is inflicted arbitrarily; its rejection by contemporary society is virtually total; and there is no reason to believe that it serves any penal purpose more effectively than the less severe punishment of imprisonment. The function of these principles is to enable a court to determine whether a punishment comports with human dignity. Death, quite simply, does not. . . .

Notes

1. Stephen, Capital Punishments, 69 Fraser's Magazine 753, 763 (1864).

2. T. Sellin, The Death Penalty, A Report for the Model Penal Code Project of the American Law Institute 15 (1959).

13

Gregg v. Georgia, 1976: The Death Penalty Is Not Per Se Unconstitutional

Judgment of the Court, and opinion of Mr. Justice Stewart, Mr. Justice Powell, and Mr. Justice Stevens, announced by Mr. Justice Stewart. . . . The Georgia statute, as amended after our decision in *Furman* v. *Georgia,* 408 U.S. 238 (1972), retains the death penalty for six categories of crime: murder, kidnapping for ransom or where the victim is harmed, armed robbery, rape, treason, and aircraft hijacking. Ga. Code Ann. §§26-1101, 26-1311, 26-1902, 26-2001, 26-2201, 26-3301 (1972). The capital defendant's guilt or innocence is determined in the traditional manner, either by a trial judge or a jury, in the first stage of a bifurcated trial.

If trial is by jury, the trial judge is required to charge lesser included offenses when they are supported by any view of the evidence. *Sims* v. *State,* 203 Ga. 668, 47 S.E. 2d 862 (1948). See *Linder* v. *State,* 132 Ga. App. 624, 625, 208 S.E. 2d 630, 631 (1974). After a verdict, finding, or plea of guilty to a capital crime, a presentence hearing is conducted before whoever made the determination of guilt. The sentencing procedures are essentially the same in both bench and jury trials. At the hearing:

> [T]he judge [or jury] shall hear additional evidence in extenuation, mitigation, and aggravation of punishment, including the record of any prior criminal convictions and pleas of guilty or pleas of nolo contendere of the defendant, or the absence of any prior conviction and pleas: Provided, however, that only such evidence in aggravation as the State has made known to the defendant prior to his trial shall be admissible. The judge [or jury] shall also hear argument by the defendant or his counsel and the prosecuting attorney . . . regarding the punishment to be imposed. § 27-2503 (Supp. 1975)

The defendant is accorded substantial latitude as to the types of evidence that he may introduce. See *Brown* v. *State,* 235 Ga. 644, 647–50, 220 S.E. 2d 922, 925–26 (1975). Evidence considered during the guilt stage may be considered during the sentencing stage without being resubmitted. *Eberheart* v. *State,* 232 Ga. 247, 253, 206 S.E. 2d 12, 17 (1974).

In the assessment of the appropriate sentence to be imposed the judge is also

Reprinted from the plurality opinion in *Gregg v. Georgia,* 428 U. S. 153 (1976) of Justice Potter Stewart. Joining in this opinion were Justices Powell and Stevens. Substantial portions of the opinion have been omitted, and the remaining footnotes renumbered.

required to consider or to include in his instructions to the jury "any mitigating circumstances or aggravating circumstances otherwise authorized by law and any of [10] statutory aggravating circumstances which may be supported by the evidence. . . ." § 27-2534.1(b) (Supp. 1975). The scope of the nonstatutory aggravating or mitigating circumstances is not delineated in the statute. Before a convicted defendant may be sentenced to death, however, except in cases of treason or aircraft hijacking, the jury, or the trial judge in cases tried without a jury, must find beyond a reasonable doubt one of the 10 aggravating circumstances specified in the statute.[1] The sentence of death may be imposed only if the jury (or judge) finds one of the statutory aggravating circumstances and then elects to impose that sentence. § 26-3102 (Supp. 1975). If the verdict is death the jury or judge must specify the aggravating circumstance(s) found. § 27-2534.1 (c) (Supp. 1975). In jury cases, the trial judge is bound by the jury's recommended sentence. §§ 26-3102, 27-2514 (Supp. 1975).

In addition to the conventional appellate process available in all criminal cases, provision is made for special expedited direct review by the Supreme Court of Georgia of the appropriateness of imposing the sentence of death in the particular case. The court is directed to consider "the punishment as well as any errors enumerated by way of appeal," and to determine:

1. Whether the sentence of death was imposed under the influence of passion, prejudice, or any other arbitrary factor, and
2. Whether, in cases other than treason or aircraft hijacking, the evidence supports the jury's or judge's finding of a statutory aggravating circumstance as enumerated in section 27.2534.1 (b), and
3. Whether the sentence of death is excessive or disproportionate to the penalty imposed in similar cases, considering both the crime and the defendant. § 27-2537 (Supp. 1975).

If the court affirms a death sentence, it is required to include in its decision reference to similar cases that it has taken into consideration. § 27-2537 (e) (Supp. 1975).[2]

A transcript and complete record of the trial, as well as a separate report by the trial judge, are transmitted to the court for its use in reviewing the sentence. § 27-2537 (a) (Supp. 1975). The report is in the form of a 6½-page questionnaire, designed to elicit information about the defendant, the crime, and the circumstances of the trial. It requires the trial judge to characterize the trial in several ways designed to test for arbitrariness and disproportionality of sentence. Included in the report are responses to detailed questions concerning the quality of the defendant's representation, whether race played a role in the trial, and, whether, in the trial court's judgment, there was any doubt about the defendant's guilt or the appropriateness of the sentence. A copy of the report is served upon defense counsel. Under its special review authority, the court may either affirm the death sentence or remand the case for resentencing. In cases in which the death sentence is affirmed there remains the possibility of executive clemency.

. . . We now consider specifically whether the sentence of death for the crime of murder is a per se violation of the Eighth and Fourteenth Amendments to the Constitution. We note first that history and precedent strongly support a negative answer to this question.

The imposition of the death penalty for the crime of murder has a long history of acceptance both in the United States and in England. The common-law rule imposed a mandatory death sentence on all convicted murderers. *McGautha* v. *California,* 402 U.S. 183, 197–98 (1971). And the penalty continued to be used into the twentieth century by most American States, although the breadth of the common-law rule was diminished, initially by narrowing the class of murders to be punished by death and subsequently by widespread adoption of laws expressly granting juries the discretion to recommend mercy. Id., at 199–200. See *Woodson* v. *North Carolina,* post, at 289–92.

It is apparent from the text of the Constitution itself that the existence of capital punishment was accepted by the Framers. At the time the Eighth Amendment was ratified, capital punishment was a common sanction in every State. Indeed, the First Congress of the United States enacted legislation providing death as the penalty for specified crimes. C. 9, 1 Stat. 112 (1790). The Fifth Amendment, adopted at the same time as the Eighth, contemplated the continued existence of the capital sanction by imposing certain limits on the prosecution of capital cases:

> No person shall be held to answer for a capital, or otherwise infamous crime, unless on a presentment or indictment of a Grand Jury . . . ; nor shall any person be subject for the same offense to be twice put in jeopardy of life or limb; . . . nor be deprived of life, liberty, or property, without due process of law. . . .

And the Fourteenth Amendment, adopted over three-quarters of a century later, similarly contemplates the existence of the capital sanction in providing that no State shall deprive any person of "life, liberty, or property" without due process of law.

For nearly two centuries, this Court, repeatedly and often expressly, has recognized that capital punishment is not invalid per se. . . .

. . . And in *Trop* v. *Dulles,* 356 U.S., at 99, Mr. Chief Justice Warren, for himself and three other Justices, wrote:

> Whatever the arguments may be against capital punishment, both on moral grounds and in terms of accomplishing the purposes of punishment . . . the death penalty has been employed throughout our history, and, in a day when it is still widely accepted, it cannot be said to violate the constitutional concept of cruelty.

Four years ago, the petitioners in *Furman* and its companion cases predicated their argument primarily upon the asserted proposition that standards of decency had evolved to the point where capital punishment no longer could be tolerated. The petitioners in those cases said, in effect, that the evolutionary process had come to an end, and that standards of decency required that the Eighth Amendment be construed finally as prohibiting capital punishment for any crime regardless of its depravity and impact on society. This view was accepted by two Justices. Three other Justices were unwilling to go so far; focusing on the procedures by which convicted defendants were selected for the death penalty rather than on the actual punishment inflicted, they joined in the conclusion that the statutes before the Court were constitutionally invalid.

The petitioners in the capital cases before the Court today renew the "standards of decency" argument, but developments during the four years since *Furman* have undercut substantially the assumptions upon which their argument rested. Despite the continuing debate, dating back to the nineteenth century, over the morality and utility of capital punishment, it is now evident that a large proportion of American society continues to regard it as an appropriate and necessary criminal sanction.

The most marked indication of society's endorsement of the death penalty for murder is the legislative response to *Furman*. The legislatures of at least 35 States have enacted new statutes that provide for the death penalty for at least some crimes that result in the death of another person. And the Congress of the United States, in 1974, enacted a statute providing the death penalty for aircraft piracy that results in death. These recently adopted statutes have attempted to address the concerns expressed by the Court in *Furman* primarily i. by specifying the factors to be weighed and the procedures to be followed in deciding when to impose a capital sentence, or ii. by making the death penalty mandatory for specified crimes. But all of the post-*Furman* statutes make clear that capital punishment itself has not been rejected by the elected representatives of the people.

In the only statewide referendum occurring since *Furman* and brought to our attention, the people of California adopted a constitutional amendment that authorized capital punishment, in effect negating a prior ruling by the Supreme Court of California in *People* v. *Anderson,* 6 Cal. 3d 628, 493 P. 2d 880, cert. denied, 406 U.S. 958 (1972), that the death penalty violated the California Constitution.

The jury also is a significant and reliable objective index of contemporary values because it is so directly involved. . . .

. . . The Court has said that "one of the most important functions any jury can perform in making . . . a selection [between life imprisonment and death for a defendant convicted in a capital case] is to maintain a link between contemporary community values and the penal system." *Witherspoon* v. *Illinois,* 391 U.S. 510, 519 n. 15 (1968). It may be true that evolving standards have influenced juries in recent decades to be more discriminating in imposing the sentence of death. But the relative infrequency of jury verdicts imposing the death sentence does not indicate rejection of capital punishment per se. Rather, the reluctance of juries in many cases to impose the sentence may well reflect the humane feeling that this most irrevocable of sanctions should be reserved for a small number of extreme cases. See *Furman* v. *Georgia, supra,* at 338 (Burger, C.J., dissenting). Indeed, the actions of juries in many States since *Furman* is fully compatible with the legislative judgments, reflected in the new statutes, as to the continued utility and necessity of capital punishment in appropriate cases. At the close of 1974 at least 254 persons had been sentenced to death since *Furman,* and by the end of March 1976, more than 460 persons were subject to death sentences.

As we have seen, however, the Eighth Amendment demands more than that a challenged punishment be acceptable to contemporary society. The Court also must ask whether it comports with the basic concept of human dignity at the core of the Amendment. *Trop* v. *Dulles,* 356 U.S., at 100. Although we cannot "invalidate a category of penalties because we deem less severe penalties adequate to serve the ends of penology," *Furman* v. *Georgia,* supra, at 451 (Powell, J., dissenting), the sanction imposed cannot be so totally without penological justification that it results in the gratuitous infliction of suffering. Cf. *Wilkerson* v. *Utah,* 99 U.S., at 135–36; *In re Kemmler,* 136 U.S., at 447.

The death penalty is said to serve two principal social purposes; retribution and deterrence of capital crimes by prospective offenders.[3]

In part, capital punishment is an expression of society's moral outrage at particularly offensive conduct. This function may be unappealing to many, but it is essential in an ordered society that asks its citizens to rely on legal processes rather than self-help to vindicate their wrongs.

> The instinct for retribution is part of the nature of man, and channeling that instinct in the administration of criminal justice serves an important purpose in promoting the stability of a society governed by law. When people begin to believe that organized society is unwilling or unable to impose upon criminal offenders the punishment they "deserve," then there are sown the seeds of anarchy—of self-help, vigilante justice, and lynch law. *Furman* v. *Georgia, supra,* at 308 (Stewart, J., concurring).

"Retribution is no longer the dominant objective of the criminal law," *Williams* v. *New York,* 337 U.S. 241, 248 (1949), but neither is it a forbidden objective nor one inconsistent with our respect for the dignity of men. *Furman* v. *Georgia,* 408 U.S., at 394–95 (Burger, C.J., dissenting); id., at 452–54 (Powell, J., dissenting); *Powell* v. *Texas,* 392 U.S., at 531, 535–36. Indeed, the decision that capital punishment may be the appropriate sanction in extreme cases is an expression of the community's belief that certain crimes are themselves so grievous an affront to humanity that the only adequate response may be the penalty of death.[4]

Statistical attempts to evaluate the worth of the death penalty as a deterrent to crimes by potential offenders have occasioned a great deal of debate. The results simply have been inconclusive. As one opponent of capital punishment has said:

> [A]fter all possible inquiry, including the probing of all possible methods of inquiry, we do not know, and for systematic and easily visible reasons cannot know, what the truth about this "deterrent" effect may be. . . .
>
> The inescapable flaw is . . . that social conditions in any state are not constant through time, and that social conditions are not the same in any two states. If an effect were observed (and the observed effects, one way or another, are not large) then one could not at all tell whether any of this effect is attributable to the presence or absence of capital punishment. A "scientific"—that is to say, a soundly based—conclusion is simply impossible, and no methodological path out of this tangle suggests itself. C. Black, Capital Punishment: The Inevitability of Caprice and Mistake 25–26 (1974).

Although some of the studies suggest that the death penalty may not function as a significantly greater deterrent than lesser penalties, there is no convincing empirical evidence either supporting or refuting this view. We may nevertheless assume safely that there are murderers, such as those who act in passion, for whom the threat of death has little or no deterrent effect. But for many others, the death penalty undoubtedly is a significant deterrent. There are carefully contemplated murders, such as murder for hire, where the possible penalty of death may well enter into the cold calculus that precedes the decision to act.[5] And there are some categories of murder, such as murder by a life prisoner, where other sanctions may not be adequate.

The value of capital punishment as a deterrent of crime is a complex factual issue the resolution of which properly rests with the legislatures, which can evaluate the results of statistical studies in terms of their own local conditions and with a flexibility of approach that is not available to the courts. *Furman* v. *Georgia,* supra, at 403–5 (Burger, C.J., dissenting). Indeed, many of the post-*Furman* statutes reflect just such a responsible effort to define those crimes and those criminals for which capital punishment is most probably an effective deterrent.

In sum, we cannot say that the judgment of the Georgia legislature that capital punishment may be necessary in some cases is clearly wrong. Considerations of federalism, as well as respect for the ability of a legislature to evaluate, in terms of its particular State, the moral consensus concerning the death penalty and its social utility as a sanction, require us to conclude, in the absence of more convincing evidence, that the infliction of death as a punishment for murder is not without justification and thus is not unconstitutionally severe.

Finally, we must consider whether the punishment of death is disproportionate in relation to the crime for which it is imposed. There is no question that death as a punishment is unique in its severity and irrevocability. *Furman* v. *Georgia,* 408 U.S., at 286–91 (Brennan, J., concurring); id., at 306 (Stewart, J., concurring). When a defendant's life is at stake, the Court has been particularly sensitive to insure that every safeguard is observed. *Powell* v. *Alabama,* 287 U.S. 45, 71 (1932); *Reid* v. *Covert,* 354 U.S. 1, 77 (1957) (Harlan, J., concurring in result). But we are concerned here only with the imposition of capital punishment for the crime of murder, and when a life has been taken deliberately by the offender,[6] we cannot say that the punishment is invariably disproportionate to the crime. It is an extreme sanction, suitable to the most extreme of crimes.

We hold that the death penalty is not a form of punishment that may never be imposed, regardless of the circumstances of the offense, regardless of the character of the offender, and regardless of the procedure followed in reaching the decision to impose it. . . .

While *Furman* did not hold that the infliction of the death penalty per se violates the Constitution's ban on cruel and unusual punishments, it did recognize that the penalty of death is different in kind from any other punishment imposed under our system of criminal justice. Because of the uniqueness of the death penalty, *Furman* held that it could not be imposed under sentencing procedures that created a substantial risk that it would be inflicted in an arbitrary and capricious manner. . . .

Furman mandates that where discretion is afforded a sentencing body on a matter so grave as the determination of whether a human life should be taken or spared, that discretion must be suitably directed and limited so as to minimize the risk of wholly arbitrary and capricious action. . . .

While some have suggested that standards to guide a capital jury's sentencing deliberations are impossible to formulate, the fact is that such standards have been developed. When the drafters of the Model Penal Code faced this problem, they concluded "that it is within the realm of possibility to point to the main circumstances of aggravation and of mitigation that should be weighed *and weighed against each other* when they are presented in a concrete case." ALI, Model Penal Code § 201.6, Comment 3, p. 71 (Tent. Draft No. 9, 1959) (emphasis in original).[7] While such standards are by necessity somewhat general, they do provide guidance to the sentencing authority and thereby reduce the likelihood that it will impose a sentence that fairly can be called capricious or arbitrary. Where the sentencing authority is required to specify the factors it relied upon in reaching its decision, the further safeguard of meaningful appellate review is available to ensure that death sentences are not imposed capriciously or in a freakish manner.

In summary, the concerns expressed in *Furman* that the penalty of death not be imposed in an arbitrary or capricious manner can be met by a carefully drafted statute that ensures that the sentencing authority is given adequate information and guidance. As a general proposition these concerns are best met by a system that provides for a bifurcated proceeding at which the sentencing authority is apprised of the information relevant to the imposition of sentence and provided with standards to guide its use of the information.

We do not intend to suggest that only the above-described procedures would be permissible under *Furman* or that any sentencing system constructed along these general lines would inevitably satisfy the concerns of *Furman,* for each distinct system must be examined on an individual basis. Rather, we have embarked upon this general exposition to make clear that it is possible to construct capital-sentencing systems capable of meeting *Furman*'s constitutional concerns. . . .

The basic concern of *Furman* centered on those defendants who were being condemned to death capriciously and arbitrarily. Under the procedures before the Court in that case, sentencing authorities were not directed to give attention to the nature or circumstances of the crime committed or to the character or record of the defendant. Left unguided, juries imposed the death sentence in a way that could only be called freakish. The new Georgia sentencing procedures, by contrast, focus the jury's attention on the particularized nature of the crime and the particularized characteristics of the individual defendant. While the jury is permitted to consider any aggravating or mitigating circumstances, it must find and identify at least one statutory aggravating factor before it may impose a penalty of death. In this way the jury's discretion is channeled. No longer can a jury wantonly and freakishly impose the death sentence; it is always circumscribed by the legislative guidelines. In addition, the review function of the Supreme Court of Georgia affords additional assurance that the concerns that prompted our decision in *Furman* are not present to any significant degree in the Georgia procedure applied here.

For the reasons expressed in this opinion, we hold that the statutory system under which Gregg was sentenced to death does not violate the Constitution. Accordingly, the judgment of the Georgia Supreme Court is affirmed.

It is so ordered.

Notes

1. The statute provides in part:

(a) The death penalty may be imposed for the offenses of aircraft hijacking or treason, in any case.

(b) In all cases of other offenses for which the death penalty may be authorized, the judge shall consider, or he shall include in his instructions to the jury for it to consider, any mitigating circumstances or aggravating circumstances otherwise authorized by law and any of the following statutory aggravating circumstances which may be supported by the evidence:

(1) The offense of murder, rape, armed robbery, or kidnapping was committed by a person with a prior record of conviction for a capital felony, or the offense of murder was committed by a person who has a substantial history of serious assaultive criminal convictions.

(2) The offense of murder, rape, armed robbery, or kidnapping was committed while the offender was engaged in the commission of another capital felony, or aggravated battery, or the offense of murder was committed while the offender was engaged in the commission of burglary or arson in the first degree.

(3) The offender by his act of murder, armed robbery, or kidnapping knowingly created a great risk of death to more than one person in a public place by means of a weapon or device which would normally be hazardous to the lives of more than one person.

(4) The offender committed the offense of murder for himself or another, for the purpose of receiving money or any other thing of monetary value.

(5) The murder of a judicial officer, former judicial officer, district attorney or solicitor or former district attorney or solicitor during or because of the exercise of his official duty.

(6) The offender caused or directed another to commit murder or committed murder as an agent or employee of another person.

(7) The offense of murder, rape, armed robbery, or kidnapping was outrageously or wantonly vile, horrible or inhuman in that it involved torture, depravity of mind, or an aggravated battery to the victim.

(8) The offense of murder was committed against any peace officer, corrections employee or fireman while engaged in the performance of his official duties.

(9) The offense of murder was committed by a person in, or who has escaped from, the lawful custody of a peace officer or place of lawful confinement.

(10) The murder was committed for the purpose of avoiding, interfering with, or preventing a lawful arrest or custody in a place of lawful confinement, of himself or another.

(c) The statutory instructions as determined by the trial judge to be warranted by the evidence shall be given in charge and in writing to the jury for its deliberation. The jury, if its verdict be a recommendation of death, shall designate in writing, signed by the foreman of the jury, the aggravating circumstance or circumstances which it found beyond a reasonable doubt. In non-jury cases the judge shall make such designation. Except in cases of treason or aircraft hijacking, unless at least one of the statutory aggravating circumstances enumerated in section 27-2534.1(b) is so found, the death penalty shall not be imposed. § 27-2534.1 (Supp. 1975).

The Supreme Court of Georgia, in *Arnold v. State,* 236 Ga. 534, 540, 224 S.E.2d 386, 391 (1976), recently held unconstitutional the portion of the first circumstance encompassing persons who have a "substantial history of serious assaultive criminal convictions" because it did not set "sufficiently 'clear and objective standards.' "

2. The statute requires that the Supreme Court of Georgia obtain and preserve the records of all capital felony cases in which the death penalty was imposed after January 1, 1970, or such earlier date that the court considers appropriate. § 27-2537 (f) (Supp. 1975). To aid the court in its disposition of these cases the statute further provides for the appointment of a special assistant and authorizes the employment of additional staff members. §§ 27-2537 (f)–(h) (Supp. 1975).

3. Another purpose that has been discussed is the incapacitation of dangerous criminals and the consequent prevention of crimes that they may otherwise commit in the future. . . .

4. Lord Justice Denning, Master of the Rolls of the Court of Appeal in England, spoke to this effect before the British Royal Commission on Capital Punishment:

> Punishment is the way in which society expresses its denunciation of wrong doing: and, in order to maintain respect for law, it is essential that the punishment inflicted for grave crimes should adequately reflect the revulsion felt by the great majority of citizens for them. It is a mistake to consider the objects of punishment as being deterrent or reformative or preventive and nothing else. . . . The truth is that some crimes are so outrageous that society insists on adequate punishment, because the wrong-doer deserves it, irrespective of whether it is a deterrent or not. Royal Commission on Capital Punishment, Minutes of Evidence, Dec. 1, 1949, p. 207 (1950)

A contemporary writer has noted more recently that opposition to capital punishment "has much more appeal when the discussion is merely academic than when the community is confronted with a crime, or a series of crimes, so gross, so heinous, so cold-blooded that anything short of death seems an inadequate response." Raspberry, Death Sentence, The Washington Post, Mar. 12, 1976, p. A27, cols. 5–6.

5. Other types of calculated murders, apparently occurring with increasing frequency, include the use of bombs or other means of indiscriminate killings, the extortion murder of hostages or kidnap victims, and the execution-style killing of witnesses to a crime.

6. We do not address here the question whether the taking of the criminal's life is a proportionate sanction where no victim has been deprived of life—for example, when capital punishment is imposed for rape, kidnapping, or armed robbery that does not result in the death of any human being.

7. The Model Penal Code proposes the following standards:

(3) Aggravating Circumstances.

(a) The murder was committed by a convict under sentence of imprisonment.

(b) The defendant was previously convicted of another murder or of a felony involving the use or threat of violence to the person.

(c) At the time the murder was committed the defendant also committed another murder.

(d) The defendant knowingly created a great risk of death to many persons.

(e) The murder was committed while the defendant was engaged or was an accomplice in the commission of, or an attempt to commit, or flight after committing or attempting to commit robbery, rape or deviate sexual intercourse by force or threat of force, arson, burglary or kidnapping.

(f) The murder was committed for the purpose of avoiding or preventing a lawful arrest or effecting an escape from lawful custody.

(g) The murder was committed for pecuniary gain.

(h) The murder was especially heinous, atrocious or cruel, manifesting exceptional depravity.

(4) Mitigating Circumstances.

(a) The defendant has no significant history of prior criminal activity.

(b) The murder was committed while the defendant was under the influence of extreme mental or emotional disturbance.

(c) The victim was a participant in the defendant's homicidal conduct or consented to the homicidal act.

(d) The murder was committed under circumstances which the defendant believed to provide a moral justification or extenuation for his conduct.

(e) The defendant was an accomplice in a murder committed by another person and his participation in the homicidal act was relatively minor.

(f) The defendant acted under duress or under the domination of another person.

(g) At the time of the murder, the capacity of the defendant to appreciate the criminality [wrongfulness] of his conduct or to conform his conduct to the requirements of law was impaired as a result of mental disease or defect or intoxication.

(h) The youth of the defendant at the time of the crime. ALI Model Penal Code § 210.6 (Proposed Official Draft 1962)

14

Woodson v. North Carolina, 1976: Mandatory Death Penalties Are Unconstitutional

Judgment of the Court, and opinion of Mr. Justice Stewart, Mr. Justice Powell, and Mr. Justice Stevens, announced by Mr. Justice Stewart. . . . At the time of this Court's decision in *Furman* v. *Georgia,* 408 U.S. 238 (1972), North Carolina law provided that in cases of first-degree murder, the jury in its unbridled discretion could choose whether the convicted defendant should be sentenced to death or to life imprisonment.[1] After the *Furman* decision the Supreme Court of North Carolina in *State* v. *Waddell,* 282 N.C. 431, 194 S.E.2d 19 (1973), held unconstitutional the provision of the death penalty statute that gave the jury the option of returning a verdict of guilty without capital punishment, but held further that this provision was severable so that the statute survived as a mandatory death penalty law.

The North Carolina General Assembly in 1974 followed the court's lead and enacted a new statute that was essentially unchanged from the old one except that it made the death penalty mandatory. The statute now reads as follows:

> *Murder in the first and second degree defined; punishment.*—A murder which shall be perpetrated by means of poison, lying in wait, imprisonment, starving, torture, or by any other kind of willful, deliberate and premeditated killing, or which shall be committed in the perpetration or attempt to perpetrate any arson, rape, robbery, kidnapping, burglary or other felony, shall be deemed to be murder in the first degree and shall be punished with death. All other kinds of murder shall be deemed murder in the second degree, and shall be punished by imprisonment for a term of not less than two years nor more than life imprisonment in the State's prison. N.C. Gen. Stat. § 14–17 (Cum. Supp. 1975).

It was under this statute that the petitioners, who committed their crime on June 3, 1974, were tried, convicted, and sentenced to death. . . .

The history of mandatory death penalty statutes in the United States . . . reveals that the practice of sentencing to death all persons convicted of a particular offense has been rejected as unduly harsh and unworkably rigid. The two crucial indicators

Reprinted from the plurality opinion in *Woodson v. North Carolina,* 428 U.S. 280 (1976) by Justice Potter Stewart. Substantial portions of the opinion have been omitted, and the remaining footnotes renumbered.

of evolving standards of decency respecting the imposition of punishment in our society—jury determinations and legislative enactments—both point conclusively to the repudiation of automatic death sentences. At least since the Revolution, American jurors have, with some regularity, disregarded their oaths and refused to convict defendants where a death sentence was the automatic consequence of a guilty verdict. . . .

. . . The consistent course charted by the state legislatures and by Congress since the middle of the past century demonstrates that the aversion of jurors to mandatory death penalty statutes is shared by society at large. . . .

Although the Court has never ruled on the constitutionality of mandatory death penalty statutes, on several occasions dating back to 1899 it has commented upon our society's aversion to automatic death sentences. In *Winston* v. *United States,* 172 U.S. 303 (1899), the Court noted that the "hardship of punishing with death every crime coming within the definition of murder at common law, and the reluctance of jurors to concur in a capital conviction, have induced American legislatures, in modern times, to allow some cases of murder to be punished by imprisonment, instead of by death." Id., at 310. Fifty years after *Winston,* the Court underscored the marked transformation in our attitudes towards mandatory sentences: "The belief no longer prevails that every offense in a like legal category calls for an identical punishment without regard to the past life and habits of a particular offender. This whole country has traveled far from the period in which the death sentence was an automatic and commonplace result of convictions. . . ." *Williams* v. *New York,* 337 U.S. 241, 247 (1949).

More recently, the Court in *McGautha* v. *California,* 402 U.S. 183 (1971), detailed the evolution of discretionary imposition of death sentences in this country, prompted by what it termed the American "rebellion against the common-law rule imposing a mandatory death sentence on all convicted murderers." Id., at 198. See id., at 198–202. Perhaps the one important factor about evolving social values regarding capital punishment upon which the Members of the *Furman* Court agreed was the accuracy of *McGautha*'s assessment of our Nation's rejection of mandatory death sentences. . . .

It is now well established that the Eighth Amendment draws much of its meaning from "the evolving standards of decency that mark the progress of a maturing society." *Trop* v. *Dulles,* 356 U.S., at 101 (plurality opinion). As the above discussion makes clear, one of the most significant developments in our society's treatment of capital punishment has been the rejection of the common-law practice of inexorably imposing a death sentence upon every person convicted of a specified offense. North Carolina's mandatory death penalty statute for first-degree murder departs markedly from contemporary standards respecting the imposition of the punishment of death and thus cannot be applied consistently with the Eighth and Fourteenth Amendments' requirement that the State's power to punish "be exercised within the limits of civilized standards." Id., at 100.[2]

A separate deficiency of North Carolina's mandatory death sentence statute is its failure to provide a constitutionally tolerable response to *Furman*'s rejection of unbridled jury discretion in the imposition of capital sentences. Central to the limited holding in *Furman* was the conviction that the vesting of standardless sentencing power in the jury violated the Eighth and Fourteenth Amendments. . . . It is argued that North Carolina has remedied the inadequacies of the death penalty statutes held unconstitutional in *Furman* by withdrawing all sentencing discretion from juries in capital cases. But when one considers the long and consistent American experience with the death penalty in first-degree murder cases, it becomes evident that mandatory statutes enacted in response to *Furman* have simply papered over the problem of unguided and unchecked jury discretion.

. . . North Carolina's mandatory death penalty statute provides no standards to guide the jury in its inevitable exercise of the power to determine which first-degree murderers shall live and which shall die. And there is no way under the North Carolina law for the judiciary to check arbitrary and capricious exercise of that power through a review of death sentences. Instead of rationalizing the sentencing process, a mandatory scheme may well exacerbate the problem identified in *Furman* by resting the penalty determination on the particular jury's willingness to act lawlessly. While a mandatory death penalty statute may reasonably be expected to increase the number of persons sentenced to death, it does not fulfill *Furman*'s basic requirement by replacing arbitrary and wanton jury discretion with objective standards to guide, regularize, and make rationally reviewable the process for imposing a sentence of death.

A third constitutional shortcoming of the North Carolina statute is its failure to allow the particularized consideration of relevant aspects of the character and record of each convicted defendant before the imposition upon him of a sentence of death. . . . A process that accords no significance to relevant facets of the character and record of the individual offender or the circumstances of the particular offense excludes from consideration in fixing the ultimate punishment of death the possibility of compassionate or mitigating factors stemming from the diverse frailties of humankind. It treats all persons convicted of a designated offense not as uniquely individual human beings, but as members of a faceless, undifferentiated mass to be subjected to the blind infliction of the penalty of death.

. . . While the prevailing practice of individualizing sentencing determinations generally reflects simply enlightened policy rather than a constitutional imperative, we believe that in capital cases the fundamental respect for humanity underlying the Eighth Amendment, see *Trop* v. *Dulles,* 356 U.S., at 100 (plurality opinion), requires consideration of the character and record of the individual offender and the circumstances of the particular offense as a constitutionally indispensable part of the process of inflicting the penalty of death.

This conclusion rests squarely on the predicate that the penalty of death is qualitatively different from a sentence of imprisonment, however long. Death, in its finality, differs more from life imprisonment than a 100-year prison term differs from one of only a year or two. Because of that qualitative difference, there is a corresponding difference in the need for reliability in the determination that death is the appropriate punishment in a specific case.

It is so ordered.

Notes

1. The murder statute in effect in North Carolina until April 1974 reads as follows:

§ 14–17. Murder in the first and second degree defined; punishment.—A murder which shall be perpetrated by means of poison, lying in wait, imprisonment, starving, torture, or by any other kind of willful, deliberate and premeditated killing, or which shall be committed in the perpetration or attempt to perpetrate any arson, rape, robbery, burglary or other felony, shall be deemed to be murder in the first degree and shall be punished with death: Provided, if at the time of rendering its verdict in open court, the jury shall so recommend, the punishment shall be imprisonment for life in the State's prison, and the court shall so instruct the jury. All other kinds of murder shall be deemed murder in the second degree, and shall be punished with imprisonment of not less than two nor more than thirty years in the State's prison. N.C. Gen. Stat. § 14–17 (1969).

2. Dissenting opinions in this case and in *Roberts* v. *Louisiana,* argue that this conclusion is "simply mistaken" because the American rejection of mandatory death sentence statutes might possibly be ascribable to "some maverick juries or jurors." (Rehnquist, J., dissenting). See *Roberts* v. *Louisiana,* (White, J., dissenting). Since acquittals no less than convictions required unanimity and citizens with moral reservations concerning the death penalty were regularly excluded from capital juries, it seems hardly conceivable that the persistent refusal of American juries to convict palpably guilty defendants of capital offenses under mandatory death sentence statutes merely "represented the intransigence of only a small minority" of jurors. (Rehnquist, Jr., dissenting). Moreover, the dissenting opinions simply ignore the experience under discretionary death sentence statutes indicating that juries reflecting contemporary community values, *Witherspoon* v. *Illinois,* 391 U.S., at 519, and n.15, found the death penalty appropriate for only a small minority of convicted first-degree murderers. . . . We think it evident that the uniform assessment of the historical record by Members of this Court beginning in 1899 in *Winston* v. *United States,* 172 U.S. 303 (1899), and continuing through the dissenting opinions of The Chief Justice and Mr. Justice Blackman four years ago in *Furman,* see supra, at 296–98, and n.32, provides a far more cogent and persuasive explanation of the American rejection of mandatory death sentences than do the speculations in today's dissenting opinions.

15

Coker v. Georgia, 1977: The Death Penalty for Rape Is Unconstitutional

Mr. Justice White announced the judgment of the Court and filed an opinion in which Mr. Justice Stewart, Mr. Justice Blackmun, and Mr. Justice Stevens, joined. Georgia Code Ann. § 26-2001 (1972) provides that "[a] person convicted of rape shall be punished by death or by imprisonment for life, or by imprisonment for not less than 20 years. Punishment is determined by a jury in a separate sentencing proceeding in which at least one of the statutory aggravating circumstances must be found before the death penalty may be imposed. Petitioner Coker was convicted of rape and sentenced to death. Both conviction and sentence were affirmed by the Georgia Supreme Court. . . .

. . . In *Gregg,* after giving due regard to such sources, the Court's judgment was that the death penalty for deliberate murder was neither the purposeless imposition of severe punishment nor a punishment grossly disproportionate to the crime. But the Court reserved the question of the constitutionality of the death penalty when imposed for other crimes. 428 U.S., at 187 n.35.

That question, with respect to rape of an adult woman, is now before us. We have concluded that a sentence of death is grossly disproportionate and excessive punishment for the crime of rape and is therefore forbidden by the Eight Amendment as cruel and unusual punishment.[1]

As advised by recent cases, we seek guidance in history and from the objective evidence of the country's present judgment concerning the acceptability of death as a penalty for rape of an adult woman. At no time in the last 50 years has a majority of the States authorized death as a punishment for rape. In 1925, 18 States, the District of Columbia, and the Federal Government authorized capital punishment for the rape of an adult female. By 1971 just prior to the decision in *Furman* v. *Georgia,* that number had declined, but not substantially, to 16 States plus the Federal Government. *Furman* then invalidated most of the capital punishment statutes in this country, including the rape statutes, because, among other reasons, of the manner in which the death penalty was imposed and utilized under those laws.

. . . In reviving death penalty laws to satisfy *Furman*'s mandate, none of the States that had not previously authorized death for rape chose to include rape

Reprinted from the plurality opinion in *Coker v. Georgia,* 433 U. S. 584 (1977) by Justice Byron White. Substantial portions of the opinion have been omitted, and the remaining footnotes renumbered.

among capital felonies. Of the 16 States in which rape had been a capital offense, only three provided the death penalty for rape of an adult woman in their revised statutes—Georgia, North Carolina, and Louisiana. In the latter two States, the death penalty was mandatory for those found guilty, and those laws were invalidated by *Woodson* and *Roberts*. When Louisiana and North Carolina, responding to those decisions, again revised their capital punishment laws, they reenacted the death penalty for murder but not for rape; none of the seven other legislatures that to our knowledge have amended or replaced their death penalty statutes since July 2, 1976, including four States (in addition to Louisiana and North Carolina) that had authorized the death sentence for rape prior to 1972 and had reacted to *Furman* with mandatory statutes, included rape among the crimes for which death was an authorized punishment. . . .

The current judgment with respect to the death penalty for rape is not wholly unanimous among state legislatures, but it obviously weighs very heavily on the side of rejecting capital punishment as a suitable penalty for raping an adult woman.[2]

It was also observed in *Gregg* that "[t]he jury . . . is a significant and reliable index of contemporary values because it is so directly involved," 428 U.S., at 181, and that it is thus important to look to the sentencing decisions that juries have made in the course of assessing whether capital punishment is an appropriate penalty for the crime being tried. . . .

According to the factual submissions in this Court, out of all rape convictions in Georgia since 1973—and that total number has not been tendered—63 cases had been reviewed by the Georgia Supreme Court as of the time of oral argument; and of these, six involved a death sentence, one of which was set aside, leaving five convicted rapists now under sentence of death in the State of Georgia. Georgia juries have thus sentenced rapists to death six times since 1973. This obviously is not a negligible number; and the State argues that as a practical matter juries simply reserve the extreme sanction for extreme cases of rape and that recent experience surely does not prove that jurors consider the death penalty to be a disproportionate punishment for every conceivable instance of rape, no matter how aggravated. Nevertheless, it is true that in the vast majority of cases, at least 9 out of 10, juries have not imposed the death sentence.

These recent events evidencing the attitude of state legislatures and sentencing juries do not wholly determine this controversy, for the Constitution contemplates that in the end our own judgment will be brought to bear on the question of the acceptability of the death penalty under the Eighth Amendment. Nevertheless, the legislative rejection of capital punishment for rape strongly confirms our own judgment, which is that death is indeed a disproportionate penalty for the crime of raping an adult woman.

We do not discount the seriousness of rape as a crime. It is highly reprehensible, both in a moral sense and in its almost total contempt for the personal integrity and autonomy of the female victim and for the latter's privilege of choosing those with whom intimate relationships are to be established. Short of homicide, it is the "ultimate violation of self."[3] It is also a violent crime because it normally involves force, or the threat of force or intimidation, to overcome the will and the capacity of the victim to resist. Rape is very often accompanied by physical injury to the female and can also inflict mental and psychological damage.[4] Because it undermines the community's sense of security, there is public injury as well.

Rape is without doubt deserving of serious punishment; but in terms of moral depravity and of the injury to the person and to the public, it does not compare with murder, which does involve the unjustified taking of human life. Although it may be accompanied by another crime, rape by definition does not include the death or even the serious injury to another person.[5] The murderer kills; the rapist, if no more than that, does not. Life is over for the victim of the murderers; for the rape victim, life may not be nearly so happy as it was, but it is not over and normally is not beyond repair. We have the abiding conviction that the death penalty, which "is unique in its severity and revocability," 428 U.S. 187, is an excessive penalty for the rapist who, as such, does not take human life.

This does not end the matter; for under Georgia law, death may not be imposed for any capital offense, including rape, unless the jury or judge finds one of the statutory aggravating circumstances and then elects to impose that sentence. Section 26-3102 (Supp. 1975); *Gregg* v. *Georgia, supra,* at 165–66. For the rapist to be executed in Georgia, it must therefore be found not only that he committed rape but also that one or more of the following aggravating circumstances were present: 1. that the rape was committed by a person with a prior record of conviction for a capital felony; 2. that the rape was committed while the offender was engaged in the commission of another capital felony, or aggravated battery; or 3. the rape "was outrageously or wantonly vile, horrible or inhuman in that it involved torture, depravity of mind, or aggravated battery to the victim."[6] Here, the first two of these aggravating circumstances were alleged and found by the jury.

Neither of these circumstances, nor both of them together, change our conclusion that the death sentence imposed on Coker is a disproportionate punishment for rape. Coker had prior convictions for capital felonies—rape, murder and kidnapping—but these prior convictions do not change the fact that the instant crime being punished is a rape not involving the taking of life.

It is also true that the present rape occurred while Coker was committing armed robbery, a felony for which the Georgia statutes authorize the death penalty.[7] But Coker was tried for the robbery offense as well as for rape and received a separate life sentence for this crime; the jury did not deem the robbery itself deserving of the death penalty, even though accompanied by the aggravating circumstance, which was stipulated, that Coker had been convicted of a prior capital crime.[8]

We note finally that in Georgia a person commits murder when he unlawfully and with malice aforethought, either express or implied, causes the death of another human being. He also commits that crime when in the commission of a felony he causes the death of another human being, irrespective of malice. But even where the killing is deliberate, it is not punishable by death absent proof of aggravating circumstances. It is difficult to accept the notion, and we do not, that the rape, with or without aggravating circumstances, should be punished more heavily than the deliberate killer as long as the rapist does not himself take the life of his victim.

The judgment of the Georgia Supreme Court upholding the death sentence is reversed and the case is remanded to that court for further proceedings not inconsistent with this opinion.

So ordered.

Notes

1. Because the death sentence is a disproportionate punishment for rape, it is cruel and unusual punishment within the meaning of the Eighth Amendment even though it may measurably serve the legitimate ends of punishment and therefore is not invalid for its failure to do so. We observe that in the light of the legislative decisions in almost all of the States and in most of the countries around the world, it would be difficult to support a claim that the death penalty for rape is an indispensable part of the States' criminal justice system.

2. In *Trop* v. *Dulles, 356* U.S. 86, 102 (1958), the Court took pains to note the climate of international opinion concerning the acceptability of a particular punishment. It is thus not irrelevant here that out of 60 major nations in the world surveyed in 1965, only 3 retained the death penalty for rape where death did not ensue. United Nations, Department of Economic and Social Affairs, Capital Punishment 40, 86 (1968).

3. Law Enforcement Assistance Administration Report, Rape and Its Victims: A Report for Citizens, Health Facilities, and Criminal Justice Agencies 1 (1975), quoting Bard & Ellison, Crisis Intervention and Investigation of Forcible Rape, The Police Chief (May 1974), Reproduced as Appendix I-B to the Report.

4. See Note, The Victim in a Forcible Rape Case: A Feminist View, 11 Am. Crim. Law Rev. 335, 338 (1973); Comment, Rape and Rape Laws: Sexism in Society and Law, 61 Calif. L. Rev. 919, 922–23 (1973).

5. [Rape is ''carnal knowledge of a female, forcibly and against her will. Carnal knowledge in rape occurs when there is any penetration of the female sex organ by the male sex organ.'' Ga. Code Ann. §26-2001 (1972)]

6. There are other aggravating circumstances provided in the statute, . . . but they are not applicable to rape.

7. In *Gregg* v. *Georgia,* the Georgia Supreme Court refused to sustain a death sentence for armed robbery because, for one reason, death had been so seldom imposed for this crime in other cases that such a sentence was excessive and could not be sustained under the statute. As it did in this case, however, the Georgia Supreme Court apparently continues to recognize armed robbery as a capital offense for the purpose of applying the aggravating circumstances provisions of the Georgia Code.

8. Where the accompanying capital crime is murder, it is most likely that the defendant would be tried for murder, rather than rape; and it is perhaps academic to deal with the death sentence for rape in such a circumstance. It is likewise unnecessary to consider the rape-felony murder—a rape accompanied by the death of the victim which was unlawfully but nonmaliciously caused by the defendant.

Where the third aggravating circumstance mentioned in the text is present—that the rape is particularly vile or involves torture or aggravated battery—it would seem that the defendant could very likely be convicted, tried and appropriately punished for this additional conduct.

16

Constitutional Interpretation, History, and the Death Penalty

DAVID A. J. RICHARDS

The argument of Raoul Berger's book, *Death Penalties: The Supreme Court's Obstacle Course,* may be easily summarized: the persons who drafted and approved the eighth and fourteenth amendments to the United States Constitution did not intend the former to limit, let alone invalidate, the use of the death penalty by the federal or state governments. Accordingly, decisions of the Supreme Court (notably, *Furman v. Georgia* and *Gregg v. Georgia*) that have limited the legitimate scope and application of the death penalty in the United States are wrong; and, a fortiori, the two Justices (Justices Brennan and Marshall) and the many lawyers and citizens who view the death penalty as per se a violation of the eighth amendment are wrong.

Berger's methodology—the use of history to criticize judicial activism—is akin to his argument in *Government by Judiciary,*[1] which similarly faults judicial construction of the fourteenth amendment. Both books claim to show a gross violation by the judiciary of what Berger views as the basic postulate of constitutional democracy: popular sovereignty. Under this view, the legitimacy of judicial supremacy derives from judicial protection of the will of the people, expressed in specific constitutional language, against the actions of temporary democratic majorities. Thus, for a judge to apply constitutional language outside the scope of what the people intended betrays the governing rationale of constitutional government—that the people should rule (pp. 77–111).

In *Government by Judiciary,* Berger is ambivalent about the destructive effect of his argument on the legitimacy of, inter alia, *Brown v. Board of Education* and its progeny, decisions whose political morality he esteems, notwithstanding their constitutional illegitimacy. In *Death Penalties,* he expresses no comparable moral or political tension. The book displays a dismissive distemper that takes a characteristic form: While Justices of the Supreme Court and commentators find some

Reprinted from *California Law Review* 71 (1983): 1372–98 by permission of the author. Portions of the text (including all of sections I and IIa) and footnotes have been deleted; the remaining footnotes have been renumerated.

aspect of the death penalty forbidden by the eighth or fourteenth amendments, the death penalty itself—clearly not constitutionally questioned by those who drafted and approved the relevant amendments—is not forbidden by the Constitution; therefore, any argument to the contrary betrays the people and their constitutional right to govern (pp. 43–58).

This argument, repeated in endless variations, is—I shall argue—fatally question begging. It assumes what, crucially, must be shown: first, that the historical evidence must be constitutionally read in the way Berger proposes; and second, that the result of this historical inquiry (what the Founders would have included in and excluded from the scope of application of the constitutional language) is the measure of legitimate constitutional interpretation by the judiciary. It is, I believe, precisely because Berger assumes this highly controversial theory of constitutional interpretation that he both reads history as he does, and gives to the readings he presents such critical force in constitutional interpretation. The consequence is, in my judgment, both bad history and bad law.

My task here is to examine the background theory of constitutional interpretation, used also by other recent constitutional theorists, that gives force and shape to Berger's historiography and constitutional argument. This theory, mislabeled interpretivism, rests, I shall argue, on an unsound conception both of interpretation in general and of legal interpretation in particular. This essentially positivist theory distorts constitutional questions and creates false and empty dilemmas about the capacity of constitutional interpretation to bring about justice through law.

Part I [not reprinted here] briefly discussed the current debate over what methods of constitutional interpretation may properly be called interpretivist. Part II [in part omitted here] analyzes the phenomenon of interpretation in general, and of legal and constitutional interpretation in particular, as the foundation for an approach to constitutional interpretation that focuses on the abstract intentions embodied in particular clauses. Part III criticizes Berger's analysis of the constitutionality of the death penalty, and presents an alternative approach, concluding that the Supreme Court was in fact correct in finding certain aspects of the death penalty unconstitutional, and should have gone farther to hold the death penalty itself unconstitutional. . . .

II Interpretation

B. Constitutional Interpretation

In the complex legal system of the United States, to determine which method of legal interpretation is appropriate to constitutional law may require nothing less than an explication of the basic premises of the political theory of constitutional democracy. The basic institutions of the American republic correspond to deep themes of democratic political theory: federalism with its complex structure of representation; the separation of powers with its controlling conception of the rule of law; judicial supremacy based on a charter of basic human rights. The question thus becomes: Which form of interpretation is metainterpretively most consistent with the beliefs, aims, and purposes defined by the democratic political theory behind American constitutional institutions? Before turning to this question, however, we must understand the philosophical inadequacy of the strict constructionist view, which does not follow—or even acknowledge—the basic principles of interpretation outlined above.

1. *The Inadequacy of Strict Constructionism*

Strict constructionism lacks the explanatory support required to justify it as the correct means of interpreting the Constitution. The unexamined assumption of the strict constructionist position, reiterated with endless rhetorical variations by Berger, is that the only proper approach to interpretation of constitutional clauses protective of human rights is to track the cases which those who wrote and approved the constitutional language would have included or excluded, and to condemn any other approach as fatally noninterpretive. But this in turn assumes that legal interpretation must proceed according to the positivist model, which defines legal concepts in terms of paradigm cases or denotative exemplars.[2]

In order to free ourselves from the intellectual inevitability which this model of interpretation assumes, we should remind ourselves that legal interpretation, as a convention directed at the understanding and elaboration of conventions (laws), is not directly about persons. A characteristic fallacy of Berger's strict constructionist model is the assimilation of legal interpretation to the explanation of the subjective purposes of the Founders, or legislators, or whomever. A more accurate description of legal interpretation is that the subjective purposes of legislators play only the role that legal conventions place upon their purposes given the governing political theory of the society.

We shall shortly see how constitutional interpretation in the United States must, consistent with this perspective, construe Founders' intent, but the point is more apparent in statutory interpretation. For example, it is a familiar principle of statutory interpretation in the United States to impute to the often conflicting and sometimes incoherent data of legislative language, context, and history the purpose of a hypothetical reasonable legislator.[3] Courts impute a hypothetical rationality to the legislative process because fundamental principles of due process of law require that both courts and legislatures pursue constitutionally reasonable purposes in rational ways. Courts must therefore frame their interpretive task accordingly. It would be a mistake to think that these features of legal interpretation wholly disengage the process from any contact with persons' intentions. Rather, the intentions of lawmakers are themselves shaped by such conventions.[4]

Legal standards are often formulated with a self-conscious understanding that tough questions regarding ambiguities and tensions in purpose have not been settled, but left to courts to resolve consistent with sound principles of legal interpretation. The normative assumptions of rationality or reasonableness which courts bring to such a task are stronger than those found in other forms of holistic explanation, for they impute a hypothetical ideal of reasonableness to a subjective process often politically haphazard and sometimes incoherent. But this is simply to mark an important truth about the metainterpretation of legal interpretation, namely, that as we have just seen in the case of statutory interpretation and shall shortly see regarding constitutional interpretation, legal interpretation is embedded in larger moral and political ideals of just and good government.

So, to the extent that the appeal of the strict constructionist model of constitutional interpretation derives from a philosophical picture of what legal interpretation must be (indeed, it does not even acknowledge an alternative conception), it rests on bad philosophy. To the extent that the model assumes there is no other plausible theory of constitutional interpretation, the assumption is simply false. An alternative model of interpretation of these general clauses focuses on the more abstract intentions that the clauses express, namely, principles concerning freedom of expression (first amendment), prohibitions on unnecessary harshness in criminal sanctions (eight amendment), and general requirements of equal dignity (fourteenth amendment). Various factors (the language used, historical context, the tradition of judicial elaboration, etc.) support the inference that the meaning of such clauses should not be bound to Founders' applications, but should be construed as embodying abstract principles of justice which, in its independent judgment, the judiciary must elaborate over time. If necessary, elaboration may involve extending, abandoning, or reinterpreting Founders' applications. We turn now to a detailed discussion of how these various factors support the abstract intention model of constitutional interpretation from the metainterpretive perspective discussed earlier.

2. *Political Theory and the Abstract Intention Approach*

From the perspective of the democratic political theory which American constitutional institutions embody, we must ask which mode of interpretation—strict constructionism or abstract intentions—is more consistent with an imputation of reasonable and coherent purposes to the Constitution. At least five convergent and interdependent considerations suggest that the relevant constitutional clauses should be construed in terms of abstract intentions.

First, the language of the clauses ("cruel and unusual punishments," "equal protection of the laws") is itself abstract. The clauses certainly do not use denoting or referring expressions that would confine meaning to some class of historic objects. This claim could perhaps be plausibly made regarding "an impartial jury"[5] on the basis of the language used, the relatively high degree of specificity that the concept of an impartial jury had acquired at the time of the Founders, and the relatively low degree of generalization that the subject matter of the phrase permits. On the other hand, the claim appears less plausible if made about "bill of attainder,"[6] because the subject matter gives rise to a principle of more general application. If "bill of attainder" is not specific enough to confine interpretation, it is hard to see how "equal protection" or "cruel and unusual punishments" could possibly be. In any event, it is not reasonable to impute to the Founders or whomever an intent to bind later interpretation by their applications of the language when the language used does not do so; when the range of such applications is often enormously controversial historically (the general language may expressly have glossed over disagreements in application); and when available conceptions of the judicial role at the time included the common law model of case-by-case elaboration of general concepts and abstract principles.[7]

Second, whatever the common sense of things included or excluded at the time the constitutional language was approved, it is not a reasonable construction of the abstract language employed to limit it forever to its historic denotations. Matters of constitutionally relevant and controlling fact and value may evolve so that applications unimaginable earlier may become reasonable, and earlier applications may become unreasonable. To bind interpretation to historic referents would impute to the constitutional design the unreasonable intent to apply abstract language counterfactually, by ignoring changes in relevant factors which would lead reasonable persons to apply the relevant language differently.

Chief Justice Hughes correctly made precisely this point in *Home Building & Loan Association v. Blaisdell.*[8] Justice Sutherland had set forth a historical argument that the contract clause was precisely intended to invalidate stay laws of the kind that Hughes, writing for the majority, had upheld.[9] Hughes suggested that the denotative exemplar of state stay laws in the 1780's, which Sutherland's theory of interpretation supposed to be controlling, could not reasonably control when the Founders would not, hypothetically, thus have construed the contract clause in modern circumstances. Hughes' point may be reformulated as follows: Since the interpretation of cultural conventions like law requires that we construe them as reasonable systems of advancing individual and collective purposes, one must hesitate to impute an irrational or self-defeating purpose in the way that counterfactual application of constitutional language may demand, unless clear evidence so requires. In the case of the American Constitution ("a constitution intended to endure for ages to come"), there is no such evidence. Indeed, few legal systems have been so much the product of rational and reflectively self-conscious design in light of the best available political theories of republican government, nor so acutely sensitive to the recognition (rife in Enlightenment thought) that human institutions change as circumstances change and that good government must accommodate to new experience.[10]

Third, the general normative clauses derived their force and meaning from a larger political and moral culture which perceived the human rights embodied in these clauses as grounded in inviolable and enduring principles of justice. General enforcement of these clauses, as abstract principles accommodated to the circumstances of evolving historic situations, would ensure a basic framework or structure of just institutions over time.[11] The interpretation of the clauses as embodying abstract intentions is more consistent with these moral norms.

Fourth, the judicial elaboration of constitutional doctrine over time coheres only with the broader interpretive approach. If we are trying to make sense of the entire constitutional design, this must include not only language, historical evidence of Founders' intent, and surrounding cultural conventions and norms, but the traditions of judicial review which have construed constitutional language over time.[12] These traditions are reflected in conventions of judicial interpretation, identification, and application of law. One should hesitate to use one kind of data (Founders' intent, for example) to undercut the legitimacy of another kind of data (traditions of judicial review over time) unless there is the strongest evidence of inconsistency and good reasons to believe that one kind of data invokes the more authoritative purposes of the system. However, aside from a question-begging appeal to one interpretation of Founders' intent (denotative exemplars) which does not even acknowledge an alternative interpretive approach, there are no such weighty reasons. Other indications of Founders' intent—language, reasonable purpose, cultural norms—support the abstract intention approach. Even if they did not, it is difficult to see why, aside from the bad philosophy which supposes strict constructionism to be the only theory of interpretation, such intent embodies more authoritative purposes than those reflected in traditions of judicial review.

Fifth, the great appeal of strict constructionism derives from an undefended and indefensible positivistic conception of popular sovereignty. Berger frequently invokes popular sovereignty in criticizing traditions of judicial interpretation which betray Founders' intent (viz., Founders' applications of constitutional language) (e.g., p. 66). According to this view, the people, the fount of political legitimacy, imposed constitutional limits on the state in terms of the Founders' sense of the application of constitutional language at the time it was drafted and approved, and any later judicial deviance from this common sense, no matter how entrenched the judicial tradition it reflects, is thus fundamentally illegitimate (Founders' intent must always prevail). But this argument cannot withstand critical examination either as a matter of jurisprudence or political theory.

As jurisprudence, positivism, which Berger's argument assumes, has had traditional problems in explaining how there can be any legal limits on the sovereign. Bentham, probably the most profound of the early proponents of positivism, struggled unsuccessfully to accommodate the existence of such legal constraints (exemplified, for example, by the enforceable constitutional guarantees of the American republic) with the requirement of his positivistic command theory that there be a sovereign who is habitually obeyed, but who habitually obeys no one.[13] The natural move, within positivistic command theory, is to fictionalize a kind of sovereign who imposes limits on the state, but is itself illimitable, namely, the people, or popular sovereignty. But, as the more perceptive positivists have always recognized,[14] such a reading of the facts of American constitutional government is strained indeed, a far cry from the European centralized bureaucracy[15] and British parliamentary supremacy[16] which positivist theories have more naturally explained.

How, for example, is this sovereign to be determinately understood? If understood as the historical persons who approved the original Constitution, why should they bind a later generation long removed in time? If understood as some current generation, how do we know who they are or what they approve of when most of them do not understand, let alone reflectively approve, constitutional institutions? Precisely because of such strain and outright distortion of facts, the most plausible contemporary forms of positivism have abandoned the kind of command theory that requires such a futile and disfiguring search for or invention of a fictionalized sovereign.[17] Indeed, these forms of positivism tend to identify valid law with the critical attitudes reflected in conventions of judicial interpretation, identification, and application of law (traditions of judicial review), not with Founders or some other sovereign. Under this contemporary view, in conflicts between judicial convention and Founders' intent it is the former, not the latter, which should govern, so that, even conceding Berger's argument that Founders' intent and judicial convention are in clear conflict, his conclusion would not follow. But, in fact, as we earlier noted, there is good reason to reject Berger's stark picture of conflict: The more reasonable construction of relevant forms of data (language, reasonable purpose, moral conventions, etc.) yields the broader interpretive approach in any event.

As political theory, popular sovereignty has long enjoyed a central place in intuitive moral conceptions of constitutional legitimacy. But it is important to understand that popular sovereignty is, if any concept in constitutional discourse is, essentially contestable, viz., a concept subject to a range of reasonable interpretations among which good political argument must reflectively choose. Accordingly, we should resist simplistic interpretations of popular sovereignty which are no more than persuasive definitions, and certainly do not deal in a principled way with the arguments supporting alternative conceptions, indeed, do not even acknowledge the fact of reasonable controversy. Berger's use of popular sovereignty is fatally flawed in precisely this way, for he uses his explanation of it—the Founders' common sense of the application of constitutional language—to dismiss alternative conceptions without addressing the basic questions of democratic political theory which his conception of popular sovereignty raises. For example, why, as previously suggested, should a contemporary generation be bound in this way to the will of a generation long dead?

Surely, there is much in the history of American constitutionalism, at least since Madison's *The Federalist* No. 10, to suggest that any purely populist interpretation of popular sovereignty, either understood as some historical moment or some continuing acclamation, is not what the most reflective explication of the values of constitutional government would suggest. Madison's conception of a republic, in contrast to popular direct democracy, suggests that the institutions of constitutional democracy (federalism, separation of powers, judicial supremacy) express a complex moral ideal resting not on populism, but on a conception of principles of justice in which democratic self-rule appears as one constitutional value among others. One of these is the value of equal liberty of religious conscience so central to Madison's conception of just government.[18] These other values restrain the untrammeled pursuit of the popular will by both procedural and substantive constraints. For example, Madison's proposal for a procedure of representation of states in a federal system argues that such representation will minimize the tendency for democratic politics in a free republic to polarize around factions, which ignore both the common interest and the rights of minorities.[19] Elsewhere, Madison defends substantive constraints on the power of religious factions intolerantly to oppress outsiders through law.[20]

The institutions of democratic self-rule—the separation of powers with its controlling conception of the rule of law, federalism, and judicial supremacy to enforce basic rights like religious toleration—reflect an attempt to design a complex system of institutions to realize a form of justice in government, in which the ultimate value of popular sovereignty reflects an idealized moral conception of persons as free, rational, and equal.[21] So understood, the institutions of constitutional government preserve a substantive moral conception of the relation of the person to other persons and to the state, one in which the equality and liberty of persons are guaranteed and maintained. If this alternative interpretation of popular sovereignty is, as I believe, much more sensible as a theory of constitutional government than any variant of populism (including Berger's),[22] the appeal of Berger's argument as political theory evaporates. . . .

III The Death Penalty as Cruel and Unusual Punishment

Once we undermine the theory of legal interpretation which Berger assumes in *Death Penalties,* both the form of his historiography and his constitutional argument lose whatever argumentative force Berger meant them to have. For Berger, constitutional history is simply a matter of deciphering the Founders' intended applications; and constitutional argument is obedience to such applications. But once we see constitutional interpretation in the more plausible way suggested above, the form of Berger's history appears confining. Berger fails to explore the ways in which historical research may clarify arguments of constitutional principle, and his conception of constitutional argument becomes a travesty of arguments of principle in constitutional law. In particular, Berger ignores the ways in which the moral growth of the community must inevitably shape the elaboration of the abstract normative intentions of the relevant clauses of the eight and fourteenth amendments.

A. Historiography

It is a striking feature of both Berger's *Government by Judiciary* and *Death Penalties* that the use of history is extremely confined and narrow. *Government by Judiciary* concentrates, for example, on the congressional debates over the proposed fourteenth amendment, with occasional allusions to secondary accounts of the history of Reconstruction. In contrast, Harold Hyman, an American historian not bound by an interpretive theory like Berger's, supplements attention to the debates with detailed and clarifying analyses of the political and social history of Reconstruction.[23] In more recent work, Hyman insists that the fourteenth amendment must be understood in the context of the egalitarian purposes of the thirteenth amendment and the larger moral aspirations of the abolitionist movement.[24]

Berger's interpretive theory directs him away from such inquiries and limits the scope of the fourteenth amendment to applications contemplated by the Reconstruction Congress that approved the fourteenth amendment. This historiographical decision leads him to ignore larger historical and cultural contexts that clarify the abstract ideals of equal respect for human dignity which the fourteenth amendment decisively introduces into the substantive values of American constitutional law. Berger's narrow use of history may also lead to serious interpretive distortions of the limited data he does consider. Plausible inferences about the common sense applications of ''equal protection of the law'' in 1868 may confuse abstract arguments of principle with historically contingent and shifting conceptions of applications and thus lead to wrong judgments about the principle involved. Similarly, focusing on the application at the time of adoption may constitutionalize one among several historically competing views of application when the abstract language chosen precisely bespeaks a warrant for independent judicial elaboration of abstract arguments of principle.

The historiographical distortion in the use of sources in *Death Penalties* is, if anything, more grave. The sources of a larger historical inquiry, which are fundamental to a reasonable discussion of the issues of constitutional principle, are omitted. The material included is thin and interpreted tendentiously.[25] A useful comparison may be made to John McManners' *Death and the Enlightenment,*[26] a broad survey of changing attitudes to death in various contexts (including natural deaths, executions, and suicides) in eighteenth century France. For Berger, the whole historiographical question is the narrow one: whether the Founders would have applied the eighth amendment or the Reconstruction Congress the fourteenth amendment to the death penalty. Once the question is resolved negatively, the matter is forever closed, and Supreme Court opinions to the contrary are simply wrong. For McManners, the historiography of death in eighteenth century France demonstrates the emergence of a distinctive modern sensibility regarding death and dying. McManners, writing of France with no particular focus on legal issues—let alone American constitutional history—profoundly illuminates the constitutionality of the death penalty in a way that Berger, the American legal historian, does not remotely approximate.

McManners' historiography casts light on the constitutionality of the death penalty in diverse but intersecting ways. First, the modern sensibility regarding death, which McManners traces to the eighteenth century, took one characteristic form as a reformist skepticism about the form and the scope of use of the death penalty as a criminal sanction.[27] This skepticism is likely to have affected the American Enlightenment and constitutionalism through the writings of Beccaria,[28] which were widely read at the time.[29] McManners makes clear that while the Enlightenment reformers, including Beccaria—the most penologically radical of them—did not intend to abolish the death penalty altogether,[30] they had severe doubts about its general use. Beccaria, for example, reserved the death penalty for treason against the state, so that Robespierre could, without inconsistency, attack the death penalty in general, yet urge the Terror and guillotine against traitors to the republic.[31] But McManners' extensive discussion of Beccaria's arguments, in contrast to Berger's narrow focus on the simple fact that the death penalty was approved, enables us to see what Berger's account obscures: that general arguments of principle justified Enlightenment concern about the extent of application of the death penalty and the grisly forms of its imposition.[32] Though these arguments did not lead them to question the death penalty as such, the arguments did suggest real moral concerns with the death penalty, indicating that the values of decency in punishment invoked by the eighth amendment could certainly be reasonably extended or elaborated to include questions about the death penalty in a way that Berger wishes to deny.[33] Indeed, these arguments of principle, elaborated in modern circumstances, might question the justifiability of the death penalty itself.

Second, the grotesque forms of the death penalty, against which Enlightenment figures reacted so violently, were importantly associated with a self-consciously elaborated drama of terror inflicted on outrageous violations of the majesty of the hierarchical order, whose patterns of deference needed to be enforced by dramatic outward shows.[34] The natural inference is that a more egalitarian, less hierarchical conception of political justice must question such uses of terror, or analogous actions.[35] If the imposition of the death penalty in modern times is ineradicably used as an instrument of freakish terror against subjugated groups to enforce a status hierarchy, it must be condemned on egalitarian grounds. Strikingly, this objection to punishments as "cruel and unusual" is supported even by the narrow range of historical material that Berger canvasses. It is, for example, probably the true significance of the *Titus Oates* affair,[36] though Berger, who lacks the perspective of principle on his own data, misses the point.

Third, extensive use of the death penalty during the eighteenth century was tolerated because death was so common and likely that the death penalty would take little that would not otherwise soon be lost.[37] Also, given the undeveloped nature of police work, there was extreme uncertainty that any form of punishment would be imposed at all, thus leading to emphasis on the severity of sanctions in order to secure any measure of deterrence.[38] When life becomes more securely valued and certainty in punishment more feasible, the death penalty should be morally more questionable.

Fourth, theological conceptions of Hell, already under attack throughout this period and earlier,[39] undoubtedly shaped conceptions of justice in punishment. The more terroristic a conception of Hell, allegedly required to bind us to the moral life, the greater the toleration for the savageries of the law courts.[40] On the other hand, the more Hell was regarded as inconsistent with the God of love and forgiveness, the more skeptical the examination of the alleged necessity of the barbarous punishments of secular law.[41] Complex countervailing relations obtained as well: The very terrors of the religious conception of Hell, before which all souls were equal, gave expression to a moral aspiration that the secular law of a hierarchical and unjust society otherwise systematically frustrated without penalty.[42]

Thus, evolving religious and moral conceptions of justice through punishment could crucially shape one's interpretation of the justice of the death penalty, precisely in the way that Berger's use of historiography fails even to contemplate. In the modern secular age, belief in a punitive and redemptive afterlife has less force, and therefore, conceptions of retributive justice in punishment, which require the death penalty, appear parochially religious.[43]

Even aside from such questions, surely the very idea of taking life by law must have a radically different moral sense and significance among people who believe in redemption in another life and those who see this life as the only life any person will have, or among people who entertain radical conceptions of free will and those who accept causal models for the explanation of human actions.[44] It is precisely such shifts in religious, metaphysical, and other beliefs which we invoked earlier in arguing that the Founders' denotations should not apply counterfactually. McManners' historiography makes this kind of inquiry possible; Berger's does not.

B. Constitutional Argument

Berger's defective theory of legal interpretation leads not only to bad history, but to an impoverished conception of constitutional argument. He dismisses all constitutional arguments against the death penalty on the same ground: that the Founders' common sense of the application of "cruel and unusual punishments" contemplated the legitimacy of the death penalty. Once we see that this argument will not do, Berger's critical strategy appears irrelevant to any serious assessment of these constitutional arguments. Certainly, no argument in *Death Penalties* even addresses the arguments of principle made in Supreme Court decisions limiting the scope and application of the death penalty. Berger's dogged appeal to Founders' applications would require the Court today to uphold all punishments acceptable in 1791, including, presumably, branding the forehead, splitting noses, and cropping ears.

The deep question is whether the Court has gone far enough, whether Justices Marshall and Brennan are not correct in questioning the very constitutional permissibility of the death penalty. Since I believe the death penalty is unconstitutional, I should like, in conclusion, to support this position and respond to one of Berger's criticisms by urging the alternative methods of interpretation earlier proposed.

This criticism is aptly summarized by Berger's descriptive heading: "Judicial Divination of the People's Will" (p. 122). In general, Berger questions the constitutional legitimacy of the judiciary finding that a form of punishment that the Founders regarded as valid is no longer consistent with the eighth and fourteenth amendments because the moral values of the people today reject it. He claims that the judiciary's divinations are often wrong, that the proper institution to register changes in moral values is the legislature, and that any judicial attempt to repudiate clear legislative expressions of moral values, as in Justice Marshall's appeal to an informed citizenry, is arrogantly elitist and antidemocratic.

In making this criticism, Berger appeals, as he does throughout *Death Penalties,* to his central political ideal—popular sovereignty. But, as I suggested earlier, it is difficult, as a matter of jurisprudence or political theory, even to make sense of American constitutionalism on Berger's populist interpretation of popular sovereignty. Indeed, it is difficult to square even Berger's strict constructionism with these values. (Why should the people now be bound by the people of some earlier time?) There is, however, as suggested above, a plausible alternative interpretation of popular sovereignty: an abstract moral ideal of free, rational, and equal persons. This view of popular sovereignty makes better sense of constitutional institutions and doctrines, including my imputation to the relevant clauses of the eighth and fourteenth amendments of an abstract intention of basic justice in the forms of punishment.

Taking this approach to popular sovereignty, we can posit that free, rational, and equal persons would be concerned with limiting when and how the state might impose severe criminal sanctions such as grave deprivations of liberty, and perhaps life.[45] Relevant constraints would include a substantive limit on the application of criminal sanctions only to conduct that has inflicted harm;[46] a principle of equal liberty requiring that sanctions be imposed so as to guarantee each person the greatest liberty, consistent with a like liberty for all, to avoid the sanctions if he chooses; a principle of proportionality with two requirements: first, a rough correspondence between severity of wrongs and gradations among punishments; and second, substantive upper limits on forms of sanction in general (prohibiting torture as inconsistent with respect for dignity) and in particular (prohibiting severe sanctions for trivial wrongs)[47] and a principle of economy and effectiveness in sanctions, that would, consistent with the underlying respect for the humanity of criminals, limit the forms of sanctions to the most economical and effective in securing general deterrence and the like.[48]

Consistent with our earlier conception of constitutional interpretation, we may construe these principles as defining a constitutionally mandated conception of just punishment in several mutually supporting ways: as abstract intentions implicit in the salient history of the relevant clauses (for example, the *Titus Oates* affair) and the general language chosen, as supported by an imputation of reasonable purpose accommodating relevant changes in facts or values; as inferred from the background norms of justice in punishment on which constitutional clauses draw; or as explicating the traditions of judicial elaboration of these constitutional values in case law over time.

To elaborate on several of these themes, the factors mentioned in our discussion of McManners' historiography provide a useful illustration. First, the ineradicable arbitrariness of the death penalty suggests it is being used as an instrument of terror and subjugation, thus violating the principle of equal liberty. Second, increasing belief in causal explanation for human action suggests that deterrence evidence must be given a salient place in the justification of forms of criminal sanctions. The greater value of life (both due to contemporary longevity and to declining belief in an afterlife) imposes a higher justificatory burden for imposition of the death penalty to demonstrate its economy and effectiveness as deterrence; furthermore, the feasibility of securing more deterrence from certain, rather than severe, sanctions imposes on proponents of the death penalty a burden of showing marginal deterrence which they cannot satisfy.[49] These considerations suggest that however the basic principles of justice in punishment would have been applied in 1791 or 1868, relevant considerations of fact or value today argue that the death penalty is either so fatally arbitrary and terroristic or so lacking in support by evidence of marginal deterrence that it violates basic constitutional principles, and should be struck down as, in principle, an unconstitutional sanction.[50]

That these principles may be traced to a plausible interpretation of the basic constitutional value of popular sovereignty supports the depth of their constitutional force. That persons in different historical periods may, consistent with the background considerations unearthed by McManners, apply them differently suggests precisely the kind of flexible application which enduring constitutional principles enjoy. These are plausible, in my view conclusive, reasons to suppose that the reasonable elaboration of these principles in modern circumstances would sharply circumscribe, indeed eliminate, the death penalty as a constitutionally permissible punishment.

From this perspective, the appeal to Founders' applications misconceives the proper role of the judiciary in the elaboration of the abstract intentions of relevant constitutional clauses precisely in ways that reinterpret Founders' applications, and sometimes abandon them entirely. In the case of the death penalty, the appeal to the Founders' applications is, as we have seen, constitutionally perverse: The mandatory form of the death penalty familiar to the Founders is a radically different institution from the discretionary and selective (even with guidelines) application of the death penalty familiar today. Indeed, enacted in discretionary forms that permit its rare application to a small number of outcasts, the death penalty enjoys acceptability precisely because of the rarity of its imposition by juries and still rarer actual infliction by public authority. This pattern suggests, if anything, that the death penalty's continuing legitimacy rests on the fact that it is not regularly, routinely, evenhandedly, and visibly applied to those for whom, given the statutory language, it is designated. Even within the narrowest historical inference of the concerns giving rise to the eighth amendment (*Titus Oates*), the legitimacy of a penalty that is dependent on its being unusually inflicted implicates the prohibition of "cruel and unusual punishments."

It was a serious constitutional misjudgment on the part of many recent Justices of the Supreme Court, in my view, ever to suppose that the legitimacy of these kinds of reasoned judgments about the unconstitutionality of the death penalty turned on popular sentiment or some kind of judicial divination about conventional morality. For this is to externalize the process of constitutional deliberation into a kind of opinion poll, on the unexamined supposition that judicial impartiality here requires this kind of external moral metric. But the supposition is false, leading judges of intelligence and integrity to abdicate what is their clear constitutional duty—to exercise their own independent consciences in the reflective elaboration of constitutional principles, which is the only authentic form of impartiality expressive of the moral powers we associate with judicial virtues. The escape from this responsibility (whether in obedience to the fictive denotations of the Founders, or the imagined demands of public opinion) is, however natural, a betrayal not only of self but of the moral integrity that we should demand from constitutional judges, and an evasion of responsibility in the service of unreal masters and invented, hystericalized dangers.

The principled elaboration of constitutional values prohibiting cruel and unusual punishment should no more track the retributive thirst of the American public than the interpretation of equal protection tracks American racism or sexism. In all these cases, the judiciary's role should be to articulate the moral sense of abstract principles of just government in contemporary circumstances. This process may require the Court independently to evaluate background constitutional facts which may, through racist or sexist science,[51] abuses of psychiatry,[52] distortions of history and religion,[53] grossly culpable ignorance of or inadvertence to marginal deterrence evidence[54] otherwise disfigure the dignified elaboration of constitutional law. Often, the consequence of unpopular decisions which expand judicial protection of human rights is not the feared loss of institutional capital,[55] but, over time, a transformation of American conventional morality in the ethically required way that constitutional principle demands.

Such judgments are neither elitist nor antidemocratic, for they express no disrespect or contempt for human dignity or equality. To the contrary, Justice Marshall's and Justice Brennan's view of the unconstitutionality of the death penalty precisely expresses the demand that populist retributivism—itself compounded of fear and ignorance and much stereotypical contempt—constrain itself by constitutional demands that criminals, even vicious ones, are to be treated as persons.

It is natural, in closing, to appeal to the value of respect for dignity—that persons should be treated as persons, not as criminal outcasts beyond the pale of humane concern. Berger finds the value of dignity without constitutional force because it requires reassessment of Founders' applications—the fount of constitutional legitimacy (see p. 12). But if his account of constitutional legitimacy is deeply defective, as I have argued, that may confirm precisely why dignity has the central place that it enjoys in the jurisprudence of the eighth and fourteenth amendments, and much other constitutional argument and discourse. For, if allegiance to Founders' denotations appears as a shallow and empty constitutional ideal, dignity is a value that endures. It enables us to understand our law and our lives as lawyers as inspirited with a living and reasonable faith in constitutional government that produces an endless demand on us for justice through law. There is no disassociative positivist alienation here (as in obedience to Founders' applications), but the more integral expression of our moral powers as lawyers to keep faith in the best of our constitutional traditions.

Notes

1. R. Berger, GOVERNMENT BY JUDICIARY: THE TRANSFORMATION OF THE FOURTEENTH AMENDMENT (1977).

2. For the classic statement of the positivist model of legal interpretation on the model of paradigm cases, see H. L. A. Hart, THE CONCEPT OF LAW ch. VII (1961). For example, a legal rule to the effect that no vehicle may be taken into the park is interpreted in terms of "the paradigm, clear cases (the motor-car, the bus, the motor-cycle)." Id. at 125.

3. See H. Hart & A. Sacks, THE LEGAL PROCESS 1414–15 (Harvard Law School tent. ed. 1958); see also R. Dickerson, THE INTERPRETATION AND APPLICATION OF STATUTES ch. 12 (1975).

4. Cf. R. Dworkin, *Law as Interpretation,* 9 CRITICAL INQUIRY 179 (1982).

5. See Williams v. Florida, 399 U.S. 78, 117 (1970) (Harlan, J., concurring).

6. See Lovett v. United States, 328 U.S. 303 (1946); United States v. Brown, 381 U.S. 437 (1965).

7. See THE FEDERALIST No. 78 (A. Hamilton).

8. 290 U.S. 398 (1934).

9. For relevant history of the period of the 1780's, see G. Wood, THE CREATION OF

THE AMERICAN REPUBLIC 1776–1787, at 393–467 (1969); C. Miller, THE SUPREME COURT AND THE USES OF HISTORY 39–51 (1969).

10. See D. Adair, FAME AND THE FOUNDING FATHERS 3–26, 93–140 (1974).

11. See generally G. Wood, supra note 9; B. Bailyn, THE IDEOLOGICAL ORIGINS OF THE AMERICAN REPUBLIC (1967); M. White, THE PHILOSOPHY OF THE AMERICAN REVOLUTION (1978); H. Commager, THE EMPIRE OF REASON 176–235 (1977); H. May, THE ENLIGHTENMENT IN AMERICA 88–101, 153–76, 197–251 (1976).

12. See Brest, *The Misconceived Quest for the Original Understanding,* 60 B.U.L. REV. 204 (1980); Fiss, *Objectivity and Interpretation,* 34 STAN. L. REV. 739 (1982). But cf. Brest, *Interpretation and Interest,* 34 STAN. L. REV. 765 (1982) (taking a more skeptical view of his earlier position); Brest, *The Fundamental Rights Controversy: The Essential Contradictions of Normative Constitutional Scholarship,* 90 YALE L.J. 1063 (1981) (same) [hereinafter cited as Brest, *The Fundamental Rights Controversy*].

13. See H. L. A. Hart, ESSAYS ON BENTHAM 220–42 (1982).

14. See H. L. A. Hart, THE CONCEPT OF LAW 49–76 (1961); H. L. A. Hart, supra note 13, at 220–68.

15. See H. Kelsen, PURE THEORY OF LAW (M. Knight trans. 1967); H. Kelsen, GENERAL THEORY OF LAW AND STATE (A. Wedberg trans. 1961).

16. See J. Austin, THE PROVINCE OF JURISPRUDENCE DETERMINED (H. L. A. Hart ed. 1954).

17. See H. L. A. Hart, supra note 14; J. Raz, THE CONCEPT OF A LEGAL SYSTEM (1970); J. Raz, PRACTICAL REASON AND NORMS (1975); J. Raz, THE AUTHORITY OF LAW (1979); N. MacCormick, LEGAL REASONING AND LEGAL THEORY (1978).

18. See Madison, *Memorial and Remonstrance, 1785,* in THE MIND OF THE FOUNDER: SOURCES OF THE POLITICAL THOUGHT OF JAMES MADISON 8–16 (M. Meyers ed. 1973).

19. For a range of commentary on Madison's argument, widely diverging in perspective, see, for example, D. Adair, FAME AND THE FOUNDING FATHERS 75–140 (1974) (way of securing moral impartiality in political leaders); G. Wills, EXPLAINING AMERICA: THE FEDERALIST 179–264 (1981) (following Adair); R. Dahl, A PREFACE TO DEMOCRATIC THEORY (1956) (defense of polyarchy); C. Beard, AN ECONOMIC INTERPRETATION OF THE CONSTITUTION OF THE UNITED STATES v–vii, 14–16, 152–88 (1935) (reduction to economic interests).

20. See Madison, supra note 18, at 8–16. In addition to his role in the history of religious freedom in Virginia, Madison was, of course, the central figure in both the drafting and approval of the free exercise and anti-establishment clauses of the first amendment. For a discussion of the pertinent historical records, see 1 A. Stokes, CHURCH AND STATE IN THE UNITED STATES 538–52 (1950).

21. See generally J. Rawls, A THEORY OF JUSTICE (1971).

22. See D. Richards, THE MORAL CRITICISM OF LAW 39–56 (1977).

23. H. Hyman, A MORE PERFECT UNION (1973). Compare the similar observation about the comparative value of constitutional historiography in Tushnet, *Following the Rules Laid Down,* 96 HARV. L. REV. 781, 795 n.39 (1983).

24. I depend here on a paper delivered to a faculty colloquium at N.Y.U. School of Law, where Harold Hyman is the Visiting Meyer Professor, 1982–83, H. Hyman, Back of Bakke: Eclectic Elements in the Creation of the Fourteenth Amendment (unpublished manuscript on file with the *California Law Review*). See also H. Hyman & W. Wiecek, EQUAL JUSTICE UNDER LAW: CONSTITUTIONAL DEVELOPMENT, 1835–1875, at 386–438 (1982). Hyman's interpretive approach converges with that of my colleague William E. Nelson; see

W. Nelson, THE ROOTS OF AMERICAN BUREAUCRACY 1830–1900 (1982), and his general work in progress on the fourteenth amendment. See also R. Cover, JUSTICE ACCUSED: ANTISLAVERY AND JUDICIAL PROCESS 154–55 (1975).

25. A striking example of this tendentiousness is Berger's dismissal of what seems to be clear and relevant evidence that the language of "cruel and unusual punishments" was understood by the Founders possibly to someday invalidate punishments conventionally supposed legitimate in 1791, namely, Livermore's objection: "it is sometimes necessary to hang a man, villains often deserve whipping, and perhaps having their ears cut off; but are we in future to be prevented from inflicting these punishments because they are cruel" (pp. 45–46). Berger's dismissal rests on what he supposes to be the clear language of the fifth amendment—that "[n]o person shall be . . . deprived of life . . . without due process of law"—which, contemplating the death penalty, must be read to express an intent that the eighth amendment should never invalidate the death penalty (pp. 45–47). But the issue posed by the language of the fifth amendment—namely, that a taking of life can only occur if it satisfies a process regarded as due—is the same kind of issue which the eighth amendment raises regarding the constitutional legitimacy of punishments in general, if anything, suggesting a higher burden of justification in the case of the imposition of capital punishment. If the imposition of a death penalty cannot satisfy the demanding requirements of the eighth amendment, a fortiori it can no longer be regarded as consistent with due process. Accordingly, there is no stronger evidence inferable from the fifth than from the eighth amendment about the permanent constitutional legitimacy of the death penalty, and Livermore's objection, which certainly was made in a context contemplating the eighth amendment as well, provides very good evidence indeed that the abstract intention approach was thought appropriate to the normative clauses of the Bill of Rights. Berger is unable to deal with historical evidence in a dispassionate way (and acknowledge weakness in his own position) precisely because he does not evaluate data as a historian, but rather as the unconscious and partisan advocate of a theory of legal interpretation which is, qua theory of interpretation, almost certainly indefensible, as we have seen. For further explorations of Berger's misinterpretations of his own data, see S. Gillers, Berger Redux 92 *Yale Law Journal* 731 (1983).

26. J. McManners, DEATH AND THE ENLIGHTENMENT (1981). See also P. Ariès, THE HOUR OF OUR DEATH (H. Weaver trans. 1981); D. Stannard, THE PURITAN WAY OF DEATH (1977).

27. J. McManners, supra note 26, at 392–408.

28. C. Beccaria, ON CRIMES AND PUNISHMENTS (H. Paolucci trans. 1963).

29. For the many American readers of Beccaria in the historical period leading to the Constitution and Bill of Rights, see H. May, THE ENLIGHTENMENT IN AMERICA 118 (1976). For the continuities between the European and American Enlightenment, see id.; H. Commager, THE EMPIRE OF REASON: HOW EUROPE IMAGINED AND AMERICA REALIZED THE ENLIGHTENMENT (1977); G. Wood, supra note 9; B. Bailyn, supra note 11, at 22–93; M. White, supra note 11.

30. J. McManners, supra note 26, at 392–408.

31. Id. at 403.

32. On its grisly forms, see id. at 368–84. For an appalling description of one of the more grotesque executions, see M. Foucault, DISCIPLINE AND PUNISH 3–6 (A. Sheridan trans. 1977).

33. Certainly, the preoccupation of Enlightenment thought with limiting both the crimes for which death was a legal penalty and the ways in which the death penalty was carried out, see J. McManners, supra note 26, at 392–408, suggests a principled continuity with the

ways in which the Supreme Court has limited the forms, procedures, and scope of the death penalty, see, e.g., Furman v. Georgia, 408 U.S. 238 (1972); Gregg v. Georgia, 428 U.S. 153 (1976); Coker v. Georgia, 433 U.S. 584 (1977).

34. J. McManners, supra note 26, at 130.

35. Cf. Hay, *Property, Authority and Criminal Law,* in ALBION'S FATAL TREE (D. Hay, P. Linebaugh, J. Rule, E. Thompson & C. Winslow eds. 1975) (arguing that in 18th century England the wealthy ruling class could afford to be benevolent and oppose the imposition of the death penalty on humanitarian grounds, since the possibility of the death penalty reinforced the social and political hierarchy).

36. Titus Oates was a minister of the Church of England, whose perjured testimony about a Catholic plot to assassinate the king led to the execution of 15 Catholics for treason. In 1685, Oates was convicted of perjury and sentenced to a fine, life imprisonment, whipping, pillorying four times a year, and defrocking. The House of Lords rejected Oates' petition to be released from the judgment; the dissenting members emphasized that defrocking by a temporal court was "unusual" because that was the function of an ecclesiastical court, and that the punishments of life imprisonment and whipping were without precedent for the crime of perjury (pp. 36–39).

37. J. McManners, supra note 26, at 374.

38. Id. at 376–79.

39. Id. at 176–90. For a discussion of comparable arguments made in the 17th century, see D. Walker, THE DECLINE OF HELL: SEVENTEENTH CENTURY DISCUSSIONS OF ETERNAL TORMENT (1964).

40. J. McManners, supra note 26, at 133.

41. Id. at 176–79.

42. Id. at 130, 134.

43. See Henkin, *Morals and the Constitution: The Sin of Obscenity,* 63 COLUM. L. REV. 391 (1963).

44. Kant's theory of punishment, which defends a strict form of *lex talionis* without any concern whatsoever with considerations of deterrence, is the clearest example in the philosophical literature, in my opinion, of the effects of a theory of radical freedom (moral freedom in action cannot for Kant, be causally explained) on conceptions of justice in punishment. See I. Kant, THE METAPHYSICAL ELEMENTS OF JUSTICE 99–107 (J. Ladd trans. 1965).

45. For further developments of this position, see D. Richards, supra note 22, at 192–259 (1977); Richards, *Human Rights and the Moral Foundations of the Substantive Criminal Law,* 13 GA. L. REV. 1395 (1979).

46. See D. Richards, SEX, DRUGS, DEATH AND THE LAW 1–20 (1982).

47. See D. Richards, THE MORAL CRITICISM OF THE LAW, at 240–44; Richards, supra note 45, at 1418 (distinguishing the two sub-principles).

48. See D. Richards, supra note 15, at 244–45; Richards, supra note 45, at 1418–19.

49. See D. Richards, supra note 45, at 225, 262 n. 72.

50. Id. at 229–59.

51. *See, e.g.,* N. Block & G. Dworkin, THE IQ CONTROVERSY (1976); J. Blum, PSEUDO-SCIENCE AND MENTAL ABILITY (1978); S. Gould, THE MISMEASURE OF MAN (1981); R. Hofstadter, SOCIAL DARWINISM IN AMERICAN THOUGHT (1944); G. Myrdal, AN AMERICAN DILEMMA (1944).

52. *See* R. Bayer, HOMOSEXUALITY AND AMERICAN PSYCHIATRY (1981).

53. *See* J. Boswell, CHRISTIANITY, SOCIAL TOLERANCE, AND HOMOSEXUALITY (1980);

A. Douglas, THE FEMINIZATION OF AMERICAN CULTURE (1977); RELIGION AND SEXISM (R. Ruether ed. 1974).

54. These cases exemplify, in my judgment, the important truth that the judiciary's constitutional role in the elaboration of constitutional values requires it independently to assess underlying factual questions which, without scrutiny, would distort and disfigure the elaboration of constitutional values. There can, consistent with the judiciary's role, be no sharp distinction between values and facts in this area: values shape facts, and facts assume values. For a telling example of distortion, see Stell v. Savannagh-Chatham County Bd. of Educ., 220 F. Supp. 667 (S.D. Ga. 1963) (upholding segregated school system on basis of alleged differential learning potentials of black and white children), rev'd, 333 F.2d 55 (5th Cir. 1964). It is a separable question, given that the judiciary must examine constitutional facts, how such facts should be raised in litigation. The general issue is brilliantly posed by the materials in P. Brest, PROCESSES OF CONSTITUTIONAL DECISIONMAKING 894–953 (1975). See also Davis, *Facts in Lawmaking,* 80 COLUM. L. REV. 931 (1980).

55. For extended use of this concept, albeit not in support of contracted interpretations of constitutional rights, see J. Choper, JUDICIAL REVIEW AND THE NATIONAL POLITICAL PROCESS (1980). For a telling criticism of the concept, see Gunther, *The Subtle Vices of the "Passive Virtues,"* 64 COLUM. L. REV. 1 (1964).

17

Why the Death Penalty Is a Cruel and Unusual Punishment

H. A. BEDAU

It is convenient to begin by examining a recent account of cruelty inspired by the great eighteenth century French opponents of the cruelties of their day. According to this account, "cruelty" is "the willful infliction of physical pain on a weaker being in order to cause anguish and fear."[1] The very ambiguity of this definition may enhance its attractiveness: In whom are the "anguish and fear" of "cruelty" willfully caused—the victim or the witnesses, or both? When this concept of cruelty is used to judge the death penalty, it certainly fits classic paradigms of cruel execution: Roman crucifixion, Tudor disembowelments, tearing asunder by *L'ancien régime*. Perhaps even the fusillade of rifle bullets that cut down Gary Gilmore in Mormon Utah or the repeated jolts of high-voltage electric current used recently by sovereign Georgia to broil Alpha Otis Stephens—these too might fall under the scope of cruelty as defined above. But capital punishment as such? Never. Where the death inflicted is not "physically" painful, it apparently cannot be cruel. Where the intention is not to cause anyone "anguish and fear"—not the condemned offender or the official witnesses or the general public—but merely to blot out the criminal once and for all, cruelty evaporates. What emerges from this plausible definition is exactly what modern friends of the death penalty have always insisted: Capital punishment is not, per se, an excessively severe, "cruel and unusual punishment," even if (as all sensible persons agree) some of its historic modes of infliction were.

But cruelty as defined above is only the first, not the last, word on the subject. Another thoughtful recent writer, equally steeped in the seminal thinking of the eighteenth century about cruelty as well as in the widespread horrors of our own time, invites us to think about the subject in a more imaginative, thematic fashion, and thus to go beyond what any typical dictionary will tell us about human cruelty. If we do this, we will see that the very "heart of cruelty" is best described as "total activity smashing total passivity."[2] Cruelty, on this view, consists of "sub-

Reprinted from "Thinking About the Death Penalty as Cruel and Unusual Punishment," *University of California–Davis Law Review* 18 (summer 1985): 873–925 by permission of the publisher. Only pages 917–24 are reprinted here; some footnotes have been omitted, others revised, and the rest renumbered.

ordination, subjection to a superior power whose will becomes the victim's law." Where cruelty reigns, therefore, there is a "power-relationship between two parties," one of whom is "active, comparatively powerful," and the other of whom, the victim, is "passive, comparatively powerless."[3] These penetrating observations, proposed originally without any explicit or tacit reference to punishment under law, much less the death penalty, nonetheless are appropriate to it. They reveal the very essence of capital punishment to be cruelty. Whether carried out by impalement or electrocution, crucifixion or the gas chamber, firing squad or hanging, with or without "due process" and "equal protection" of the law, there is always present that "total activity" of the executioner and the "total passivity" of the condemned. The state, acting through its local representatives in the execution chamber, smashes the convicted criminal into oblivion. The one annihilates—reduces to inert lifeless matter—the other. If this is a fair characterization of cruelty, then the death penalty was, is, and always will be a cruel punishment.

What is most compelling about the concept of cruelty understood as a "power-relationship" in the foregoing manner is that it focuses our attention on the salient common factor in all situations where the death penalty is inflicted, however painlessly and whatever the condemned has done. For western philosophy, the classic example of capital punishment is provided by the case of Socrates, whose death (if we may believe Plato and Xenophon) was painless and administered by his own hand from the cup of hemlock, which he drank by order of the Athenian court that sentenced him to death. If such a method of execution were revived today it could not easily be condemned as "undignified" and thus an assault on "the dignity of man," said to be the central value protected by the constitutional prohibition of "cruel and unusual punishments."[4] Today, with the growing use of lethal injection, and when even more acceptable modes of execution are invented and adopted in the future, the same difficulty arises. With death carried out by the state in a manner that does not disfigure the offender's body, apparently causes no pain whatever, and brings about death within a few minutes, it is extremely difficult and maybe even impossible to construct a convincing argument that condemns the practice based on its "indignity." These are awkward facts for those who oppose capital punishment. But they are completely outflanked when cruelty is viewed as a "power-relationship" in the manner indicated. Cruelty seen in this fashion enables us to recognize that the death penalty is and will remain cruel no matter how or on whom it is inflicted.

The idea of such total obliteration offends our moral imagination, however, only if we grant that using the death penalty destroys something of value. We must explain what is wrong about cruel punishments and why it matters so much. The only kind of answer worth seeking is one that reveals the worth to us (and not only or even primarily to the person cruelly punished) of what cruelty destroys. But what value is there in a deservedly condemned criminal? It does not suffice to say, even if it is true, that "there is a nonwaivable, nonforfeitable, nonrelinquishable right—the right to one's status as a moral being, a right that is implied in one's being a possessor of any rights at all."[5] Traditional theories of "natural rights" in the seventeenth and eighteenth centuries fully acknowledged that a person's "natural rights" included a "right to life."[6] But according to these theories this right is "forfeited" by any act of killing another person without excuse or justification.[7] There are, to be sure, difficulties with the idea of forfeiture of natural rights. Whether they are any graver than the difficulties in the alternative is not obvious. The alternative holds that there is nothing a person can do or become by virtue of which the person loses the status of a moral agent. This is one way to express the underlying conception of the person as shielded by fundamental rights, including the right to life. The essence-relative argument [details of which are omitted here] against the death penalty as a "cruel and unusual punishment" turns on it. Without such a conception, we cannot resist the obvious inference: Once a person is fairly found guilty of a ghastly crime (for example, mass or serial murder, or genocidal murder), then the offender has no moral "worth" or residual "dignity," and deserves no minimal "respect" from society. Only with such a conception of fixed rights can we avoid such an inference.

The argument can be advanced from each of three directions. The first draws upon familiar constitutional principles. According to these principles, even the persons convicted of the gravest crimes retain their fundamental rights of "due process of law" and "equal protection of the laws." These rights are not forfeitable and cannot be waived. If government officials violate them, that is sufficient to nullify whatever legal burdens were placed on the person arising out of that violation and quite apart from whatever consequences may ensue. What this shows is that our society already has in place, and fully acknowledges, the principle that the individual *cannot* do anything that utterly nullifies his or her "moral worth" and standing as a person. The essence-relative argument against the death penalty thus does not aim to invent an unfamiliar type of reasoning and then inject it into constitutional thinking. It merely extends something that has long been done into the area of the substantive constitutional law of punishments.

The second line of reasoning draws upon quotidian experience. This assures us that those persons actually condemned by law to die for their crimes are not merely living members of *homo sapiens* but are also persons capable of the full range of moral action and passion indigenous to moral creatures. However dangerous, irrational, self-centered, stupid, or beyond improvement such a person may in fact be, these deficiencies do not overwhelm all capacity for moral agency—for responsible action, thought, and judgment, in solitude and in relationship with other persons.[8] In particular, none of these capacities vanishes as a result of the person's being at fault for causing wilful, deliberate homicide. The act of murder does not cause the varying moral capacities of murderers that experience amply reveals.[9] No plausible empirical argument can support an alleged loss of moral agency in a convicted murderer as a result of the act of murder. Even more to the point, so far as moral agency is concerned, there is no evidence to show that convicted murderers are different from other convicts.[10] So the doctrine that certain persons, who had basic human rights prior to any criminal acts, forfeit or relinquish all those rights by such acts and thereby cease to be moral persons, receives no support from experience.

The third direction in which to look for support is more obscure and controversial; it concerns moral theory and the nature of the person. Despite recent remarks from the federal bench[11] expressing hostility to all such theories, they cannot be ignored. Human beings are not merely biological specimens of the species *homo sapiens;* nor are we merely self-motivating information-processing creatures. We are moral beings; the meaning of this proposition cannot be intuitively grasped or read off from any value-neutral set of descriptions about our behavioral capacities.[12] It can be understood only as the product of reflective thought about our own capacities as agents and patients, and any remotely adequate account will embody or rely upon moral theory. As a consequence, the nature of the person (as well as any account of that nature) itself changes over time as a result of changes in our self-perceptions. History assures us that we are permanently engaged in our own progressive self-understanding as individuals and as societies. For several centuries—and in particular, since the Age of Enlightenment—philosophers have struggled to enunciate a conception of the person as fundamentally social, rational, and autonomous, and as immune to change in these respects by virtue of any contingencies of history or circumstance. Such personal traits and capacities are no guarantee against immorality in private or public conduct. Nor do they protect us from mortality; they decay with senescence and can vanish prior to biological death. It is also true that in particular cases illness, abnormality, and other misfortunes can prevent their normal development in otherwise "normal" persons. Yet these capacities are not, and cannot be thought of as, vulnerable to destruction by the agent's own acts that are deliberate, intentional, responsible—the very qualities properly deemed necessary in a person's conduct before the criminal law subjects a person's harmful conduct to judgment, condemnation, and punishment. On such a theory, even the worst and most dangerous murderer is not a fit subject for annihilation by others. Not even the convicted criminal is a mere object, a thing, to be disposed of by the decision of others, as though there were no alternative. Society has no authority to create and sustain any institution whose nature and purpose is to destroy some of its own members. So cruelty, which does this, matters—because our own status as moral creatures matters. Accordingly, deliberate, institutionalized, lethally punitive cruelty matters, too. Bringing it to an end in all human affairs heads the list of desiderata for any society of persons who understand themselves as moral agents.

Why a theory with the consequences sketched above should be accepted in preference to alternative theories of the person is far too large a question to try to answer here. Until it is answered satisfactorily, however, its conception of the person will not convince the unconverted. Today's handful of literate friends of the death penalty are unaware of or unpersuaded by it; one can only speculate about what they would offer in its place. Fortunately, during the past decade or so (indeed, coincident with but wholly independent of the Supreme Court's death penalty cases beginning with *Furman*) several philosophers have begun thorough and systematic work toward developing versions of this theory,[13] including versions that connect it with our constitutional tradition in general and with the concepts employed in the Bill of Rights and fourteenth amendment in particular.[14] It must suffice here to point in this direction and leave to others and for other occasions the detailed characterization and evaluation of this theory.[15]

If the death penalty is an excessively severe punishment, as I believe, then it is in part because the best conception of the person is the one sketched above. According to that conception of the person, given the familiar facts of our society in this century, and given the unalterable nature of the death penalty itself, this kind of punishment—even when carried out in the most dignified fashion, on the most hardened offenders, for the most heinous crimes—exceeds the severity that society acting through its government may employ. Translated into the terms of the severity-limiting language of the Constitution, the death penalty thus is a "cruel and unusual punishment."

Notes

1. J. Shklar, ORDINARY VICES, 7–44 (1984).
2. P. Hallie, CRUELTY (1982).
3. Id. at 34.
4. Trop v. Dulles, 356 U.S. 86, 100 (1958), quoted in *Furman,* 408 U.S. at 270 (Brennan, J., concurring). While I do not wish to rely in my argument on this concept, I do not wish to hold it up to contempt, either, as some have done, see, e.g., R. Berger, DEATH PENALTIES: THE SUPREME COURT'S OBSTACLE COURSE (1984) at 118 ("empty rhetoric"); id. at 118 n.30 ("arrant nonsense"), nor repeat the pusillanimities of others. See, e.g., E. van den Haag & J. Conrad, THE DEATH PENALTY: A DEBATE (1983) at 262, 276, 297–98. Much the most serious treatment of this concept is given in W. Berns, FOR CAPITAL PUNISHMENT: CRIME AND THE MORALITY OF THE DEATH PENALTY (1979) at 24–28, 162–63. However, Berns balks (rhetorically?) at the idea that even "the vilest criminal" retains *some* "human dignity." Id. at 189.
5. H. Morris, *A Paternalistic Theory of Punishment,* 18 AM. PHIL. Q. 263 (1981) at 270.
6. There is no adequate study of the historical sources and content of the "natural right to life." It is, for instance, virtually unmentioned in the otherwise valuable monograph by R. Tuck, NATURAL RIGHTS THEORIES: THEIR ORIGIN AND DEVELOPMENT (1979). For discussion of current themes and references to the standard sources, from Hobbes to Kant, see M. White, THE PHILOSOPHY OF THE AMERICAN REVOLUTION 185–228 (1981); Bedau, *The Right to Life,* 52 THE MONIST 550 (1968); Fletcher, *The Right to Life,* 63 THE MONIST 135 (1980).
7. See, e.g., J. Locke, TWO TREATISES OF GOVERNMENT (P. Laslett 2d ed.) at 172.
8. Anyone who doubts the claims in the text will put doubt aside after reading recent accounts of men on America's "death rows." See R. Johnson, CONDEMNED TO DIE: LIFE UNDER SENTENCE OF DEATH (1981). For a discussion of this and other recent studies of life on death row, see Bedau, Book Review, 28 CRIM. & DELINQ. 482 (1982).
9. See, e.g., Danto, *A Psychiatric View of Those Who Kill,* in THE HUMAN SIDE OF HOMICIDE 3–20 (B. Danto, J. Bruhns & A. Kutscher eds. 1982), and the extensive literature cited therein. No doubt, as Danto notes, "murderers have defective super egos, that is, they have defective consciences," id. at 7, incontestably proved by their criminal acts. But he cites no evidence in the research he surveys to contradict the claims in the text.
10. Whether the issue has ever been tested directly is not clear, but it is clear that some

of those who have studied convicted murderers agree with the statement in the text. See, e.g., A. Morris, HOMICIDE: AN APPROACH TO THE PROBLEM OF CRIME 18–19 (1955) ("[T]he murderer's mental processes are those common to all of us."). Other research shows that the murderer is typically male, young, and in other ways like those who commit non-homicidal crimes of violence against the person. STUDIES IN HOMICIDE 3–4 (M. Wolfgang ed. 1967). Thus, murderers as a class may well be like other violent offenders and unlike most non-violent offenders.

11. Thus, Judge Robert R. Bork declared that "contractarian . . . philosophy" (along with others) is unsuitable as a "constitutional ideolog[y]" because it is "abstract," lacks "democratic legitimacy," and because "[o]ur constitutional liberties . . . do not rest on any general theory." N.Y. Times, Jan. 4, 1985, at A16, col. 5. "Contractarian philosophy" is a generic term the best specific instance of which is the moral philosophy of J. Rawls, A THEORY OF JUSTICE (1972). Judge Bork also condemned what he described as the attempt to "substitute" the "abstractions of moral philosophy" for "our constitutional freedoms." N.Y. Times, Jan. 4, 1985, at A16, col. 5. Rawls and other contractarians do not argue for such a "substitution"; they do argue that the best theory of these "freedoms" is to be found in their "moral philosophy"—a very different thesis.

12. It has become standard practice to distinguish several concepts of the person, the most primitive of which is that of a biological member of *homo sapiens* and the most complex of which is that of an autonomous rational claimer of rights. See J. Rosenberg, THINKING CLEARLY ABOUT DEATH 108–23 (1984). Various commentators believe that a moral dimension to personhood is necessary to any adequate account of the person. See, e.g., Dennett, *Conditions of Personhood,* in THE IDENTITIES OF PERSONS 175–96 (A. Rorty ed. 1976); see also S. Hampshire, THOUGHT AND ACTION (1959).

13. B. Ackerman, SOCIAL JUSTICE AND THE LIBERAL STATE (1980); A. Gewirth, REASON AND MORALITY (1978); A. I. Melden, RIGHTS AND PERSONS (1977); J. Rawls, supra note. 11; D. Richards, A THEORY OF REASONS FOR ACTIONS (1971).

14. H. Gross, A THEORY OF CRIMINAL JUSTICE (1979); R. Dworkin, TAKING RIGHTS SERIOUSLY (1977); D. Richards, THE MORAL CRITICISM OF LAW (1977); D. Richards, SEX, DRUGS, DEATH AND THE LAW (1982); D. Richards, *Human Rights and the Moral Foundations of the Substantive Criminal Law,* 13 GA. L. REV. 1395 (1979). Hart has rightly pointed out that Dworkin "does not appeal to any theory of human nature" to ground his defense of unwritten constitutional rights. H. L. A. Hart, ESSAYS IN JURISPRUDENCE AND PHILOSOPHY 210 (1983). Nevertheless, there is no way to explain Dworkin's position without eventually appealing to a "theory" of precisely this sort. See also *Respect for Persons,* 31 TULANE STUDIES IN PHILOSOPHY (O. Green ed. 1982).

15. The central figure around whose thought these reflections focus is Rawls. See J. Rawls, supra note 11. His work has received extensive and varied criticism. See B. Barry, THE LIBERAL THEORY OF JUSTICE: A CRITICAL EXAMINATION OF THE PRINCIPAL DOCTRINES IN A THEORY OF JUSTICE BY JOHN RAWLS (1973); H. Blocker & E. Smith, JOHN RAWLS' THEORY OF SOCIAL JUSTICE: AN INTRODUCTION (1980); N. Daniels, READING RAWLS: CRITICAL STUDIES ON RAWLS' A THEORY OF JUSTICE (1975); R. Wolff, UNDERSTANDING RAWLS (1977). However, little or none of this criticism is aimed at or touches the conception of the person central to Rawls' (and allied) moral theory. For an exploration of some of the issues here, see Daniels, *Moral Theory and the Plasticity of Persons,* 62 THE MONIST 265 (1979).

18

Habeas Corpus and Other Constitutional Controversies

H. A. BEDAU

No sooner had the Supreme Court ruled in 1976 that the death penalty was in principle not an unconstitutionally "cruel and unusual punishment" than attorneys for death row convicts began to pursue a wide range of other constitutional challenges to the procedures being followed under the new death penalty laws as they were applied in particular cases. Such litigation has continued for twenty years and shows no signs of coming to an end. Most of these cases found their way to the Supreme Court (even if only to be summarily dismissed) because the federal courts, however reluctantly, cannot really avoid reviewing complaints that raise federal constitutional issues. The proof that many of these claims have merit is found in the high percentage of cases where the federal courts have overturned the state courts.

Some of these rulings have had sweeping effect on all death row inmates; others (because of the special peculiarities of the facts of the case) had little or no impact apart from benefiting the particular death row prisoner who brought the suit in question. A crucial factor in the impact of any decision is its retroactivity: Will it be extended to benefit other death row prisoners to whom it could be applied but who entered death row before the litigating prisoner did? Or will the new ruling be limited so that its benefits accrue only to those who arrived on death row after the litigating prisoner? Since 1990 the Supreme Court has refused to grant retroactive application of any of its new rulings establishing the rights of death row prisoners, unless very stringent exceptions apply. The denial of retroactive application is only one of several ways the Court in its post-*Gregg* decisions in capital cases has ruled against the interests of death row prisoners.

Supreme Court Decisions, 1978–1995

In the quarter century since the decision in *Furman* (and leaving to one side the post-*Furman* cases already discussed in part IV), hundreds of death penalty cases have appeared on the docket of the Supreme Court, leading to several score significant decisions.[1] These rulings touch all the main aspects of the procedures in capital trials, from impaneling the jury to postsentencing appeals. (Untouched by any Court decisions, however, are prosecutorial discretion and executive clemency—the alpha and omega of the death penalty system.) One cannot understand the present death penalty system in the United States without some knowledge of this decisional law. (A selective discussion may be found in *The Death Penalty in the Nineties* [1991], by law professor Welsh S. White. For a fuller and more recent account see *Capital Punishment and the Judicial Process* [1994], by law professor Randall Coyne and judicial law clerk Lyn Entzeroth.) Here it is possible to do no more than summarize the Court's holdings in some two dozen of these cases:

Lockett v. Ohio, 1978. Mitigating circumstances are not confined to those specifically cited as such in the statute. Rather, the jury must be allowed to hear "any aspect of the defendant's character or record and any of the circumstances of the offense that the defendant proffers as a basis for a sentence less than death."[2]

Presnell v. Georgia, 1978. A death sentence is invalid if it is imposed by a jury that failed to specify any statutory aggravating circumstance during the penalty phase.

Godfrey v. Georgia, 1980. The aggravating circumstance specified in Georgia's statute as "outrageously or wantonly vile, horrible or inhuman in that it involved torture, depravity of mind or an aggravated battery to the victim," is too vague to be constitutionally permissible. In *Walton v. Arizona* (1990), however, the Court held that the aggravating circumstances defined by Arizona's statute as "especially heinous, cruel or depraved" is not so vague as to be unconstitutional.

Enmund v. Florida, 1982. The death penalty is disproportionate for one who only aids and abets a murder but does not kill, attempt to kill, or intend to kill the victim. However, in *Tison v. Arizona* (1987) the Court ruled that a death sentence is not disproportionate if the defendant participated in a major way in a felony involving a homicide and acted with "reckless indifference to the value of human life."[3]

Barefoot v. Estelle, 1983 [Texas]. Psychiatric testimony regarding the future dangerousness of a defendant, placed before the jury by the prosecution seeking a death sentence, is admissible at the sentencing hearing even if the expert testimony is not based on any interview with or examination of the defendant. The rules governing habeas corpus appeal provide no special exceptions in favor of death penalty petitioners; courts of appeal may apply "expedited procedures" in evaluating such petitions, and stays of execution are not "automatic" pending the filing and review in this Court of a denial of such a petition by the Court of Appeals.[4]

Pulley v. Harris, 1984 [California]. Establishing that a death sentence was fairly imposed by affording "proportionality review," comparing it with other cases in which death was (and was not) imposed, is not a requirement under the federal Constitution.[5]

Spaziano v. Florida, 1984. Florida's statute allowing the trial judge to override the jury's recommendation of a life sentence and impose a death sentence instead is not unconstitutional.[6]

Strickland v. Washington, 1984. Ineffective assistance of counsel will not serve as a ground for review of the conviction or sentence in a capital case unless counsel failed to give "reasonably effective assistance" and counsel's errors resulted in a reasonable probability of a different outcome.[7] However, counsel's failure to develop and present mitigating evidence during the sentencing phase was not ineffective assistance; *Burger v. Kemp,* 1987 [Georgia].

Ford v. Wainwright, 1986 [Florida]. Execution of the insane is unconstitutional, and state procedures must accommodate the condemned person's right to submit evidence of insanity.[8]

McCleskey v. Kemp, 1987 [Georgia]. Racial disparities in death sentences, however well established statistically, are insufficient to warrant intervention by the federal courts, unless those disparities can be traced to intentional discrimination on racial grounds against the defendant in question. (For a fuller discussion, see part V.)

Booth v. Maryland, 1987. Victim-impact evidence, showing the pain and loss suffered by surviving relatives and friends of a murder victim, offered in support of the prosecution's argument for a death sentence, is inadmissible during the sentencing phase of a capital trial. Overruled in *Payne v. Tennessee,* 1991.[9]

Thompson v. Oklahoma, 1988. Oklahoma's statute that permits execution of a prisoner under age sixteen at the time of the crime is unconstitutional. However, there is nothing "cruel and unusual" in Kentucky's law that authorizes a death sentence and execution for a person at least sixteen years old at the time of the crime; *Stanford v. Kentucky,* 1989.[10]

Teague v. Lane, 1989 [Illinois]. The constitutional ban on race-based peremptory challenges during the voir dire does not apply retroactively to a prisoner whose conviction is otherwise final and who raises this issue on collateral review. In general, "new constitutional rules of criminal procedure will not be applicable to those cases which have become final before the new rules are announced."[11] This holding was promptly extended to death penalty cases in *Penry v. Lynaugh.*

Penry v. Lynaugh, 1989 [Texas]. The Eighth Amendment does not prohibit execution of a mentally retarded defendant; however, mental retardation is a mitigating factor the trial jury is entitled to consider during its postconviction deliberations prior to sentencing.[12]

Murray v. Giarrantano, 1989 [Virginia]. States are not required to provide counsel to indigent death row prisoners seeking postconviction relief in state courts. However, *McFarland v. Texas,* 1994, held that federal courts must provide counsel for such defendants in federal litigation.

Blystone v. Pennsylvania, 1990; *Boyde v. California,* 1990. A death sentence imposed under a quasi-mandatory capital statute (requiring the jury to mete out a death sentence if it finds even one aggravating circumstance and has not received from defense counsel any evidence of a mitigating circumstance) is not unconstitutional.

Clemons v. Mississippi, 1990. Despite the sentencing jury's reliance on an unconstitutional aggravating circumstance in sentencing the defendant to death, the state appellate court may reevaluate the evidence heard during the sentencing phase of the trial and sustain the death sentence without returning the case to the trial court for a new sentencing hearing.

McCleskey v. Zant, 1991 [Georgia]. No successor federal habeas corpus petition will be granted unless the prisoner can demonstrate "cause and prejudice" for failure to raise the new claim in his original petition. To do otherwise constitutes an "abuse of the writ."

Coleman v. Thompson, 1991 [Virginia]. Defendant's counsel's failure to file a timely notice of appeal in state court does not excuse procedural default unless the defendant can show "cause and prejudice" in his failure to meet notice deadlines.

Herrera v. Collins, 1993 [Texas]. A death row prisoner convicted under state law has no right to a hearing in federal courts on grounds of newly discovered evidence purporting to show the defendant's innocence if the evidence is belated according to a state statute of limitations, unless the defendant can present a "truly persuasive show by clear and convincing evidence . . . that no reasonable juror would have found the defendant eligible for the death penalty."[13]

Simmons v. South Carolina, 1994. If the prosecution argues in favor of a death sentence, on the ground that the convicted murderer is too dangerous ever to be released, then the prosecution must also inform the jury whether the state provides, as an alternative to a death sentence, life in prison without possibility of parole.

Felker v. Turpin, 1996 [Georgia]. The tighter standards for federal habeas corpus relief, enacted by Congress in the Antiterrorisim and Effective Death Penalty Act of 1996, which prevent the Supreme Court from reviewing a lower court order denying a prisoner's second habeas petition, are not unconstitutional (for further discussion, see below, p. 244).

These cases, whose blunt abstracts here barely scratch the surface of the complexity of the issues raised and decided, at least suggest two important generalizations. First, since 1976 the Court has become an active referee in the ongoing conflicts between the state (seeking a death penalty and then seeking to carry it out) and the defendant (trying to avoid both). The Court has not, however, walked a very straight and predictable line in its capital decisions and thus has endured steady criticism from all sides. More than a decade ago, some critics complained that the overall effect of the Court's death penalty rulings was to give the states more and more authority over their own death sentencing practices, amounting to a federal "deregulation of death"; a majority of the Court had simply lost interest in "telling the states how to administer the death penalty phase of capital murder trials" (Weisberg 1984:305). More recent observers see no improvements: "the Supreme Court's chosen path of constitutional regulation of the death penalty has been a disaster, an enormous regulatory effort with almost no rationalizing effect" (Steiker & Steiker 1995:426).

Surely this conclusion is strengthened by such decisions as *Penry, Giarrantano, Payne, Coleman,* and especially *Herrera*—"one of those infamous Supreme Court [decisions] like *Lochner* and *Plessey,* that is utterly repugnant to any basic sense of fairness" (Newton 1994:34). And the upshot? As one recent observer put it, "[T]hese decisions will increase the likelihood that life and death will be determined in some cases not by the merits of an individual's claims but by the fortuities in the timing and pace of litigation which are beyond the individual [defendant's] control'' (Goldstein 1990–91:401–2). Other observers have bluntly described the situation developing over the past decade as ''the death of fairness''[14] in death penalty jurisprudence.

What accounts for this pattern of decisions by the Supreme Court? Surely, in part it is owing to the transformation of the Court's personnel from the liberal era under Chief Justice Earl Warren, through the centrist Court under Chief Justice Warren E. Burger, to the current Court with its libertarian-conservative bent under Chief Justice William H. Rehnquist.[15] Since 1991 Rehnquist and two recent appointees to the Court, Antonin Scalia[16] and Clarence Thomas, have formed the nucleus around which a majority frequently gathers where twenty years ago Rehnquist stood alone. He and these two closest colleagues on the bench profess belief in federalism, which imposes constraints on federal interference with state prerogatives, and in judicial self-restraint when evaluating legislative enactments. There is no small irony here, in that some of the most sweeping rulings affecting procedures in important recent capital cases were announced by the Court ''without briefing and argument,'' without ''sufficient explanation,'' and ''with no deference at all to the traditional requirement that judges confine themselves to the issue as narrowly framed by the facts of the particular case'' (Liebman 1990–91:544–45). And, finally, it may even be that these conservative justices strongly believe in the substantive merits of capital punishment. In 1953, as a clerk to Justice Robert H. Jackson, Rehnquist was prompted by the imminent execution of Julius and Ethel Rosenberg to note in a memorandum that, in his view, the Rosenbergs were ''fitting candidates'' for the electric chair and that ''[i]t is too bad that drawing and quartering has been abolished.''[17]

But perhaps the chief reason for the unsatisfactory state of the Supreme Court's death penalty jurisprudence lies elsewhere, in the inherent difficulties in legislatively fabricating and judicially policing three dozen different death penalty systems so that each is both fair and efficient. The record of the past two decades shows that the Court vastly underestimated the difficulty of this task when it decided *Gregg* and allied cases in 1976. We now have the most complex and cumbersome system for administering the death penalty the world has ever seen; it is neither fair nor efficient. Few like it, and the more familiarity one has with it, the less one finds to like about it.[18]

Expressions of despair are even heard from the Supreme Court. Recently, two Supreme Court justices—Lewis F. Powell Jr. (then retired) and Harry A. Blackmun (since retired), both of whom supported the death penalty without flinching from *Furman* to *Gregg* and beyond—have now reversed themselves and are on public record favoring its abolition, thus joining retired Justices Brennan and Marshall in categorical opposition to the death penalty on constitutional grounds. In 1994 Powell's biographer reported that when he asked the retired justice whether he would now change any of his votes in the cases he decided while on the Court, Powell cited his crucial vote in *McCleskey* and added, ''I would [now] vote the other way in *any* capital case'' (emphasis added).[19] A few months earlier, in his dissent in *Callins v. Collins,* Justice Blackmun had written:

> From this day forward, I no longer shall tinker with the machinery of death. For more than 20 years I have endeavored . . . along with a majority of this Court, to develop procedural and substantive rules that would lend more than the mere appearance of fairness to the death penalty endeavor. Rather than continue to coddle the Court's delusion that the desired level of fairness has been achieved and the need for regulation eviscerated, I feel morally and intellectually obligated simply to concede that the death penalty experiment has failed. It is virtually self-evident to me now that no combination of procedural rules or substantive regulations ever can save the death penalty from its inherent constitutional deficiencies.[20]

The Quarrel over Federal Habeas Corpus

For a decade or so, the focus of complaint has been on the way state death row prisoners have used the federal writ of habeas corpus to seek review in federal court of a wide variety of complaints affecting either their conviction or their sentence.[21] Traditionally, a writ of habeas corpus empowered a judge to ''inquire into the legitimacy of any form of loss of personal liberty.''[22] No statute of limitations governs a prisoner's access to this writ, nor does a failed application for the writ preclude the prisoner from filing a subsequent application. In 1867 Congress passed the Habeas Act, empowering state prisoners to obtain federal review of alleged violations of federal constitutional rights. By the early 1960s a petition for habeas corpus to the federal courts had become the chief device for attacking a state court death sentence. Since 1976, with debate over the constitutionality of the death penalty per se settled adverse to the interests of death row prisoners, their attorneys increasingly sought habeas relief for their clients in federal courts after exhausting legal remedies in the state courts (including the remedy of state habeas corpus). Since it was in principle open to a prisoner to file a habeas petition at any time on new issues, even if a court had ruled against him in a prior habeas petition on other issues, so-called successor habeas petitions soon become a hallmark of postconviction capital litigation.

However, troubled by the lack of finality in state criminal proceedings as well as ''abuse of the writ'' by prisoners filing allegedly frivolous claims, both the Supreme Court and Congress began to consider limits to the availability of such relief. Experienced death penalty defense lawyers were acutely distressed; they were quick to point out that between 1972 and 1980, some 60 percent of all state death penalty convictions or sentences were invalidated by the federal courts in response to habeas petitions;[23] in the years 1976 through 1991, the reversal rate in capital cases was between 40 and 60 percent of all cases involving such petitions.[24] Many of these reversals were granted not on the first but on a successor habeas petition. No wonder capital defense lawyers have viewed with alarm the mood of Congress in the mid-1990s on this issue. Case in point: In Missouri, Lloyd Schlup had served eleven years on death row for a murder he claimed he didn't commit. On 2 May 1996 a federal district judge granted him relief, thanks to a persuasive second petition for habeas corpus which will result in a hearing to assess his claims. Under the new 1996 habeas "reform," however, Schlup's second petition probably would have been denied.[25]

On 24 April 1996, President Clinton signed the Anti-Terrorism and Effective Death Penalty Act, which incorporated severe restrictions on the availability of federal habeas corpus to state prisoners—including death row prisoners. As *New York Times* correspondent Stephen Labaton noted, by signing this bill the president "impos[ed] the most rigorous constraints on the constitutional right to seek Federal review of convictions since Lincoln suspended the writ of habeas corpus in the Civil War" (1996:B9).[26] The National Legal Aid and Defender Association's newsletter, *Capital Report,* summarized the main features of the new law: "only claims of actual innocence can yield an evidentiary hearing;" only "unreasonable" unconstitutional state court rulings can be overturned; and filing deadlines have been curtailed to [. . .] six months in death cases" (1996:1)—that is, any federal habeas petition must be filed by the capital defendant within six months after his final state court proceeding.

Although the new law requires states to provide competent post-conviction counsel for the defense, it imposes no such requirement on the states regarding trial counsel in capital cases. Yet it is at trial, not on appeal, that the gravest errors typically occur, errors hitherto remediable—at least in principle, if not always in practice—by federal habeas corpus. As for the new laws lightening the burden on the federal courts and speeding up the appellate process, the National Center for State Courts reported in 1992 that death row inmates filed only about 1 percent of all habeas petitions and that these petitions constituted only 4 percent of the civil caseload of the district courts.[27] Substantial litigation over the application and interpretation of the new law lies ahead.

Notes

1. In the discussion that follows, I have relied in part on an unpublished memorandum; see Southern Center for Human Rights 1995.
2. See Bilionis 1991.
3. See Wickert 1983.
4. Regarding the difficulties in predicting future dangerousness, see Dix 1981; Marquart, Ekland-Olson, and Sorensen 1989a; on the procedural aspects of the decision in *Barefoot,* see Ita 1983; Levine 1984; Boaz 1985.
5. See Mayell 1984; Liebman 1985.
6. See Wellek 1984; Mello and Robson 1985; Mello 1991.
7. Contrast the pre-*Strickland* discussion of this issue in Goodpaster 1983 with the post-*Strickland* discussion in White 1993.
8. For a book-length discussion of the Ford case and the issues it raised, see Miller and Radelet 1993.
9. See V. Berger 1992 and Bedau 1994a.
10. See Streib 1988. It is useful to compare U.S. law on the execution of juveniles with

the practice of foreign nations (see Hood 1989:59–61) and with international law (see Schabas 1993:123–26, 193–95, 255–59, 270–71, 278–79).

11. See Blume and Pratt 1990–91.

12. See Denno 1994b.

13. See Steiker 1993a; V. Berger 1994; Newton 1994.

14. The phrase first appears in the title of Tabak 1986.

15. For a sympathetic review of Chief Justice Rehnquist's capital punishment jurisprudence, see Bigel 1991.

16. For a cool review of Justice Scalia's death penalty jurisprudence, see Gey 1992.

17. Sharlitt 1989:131 n.

18. For general book-length discussions of the current death penalty system see Zimring and Hawkins 1986; Amnesty International 1987; White 1991; Paternoster 1991; Streib ed. 1993; Coyne and Entzeroth 1994. In 1993 Amnesty International USA held a public hearing in Boston in which the death penalty in America was subjected to international scrutiny; see Harlow, Matas, and Rocamora 1995.

19. Jeffries 1994:451; von Drehle 1994.

20. *Callins v. Collins,*—U.S.—(1994), at p. 4 (slip opinion).

21. The literature on revision of federal habeas corpus in the 1990s is considerable; see especially V. Berger 1990; Goldstein 1990 and 1990–91; Liebman 1990–91 and 1992; Tabak and Lane 1991; and Bright 1993.

22. Fellman 1992:357.

23. Greenberg 1986:1671.

24. Liebman 1990–91:541 n. 15. See also his letter in the New York Times, 1 April 1996, p. A16. The high percentage of reversals he reports has been challenged (see the letter by Barry Latzer, 27 March 1996, p. A20), claiming that the National Center for State Courts reported only 15–17% reversals. The discrepacy arose because NCSC did not count habeas petitions granted on appeal from denial in the federal district courts, whereas Liebman's total did. See also Greenhouse 1992, reporting an ABA source to the effect that "[f]ederal judges overturned more than 40% of all death penalty cases they reviewed between July 1976 and May [1991]."

25. National Law Journal, 20 May 1996, p. 1. On the recent revisions in habeas corpus, see New York Times, 8 April 1996, 25 April 1996, p. A18, 4 June 1966, p. D23, and the editorial of 9 May 1966, p. A26.

26. For further discussion see Conference 1995 and Panel Discussion 1996.

27. National Law Journal, 1 April 1996, p. a14., and 25 September 1995, p. A14.

19

International Human Rights Law and the Death Penalty in America

H. A. BEDAU

In 1948 the Universal Declaration of Human Rights affirmed that "everyone has the right to life" (Article 3) and that "no one shall be subjected to torture or to cruel, inhuman or degrading treatment or punishment" (Article 5). Exactly how these provisions would affect the worldwide practice of the death penalty was unclear at the time. The International Covenant on Civil and Political Rights was adopted by the General Assembly in 1966, incorporating this language in Articles 6.1 and 7, respectively. With the coming into force of the Covenant in 1976, there was little doubt that the developing thrust of interpretation of these provisions was in the direction of outlawing the death penalty. However, the only explicit prohibitions affecting the death penalty were in Article 6.5, outlawing the execution of juveniles (persons under eighteen at the time of the crime) and pregnant women.

Not until 1992 did the United States ratify the Covenant. It did so only with several reservations, including ones directed at the death penalty implications of Articles 6 and 7. Obviously, the United States could not ratify the Covenant and remain silent on these provisions, when the death penalty for juveniles (if not for pregnant women) was then allowed in over two dozen states and the death penalty in general enjoyed open support from the Bush administration. No other nation ratifying the Covenant (except Ireland and Norway, for purely technical reasons) filed any reservations concerning Article 6 and its assertion of an "inherent right to life" for all persons. It is the status of these provisions and the reservations by the United States that are particularly troubling.

In 1993, eleven European nations, all of which had ratified the Covenant and also abolished the death penalty under their domestic law, reported that they found U.S. reservations concerning Articles 6 and 7 to be illegal, on the grounds that they were essentially incompatible with the spirit of ratification of the Covenant. (Such an objection by ratifying states to the reservations of another state's ratification was, if not unique, certainly rare.) A year later, the Human Rights Committee (a creature of the Covenant, consisting of eighteen persons appointed from among those nominated by the ratifying nations) declared that it had the authority to determine the validity of reservations.[1]

Under the provisions of the Covenant, nations must supply periodic reports evaluating their own compliance with the terms of the Covenant. The United States did not file its first report until 1994, devoting only a few paragraphs to the current practice and legal provisions affecting the death penalty. In March 1995 John Shattuck, assistant secretary of state for human rights, officially presented the nation's report to the Human Rights Committee. After reviewing the report and the presentation, a majority of the committee declared the U.S. reservations to be illegal (the U.S. representative on this committee, Professor Thomas Buergenthal, was recused); this was followed by a consensus report of the committee affirming the judgment of the majority.

Thus it appears as of the summer of 1995 that the United States, with its constitutional toleration of the death penalty and its attempt to protect this punishment from international scrutiny, has in fact been judged to be in violation of international law. Just how this conflict will unfold and be resolved is unclear. But it is clear that the United States faces a dilemma: Either the State Department, on behalf of the government, refuses to respond to this judgment or it responds. If it chooses not to respond, then the United States risks being judged after the passage of a year or so to have acquiesced in the committee's verdict under the familiar principle that silence argues consent. If it chooses to respond, however, it will have to decide whether to challenge the authority of the Human Rights Committee to render a verdict on the legitimacy of national reservations. On what grounds would an argument to this effect be based? Or should the government consider rescinding our nation's ratification of the Covenant? That step seems unthinkable, given the worldwide importance of the Covenant and the leadership of the United States in propagating an international consciousness of the role of human rights in domestic law.[2]

A straw in the wind, indicating the kind of effect our nation's support for the death penalty can have on the behavior of other nations toward us, occurred late in June 1996, when the Italian government "blocked the extradition to the United States of an Italian wanted in Florida on first degree murder charges because Florida law includes capital punishment among the possible penalties" (Tagliabue 1996).

In addition to the provisions of articles 6 and 7 of the International Covenant on Civil and Political Rights, discussed above, two other international legal instruments deserve mention here. One is the Second Optional Protocol to the International Covenant Aiming at the Abolition of the Death Penalty, adopted by the U.N. General Assembly on 15 December 1989. It declares (Article 1.1) that "No one within the jurisdiction of a State party to the present Optional Protocol shall be executed," and (Article 1.2) that "Each State party shall take all necessary measures to abolish the death penalty within its jurisdiction." This Protocol entered into force on 11 July 1991, following ratification by the tenth nation (Schabas 1993:170).

The other is the Protocol to the American Convention on Human Rights to Abolish the Death Penalty, adopted by the Organization of American States on 8 June 1990. As of 1994, four states had signed the Protocol and three ratified it (Amnesty International 1995a:333).

The United States has neither signed nor ratified either of these Protocols.

Notes

1. For discussion, see U.N. Human Rights Committee, "General Comment No. 24 (52) relating to reservations," Human Rights Law Journal 15 (1994):464–67.

2. This essay was developed through conversation with William A. Schabas; see also Schabas 1994, 1995.

PART V

The Controversy over Race and Class

If one reads through the five concurring opinions in *Furman v. Georgia,* searching for common threads holding together those otherwise independent opinions, one is likely to seize on the twin themes of *arbitrariness* and *discrimination.*[1] The argument from arbitrariness is that the death penalty as applied, beginning with the prosecutor's decision whether to seek it in a particular case to the chief executive's decision whether to grant clemency, fails to show any coherent, rational, principled pattern. Instead, the results, as Justice Stewart observed in *Furman,* are random, like "being struck by lightning."[2] The argument from discrimination is that the death penalty is not administered entirely randomly; on the contrary, its actual administration takes into account legally and morally irrelevant factors—notably race, class, and gender. Implicit in this pair of arguments is the fact that however much the rest of the criminal justice system also exhibits arbitrariness and discrimination, these two grave faults loom much larger when the defendant's life and not only his liberty is at stake. Death, after all, *is* different from other punishments.

Race

Opposition to the death penalty in this country, at least since the 1950s, has been based in part on the belief that this penalty is enforced in a racially discriminatory manner. The basis for this belief need not be reviewed here,[3] but it unquestionably played an important role in motivating the LDF attorneys to launch their attack in the mid-1960s on the constitutionality of capital punishment. The plight of their clients—whether as victims of attempted lynching in earlier years or as latter-day victims of yesterday's racist criminal procedures—brought them face-to-face with the worst aspects of racism in the South.[4] Worry about the impact of the death penalty on African Americans certainly played a role in the Supreme Court's decision in *Furman,* and perhaps in some subsequent cases as well (*Woodson, Roberts,* and *Coker* each involved a black defendant and one or more white victims). Most opponents of the death penalty believe that such racist effects occur throughout the system, not only in the South, and that they cannot be eradicated in the foreseeable future.

Today, few defenders of the death penalty are indifferent to the charge that as administered the death penalty in America is fundamentally a racist institution. On the contrary, some might concede that if the charge can be sustained, and if there is no effective remedy short of abolishing the death penalty, then abolish it we must.[5] Others insist that racism in the administration of the death penalty is no worse than the racism elsewhere in the criminal justice system—yet no one proposes to abolish life imprisonment just because its administration, too, may be racially unfair. Still others concede the charge and propose remedying it by executing more whites (especially whites who kill blacks), not by abolition of the death penalty—the argument of Ernest van den Haag, for instance (see his essay in chapter 32). But most defenders of capital punishment probably contest the charge. Whatever one's opinion, the argument for the racist effects of the death penalty depends on empirical evidence analyzed statistically in ways that the untrained reader finds difficult to grasp—especially when apparently qualified experts can be found on both sides of the issue.

In this part we first look at central portions of the Supreme Court's decision in *McCleskey v. Kemp* (1987), the principal case in which statistically based evidence of racial discrimination was introduced to challenge the death penalty. The argument advanced by McCleskey's attorneys was essentially a vastly more elaborate version of the argument that inaugurated the constitutional attack on the death penalty two decades earlier in *Maxwell v. Bishop.* The Court's decision in *McCleskey,* too, was much the same as in *Maxwell,* except that *McCleskey* was decided by a five-to-four vote. (Justice Harry Blackmun, who joined the Supreme Court five years after his opinion for the appeals court in *Maxwell,* switched sides in *McCleskey* and voted with the dissenters.) The majority opinion for the Court by Justice Lewis F. Powell Jr. (excerpts of which are reprinted here as chapter 20) argued that racial discrimination had not been adequately shown to be among the explanatory factors governing prosecution, conviction, and sentencing in Georgia's post-*Furman* capital cases. Furthermore, even if race of victim and defendant could serve as significant predictors of sentencing outcomes in death penalty cases, there was no constitutional violation of "equal protection of the laws" because such evidence does not show *intentional* discrimination by anybody against defendant McCleskey or against any other given defendant.[6]

Much, of course, turns on exactly what the empirical evidence was. At least the following can be said without fear of contradiction: It was the most elaborate attempt ever made to show the disproportionately racial impact of any public policy. The research was directed by law professor David C. Baldus and two associates—statistician George G. Woodworth and attorney Charles A. Pulaski Jr.—and is presented in exquisite detail in their treatise, *Equal Justice and the Death Penalty: A Legal and Empirical Analysis* (1990). At the same time this book was published, Congress's General Accounting Office (GAO) released its own review of death sentencing research, evaluating more than two dozen empirical studies by a wide variety of investigators, including the Baldus-Woodworth-Pulaski research. The GAO's report is reprinted here as chapter 21; its conclusion? "Our synthesis . . . shows a pattern of evidence indicating racial disparities in the charging, sentencing, and imposition of the death penalty after the *Furman* decision.'' Of course, a ''disparity'' is not necessarily a result of unfair discrimination, as all would agree. It becomes discrimination to the extent that the disparity can be explained only by racial factors having nothing to do with the gravity of the crime or other relevant features that should govern prosecutorial and judicial decisions.[7]

The Court's opinion in *McCleskey* ended by declaring that ''McCleskey's argument is best presented to the legislative bodies.'' That is, any wholesale revision of the nation's death penalty system intended to remove the infection of racism (if such there was) must be designed by the state and national legislatures, not by the federal appellate courts. In response to that challenge, the Racial Justice Act was proposed for congressional enactment. The act would empower the federal courts to review capital cases for possible racial bias by prosecutors and juries and would put the burden on the government to overcome a prima facie case of racial bias. Between 1988 and 1994, different versions of the Racial Justice Act were formulated. During the summer of 1994, as the Omnibus Crime Control Bill was in its final stages, the Racial Justice Act (in the version then known as the Fairness in Sentencing Act) was quietly dropped by the House-Senate conference committee from the proposed legislation after having been adopted in the House; it is unlikely soon to be revived.[8]

When hearings were first held on the Racial Justice Act in 1990, the Department of Justice strongly argued against its adoption, as did the Washington Legal Foundation (a conservative counterpart to the American Civil Liberties Union) and many others. The kinds of reasons offered were essentially those repeated by the department and other critics in both the 1991 and 1994 debates in Congress.[9] Perhaps the most accessible version of that critique appeared in the summer of 1994 at the height of political maneuvering over the proposed act. Provocatively entitled ''Execution by Quota?'' and published in the neoconservative journal *The Public Interest,* it was written by Stanley Rothman and Stephen Powers of the Center for the Study of Social and Political Change at Smith College.

A more popular version of some of the Rothman-Powers charges, ''A Capitol Offense,'' appeared in May 1994 in the nationally syndicated column of George F. Will. Baldus and his two associates wrote a succinct reply to Will's column and implicitly replied to the Rothman-Powers critique as well (a fuller rebuttal appears in their law review article on the subject published later in 1994). Given the Republican control of Congress since November 1994, we are not likely to hear more of the Racial Justice Act in the near future.

Class

Justice William O. Douglas in his concurring opinion in *Furman* remarked, ''One searches our chronicles in vain for the execution of any member of the affluent strata of this society. The Leopolds and Loebs[10] are given prison terms, not sentenced to death.'' Today, the plight of an impoverished defendant in a murder trial is serious, indeed. Court-appointed attorneys, often inexperienced, underpaid, and overworked—especially in the southern states, where most death sentences and executions take place—hardly offer the prospect of a truly fair trial and a vigorous, resourceful defense. Complaints regularly are heard on all sides about the deficient quality of counsel representing defendants on trial for their lives.[11] If one had to single out a recent discussion of this problem as seen through the eyes of a highly experienced observer, one could not do better than to read the essay by Stephen B. Bright, director, Southern Center for Human Rights, in Atlanta, Georgia, reprinted here as chapter 22. Bright is one of the two dozen or so attorneys around the nation who directs litigation on behalf of state death row clients; no one has a better view of the day-to-day events surrounding capital trials and appeals than do these lawyers. What Bright and his colleagues engaged in death penalty litigation have to report is not very reassuring.

It may be helpful to note how others view the issues of arbitrariness and discrimination in our administration of the death penalty. In July 1996 the Geneva-based International Commission of Jurists released a 260 page report on the subject authored by four judges and lawyers from India, Sweden, Nigeria, and Australia. Their conclusion? The death penalty as administered today is "arbitrary, and racially discriminatory, and prospects of a fair hearing for capital offenders cannot . . . be assured" (Evans 1996; cf. also the conclusions of the Commission of Inquiry into the Death Penalty as Practiced in the United States, held in Boston in August 1993 and convened by Amnesty International, in Harlow, Matas, and Rocamora 1995).

Notes

1. See Nakell and Hardy 1987:16.

2. See Bentele 1985, V. Berger 1988, and especially Berk, Weiss, and Boger 1993a for a mathematically sophisticated discussion of the problem; see also the subsequent discussion between Paternoster 1993 and Berk, Weiss, and Boger 1993b.

3. The classic source is, of course, Myrdal 1944. The most recent discussion is in Tonry 1995. For a more general attack on the claim of racism in the criminal justice system, see Wilbanks 1986.

4. See Meltsner 1973, Kluger 1976, Brundage 1993, and Marquart, Ekland-Olson, and Sorensen 1994. From among many individual case studies, see especially McGovern 1982, Smead 1986, Cortner 1988, and Rise 1995.

5. Walter Berns, one of the most thoughtful defenders of the death penalty, verges on this position; see Berns 1979:186–87.

6. Among the many critical discussions of this case, see Berger et al. 1989, Kennedy 1988, and Amsterdam 1988. Willbanks 1988, criticizing the Baldus research, supported the Court's reasoning in *McCleskey.* For a discussion of the Rehnquist Court's struggle in reaching the 5 to 4 decision in *McCleskey,* see Simon 1995:172–211.

7. Subsequent to the GAO report and the Baldus research, there is a considerable literature on racial aspects of the death penalty. See, for example, Amnesty International 1996b, Bright 1995a, Eckholm 1995; Russell 1993; Radelet and Pierce 1991; Winn 1991a, 1991b, 1991c; Death Penalty Information Center 1991, Johnson 1988. One of the rare studies finding no evidence of racial discrimination is Klein and Rolph 1991; they argue that at least in California, race plays no role in capital sentencing.

8. The Fairness in Sentencing Act (1994) provided in part that "An inference that race was the basis of a death sentence is established if valid evidence is presented demonstrating that, at the time the death sentence was imposed, race was a statistically significant factor in decisions to seek or to impose the sentence of death in the jurisidiction in question.... Evidence relevant to establish [such an] inference ... may include evidence that death sentences were, at the time ..., being imposed significantly more frequently in the jurisdiction in question—(1) upon persons of one race than upon persons of another race; or (2) as punishment for capital offenses against persons of one race than as punishment for capital offenses against persons of another race.... If statistical evidence is presented to establish an inference that race was the basis of a sentence of death, the court shall determine the validity of the evidence.... If an inference that race was the basis of a death sentence is established ..., the death sentence may not be carried out unless the government rebuts the inference by a preponderance of the evidence.... [T]he government cannot rely on mere assertions that it did not intend to discriminate or that the cases in which death was imposed fit the statutory criteria for imposition of the death penalty." The text of the proposed Act is reprinted in full in Baldus, Woodworth, and Pulaski 1994b:424–25.

For further discussion of this proposed legislation, see Lungren and Krotoski 1995, Edwards and Conyers 1995, Tabak 1990–91, and especially Baldus, Woodworth, and Pulaski 1994b.

9. See House Hearings 1990a, 1991a, Baldus, Woodworth, and Pulaski 1994b:426–27.

10. Editor's note: In 1924, Nathan Leopold and Richard Loeb were high school students from wealthy Chicago families; they were charged with the "thrill killing" of 14 year-old Bobby Frank. The famous civil liberties attorney, Clarence Darrow, served as their defense counsel and persuaded them to plead guilty. The sole issue before the trial court was their sentence; in his most famous (and longest) oration to a trial court, Darrow managed to get his clients sentenced to life plus 99 years in prison, thus saving them from the electric chair. See Darrow 1991. Loeb was later killed by a fellow prisoner; Leopold went on to a successful career as a medical technician, first in prison and then, after serving three decades of his sentence, in Haiti.

11. See Robbins 1990 and Spangenberg Group 1994.

20

McCleskey v. Kemp, 1987: A Racially Disproportionate Death Penalty System Is Not Unconstitutional

Justice Powell delivered the opinion of the Court.

This case presents the question whether a complex statistical study that indicates a risk that racial considerations enter into capital sentencing determinations proves that petitioner McCleskey's capital sentence is unconstitutional under the Eighth or Fourteenth Amendment. . . .

McCleskey . . . filed a petition for a writ of habeas corpus in the Federal District Court for the Northern District of Georgia. His petition raised 18 claims, one of which was that the Georgia capital sentencing process is administered in a racially discriminatory manner in violation of the Eighth and Fourteenth Amendments to the United States Constitution. In support of his claim, McCleskey proffered a statistical study performed by Professors David C. Baldus, Charles Pulanski, and George Woodworth (the Baldus study) that purports to show a disparity in the imposition of the death sentence in Georgia based on the race of the murder victim and, to a lesser extent, the race of the defendant. The Baldus study is actually two sophisticated statistical studies that examine over 2,000 murder cases that occurred in Georgia during the 1970's. The raw numbers collected by Professor Baldus indicate that defendants charged with killing white persons received the death penalty in 11% of the cases, but defendants charged with killing blacks received the death penalty in only 1% of the cases. The raw numbers also indicate a reverse racial disparity according to the race of the defendant: 4% of the black defendants received the death penalty, as opposed to 7% of the white defendants. . . .

Baldus subjected his data to an extensive analysis, taking account of 230 variables that could have explained the disparities on nonracial grounds. One of his models concludes that, even after taking account of 39 nonracial variables, defendants charged with killing white victims were 4.3 times as likely to receive a death

Reprinted from the plurality opinion for the Court in *McCleskey v. Kemp,* 481 U.S. 279 (1987), by Justice Lewis F. Powell Jr. Substantial portions of the opinion (including all of sections I and IV) have been omitted, and the remaining footnotes renumbered. Justice Powell was joined by Chief Justice Rehnquist and Justices White, O'Connor, and Scalia. Filing dissenting opinions were Justices William Brennan Jr. (joined by Thurgood Marshall), Harry A. Blackmun, and John Paul Stevens; none of their opinions is reprinted here.

sentence as defendants charged with killing blacks. According to this model, black defendants were 1.1 times as likely to receive a death sentence as other defendants. Thus, the Baldus study indicates that black defendants, such as McCleskey, who kill white victims have the greatest likelihood of receiving the death penalty.[1]

The District Court held an extensive evidentiary hearing on McCleskey's petition. Although it believed that McCleskey's Eighth Amendment claim was foreclosed by the Fifth Circuit's decision in Spinkellink v Wainwright, 578 F2d 582, 612, 616 (1978), cert denied, 440 US 976 (1979), it nevertheless considered the Baldus study with care. It concluded that McCleskey's "statistics do not demonstrate a prima facie case in support of the contention that the death penalty was imposed upon him because of his race, because of the race of the victim, or because of any Eighth Amendment concern." McCleskey v Zant, 580 F Supp 338, 379 (ND Ga 1984). As to McCleskey's Fourteenth Amendment claim, the court found that the methodology of the Baldus study was flawed in several respects.[2] Because of these defects, the court held that the Baldus study "fail[ed] to contribute anything of value" to McCleskey's claim. Id., at 372 (emphasis omitted). Accordingly, the court denied the petition insofar as it was based upon the Baldus study.

The Court of Appeals for the Eleventh Circuit, sitting en banc, carefully reviewed the District Court's decision on McCleskey's claim. 753 F2d 877 (1985). It assumed the validity of the study itself and addressed the merits of McCleskey's Eighth and Fourteenth Amendment claims. That is, the court assumed that the study "showed that systematic and substantial disparities existed in the penalties imposed upon homicide defendants in Georgia based on race of the homicide victim, that the disparities existed at a less substantial rate in death sentencing based on race of defendants, and that the factors of race of the victim and defendant were at work in Fulton County." Id., at 895. Even assuming the study's validity, the Court of Appeals found the statistics "insufficient to demonstrate discriminatory intent or unconstitutional discrimination in the Fourteenth Amendment context, [and] insufficient to show irrationality, arbitrariness and capriciousness under any kind of Eighth Amendment analysis." Id., at 891. The court noted:

> The very exercise of discretion means that persons exercising discretion may reach different results from exact duplicates. Assuming each result is within the range of discretion, all are correct in the eyes of the law. It would not make sense for the system to require the exercise of discretion in order to be facially constitutional, and at the same time hold a system unconstitutional in application where that discretion achieved different results for what appear to be exact duplicates, absent the state showing the reasons for the difference. . . .
>
> The Baldus approach . . . would take the cases with different results on what are contended to be duplicate facts, where the differences could not be otherwise explained, and conclude that the different result was based on race alone. . . . This approach ignores the realities. . . . There are, in fact, no exact duplicates in capital crimes and capital defendants. The type of research submitted here tends to show which of the directed factors were effective, but is of restricted use in showing what undirected factors control the exercise of constitutionally required discretion. Id., at 898–99.

The court concluded:

> Viewed broadly, it would seem that the statistical evidence presented here, assuming its validity, confirms rather than condemns the system. . . . The marginal disparity based on the race of the victim tends to support the state's contention that the system is working far differently from the one which Furman condemned. In pre-Furman days, there was no rhyme or reason as to who got the death penalty and who did not. But now, in the vast majority of cases, the reasons for a difference are well documented. That they are not so clear in a small percentage of the cases is no reason to declare the entire system unconstitutional. Id., at 899.

The Court of Appeals affirmed the denial by the District Court of McCleskey's petition for a writ of habeas corpus insofar as the petition was based upon the Baldus study, with three judges dissenting as to McCleskey's claims based on the Baldus study. We granted certiorari, . . . and now affirm.

II

McCleskey's first claim is that the Georgia capital punishment statute violates the Equal Protection Clause of the Fourteenth Amendment.[3] He argues that race has infected the administration of Georgia's statute in two ways: persons who murder whites are more likely to be sentenced to death than persons who murder blacks, and black murderers are more likely to be sentenced to death than white murderers. As a black defendant who killed a white victim, McCleskey claims that the Baldus study demonstrates that he was discriminated against because of his race and because of the race of his victim. In its broadest form, McCleskey's claim of discrimination extends to every actor in the Georgia capital sentencing process, from the prosecutor who sought the death penalty and the jury that imposed the sentence, to the State itself that enacted the capital punishment statute and allows it to remain in effect despite its allegedly discriminatory application. We agree with the Court of Appeals, and every other court that has considered such a challenge, that this claim must fail.

A

Our analysis begins with the basic principle that a defendant who alleges an equal protection violation has the burden of proving "the existence of purposeful discrimination." Whitus v Georgia, 385 US 545 (1967). A corollary to this principle is that a criminal defendant must prove that the purposeful discrimination "had a discriminatory effect" on him. Wayte v United States, 470 US 598, 608 (1985). Thus, to prevail under the Equal Protection Clause, McCleskey must prove that the decisionmakers in *his* case acted with discriminatory purpose. He offers no evidence specific to his own case that would support an inference that racial considerations played a part in his sentence. Instead, he relies solely on the Baldus study. McCleskey argues that the Baldus study compels an inference that his sentence rests on purposeful discrimination. McCleskey's claim that these statistics are sufficient proof of discrimination, without regard to the facts of a particular case, would extend to all capital cases in Georgia, at least where the victim was white and the defendant is black.

The Court has accepted statistics as proof of intent to discriminate in certain limited contexts. First, this Court has accepted statistical disparities as proof of an equal protection violation in the selection of the jury venire in a particular district. Although statistical proof normally must present a "stark" pattern to be accepted as the sole proof of discriminatory intent under the Constitution,[4] "[b]ecause of the nature of the jury-selection task, . . . we have permitted a finding of constitutional violation even when the statistical pattern does not approach [such] extremes." Id., at 266, n 13. Second, this Court has accepted statistics in the form of multiple-regression analysis to prove statutory violations under Title VII of the Civil Rights Act of 1964. Bazemore v Friday, 478 US 385 (1986) (opinion of Brennan, J., concurring in part).

But the nature of the capital sentencing decision, and the relationship of the statistics to that decision, are fundamentally different from the corresponding elements in the venire-selection or Title VII cases. Most importantly, each particular decision to impose the death penalty is made by a petit jury selected from a properly constituted venire. Each jury is unique in its composition, and the Constitution requires that its decision rest on consideration of innumerable factors that vary according to the characteristics of the individual defendant and the facts of the particular capital offense. Thus, the application of an inference drawn from the general statistics to a specific decision in a trial and sentencing simply is not comparable to the application of an inference drawn from general statistics to a specific venire-selection or Title VII case. In those cases, the statistics relate to fewer entities, and fewer variables are relevant to the challenged decisions.[5]

Another important difference between the cases in which we have accepted statistics as proof of discriminatory intent and this case is that, in the venire-selection and Title VII contexts, the decisionmaker has an opportunity to explain the statistical disparity. . . . Here, the State has no practical opportunity to rebut the Baldus study. "[C]ontrolling considerations of . . . public policy," . . . dictate that jurors "cannot be called . . . to testify to the motives and influences that led to their verdict." . . . Similarly, the policy considerations behind a prosecutor's traditionally "wide discretion" suggest the impropriety of our requiring prosecutors to defend their decisions to seek death penalties, "often years after they were made." See Imbler v Pachtman, 424 US 409, 425–426 (1976).[6] Moreover, absent far stronger proof, it is unnecessary to seek such a rebuttal, because a legitimate and unchallenged explanation for the decision is apparent from the record: McCleskey committed an act for which the United States Constitution and Georgia laws permit imposition of the death penalty.

Finally, McCleskey's statistical proffer must be viewed in the context of his challenge. McCleskey challenges decisions at the heart of the State's criminal justice system. "[O]ne of society's most basic tasks is that of protecting the lives of its citizens and one of the most basic ways in which it achieves the task is through criminal laws against murder." Gregg v Georgia, 428 US 153 (1976) (White, J., concurring). Implementation of these laws necessarily requires discretionary judgments. Because discretion is essential to the criminal justice process, we would demand exceptionally clear proof before we would infer that the discretion has been abused. The unique nature of the decisions at issue in this case also counsels against adopting such an inference from the disparities indicated by the Baldus study. Accordingly, we hold that the Baldus study is clearly insufficient to support an inference that any of the decisionmakers in McCleskey's case acted with discriminatory purpose.

B

McCleskey also suggests that the Baldus study proves that the State as a whole has acted with a discriminatory purpose. He appears to argue that the State has violated the Equal Protection Clause by adopting the capital punishment statute and allowing it to remain in force despite its allegedly discriminatory application. But " '[d]iscriminatory purpose' . . . implies more than intent as volition or intent as awareness of consequences. It implies that the decisionmaker, in this case a state legislature, selected or reaffirmed a particular course of action at least in part 'because of,' not merely 'in spite of,' its adverse effects upon an identifiable group." Personnel Administrator of Massachusetts v Feeney, 442 US 256 (1979). . . . For this claim to prevail, McCleskey would have to prove that the Georgia Legislature enacted or maintained the death penalty statute *because of* an anticipated racially discriminatory effect. In Gregg v Georgia, supra, this Court found that the Georgia capital sentencing system could operate in a fair and neutral manner. There was no evidence then, and there is none now, that the Georgia Legislature enacted the capital punishment statute to further a racially discriminatory purpose.[7]

Nor has McCleskey demonstrated that the legislature maintains the capital punishment statute because of the racially disproportionate impact suggested by the Baldus study. As legislatures necessarily have wide discretion in the choice of criminal laws and penalties, and as there were legitimate reasons for the Georgia Legislature to adopt and maintain capital punishment, see Gregg v Georgia. . . . (joint opinion of Stewart, Powell, and Stevens, JJ.), we will not infer a discriminatory purpose on the part of the State of Georgia.[8] Accordingly, we reject McCleskey's equal protection claims.

III

McCleskey also argues that the Baldus study demonstrates that the Georgia capital sentencing system violates the Eighth Amendment. . . .

B

Although our decision in Gregg as to the facial validity of the Georgia capital punishment statute appears to foreclose McCleskey's disproportionality argument, he further contends that the Georgia capital punishment system is arbitrary and capricious in *application,* and therefore his sentence is excessive, because racial considerations may influence capital sentencing decisions in Georgia. We now address this claim.

To evaluate McCleskey's challenge, we must examine exactly what the Baldus study may show. Even Professor Baldus does not contend that his statistics *prove* that race enters into any capital sentencing decisions or that race was a factor in McCleskey's particular case.[9] Statistics at most may show only a likelihood that a particular factor entered into some decisions. There is, of course, some risk of racial prejudice influencing a jury's decision in a criminal case. There are similar risks that other kinds of prejudice will influence other criminal trials. . . . The question "is at what point that risk becomes constitutionally unacceptable," Turner v Murray, 476 US 28 (1986). McCleskey asks us to accept the likelihood allegedly shown by the Baldus study as the constitutional measure of an unacceptable risk of racial prejudice influencing capital sentencing decisions. This we decline to do.

Because of the risk that the factor of race may enter the criminal justice process, we have engaged in "unceasing efforts" to eradicate racial prejudice from our criminal justice system. Batson v Kentucky, 476 US (1986).[10] Our efforts have been guided by our recognition that "the inestimable privilege of trial by jury . . . is a vital principle, underlying the whole administration of criminal justice," Ex parte Milligan, 4 Wall 2, 123 (1866). See Duncan v Louisiana, 391 US 145 (1968). Thus, it is the jury that is a criminal defendant's fundamental "protection of life and liberty against race or color prejudice." Strauder v West Virginia, 100 US 303 (1880). Specifically, a capital sentencing jury representative of a criminal defendant's community assures a " 'diffused impartiality,' " Taylor v Louisiana, 419 US 522. . . .[11]

Individual jurors bring to their deliberations "qualities of human nature and varieties of human experience, the range of which is unknown and perhaps unknowable." Peters v Kiff, 407 US 493 (1972) (opinion of Marshall, J.). The capital sentencing decision requires the individual jurors to focus their collective judgment on the unique characteristics of a particular criminal defendant. It is not surprising that such collective judgments often are difficult to explain. But the inherent lack of predictability of jury decisions does not justify their condemnation. On the contrary, it is the jury's function to make the difficult and uniquely human judgments that defy codification and that "buil[d] discretion, equity, and flexibility into a legal system." H. Kalven & H. Zeisel, The American Jury 498 (1966).

McCleskey's argument that the Constitution condemns the discretion allowed decisionmakers in the Georgia capital sentencing system is antithetical to the fundamental role of discretion in our criminal justice system. Discretion in the criminal justice system offers substantial benefits to the criminal defendant. Not only can a jury decline to impose the death sentence, it can decline to convict or choose to convict of a lesser offense. Whereas decisions against a defendant's interest may be reversed by the trial judge or on appeal, these discretionary exercises of leniency are final and unreviewable. Similarly, the capacity of prosecutorial discretion to provide individualized justice is "firmly entrenched in American law." 2 W. LaFave & D. Israel, Criminal Procedure § 13.2(a), p 160 (1984). As we have noted, a prosecutor can decline to charge, offer a plea bargain,[12] or decline to seek a death sentence in any particular case. . . . Of course, "the power to be lenient [also] is the power to discriminate," K. Davis, Discretionary Justice 170 (1973), but a capital punishment system that did not allow for discretionary acts of leniency "would be totally alien to our notions of criminal justice." Gregg v Georgia, 428 US, at 200, n 50. . . .

C

At most, the Baldus study indicates a discrepancy that appears to correlate with race. Apparent disparities in sentencing are an inevitable part of our criminal justice system.[13] The discrepancy indicated by the Baldus study is "a far cry from the major systemic defects identified in Furman," Pulley v Harris, 465 US, at 54.[14] As this Court has recognized, any mode for determining guilt or punishment "has its weaknesses and the potential for misuse." Singer v United States, 380 US 24 (1965). . . . Specifically, "there can be 'no perfect procedure for deciding in which cases governmental authority should be used to impose death.' " Zant v Stephens, 462 US 862 (1983) (quoting Lockett v Ohio, 438 US, at 605, (plurality opinion of Burger, C. J.)). Despite these imperfections, our consistent rule has been that constitutional guarantees are met when "the mode [for determining guilt or punishment] itself has been surrounded with safeguards to make it as fair as possible." Singer v United States, supra, at 35. . . .

Where the discretion that is fundamental to our criminal process is involved, we decline to assume that what is unexplained is invidious. In light of the safeguards designed to minimize racial bias in the process, the fundamental value of jury trial in our criminal justice system, and the benefits that discretion provides to criminal defendants, we hold that the Baldus study does not demonstrate a constitutionally significant risk of racial bias affecting the Georgia capital sentencing process.[15]

V

Two additional concerns inform our decision in this case. First, McCleskey's claim, taken to its logical conclusion, throws into serious question the principles that underlie our entire criminal justice system. The Eighth Amendment is not limited in application to capital punishment, but applies to all penalties. Solem v Helm, 463 US 277 (1983). . . . Thus, if we accepted McCleskey's claim that racial bias has impermissibly tainted the capital sentencing decision, we could soon be faced with similar claims as to other types of penalty.[16] Moreover, the claim that his sentence rests on the irrelevant factor of race easily could be extended to apply to claims based on unexplained discrepancies that correlate to membership in other minority groups,[17] and even to gender.[18] Similarly, since McCleskey's claim relates to the race of his victim, other claims could apply with equally logical force to statistical disparities that correlate with the race or sex of other actors in the criminal justice system, such as defense attorneys or judges. Also, there is no logical reason that such a claim need be limited to racial or sexual bias. If arbitrary and capricious punishment is the touchstone under the Eighth Amendment, such a claim could—at least in theory—be based upon any arbitrary variable, such as the defendant's facial characteristics,[19] or the physical attractiveness of the defendant or the victim,[20] that some statistical study indicates may be influential in jury decisionmaking. As these examples illustrate, there is no limiting principle to the type of challenge brought by McCleskey.[21] The Constitution does not require that a State eliminate any demonstrable disparity that correlates with a potentially irrelevant factor in order to operate a criminal justice system that includes capital punishment. As we have stated specifically in the context of capital punishment, the Constitution does not ''plac[e] totally unrealistic conditions on its use.'' Gregg v Georgia, 428 US, at 199. . . .

Second, McCleskey's arguments are best presented to the legislative bodies. It is not the responsibility—or indeed even the right—of this Court to determine the appropriate punishment for particular crimes. It is the legislatures, the elected representatives of the people, that are ''constituted to respond to the will and consequently the moral values of the people.'' Furman v Georgia, 408 US, at 383 (Burger, C.J., dissenting). Legislatures also are better qualified to weigh and ''evaluate the results of statistical studies in terms of their own local conditions and with a flexibility of approach that is not available to the courts,'' Gregg v Georgia, supra, at 186. . . . Capital punishment is now the law in more than two-thirds of our States. It is the ultimate duty of courts to determine on a case-by-case basis whether these laws are applied consistently with the Constitution. Despite McCleskey's wide-ranging arguments that basically challenge the validity of capital punishment in our multiracial society, the only question before us is whether in his case, . . . the law of Georgia was properly applied. We agree with the District Court and the Court of Appeals for the Eleventh Circuit that this was carefully and correctly done in this case.

VI

Accordingly, we affirm the judgment of the Court of Appeals for the Eleventh Circuit.

It is so ordered.

Notes

1. Baldus' 230-variable model divided cases into eight different ranges, according to the estimated aggravation level of the offense. Baldus argued in his testimony to the District Court that the effects of racial bias were most striking in the midrange cases. ''[W]hen the cases become tremendously aggravated so that everybody would agree that if we're going to have a death sentence, these are the cases that should get it, the race effects go away. It's only in the mid-range of cases where the decision-makers have a real choice as to what to do. If there's room for the exercise of discretion, then the [racial] factors begin to play

a role.'' App 36. Under this model, Baldus found that 14.4% of the black-victim midrange cases received the death penalty, and 34.4% of the white-victim cases received the death penalty. See Exhibit DB 90, *reprinted in* Supplemental Exhibits 54. According to Baldus, the facts of McCleskey's case placed it within the midrange. App 45–46.

2. Baldus, among other experts, testified at the evidentiary hearing. The District Court ''was impressed with the learning of all of the experts.'' 580 F Supp, at 353 (emphasis omitted). Nevertheless, the District Court noted that in many respects the data were incomplete. In its view, the questionnaires used to obtain the data failed to capture the full degree of the aggravating or mitigating circumstances. Id., at 356. The court criticized the researcher's decisions regarding unknown variables. Id., at 357–58. The researchers could not discover whether penalty trials were held in many of the cases, thus undercutting the value of the study's statistics as to prosecutorial decisions. Id., at 359. In certain cases, the study lacked information on the race of the victim in cases involving multiple victims, on whether or not the prosecutor offered a plea bargain, and on credibility problems with witnesses. Id., at 360. The court concluded that McCleskey had failed to establish by a preponderance of the evidence that the data were trustworthy. ''It is a major premise of a statistical case that the data base numerically mirrors reality. If it does not in substantial degree mirror reality, any inferences empirically arrived at are untrustworthy.'' Ibid.

The District Court noted other problems with Baldus' methodology First, the researchers assumed that all of the information available from the questionnaires was available to the juries and prosecutors when the case was tried. The court found this assumption ''questionable.'' Id., at 361. Second, the court noted the instability of the various models. Even with the 230-variable model, consideration of 20 further variables caused a significant drop in the statistical significance of race. In the court's view, this undermined the persuasiveness of the model that showed the greatest racial disparity, the 39-variable model. Id., at 362. Third, the court found that the high correlation between race and many of the nonracial variables diminished the weight to which the study was entitled. Id., at 363–64.

Finally, the District Court noted the inability of any of the models to predict the outcome of actual cases. As the court explained, statisticians use a measure called an ''r^2'' to measure what portion of the variance in the dependent variable (death sentencing rate, in this case) is accounted for by the independent variables of the model. A perfectly predictive model would have an r^2 value of 1.0. A model with no predictive power would have an r^2 value of 0. The r^2 value of Baldus' most complex model, the 230-variable model, was between .46 and .48. Thus, as the court explained, ''the 230-variable model does not predict the outcome in half of the cases.'' Id., at 361.

3. Although the District Court rejected the findings of the Baldus study as flawed, the Court of Appeals assumed that the study is valid and reached the constitutional issues. Accordingly, those issues are before us. As did the Court of Appeals, we assume the study is valid statistically without reviewing the factual findings of the District Court. Our assumption that the Baldus study is statistically valid does not include the assumption that the study shows that racial considerations actually enter into any sentencing decisions in Georgia. Even a sophisticated multiple regression analysis such as the Baldus study can only demonstrate a *risk* that the factor of race entered into some capital sentencing decisions and a necessarily lesser risk that race entered into any particular sentencing decision.

4. Gomillion v Lightfoot, 364 US 339 (1960), and Yick Wo v Hopkins, 118 US 356 (1886), are examples of those rare cases in which a statistical pattern of discriminatory impact demonstrated a constitutional violation. In Gomillion, a state legislature violated the Fifteenth Amendment by altering the boundaries of a particular city ''from a square to an

uncouth twenty-eight-sided figure.'' 364 US, at 340. The alterations excluded 395 of 400 black voters without excluding a single white voter. In Yick Wo, an ordinance prohibited operation of 310 laundries that were housed in wooden buildings, but allowed such laundries to resume operations if the operator secured a permit from the government. When laundry operators applied for permits to resume operation, all but one of the white applicants received permits, but none of the over 200 Chinese applicants were successful. In those cases, the Court found the statistical disparities ''to warrant and require,'' Yick Wo v Hopkins, supra, at 373, a ''conclusion [that was] irresistible, tantamount for all practical purposes to a mathematical demonstration,'' Gomillion v Lightfoot, supra, at 341, that the State acted with a discriminatory purpose.

5. We refer here not to the number of entities involved in any particular decision, but to the number of entities whose decisions necessarily are reflected in a statistical display such as the Baldus study. The decisions of a jury commission or of an employer over time are fairly attributable to the commission or the employer. Therefore, an unexplained statistical discrepancy can be said to indicate a consistent policy of the decisionmaker. The Baldus study seeks to deduce a state ''policy'' by studying the combined effects of the decisions of hundreds of juries that are unique in their composition. It is incomparably more difficult to deduce a consistent policy by studying the decisions of these many unique entities. It is also questionable whether any consistent policy can be derived by studying the decisions of prosecutors. The District Attorney is elected by the voters in a particular county. See Ga Const, Art 6, § 8, ¶ 1. Since decisions whether to prosecute and what to charge necessarily are individualized and involve infinite factual variations, coordination among district attorney offices across a State would be relatively meaningless. Thus, any inference from statewide statistics to a prosecutorial ''policy'' is of doubtful relevance. Moreover, the statistics in Fulton County alone represent the disposition of far fewer cases than the statewide statistics. Even assuming the statistical validity of the Baldus study as a whole, the weight to be given the results gleaned from this small sample is limited.

6. Although Imbler was decided in the context of damages under 42 USC § 1983 [42 USCS § 1983] actions brought against prosecutors, the considerations that led the Court to hold that a prosecutor should not be required to explain his decisions apply in this case as well: ''[I]f the prosecutor could be made to answer in court each time . . . a person charged him with wrongdoing, his energy and attention would be diverted from the pressing duty of enforcing the criminal law.'' 424 US, at 425. Our refusal to require that the prosecutor provide an explanation for his decisions in this case is completely consistent with this Court's longstanding precedents that hold that a prosecutor need not explain his decisions unless the criminal defendant presents a prima facie case of unconstitutional conduct with respect to his case. See, e.g., Batson v Kentucky, supra; Wayte v United States, supra.

7. McCleskey relies on ''historical evidence'' to support his claim of purposeful discrimination by the State. This evidence focuses on Georgia laws in force during and just after the Civil War. Of course, the ''historical background of the decision is one evidentiary source'' for proof of intentional discrimination. Arlington Heights v Metropolitan Housing Dev. Corp., 429 US, at 267. But unless historical evidence is reasonably contemporaneous with the challenged decision, it has little probative value. Cf. Hunter v Underwood, 471 US 222 (1985) (relying on legislative history to demonstrate discriminatory motivation behind state statute). Although the history of racial discrimination in this country is undeniable, we cannot accept official actions taken long ago as evidence of current intent.

8. Justice Blackmun suggests that our ''reliance on legitimate interests underlying the Georgia Legislature's enactment of its capital punishment statute is . . . inappropriate [be-

cause] it has no relevance in a case dealing with a challenge to the Georgia capital sentencing system *as applied* in McCleskey's case.'' Post, at 349 (emphasis in original). As the dissent suggests, this evidence is not particularly probative when assessing the application of Georgia's capital punishment system through the actions of prosecutors and juries, as we did in Part II-A, supra. But that is not the challenge that we are addressing here. As indicated above, the question we are addressing is whether the legislature maintains its capital punishment statute because of the racially disproportionate impact suggested by the Baldus study. McCleskey has introduced no evidence to support this claim. . . .

9. According to Professor Baldus: ''McCleskey's case falls in [a] grey area where . . . you would find the greatest likelihood that some inappropriate consideration may have come to bear on the decision.

''In an analysis of this type, obviously one cannot say that we can say to a moral certainty what it was that influenced the decision. We can't do that.'' App 45–46.

10. This Court has repeatedly stated that prosecutorial discretion cannot be exercised on the basis of race. Wayte v United States, 470 US, at 608; United States v Batchelder, 442 US 114 (1979); Oyler v Boles, 368 US 448 (1962). . . .

11. In Witherspoon, Justice Brennan joined the opinion of the Court written by Justice Stewart. The Court invalidated a statute that permitted a prosecutor to eliminate prospective jurors by challenging all who expressed qualms about the death penalty. The Court expressly recognized that the purpose of the ''broad discretion'' given to a sentencing jury is ''to decide whether or not death is 'the proper penalty' in a given case,'' noting that ''a juror's general views about capital punishment play an inevitable role in any such decision.'' 391 US, at 519 (emphasis omitted). Thus, a sentencing jury must be composed of persons capable of expressing the ''conscience of the community on the ultimate question of life or death.'' Ibid. The Court referred specifically to the plurality opinion of Chief Justice Warren in Trop v Dulles, 356 US 86 (1958), to the effect that it is the jury that must ''maintain a link between contemporary community values and the penal system . . .'' 391 US, at 519, n 15.

Justice Brennan's condemnation of the results of the Georgia capital punishment system must be viewed against this background. As to community values and the constitutionality of capital punishment in general, we have previously noted, supra, . . . that the elected representatives of the people in 37 States and the Congress have enacted capital punishment statutes, most of which have been enacted or amended to conform generally to the Gregg standards, and that 33 States have imposed death sentences thereunder. In the individual case, a jury sentence reflects the conscience of the community as applied to the circumstances of a particular offender and offense. We reject Justice Brennan's contention that this important standard for assessing the constitutionality of a death penalty should be abandoned.

12. In this case, for example, McCleskey declined to enter a guilty plea. According to his trial attorney: ''[T]he Prosecutor was indicating that we might be able to work out a life sentence if he were willing to enter a plea. But we never reached any concrete stage on that because Mr. McCleskey's attitude was that he didn't want to enter a plea. So it never got any further than just talking about it.'' Tr in No. 4909, p 56 (Jan. 30, 1981).

13. Congress has acknowledged the existence of such discrepancies in criminal sentences, and in 1984 created the United States Sentencing Commission to develop sentencing guidelines. The objective of the guidelines ''is to avoid *unwarranted* sentencing disparities among defendants with similar records who have been found guilty of similar criminal conduct, while maintaining sufficient flexibility to permit individualized sentencing when warranted by mitigating or aggravating factors not taken into account in the guidelines.'' 52 Fed Reg 3920 (1987) (emphasis added). No one contends that all sentencing disparities

can be eliminated. The guidelines, like the safeguards in the Gregg-type statute, further an essential need of the Anglo American criminal justice system—to balance the desirability of a high degree of uniformity against the necessity for the exercise of discretion.

14. The Baldus study in fact confirms that the Georgia system results in a reasonable level of proportionality among the class of murderers eligible for the death penalty. As Professor Baldus confirmed, the system sorts out cases where the sentence of death is highly likely and highly unlikely, leaving a midrange of cases where the imposition of the death penalty in any particular case is less predictable. App 35–36. See n 1, supra.

15. Justice Brennan's eloquent dissent of course reflects his often repeated opposition to the death sentence. His views, that also are shared by Justice Marshall, are principled and entitled to respect. Nevertheless, since Gregg was decided in 1976, seven Members of this Court consistently have upheld sentences of death under Gregg-type statutes providing for meticulous review of each sentence in both state and federal courts. The ultimate thrust of Justice Brennan's dissent is that Gregg and its progeny should be overruled. He does not, however, expressly call for the overruling of any prior decision. Rather, relying on the Baldus study, Justice Brennan, joined by Justices Marshall, Blackmun, and Stevens, questions the very heart of our criminal justice system: the traditional discretion that prosecutors and juries necessarily must have.

We have held that discretion in a capital punishment system is necessary to satisfy the Constitution. Woodson v North Carolina, 428 US 280 (1976). See supra, at 303–6. Yet, the dissent now claims that the "discretion afforded prosecutors and jurors in the Georgia capital sentencing system" violates the Constitution by creating "opportunities for racial considerations to influence criminal proceedings." Post, at 333.

The dissent contends that in Georgia "[n]o guidelines govern prosecutorial decisions . . . and that Georgia provides juries with no list of aggravating and mitigating factors, nor any standard for balancing them against one another." Post, at 333.

Prosecutorial decisions necessarily involve both judgmental and factual decisions that vary from case to case. See ABA Standards for Criminal Justice 3-3.8, 3-3.9 (2d ed 1982). Thus, it is difficult to imagine guidelines that would produce the predictability sought by the dissent without sacrificing the discretion essential to a humane and fair system of criminal justice. Indeed, the dissent suggests no such guidelines for prosecutorial discretion.

The reference to the failure to provide juries with the list of aggravating and mitigating factors is curious. The aggravating circumstances are set forth in detail in the Georgia statute. . . . The jury is not provided with a list of aggravating circumstances because not all of them are relevant to any particular crime. Instead, the prosecutor must choose the relevant circumstances and the State must prove to the jury that at least one exists beyond a reasonable doubt before the jury can even consider imposing the death sentence. It would be improper and often prejudicial to allow jurors to speculate as to aggravating circumstances wholly without support in the evidence.

The dissent's argument that a list of mitigating factors is required is particularly anomalous. We have held that the Constitution requires that juries be allowed to consider "any relevant mitigating factor," even if it is not included in a statutory list. Eddings v Oklahoma, 455 US 104 (1982). See Lockett v Ohio, 438 US 586 (1978). The dissent does not attempt to harmonize its criticism with this constitutional principle. The dissent also does not suggest any standard, much less a workable one, for balancing aggravating and mitigating factors. If capital defendants are to be treated as "uniquely individual human beings," Woodson v North Carolina, supra, at 304, then discretion to evaluate and weigh the circumstances relevant to the particular defendant and the crime he committed is essential.

The dissent repeatedly emphasizes the need for "a uniquely high degree of rationality in imposing the death penalty.'' Post, at 335. Again, no suggestion is made as to how greater ''rationality'' could be achieved under any type of statute that authorizes capital punishment. The Gregg-type statute imposes unprecedented safeguards in the special context of capital punishment. These include: (i) a bifurcated sentencing proceeding; (ii) the threshold requirement of one or more aggravating circumstances; and (iii) mandatory State Supreme Court review. All of these are administered pursuant to this Court's decisions interpreting the limits of the Eighth Amendment on the imposition of the death penalty, and all are subject to ultimate review by the Court. These ensure a degree of care in the imposition of the sentence of death that can be described only as unique. Given these safeguards already inherent in the imposition and review of capital sentences, the dissent's call for greater rationality is no less than a claim that a capital punishment system cannot be administered in accord with the Constitution. As we reiterate, infra, the requirement of heightened rationality in the imposition of capital punishment does not ''plac[e] totally unrealistic conditions on its use.'' Gregg v Georgia, 428 US, at 199, n 50.

16. Studies already exist that allegedly demonstrate a racial disparity in the length of prison sentences. See, e.g., Spohn, Gruhi, & Welch, The Effect of Race on Sentencing: A Reexamination of an Unsettled Question, 16 Law & Soc Rev 71 (1981–1982); Unnever, Frazier, & Henretta, Race Differences in Criminal Sentencing, 21 Sociological Q 197 (1980).

17. In Regents of the University of California v Bakke, 438 US 265 (1978) (opinion of Powell, J.), we recognized that the national ''majority'' ''is composed of various minority groups, most of which can lay claim to a history of prior discrimination at the hands of the State and private individuals.'' Increasingly whites are becoming a minority in many of the larger American cities. There appears to be no reason why a white defendant in such a city could not make a claim similar to McCleskey's if racial disparities in sentencing arguably are shown by a statistical study.

Finally, in our heterogeneous society the lower courts have found the boundaries of race and ethnicity increasingly difficult to determine.

18. See Chamblin, The Effect of Sex on the Imposition of the Death Penalty (speech given at a symposium of the American Psychological Association, entitled ''Extra-legal Attributes Affecting Death Penalty Sentencing,'' New York City, Sept., 1979); Steffensmeier, Effects of Judge's and Defendant's Sex on the Sentencing of Offenders, 14 Psychology, Journal of Human Behavior, 3 (Aug. 1977).

19. See Kerr, Bull, MacCoun, & Rathborn, Effects of Victim Attractiveness, Care and Disfigurement on the Judgements of American and British Mock Jurors, 24 Brit J Social Psych 47 (1985); Johnson, Black Innocence and the White Jury, 83 Mich. L. Rev. 1611 (1985), at 1638, n 128 (citing Shoemaker, South, & Lowe, Facial Stereotypes of Deviants and Judgments of Guilt or Innocence, 51 Social Forces 427 (1973)).

20. Some studies indicate that physically attractive defendants receive greater leniency in sentencing than unattractive defendants, and that offenders whose victims are physically attractive receive harsher sentences than defendants with less attractive victims. Smith & Hed, Effects of Offenders' Age and Attractiveness on Sentencing by Mock Juries, 44 Psychological Rep 691 (1979); Kerr, Beautiful and Blameless: Effects of Victim Attractiveness and Responsibility on Mock Jurors' Verdicts, 4 Personality and Social Psych Bull 479 (1978). But see Baumeister & Darley, Reducing the Biasing Effect of Perpetrator Attractiveness in Jury Simulation, 8 Personality and Social Psych Bull 286 (1982); Schwibbe & Schwibbe, Judgment and Treatment of People of Varied Attractiveness, 48 Psychological Rep 11 (1981); Weiten, The Attraction-Leniency Effect in Jury Research: An Examination of External Validity, 10 J Applied Social Psych 340 (1980).

21. Justice Stevens, who would not overrule Gregg, suggests in his dissent that the infirmities alleged by McCleskey could be remedied by narrowing the class of death-eligible defendants to categories identified by the Baldus study where "prosecutors consistently seek, and juries consistently impose, the death penalty without regard to the race of the victim or the race of the offender." This proposed solution is unconvincing. First, "consistently" is a relative term, and narrowing the category of death-eligible defendants would simply shift the borderline between those defendants who received the death penalty and those who did not. A borderline area would continue to exist and vary in its boundaries. Moreover, because the discrepancy between borderline cases would be difficult to explain, the system would likely remain open to challenge on the basis that the lack of explanation rendered the sentencing decisions unconstitutionally arbitrary.

Second, even assuming that a category with theoretically consistent results could be identified, it is difficult to imagine how Justice Stevens' proposal would or could operate on a case-by-case basis. Whenever a victim is white and the defendant is a member of a different race, what steps would a prosecutor be required to take—in addition to weighing the customary prosecutorial considerations—before concluding in the particular case that he lawfully could prosecute? In the absence of a current, Baldus-type study focused particularly on the community in which the crime was committed, where would he find a standard? Would the prosecutor have to review the prior decisions of community prosecutors and determine the types of cases in which juries in his jurisdiction "consistently" had imposed the death penalty when the victim was white and the defendant was of a different race? And must he rely solely on statistics? Even if such a study were feasible, would it be unlawful for the prosecutor, in making his final decision in a particular case, to consider the evidence of guilt and the presence of aggravating and mitigating factors? However conscientiously a prosecutor might attempt to identify death-eligible defendants under the dissent's suggestion, it would be a wholly speculative task at best, likely to result in less rather than more fairness and consistency in the imposition of the death penalty.

21

Death Penalty Sentencing: Research Indicates Pattern of Racial Disparities

U.S. GENERAL ACCOUNTING OFFICE

The Anti-Drug Abuse Act of 1988 (Public Law 100–690) requires us to study capital sentencing procedures to determine if the race of either the victim or the defendant influences the likelihood that defendants will be sentenced to death. We did an evaluation synthesis—a review and critique of existing research—on this subject to fulfill the mandate. This report provides a summary of our findings and a discussion of our approach and data limitations.

Approach

An evaluation synthesis is a critical integration of findings from existing empirical research on a given topic—in this case death penalty sentencing after the *Furman* decision. First, we identified and collected all potentially relevant studies done at national, state, and local levels from both published and unpublished sources. Computer-generated bibliographic searches and manual reviews of the bibliographies of studies that we obtained contributed to our list of potentially relevant material. We also surveyed 21 criminal justice researchers and directors of relevant organizations whose work relates to death penalty sentencing to identify additional research. We screened more than 200 annotated citations and references to determine relevance to our review. We excluded studies that (1) were based primarily on data collected prior to the *Furman* decision and (2) did not examine race as a factor that might influence death penalty sentencing. From this initial screening we obtained 53 studies that we determined to be relevant.

We then reviewed each of the 53 studies to determine both appropriateness and overall quality of the research. We excluded studies that did not contain empirical data or were duplicative (a few researchers published several articles, with the most

Reprinted from GAO/GGD-90-57, 26 February 1990. Contributors to this report include Lowell Dodge, Director, Administration of Justice Issues; Laurie E. Ekstrand, Chief Social Scientist; Harriet C. Ganson, Analyst-in-Charge; Lisa Cassady, Social Science Analyst; James L. Fremming, Consultant; and Douglas M. Sloane, Statistical Consultant. Some footnotes have been deleted and the rest renumbered.

current including data and findings cited in earlier versions). Twenty-eight studies remained after this assessment. The information included in these studies forms the basis for our findings.

Next, we rated the 28 studies according to research quality. [The studies are listed in the Appendix.] Two social science analysts independently rated each study in five dimensions: (1) study design, (2) sampling, (3) measurement, (4) data collection, and (5) analysis techniques. A rating for overall quality was also given. A third analyst reviewed the raters' assessments to ensure consistency. In addition, a statistician reviewed the studies that used specialized analytic techniques to assess whether the techniques were applied correctly and whether the analyses fully supported the researchers' conclusions.

Finally, we extracted all relevant information on the relationship of race to death penalty sentencing from each of the studies. This information was compared and contrasted across studies to identify similarities and differences in the findings.

Evaluation synthesis has benefits and limitations. The major benefit is that evidence from multiple studies can provide greater support for a finding than evidence from an individual study. The major limitation is that this approach depends on the quantity and quality of the design and methodology of available studies and the comprehensiveness of their reporting. In this case, the body of research concerning discrimination in death penalty sentencing is both of sufficient quality and quantity to warrant the evaluation synthesis approach.

Description of the Studies

We evaluated 28 studies which were done by 21 sets of researchers. The studies covered homicide cases for different time periods through 1988, many states that have the death penalty, and different geographic regions of the country. In three instances, two or more articles were generated from a single database, with each article focusing on a different aspect of the sentencing process. A few researchers used data from other studies in their analyses. Overall, the 28 studies constitute 23 different data sets.

We rated almost half of the studies as high or medium quality; the remainder were rated as low. It is important to evaluate research quality for two reasons: (1) the results of the synthesis should be based on a sufficient number of medium or high quality studies; and (2) it is important to note differences in studies' findings, if any, by the quality of the studies. By quality we mean the strength of the design and the rigor of the analytic technique that leads to a level of confidence we have in the study findings. We judged a study to be high quality if it

- was characterized by a sound design that analyzed homicide cases throughout the sentencing process;
- included legally relevant variables (aggravating and mitigating circumstances); and

- used statistical analysis techniques to control for variables that correlate with race and/or capital sentencing.

We judged a study as medium quality if we found it to be lacking in one or more of the above characteristics. However, the medium quality studies generally were more similar to high quality studies than to low quality studies. Low quality studies typically had weak or flawed designs, relied on less reliable statistical analysis, and were simplistic in interpretation of the data. Studies published before 1985 comprised a larger proportion of lower quality studies than those published subsequently. This coincides with the relatively recent development and use of a more sophisticated statistical technique appropriate for use with data such as those in death penalty studies.

Limitations of the Studies

We critiqued all of the studies to identify methodological limitations in the design and analysis of the research. We identified three major limitations among these studies: (1) the threat of sample selection bias, (2) the problem of omitted variables, and (3) the small sample sizes.

Sample selection bias implies that the cases under consideration are not representative of all the cases of interest. The criminal justice system is characterized by discretionary processes of selection at different points in the system. Racial factors may influence decisions at different stages of the process. A study that considered only whether persons convicted were sentenced to death was especially prone to the biasing effect of sample selection. Racial factors may have influenced decisions earlier in the process, such as whether the prosecutor requested that an offender be charged with capital murder. This discretion exercised early in the process may have the effect of concealing (masking) race effects if analysis is limited only to the later stages.

We found sample selection bias in more than half of the low quality studies; these studies typically analyzed only those cases in which the defendant was convicted of capital murder or received the death penalty. Studies that included all reported homicides and followed the disposition of these defendants from initial charge through subsequent stages of the judicial process are not likely to have been affected by this bias. More than two-thirds of the studies we rated high or medium quality picked up cases prior to conviction and followed these cases through the judicial process.

Another limitation is the problem of omitted variables. This limitation is especially important in studies examining racial discrimination. This is because the effect of race is considered the residual—after all relevant and important variables have been controlled, the effect that remains, the residual, is interpreted to be racial disparity. Omitting relevant variables can affect results by failing to reduce the residual appropriately, thus enhancing the perceived racial disparity. Omitted variables in death penalty research are potentially of two types: (1) variables that were known and were believed to be correlated with race or the death penalty and (2) variables that were not known and may be correlated with race or the death penalty outcome.

Several of the higher quality studies controlled for many variables. For example, one high quality study controlled for more than 200 variables. Only a few variables are shown to be highly explanatory. Most of these are controlled for in the better quality studies. However, there are variables such as strength of evidence or socioeconomic status of the victim and defendant which are difficult to measure or obtain. If there are important omitted variables (either because they are difficult to measure or because they are unknown), other explanations for the differences in death penalty outcomes cannot be excluded. But for another variable to influence the existing disparity it would have to (1) be jointly correlated with both race and the death penalty outcome and (2) operate independently of the factors already included in the analysis.

A third limitation relates to the consequences of the small sample sizes in the analyses of death penalty imposition. The imposition of the death penalty is a relatively rare event. As such, in most studies there were very few cases at the end of the process—the sentencing and imposition stages. The small sample size places limits on the usefulness of statistical techniques for analysis at these final stages and thus limits the rigor of analyses at these stages.

While the severity of the limitations varied, as reflected in the studies' ratings, these limitations do not preclude a meaningful analysis of the studies. We have considered quality in evaluating the studies and arriving at our findings.

Findings

Our synthesis of the 28 studies shows a pattern of evidence indicating racial disparities in the charging, sentencing, and imposition of the death penalty after the *Furman* decision.

In 82 percent of the studies, race of victim was found to influence the likelihood of being charged with capital murder or receiving the death penalty, i.e., those who murdered whites were found to be more likely to be sentenced to death than those who murdered blacks.[1] This finding was remarkably consistent across data sets, states, data collection methods, and analytic techniques. The finding held for high, medium, and low quality studies.

The race of victim influence was found at all stages of the criminal justice system process, although there were variations among studies as to whether there was a race of victim influence at specific stages. The evidence for the race of victim influence was stronger for the earlier stages of the judicial process (e.g., prosecutorial decision to charge defendant with a capital offense, decision to proceed to trial rather than plea bargain) than in later stages. This was because the earlier stages were comprised of larger samples allowing for more rigorous analyses. However, decisions made at every stage of the process necessarily affect an individual's likelihood of being sentenced to death.

Legally relevant variables, such as aggravating circumstances, were influential but did not explain fully the racial disparities researchers found. In the high or medium quality studies, researchers used appropriate statistical techniques to control for legally relevant factors, e.g., prior criminal record, culpability level, heinousness of the crime, and number of victims. The analyses show that after controlling statistically for legally relevant variables and other factors thought to influence death penalty sentencing (e.g., region, jurisdiction), differences remain in the likelihood of receiving the death penalty based on race of victim.

The evidence for the influence of the race of defendant on death penalty outcomes was equivocal. Although more than half of the studies found that race of defendant influenced the likelihood of being charged with a capital crime or receiving the death penalty,[2] the relationship between race of defendant and outcome varied across studies. For example, sometimes the race of defendant interacted with another factor. In one study researchers found that in rural areas black defendants were more likely to receive death sentences, and in urban areas white defendants were more likely to receive death sentences. In a few studies, analyses revealed that the black defendant/white victim combination was the most likely to receive the death penalty. However, the extent to which the finding was influenced by race of victim rather than race of defendant was unclear.

Finally, more than three-fourths of the studies that identified a race of defendant effect found that black defendants were more likely to receive the death penalty. However, the remaining studies found that white defendants were more likely to be sentenced to death.

To summarize, the synthesis supports a strong race of victim influence. The race of offender influence is not as clear cut and varies across a number of dimensions. Although there are limitations to the studies' methodologies, they are of sufficient quality to support the synthesis findings.

We are sending copies of this report to cognizant congressional committees, the Attorney General, and other interested parties.

Notes

1. When we refer to a finding of racial disparities at the sentencing and imposition stages we are, in fact, including disparities that occurred in earlier stages of the judicial process, e.g., charging and decision to proceed to trial.
2. About two-thirds of these studies were of high or medium quality.

Appendix: List of Studies

Arkin, Stephen. "Discrimination and Arbitrariness in Capital Punishment: An Analysis of Post-Furman Murder Cases in Dade County, Florida, 1973–1976." *Stanford Law Review,* Vol. 33 (November 1980) 75–101.

Baldus, David, George Woodworth, and Charles Pulaski. *Equal Justice and the Death Penalty: A Legal and Empirical Analysis.* Boston: Northeastern University Press, 1990.

Barnett, Arnold. "Some Distribution Patterns for the Georgia Death Sentence." *University of California Davis Law Review,* Vol. 18, No. 4 (Summer 1985) 1327–74.

Berk, Richard and Joseph Lowery. "Factors Affecting Death Penalty Decisions in Mississippi." Unpublished manuscript, June 1985.

Bienen, Leigh et al. "The Reimposition of Capital Punishment in New Jersey: The Role of Prosecutorial Discretion." *Rutgers Law Review* (Fall 1988) 27–372.

Bowers, William. "The Pervasiveness of Arbitrariness and Discrimination Under Post-Furman Capital Statutes." *Journal of Criminal Law & Criminology,* Vol 74. No. 3 (Fall 1983) 1067–100.

Bowers, William and Glenn Pierce. "Arbitrariness and Discrimination Under Post-Furman Capital Statutes." *Crime and Delinquency* (October 1980) 563–635.

Ekland-Olson, Sheldon. "Structured Discretion, Racial Bias and the Death Penalty: The First Decade After Furman in Texas." *Social Science Quarterly,* Vol. 69 (December 1988) 853–73.

Foley, Linda. "Florida After the Furman Decision: The Effect of Extralegal Factors on the Processing of Capital Offense Cases." *Behavioral Sciences & the Law,* Vol. 5, No. 4 (Autumn 1987) 457–65.

Foley, Linda and Richard Powell. "The Discretion of Prosecutors, Judges, and Juries in Capital Cases." *Criminal Justice Review* Vol. 7, No. 2 (1982) 16–22.

Gross, Samuel and Robert Mauro. "Patterns of Death: An Analysis of Racial Disparities in Capital Sentencing and Homicide Victimization." *Stanford Law Review,* Vol. 37 (1984) 27–153.

Keil, Thomas and Gennaro Vito. "Race and the Death Penalty in Kentucky Murder Trials: An Analysis of Post-Gregg Outcomes." Forthcoming in *Justice Quarterly.*

Keil, Thomas and Gennaro Vito. "Race, Homicide Severity, and Application of the Death Penalty: A Consideration of the Barnett Scale." *Criminology,* Vol. 27, No. 3 (1989) 511–35.

Kleck, Gary. "Racial Discrimination in Criminal Sentencing: A Critical Evaluation of the Evidence with Additional Evidence on the Death Penalty." *American Sociological Review,* Vol. 46 (1981) 783–805.

Klein, Stephen. "Relationship of Offender and Victim Race to Death Penalty Sentences in California." Unpublished manuscript, The Rand Corporation (1989).

Klein, Stephen, Allen Abrahamse, and John Rolph. "Racial Equity in Prosecutor Requests for the Death Penalty." Unpublished manuscript, The Rand Corporation (1987).

Klemm, Margaret F. "The Determinants of Capital Sentencing in Louisiana, 1975–1984." Dissertation, University of New Orleans (1986).

Lewis, Peter, Henry Mannle, and Harold Vetter. "A Post-Furman Profile of Florida's Condemned—A Question of Discrimination in Terms of Race of the Victim and a Comment on Spenkelink v. Wainwright." *Stetson Law Review,* Vol. IX, No. 1 (1979) 1–45.

Murphy, Elizabeth. "The Application of the Death Penalty in Cook County." *Illinois Bar Journal,* Vol. 93 (1984) 90–95.

Nakell, Barry and Kenneth Hardy. *The Arbitrariness of the Death Penalty.* Philadelphia: Temple University Press, 1987.

Paternoster, Raymond and Ann Marie Kazyaka. "The Administration of the Death Penalty in South Carolina: Experiences over the First Few Years." *South Carolina Law Review,* Vol. 39, No. 2 (1988) 245–414.

Radelet, Michael. "Racial Characteristics and the Imposition of the Death Penalty." *American Sociological Review,* Vol. 46 (1981) 918–27.

Radelet, Michael and Margaret Vandiver. "The Florida Supreme Court and Death Penalty Appeals." *Journal of Criminal Law and Criminology,* Vol. 74, No. 3 (1983) 913–26.

Radelet, Michael and Glenn Pierce. "Race and Prosecutorial Discretion in Homicide Cases." *Law and Society Review,* Vol. 19, No. 4 (1985) 587–621.

Riedel, Marc. "Discrimination in the Imposition of the Death Penalty: A Comparison of the Characteristics of Offenders Sentenced Pre-Furman and Post-Furman." *Temple Law Quarterly,* Vol. 49, No. 2 (1976) 261–87.

Smith, Dwayne M. "Patterns of Discrimination in Assessments of the Death Penalty: The Case of Louisiana." *Journal of Criminal Justice,* Vol. 15 (1987) 279–86.

Vito, Gennaro and Thomas Keil. "Capital Sentencing in Kentucky: An Analysis of the Factors Influencing Decision Making in the Post-Gregg Period." *Journal of Criminal Law & Criminology,* Vol. 79, No. 2 (Summer 1988) 483–508.

Zeisel, Hans. "Race Bias in the Administration of the Death Penalty: The Florida Experience." *Harvard Law Review,* Vol. 95, No. 2 (December 1981) 456–68.

22

Counsel for the Poor: The Death Sentence Not for the Worst Crime but for the Worst Lawyer

STEPHEN B. BRIGHT

After years in which she and her children were physically abused by her adulterous husband, a woman in Talladega County, Alabama, arranged to have him killed. Tragically, murders of abusive spouses are not rare in our violent society, but seldom are they punished by the death penalty. Yet this woman was sentenced to death. Why?

It may have been in part because one of her court-appointed lawyers was so drunk that the trial had to be delayed for a day after he was held in contempt and sent to jail. The next morning, he and his client were both produced from jail, the trial resumed, and the death penalty was imposed a few days later.[1] It may also have been in part because this lawyer failed to find hospital records documenting injuries received by the woman and her daughter, which would have corroborated their testimony about abuse. And it may also have been because her lawyers did not bring their expert witness on domestic abuse to see the defendant until 8 P.M. on the night before he testified at trial.[2]

Poor people accused of capital crimes are often defended by lawyers who lack the skills, resources, and commitment to handle such serious matters. This fact is confirmed in case after case. It is not the facts of the crime, but the quality of legal representation,[3] that distinguishes this case, where the death penalty was imposed, from many similar cases, where it was not.

The woman in Talladega, like any other person facing the death penalty who cannot afford counsel, is entitled to a court-appointed lawyer under the Supreme Court's decision in *Powell v. Alabama.* But achieving competent representation in capital and other criminal cases requires much more than the Court's recognition, in *Powell* and in *Gideon v. Wainwright,* of the vital importance of counsel and of "thoroughgoing investigation and preparation." Providing better representation to-

Reprinted from *Yale Law Journal* 103, no. 7 (May 1994): 1835–83 and by permission of the author. Some footnotes have been omitted and the rest renumbered.

day than the defendants had in Scottsboro in 1931 requires money, a structure for providing indigent defense that is independent of the judiciary and prosecution, and skilled and dedicated lawyers. As Anthony Lewis observed after the *Gideon* decision extended the right to counsel to all state felony prosecutions:

> It will be an enormous task to bring to life the dream of *Gideon v. Wainwright*—the dream of a vast, diverse country in which every person charged with a crime will be capably defended, no matter what his economic circumstances, and in which the lawyer representing him will do so proudly, without resentment at an unfair burden, sure of the support needed to make an adequate defense.[4]

More than sixty years after *Powell* and thirty years after *Gideon,* this task remains uncompleted, the dream unrealized. This essay describes the pervasiveness of deficient representation, examines the reasons for it, and considers the likelihood of improvement.

I. The Difference a Competent Lawyer Makes in a Capital Case

Arbitrary results, which are all too common in death penalty cases, frequently stem from inadequacy of counsel. The process of sorting out who is most deserving of society's ultimate punishment does not work when the most fundamental component of the adversary system, competent representation by counsel, is missing.[5] Essential guarantees of the Bill of Rights may be disregarded because counsel failed to assert them, and juries may be deprived of critical facts needed to make reliable determinations of guilt or punishment. The result is a process that lacks fairness and integrity.

For instance, the failure of defense counsel to present critical information is one reason that Horace Dunkins was sentenced to death in Alabama. Before his execution in 1989, when newspapers reported that Dunkins was mentally retarded, at least one juror came forward and said she would not have voted for the death sentence if she had known of his condition.[6] Nevertheless, Dunkins was executed.

This same failure of defense counsel to present critical information also helps account for the death sentences imposed on Jerome Holloway—who has an IQ of 49 and the intellectual capacity of a 7-year old—in Bryan County, Georgia, and William Alvin Smith—who has an IQ of 65—in Oglethorpe County, Georgia. It helps explain why Donald Thomas, a schizophrenic youth, was sentenced to death in Atlanta, where the jury knew nothing about his mental impairment because his lawyer failed to present any evidence about his condition. In each of these cases, the jury was unable to perform its constitutional obligation to impose a sentence based on "a reasoned *moral* response to the defendant's background, character and crime."[7] because it was not informed by defense counsel of the defendant's background and character.

It can be said confidently that the failure to present such evidence made a difference in the Holloway, Smith, and Thomas cases. After each was reversed—

one of them for reasons having nothing to do with counsel's incompetence—the pertinent information was presented to the court by new counsel, the death sentence was not imposed. But for many sentenced to death, such as Horace Dunkins, there is no second chance.

Quality legal representation also made a difference for Gary Nelson and Federico Martinez-Macias, but they did not receive it until years after they were wrongly convicted and sentenced to death. Nelson was represented at his capital trial in Georgia in 1980 by a sole practitioner who had never tried a capital case. The court-appointed lawyer, who was struggling with financial problems and a divorce, was paid at a rate of only $15 to $20 per hour. His request for co-counsel was denied. The case against Nelson was entirely circumstantial, based on questionable scientific evidence, including the opinion of a prosecution expert that a hair found on the victim's body could have come from Nelson. Nevertheless, the appointed lawyer was not provided funds for an investigator and, knowing a request would be denied, did not seek funds for an expert. Counsel's closing argument was only 255 words long. The lawyer was later disbarred for other reasons.

Nelson had the good fortune to be represented pro bono in postconviction proceedings by lawyers willing to spend their own money to investigate Nelson's case.[8] They discovered that the hair found on the victim's body, which the prosecution expert had linked to Nelson, lacked sufficient characteristics for microscopic comparison. Indeed, they found that the Federal Bureau of Investigation had previously examined the hair and found that it could not validly be compared. As a result of such inquiry, Gary Nelson was released after eleven years on death row.

Federico Martinez-Macias was represented at his capital trial in El Paso, Texas, by a court-appointed attorney paid only $11.84 per hour. Counsel failed to present an available alibi witness, relied upon an incorrect assumption about a key evidentiary point without doing the research that would have corrected his erroneous view of the law, and failed to interview and present witnesses who could have testified in rebuttal of the prosecutor's case. Martinez-Macias was sentenced to death.

Martinez-Macias received competent representation for the first time when a Washington, D.C., firm took his case pro bono. After a full investigation and development of facts regarding his innocence, Martinez-Macias won federal habeas corpus relief. An El Paso grand jury refused to re-indict him and he was released after nine years on death row.[9]

Inadequate representation often leaves the poor without the protections of the Bill of Rights. An impoverished person was sentenced to death in Jefferson County, Georgia, in violation of one of the most basic guarantees of our Bill of Rights—the right to a representative jury selected without discrimination on the basis of race. African-Americans make up 54.5% of the population of that county, but the jury pool was only 21.6% black, a severe underrepresentation of over 50%. But this issue was not properly raised and preserved by the court-appointed lawyer for the accused. The defendant had the extreme misfortune of being represented—over his protests—by a court-appointed lawyer who, when later asked to name the criminal law decisions from any court with which he was familiar, could name only two: "*Miranda* and *Dred Scott.*" As a result of the lawyer's failure to challenge the racial discrimination at or before trial, the reviewing courts held that the defendant was barred from vindication of his constitutional rights.

The difference that representative juries and competent counsel make in capital cases is illustrated by the cases of two codefendants, John Eldon Smith and Rebecca Machetti. They were sentenced to death by unconstitutionally composed juries within a few weeks of each other in Bibb County, Georgia. Machetti's lawyers challenged the jury composition in state court; Smith's lawyers did not because they were unaware of the Supreme Court decision prohibiting gender discrimination in juries.

A new trial was ordered for Machetti by the federal court of appeals. At that trial, a jury which fairly represented the community imposed a sentence of life imprisonment. The federal courts refused to consider the identical issue in Smith's case because his lawyers had not preserved it. He was executed, becoming the first person to be executed under the Georgia death penalty statute upheld by the U.S. Supreme Court in 1976. Had Machetti been represented by Smith's lawyers in state court and Smith by Machetti's lawyers, Machetti would have been executed and Smith would have obtained federal habeas corpus relief.

In these examples, imposition of the death penalty was not so much the result of the heinousness of the crime or the incorrigibility of the defendant—the factors upon which imposition of capital punishment supposedly is to turn—but rather of how bad the lawyers were. In consequence, a large part of the death row population is made up of people who are distinguished by neither their records nor the circumstances of their crimes, but by their abject poverty, debilitating mental impairments, minimal intelligence, and the poor legal representation they received.

A member of the Georgia Board of Pardons and Paroles has said that if the files of 100 cases punished by death and 100 punished by life were shuffled, it would be impossible to sort them out by sentence based upon information in the files about the crime and the offender.[10] A justice of the Mississippi Supreme Court made the same observation about the imposition of death sentences in his state in testimony before the U.S. Senate Judiciary Committee:

> I dare say I could take every death sentence case that we have had where we have affirmed, give you the facts and not tell you the outcome, and then pull an equal number of murder cases that have been in our system, give you the facts and not tell you the outcome, and challenge you to pick which ones got the death sentence and which ones did not, and you couldn't do it.[11]

Although it has long been fashionable to recite the disgusting facts of murder cases to show how deserving of death particular defendants may be, such renditions fail to answer whether the selection process is a principled one based on neutral, objective factors that provide a "meaningful basis for distinguishing the few cases in which the [death] penalty is imposed from the many cases in which it is not."[12] Virtually all murders involve tragic and gruesome facts. However, the death penalty is imposed, on average, in only 250 cases of the approximately 20,000 homicides that occur each year in the United States. Whether death is imposed frequently turns on the quality of counsel assigned to the accused.

II. The Pervasive Inadequacy of Counsel for the Poor and the Reasons for it

Inadequate legal representation does not occur in just a few capital cases. It is pervasive in those jurisdictions which account for most of the death sentences. The American Bar Association concluded after an exhaustive study of the issues that "the inadequacy and inadequate compensation of counsel at trial" was one of the "principal failings of the capital punishment systems in the states today."[13] Justice Thurgood Marshall observed that "capital defendants frequently suffer the consequences of having trial counsel who are ill equipped to handle capital cases."[14] The *National Law Journal,* after an extensive study of capital cases in six Southern states, found that capital trials are "more like a random flip of the coin than a delicate balancing of the scales" because the defense lawyer is too often "ill trained, unprepared . . . [and] grossly underpaid."[15] Many observers from a variety of perspectives and from different states have found the same scandalous quality of legal representation.

These assessments are supported by numerous cases in which the poor were defended by lawyers who lacked even the most rudimentary knowledge, resources, and capabilities needed for the defense of a capital case. Death sentences have been imposed in cases in which defense lawyers had not even read the state's death penalty statute or did not know that a capital trial is bifurcated into separate determinations of guilt and punishment.[16] State trial judges and prosecutors—who have taken oaths to uphold the law, including the Sixth Amendment—have allowed capital trials to proceed and death sentences to be imposed even when defense counsel fought among themselves or presented conflicting defenses for the same client,[17] referred to their clients by a racial slur,[18] cross-examined a witness whose direct testimony counsel missed because he was parking his car,[19] slept through part of the trial,[20] or was intoxicated during trial.[21] Appellate courts often review and decide capital cases on the basis of appellate briefs that would be rejected in a first-year legal writing course in law school.

There are several interrelated reasons for the poor quality of representation in these important cases. Most fundamental is the wholly inadequate funding for the defense of indigents. As a result, there is simply no functioning adversary system in many states. Public defender programs have never been created or properly funded in many jurisdictions. The compensation provided to individual court-appointed lawyers is so minimal that few accomplished lawyers can be enticed to defend capital cases. Those who do take a capital case cannot afford to devote the time required to defend it properly. As a result, the accused are usually represented by lawyers who lack the experience, expertise, and resources of their adversaries on the prosecution side.

Many state court judges, instead of correcting this imbalance, foster it by intentionally appointing inexperienced and incapable lawyers to defend capital cases, and denying funding for essential expert and investigative needs of the defense. The minimal standard of legal representation in the defense of poor people, as currently interpreted by the Supreme Court, offers little protection to the poor person stuck with a bad lawyer.

A. *The Lack of a Functioning Adversary System*

Many death penalty states have two state-funded offices that specialize in handling serious criminal cases. Both employ attorneys who generally spend years—some even their entire careers—handling criminal cases. Both pay decent annual salaries and provide health care and retirement benefits. Both send their employees to conferences and continuing legal education programs each year to keep them up to date on the latest developments in the law. Both have at their disposal a stable of investigative agencies, a wide range of experts, and mental health professionals anxious to help develop and interpret facts favorable to their side. Unfortunately, however, in many states both of these offices are on the same side: the prosecution.

One is the District Attorney's office in each judicial district, whose lawyers devote their time exclusively to handling criminal matters in the local court systems. These lawyers acquire considerable expertise in the trial of criminal cases, including capital cases. There are, for example, prosecutors in the District Attorney's office in Columbus, Georgia, who have been trying death penalty cases since the state's current death penalty statute was adopted in 1973.

The other office is the state Attorney General's office, which usually has a unit made up of lawyers who specialize in handling the appeals of criminal cases and habeas corpus matters. Here, too, lawyers build expertise in handling capital cases. For example, the head of the unit that handles capital litigation for the Georgia Attorney General has been involved in that work since 1976, the same year the Supreme Court upheld Georgia's death penalty statute. She brings to every case a wealth of expertise developed in seventeen years of litigating capital cases in all the state and federal courts involved in Georgia cases. She and her staff are called upon by district attorneys around the state for consultation on pending cases and, on occasion, will assist in trial work. It is the normal practice in Georgia that briefs by *both* the district attorney and the attorney general are filed with the Georgia Supreme Court on the direct appeal of a capital case.

The specialists in the offices of both the district attorneys and the attorneys general have at their call local, state, and, when needed, federal investigative and law enforcement agencies. They have a group of full-time experts at the crime laboratory and in the medical examiner's offices to respond to crime scenes and provide expert testimony when needed. If mental health issues are raised, the prosecution has a group of mental health professionals at the state mental facilities. No one seriously contends that these professional witnesses are objective. They routinely testify for the prosecution as part of their work, and prosecutors enjoy longstanding working relationships with them.

In Alabama, Georgia, Mississippi, Louisiana, Texas, and many other states with a unique fondness for capital punishment, there is no similar degree of specialization or resources on the other side of capital cases. A poor person facing the death penalty may be assigned an attorney who has little or no experience in the defense of capital or even serious criminal cases, one reluctant or unwilling to defend him, one with little or no empathy or understanding of the accused or his particular plight, one with little or no knowledge of criminal or capital punishment law, or one with no understanding of the need to document and present mitigating circumstances. Although it is widely acknowledged that at least two lawyers, supported by investigative and expert assistance, are required to defend a capital case, some of the jurisdictions with the largest number of death sentences still assign only one lawyer to defend a capital case.[22]

In contrast to the prosecution's virtually unlimited access to experts and investigative assistance, the lawyer defending the indigent accused in a capital case may not have any investigative or expert assistance to prepare for trial and present a defense. A study of twenty capital cases in Philadelphia in 1991 and 1992 found that the court "paid for investigators in eight of the twenty cases, spending an average of $605 in each of the eight" and that the court "paid for psychologists in two of them, costing $400 in one case, $500 in the other."[23] It is impossible even to begin a thorough investigation or obtain a comprehensive mental health evaluation for such paltry amounts.

Although the Supreme Court has held that indigent defendants may be entitled to expert assistance in certain circumstances, defense attorneys often do not even request such assistance because they are indifferent or know that no funds will be available.[24] Courts often refuse to authorize funds for investigation and experts by requiring an extensive showing of need that frequently cannot be made without the very expert assistance that is sought. Many lawyers find it impossible to maneuver around this "Catch 22," but even when a court recognizes the right to an expert, it often authorizes so little money that no competent expert will get involved.

An indigent accused facing the death penalty in Columbus, Georgia, was assigned counsel by the local trial judge, a former district attorney who had tried high profile capital cases on the way to becoming a judge.[25] Neither of the two lawyers appointed had ever tried a capital case before. The lawyers were denied any funds for an investigator or expert assistance. The case was prosecuted by an assistant district attorney with over fifteen years of experience in trying capital and other criminal cases. The defense was unable to investigate the case or present any expert testimony in response to the state's fingerprint and identification technicians, ballistics expert, coroner, and medical examiner.

An Alabama attorney, appointed without co-counsel and granted only $500 for expert and investigative expenses to defend a highly publicized capital case, facing three prosecutors and an array of law enforcement agencies and expert witnesses, described his situation:

> Without more than $500, there was only one choice, and that is to go to the bank and to finance this litigation, myself, and I was just financially unable to do that. It would have cost probably in excess of thirty to forty thousand dollars, and I just could not justify taking those funds from my practice, or my family at that time.[26]

Not surprisingly, the attorney was simply unable to investigate the case properly:

> I could not take days at a time out of my office to do essentially non-legal work. And investigation is necessary, certainly, to prepare a case, but it is non-legal. . . . You're actually pounding the pavement, trying to come up with the same information that a person who is paid substantially less per hour could take care of, I mean,

> whether it be the investigator for the Sheriff's Department or the District Attorney's office or the F.B.I., or the U.S. Attorney's office. You don't find the U.S. Attorney pounding the pavement, trying to investigate facts. . . . And it just creates a terrible situation when you have to do everything for yourself.[27]

As a result, much of the investigation simply was not done and critical evidence was not presented. With regard to the lack of funds for expert witnesses, the lawyer testified that in civil cases, which constituted 90% of his caseload, he would have hired the required experts because failure to do so would have constituted malpractice.

An attorney involved in the defense of many capital cases in Arkansas has described how lawyers in that state are forced to perform "a sort of uninformed legal triage," ignoring some issues, lines of investigation, and defenses because of the lack of adequate compensation and resources. He described the costs of such an approach: "The lawyer pays some in reputation, perhaps, but it is his client who must pay with his liberty or life."[28]

The adversary system often breaks down at the appellate level as well. The poor defendant usually does not receive representation equal to that of the prosecution in a state like Georgia, where on direct appeal of capital cases, specialists in the offices of the Attorney General and District Attorney both file briefs for the state. The poor person sentenced to death may be represented by a lawyer with little or no appellate experience, no knowledge of capital punishment law, and little or no incentive or inclination to provide vigorous advocacy. For example, in one Georgia case, the court-appointed attorney filed a brief containing only five pages of argument, and that only after the Georgia Supreme Court threatened to impose sanctions.[29] The lawyer did not raise as an issue the trial court's charge to the sentencing jury, which was later found by the U.S. Court of Appeals to have violated the Constitution, did not appear for oral argument, and did not file a supplemental brief on the jury instruction issue even after requested to do so by the court. Nevertheless, the Georgia Supreme Court did not appoint other counsel or require adequate briefing. Instead, with nothing more before it than counsel's deficient performance, the court upheld the conviction and death sentence. The death sentence was later set aside by the U.S. Court of Appeals. There have been numerous other instances of grossly deficient representation on appeal in cases of those condemned to die.

B. The Lack of Indigent Defense Programs

In many jurisdictions where capital punishment is frequently imposed, there are no comprehensive public defender systems whose resources can parallel the prosecutorial functions of the district attorneys' offices.[30] There are no appellate defender offices that parallel the function of the capital litigation sections of the attorneys general's offices. In fact, there is no coherent system at all, but a hodgepodge of approaches that vary from county to county.

In many jurisdictions, judges simply appoint members of the bar in private practice to defend indigents accused of crimes. The lawyers appointed may not want the cases, may receive little or no compensation for the time and expense of handling them, may lack any interest in criminal law, and may not have the skill to defend those accused of a crime. As a result, the poor are often represented by inexperienced lawyers who view their responsibilities as unwanted burdens, have no inclination to help their clients, and have no incentive to develop criminal trial skills. Lawyers can make more money doing almost anything else. Even many lawyers who have an interest in criminal defense work simply cannot afford to continue to represent indigents while also repaying their student loans and meeting their familial obligations.

Some counties employ a "contract system" in which the county contracts with an attorney in private practice to handle all of the indigent cases for a specified amount. Often contracts are awarded to the lawyer—or group of lawyers—who bids the lowest. The lawyer is still free to generate other income through private practice. Any money spent on investigation and experts comes out of the amount the lawyer receives. These programs are well known for the exceptionally short shrift that the poor clients receive and the lack of expenditures for investigative and expert assistance.[31]

A third system is the employment of a group of lawyers or an organization to handle all indigent criminal cases while not engaging in any outside practice. These lawyers are usually called "public defenders," although in some jurisdictions they lack the investigative and support staff that is considered part of a genuine public defender program. Some of these offices employ remarkably dedicated attorneys, whose jobs are nonetheless made almost impossible by overwhelming caseloads and low funding.

For example, the Fulton County Public Defender program, which serves the courts in Atlanta, has achieved nationwide notoriety for its high caseloads—an average of 530 felony cases per attorney for each year plus extraditions, probation revocations, commitment, and special hearings—and grossly inadequate funding. A public defender in Atlanta may be assigned as many as forty-five new cases at one arraignment. At that time, upon first meeting these clients—chained together—for a nonprivate, nonconfidential "interview" in a holding area near the courtroom, she may plead many of them guilty and have them sentenced on the spot. As one public defender described disposing of seventeen indigent defendants: "I met 'em, pled 'em and closed 'em—all in the same day."[32] This system of criminal procedure is known as "slaughterhouse justice." When one lawyer in the office, after closing 476 cases in ten months and still carrying a caseload of 122, asserted her ethical obligation to limit her caseload, she was berated by the trial judge, who refused her request; she was eventually demoted to juvenile court by the director of her office.

A public defender in New Orleans represented 418 defendants during the first seven months of 1991. During this time, he entered 130 guilty pleas at arraignment and had at least one serious case set for trial on every single trial date during the period. In "routine cases," he received no investigative support because the three investigators in the public defender's office were responsible for more than 7000 cases per year. No funds were available for expert witnesses. The Louisiana Supreme Court found that, because of the excessive caseloads and insufficient resources of the public defender's office, the clients served by this system are "not provided with the effective assistance of counsel the [C]onstitution requires."[33]

The structure of indigent defense not only varies among states, it varies within many states from county to county. Some localities employ a combination of these programs. All of these approaches have several things in common. They evince the gross underfunding that pervades indigent defense. They are unable to attract and keep experienced and qualified attorneys because of lack of compensation and overwhelming workloads. Just when lawyers reach the point when they have handled enough cases to begin avoiding basic mistakes, they leave criminal practice and are replaced by other young, inexperienced lawyers who are even less able to deal with the overwhelming caseloads. Generally, no standards are employed for assignment of cases to counsel or for the performance of counsel. And virtually no resources are provided for investigative and expert assistance or defense counsel training.

The situation has further deteriorated in the last few years. This is largely due to the increased complexity of cases and the increase in the number of cases resulting from expanded resources for police and prosecution and the lack of a similar increase, and perhaps even a decline, in funding for defense programs. The quality and funding for defense programs often varies greatly from one county or judicial district to another in the same state. Texas, which has one of the largest death row populations and has carried out the most executions since the resumption of capital punishment in 1976, is one of eight states in which indigent defense is handled at the county level with no state funding. Funding for indigent defense varies significantly from county to county. In Louisiana, the indigent defense system is funded by assessments from traffic tickets. As a result, there have been "wide variations in levels of funding," adding to a "general pattern . . . of chronic underfunding of indigent defense programs in most areas of the state."[34] Alabama finances its indigent defense system through a tax on all civil and criminal filings in the court system.

The deficiencies in representation resulting from such haphazard and underfunded approaches have been acknowledged. The vice president of the Georgia Trial Lawyers Association once described the simple test used in that state to determine whether a defendant receives adequate counsel as "the mirror test." "You put a mirror under the court-appointed lawyer's nose, and if the mirror clouds up, that's adequate counsel."[35] It is not surprising that such a dysfunctional system is incapable of providing legal representation in capital cases. Unlike the offices of the district attorneys and attorneys general, there is no structure in many states for training and supervising young lawyers in their initial years of practice to develop a cadre of attorneys who specialize in the defense of complex cases. There are no job opportunities in indigent defense for the young law graduates who want to become criminal lawyers. And, because of the financial incentives, most of those who have or develop good trial skills quickly move on to personal injury work or, if they remain in criminal law, the more lucrative defense of drug, pornography, and white collar cases.

C. Compensation of Attorneys: The Wages of Death

The United States Court of Appeals for the Fifth Circuit, finding that Federico Martinez-Macias "was denied his constitutional right to adequate counsel in a capital case in which [his] actual innocence was a close question," observed that, "The state [Texas] paid defense counsel $11.84 per hour. Unfortunately, the justice system got only what it paid for."[36] What is unusual about the case is not the amount paid to counsel, but the court's acknowledgement of its impact on the quality of services rendered.

As we have seen, in many jurisdictions poor people facing the death penalty are not assigned specialists who work for indigent defense programs, but individual attorneys, often sole practitioners. In some jurisdictions, the hourly rates in capital cases may be below the minimum wage or less than the lawyer's overhead expenses. Many jurisdictions limit the maximum fee for a case. At such rates it is usually impossible to obtain a good lawyer willing to spend the necessary time.

Alabama limits compensation for out-of-court preparation to $20 per hour, up to a limit of $1000. In one rare Alabama case where two lawyers devoted 246.86 and 187.90 hours respectively to out-of-court preparation, they were still paid $1000 each, or $4.05 and $5.32 per hour.

In some rural areas in Texas, lawyers receive no more than $800 to handle a capital case. Generally, the hourly rate is $50 or less. Attorneys appointed to defend capital cases in Philadelphia are paid an average of $6399 per case. In the few cases where a second attorney has been appointed, it is often at a flat rate of $500. A study in Virginia found that, after taking into account an attorney's overhead expenses, the effective hourly rate paid to counsel representing an indigent accused in a capital case was $13. In Kentucky, the limit for a capital case is $2500.

Sometimes even these modest fees are denied to appointed counsel. A capital case in Georgia was resolved with a guilty plea only after the defense attorneys, a sole practitioner and this author, agreed not to seek attorneys fees as part of the bargain in which the state withdrew its request for the death penalty.

In cases involving financial as opposed to moral bankruptcy, Atlanta law firms charge around $125 per hour for their associates, $200 per hour for partners, and $50 to $80 per hour for paralegals. In civil rights and other civil litigation, courts routinely order attorneys fees much higher than those paid to appointed lawyers in capital cases. Paralegals and law clerks in civil rights cases may be compensated at rates equal to or better than what experienced attorneys are paid in capital cases. A new attorney at the Southern Center for Human Rights, straight out of law school, was awarded $65 per hour by a federal court in 1990 for work on a prison conditions case. More experienced lawyers on that case were paid at rates of $90, $100, and $150 per hour. Attorneys appointed to death penalty cases in state courts can never expect compensation at such rates.

A justice of the Georgia Supreme Court recently criticized that court's limitation of attorneys fees in an employment discrimination case. Limiting the attorney to $50 per hour instead of providing the opportunity to recover reasonable attorneys fees would, the justice argued, make it unduly difficult to find lawyers for those who were victims of discrimination and "effectively den[y] many Georgians the key to the courthouse door." At lower rates it is even more difficult to find attorneys for capital cases.

Thus, it is unlikely that lawyers will seek appointments in capital cases when they can earn more handling other types of cases. It is undeniable that "[i]n our pecuniary culture the caliber of personal services rendered usually has a corresponding relationship to the compensation provided."[37] Lawyers who have been appointed to defend the poor in capital trials often vow never to handle another. It is financially disastrous, emotionally draining, and, for the small-town sole practitioner, it may be very damaging to relations with paying clients. Even at $200 an hour, it would be difficult to attract lawyers to handle these cases.

Not surprisingly, a recent study in Texas found that "more experienced private criminal attorneys are refusing to accept court appointments in capital cases because of the time involved, the substantial infringement on their private practices, the lack of compensation for counsel fees and expert expenses and the enormous pressure that they feel in handling these cases." "In many counties, the most qualified attorneys often ask not to be considered for court appointments in capital cases due to the fact that the rate of compensation would not allow them to cover the expense of running a law practice."[38] The same unwillingness to take cases because of the low fees has been observed in other states. Consequently, although capital cases require special skills, the level of compensation is often not enough even to attract those who regularly practice in the indigent defense system.

D. The Role of Judges: Appointment and Oversight of Mediocrity and Incompetence

Even if, despite the lack of indigent defense programs and adequate compensation, capable lawyers were willing to move to jurisdictions with many capital cases, forego more lucrative business, and take appointments to capital cases, there is still no assurance that those lawyers would be appointed to the cases. It is no secret that elected state court judges do not appoint the best and brightest of the legal profession to defend capital cases. In part, this is because many judges do not want to impose on those members of the profession they believe to have more important, financially lucrative things to do. But even when choosing from among those who seek criminal appointments, judges often appoint less capable lawyers to defend the most important cases.

Judges have appointed to capital cases lawyers who have never tried a case before. A study of homicide cases in Philadelphia found that the quality of lawyers appointed to capital cases in Philadelphia is so bad that "even officials in charge of the system say they wouldn't want to be represented in Traffic Court by some of the people appointed to defend poor people accused of murder."[39] The study found that many of the attorneys were appointed by judges based on political connections, not legal ability. "Philadelphia's poor defendants often find themselves being represented by ward leaders, ward committeemen, failed politicians, the sons of judges and party leaders, and contributors to the judge's election campaigns.''

An Alabama judge refused to relieve counsel even when they filed a motion to be relieved of the appointment because they had inadequate experience in defending criminal cases and considered themselves incompetent to defend a capital case. Georgia trial judges have repeatedly refused to appoint or compensate the experienced attorneys who, doing pro bono representation in postconviction stages of review, had successfully won new trials for clients who had been sentenced to death. In several of those cases, the Georgia Supreme Court ordered continued representation at the new trials by the lawyers who were familiar with the case and the client. Despite those precedents, a Georgia judge refused to appoint an expert capital litigator from the NAACP Legal Defense and Educational Fund to continue representation of an indigent defendant, even though the Legal Defense Fund lawyer had won a new trial for the client by showing in federal habeas corpus proceedings that he had received ineffective assistance from the lawyer appointed by the judge at the initial capital trial. And the lower court judges who have been reversed for failing to allow continuity in representation are still appointing lawyers when new cases come through the system. Those new defendants have no one to assist them in securing competent representation.

A newly admitted member of the Georgia bar was surprised to be appointed to handle the appeal of a capital case on her fifth day of practice in Columbus, Georgia. Two days earlier she had met the judge who appointed her when she accompanied her boss to a divorce proceeding. Only after she asked for help was a second attorney brought onto the case. Another lawyer in that same circuit was appointed to a capital case, but after submitting his first billing statement to the judge for approval was told by the judge that he was spending too much time on the case. He was summarily replaced by another lawyer and the defendant was ultimately sentenced to death. For a number of years, judges in that circuit appointed a lawyer to capital cases who did not challenge the underrepresentation of black citizens in the jury pools for fear of incurring hostility from the community and alienating potential jurors. As a result, a number of African-Americans were tried by all-white juries in capital cases even though one-third of the population of the circuit is African-American.

The many other examples of exceptionally poor legal representation documented by the American Bar Association (ABA), the *National Law Journal,* and others indicate that judges either are intentionally appointing lawyers who are not equal to the task or are completely inept at securing competent counsel in capital cases. The reality is that popularly elected judges, confronted by a local community that is outraged over the murder of a prominent citizen or angered by the facts of a crime, have little incentive to protect the constitutional rights of the one accused in such a killing. Many state judges are former prosecutors who won their seats on the bench by exploiting high-publicity death penalty cases. Some of those judges have not yet given up the prosecutorial attitude.

United States Congressman William J. Hughes, a former New Jersey prosecutor and leader on crime issues in the Congress, observed: ''With some of the horror stories we've heard—lawyers who didn't call witnesses, who waived final argument—it is incredible that the courts allowed these cases to move forward.''[40] What is even more incredible is that in most of these instances the judges appointed the lawyers to the case.

E. The Minimal Standard of Legal Representation Tolerated in Capital Cases

This sad state of affairs is tolerated in our nation's courts in part because the United States Supreme Court has said that the Constitution requires no more. Instead of actually requiring *effective* representation to fulfill the Sixth Amendment's guarantee of counsel, the Court has brought the standard down to the level of ineffective practice. Stating that ''the purpose of the effective assistance guarantee of the Sixth Amendment is not to improve the quality of legal representation,'' the Court in *Strickland v. Washington* adopted a standard that is ''highly deferential'' to the performance of counsel. To prevail on a claim of ineffective assistance of counsel, a defendant must overcome ''a strong presumption that counsel's conduct falls within the wide range of reasonable professional assistance,'' show that the attorney's representation ''fell below an objective standard of reasonableness,'' and establish ''prejudice,'' which is defined as a reasonable probability that counsel's errors affected the outcome.[41]

As Judge Alvin Rubin of the Fifth Circuit concluded:

> The Constitution, as interpreted by the courts, does not require that the accused, even in a capital case, be represented by able or effective counsel. . . . Consequently, accused persons who are represented by ''not-legally-ineffective'' lawyers may be condemned to die when the same accused, if represented by *effective* counsel, would receive at least the clemency of a life sentence.[42]

Much less than mediocre assistance passes muster under the *Strickland* standard. Errors in judgment and other mistakes may readily be characterized as ''strategy'' or ''tactics'' and thus are beyond review. Indeed, courts employ a lesser standard for judging the competence of lawyers in a capital case than the standard for malpractice for doctors, accountants, and architects.

The defense lawyer in one Texas case failed to introduce any evidence about his client at the penalty phase of the trial. The attorney's entire closing argument regarding sentencing was: ''You are an extremely intelligent jury. You've got that man's life in your hands. You can take it or not. That's all I have to say.''[43] A United States district court granted habeas corpus relief because of the lawyer's failure to present and argue evidence in mitigation, but the Fifth Circuit, characterizing counsel's nonargument as a ''dramatic ploy,'' found that the attorney's performance satisfied *Strickland.* The lawyer was later suspended for other reasons. The defendant was executed.

Numerous other cases in which executions have been carried out demonstrate that the minimal standard for attorney competence employed in death penalty cases provides little protection for most poor persons accused of capital crimes. The case of John Eldon Smith, the first person executed in Georgia since the death penalty was restored, is not exceptional. Smith's sentence was upheld and he was killed despite a constitutional violation because of his lawyer's ignorance of the law, while his codefendant won a new trial due to the same constitutional violation and later received a life sentence. The *second* person executed in Georgia after Smith was a mentally retarded offender, convicted despite a jury instruction that unconstitutionally shifted the burden of proof on intent; he was denied relief because his attorney did not preserve the issue for review. The more culpable codefendant was granted a new trial on the very same issue. Again, as with Smith and Machetti, switching the lawyers would have reversed the outcomes of the case.

John Young was sentenced to death in the same county as Smith. Young was represented at his capital trial by an attorney who was dependent on amphetamines and other drugs which affected his ability to concentrate. At the same time, the lawyer was physically exhausted, suffering severe emotional strain, and distracted from his law practice because of marital problems, child custody arrangements, difficulties in a relationship with a lover, and the pressures of a family business. As a result, the lawyer made little preparation for Young's trial, where his performance was inept. Young was sentenced to death. A few weeks later, Young met his attorney at the prison yard in the country jail. The lawyer had been sent there after pleading guilty to state and federal drug charges. Georgia executed John Young on March 20, 1985.

James Messer was "represented" at trial by an attorney who, at the guilt phase, gave no opening statement, presented no defense case, conducted cursory cross-examination, made no objections, and then emphasized the horror of the crime in some brief closing remarks that could not be fairly described as a "closing argument."[44] Even though severe mental impairment was important to issues of mitigation at both the guilt and penalty phases, the lawyer was unable to present any evidence of it because he failed to make an adequate showing to the judge that he needed a mental health expert. He also failed to introduce Messer's steady employment record, military record, church attendance, and cooperation with police. In closing, the lawyer repeatedly hinted that death was the most appropriate punishment for his own client. This too was good enough for a capital case in Georgia. Messer was executed July 28, 1988.

In light of Messer's case, one cannot help but wonder what progress has been made since the Supreme Court held that there is a right to counsel in capital cases in *Powell v. Alabama.* The nine black youths tried in Scottsboro, Alabama, in 1931 for the rapes of two white girls were represented by a lawyer described as "an able member of the local bar of long and successful experience in the trial of criminal as well as civil cases" who conducted "rigorous and rigid cross-examination" of the state's witnesses.[45] That is more than James Messer received at his capital trial.

Another case in which the attorney did nothing was that of Billy Mitchell, executed by Georgia on September 1, 1987. Following a guilty plea, Mitchell was sentenced to death at a sentencing hearing at which defense counsel called no witnesses, presented no mitigating evidence, and made no inquiries into his client's academic, medical, or psychological history. A great deal of information of this kind was available and, if presented, could well have reduced the sentence imposed on Mitchell. In postconviction proceedings, new counsel submitted 170 pages of affidavits summarizing the testimony of individuals who could have appeared on Mitchell's behalf. Among them were family members, a city council member, a former prosecutor, a professional football player, a bank vice president, and several teachers, coaches, and friends.

The same ineptitude is frequently tolerated on appeal. The brief on direct appeal to the Alabama Supreme Court in the case of Larry Gene Heath, executed by Alabama on March 20, 1992, consisted of only one page of argument and cited only one case, which it distinguished.[46] Counsel, who had filed a six-page brief on the same issue in the Alabama Court of Criminal Appeals, did not appear for oral argument in the case. Although the United States Court of Appeals later found counsel's performance deficient for failing to raise issues regarding denial of a change of venue, denial of sixty-seven challenges for cause of jurors who knew about the defendant's conviction in a neighboring state arising out of the same facts, and use of the defendant's assertion of his Fifth Amendment rights against him, it found no prejudice.

While such incompetence as has been described here passes muster as "effective assistance of counsel" under the Supreme Court's view of the Sixth Amendment, counsel's performance often fails to satisfy the increasingly strict procedural doctrines developed by the Supreme Court since 1977. Failure of counsel to recognize and preserve an issue, due to ignorance, neglect, or failure to discover and rely upon proper grounds or facts, even in the heat of trial, will bar federal review of that issue. A lawyer whose total knowledge of criminal law is *Miranda* and *Dred Scott* may be "not-legally-ineffective" counsel under *Strickland,* but such a lawyer will of course not recognize or preserve many constitutional issues. The result has been what Justice Thurgood Marshall described as an "increasingly pernicious visegrip" for the indigent accused: courts refuse to address constitutional violations because they were not preserved by counsel, but counsel's failure to recognize and raise those issues is not considered deficient legal assistance.

Together, the lax standard of *Strickland* and the strict procedural default doctrines reward the provision of deficient representation. By assigning the indigent accused inadequate counsel, the state increases the likelihood of obtaining a conviction and death sentence at trial and reduces the scope of review. So long as counsel's performance passes muster under *Strickland,* those cases in which the accused received the poorest legal representation will receive the least scrutiny on appeal and in postconviction review because of failure of the lawyer to preserve issues.

In applying *Strickland,* courts indulge in presumptions and assumptions that have no relation to the reality of legal representation for the poor, particularly in capital cases. One scholar has aptly called the idea that bar membership automatically qualifies one to defend a capital case "lethal fiction." The reality is that most attorneys are not qualified to represent criminal defendants and certainly not those accused of capital crimes.[47]

There is no basis for the presumption of competence in capital cases where the accused is represented by counsel who lacks the training, experience, skill, knowledge, inclination, time, and resources to provide adequate representation in a capital case. The presumption should be just the opposite—where one or more of these deficiencies exist, it is reasonable to expect that the lawyer is not capable of rendering effective representation. Indeed, the presumption of competence was adopted even though the Chief Justice of the Supreme Court, who joined in the majority in *Strickland,* had written and lectured about the *lack* of competence of trial attorneys.[48]

Another premise underlying *Strickland* is that "[t]he government is not responsible for, and hence not able to prevent, attorney errors." However, the notion of government innocence is simply not true in cases involving poor people accused of crimes. The poor person does not choose an attorney; one is assigned by a judge or some other government official. The government may well be responsible for attorney errors when it appoints a lawyer who lacks the experience and skill to handle the case, or when it denies the lawyer the time and resources necessary to do the job. In addition, as observed by Justice Blackmun:

> The county's control over the size of and funding for the public defender's office, as well as over the number of potential clients, effectively dictates the size of an individual attorney's caseload and influences substantially the amount of time the attorney is able to devote to each case. The public defender's discretion in handling individual cases—and therefore his ability to provide effective assistance to clients—is circumscribed to an extent not experienced by privately retained attorneys.[49]

The assumption that deficient representation makes no difference, which underlies a finding of lack of prejudice under *Strickland,* is also flawed. In cases where constitutional violations were not preserved and the defendant was executed while an identically situated defendant received relief for the same constitutional violation, it is apparent that the ineptitude of the lawyer did make a difference in the outcome of the case. In other more subtle but equally determinative ways, competent legal assistance can make a difference in the outcome which may not be detectable by reviewing courts.

A lawyer may muddle through a case with little or no preparation, but it is impossible to determine how the case might have been handled differently if he had investigated and prepared. Other difficulties may be even more difficult to detect. Rapport with the client and the family may lead to cooperation and the disclosure of compelling mitigating evidence that might not be found by a less skillful attorney. Good negotiating skills may bring about a plea offer to resolve the case with a sentence less than death, and a good relationship with the client may result in acceptance of an offer that might otherwise be rejected. Nor are reviewing courts able to determine after the fact the difference made by other skills that are often missing in the defense of criminal cases—such as conducting a good voir dire examination of jurors, effective examination and cross-examination of witnesses, and presenting well-reasoned and persuasive closing arguments.

The prejudice standard is particularly inappropriate for application to deficient representation at the penalty phase of a capital case. It is impossible for reviewing courts to assess the difference that investigation into mitigating circumstances and the effective presentation of mitigating evidence might make on a jury's sentencing decision.

The Supreme Court has consistently reaffirmed that in a capital case any aspect of the life and background of the accused offered by the defense must be considered as "mitigating circumstances" in determining punishment. Those who have tried capital cases have found that the competent presentation of such evidence often results in sentences less than death. But the right to have any of the "diverse frailties of humankind" taken into account is meaningless if the accused is not provided with counsel capable of finding and effectively presenting mitigating circumstances.

A court-appointed defense lawyer's only reference to his client during the penalty phase of a Georgia capital case was: "You have got a little ole nigger man over there that doesn't weigh over 135 pounds. He is poor and he is broke. He's got an appointed lawyer. . . . He is ignorant. I will venture to say he has an IQ of not over 80."[50] The defendant was sentenced to death.

Had that lawyer done any investigation into the life and background of his client, he would have found that his client was not simply "ignorant." Instead, he was mentally retarded. For that reason, he had been rejected from military service. And he had been unable to function in school or at any job except the most repetitive and menial ones. His actual IQ was far from 80; it was 68. He could not do such basic things as make change or drive an automobile. After his death sentence was set aside because of failure to grant a change of venue, an investigation was conducted, these facts were documented, and the defendant received a life sentence.

In another case, an attorney, obviously under the influence of alcohol, came to the Southern Center for Human Rights, in Atlanta, after business hours on a Friday evening. He was clutching part of a trial transcript and said that he needed help preparing his brief to the Georgia Supreme Court for the direct appeal of a mentally retarded man he had represented at trial who had been sentenced to death. The brief was due the following Monday. Nothing had been written for the appeal. It was impossible even to assemble the entire record by Monday. Fortunately, an extension of time was obtained and eventually the case was remanded to the trial court. New counsel subsequently negotiated a life sentence.

In these and other cases previously discussed in Section I, once the facts were discovered and brought out, life sentences were obtained for people previously sentenced to death. But these were cases where by sheer luck the defendants later received adequate representation on appeal or in postconviction proceedings. Many of these cases were returned for retrials for reasons having nothing to do with the poor legal representation at the original trials. But, as shown by the many cases summarized here in which executions were carried out, many of those facing the death penalty never receive the representation that would make such a difference.

III. The Failure to Keep the Promise of Gideon

The right to counsel is essential to protect all other rights of the criminally accused. Yet this most fundamental right has received the least protection. Nevertheless, many members of the judiciary and the bar—who have a special responsibility to uphold the rule of law in the face of public outrage and revulsion—stand by year after year, case after case, looking the other way, pretending that nothing is amiss, or calling upon someone else to solve the problem, but never engaging in a concerted and effective effort to change the situation. The United States Department of Justice, the state District Attorneys, and state Attorneys General, all of whom should have some concern about the fairness and integrity of the judicial process, use their power and influence to make the situation even worse. As a result, although some solutions to the problem are apparent, the situation continues to deteriorate and, tragically, to be increasingly accepted as the inevitable lot of the poor.

A. Minimal Reforms in Response to Major Crisis

Over ten years ago, the ABA and the National Legal Aid and Defender Association found the funding for indigent defense inadequate and deemed the promise of *Gideon v. Wainwright* unrealized, stating: "we must be willing to put our money where our mouth is; we must be willing to make the constitutional mandate a reality."[51] However, despite many reports with similar warnings, another ABA report in 1993 still found that "long-term neglect and underfunding of indigent defense has created a crisis of extraordinary proportions in many states throughout the country."[52]

In Alabama, ten reports over eleven years pointed out the many defects in representation of indigent defendants. Judges, court administrators, and the bar have recommended reform. A commission proposed in 1988 that the limits on attorneys fees in capital cases be eliminated or raised, but the legislature has done nothing to change the limit on compensation for out-of-court time expended by attorneys in capital cases. As a result, and despite repeated acknowledgement of the problem, the quality of indigent defense in Alabama remains a disgrace.

Limits on compensation have been struck down by courts in a number of states. However, even as courts have recognized the unreasonableness of the low fees, the adverse impact of such low fees on the right to counsel and a fair trial, and their own constitutional duty to do something about it, they have often ordered only minimal, inadequate reforms.

A challenge to Mississippi's limit of $1000 for compensation to lawyers appointed to defend capital cases was rejected by the state's supreme court. The court held that lawyers were entitled to reimbursement for actual costs, including the overhead cost of operating a law office, so that "the attorney will not actually lose money," but characterized the $1000 fee as "an 'honorarium' or pure profit."[53] One justice published a dissent, which had initially been prepared as the majority opinion, that carefully analyzed how the statutory limit on compensation adversely affected the right to counsel and the administration of justice in violation of the Constitution. However, because that opinion was not supported by a majority of the court, an attorney appointed to defend a capital case in Mississippi, while no longer required to lose money, may still make less than the minimum wage.

The Louisiana Supreme Court, considering a capital case in which assigned counsel was neither compensated nor reimbursed for expenses, held that counsel were entitled to reimbursement for out-of-pocket and overhead costs, overruling contrary state precedent, but held that a "fee for service need not be paid" as long as the time required to defend the case does not reach "unreasonable levels."

The South Carolina Supreme Court struck down that state's statutory limitations on compensation of appointed counsel in capital cases. The statutes provided for $15 per hour of in-court time and $10 per hour of out-of-court time for attorneys, with a limit of $5000 per case for attorneys fees, expert and investigative services, and costs. Even in doing so, however, the court discussed the fee limitations in the context of "the legal profession's traditional and historic role in the general society. It is a role anchored to the postulate that the practice of law is not a marketplace business or commercial venture but, rather, a profession dedicated primarily to service." The court accordingly held that "[t]he appointed attorney should not expect to be compensated *at market rate,* rather at a reasonable, but lesser rate" to be fixed in the court's discretion at the conclusion of the trial.

One would hope that such an undesirable assignment as defending a person in a capital case would be compensated at rates *greater* than market rates, not less. In civil rights cases, the undesirability of a case is a factor used to multiply or enhance an attorneys fee award. For example, prison conditions cases have been found to be "undesirable" for purposes of determining whether to enhance attorneys fees. However, legislatures and courts have simply been unwilling to pay sufficient rates to attract lawyers to handle capital cases.

There have been few systematic challenges to the inadequacy of legal representation for the poor, and they have produced only limited results. Some hope of reforming Georgia's indigent defense system appeared when a federal court of appeals held that a challenge to deficiencies in the system stated a claim and should not have been dismissed. However, after a change in the composition of the court, the case was dismissed on abstention grounds. The federal courts also refused on abstention grounds to examine Kentucky's limit on attorneys' compensation in capital cases.

Despite abundant documentation of the enormity of the need for substantive changes, some continue to suggest that the burden of providing counsel to the poor—even in capital cases—may be satisfied by the conscription of members of the legal profession. However, it is the constitutional duty of the state, not of members of the legal profession, to provide indigent defendants with counsel. Responses to the problems posed by ineffective assistance of counsel should be conceived in a way that gives effect to this principle. Georgia, a state in which there have been numerous egregious examples of deficient representation, has no difficulty coming up with local, state, and federal money to prepare for the Olympic

Games, but it does not secure or appropriate funding to assure competent representation and equal justice in its courts.

Though it is desirable for more members of the legal profession to shoulder their ethical obligations to provide legal assistance for the poor, the defense of capital cases often requires more expertise, commitment, and resources than individual lawyers are able to offer. And there are too many cases for the lawyers who do respond. Moreover, the absence of indigent defense programs limits the opportunity for young, committed lawyers to enhance their skills and learn to do the job properly. Beyond these difficulties, even the most conscientious lawyer needs proper investigative and expert assistance to defend a capital case.

Moreover, to ask for such major sacrifices for such an overwhelming and thankless job as defending a capital case from a few members of the profession is unreasonable. Judges are not presiding without compensation, and district attorneys are not prosecuting without decent salaries. And most members of the legal profession—particularly those at the high income law firms which have the litigation skills and resources equal to the task—are not being asked to share the burden of defending the poor. The supply of lawyers who are willing to make the sacrifice has never come close to satisfying the desperate needs of the many poor who face the death penalty throughout the country today.

Georgia Chief Justice Harold Clarke's description of Georgia's response to the need for indigent defense applies to most other states as well: "[W]e set our sights on the embarrassing target of mediocrity. I guess that means about halfway. And that raises a question. Are we willing to put up with halfway justice? To my way of thinking, one-half justice must mean one-half injustice, and one-half injustice is no justice at all."[54]

B. The Politics of Crime and the Lack of Leadership to Remedy the Situation

At this time, there appears to be little prospect of achieving even the level of mediocrity that Chief Justice Clarke described. What is needed to provide competent legal representation to any litigant, rich or poor, is no secret. But significant improvement in the quality of representation for the poor is unlikely because of the unpopularity of those accused and the lack of leadership and commitment to fairness of those entrusted with responsibility for the justice system.

A properly working adversary system will never be achieved unless defender organizations are established and properly funded to employ lawyers at wages and benefits equal to what is spent on the prosecution, to retain expert and investigative assistance, to assign lawyers to capital cases, to recruit and support local lawyers, and to supervise the performance of counsel defending capital cases. Judges are not equipped to do this. Management of the defense is not a proper judicial function. And, as previously described, all too often political and other improper considerations influence elected state court judges in their appointment of lawyers to defend those facing the death penalty.

What is needed is a system in which defense counsel's loyalty is to the client and not the judge; and in which defense counsel, as well as the prosecutor, understands the scientific and legal issues in the case and has access to the investigative and expert assistance needed to prepare and present the case. The ABA has promulgated standards for the appointment and performance of counsel in capital cases, which are seldom followed today, but standards mean nothing without capable attorneys and well-funded defender organizations to implement them.[55]

Moreover, it must be recognized that defending capital cases is a most unattractive responsibility for most members of the legal profession. With the increasing number of state and federal capital prosecutions, it will be more and more difficult to find enough capable lawyers willing to defend the cases. It should be recognized that, as in other difficult and undesirable areas of practice, a significant financial incentive, considerably beyond what lawyers receive for far less demanding legal work, will be required.

Such a system would require a substantial commitment of resources. The argument has been made that some jurisdictions do not have the money to attract qualified lawyers and that in some areas, particularly rural areas, qualified counsel is simply not available.[56] But these considerations should not excuse the lack of adequate legal representation in capital cases. There are communities that have no pathologists, hair and fiber experts, evidence technicians, and others needed for the investigation and prosecution of homicide cases. However, when a murder occurs in those communities and is followed by a capital prosecution, the prosecution invariably brings in the experts needed and pays what it costs to do so.

There was a time when many localities did not have capable law enforcement agencies or pathologists, fingerprint examiners, ballistics experts, serologists, and other forensic scientists needed to investigate and prosecute crime. These deficiencies were remedied in most places, often with funding from the Federal Law Enforcement Assistance Administration as well as state and local governments. Crime laboratories were built, local police officers were sent to FBI training programs, and pools of experts were developed who travel around states to investigate crime scenes and testify in local prosecutions.

These jurisdictions could also establish defender organizations to provide lawyers with the expertise required to defend capital cases, and the investigators and expert assistance needed to prepare the defense of these cases. What is lacking is not money, but the political will to provide adequate counsel for the poor in capital and other criminal cases. Adequate representation and fairness will never be achieved as long as it is accepted that states can pay to *prosecute* a capital case without paying to defend one. Adequate representation and fairness will never be achieved until ensuring justice in the courts becomes a priority equal to public concern for roads, bridges, schools, police protection, sports, and the arts.

But the leadership needed to help bring about justice is missing. There was a time when the Attorney General of the United States and the attorneys general in many of the states were concerned not just with getting convictions, but also with fairness, integrity, and the proper functioning of the adversary system.

In that spirit, Attorneys General Walter F. Mondale of Minnesota and Edward

J. McCormack, Jr., of Massachusetts, and twenty-one of their fellow attorneys general filed a brief *in support* of Clarence Earl Gideon's right to counsel in *Gideon v. Wainwright.* It was out of that same concern that Attorney General Robert F. Kennedy helped secure passage of the federal Criminal Justice Act in 1963. But those days are gone.

Today, the United States Department of Justice, state district attorneys, and state attorneys general use their power and influence to make this shameful situation even worse. They take every advantage of the ignorant, incompetent lawyers foisted upon the poor.[57] They have defended in the courts even the most outrageous instances of incompetence on the part of defense counsel previously described and used the ineptness of counsel as a barrier to prevent courts from addressing constitutional violations in capital cases.

Despite abundant evidence of poor lawyering and egregious constitutional violations in capital cases, the Justice Department and many prosecutors have proposed shortcuts and procedural traps to paper over the problems and speed up the process of sending those sentenced to death at unconstitutional trials to their executions. In response to findings by federal courts of constitutional violations in state capital cases, prosecutors have urged stricter enforcement of procedural default rules to avoid dealing with the violations, not better counsel to avoid those unconstitutional trials in the first place. Justice James Robertson of the Mississippi Supreme Court described as "unseemly" the arguments of that state's attorney general that the court "should hold [the defendant's] claims procedurally barred, not because such would promote the interests of justice, but rather that such would pull the rug out from under [him] when he ultimately seeks federal review of his case."[58] An accommodating Supreme Court has been willing to cut back drastically on the availability of the once great writ of habeas corpus,[59] and prosecutors have supported even more drastic legislative proposals to restrict it further.

Many prosecutors have been unwilling to agree to even the most minor reforms to improve the quality of legal representation received by the poor. Federal legislation was proposed in 1990 that would have restricted imposition of the procedural default doctrines unless states improved the quality of defense counsel. One proposal would have required the establishment of an appointing authority for counsel in capital cases composed either of a statewide defender organization or of a death penalty resource center. The appointing authority would have been responsible for securing qualified counsel and engaging in periodic review to ensure the competence of representation. The legislation would also have set standards for counsel and required payment for counsel "at a reasonable rate in light of the attorney's qualifications and experience and the local market for legal representation in cases reflecting the complexity and responsibility of capital cases."[60]

This modest proposal evoked vehement opposition from the U.S. Department of Justice and state prosecutors. William P. Barr, then–Deputy Attorney General and later Attorney General, characterized the counsel provisions as "an elaborate and expensive system for appointing counsel" that were "inimical to the principles of federalism inherent in our constitutional system, and to the need for reasonable finality of state criminal judgments."[61] A letter signed by the attorneys general of twenty-three states which have the death penalty described the provisions as "so extreme as to be absurd." The twenty-three attorneys general asserted: "The current problems which beset capital cases are not caused by the quality of representation they receive" and that "the focus in capital cases should be on the guilt or innocence of the defendant and the sentence he should receive" and not "how many seminars a defense attorney has attended, how well he is paid, and other collateral matters."[62] The National Association of District Attorneys adopted a resolution opposing the legislation, reiterating its support for the procedural default doctrines and "strongly oppos[ing] any legislation" which would "create new requirements concerning the experience, competency, or performance of counsel" beyond *Strickland v. Washington.*[63]

A bill introduced in 1993 would have required only a "certifying" authority to identify lawyers to defend capital cases, allowing judges to continue to appoint counsel and setting only minimal standards measured in terms of years of practice and number of cases with no inquiry into quality of work. Although representatives of the state attorneys general and district attorneys associations were involved in drafting the legislation, which would, in fact, do little to improve the quality of representation and could even worsen the situation, it was opposed by many prosecutors.[64] One letter circulated among Senators criticized its "expansive and costly appointment of counsel provisions" and quoted the Attorney General of Georgia as saying that, if enacted, the bill would "effectively repeal the death penalty."

Such hyperbolic statements have repeatedly greeted other efforts to improve the quality of legal representation in capital cases. When the Georgia legislature, after years of refusing to appropriate any funds for indigent defense, finally responded grudgingly to the eloquent appeals of the chief justice of the state's supreme court by creating in 1992 a small capital defender program that employed only four attorneys, one district attorney criticized it as a step toward abolishing the death penalty in Georgia. When a report to the Texas Bar described the serious deficiencies of the representation in capital cases in that state, the district attorney in Houston dismissed it as an argument against the death penalty.

The enthusiasm of prosecutors to continue to take every advantage has not been tempered by the poverty and powerlessness of those accused of capital crimes. Nor has the situation motivated a new presidential administration or a new Attorney General to rein in the assaults on the Bill of Rights and habeas corpus or question the power that state courts should be allowed to exercise over the lives of persons who are not provided adequate representation. Instead, the country is engaged in a crime debate in which politicians try to outdo one another in proposing crime bills which simultaneously expand the use of the death penalty and other severe penalties while restricting or eliminating procedural protections. Those who are supposedly leaders dismiss the Bill of Rights as a mere collection of technicalities. The debate is exceptionally one-sided. For, as Robert F. Kennedy said long ago, the poor person accused of a crime has no lobby. No member of Congress or a state legislature is likely to receive complaints about the quality of counsel for poor people accused of crimes. But lost in the effort to get tough on crime is concern about the fairness and integrity of the criminal justice system.

Completely missing from the crime debate and from the courts is the notion that if it is too expensive or impractical for some jurisdictions to provide competent counsel and the fairness and reliability that should accompany a judicial decision to take a human life, their power should be limited. If a local trial court cannot comply with the most fundamental safeguard of the Constitution by providing a capable attorney to one whose life is at stake, it should not be authorized to extinguish life. The solution is not to depreciate human life and the Bill of Rights by accepting what is available. Many small communities do not have surgeons, yet they do not rely on chiropractors to perform heart surgery.

Pronouncements about the importance of and the need for counsel do not make quality representation a reality. It has become apparent that the legislatures of most states, particularly those where the death penalty is frequently imposed, are not going to discharge their constitutional duty to appropriate funds and provide competent legal assistance for poor persons in criminal cases. It is also unlikely that the judiciary and bar, after years of neglect, punctuated by occasional moments of hand wringing, will respond effectively to this worsening situation.

IV. The Need for Individual Responses and Limits on the Power of the Courts

The quality of legal representation in capital cases in many states is a scandal. However, almost no one cares. Those facing the death penalty are generally poor, often members of racial minorities, often afflicted with substantial mental impairments, and always accused of serious, terrible crimes. The crimes of which they are accused bring out anger, hatred, and a quest for vengeance on the part of most people, including judges, prosecutors, and, quite often, even those appointed to represent the accused. All of this leads to, at best, indifference and, more often, hostility toward the plight of those accused. And many outside the criminal justice system are indifferent because they are unaware of what passes for justice in the courts. There is a growing cynicism about the importance of due process and the protections of the Bill of Rights. Many of those who hold or aspire to public office find it impossible to resist the temptation to resort to demagoguery to exploit these sentiments.

But this reality does not excuse the constitutional responsibility of the judiciary and members of the legal profession to ensure that even the most despised defendants still receive the highest quality legal representation in proceedings that will determine whether they live or die. Justice William Brennan, with his usual eloquence, once observed in another context,

> It is tempting to pretend that [those] on death row share a fate in no way connected to our own, that our treatment of them sounds no echoes beyond the chambers in which they die. Such an illusion is ultimately corrosive, for the reverberations of injustice are not so easily confined. . . . [T]he way in which we choose those who will die reveals the depth of moral commitment among the living.[65]

Unfortunately, what has been revealed about the depth of moral commitment among legislators, members of the bar, and the judiciary is very discouraging. It is unlikely that the promise of *Powell* and *Gideon* will ever be fulfilled for most of those accused of criminal violations. Legislatures are unwilling to pay the price for adequate representation, most courts are unwilling to order it, and most members of the bar are unwilling or unable to take on the awesome responsibility of providing a vigorous defense without adequate compensation.

The best hope for most of those facing the death penalty is that capable lawyers will volunteer to take their cases and provide proper representation regardless of whether they are paid adequately or at all. A member of the New York Court of Appeals, citing the ethical obligation of lawyers to recognize deficiencies in the legal system and initiate corrective measures, has urged lawyers to respond to the challenge of seeing that those who face the worst penalty receive the best representation.

> During the civil rights movement of the fifties and especially the sixties, inspired attorneys, not all young neophytes, travelled often at great personal expense and real risk, including their own deaths, to make a difference. That spirit needs to be revived. Right now, it fuels only a few who are to be commended for what they are trying to do, but it has not motivated a sufficient number of people in our profession to do their needed parts, too. Until that conversion comes about, Lady Justice may as well keep her eyes blindfolded so as not to notice with shame the grotesque imbalance in the scales of justice that hang from her fingertips, because of the growing numbers of death penalty cases in this great country that are finally, really finally, resolved under such disproportionate odds and resources.[66]

Such spirit and commitment are desperately needed. When achieved, they will undoubtedly make a difference for those persons represented. Indeed it is hard to imagine how a member of the legal profession could make a greater difference than by saving a client from execution. But the response of individual lawyers will not be nearly enough to end the systemic problems previously described and provide adequate representation to the thousands of people facing the death penalty in this country.

Lawyers must not only respond, but in doing so they must litigate aggressively the right to adequate compensation, to the funds necessary to investigate, and for the experts needed to prepare and present a defense. Lawyers must also bring systemic challenges to indigent defense systems. Attorneys for the poor—whether in assigned counsel, contract, or public defender systems—must refuse unreasonable caseloads and insist upon the training and resources to do the job right. Where these problems make it impossible for attorneys to discharge their constitutional and ethical obligations, attorneys should frankly declare their inability to render effective assistance.

And lawyers must continue to bear witness to the shameful injustices which are all too routine in capital cases. The uninformed and the indifferent must be educated and reminded of what is passing for justice in the courts. The substandard quality of counsel for the poor and the lack of a structure and funding for indigent defense must become part of the debate on crime. The state and federal legislatures should not continue to enact capital crimes without considering the costs of adequate representation for the defendant and, even if the costs are met, whether there is anyone to defend those accused. Lawyers and law students need to be reminded that there continue to be people with desperate, unmet needs for competent representation.[67] They need to be informed that the protections of the Bill of Rights are often denied those most in need of them—poor, minority, and disadvantaged persons facing the death penalty. The danger of silence is not only that lawyers will be unaware of the need, but also that many in society will mistakenly assume that there is a properly working adversary system in the criminal courts.

It is only by the witness of those who observe the injustices in capital cases firsthand that others in society can be accurately informed. This knowledge may prompt questions about the system and its limits such as: whether the quest for vengeance receives too high a priority over the pursuit of justice in the courts; whether criminal courts should be allowed to dispatch people to their deaths without providing capable lawyers or even one penny for the investigators and experts necessary to present evidence that is constitutionally indispensable to the punishment decision; whether indigent and often mentally limited persons accused of crimes should continue to be denied the protections of the Bill of Rights under the procedural default doctrines because of the ineptness of lawyers they had no voice in choosing; whether the assignment of lawyers to defend the poor should be made by judges who must keep one eye on the next election and, with the other, often wink at the Constitution; and whether courts should continue to demean the Sixth Amendment by employing the *Strickland v. Washington* standard for "legally effective counsel."

These questions must be raised vigorously until courts and leaders of the bar realize that the judgments of the criminal courts cannot be seen as legitimate and entitled to respect so long as such poor quality of representation is tolerated. It is only by dealing squarely with these questions that there is hope that the courts will face reality and deliver on the promise of *Powell* and *Gideon* instead of indulging in wishful thinking and hollow pronouncements about the right to counsel. One must hope that a frank discussion of the deficiencies of the system will prompt courts to take their eyes off the embarrassing target of mediocrity and take aim at a full measure of justice for all citizens, especially those whose lives and freedom hang in the balance. One must also hope that some prosecutors, who recognize a higher calling in seeing that justice is done and making the adversary system work than in simply getting convictions and death sentences against inept lawyers, will add their voices regarding the need for adequate representation and limits on the power of the courts. And finally, some law schools must respond and prepare students better for defending criminal cases.

The Louisiana Supreme Court recently faced reality and created a presumption of incompetence of counsel where provision of indigent defense services are so lacking that defendants are not likely to be receiving effective representation. Unless the state is able to rebut the presumption at a pretrial hearing, a trial court is not to let the prosecution go forward until the defendant is provided with reasonably effective counsel. This approach responds much better to the reality of representation for indigents than *Strickland.* Nevertheless, Justice Dennis pointed out that the court could have done more:

> This court should establish standards by setting limits on the number of cases handled by indigent defense attorneys, by requiring a minimum number of investigators to be assigned to each [public] defender, and by requiring specified support resources for each attorney. If a defendant demonstrates further error due to funding and resource deficiencies, the courts should be instructed to view the harm as state-imposed error, which would require reversal of the conviction unless the state demonstrates that the error was harmless.[68]

If systemic reforms are not attainable, other state courts could follow the example of the Louisiana Supreme Court and prohibit the prosecution from going forward in the absence of competent counsel. In addition, as long as trial judges remain in the business of appointing defense counsel, conscientious judges who are concerned about fairness can order the appointment of experienced, competent lawyers, and just compensation at enhanced rates for those lawyers. Trial judges could obtain the services of the best members of the profession, those equal to the task of handling the highest stakes in our legal system, but whose time generally is spent in more lucrative pursuits. The appointment of the top litigators, managing partners, and bar leaders from firms in Atlanta, Birmingham, Jackson, New Orleans, Philadelphia, Houston, and Dallas to defend capital cases would undoubtedly change the quality of indigent defense representation in those areas. It is remarkable that courts do not call upon those lawyers to respond to the need. In addition to introducing litigation skills to the cases, the involvement of such lawyers might also result in some of them bringing their considerable power and influence to bear upon the systemic problems, if for no other reason than to avoid future appointments.

Such efforts, while urgently needed, will assure competent representation to only a small percentage of those facing death and, at best, may prompt reforms that will take years to accomplish. In the meantime, many will continue to be sentenced to death at trials where they will receive only perfunctory representation by lawyers who are not equal to the task of defending a capital case and are denied the resources to do the job properly. It is those poor people who will suffer the consequences of the failure of the legislatures and the judiciary to discharge their constitutional responsibilities.

The death penalty will continue to be imposed and new capital statutes enacted with the continuing promise that efforts will be made to improve the quality of counsel *in the future.* But this is surely backwards. A very high quality of counsel—instead of minimal representation—should not only be the goal, but the reality *before* a jurisdiction is authorized to take life. Moreover, the promise of adequate counsel is continually broken. It has been over sixty years since the Supreme Court held in *Powell v. Alabama* that those accused in Scottsboro and all poor people were entitled to a higher level of representation in capital cases than merely being accompanied to their trials by a member of the bar. Yet the representation in many trials today is no better than that provided to the accused in Scottsboro in 1931. This longstanding lack of commitment to counsel for the poor is one of the many reasons that the effort to achieve fairness and consistency in the administration of the death penalty is "doomed to failure."[69]

V. Conclusion

Courts have issued many pronouncements about the importance of the guiding hand of counsel, but they have failed to acknowledge that most state governments are unwilling to pay for an adequate defense for the poor person accused of a crime. Unfortunately, the Supreme Court has not been vigilant in enforcing the promise of *Powell* and *Gideon.* Its acceptance of the current quality of representation in capital cases as inevitable or even acceptable demeans the Sixth Amendment. It undermines the legitimacy of the criminal courts and the respect due their judgments. No poor person accused of *any* crime should receive the sort of representation that is found acceptable in the criminal courts of this nation today, but it is particularly indefensible in cases where life is at stake. Even one of the examples of deficient representation described in this Essay is one more than should have occurred in a system of true justice.

Providing the best quality representation to persons facing loss of life or imprisonment should be the highest priority of legislatures, the judiciary, and the bar. However, the reality is that it is not. So long as the substandard representation that is seen today is tolerated in the criminal courts, at the very least, this lack of commitment to equal justice should be acknowledged and the power of courts should be limited. So long as juries and judges are deprived of critical information and the Bill of Rights is ignored in the most emotionally and politically charged cases due to deficient legal representation, the courts should not be authorized to impose the extreme and irrevocable penalty of death. Otherwise, the death penalty will continue to be imposed, not upon those who commit the worst crimes, but upon those who have the misfortune to be assigned the worst lawyers.

Notes

1. Record at 846–49, State v. Haney, No. 7 Div. 148 (Ala. Crim. App. 1989).

2. Nevertheless, both the Alabama Court of Criminal Appeals, Haney v. State, 603 So. 2d 368 (Ala. Crim. App. 1991), and the Alabama Supreme Court, *Ex parte* Haney, 603 So. 2d 412 (Ala. 1992), upheld the conviction and death sentence in the case.

3. The defendant's other court-appointed lawyer was later disciplined by the Alabama Bar for neglect in two worker's compensation cases, allowing the statute of limitations to run in both cases. *Disciplinary Report,* ALA. LAW., Nov. 1993, at 401.

4. Anthony Lewis, GIDEON'S TRUMPET 205 (1964).

5. This Essay deals primarily with the problem at trial and on direct appeal where the state is required to provide counsel for the indigent accused. It does not analyze the equally serious crisis regarding lack of representation and inadequate representation in postconviction review. For such a review, see American Bar Ass'n, *Toward a More Just and Effective*

System of Review in State Death Penalty Cases, 40 AM. U. L. REV, 1, 79–92 (1990). The Supreme Court has held there is no right to counsel, even in capital cases in postconviction review. Murray v. Giarratano, 492 U.S. 1 (1989) (plurality opinion).

6. Peter Applebome, *Two Electric Jolts in Alabama Execution.* N.Y. TIMES, July 15, 1989, at A6.

7. Penry v. Lynaugh, 492 U.S. 302, 319 (1989) (quoting California v. Brown, 479 U.S. 538, 545 (1987) (O'Connor, J., concurring)).

8. David Lundy, *Bondurant's Costly Death Appeal,* FULTON COUNTY DAILY REP., Aug. 18, 1989, at 6.

9. Gordon Dickinson, *Man Freed in Machete Murder Case,* EL PASO TIMES, June 24, 1993, at 1.

10. Tracy Thompson, *Once "Unfit To Live," Ex-Death-Row Inmates Winning Parole,* ATLANTA CONST. Mar. 12, 1987, at A1.

11. *Habeas Corpus Reform: Hearings Before the Comm. on the Judiciary,* 101st Cong., 1st & 2d Sess. 349 (1989–90) (statement of Justice James Robertson of the Supreme Court of Mississippi).

12. Godfrey v. Georgia, 446 U.S. 420, 427–28 (1980) (quoting Gregg v. Georgia, 428 U.S. 153, 188 (1976) (quoting Furman v. Georgia, 408 U.S. 238, 313 (1972) (White, J., concurring))).

13. American Bar Ass'n, supra note 5, at 16. The ABA's report illustrates the pervasiveness of the problem:

> Georgia's recent experience with capital punishment has been marred by examples of inadequate representation ranging from virtually no representation at all by counsel, to representation by inexperienced counsel, to failures to investigate basic threshold questions, to lack of knowledge of governing law, to lack of advocacy on the issue of guilt, to failure to present a case for life at the penalty phase. . . .
>
> . . . Defense representation is not necessarily better in other death penalty states. In Tennessee, for another example, defense lawyers offered no evidence in mitigation in approximately one-quarter of all death sentences affirmed by the Tennessee Supreme Court since the Tennessee legislature promulgated its current death penalty statute.

Id. at 65–67. . . .

14. Thurgood Marshall, *Remarks on the Death Penalty Made at the Judicial Conference of the Second Circuit,* 86 COLUM. L. REV. 1, 1–2 (1986). Justice Marshall noted that "[t]he federal reports are filled with stories of counsel who presented *no* evidence in mitigation of their clients' sentences because they did not know what to offer or how to offer it, or had not read the state's sentencing statute." Id.

15. Marcia Coyle et al., *Fatal Defense: Trial and Error in the Nation's Death Belt,* NAT. L.J., June 11, 1990, at 30. Twelve articles examining the quality of representation in numerous cases in the six states appear in Id. at 30–44.

16. A lawyer in one Georgia case conceded his client's guilt and argued for a life sentence at the guilt phase; he continued to plead for mercy even after he was admonished by the trial judge to save his argument on punishment for the sentencing phase. Young v. Zant, 677 F.2d 792, 797 (11th Cir. 1982). A judge in a Florida case took a defense lawyer in chambers during the penalty phase to explain what it was about. The lawyer responded: "I'm at a loss. I really don't know what to do in this type of proceeding. If I'd been through one, I would, but I've never handled one except this time." Douglas v. Wainwright, 714 F.2d 1532, 1556 (11th Cir. 1983), *vacated and remanded,* 468 U.S. 1206 (1984), *on remand,* 739 F.2d 531 (11th Cir. 1984), *and cert. denied,* 469 U.S. 1208 (1985). An Alabama defense

lawyer asked for time between the guilt and penalty phases so that he could read the state's death penalty statute. Record at 1875–76, State v. Smith, 581 So. 2d 497 (Ala. Crim. App. 1990). The lawyer in a Pennsylvania case tailored his presentation of evidence and argument around a death penalty statute that had been declared unconstitutional three years earlier because it limited the arguments on which the defense could rely as to mitigating circumstances. Frey v. Fulcomer, 974 F.2d 348, 359 (3d Cir. 1992) (reversing finding of ineffective assistance of counsel).

17. In one Alabama case, one defense lawyer sued co-counsel over attorneys fees before trial and the attorneys were in conflict over personal differences during trial. Daniel v. Thigpen, 742 F. Supp. 1535, 1558–59 (M.D. Ala. 1990); Friedman & Stevenson. Ruth E. Friedman and Bryan A. Stevenson, *Solving Alabama's Capital Defense Problems: It's a Dollars and Sense Thing,* 44 Ala. L. Rev. 1 (1992), at 34. In a Georgia case, one attorney presented an incredible alibi defense while the other asserted a mental health defense that acknowledged the accused's participation in the crime. Ross v. Kemp, 393 S.E.2d 244, 245 (Ga. 1990).

18. Goodwin v. Balkcom, 684 F.2d 794, 805 n.13 (11th Cir. 1982) (defendant called a "little old nigger boy" in closing argument by defense counsel); *Ex parte* Guzmon, 730 S.W.2d 724, 736 (Tex. Crim. App. 1987) (Mexican client referred to as "wet back" in front of all-white jury by defense counsel); Record Excerpts at 102, Dungee v. Kemp, No. 85-8202 (11th Cir.) (defendant called "nigger" by defense counsel), *decided sub nom.* Isaacs v. Kemp, 778 F.2d 1482 (11th Cir. 1985), *cert. denied,* 476 U.S. 1164 (1986).

19. House v. Balkcom, 725 F.2d 608, 612 (11th Cir. 1984), *cert. denied,* 469 U.S. 870 (1984).

20. A judge in Harris County, Texas, responding to a capital defendant's complaints about his lawyer sleeping during the trial at which death was imposed, stated: "The Constitution does not say that the lawyer has to be awake." John Makeig, *Asleep on the Job; Slaying Trial Boring, Lawyer Said,* HOUS. CHRON., Aug. 14, 1992, at A35. Defense counsel was found to have slept during a capital trial in Harrison v. Zant, No. 88-V-1640. Order at 2 (Super. Ct. Butts County, Ga. Oct. 5, 1990), *aff'd,* 402 S.E.2d 518 (Ga. 1991).

21. People v. Garrison, 254 Cal. Rptr. 257 (1986). Counsel, an alcoholic, was arrested en route to court one morning and found to have a blood alcohol level of 0.27. Yet the court was unwilling to create a presumption against the competence of attorneys under the influence of alcohol.

22. In Texas, which has the second largest death row in the nation and has carried out more executions than any other state, the accused is given only one lawyer in many cases. The Spangenberg Group, A STUDY OF REPRESENTATION IN CAPITAL CASES IN TEXAS 156, 157 (1993) (prepared for the State Bar of Texas). In Philadelphia, where the number of people sentenced to death is greater than the combined death rows of 21 of the 36 states which have the death penalty, a capital case is often defended by a single attorney. See Michael DeCourcy Hinds, *Circumstances in Philadelphia Consign Killers,* N.Y. TIMES, June 8, 1992, at K1; Frederic N. Tulsky, *What Price Justice? Poor Defendants Pay the Cost as Courts Save on Murder Trials,* PHILA. INQUIRER, Sept. 13, 1992, at A18.

23. Frederick N. Tulsky, *What Price Justice? Poor Defendants Pay the Cost as Courts Save on Murder Trials,* Phila. Inquirer, Sept. 13, 1992, at A18.

24. A survey of lawyers and judges in Texas found that approximately one-half of the attorneys who had handled a capital case and 33% of judges who had recently presided over a capital case indicated that resources were inadequate to pay expert witnesses and attorneys. The Spangenberg Group, supra note 60, at 159; see, e.g., Jeff Rosenzweig, *The Crisis in*

Indigent Defense: An Arkansas Commentary, 44 ARK. L. REV. 409, 410 (1991) (describing the dilemma of an Arkansas attorney in a capital case who needed a psychiatrist to examine a defendant who had previously been diagnosed as schizophrenic; the lawyer was first told by the judge to find a mental health expert closer to home and then denied funds after he located a local psychologist).

25. State v. Walker, No. 89 CR 56742-2 (Super. Ct. Muscogee County, Ga. 1991), *rev'd on other grounds,* 424 S.E.2d 782 (Ga. 1993).

26. Deposition of Richard Bell at 24–25, Grayson v. State (Cir. Ct. Shelby County, Ala. Oct. 10, 1991) (No. CV 86–193).

27. Id. at 62–63.

28. Rosenzweig, supra note 24, at 412.

29. Morgan v. Zant, 743 F.2d 775, 780 (11th Cir. 1984).

30. Only 11 of the 36 states which have the death penalty have statewide public defender programs. The Spangenberg Group, supra note 22, at 122, 125. Some of those state public defender programs have specialized full-time capital litigation groups that provide representation in capital cases at trial. Id. Two of those states, New Hampshire and Wyoming, have no one under death sentence. Id. at 119; NAACP Legal Defense & Educational Fund, DEATH ROW USA 1 (Winter 1993). Eight of the states with statewide defense programs have death rows that are comparatively small: Connecticut (5); Delaware (16); Maryland (14); New Jersey (9); New Mexico (1). Id. at 17, 27, 25, 38, 29. This leaves two states with large death row populations, Ohio (127) and Missouri (83), with statewide programs and capital litigation sections. Id. at 26, 29; The Spangenberg Group, supra note 22, at 122. Florida and California, which have two of the country's three largest death rows, have public defender programs, but many capital cases in those states are handled by assigned counsel outside of the public defender system. Florida has an elected public defender in each judicial circuit. Id. at 122–23. California has county public defender agencies in all of its major counties. Id. at 123. Even though these programs cannot handle the huge volume of capital cases in those states, they have annual training programs and provide materials which improve the quality of representation in those states. No similar programs exist in Texas or many other states with large death row populations.

31. Id. at 680. A contract arrangement in one Georgia county required that the attorney pay any investigative and expert expenses out of the $4265 he was to be paid that year for representing all of the county's indigent defendants. Not surprisingly, often not one penny is spent on either investigative or expert assistance in an entire year in some Georgia counties.

32. Trisha Renaud & Ann Woolner, *Meet Em and Plead Em: Slaughterhouse Justice in Fulton's Decaying Indigent Defense System,* FULTON COUNTY DAILY REP., Oct. 8, 1990, at 1.

33. State v. Peart, 621 So. 2d 780, 790 (La. 1993).

34. State v. Peart, 621 So. 2d 780, 789 (La. 1993). A study of the system found that there is a "desperate need to double the budget for indigent defense in Louisiana in the next two years." Id. (quoting The Spangenberg Group, STUDY OF THE INDIGENT DEFENDER SYSTEM IN LOUISIANA 50 (1992)).

35. Hal Strauss, *Indigent Legal Defense Called "Terrible,"* ATLANTA J.-CONST., July 7, 1985, at 12A.

36. Martinez-Macias v. Collins, 979 F.2d 1067 (5th Cir. 1992).

37. Makemson v. Martin County, 491 So. 2d 1109, 1114–15 (Fla. 1986), *cert. denied,* 479 U.S. 1043 (1987) (quoting MacKenzie v. Hillsborough County, 288 So. 2d 200, 202 (Fla. 1973) (Ervin, J., dissenting)).

38. The Spangenberg Group, supra note 22, at 157.

39. Frederic N. Tulsky, *Big-Time Trials, Small Time Defenses,* PHILADELPHIA INQ., Sept. 14, 1992, at A8.

40. Marcia Coyle et al., *Washington Brief: High Noon for Congressional Habeas,* NAT. L.J., July 9, 1990, at 5.

41. 466 U.S. 668, 694 (1984).

42. Riles v. McCotter, 799 F.2d 947, 955 (5th Cir. 1986) (Rubin, J., concurring).

43. Romero v. Lynaugh, 884 F.2d 871, 875 (5th Cir. 1989).

44. Messer v. Kemp, 474 U.S. 1008, 1090 (1986) (Marshall, J., dissenting from denial of certiorari).

45. Powell v. Alabama, 287 U.S. 45, 75 (1932) (Butler, J., dissenting) (quoting decision of Alabama Supreme Court).

46. What follows is the brief in its entirety. The only parts of the brief not set out below are the cover page and certificate of service:

> THE RECORD AFFIRMATIVELY SHOWS THAT THE APPELLANT WAS CONVICTED OF THE SAME OFFENSE, WHICH IS PRECISELY THE SAME IN LAW AND FACT IN VIOLATION OF THE 5th AMENDMENT OF THE UNITED STATES CONSTITUTION.

47. Bruce A. Green, *Lethal Fiction: The Meaning of "Counsel" in the Sixth Amendment,* 78 IOWA L. REV. 433, 454 (1993).

48. See, e.g., Warren E. Burger, *Remarks on Trial Advocacy: A Proposition,* 7 WASHBURN L.J. 15 (1967); Warren E. Burger, *The Special Skills of Advocacy: Are Specialized Training and Certification of Advocates Essential to Our System of Justice,* 42 FORDHAM L. REV. 227 (1973).

49. Polk County v. Dodson, 454 U.S. 312, 332 (1981) (Blackman, J., dissenting).

50. Transcript of Opening and Closing Arguments at 39, State v. Dungee, Record Excerpts at 102. (11th Cir.) (No. 85-8202), *decided sub nom.* Isaacs v. Kemp, 778 F.2d 1482 (11th Cir. 1985), *cert. denied,* 476 U.S. 1164 (1986).

51. American Bar Ass'n & the Nat'l Legal Aid & Defender Ass'n, *GIDEON* UNDONE! THE CRISIS OF INDIGENT DEFENSE FUNDING 3 (1982).

52. Many of the reports are summarized in Richard Klein & Robert Spangenberg, THE INDIGENT DEFENSE CRISIS 5 (1993) (prepared for the American Bar Association Section of Criminal Justice Ad Hoc Committee on the Indigent Defense Crisis), at 10; Richard Klein, *The Eleventh Commandment: Thou Shalt Not Be Compelled to Render the Ineffective Assistance of Counsel,* 68 IND. L.J. 363, 393 (1993).

53. Wilson v. State, 574 So. 2d 1338, 1341 (Miss. 1990).

54. Chief Justice Harold G. Clarke, Annual State of the Judiciary Address, *reprinted in* FULTON COUNTY DAILY REP., Jan. 14, 1993, at 5.

55. Standards for the appointment of counsel, which are defined in terms of number of years in practice and number of trials, do very little to improve the quality of representation since many of the worst lawyers are those who have long taken criminal appointments and would meet the qualifications. Such standards can actually be counterproductive because they may provide a basis for denying appointment to some of the most gifted and committed lawyers who lack the number of prior trials but would do a far better job in providing representation than the usual court-appointed hacks with years of experience providing deficient representation.

56. See, e.g., *Report of Malcolm Lucas to ABA Task Force Report on the Death Penalty,* 40 AM. U. L. REV. 195, 197 (1990). The expense of providing more qualified counsel is

repeatedly argued as a reason to defeat legislation aimed at improving representation in capital cases.

57. At the urging of prosecutors, the federal courts and many state courts have increasingly refused to consider constitutional issues even where the failure to raise them was the result of ignorance, neglect, or inadvertent failure to raise and preserve an issue by a court-appointed lawyer. Coleman v. Thompson, 111 S. Ct. 2546 (1991) ("[A]ttorney ignorance or inadvertence is not 'cause' " to excuse filing of notice of appeal three days late, as indigent prisoner "must bear the risk of attorney error") (quotation omitted); Dugger v. Adams, 489 U.S. 401, 406–8 (1989) (barring relief because trial lawyer did not object to jury instructions even though court of appeals had unanimously concluded that death penalty was unconstitutionally imposed due to those instructions); Smith v. Murray, 477 U.S. 527, 539 (1986) (Stevens, J., dissenting) (barring issue not properly raised on appeal even though "[t]he record . . . unquestionably demonstrates that petitioner's constitutional claim is meritorious, and that there is a significant risk that he will be put to death because his constitutional rights were violated"); Murray v. Carrier, 477 U.S. 478, 488 (1986) (holding that attorney "ignorance or inadvertence" does not constitute cause to excuse failure to raise Fourteenth Amendment claim in earlier proceeding). Three of these cases—all except *Murray v. Carrier*—were capital cases. In each of those cases, the defendant has been executed without a determination of the constitutional issue because of the attorney error.

As a result of the complexity of the procedural rules and the lack of familiarity with them by many of the lawyers appointed to defend the poor, executions are now routinely carried out without review by any court of significant constitutional issues because of errors by counsel. See, e.g., Whitley v. Bair, 802 F.2d 1487, 1496 n. 17 (4th Cir. 1986) (finding that all 15 issues raised on behalf of Whitley were barred because they had not been properly raised by his trial lawyer), *cert. denied,* 480 U.S. 951 (1987). Today, it is unusual to see a capital case in which one or more issues presented in federal habeas corpus review is not found to be procedurally barred.

58. Evans v. State, 441 So. 2d 520, 531 (Miss. 1983) (Robertson, J., dissenting), *cert. denied,* 467 U.S. 1264 (1984); see also Hill v. State, 432 So. 2d 427, 444–51 (Miss. 1983) (Robertson, J., dissenting).

59. Justice Stevens has expressed the view that the Supreme Court has "grossly misevaluate[d] the requirements of 'law and justice' that are the federal court's statutory mission under the federal habeas corpus statute" and instead "lost its way in a procedural maze of its own creation." Smith v. Murray, 477 U.S. 527, 541 (1986) (Stevens, J., dissenting). Justice Blackmun, writing for four members of the Court in *Dugger v. Adams,* accused the majority of "arbitrarily impos[ing] procedural obstacles to thwart the vindication of what apparently is a meritorious Eighth Amendment claim." Dugger v. Adams, 489 U.S. 401, 412–13 (1989). . . .

60. H.R. 4737, § 8(e)–(g)(1990), *reprinted in Hearings Before Subcomm. on Courts, Intellectual Property and the Administration of Justice of the House Judiciary Comm. on H.R. 4737, H.R. 1090, H.R. 1953, and H.R. 3584,* 101st Cong., 2d Sess. 3, 11 (1990), at 14–16; see also H.R. 5269, § 1307(e)–(g) (1990), *House Hearings,* supra at 486–91.

61. Detailed Comments on H.R. 5269 Submitted with Letter from William P. Barr to Thomas S. Foley, Speaker of the U.S. House of Representatives (Sept. 10, 1990), *reprinted in House Hearings,* supra note 60, at 723, 746–47.

62. Letter from Don Siegelman, Attorney General of Alabama et al., to Jack Brooks, Chairman of the House Judiciary Committee (July 13, 1990), *reprinted in House Hearings,* supra note 60, at 654, 656.

63. Resolution Opposing Habeas Reform Legislation, *reprinted in House Hearings,* supra note 60, at 649.

64. California Attorney General Daniel E. Lungren asserted that the bill "could appropriately be called the 'Capital Defense Attorney Employment Act of 1993' " and urged its defeat because it would "raise the overall cost of capital litigation by imposing new federal standards" and result in additional litigation. Letter from Daniel E. Lungren to Senator Diane Feinstein (Aug. 13, 1993) at 15 (on file with author). . . .

65. McCleskey v. Kemp, 481 U.S. 279, 344 (1987) (Brennan, J., dissenting).

66. Joseph W. Bellacosa, Ethical Impulses from the Death Penalty: "Old Sparky's" Jolt to the Legal Profession 29 (Dyson Distinguished Lecture, Oct. 26, 1993) (unpublished manuscript, on file with the Pace University School of Law).

67. See, e.g., Stephen B. Bright, *In Defense of Life: Enforcing the Bill of Rights on Behalf of Poor, Minority and Disadvantaged Persons Facing the Death Penalty,* 57 Mo. L. Rev. 849 (1992).

68. State v. Peart, 621 So. 2d 780 (La. 1993) at 795 (Dennis, J., dissenting). . . .

69. Callins v. Collins, 62 U.S.L.W. 3546 (U.S. Feb. 22, 1994) (No. 93-7054) (Blackmun, J., dissenting from denial of certiorari).

PART VI

Controversies from Prosecution to Execution

The complex interaction of public attitudes and values, statutory and case law, plus a wide variety of empirical facts and hypotheses, has given rise to numerous controversies over the current administration of the death penalty. Especially during the past decade, as the number of persons on the nation's death rows has steadily increased, tensions have been felt throughout the system at every crucial decision point: among them the prosecutor's decision to seek the death penalty, the jury's decision to sentence, and the chief executive's decision to consider clemency. Controversy also surrounds possible reforms and revisions in the current system. From among many that ought to be at least briefly mentioned, here are five.

Availability of Defense Counsel for Death Row Inmates

At least since the infamous Scottsboro Boys capital trial in Alabama in 1931, in which the rape convictions and death sentences of the innocent defendants were overturned because of the failure of the state to provide adequate defense counsel,[1] critics of the death penalty (such as Stephen Bright, in Chapter 22) have pointed out how difficult it is to get competent counsel—indeed, *any* counsel—for indigent death penalty defendants. A decade after *Gregg,* with 1,800 persons on death row, complaints were already being heard about how the capital defense bar was stretched thin. "Many lawyers who used to take such cases are shunning them now, discouraged by the enormous financial and emotional cost of pressing such cases. . . ." (Reinhold 1986).[2] In 1990, responding to the growing crisis, the Criminal Justice Section of the American Bar Association urged "the state and federal governments . . . to provide competent and adequately compensated counsel for capital defendants/appellants/petitioners, as well as to provide sufficient resources for investigation, expert witnesses, and other services, at all stages of capital punishment litigation" (Robbins 1990).

Acknowledging the legitimacy of the complaints from the legal community, Congress undertook to fund some twenty death penalty resource centers; in 1993 the operating costs of these centers came to eighteen million dollars.[3] Meanwhile, the population on the nation's death rows continued to increase faster than did available counsel. In 1992 Bryan A. Stevenson, executive director of the newly created Alabama Capital Representation Resource Center, voiced a note of despair:

> The Justices treat us as legal terrorists abusing the Federal courts toward unlawful ends. . . . It used to be that if you took these cases, the judiciary would congratulate you on your commitment. . . . But it's burdensome, emotionally and financially. . . . Partners [in private law firms in a position to underwrite pro bono services to death row clients] are concerned about public image and expense, and these clients are society's most despised people. The firms had their one case and they're not willing to do another. (Jan Hoffman 1992)[4]

With prisoners entering death row at the rate of roughly 250 per year at present, and fewer than 100 exiting annually (whether by execution, suicide, retrial, or other release), the need for qualified lawyers steadily increases. However, in the summer of 1995, under pressure from radical Republicans seeking to balance the federal budget and hostile to delays in processing death penalty cases, Congress voted to zero-fund these centers, leaving the availability of trained counsel for indigent defendants in future death penalty cases up in the air. This defunding, unless reversed, or replaced by the states or by private sources, virtually guarantees that before long some prisoner will be executed despite good grounds for invalidating either his conviction or his death sentence or both.[5]

Conditions on Death Row

The physical and psychological conditions on death row continue to raise the question whether confinement there for years is itself "cruel and unusual" in the sense of that phrase used in the Eighth Amendment.[6] Defenders of the death penalty are typically unsympathetic to any argument about poor prison conditions—even unconstitutionally "cruel and unusual" conditions—on the grounds that prolonged life on death row, however wretched and painful, is a direct consequence of the defendant's own choices, since it always is open to him to drop all appeals and accept his death sentence.

Opponents of the death penalty disagree, and now they can point to the decision in 1993 by the Judicial Committee of the Privy Council in England (the final court of appeal in death penalty cases arising in erstwhile Commonwealth jurisdictions) in the case of *Pratt et al. v. Attorney General of Jamaica.* In this case the law lords held that the government of Jamaica has only five years after pronouncing a death sentence on a convict in which to hear all the issues raised by the defendant on appeal; if in that time these issues cannot be adjudicated, the defendant must be resentenced to life in prison. "If the appellate procedure enables the prisoner to prolong the appellate hearings over a period of years," the judges argued, "the fault is to be attributed to the appellate system that permits such delay and not to the prisoner who takes advantage of it" (Schabas 1994:189). What is true for processing death penalty cases in Jamaica is arguably true as well for such cases elsewhere, including in this country.

Whether these delays should nonetheless be laid at the defendant's door, because they result from "frivolous" or otherwise ill-advised appeals, can be tested in part by the reports from death row in Florida presented with cool insight by journalist David von Drehle in his book *Among the Lowest of the Dead* (1995) or with more passion by death row convict Mumia Abu-Jamal in *Life on Death Row* (1996).

Physician Participation in Executions

In recent years—especially since the advent of execution by lethal injection—attention has focused on the proper role of doctors and other medically trained personnel before, during, and after an execution.[7] Some have insisted that any participation is a direct violation of the professional obligations of physicians, since any involvement in an execution is to that extent cooperation in bringing about an unnecessary and nonconsensual death.[8] Others, including many doctors, see the matter in a different light altogether, viewing medical participation in executions both as a personal and professional right and as an effective way to reduce the likelihood of discomfort (or worse) for the condemned prisoner during the execution process.[9]

Methods of Execution

Another chronic controversy concerns the moral and empirical factors favoring different modes of execution, especially since death by lethal injection has become so popular. Is lethal injection really no more painful than what our aged household pets undergo at the hands of a skillful and considerate veterinarian? Or is the impact on a conscious human person of the standard lethal drugs really unknown? Or is it known to cause unacceptable distress of various sorts in at least some prisoners? And where does this leave the firing squad, hanging, the gas chamber, and especially the electric chair, with its century-long history of misfirings, flash fires, unreliable voltage, all in the service of cooking the human brain and nervous system until the person dies?[10] How can anyone familiar with the details of the way the electric chair works not conclude that it is a "cruel" punishment even if, after a hundred years of widespread use in the United States, it is not "unusual"?[11]

What I have elsewhere called Schwarzschild's Paradox—some methods of execution are worse than others, but none is better—continues to haunt the practice of capital punishment in this country.[12]

Victim-Impact Testimony

Under the *Lockett* ruling (1978) the defense in a capital case is allowed to introduce "any" evidence it deems relevant to persuade a jury to bring in less than a death sentence. The prosecution, however, was kept on a shorter tether and confined strictly to introducing evidence relevant under one or more of the specific "aggravating'' circumstances in the relevant statutes. But in *Payne v. Tennessee* (1991), the Supreme Court ruled that the prosecution may now bring in so-called victim-impact evidence to show the jury just how valuable and loved the victim was and thus, by implication, how deserving of a death sentence the convicted murderer is. This is a troubling development; as I have remarked elsewhere:

> [C]riminal desert is supposed to be measured by the offender's culpability and the harm caused by the crime. . . . [W]hile in theory the harm caused in crimes such as arson or robbery will vary with the value of the property destroyed or money stolen, the harm caused in criminal homicide is deemed uniform in all cases, on the tacit ground that all human lives are of equal worth. . . . Now, however, it will be up to each capital trial jury to decide for itself whether the murder of which the defendant has been found guilty is deserving of a death penalty because of some special features about the victim, features not defined by any statute, possibly not evident to the defendant at the time of the crime, and not specifiable by the trial court or in any uniform manner from case to case. (Bedau 1994a:299–300)[13]

With this brief discussion of these five topics behind us, we can turn to several perhaps more important issues concerning the administration of capital punishment. These topics take us from the beginnings of a death penalty case in the prosecutor's office, through the trial and sentencing, to the clemency hearing and an actual execution, and end by confronting us with the question whether the system we have just examined is worth the costs.

Prosecutorial Discretion

Although the Supreme Court in *Gregg, Proffitt,* and *Jurek* insisted that capital trial juries be given some form of statutory guidance in deciding whether to sentence the convicted defendant to life or to death, the Court has not insisted that comparable guidance be imposed on prosecutors. Yet the decision whether to seek the death sentence is perhaps the most far-reaching decision to be made in the whole arena of criminal justice. How do prosecutors make such decisions? Why do some prosecutors seek and others shun the death penalty in the murder cases they bring to trial? These questions and their answers are examined in the research by legal scholar Leigh Bienen on the experience in New Jersey, in an article reprinted here as chapter 23. Longtime Manhattan (N.Y.) district attorney Robert M. Morgenthau drawing on his own experience, agrees with Bienen's conclusions. As New York was about to reenact the death penalty early in 1995, he argued that ''[t]he death penalty actually hinders the fight against crime,'' but ''fear of political repercussion keeps [many district attorneys] from saying so publicly.''[14]

Capital Jury Decision Making

Occasionally a person indicted for first-degree murder will plead guilty before the judge and be sentenced forthwith (in some states, a plea of guilty nullifies the possibility of a death sentence). But the usual practice is for the defendant to plead not guilty and then go to trial, taking his chances with the jury. Prior to *Furman,* juries were left entirely on their own in deciding between a life and a death sentence. Since *Furman,* juries have been helped (at least in theory) by statutory guidelines specifying the relevant aggravating and mitigating circumstances governing their choice of sentence.

But how effective is that help? The classic example is in the statutory language specifying as an aggravating circumstance that the murder was "especially heinous, cruel, or depraved" (or words to that effect). Just how is a jury to tell when a murder is, and when it is not, covered by such language?[15] What kind of guidance does such language actually provide to the jury? In general, do jurors really understand the language in which the judge instructs them in the law of capital sentencing? Furthermore, do jurors really make up their minds on the basis of these legal criteria and the evidence submitted during the penalty phase? No one knows.

Or, at least no one did prior to the creation of the Capital Jury Project in 1991 and its uniquely informative results to date. Under the direction of William J. Bowers at Northeastern University, the project has arranged for interviews with hundreds of former capital trial jurors across the nation in an effort to learn more about their deliberations prior to sentencing. What emerges from these investigations is little short of shocking; the confusion, irrationality, and willful indifference to relevant mitigating conditions among these jurors must undermine confidence in the ability of the typical capital jury to make responsible sentencing decisions.[16] Although the project in 1995 is only midway in its career, more than two hundred pages of a recent law journal are devoted to discussing the preliminary results.[17] A brief essay by law professor Joseph L. Hoffman, surveying some of the findings of the project so far, is reprinted here as Chapter 24.

Convicting the Innocent

Probably no single issue so fortifies abolitionists as does worry over the possibility of executing an innocent person. At least since 1762, when the innocent Jean Calas was hanged in Toulouse, France, the abolition movement in Europe and the Americas has been influenced by documented cases of wrongful executions—not an execution of someone merely denied due process (such cases, historically at least, are legion), nor merely cases in which the defendant's killing in self-defense is wrongly judged to be murder (such cases, too, are not unknown), but rather where a person entirely innocent of any role in the crime is nonetheless tried, found guilty, sentenced to death, and executed. Abolitionists and retentionists alike agree that this is a terrible injustice, but they disagree over whether it actually happens—or happens now, or happens frequently—and whether avoiding the risk of it happening at all is worth the possible cost (in reduced deterrence, incapacitation, and retribution) of not executing at least the many who are guilty.

The most extensive attempt to document such cases has been carried out by University of Florida sociologist Michael L. Radelet and me. Our research was initially made public in 1985 at the annual meeting of the American Society of Criminology, published in the *Stanford Law Review* (1987), and then expanded with the assistance of writer Constance E. Putnam into a book, *In Spite of Innocence* (1992, new preface 1994). My coauthors and I argue that serious miscarriages do happen in capital cases, and are bound to continue to happen, and we claim that in the more than four hundred cases we discuss—stretching over the whole of this century, from one end of the country to the other—some two dozen cases at least involve the execution of an innocent person.

Even before the research was published it was put under the microscope by the Department of Justice in Washington, D.C., a backhanded tribute to how important some members of the Reagan administration viewed our findings and an unprecedented step for the federal government to take in evaluating scholarly research on the death penalty prior to its formal publication. The task of criticism fell to Paul G. Cassell and Stephen Markman, two lawyers in the office of then–Attorney General Edwin Meese III. The first version of their critique appeared as a memorandum to the attorney general. Then, in 1988, having failed to persuade the Stanford Law Review editors to reverse their decision to publish our research, or at least to give equal space for their rebuttal in the same issue of the review in which our article was scheduled to appear, they published an abbreviated and revised edition of their criticism in the review;[18] our even briefer reply appeared in the same issue.[19] Since then, Cassell and Markman have left the Department of Justice, but each continues to restate for publication in various sources their criticisms of our research.[20] Rather than reproduce here any of the exchange between us and our two critics, I have reprinted as chapter 25 the staff report of the House Subcommittee on Civil and Constitutional Rights, *Innocence and the Death Penalty* (1993).

Executions "Live" on Television

In the days of public executions, defenders of the death penalty convinced themselves that actually seeing convicts put to death would enhance the deterrent effect of the penalty. Critics were not so sure; by the mid-1800s in this country and in England,[21] many observers thought the spectacle aroused the public to no good end by making those in attendance either more angry at the authorities for failing to grant clemency (if the condemned was a sympathetic character despite his or her crimes) or else coarsened by their own misbehavior (excessive public drunkenness, especially). Over the past two decades the modern version of this controversy takes the form of whether executions should be shown on television.[22]

Playwright Arthur Miller has proposed an even more dramatic way to teach the nation about the death penalty. With tongue in cheek he argued that we need to "privatize executions," holding them in football stadiums, selling box seats at two hundred dollars each—in short, making executions part of the regular entertainment offerings in major cities across America. Eventually, he mused, the public would become bored with the spectacle, "just as it seizes on all kinds of entertainment only to lose interest once their repetitiousness becomes too tiresomely apparent'' (Miller 1992).

Defenders of the death penalty have not participated in the debate over public executions to the extent that abolitionists have. And, Miller's irony aside, abolitionists are sharply divided over whether televising executions would advance or retard their cause. Perhaps the best example of this debate is in the brief exchange reprinted here as chapter 27, between two of the nation's most prominent death penalty opponents, provoked by the attempt made by station KQED in San Francisco to televise the execution of Robert Alton Harris. Arguing against televising executions is Robert R. Bryan, a former chairman of the board of the NCADP and an experienced death penalty attorney practicing in San Francisco. Arguing the other side, largely on grounds of free speech, is Henry Schwarzschild, the founder of the NCADP in 1976 and for fifteen years the director of the Capital Punishment Project of the ACLU in New York. So far the courts have refused to allow television cameras into the death chamber, but this controversy is by no means settled.

Failed Clemency Efforts

As noted in chapter 1, the practice of clemency in capital cases—commutation by the governor (or other authority) of a death sentence to a long term of imprisonment—has fallen virtually into desuetude,[23] but not for lack of effort by defense counsel searching for a way to strike a sympathetic chord. Clemency efforts, whether successful or not, are not often recorded for the general public.[24] Obviously, some death row prisoners are better candidates for clemency than others even if, like many who are not, they fail to obtain it. The case of Harold Lamont (''Wili'') Otey, presented in chapter 26, is not atypical of those where good (though not the best) grounds for commutation existed. The Otey case stretched out for many years and in its entirety is fairly complex; published here for the first time is an account by Larry Myers, one of his attorneys, focused exclusively on the political and legal setting of the clemency efforts on Otey's behalf. Despite the patient efforts of his legal counsel and many friends, Otey was executed in 1994.

Witnessing an Execution

Each side in the death penalty controversy frequently insists that if only we gave our attention to the central events in a capital case—the horrible murder of the innocent, the helpless prisoner's needless execution—we could more easily make up our minds where we stand on the issue, as if rage or disgust were the ultimate arbiters. The only contribution in this vein to be found in this book is the personal account by journalist Susan Blaustein of the execution she witnessed in Texas in 1993, reprinted here as chapter 28. ''We have perfected the art of institutional killing,'' she concludes, ''to the degree that it has deadened our natural, quintessential human response to death.''[25] The reader who seeks a fuller account of personal involvement with prisoners on death row that culminates with witnessing the death of a prisoner ought to read Sister Helen Prejean's *Dead Man Walking* (1993), the book on which the provocative movie of the same title, starring Susan Sarandon and Sean Penn, was based. A very different approach, in which the grim setting for an actual execution is examined in great detail, will be found in two recent books: *Death Work: A Study of the Modern Execution Process* (1990), by criminologist Robert Johnson; and *Death At Midnight: The Confession of An Executioner* (1996), by Donald A. Cabana, formerly warden at Mississippi State Prison in Parchman.

Estimating the Costs of a Modern Death Penalty System

How expensive is the death penalty? Does the taxpayer—who, with family and friends, is also a potential victim of murder—get benefits worth the cost? For more than a decade abolitionists have argued that however cheap it may be to carry out the purely physical or technical aspects of an execution (a little electricity, cyanide gas, or sodium pentothal), a death penalty *system* of criminal justice for any crime in a civilized society is enormously expensive. Whether those costs could be reduced dramatically by curbing the right of appeal (especially through limiting federal habeas corpus) and underfunding or abolishing the death penalty resource centers around the nation, strategies pursued in Congress during 1994 and 1995, remains controversial.

The most recent (1993) and precise research on the point was conducted in North Carolina at Duke University; the authors summarize their results in three conclusions: First, "The extra costs to the North Carolina public of adjudicating a case capitally through to execution, as compared with a noncapital adjudication that results in conviction for first-degree murder and a 20-year prison term, is about *$163 thousand.*" Second, "The extra cost to the North Carolina public of prosecuting a case capitally, as compared with a noncapital prosecution, is more than the *$216 thousand* per death penalty imposed. This estimate takes into account the likelihood that the jury will actually impose the death penalty, and if so, that the appellate courts will return the case to Superior Court for retrial or resentencing." Finally, "The extra cost *per execution* of prosecuting a case capitally is more than $2.16 million" (Cook and Slawson 1993:97, and Verhovek 1995).

Reprinted here as chapter 29 is a broader survey of the whole issue, conducted and originally published in 1993 by the Death Penalty Information Center. Earlier studies on this subject may be traced through the references in this report.

Notes

1. See Carter 1979.
2. See also Stout 1988; Coyle, Strasser, and Lavelle 1990.
3. Berkman 1995.
4. See also Margolick 1993; Smothers 1993.
5. See also Lewis 1995; Wiehl 1995; and Dieter 1995b. The crisis in representing death row convicts has been widely reported in the press; see, for example, *San Francisco Chron-*

icle, 23 Jan. 1996, p. 1; *Dallas Morning News,* 19 Feb. 1996, p. 6A; *Boston Globe,* 4 April 1996, p. As of early 1996 it appears that some, if not all, of the resource centers will be "reborn as private groups," though on a significantly smaller scale and without any guarantee of funding. See Coyle 1996.

6. The debate was initiated by Curran and Casscells 1980.

7. See the report by the American College of Physicians et al. 1994.

8. See Davis 1995. For a general discussion of the whole issue not confined to the United States, see Radelet 1996.

9. See R. Johnson 1990; Holland 1985; Carroll 1988.

10. See especially Hillman 1993.

11. See Denno 1994a, 1996.

12. Bedau 1990b.

13. For fuller details, see V. Berger 1992; Vitiello 1994.

14. See also Nossiter 1995. In Massachusetts, when Governor William Weld announced the filing of his bill to restore the death penalty, Attorney General Scott Harshbarger opposed it, saying in part: "It is a simplistic, bumper sticker response to a complex problem." *Worcester Telegram & Gazette,* 11 March 1995, p. A11.

15. See Garnett 1994; Rosen 1986.

16. Since 1991, Bowers and his associates have released several unpublished working papers, including " 'Proof Beyond a Reasonable Doubt': A Review of Jurors Thoughts" (1992) and "Juror's Response to the Defendant's Testimony, or Lack Thereof" (1992). For a full list, see the Bibliography.

17. See Baldus 1995; Bowers 1995; Sarat 1995; Hoffman 1995; Luginbuhl and Howe 1995; Sandys 1995; Haney 1995; Hans 1995; Sherman 1995; Slobogin 1995.

18. Markman and Cassell 1988.

19. Bedau and Radelet 1988.

20. See Cassell 1994; Markman 1994. For a thorough review of *In Spite of Innocence,* see Marshall 1994. For the most recent compilation of innocent defendants released from death row, see Radelet, Lofquist, and Bedau 1996.

21. See Gattrell 1994.

22. For further discussion of the efforts to televise this and other executions in California, see Hentoff 1991; Quindlen 1991; Kroll 1991; Kaplan 1991; Sherman 1991. See also Lesser 1993:24–46. A videotape of the Harris execution was made but was later destroyed; see *New York Times,* 23 February 1994, p. 35. Other death row convicts—James Autrey in Texas in 1984 and John Thanos in Maryland in 1994—have sought to have their executions videotaped; see Goodman 1984; Chartrand 1994. Talk show host Phil Donahue was unsuccessful in his suit against the State of North Carolina, in which he sought to broadcast the execution of David Lawson in 1994; see Biddle 1994.

23. For a digest of the law on executive clemency, see National Governors' Association 1988.

24. The most extensive discussion of death penalty commutations, during the years 1959–66, is by former California Governor Edmund (Pat) Brown; see Brown 1989. For accounts of more recent clemency hearings that failed, see Ingle 1990:51–54; von Drehle 1994:29–41 (both on John Spenkelink, Florida, 1979). See also Prejean 1993:157–69 (Robert Willie, Louisiana, 1984). For an account of a successful clemency hearing, see NCADP *Lifelines,* no. 50 (September/October 1990), pp. 1, 5 (Billy Neal Moore, Georgia, 1990).

25. For other eyewitness descriptions of recent executions, see Cabana 1995; von Drehle 1995:104–13, 393–401; Moran 1985. For a journalistic account, see Solotaroff 1995. See also Johnson 1990; Ingle 1990; Trombley 1992.

23

"A Good Murder"

LEIGH B. BIENEN

> A good murder, a genuine murder, a fine murder, as fine as you could hope to see, we haven't had one like it for a long time."
>
> Georg Büchner, *Woyzeck* (1836)

I

. . . Every culture has its own way of portraying death, of ritualizing murder. In America, representations of violent and ghoulish murders are pervasive in our entertainment and news. The reports of murders, especially capital murders, do not only tell us what is out there and what happened; they tell us what to think and how to feel. Portrayals of murder cases communicate important messages about who is in charge and who is a threat.

Sometimes the message is that the people who are convicted of capital murder are beneath contempt, unworthy of anything more than summary justice. They are so threatening to our lives and property that they can be kept in prisons which are brutal and inhumane, or, better, executed. Sometimes the message is that the society needs to continue to spend large amounts of money on law enforcement and the establishment and maintenance of prisons. Another frequently heard theme is that it is unfair for police and prosecutors to be forced into battle using laws which give an unfair advantage to the accused, that the courts have been sentimental and foolish in restricting the police in the area of search and seizure and in the use of evidence from confessions.

If the news presented its message in terms of those kinds of abstractions, no copies of newspapers would be sold, and no one would watch dramatizations of the day's events on television. So the news carries its cultural burden the way societies have always transmitted their most important messages, through stories and drama. Some dramatizations may airbrush out those facts of the case which do not fit within the stock script. Yet the dramatization will retain enough details from the actual crime so that the viewer's pleasure is heightened by the illusion of verisimilitude. It is no longer even necessary to change the names of the principals

Reprinted from *Fordham Urban Law Journal* 20 (1993), pp. 585–607 by permission. Portions of the text and footnotes have been omitted and the remaining footnotes renumbered.

of the crime which catches the fancy of the public before it becomes the subject of a television movie.

Murder, in other words, sells soap and beer and cars and newspapers. A good murder, that is, one the public wants to read about, will generate dozens of stories. The formerly prim Metropolitan section of the New York Times has become a daily reading of our cultural attitudes towards violence in general and murder in particular. New York City reports over a thousand homicides a year, the vast majority of which do not occur in Manhattan. Almost every day in the Manhattan daily newspapers, there is a story about murder. There are also many stories about capital murder prosecutions and detailed reports of executions in other states, since [as of 1997] New York state has no capital punishment statute.

. . . The prosecution of murder cases, especially the prosecution of capital cases, has much to do with cultural stereotypes and dreams of revenge. Capital prosecutions are supposed to be reserved for the worst people, people who have committed crimes so terrible that society does not think they deserve to live. The need for vengeance and cultural expiation are central to justifications for the death penalty. Dramatizations of murders and capital trials are very effective in feeding people's desire for revenge. The prospect of an impending execution, as was recently seen in the Wesley Dodd case in Washington state, gives the media an opportunity to focus again and again upon the repellent and horrifying details of a murder. The public response is one of outrage and frustration, and this sense of rage is fueled by the daily repetition of details of brutality as the execution draws closer. The murder occurred once, but the public is presented with it again and again to justify the execution.

Choices about how and what to report in a crime story anticipate and play against assumptions concerning the expectations of an audience conditioned by heavily stereotyped dramatizations of violence. One scenario of urban murder which is seen frequently includes a black male defendant, perhaps an illegal immigrant, possibly high on drugs or mentally unbalanced, or mentally deficient, or previously institutionalized, someone who is without a job, has a criminal record, possibly on parole or probation for another offense, who kills a middle class victim, male or female, but often white. In these murders, which may briefly become obsessions for a community, the victim not only works, but symbolizes the values of the meritocracy. Often the victim is an incarnation of the myth of self-made success, a model which is a cruel rebuke to many citizens. The message of such stories is clear: someone who is worthless killed someone who was of value.

Reports of murders in the tabloids tend to be the comic book version, complete with bubble quotes and illustrations. And the level of tolerance for details of brutality and violence in the news continues to rise. The accepted level of the brutality in entertainment has escalated to the point where two or three murders in a movie are considered trivial. The target audience of teenage boys pays to see graphic dismembering or explicit slashing of what is called in rape reform legislation the initimate parts. In a quiet evening at home the viewer can vicariously participate in a dozen homicides, identifying in turn with the victim, slayer, investigator, police or prosecutor. The young men who are the target audience for action movies are especially death-obsessed, and they account for an increasingly large proportion of all murders committed.

Granting that the criminal justice system may be misrepresented in high profile and high action news stories, what do these dramatizations of murders have to do with actual homicides, with what murder in the cities really looks like? A single sensational murder has been known to be the impetus for changing the penalty for murder, but aside from that kind of isolated impact, can it be said that whether stereotyped or not, media representations of murder have any effect upon the criminal justice system? . . .

II

This essay will describe a pattern which emerged when researchers examined all homicide cases in the state of New Jersey during the years immediately after the reimposition of capital punishment in 1982. Particularly relevant is the pattern of capital prosecution for urban and suburban murders, and how those cases were regarded by law enforcement, the media, and the public.

In 1982 the New Jersey legislature reinstated capital punishment with a statute which identified eight aggravating factors that could be used to elevate the crime of ordinary murder to a capital offense. The capital statute in New Jersey is similar to capital statutes in effect in a number of other jurisdictions; indeed, it is similar to the statute which was proposed to reenact the death penalty in New York in 1991.

Several aspects of the New Jersey situation, however, are unusual. First, the New Jersey Supreme Court has had a history of being a leader in the development of state constitutional doctrine. Second, the Office of the Public Defender in New Jersey is unusual in that it is administered by a single administrative agency at both the trial and appellate level. Immediately after reenactment, the Office of the Public Defender was able to commit itself to a coordinated statewide challenge to the reimposition of capital punishment at both the trial and appellate level. This challenge included a data collection and analysis project dedicated to tracking all homicide cases and capital prosecutions in the state after reenactment. The atypical institutional structure of the Public Defender's Office at the time made such a comprehensive, statewide data collection effort possible. The Public Defender data base was eventually taken over by the Administrative Office of the New Jersey Supreme Court, and subsumed within the research of the New Jersey Supreme Court's Proportionality Review Project.

Data were collected on all final dispositions of homicide indictments at the trial court stage, a process which takes about two years for most murders and longer for cases which are declared capital. The Proportionality Review Project presented an analysis of dispositions in over 1350 homicide cases to the New Jersey Supreme Court in the capital appeal of *State v. Marshall.* This case involved the first person in New Jersey to have a death sentence upheld by the state supreme court. The Report presented to the *Marshall* court included a detailed analysis and description of over 260 death eligible murder cases which had resulted in thirty-five death sentences actually being imposed, during the period of 1982-1989.

In New Jersey and most other capital jurisdictions, capital murders are a small proportion of all murders and only a fractional proportion of all homicides. The proponents of reenactment in New Jersey repeatedly stated that they intended the capital punishment statute to apply to few cases, that is, to the exceptional case. Only a few defendants have been sentenced to death in New Jersey since reenactment in 1982, a total of thirty-nine; and of these thirty-nine who were sentenced to death, only one person, Robert Marshall, has had his death sentence upheld through all stages of the state appeals process. The New Jersey Supreme Court reversed twenty-six death sentences in a row, an unprecedented series of reversals by any state supreme court, before upholding Mr. Marshall's death sentence on direct appeal. The court then ordered a special and separate set of arguments to address the question of whether imposing the death sentence in this case was fair in comparison to the sentences imposed upon similar defendents for similar crimes.

Although there were over 250 cases where the death penalty could have been sought, and over 120 cases which went to a capital penalty trial after a verdict of guilty of capital murder, less than a quarter of all aggravated murders and less than a third of the cases which reached the second stage of a penalty trial resulted in the jury imposing a death sentence. In spite of the high level of support for capital punishment in the opinion polls, and in spite of the fact that the cases which reached penalty phase were typically very aggravated murders actual jurors were reluctant to impose the death sentence when faced with that option in sentencing a real defendant who had murdered a real victim. National opinion polls reported that about 80% of the people in the state were in favor of capital punishment during this period, yet the death sentence, in New Jersey at least, has been imposed in a very small number of actual cases. Some take that as a sign that the law is being applied justly.

The reason why there are a few capital prosecutions in New Jersey and elsewhere is not because there are few killings which meet the legal criteria for capital prosecution. In New Jersey and elsewhere, the definition of death eligible murder is broad enough to encompass many more cases than will ever be prosecuted as capital murders. Local prosecutors have a great deal of discretion in the cases they select for capital prosecution. The decision to prosecute for capital murder is usually not determined by limitations on the statutory definition of death eligible murder. One statutory factor alone, the felony factor, which declares capital all murders associated with the commission of another felony, regularly presents a large number of death eligible homicides.

When capital murder prosecutions in New Jersy were examined over a seven year period immediately after reenactment, it became apparent that the number of potentially capital murders in urban areas is far larger than the number of such murders in rural and nonurban jurisdictions. Yet in New Jersey, prosecutions for capital murder are far less likely to occur in some urban jurisdictions.

Historically, in both the South and the North, racial disparities in the application of the death penalty have resulted in a disproportionate number of blacks being sentenced to death and executed. Recently there has been a widespread and well documented pattern of defendants being more likely to be sentenced to death if their victims are white, irrespective of the race of the defendant. In addition to race, many believe that factors of class and social status are influential in determining who is prosecuted for capital murder and sentenced to death.

Those who argue for capital murder as a way of championing the victims of homicide overlook the fact that there are so many victims. During the period of the New Jersey Proportionality Review Project, there were thirty-five death sentences imposed. During that same period, from over 1300 homicides, 264 cases almost certainly could have been declared death eligible by the prosecutor, and 119 cases actually resulted in a conviction at trial for capital murder. What was distinctive about the small number of cases where the death sentence was actually imposed? What characteristics did the capital cases have in common?

In New Jersey and most other states, the important unit is the county. The county defines the limits of trial court jurisdiction: prosecutors are county, not city, officials who may or may not be elected; and jurors are selected according to county vicinage. New Jersey is unusual in that a very large proportion of the state is classified by the U.S. Census Bureau as being within a metropolitan area, but New Jersey also has suburban and rural counties.

There are significant county-by-county disparities in income and economic vitality in New Jersey. Six counties have been identified by state urban planners as having large urban centers which are economically distressed: Essex, Camden, Hudson, Passaic, Mercer and Union. Not surprisingly, these counties also have a high proportion of blacks and Hispanics, a high unemployment rate, and a relatively low per capita income. Together these six counties accounted for over 68% of all homicides and over 60% of all aggravated, potentially capital murders in the state. Some rural counties are also relatively poor, however, and not all suburban counties are wealthy.

Murder is overwhelmingly a crime which involves people of the same race. As a result, more often than not, the greater proportion of murders in the cities consist of black and Hispanics killing one another. Specifically, murders in the cities typically consist of black and Hispanic men between the ages of eighteen and twenty-six killing one another.

Essex County, which reported the largest number of homicides in the state, had a large proportion, seven out of thirty-five, of all death sentences in the study period. But those seven cases in Essex county in which the death sentence was imposed represented less than 2% of all homicides in the county and only 13% of all of the homicides in the county where there was a clear factual basis for the imposition of the death penalty under the statute.

Essex County had over 20% of all of the death eligible cases in the state, yet the death sentence was imposed in only 13% of those cases. Over a fifth of all potentially capital homicides were disposed of in Essex County courts, yet capital prosecutions in Essex County accounted for less than 14% of all homicide dispositions. In other words, many serious highly aggravated murders occurred in Essex County, but a very small proportion of them were prosecuted as capital cases.

In contrast, the Ocean County courts, which adjudicated a total of twenty-seven homicides in the entire study period of over seven years, imposed *three* death sentences from a pool of seven death eligible cases. Ocean County, which accounted for 3% of all death eligible homicides, imposed the death penalty in 38% of those cases, in comparison to Essex County's 13%. Hudson County had the same number of penalty trials as Ocean County, seven, and no death sentences were imposed in Hudson County during the period. Yet Hudson County, which includes Jersey City, had 159 homicides during the period, of which nineteen were eligible for capital prosecution of their facts.

There is some evidence that this pattern of widely varying rates of prosecution from one prosecutorial jurisdiction to another is not atypical. A recent report on capital case prosecutions in adjoining rural and urban jurisdictions in Georgia found striking differences between the Chattahoochee and Atlanta judicial districts.[1] The rural district of Chattahoochee imposed 75% more death sentences than Atlanta, a city with nearly three times its population and many more homicides. In potentially capital cases in Chattahoochee, the prosecutor sought the death penalty in 34% of the cases when the victim was white, but only 6% of the time when the victim was black. Although black victim cases constituted 65% of all murder cases in the district, they accounted for only 15% of all cases which were prosecuted capitally in Chattahoochee.

Pennsylvania now has one of the larger death row populations. As elsewhere, race seems to be relevant to sentencing patterns. One Philadelphia judge has sentenced twenty-six men to death, twenty-four of them African-American. The sentences of this Philadelphia judge alone account for about a fifth of the death row population in the state. Yet, another type of pattern has been observed in Pennsylvania—one which suggests that race may be only one factor in creating large county-by-county disparities in patterns of capital sentencing.

Philadelphia, which does not allow public defenders to represent capital defendants, accounts for 14% of the state population and over 50% of all death sentences.[2] Allegheny County, which includes Pittsburgh and 12% of the state

1. DEATH PENALTY INFORMATION CENTER, CHATTAHOOCHEE JUDICIAL DISTRICT: THE BUCKLE OF THE DEATH BELT (1991) (With the support of the Southern Christian Leadership Conference, this organization (based in Washington, DC) reports statistics on the imposition of the death penalty in Chattahoochee and Atlanta.).

2. MICHAEL KROLL, DEATH PENALTY INFORMATION CENTER, JUSTICE ON THE CHEAP: THE PHILADELPHIA STORY (1992) (reports statistics on the imposition of capital punishment in Philadelphia, Allegheny County and all Pennsylvania).

population, accounts for less than 5% of all the death sentences. Allegheny County does provide public defender representation in capital cases. In Philadelphia, capital cases are assigned at very low fees to the private bar.

The first case in which the New Jersey Supreme Court upheld a death sentence after reversing twenty six in a row was a case in which a white male insurance executive from Monmouth County, a high income suburban county, murdered his wife after taking out a million dollar insurance policy on her life. Mr. Marshall paid two accomplices to commit the murder, and there is little doubt either that he planned the murder, that he paid his accomplices to commit the murder, or that his motive was to kill his wife for the insurance. Mr. Marshall is now the only person in New Jersey who has a death sentence which has been upheld through all stages of state appellate review process, including proportionality review, and his appeal is now pending in the federal and state systems.

III

The capital prosecution of Robert Marshall was portrayed in a series of widely popular retellings. A book about the case, Joseph McGinnis' *Blind Faith,* remained high on the best seller list, and it then became the basis for a television mini-series watched by an audience which numbered in the millions. The television mini-series left the audience with the impression that justice was done because a bad man who killed an innocent person was sentenced to death and will be executed. And at some simple level that is true. On the other hand, if that were the standard for justifiable legal executions, there would have been a least a hundred executions in the state of New Jersey alone since reenactment in 1982.

The verdict appeared fair to many because Mr. Marshall was clearly guilty: and ambiguities, contradictions and complexities in the case were either lied about or omitted from the book and other versions retelling this story. A general audience would have no sense of how Mr. Marshall's culpability compared with that of others who may or may not have been sentenced to death. The popular audience was left with two misleading impressions: that every murder case is treated like Mr. Marshall's case, and that his case was especially and uniquely aggravated. The dramatizations and news reports led the public to believe that a white middle class person is as likely to be sentenced to death as a black person, or a poor person, because this particular capital trial did not fit the former stereotype of a poor black illiterate man being railroaded to the death sentence.

Partly because of the enormous media attention given to the *Marshall* case, the challenge to his death sentence became more than usually politically charged, especially since the New Jersey Supreme Court had already inspired the wrath of the legislature and some of the public by overturning twenty-six death sentences in a row before upholding the first one in the case of Mr. Marshall.

Mr. Marshall's murder was atypical of murders in New Jersey, and it would have been an unusual case in any jurisdiction. But, the *Marshall* case did bear some resemblance to other capital murders. It was a made-for-media murder, and those who had the wit to recognize its commercial potential made substantial profits. It was not by chance that the case became the subject of a best selling book and a television mini-series. The circumstances of Mr. Marshall's case contained many standard features of Hollywood melodramas involving murder, and that made this murder especially appealing to the entertainment industry.

To imply that a murder must be Hollywood-worthy before it will be prosecuted capitally is only partially facetious. Cases will be selected for capital prosecution according to factors which demonstrate patterns of bias related to class and race and reflect the unchecked discretion of local prosecutors.

The *Marshall* case is an extreme example: the reasons why the circumstances of this case became the plot for a best selling book and a mini-series were not irrelevant to why and how Mr. Marshall was prosecuted for capital murder. The *Marshall* case had a recognizable villain who could have been a character in a melodrama from the fifties. He had a clearly discernible motive, which identified him as a bad guy, deserving of punishment. His victim could not have been more heroic or blameless, always a relevant factor for audience indentification. Mrs. Marshall was a model mother and wife, and she devoted herself selflessly to her sons and her foolish and errant husband, who showed his gratitude by murdering her. There were circumstances in this case which made for a saga of injustice.

Not only did Mr. Marshall have a comprehensible motive for killing his wife, but he was killing her for an insurance policy he took out on her life, without her knowledge, because he had gambling debts and wanted to run away with his mistress, who became, after some prosecutorial maneuvering, the state's star witness. Mr. Marshall had a motive everyone could understand, and he articulated that motive to people who testified about it at trial. Ineptly he tried again and again to persuade marginal and incompetent petty criminals to kill his wife for him. Finally, they did it, by shooting her at a turnpike rest stop where Mr. Marshall had pulled off the road and delivered her to be murdered, as prearranged.

The story aspects of the case were compelling. Interesting and colorful types were tangled up in the action, and this was capitalized upon in the various dramatizations and retellings of the murder. There were many ironic twists to the plot, and a dramatic ending, the imposition of the death sentence. The hit man, the person who allegedly fired the gun which killed the victim, was acquitted of murder at trial, and his partner at the killing was released pursuant to a plea bargain shortly after testifying for the prosecution at trial. By contrast, a marginal participant who had never set foot in New Jersey at the time of the murder, whose role was allegedly no more than passing on phone messages in Louisiana, was sentenced to thirty calendar years without parole. The mistress took the stand for the prosecution and testified at length about her clandestine love affair and that Mr. Marshall told her he wanted to get rid of his wife. Her own role in the case could have been the subject of a whole other movie. Mr. Marshall himself, the audience agreed, was villainous, cowardly, despicable, and stupid. He was sentenced to death by the jury after a very short penalty trial.

Is this an unjust result? Mr. Marshall certainly committed murder, and there was little in his character or actions to excuse him. But he is no worse than several dozen others who committed equally cold blooded murders, but who will not be executed for reasons which have nothing to do with the seriousness of their murders or the harm they caused to innocent victims or their threat to the public peace. Not only were there several cases which were very similar to the Marshall case in their circumstances, but there were other spousal murders in New Jersey which were at least as aggravated, where the death penalty was not imposed or even considered.

As reprehensible as Mr. Marshall's motives were, and as blameless as his victim was, his case probably would not have been prosecuted capitally if it had occurred in Newark, Jersey City or Camden. Wicked, foolish men kill their wives and get caught in those jurisdictions too, but rarely are they prosecuted for capital murder. . . .

The pattern in New Jersey is an inversion of an earlier sterotype. This pattern may or may not persist, although there is some evidence that parts of this pattern are repeated in other jurisdictions. The former sterotype was that if you were poor and black and male, and represented by a public defender or assigned counsel, you were likely to be railroaded into a death sentence by an all white prosecutorial system. And that may still be the case in some jurisdictions or in places where courts and legislatures refuse to allocate resources to the defense of capital cases, in spite of the constitutional requirement to provide indigents with adequate representation.

However, in New Jersey during the period studied, it was an advantage to be represented by the Public Defender, counter to the earlier popular stereotype. In some jurisdictions it may still be the case that black defendants are significantly more likely to be sentenced to death than whites, other things being equal, although this effect is not seen in recent national studies. It is difficult to comprehend discrepancies such as those cited for Philadelphia and Chattahoochee outside of a racial context. The racial effect that recently has been documented independently in a number of states is a white victim effect: a person who kills a white victim is more likely to be prosecuted capitally and sentenced to death, other things being equal.

Since the reenactment of the death penalty in New Jersey the following pattern emerged: if you were poor and black and committed a murder, *and* if your victim was poor and black *and* your case was processed in an urban jurisdiction, *and* if you were represented by the Public Defender, you were less likely to be prosecuted and convicted for capital murder or to be sentenced to death, than if your crime was committed in a rural or suburban jurisdiction and your victim was white, especially if your victim was white and middle class. Having a private attorney was no advantage, and the presence of a white victim was statistically significant. In part, this pattern in New Jersey reflects the same "white victim effect" which has been independently documented and verified in many other states in the North and South. Partly it is the result of other factors, such as the differential economic resources available to the prosecutor's office in urban and suburban counties.

Certainly the resources available to the prosecutors is one explanation for county disparities in capital case processing. Even though Essex County regularly reported over 140 homicides a year, it had no new capital prosecution for over a year during the middle of the period studied. Part of the reason for the lack of such prosecutions was that the financial resources of the prosecutor's office were strained due to a county budgetary crisis. And a backlog in the county courts existed to the point where several judges in the Essex County court house only heard cases which had been indicted prior to 1982. Neither political nor institutional forces in Essex County at that time were pressing for expensive and lengthy capital trials.

Essex County juries are also different from the juries in Ocean County and Monmouth County: Essex County juries have more black people on them, more Hispanics, and the jurors are younger. We know that younger people, blacks and women and Hispanics, are less likely to be in favor of capital punishment than older white men, the group most likely to support capital punishment and to see it as in their interest. We also know that blacks have more skepticism about the fairness of the criminal justice system generally, and the system for imposing capital punishment in particular. The polls consistently indicate that black men and women are significantly more likely than whites to believe that the imposition of the death penalty is racially biased.

These may be some of the reasons why relatively few death sentences come from Essex County, even though many of the aggravated murders come from Essex County. So when the prosecutors are not charging capital murder in Essex County, it may not only be that the county's prosecutors are overburdened and underfunded, although that is certainly not irrelevant in spite of the county prosecutor's official protestations to the contrary. The Essex County prosecutors may know that an Essex County jury is unlikely to return a death verdict against some defendants, even though the circumstances of the murder theoretically meet the objective, legal criteria for death eligibility. There is another intangible factor which should not be discounted. Murders in Newark do not even make the front pages of the major newspapers any more. There are so many of them.

What about Hudson County, a county which includes Jersey City and accounts for quite a few murders? During the entire first decade that capital punishment has been in effect in New Jersey, there has not been a death sentence imposed in Hudson County. Yet Hudson County had fifteen death eligible cases and seven penalty trials during the period studied, twice as many as Ocean County, and Hudson County accounted for a total of 159 homicide cases in the data base of over 1300 cases. There were rumors that the county prosecutor in that county did not much like the death penalty, and that he did not believe the death penalty should be imposed upon minorities.

Is it credible to suggest that there was no case as aggravated or as serious as the murder of Mrs. Marshall among those 159 Hudson County cases? In the state as a whole there were over a hundred cases that involved a man killing his wife or sex partner during the period. There must have been at least one other wife as blameless as Mrs. Marshall. Some of the cases documented involved dismembering, over fifty stab wounds, and tortuous homicidal incidents in which the victim suffered over a considerable period of time. Yet these cases did not result in the death sentence being imposes, or even sought.

The lesson here is that murder is ultimately a personal crime, in addition to being a crime against the person. A very particular person is the victim of murder. Of course the individual circumstances of the crime are important. A jury is going to be more likely to find an unsympathetic defendant guilty of capital murder if the victim is victuous, blameless, educated, good looking, and a parent, and everyone involved is prosecutorial decision-making along the way knows this and plays upon it.

IV

The way crime is reported, where some stories are selected over others, some tales told and some not, and the way murders are prosecuted, reveals who and what society values. Characterizations of killers and how they are brought to justice is an important part of our national identity, the reflection we get back from the cultural mirror. As Americans, one of our most dearly held self images is that in the United States there is equality before law, that the poor, racial minorities, the mentally retarded and the illiterate receive as fair a trial as the rich. Whether or not it is true in each individual case, it comforts us as a people to believe our criminal justice system treats everyone alike. There is certainly no other society where both the state and federal government devote so many resources to providing poor people with lawyers.

What is frequently expressed now both in news stories and their dramatizations is a portrait of the criminal justice system as an ineffective and overwhelmed parent, sometimes a parent who is corrupt, sometimes just a bumbling parent who is well-intentioned but cannot cope. Sometimes the message is that the system is so badly broken that no one should even care about fixing it. The criminal justice system in this portrayal begins to resemble the nuclear arms industry: it costs too much, it does not do what we want, but we cannot do anything about it.

This orchestrated view absolves the rest of us from responsibility, and lets us believe that justice has nothing to do with us. Law abiding citizens should stay away from the criminal courts and let the police and the prosecutors do the nasty job of protecting the hard working, taxpaying people, who bear little resemblance to those who end up in jail. It is us against the monsters out there. If the police have to be nasty, if prison conditions are inhuman, it is to protect the lives and property of the law abiding.

In this scenario, defense attorneys and civil libertarians are naive do-gooders, troublemakers, or cynics who take advantage of a system in disrepair or dishonestly manipulate the law to try to bring about an unjust result, the acquittal of a guilty person. And since jobs are involved, we had better just leave the system as it is. The threat from criminals on the loose is too large and important for the ordinary citizen to understand: better let the men in uniforms and dark suits make all the decisions. It is probably good if middle class people do not know too much about what goes on in our criminal courts and prisons. It is certainly better not to object when we suspect things are not as they ought to be, especially if we can tell ourselves that the experts are in charge.

If capital murder cases are no more than the good guys chasing down the bad guys, and homicidal maniacs are threatening my job, my house and my kids, and it's all a mess anyway, why not call in Clint Eastwood or Charles Bronson. The death penalty, after all, just catches and stops one of those bad guys; there are so many of them and so few of us. Sentencing a person to death acts as a catharsis for everyone's general sense of overwhelming frustration.

This is not to suggest that the dramatized representations of crime in the news do not respond to real public concerns about crime and violence. News reports of murder are real, and important. The question is, how do emotionally heightened representations of murder cases influence how actual murder cases, and especially capital murders, are handled in the real criminal justice system? How do reports of murders justify the maintenance of the criminal justice system in its present form? Dramatizations, and the way in which murders are reported, have a powerful effect upon the selection of actual cases for capital prosecution and upon public perception. The portrayal of murders in the media shapes what the society believes to be important.

The pattern which emerges from an analysis of homicides over a decade in New Jersey suggests that urban homicides, especially those in which young blacks kill other blacks, mostly men but women too, or Hispanics kill Hispanics, are likely to be plea bargained to relatively light sentences. Perhaps the likelihood of plea bargaining reflects the fact that the society does not care about these victims, perhaps it is because these cases are not newsworthy. Or, perhaps it is the other way around, the cases are not newsworthy because they are plea bargained. Or, the cases are downgraded, both literally and procedurally, because we have no framework for the stories of the defendant or victim. Or, is it because the urban counties have fewer resources, or more forgiving juries, or just because there are so many murders there?

Whatever the reason, this does not seem to be a random or isolated pattern. Rarely do urban homicides involving minorities result in a capital prosecution, even though their circumstances may be highly aggravated, and in spite of the fact that minorities in the cities ara legitimately worried about the threat of crime and are disturbed by the reality that entire groups of young men are being removed from the community by homicide and the imprisonment for it. The public minded citizens of the city do not think these murders among young men are trivial.

The media, both the commercialized entertainment industry and its cousin the news industry, continue to dramatize capital murder either as an old fashioned detective melodrama, as in the *Marshall* case, or as the hunting and banishment of monsters, because that is what a conditioned audience expects. The *Marshall* case was an atypical spouse murder. Most men who kill their wives do so in a fit of drunken rage, after a pattern of repeated, serious beatings. Audiences are pleasurably terrified by portrayals of murderers as Hollywood villains or lurking strangers. These scare tactics do not even serve a useful educational purpose. For self-protection women should receive the message that the man to fear is their abusive husband, or a familiar acquaintance, not the stranger in the alley.

By making monsters out of marginal or mentally ill murderers, by insisting that they are the threat, emotionally charged dramatizations of crime justify depriving many other people of their rights; they make brutal and inhumane conditions of imprisonment seem legitimate. Focusing on the high profile, talismanic urban or suburban murders in which a minority person kills a middle class white also justifies incarcerating large numbers of minorities for other types of offenses that are often relatively minor. The United States has more people absolutely, and more people per capita, in prison than any other country in the world, including Pakistan and South Africa. The Hollywood version of capital murder cases—which implies that the good guy cops are catching bad guy murderers, and that it all ends up all right when a bad person is executed—is reassuring, but inaccurate. . . .

Dramatizations like those of the *Marshall* case portray a criminal justice system which is comprehensible and fair, even if harsh. This conforms to what many white suburbanites and some middle class blacks would like to believe. The death penalty is put in a context which both of these audiences find acceptable, and even desirable. Stories about murders which are not prosecuted, or murders where guilty defendants get off lightly, or where a retarded person, or a person who might not be guilty, is executed, imply that the system is unjust, is not working effectively. That does not make any one feel good. So capital murders continue to be presented as revenge dramas, as westerns, good guys versus bad guys shooting it out at the OK corral. This characterization of capital prosecutions tells us the criminal justice system is fine. It is effective. Justice is being done.

The death penalty is not about deterring murder. If law makers really wanted to prevent the deaths of innocent, helpless victims, lowering the speed limit to fifty-five miles per hour and vigorously prosecuting drunk drivers would result in a predictable reduction of highway fatalities. There is no reliable empirical evidence that reinstating capital punishment has any effect upon the homicide rate, or that it removes the worst murderers, although it is certain that reintroducing the death penalty will push up the costs of prosecuting murders.

There is something fundamentally wrong with a capital punishment system which selects people for execution on a random basis, or on the basis of whether the circumstances of their murders tell a story which will sell newspapers or television advertising. There is something very wrong with a society which allows its criminal justice system to seek vengeance for only a few who are murdered, especially if those few also happen to be the privileged in the society.

Our system for prosecuting murders is not working. We do not do ourselves a favor by lying to ourselves about this. The death penalty solves nothing, is nothing but a ghoulish entertainment, a distraction which keeps us from addressing the more serious structural problems of the entire criminal justice system. As law students, lawyers, judges, and most importantly citizens, we have been taken in, and we know better.

24

How American Juries Decide Death Penalty Cases: The Capital Jury Project

JOSEPH L. HOFFMAN

In the United States, the jury system is becoming a matter of controversy. Most Americans still support the basic concept of the jury trial, especially in criminal cases, believing juries composed of average citizens to be an important bulwark against the potential tyranny of government. At the same time, widely publicized cases like the Menendez case, the Hattori case, the two Rodney King trials, and now the O. J. Simpson case have led many Americans to question whether juries can be trusted to make wise decisions. Emotional arguments by lawyers, pressures from the mass media, and personal disagreements within the jury room often seem to distort jury decision making.

Unfortunately, much of the debate about the jury system has taken place in the dark, because juries conduct their business in a "black box"—no one else is allowed in the jury room during jury deliberations. More than thirty years ago, the Chicago Jury Project, headed by Harry Kalven and Hans Zeisel, tried to observe juries by using hidden cameras and microphones. This part of the research was quickly banned, however, and ever since, researchers have been unable to study jury behavior by direct observation.

In the absence of direct observation, jury research has relied largely on either "mock jury" studies (using volunteers, often university students, who pretend to be jurors in a real or imaginary case) or inferences about jury behavior from the end results of actual cases. These methods have produced important knowledge about juries, providing an empirical foundation for the theoretical work of Phoebe Ellsworth, Shari Seidman Diamond, Valerie Hans, Reid Hastie, Nancy Pennington, Vicki Smith, and other leaders in jury research. Yet these methods often seem to be missing a crucial connection with the "real world" of jury decision making. Jury researchers have lacked the opportunity to learn, as Kalven and Zeisel tried to do, what really happens in the jury room.

The Capital Jury Project is an attempt to fill this research gap in the specific

This is a slightly revised version of a paper presented at the 1995 annual meeting of the Research Committee on the Sociology of Law, International Sociological Association, held in August 1995 at the University of Tokyo.

context of death penalty trials. Death penalty trials are certainly the most important cases a jury is ever asked to decide—they involve, quite literally, a matter of life and death. I will begin by explaining some of the basic procedures of an American death penalty trial. Then I will describe the Capital Jury Project and its methodology. Finally, I will report some of the interim findings of the Capital Jury Project.

American Death Penalty Cases

There are both similarities and differences in the basic procedures that are used in an average American criminal trial and in the trial of a death penalty case. One important difference is in the selection of the jury. In an average criminal trial, jury selection deals primarily with identifying any potential jurors who might have prior knowledge about the case, or who might have a relationship with one of the parties; often, it takes only a few minutes to select a jury.

In a death penalty trial, on the other hand, any person whose personal views about capital punishment are strong enough to substantially influence his or her behavior as a juror is excluded from service. In other words, each potential juror must be capable of giving full and fair consideration to both a life sentence and a death sentence. This legal standard creates an opportunity for the lawyers to battle over each potential juror, based on their feelings about whether the potential juror is likely to favor one sentence or the other. For this reason, jury selection in a death penalty case often takes several weeks; during that period, potential jurors are probed for their views about capital punishment, before they have even begun to hear any evidence about whether the defendant committed the crime.

After the jury is finally selected, the next part of an American death penalty trial—which is called the "guilt phase"—proceeds much like any other criminal trial. The prosecution presents its case first, followed by any evidence the defense wishes to present. The defense need not present any evidence at all; the prosecution must always bear the burden of convincing the jury, beyond a reasonable doubt, that the defendant is guilty of the crime. The defendant need not take the stand as a witness, and no inference of guilt may be based on the defendant's silence in the courtroom. The trial judge is a largely passive observer of the proceedings, ruling on procedural matters but otherwise letting the jury make up its own mind based on the evidence and the arguments of the lawyers. After the close of evidence and arguments, the jury receives legal instructions from the judge and then retires to the jury room to deliberate, in private, about the defendant's guilt.

In the average criminal trial, if the defendant is found guilty, then the jury's role is over. The trial judge reads the jury's verdict aloud in open court, the jury is dismissed, and the case is scheduled for a sentencing hearing at a future date. The trial judge then determines an appropriate sentence for the defendant (within the range set by the statute) after receiving information about the defendant's background and circumstances.

In a death penalty case, however, the guilt phase of the trial is only a prelude to the main event. In most instances a prosecutor will not ask for the death penalty unless the evidence of the defendant's guilt is quite strong. Therefore, in a death penalty case, it is often a foregone conclusion that the defendant will be found guilty by the jury.

After the guilt phase of a capital trial, the trial reconvenes for what is called the "sentencing phase." This phase is basically a completely separate trial, except that the same parties, the same trial judge, and (in most states) the same jury are still involved. At the guilt phase of the trial, the jury is told to focus only on whether or not the defendant committed the crime. At the sentencing phase, the defendant's guilt is no longer the issue; the only question is whether or not the defendant should receive the death penalty. In all but two of the states where the death penalty exists, the same jury that decided the defendant's guilt must go ahead and try to reach a verdict (either final or advisory, depending on the state) about whether the defendant should live or die.

Although the guilt phase and the sentencing phase of a capital trial may seem to be similar in their basic procedures, they are quite different in substance. The most important difference is in the role of the jury. In the guilt phase (as well as in an average criminal trial), the jury's role is to be the finder of fact. The jury decides who is telling the truth and what really happened. There is (at least in theory) a true story about what happened, and maybe one or more false stories. It is the jury's fundamental role to determine the truth.

At the sentencing phase of a capital trial, on the other hand, the jury is no longer deciding a question that has a "true" or "false" answer. Instead, the jury is being asked to decide a moral question that has no "true" or "false" answer: Is the defendant a person who deserves to live or to die?

This is not a question of fact but one of moral judgment. There are no rules for making this kind of decision, and the law gives the jury no definitive guidance. The prosecution presents its evidence in support of a death sentence, usually emphasizing the brutality of the defendant's crime; the defense presents its case for mitigation, usually trying to explain how the defendant came to be the kind of person he is. The trial judge instructs the jury about the factors to consider, but in the end the jury is told to exercise its sound discretion and do whatever it believes to be just. If the jury unanimously votes for a death sentence, then (in most states) the trial judge must impose such a sentence. The trial judge's power to override the jury's sentencing verdict is (in most states) extremely limited.

The Capital Jury Project

In 1990 a group of researchers from over a dozen different American universities in the widespread fields of law, sociology, political science, psychology, and criminology came together to begin a research project to interview jurors who had served in death penalty cases. The Capital Jury Project is being funded by the National Science Foundation of the U.S. government. We are now near the end of our data collection, and we will soon have completed over one thousand juror interviews.

The project is under way in more than a dozen states, representing more than one-third of the states where the death penalty exists. The states were chosen in order to permit useful comparisons based on different kinds of death penalty statutes, as well as regional and demographic variations. Within each state our sample includes all recent cases in which a jury was asked to decide whether or not to impose a death sentence; half of our interviews come from cases in which the jury voted for life, and half come from cases in which death was imposed. We interview at least three of the jurors in each case.

The interviews, which are all based on the same data collection instrument and protocol, cover the entire experience of the juror, from the jury selection phase through the juror's emotional reactions after the trial ended. The interviews are audiotaped and range in length from two to eight hours. The interview data are being entered into a computer for quantitative analysis, and the audiotapes are providing rich material for qualitative analysis.

Interim Findings of the Capital Jury Project

As an original member of the Capital Jury Project, with responsibility for the project in my home state of Indiana, I am glad to have this chance to report some of its interim findings. The quantitative findings I will report are based on the completed sets of juror interviews from seven states; I will also refer to qualitative information from juror interviews in other states, where data collection is still ongoing.

My report will focus on two areas of interest. First, what specific factors exert the greatest influence on jurors as they try to decide whether the defendant should live or die? Second, how do jurors feel about the responsibility they bear for the fate of the defendant, and how do those feelings affect their behavior?

Factors That Influence the Sentencing Decision

Perhaps the most important question we hope to explore asks which specific factors most strongly influence the jury's sentencing decision. Because the jury is not given a rigid legal formula for the decision but is free to exercise discretion, we are curious about the factors that determine whether a defendant lives or dies. We hope eventually to develop tentative models of jury decision making in capital cases, which may also help us understand jury decision making in other kinds of cases.

So far, several observations can be made about this subject. The most extensive analysis has been conducted by Ted Eisenberg of Cornell University, who supervised the juror interviews in South Carolina, and his research colleague Martin Wells. Table 24-1 identifies the relative importance of various factors in the deliberations of over one hundred South Carolina jurors.

As can be seen from Table 24-1, where lower numbers represent greater amounts of discussion about that factor, one of the most important issues for jurors—more

Table 24-1.
"How much did the discussion among the jurors [at the sentencing phase of the trial] focus on the following topics?"

	Mean in life cases	Mean in death cases
Factors about future dangerousness		
Defendant's dangerousness in society	1.84	1.78
How likely to be a parole or pardon	1.66	2.15
How long before a parole or pardon	1.79	2.23
Prevent defendant from killing again	1.59	1.70
Factors about the crime		
Defendant's role or responsibility	1.25	1.23
Defendant's motive for the crime	1.50	1.67
Planning or premeditation	1.68	1.54
Alcohol as a factor in crime	2.81	2.88
Drugs as a factor in crime	2.98	2.98
Mental illness as a factor in crime	2.55	2.99
Insanity as a factor in crime	2.95	2.43
Victim's role or responsibility	2.71	2.51
Innocence or helplessness of victim	1.70	1.78
Pain and suffering of victim	1.80	1.82
The way the victim was killed	1.52	1.37
Strength of the evidence of guilt	1.41	1.54
What punishment the law requires	1.75	1.76
What punishment the defendant deserved	1.74	1.49
Other factors		
Defendant's background or upbringing	2.25	2.22
Defendant's history of crime/violence	2.11	2.10
Defendant's IQ or intelligence	2.20	2.33
Defendant's remorse or lack of it	2.16	1.94
Defendant's appearance in court	2.55	2.55
Defendant's dangerousness in prison	3.39	3.39
Death penalty as a deterrent to others	2.45	2.81
Reputation or character of victim	2.48	2.49
Loss or grief of victim's family	2.27	2.09
Punishment wanted by victim's family	2.86	3.16
Performance of the lawyers	1.98	1.96
Jurors' attitudes about death penalty	2.12	2.01
Jurors' feelings about victim's family	2.55	2.49
Jurors' feelings about defendant	2.30	2.40
Jurors' feelings about defendant's family	2.84	2.55
What religious beliefs require	2.93	2.85
What moral values require	2.49	2.34
What community feelings require	2.88	3.06
Similarity to other murders	3.35	3.39

*1 = great deal, 2 = fair amount, 3 = not much, 4 = not at all; N of South Carolina jurors ranged from 104 to 114.

Source: Theodore Eisenberg and Martin T. Wells, "Deadly Confusion: Juror Instructions in Capital Cases," 79 *Cornell Law Review* 1 (1993).

Table 24-2.
"How much did the discussion [about the defendant's guilt] among the jurors focus on the following topics?"*

	Great deal	Fair amount	Not much	Not at all	N of jurors
Defendant's dangerousness if ever back in society	35.7%	26.4%	19.0%	18.9%	(641)
Jurors' feelings about the right punishment	49.7%	15.2%	11.0%	24.1%	(630)

*Based on complete results from seven states.

Source: William J. Bowers, "The Capital Jury Project: Rationale, Design, and Preview of Early Findings," 70 *Indiana Law Journal* 1043 (1995).

Table 24-3.
"After hearing the judge's instructions, did you believe that the law required you to impose a death sentence if the evidence proved that . . . ?"*

	Yes	No	Undecided	N of jurors
Defendant would be dangerous in the future	31.9%	66.6%	1.5%	(652)

*Based on complete results from seven states.

Source: William J. Bowers, "The Capital Jury Project: Rationale, Design, and Preview of Early Findings," 70 *Indiana Law Journal* 1043 (1995).

important than the defendant's criminal history, background and upbringing, and remorse—is whether the defendant, if he is allowed to live, is likely to pose a danger to society in the future. Most states provide for either life imprisonment or a very long term of years in prison (for example, fifty years) as the alternative to a death sentence. In many states, however, the jury is not told about the nature of these alternative sentences. Therefore, the impact of the factor of "future dangerousness" depends on what jurors believe—rightly or wrongly—about the likelihood that a defendant who is not sentenced to death will remain in prison for a long time.

Table 24-2 shows that over 60 percent of the jurors we interviewed reported discussing this factor "a great deal" or "a fair amount" *even during the guilt phase deliberations,* at a time when they were not supposed to be thinking about the defendant's sentence at all. Nearly 65 percent also reported discussing their feelings about the right punishment during the same guilt phase deliberations.

Another measure of the importance of the "future dangerousness" factor appears in Table 24-3. Under the law of almost all states, a jury is *never* required to impose a death sentence on a defendant; the trial judge instructs the jury that the proper sentence in a capital case is *always* a matter of jury discretion. Yet 31.9 percent of the jurors we interviewed said that, based on their understanding of the

Table 24-4.
''After hearing all of the evidence [at the punishment phase of the trial,] did you believe it proved that . . . ?''*

	Yes	No	Undecided	N of jurors
Defendant would be dangerous in the future	75.6%	18.0%	6.4%	(672)

*Based on complete results from seven states.

Source: William J. Bowers, ''The Capital Jury Project: Rationale, Design, and Preview of Early Findings,'' 70 *Indiana Law Journal* 1043 (1995).

judge's instructions, the law ''required'' a death sentence if the defendant would be ''dangerous in the future.''

As Table 24-4 reveals, more than three out of four jurors *did* find that the defendant would be ''dangerous in the future.'' This figure may reflect the tendency of jurors to underestimate how many years a defendant will serve in prison if not given a death sentence. Jurors who underestimate the severity of alternative sentences and worry about the defendant's ''future dangerousness'' tend to vote for death (see Tables 24-5 and 24-6, North Carolina and South Carolina data). Results similar to those in Table 24-6 have also been found by our researchers in California and Florida; however, the difference in California was less significant because about one out of three California jurors knew that a defendant not sentenced to death would receive an alternative of life without parole. In South Carolina, less than 15 percent of the jurors were aware of this important fact.

To summarize, data from the Capital Jury Project reveal that one of the primary influences on jury behavior in capital cases is the fear—often based on misunderstanding—that a defendant who does not receive a death sentence might return to society in a relatively short time and commit more crimes of violence. This finding, which both Ted Eisenberg and Bill Bowers have reported in recently published articles, was cited by the U.S. Supreme Court in the recent case of *Simmons v. South Carolina,* 114 S.Ct. 2187 (1994). In *Simmons,* the Court held that it was a violation of a capital defendant's constitutional rights for the trial judge to bar the jury from receiving accurate information about alternatives to a death sentence. Although the direct effect of the decision in *Simmons* is limited to South Carolina capital cases, *Simmons* holds the promise that future Court decisions might reduce the influence of the ''future dangerousness'' factor upon juries.

Juror Responsibility for the Defendant's Fate

Another issue that has emerged as crucial to understanding the decision making of capital juries is the degree of responsibility that jurors feel for the fate of the defendant. Based on my interviews with jurors in Indiana, I can report that in most cases, jurors began their sentencing deliberations by discussing—often quite emo-

Table 24-5.
"How long did you think someone not given the death penalty for a capital murder in this state usually spends in prison before returning to society?"

	Less than 20 years	20 to 30 years	More than 30 years	(N of jurors)
Voted for death	74	12	14	43
Voted for life	28	67	5	40

"When you were considering the punishment, were you concerned that [the defendant] might get back into society someday, if not given the death penalty?"

	Level of concern		
	Great or somewhat	Slight or not at all	(N of jurors)
Voted for death	76	24	49
Voted for life	41	59	17

*Based on complete results from North Carolina only.

Source: James Luginbuhl and Julie Howe, "Discretion in Capital Sentencing Instructions: Guided or Misguided?" 70 *Indiana Law Journal* 1161 (1995)

Table 24-6.
"How long did you think someone not given the death penalty for a capital murder in this state usually spends in prison before returning to society?"*

Mean in life cases	Mean in death cases
23.8 years	16.8 years

*Based on complete results from South Carolina only; N of jurors = 86; difference between life and death cases is statistically significant at the level of .001.

Source: Theodore Eisenberg and Martin T. Wells, "Deadly Confusion: Juror Instructions in Capital Cases," 79 Cornell *Law Review* 1 (1993).

Table 24-7.
"Rank the following from 'most' through 'least' responsible for [the defendant's] punishment."*

	Most–Least					
	1	2	3	4	5	(N)
Defendant—because his conduct determined the punishment	46.1	10.7	6.4	7.6	29.1	(605)
Law—states what punishment applies	34.4	39.2	7.8	11.2	7.4	(605)
Jury—votes for sentence	8.8	23.3	38.8	25.5	3.6	(605)
Individual juror—since jury's decision depends on the vote of each juror	6.4	13.7	26.8	29.4	23.6	(605)
Judge—imposes sentence	4.5	12.9	20.2	26.1	36.4	(605)

*Based on complete data from seven states.

Source: William J. Bowers, "The Capital Jury Project: Rationale, Design, and Preview of Early Findings," 70 *Indiana Law Journal* 1043 (1995).

tionally—whether they should have this responsibility at all. One juror said: "The first thing we did was everybody just collapsed literally in each others' arms and cried, knowing that we had to do that. . . . Somebody just said, what right do we have to decide if somebody should live or die? And then we had a large discussion about that, about whether we as people had that right."[1]

For obvious reasons, most average citizens who are pressed into service as jurors in capital cases are extremely uncomfortable with the responsibility of making a decision about whether to put a defendant to death. Jurors cope with these overwhelming feelings in a variety of ways: Some try to joke about the situation or otherwise distract themselves from thinking about it; some pray in an attempt to find guidance from a higher authority; and some even turn to alcohol or other similar diversions during the hours they are not required to be in the courtroom.

One of the most common reactions, however, is for jurors to look to "the law" for guidance in making the sentencing decision. Even though "the law" does not actually purport to tell the jury which sentence to choose, many jurors misinterpret the trial judge's legal instructions and manage to convince themselves that "the law" dictates a certain sentencing result. This apparently allows the jurors to avoid feeling personally responsible for the sentence. As one Indiana juror described the sentencing decision: "I think it more or less was a procedure. I had a feeling [the judge] was giving us a procedure and we needed to go through these certain steps. And then if all the pieces fit, then you have a responsibility to come back with a death sentence."

Table 24-7 reveals that many of the jurors we interviewed managed to avoid

Table 24-8.
"Who was 'most responsible' for the defendant's sentence?"*

	"Judge override"	Jury verdict binding
Defendant	42.6%	47.3%
Law	36.8%	33.6%
Jury	7.1%	9.3%
Individual juror	3.2%	7.6%
Judge	10.3%	2.4%
(N of jurors)	(155)	(450)

*Based on complete data from seven states.

Source: William J. Bowers, "The Capital Jury Project: Rationale, Design, and Preview of Early Findings," 70 *Indiana Law Journal* 1043 (1995).

feeling personally responsible for the sentencing decision—despite the fact that the trial judge directly instructed them that the sentencing decision rested in their discretion. The jurors were asked to rank, on a scale of 1 to 5, who was the "most" (1) or "least" (5) responsible for the defendant's sentence.

Table 24-8 shows that the avoidance of personal responsibility is even greater in those few states where the trial judge has the legal authority to override the jury's sentencing verdict; in these "judge override" states, the "individual juror" ranked last in the jury's perception of responsibility for the defendant's sentence.

At present, we cannot say whether capital jurors reach better sentencing decisions when they feel personally responsible for those decisions. However, we can speculate that avoidance of personal responsibility might have the effect of making jurors more likely to choose a death sentence; it may be easier for jurors to live with the knowledge that a defendant will be executed, based on their sentencing verdict, if they do not feel they had freedom to choose otherwise. If this speculation is correct, then the findings of the Capital Jury Project may establish a need for our legal system to try to overcome this tendency among capital jurors.

Conclusion

The Capital Jury Project is the most extensive research project of its kind that has ever been undertaken in the United States. Although the findings reported here are tentative, they represent the kinds of information we are gathering from our juror interviews. Those of us who are part of the project are thankful for the opportunity to participate in such an effort.

Appendix
Citations to Selected Capital Jury Project Articles

SYMPOSIUM ISSUE: THE CAPITAL JURY PROJECT, 70 *Indiana Law Journal* no. 4 (1995) (contains Capital Jury Project articles by William Bowers, Austin Sarat, Joseph Hoffmann, James Luginbuhl and Julie Howe, and Marla Sandys, along with commentaries by other jury researchers who are not part of the Capital Jury Project).

William Bowers, "Research Note," 27 *Law & Society Review* 157 (1993).

Theodore Eisenberg and Martin Wells, "Deadly Confusion: Juror Instructions in Capital Cases," 79 *Cornell Law Review* 1 (1993).

Austin Sarat, "Speaking of Death: Narratives of Violence in Capital Trials," 27 *Law & Society Review* 19 (1993).

Note

1. This comment, and other juror comments on sentencing responsibility quoted in this paper, appear in Joseph L. Hoffman, "Where's the Buck—Juror Misperception of Sentencing Responsibility in Death Penalty Cases," 70 Indiana L.J. 1137 (1995) (Capital Jury Project Symposium Issue). See also Austin Sarat, "Violence, Representation, and Responsibility in Capital Trials: The View From the Jury," 70 Indiana L.J. 1103 (1995) (Capital Jury Project Symposium Issue); Marla Sandys, "Cross-Overs—Capital Jurors Who Change Their Minds About the Punishment: A Litmus Test for Sentencing Guidelines," 70 Indiana L.J. 1183 (1995) (Capital Jury Project Symposium Issue).

25

Innocence and the Death Penalty: Assessing the Danger of Mistaken Executions

No matter how careful courts are, the possibility of perjured testimony, mistaken honest testimony, and human error remain all too real. We have no way of judging how many innocent persons have been executed, but we can be certain that there were some.

Furman v. *Georgia,* 408 U.S. 238, 367–68 (1972) (Marshall, J., concurring)

I. Introduction

In 1972, when the Supreme Court ruled in *Furman* v. *Georgia* that the death penalty as then applied was arbitrary and capricious and therefore unconstitutional, a majority of the Justices expected that the adoption of narrowly crafted sentencing procedures would protect against innocent persons being sentenced to death. Yet the promise of *Furman* has not been fulfilled: innocent persons are still being sentenced to death, and the chances are high that innocent persons have been or will be executed.

No issue posed by capital punishment is more disturbing to the public than the prospect that the government might execute an innocent person. A recent national poll found that the number one concern raising doubts among voters regarding the death penalty is the danger of a mistaken execution.[1] Fifty-eight percent of voters are disturbed that the death penalty might allow an innocent person to be executed.

Earlier this year, the Subcommittee on Civil and Constitutional Rights heard testimony from four men who were released from prison after serving years on death row—living proof that innocent people are sentenced to death.[2] The hearing raised two questions: (1) just how frequently are innocent persons convicted and sentenced to death; and (2) what flaws in the system allow these injustices to occur? In order to answer these questions, Subcommittee Chairman Don Edwards called

Reprinted from Staff Report, Subcommittee on Civil and Constitutional Rights, House Judiciary Committee 103d Congress, 1st Session, October 21, 1993. Some footnotes have been deleted, and the rest renumbered. The staff notes that the report was prepared at the direction of Chairman Don Edwards (D-Calif.) by the "majority staff" and "has not been reviewed or approved by other members of the subcommittee."

upon the Death Penalty Information Center to compile information on cases in the past twenty years where inmates had been released from death row after their innocence had been acknowledged. This staff report is based on the research of the Center.

Section II of the report briefly describes each of the 48 cases in the past twenty years where a convicted person has been released from death row because of innocence. Sections III and IV examine why the system of trials, appeals, and executive clemency fails to offer sufficient safeguards in protecting the innocent from execution. The role of current legal protections is addressed by looking closely at a few of the cases where death row inmates were later found to be innocent or were executed with their guilt still in doubt. The report concludes that there is a real danger of innocent people being executed in the United States.

II. Recent Cases Involving Innocent Persons Sentenced to Death

The most conclusive evidence that innocent people are condemned to death under modern death sentencing procedures comes from the surprisingly large number of people whose convictions have been overturned and who have been freed from death row. Four former death row inmates have been released from prison just this year after their innocence became apparent: Kirk Bloodsworth, Federico Macias, Walter McMillian, and Gregory Wilhoit.

At least 48 people have been released from prison after serving time on death row since 1973 with significant evidence of their innocence.[3] In 43 of these cases, the defendant was subsequently acquitted, pardoned, or charges were dropped. In three of the cases, a compromise was reached and the defendants were immediately released upon pleading to a lesser offense. In the remaining two cases, one defendant was released when the parole board became convinced of his innocence, and the other was acquitted at a retrial of the capital charge but convicted of lesser related charges. These five cases are indicated with an asterisk (*).

YEAR OF RELEASE

1973

1. David Keaton — Florida — Conviction: 1971

Sentenced to death for murdering an off-duty deputy sheriff during a robbery. Charges were dropped and Keaton was released after the actual killer was convicted.

1975

2. Wilber Lee — Florida — Conviction: 1963
3. Freddie Pitts — Florida — Conviction: 1963

Lee and Pitts were convicted of a double murder and sentenced to death.

They were released when they received a full pardon from Governor Askew because of their innocence. Another man had confessed to the killings.

1976

4. Thomas Gladish	New Mexico	Conviction: 1974
5. Richard Greer	New Mexico	Conviction: 1974
6. Ronald Keine	New Mexico	Conviction: 1974
7. Clarence Smith	New Mexico	Conviction: 1974

The four were convicted of murder, kidnapping, sodomy, and rape and were sentenced to death. They were released after a drifter admitted to the killings and a newspaper investigation uncovered lies by the prosecution's star witness.

1977

8. Delbert Tibbs — Florida — Conviction: 1974

Sentenced to death for the rape of a sixteen-year-old and the murder of her companion. The conviction was overturned by the Florida Supreme Court because the verdict was not supported by the weight of the evidence. Tibbs' former prosecutor said that the original investigation had been tainted from the beginning.

1978

9. Earl Charles — Georgia — Conviction: 1975

Convicted on two counts of murder and sentenced to death. Charles was released when evidence was found that substantiated his alibi. After an investigation, the district attorney announced that he would not retry the case. Charles won a substantial settlement from city officials for misconduct in the original investigation.

10. Jonathan Treadway — Arizona — Conviction: 1975

Convicted of sodomy and first degree murder of a six-year-old and sentenced to death. He was acquitted of all charges at retrial by the jury after 5 pathologists testified that the victim probably died of natural causes and that there was no evidence of sodomy.

1979

11. Gary Beeman — Ohio — Conviction: 1976

Convicted of aggravated murder and sentenced to death. Acquitted at the retrial when evidence showed that the true killer was the main prosecution witness at the first trial.

1980

12. Jerry Banks — Georgia — Conviction: 1975

Sentenced to death for two counts of murder. The conviction was overturned because the prosecution knowingly withheld exculpatory evidence. Banks committed suicide after his wife divorced him. His estate won a settlement from the county for the benefit of his children.

13. Larry Hicks Indiana Conviction: 1978
Convicted on two counts of murder and sentenced to death, Hicks was acquitted at the retrial when witnesses confirmed his alibi and when the eyewitness testimony at the first trial was proved to have been perjured. The Playboy Foundation supplied funds for the reinvestigation.

1981

14. Charles Ray Giddens Oklahoma Conviction: 1978
Conviction and death sentence reversed by the Oklahoma Court of Criminal Appeals on the grounds of insufficient evidence. Thereafter, the charges were dropped.

15. Michael Linder South Carolina Conviction: 1979
Linder was acquitted at retrial on the grounds of self-defense.

16. Johnny Ross Louisiana Conviction: 1975
Sentenced to death for rape, Ross was released when his blood type was found to be inconsistent with that of the rapist's.

1982

17. Anibal Jarramillo Florida Conviction: 1981
Sentenced to death for two counts of first degree murder; released when the Florida Supreme Court ruled the evidence did not sustain the conviction.

18. Lawyer Johnson Massachusetts Conviction: 1971
Sentenced to death for first degree murder. The charges were dropped when a previously silent eyewitness came forward and implicated the state's chief witness as the actual killer.

1986

19. Anthony Brown Florida Conviction: 1983
Convicted of first degree murder and sentenced to death. At the retrial, the state's chief witness admitted that his testimony at the first trial had been perjured and Brown was acquitted.

20. Neil Ferber Pennsylvania Conviction: 1982
Convicted of first degree murder and sentenced to death. He was released at the request of the state's attorney when new evidence showed that the conviction was based on the perjured testimony of a jail-house informant.

1987

21. Joseph Green Brown (Shabaka Waglini) Florida Conviction: 1974
Charges were dropped after the 11th Circuit Court of Appeals ruled that the prosecution had knowingly allowed false testimony to be introduced at trial. At one point, Brown came within 13 hours of execution.

22. Perry Cobb Illinois Conviction: 1979
23. Darby Williams Illinois Conviction: 1979
Cobb and Williams were convicted and sentenced to death for a double

murder. They were acquitted at retrial when an assistant state attorney came forward and destroyed the credibility of the state's chief witness.

24. Henry Drake* Georgia Conviction: 1977
Drake was resentenced to a life sentence at his second retrial. Six months later, the parole board freed him, convinced he was exonerated by his alleged accomplice and by testimony from the medical examiner.

25. John Henry Knapp* Arizona Conviction: 1974
Knapp was originally sentenced to death for the arson murder of his two children. He was released in 1987 after new evidence about the cause of the fire prompted a judge to order a new trial. In 1991, his third trial resulted in a hung jury. Knapp was again released in 1992 after an agreement with the prosecutors in which he pleaded no contest to second degree murder. He has steadfastly maintained his innocence.

26. Vernon McManus Texas Conviction: 1977
After a new trial was ordered, the prosecution dropped the charges when a key prosecution witness refused to testify.

27. Anthony Ray Peek Florida Conviction: 1978
Convicted of murder and sentenced to death. His conviction was overturned when expert testimony was shown to be false. He was acquitted at his second retrial.

28. Juan Ramos Florida Conviction: 1983
Sentenced to death for rape and murder. The decision was vacated by the Florida Supreme Court because of improper use of evidence. At his retrial, he was acquitted.

29. Robert Wallace Georgia Conviction: 1980
Sentenced to death for the slaying of a police officer. The 11th Circuit ordered a retrial because Wallace had not been competent to stand trial. He was acquitted at the retrial because it was found that the shooting was accidental.

1988

30. Jerry Bigelow California Conviction: 1980
Convicted of murder and sentenced to death after acting as his own attorney. His conviction was overturned by the California Supreme Court and he was acquitted at the retrial.

31. Willie Brown Florida Conviction: 1983
32. Larry Troy Florida Conviction: 1983
Originally sentenced to death after being accused of stabbing a fellow prisoner, Brown and Troy were released when the evidence showed that the main witness at the trial had perjured himself.

33. William Jent* Florida Conviction: 1980
34. Earnest Miller* Florida Conviction: 1980
A federal district court ordered a new trial because of suppression of exculpatory evidence. Jent and Miller were released immediately after agreeing to plead guilty to second degree murder. They repudiated their plea upon leaving the courtroom and were later awarded compensation by the Pasco County Sheriff's Dept. because of official errors.

1989

35. Randall Dale Adams Texas Conviction: 1977
Adams was ordered to be released pending a new trial by the Texas Court of Appeals. The prosecutors did not seek a new trial due to substantial evidence of Adams' innocence. Subject of the movie *The Thin Blue Line.*

36. Jesse Keith Brown* South Carolina Conviction: 1983
The conviction was reversed twice by the state Supreme Court. At the third trial, Brown was acquitted of the capital charge but convicted of related robbery charges.

37. Robert Cox Florida Conviction: 1988
Released by a unanimous decision of the Florida Supreme Court on the basis of insufficient evidence.

38. Timothy Hennis North Carolina Conviction: 1986
Convicted of three counts of murder and sentenced to death. The state Supreme Court granted a retrial because of the use of inflammatory evidence. At the retrial, Hennis was acquitted.

39. James Richardson Florida Conviction: 1968
Released after reexamination of the case by prosecutor Janet Reno, who concluded Richardson was innocent.

1990

40. Clarence Brandley Texas Conviction: 1980
Awarded a new trial when evidence showed prosecutorial suppression of exculpatory evidence and perjury by prosecution witnesses. All charges were dropped. Brandley is the subject of the book *White Lies* by Nick Davies.

41. Patrick Croy California Conviction: 1979
Conviction overturned by state Supreme Court because of improper jury instructions. Acquitted at retrial after arguing self-defense.

42. John C. Skelton Texas Conviction: 1982
Convicted of killing a man by exploding dynamite in his pickup truck. The conviction was overturned by the Texas Court of Criminal Appeals due to insufficient evidence.

1991

43. Gary Nelson Georgia Conviction: 1980
Nelson was released after a review of the prosecutor's files revealed that material information had been improperly withheld from the defense. The district attorney acknowledged: "There is no material element of the state's case in the original trial which has not subsequently been determined to be impeached or contradicted."

44. Bradley P. Scott Florida Conviction: 1988
Convicted of murder ten years after the crime. On appeal, he was released by the Florida Supreme Court because of insufficiency of the evidence.

1993

45. Kirk Bloodsworth Maryland Conviction: 1984
Convicted and sentenced to death for the rape and murder of a young girl. Bloodsworth was granted a new trial and given a life sentence. He was released after subsequent DNA testing confirmed his innocence.

46. Federico M. Macias Texas Conviction: 1984
Convicted of murder, Macias was granted a federal writ of habeas corpus because of ineffective assistance of counsel and possible innocence. A grand jury refused to reindict because of lack of evidence.

47. Walter McMillian Alabama Conviction: 1988
McMillian's conviction was overturned by the Alabama Court of Criminal Appeals and he was freed after three witnesses recanted their testimony and prosecutors agreed case had been mishandled.

48. Gregory R. Wilhoit Oklahoma Conviction: 1987
Wilhoit was convicted of killing his estranged wife while she slept. He was acquitted at a retrial after 11 forensic experts testified that a bite mark found on his dead wife did not belong to him.

III. Where Did the System Break Down?

These 48 cases illustrate the flaws inherent in the death sentencing systems used in the states. Some of these men were convicted on the basis of perjured testimony or because the prosecutor improperly withheld exculpatory evidence. In other cases, racial prejudice was a determining factor. In others, defense counsel failed to conduct the necessary investigation that would have disclosed exculpatory information.

Racial Prejudice: Clarence Brandley

> The court unequivocally concludes that the color of Clarence Brandley's skin was a substantial factor which pervaded all aspects of the State's capital prosecution of him.
>
> Judge Perry Pickett

Sometimes racial prejudice propels an innocent person into the role of despicable convict. In 1980, a 16-year-old white girl named Cheryl Dee Ferguson was raped and murdered at a Texas high school. Suspicion turned to the school's five janitors. One of the janitors later testified that the police looked at Clarence Brandley, the only black in the group, and said, "Since you're the nigger, you're elected."[4]

Brandley was convicted and sentenced to death by an all-white jury after two trails. The prosecutor used his peremptory strikes to eliminate all blacks in the jury pool. Eleven months after the conviction, Brandley's attorneys learned that 166 of the 309 exhibits used at trial, many of which offered grounds for appeal, had vanished.

After six years of fruitless appeals and civil rights demonstrations in support of Brandley, the Texas Court of Criminal Appeals ordered an evidentiary hearing to investigate all the allegations that had come to light. The presiding judge wrote a stinging condemnation of the procedures used in Brandley's case, and stated that "The court unequivocally concludes that the color of Clarence Brandley's skin was a substantial factor which pervaded all aspects of the State's capital prosecution of him." Brandley was eventually released in 1990 and all charges were dismissed.

It took many years and a tremendous effort by outside counsel, civil rights organizers, special investigators, and the media to save Brandley's life. For others on death row, it is nearly impossible to even get a hearing on a claim of innocence.

The Pressure to Prosecute: Walter McMillian

> I was wrenched from my family, from my children, from my grandchildren, from my friends, from my work that I loved, and was placed in an isolation cell, the size of a shoe box, with no sunlight, no companionship, and no work for nearly six years. Every minute of every day, I knew I was innocent. . . .
>
> Walter McMillian, Written testimony at
> Subcommittee Hearing, July 23, 1993

In 1986, in the small town of Monroeville, Alabama, an 18-year-old white woman was shot to death in the dry cleaners around 10 AM. Although the town was shocked by the murder, no one was arrested for eight months. Johnny D. (Walter) McMillian was a black man who lived in the next town. He had been dating a white woman and his son had married a white woman, none of which made McMillian popular in Monroeville.[5]

On the day of the murder, McMillian was at a fish fry with his friends and relatives. Many of these people gave testimony at trial that McMillian could not have committed the murder of Ronda Morrison because he was with them all day. Nevertheless, he was arrested, tried and convicted of the murder. Indeed, McMillian was placed on death row upon his *arrest,* well before his trial. No physical evidence linked him to the crime but three people testifying at his trail connected him with the murder. All three witnesses received favors from the state for their incriminating testimony.[6] All three later recanted their testimony, including the only "eyewitness," who stated that he was pressured by the prosecutors to implicate McMillian in the crime.

The jury in the trial recommended a life sentence for McMillian but the judge overruled this recommendation and sentenced him to death. His case went through four rounds of appeal, all of which were denied. New attorneys, not paid by the State of Alabama, voluntarily took over the case and eventually found that the prosecutors had illegally withheld evidence which would have pointed to McMillian's innocence. A story about the case appeared on CBS-TV's program, *60 Minutes,* on Nov. 22, 1992. Finally, the State agreed to investigate its earlier handling of the case and then admitted that a grave mistake had been made.[7] Mr. McMillian was freed into the welcoming arms of his family and friends on March 3, 1993.

Inadequate Counsel: Federico Macias

Federico Macias' court-appointed lawyer did virtually nothing to prepare the case for trial. Macias was sentenced to death in Texas in 1984. Two days before his scheduled execution, Macias received a stay. New counsel from the large Skadden, Arps law firm had entered the case and devoted to it the firm's considerable resources and expertise. Mr. Macias' conviction was overturned via a federal writ of habeas corpus, which was upheld by a unanimous panel of the U.S. Court of Appeals for the Fifth Circuit in December, 1992. The court found that not only was Macias' original counsel grossly ineffective, but also that he had missed considerable evidence pointing to Macias' innocence. The court concluded:

> We are left with the firm conviction that Macias was denied his constitutional right to adequate counsel in a capital case in which actual innocence was a close question. The state paid defense counsel $11.84 per hour. Unfortunately, the justice system got only what it paid for.[8]

Thereafter, Macias was freed when the grand jury, which now had access to the evidence developed by the Skadden, Arps attorneys, refused to re-indict him.

There are many similar stories of defendants who have spent years on death row, some coming within hours of their execution, only to be released by the courts with all charges dropped. What is noteworthy about the cases outlined above is that they are very recent examples which illustrate that mistaken death sentences are not a relic of the past.

Official Misconduct: Chance and Powell

While Clarence Chance and Benny Powell were not sentenced to death, their convictions for murder illustrate the dangers of overzealous police work. They were released from prison last year after Jim McCloskey of Centurion Ministries took on their case and demonstrated their innocence. The City of Los Angeles awarded them $7 million and the judge termed the police department's conduct ''reprehensible'' while apologizing for the ''gross injustices'' that occurred.[9]

IV. Are the Protections in the Legal System Adequate to Prevent Executing Innocent Persons?

To some degree, the cases discussed in Section III illustrate the inherent fallibility of the criminal justice system. (Sensational murder cases often tend, however, to amplify the flaws of the system.) Mistakes and even occasional misconduct are to be expected. The cases outlined above might convey a reassuring impression that, although mistakes are made, the system of appeals and reviews will ferret out such cases prior to execution. In one sense, that is occasionally true: the system of appeals sometimes allows for correction of factual errors.

But there is another sense in which these cases illustrate the inadequacies of the system. These men were found innocent *despite the system* and only as a result of extraordinary efforts not generally available to death row defendants.

Indeed, in some cases, these men were found innocent as a result of sheer luck. In the case of Walter McMillian, his volunteer outside counsel had obtained from the prosecutors an audio tape of one of the key witnesses' statements incriminating Mr. McMillian. After listening to the statement, the attorney flipped the tape over to see if anything was on the other side. It was only then that he heard the same witness complaining that he was being pressured to frame Mr. McMillian.[10] With that fortuitous break, the whole case against McMillian began to fall apart.

Similarly, proving the innocence of Kirk Bloodsworth was more a matter of chance than the orderly working of the appeals' process. Only a scientific breakthrough, and an appellate lawyer's initiative in trying it, after years of failed appeals, allowed Bloodsworth to prove his innocence. And even then, the prosecutor was not bound under Maryland law to admit this new evidence.[11]

Furthermore, not every death row inmate is afforded, after conviction, the quality of counsel and resources which Walter McMillian and Federico Macias were fortunate to have during their post-conviction proceedings. Many of those on death row go for years without any attorney at all.

Most of the releases from death row over the past twenty years came only after many years and many failed appeals. The average length of time between conviction and release was almost 7 years for the 48 death row inmates released since 1970.

Innocence Is Not Generally Reviewed

Too often, the reviews afforded death row inmates on appeal and habeas corpus simply do not offer a meaningful opportunity to present claims of innocence. As will be discussed more fully below, in many states there simply is no formal procedure for hearing new evidence of a defendant's innocence prior to his execution date. After trial, the legal system becomes locked in a battle over procedural issues rather than a reexamination of guilt or innocence. The all-night struggle to stay the execution of Leonel Herrera in 1992, even *after* the U.S. Supreme Court had agreed to hear his constitutional challenge, is an example of how much pressure is exerted to proceed with executions.[12]

Accounts which report that a particular case has been appealed numerous times before many judges may be misleading. In fact, most often, procedural issues, rather than the defendant's innocence are being argued and reviewed in these appeals. For example, when Roger Keith Coleman was executed in Virginia last year, it was reported that his last appeal to the Supreme Court "was Coleman's 16th round in court."[13] However, the Supreme Court had earlier declared that Coleman's constitutional claims were barred from any review in federal court because his prior attorneys had filed an appeal too late in 1986.[14] His evidence was similarly excluded from review in state court as well. Instead, Coleman's innocence was debated only in the news media and considerable doubt concerning his guilt went with him to his execution.[15]

This section will examine some of the means, both extra-judicial and within the system, by which the cases of innocence are uncovered. But first, it is necessary to clarify what is meant in this report by the term "innocent."

Meaning of "Innocent"

In the criminal justice system, defendants are presumed to be innocent until proven guilty beyond a reasonable doubt. Thus, a person is fully entitled to a claim of innocence if charges are not brought against him or if the charges brought are not proven. A person may be guilty of other crimes or there may be some who still insist he is guilty, but with respect to the charge in question, he is innocent.

In some cases, the investigative process does conclusively determine innocence. A piece of evidence may demonstrate that a suspect or defendant could not have been the perpetrator, or someone else confesses, eliminating other suspects. Under the law, there is no distinction between the definitively innocent and those found innocent after a trial but about whom there may remain a lingering doubt.

Extra-Judicial Redress

In the absence of adequate legal mechanisms, the most serious errors in the criminal justice system are sometimes uncovered as a result of such extra-judicial factors as the media and the development of new scientific techniques. These following cases illustrate the randomness of how the legal system works.

Role of the Media: Randall Dale Adams

One unpredictable element that can affect whether an innocent person is released is the involvement of the media. In Randall Dale Adams' case, film producer Errol Morris went to Texas to make a documentary on Dr. James Grigson, the notorious "Dr. Death." Grigson would claim 100% certainty for his courtroom predictions that a particular defendant would kill again, and he made such a prediction about Randall Adams.

In the course of his investigation of Grigson, Morris became interested in Adams' plight and helped unearth layers of prosecutorial misconduct in that case. He also obtained on tape a virtual confession by another person. Morris' movie, *The Thin Blue Line,* told Randall Adams' story in a way no one had seen before. The movie was released in 1988 and Adams was freed the following year.

Role of the Media: Other Cases

Similarly, all charges and death sentences against Thomas Gladish, Richard Greer, Ronald Keine, and Clarence Smith were dropped in 1976 thanks, in part, to the *Detroit News* investigation of lies told by the prosecution's star witness.[16]

Walter McMillian's case was featured on *60 Minutes* shortly before his release. So was the case of Clarence Brandley. Brandley was also aided by the civil rights community, which organized opposition to his execution. Supporters were able to raise $80,000 for his defense. Obviously, these advantages are not available to everyone on death row who may have been wrongly convicted.

Unpredictable Emergence of New Scientific Tests: Kirk Bloodsworth

In 1984, a 9-year-old girl named Dawn Hamilton was raped and murdered in Baltimore County, Maryland. Two young boys and one adult said they had seen Dawn with a man prior to her death. They thought that Kirk Bloodsworth looked like the man who had been with her. Again, no physical evidence linked Bloodsworth to the crime. He was convicted and sentenced to death because he looked like someone who might have committed the crime.[17]

There was some evidence taken from the crime scene, but it gave the police no clue as to who the killer was. Tests were conducted on the girl's underwear, but the tests were not sophisticated enough at that time to detect and identify DNA material from the likely assailant. Fortunately for Mr. Bloodsworth, he was granted a new trial when a judge ruled that the state had withheld evidence from the defense attorneys about another suspect. This time he received a life sentence. Bloodsworth, however, continued to maintain his innocence and the life sentence gave him the time to prove it.[18]

When a new volunteer lawyer agreed to look into Bloodsworth's case, he decided to try one more time to have the evidence in the case tested. He sent the underwear to a laboratory in California that used newly developed DNA techniques. The defense attorney was astonished when he learned that there was testable DNA material. The tests showed that the semen stain on the underwear could not possibly have come from Mr. Bloodsworth. The prosecution then agreed that if these results could be duplicated by the FBI's crime laboratory, it would consent to Mr. Bloodsworth's release. On Friday, June 25, the FBI's results affirmed what Bloodsworth had been saying all along: he was innocent of all charges. On June 28, he was released by order of the court from the Maryland State Correctional facility in Jessup, after nine years in prison—two of which were on death row.

The next section of the report will look at the traditional avenues which an innocent defendant can use to prevent or overturn a sentence of death.

Trial Is Critical, but Often Hampered by Poor Legal Representation

The trial is obviously the critical time for the defendant to make his or her case for innocence. Unfortunately, the manner in which defense counsel are selected and compensated for death penalty trials does not always protect the defendant's rights at this pivotal time. Most defendants facing the death penalty cannot afford to hire their own attorney and so the state is required to provide them with one. Some states have public defender offices staffed by attorneys trained to handle such cases. In other states, attorneys are appointed from the local community and the quality of representation is spotty.[19]

Federico Macias is certainly not alone with respect to ineffective counsel. The stories regarding deficient representation in death penalty cases are rampant.[20] The Subcommittee has held several hearings documenting this problem.[21] Although death penalty law is a highly specialized and complex form of litigation, there is no guarantee that the attorney appointed to this critical role will have the necessary expertise. There is no independent appointing authority to select only qualified counsel for these cases and attorneys are frequently underpaid and understaffed, with few resources for this critical undertaking.

Proving Innocence After Trial: Defendant's Burden

Before trial, the arrested defendant need do nothing to prove his innocence. The burden is completely on the prosecution to prove that the individual is guilty of the crimes charged beyond a reasonable doubt. However, *after* someone has been found guilty, the presumption shifts in favor of the state. The burden is now on the defendant to prove to a court that something went wrong in arriving at the determination of guilt. It is no longer enough to raise a reasonable doubt. To overturn a conviction, the evidence must be compelling, and violations of constitutional rights by the state will be forgiven as long as they were "harmless."[22]

The Appellate Process

If an innocent defendant is convicted, he generally has little time to collect and present new evidence which might reverse his conviction. In Texas, for example, a defendant has only 30 days after his conviction to present new evidence, and the state strictly adheres to that rule. Sixteen other states also require that a new trial motion based on new evidence be filed within 60 days of judgment. Eighteen jurisdictions have time limits between 1 and 3 years, and only 9 states have no time limits.[23]

Thus, even a compelling claim of innocence, such as a videotape of someone else committing the crime (as recently hypothesized by Justice Anthony Kennedy in oral arguments of Herrera,[24] discussed below), does not guarantee a review in state or federal court.

All death row inmates are assured representation to make one direct appeal in their state courts. If that appeal is denied, representation is no longer assured.[25] In states like Texas and California with large death rows, many defendants sentenced to death are not currently being represented by any attorney. Obviously, such a defendant's opportunity to uncover evidence to prove his innocence is greatly reduced, even assuming a court would hear the evidence if it was found.

Habeas Corpus: The Great Writ

When someone has been unjustly convicted under circumstances similar to those described above, he can challenge that conviction in federal court through the writ of habeas corpus. Although numerous legislative proposals to limit habeas corpus in the past few years have failed, the opportunity for using this writ has already been stringently narrowed by recent Supreme Court decisions. The following cases illustrate some of the barriers erected by the Court to claims of innocence in habeas cases.

Leonel Herrera

The Supreme Court has denied habeas review of claims from prisoners on death row with persuasive, newly discovered evidence of their innocence. Leonel Herrera presented affidavits and positive polygraph results from a variety of witnesses, including an eyewitness to the murder and a former Texas state judge, both of whom stated that someone else had committed the crime. However, the Supreme Court ruled that Herrera was not entitled to a federal hearing on this evidence and was told that his only recourse was the clemency process of the state of Texas. Herrera was executed in May of this year.

Gary Graham

Death row inmates who claim their innocence are therefore often forced to rely on procedural claims. But those, too, are being foreclosed by the Supreme Court.

For example, Gary Graham's case has gained national attention because he has made a substantial claim of innocence. However, the barriers to getting such new evidence before the courts has necessitated that the defense pursue other claims which only affect his sentence. Death penalty attorneys realize that proving their client innocent after he is executed is of no value to him.

But when Gary Graham claimed that the Texas death penalty procedures did not allow consideration of his youth at the time of the crime, the U.S. Supreme Court refused to even consider the question. The Court said that even if he was right in his claim, ruling in his favor would create a "new rule" of law and no such rule could apply retroactively to his case.[26]

Another recent narrowing of the writ requires federal courts to reject all claims if the proper procedures were not followed by the defendant in state court. Roger Coleman, for example, filed his Virginia state appeal three days late and this error *by his attorneys* barred any consideration of his federal constitutional claims.[27] Coleman was executed without a federal court hearing his claim. Similarly, if a claim is not raised on a defendant's first habeas petition, the claim (with rare exceptions) is automatically rejected, even if the government withheld the very evidence the defendant would have needed to raise the claim in his first petition.[28]

Clemency

For the innocent defendant, the last avenue of relief is clemency from the executive branch. All death penalty states have some form of pardon power vested either in the governor or in a board of review. However, clemencies in death penalty cases are extremely rare. Since the death penalty was re-instated in 1976, 4,800 death sentences have been imposed but less than three dozen clemencies have been granted on defendants' petitions.[29] In Texas, the state with the greatest number of executions, no clemencies have been granted.

The procedures for clemency are as varied as the states. In many states the governor has the final say on granting a commutation of a death sentence. Since the governor is an elected official and since there is virtually no review of his or her decision, there is the danger that political motivations can influence the decisions.[30] Many of the commutations which have been granted in the past 20 years were granted by governors only as they were leaving office.

Other arrangements are also subject to political pressures. In Texas, a board must first recommend a clemency to the governor. However, the board is appointed by the governor and is not required to meet or hear testimony to review a case. Recently, a judge in Texas held that this lack of process violated Gary Graham's constitutional rights and ordered a hearing to review his claims of innocence.[31]

In Nebraska, Nevada and Florida, the chief state prosecutor sits on the clemency review board. And generally, there are no procedural guarantees to assure that a claim of innocence which has been barred review by the courts will be fully aired for clemency. As Justice Blackmun recently pointed out:

> Whatever procedures a State might adopt to hear actual innocence claims, one thing is certain: The possibility of executive clemency is *not* sufficient to satisfy the requirements of the Eighth and Fourteenth Amendments.[32]

Thus, the prospect of clemency provides only the thinnest thread of hope and is certainly no guarantee against the execution of an innocent individual.

IV. Conclusion

It is an inescapable fact of our criminal justice system that innocent people are too often convicted of crimes. Sometimes only many years later, in the course of a defendant's appeals, or as a result of extra-legal developments, new evidence will emerge which clearly demonstrates that the wrong person was prosecuted and convicted of a crime.

Americans are justifiably concerned about the possibility that an innocent person may be executed. Capital punishment in the United States today provides no reliable safeguards against this danger. Errors can and have been made repeatedly in the trial of death penalty cases because of poor representation, racial prejudice, prosecutorial misconduct, or simply the presentation of erroneous evidence. Once convicted, a death row inmate faces serious obstacles in convincing any tribunal that he is innocent.

The cases discussed in this report are the ones in which innocence was uncovered before execution. Once an execution occurs, the small group of lawyers who handle post-conviction proceedings in death penalty cases in the United States move on to the next crisis. Investigation of innocence ends after execution. If an innocent person was among the 222 people executed in the United States since *Furman,* nobody in the legal system is any longer paying attention.

Many death penalty convictions and sentences are overturned on appeal, but too frequently the discovery of error is the result of finding expert appellate counsel, a sympathetic judge willing to waive procedural barriers, and a compelling set of facts which can overcome the presumption of guilt. Not all of the convicted death row inmates are likely to have these opportunities.

Judging by past experience, a substantial number of death row inmates are indeed innocent and there is a high risk that some of them will be executed. The danger is inherent in the punishment itself and the fallibility of human nature. The danger is enhanced by the failure to provide adequate counsel and the narrowing of the opportunities to raise the issue of innocence on appeal. Once an execution occurs, the error is final.

Notes

1. See *Sentencing for Life: Americans Embrace Alternatives to the Death Penalty 6,* Death Penalty Information Center (April, 1993).

2. Hearings on innocence and the death penalty were also held before the Senate Judiciary Committee on April 1, 1993.

3. The principal sources for this information are news articles, M. Radelet, H. Bedau, & C. Putnam, *In Spite of Innocence* (1992), H. Bedau & M. Radelet, *Miscarriages of Justice in Potentially Capital Cases,* 40 Stanford L. Rev. 21 (1987), and the files of the National Coalition to Abolish the Death Penalty.

4. M. Radelet, H. Bedau, & C. Putnam, *In Spite of Innocence* 121 (1992).

5. See P. Applebome, *Black Man Freed After Years on Death Row in Alabama,* The New York Times, Mar. 3, 1993, at A1.

6. See *Five Years on Death Row,* The Washington Post, Mar. 6, 1993, at A20.

7. See P. Applebome, note 5 above, at B11.

8. Martinez-Macias v. Collins, 979 F.2d 1067 (5th Cir. 1992).

9. M. Lacey & S. Hubler, *L.A. Awards 2 Freed Inmates $7 Million,* The Los Angeles Times, Jan. 27, 1993, at B1.

10. C. Carmody, *The Brady Rule: Is It Working?* The National Law Journal, May 17, 1993, at 1.

11. See, e.g., S. Skowron, *New DNA Testing Provides Hope for Some Inmates,* The Los Angeles Times, July 4, 1993, at A26 (Maryland's time limit for admitting new evidence is one year after the judgment becomes final).

12. See R. Marcus, *Execution Stalled on 11th-Hour Claim of Innocence,* The Washington Post, Feb. 25, 1992, at A3: "Lawyers for the state of Texas and a death row prisoner engaged

in a last-minute sprint through the federal court system over the execution, which had been scheduled to take place before sunrise.'' The execution did not take place that night because a Texas state court decided to issue a stay. Herrera's case was argued before the Supreme Court on Oct. 7, 1992. The Court decided Herrera was not entitled to a hearing on his innocence claims, and he was executed in May, 1993.

13. M. Allen, *Coleman Is Electrocuted,* Richmond Times-Dispatch, May 21, 1992, at A11.

14. Coleman v. Thompson, 111 S. Ct. 2546 (1991).

15. See, e.g., J. Smolowe, *Must This Man Die?,* Time Magazine, May 18, 1992, at 41 (cover story).

16. See Radelet, et al., supra note 3 at 56–57.

17. See G. Small, *Nine-year Prison ''Nightmare'' Comes to an End as Accused Killer Is Exonerated,* The Baltimore Sun, June 29, 1993, at 1A.

18. See also P. Valentine, *Jailed for Murder, Freed by DNA,* The Washington Post, June 29, 1993, at A1.

19. See *A Study of Representation in Capital Cases in Texas,* The Spangenberg Group (1993), at vi (''the rate of compensation provided to court-appointed attorneys in capital cases in absurdly low and does not cover the cost of providing representation'').

20. See, e.g., S. Bright, *In Defense of Life: Enforcing the Bill of Rights on Behalf of Poor, Minority and Disadvantaged Persons Facing the Death Penalty,* 57 Missouri L. Rev. 849 (1992).

21. See Subcommittee hearings May 22, June 27, and July 17, 1991.

22. See, e.g., Brecht v. Abrahamson, 123 L.Ed.2d 353 (1992) (relaxing the standard in federal habeas for finding error to be harmless).

23. See Herrera v. Collins, slip op. No. 91-7328 (Jan. 25, 1993), at 19–20, n.9–11.

24. See D. Savage, *Court Urged to OK Execution Despite Evidence,* The Los Angeles Times, Oct. 8, 1992, at A1: '' 'Let's say you have a videotape which conclusively shows the suspect is innocent,' said Justice Anthony M. Kennedy, addressing the state's attorney. 'Is it a federal constitutional violation to execute that person?'

'' 'No. It would not be violative of the Constitution,' replied Texas Assistant Attorney Gen. Margaret P. Griffey.''

25. See Murray v. Giarratano, 492 U.S. 1 (1989) (states not required to provide counsel to indigent death row prisoners after direct appeal). Once a case moves into federal habeas litigation, federal law allows for the appointment of counsel but crucial issues may have been waived before then.

26. Graham v. Collins, 122 L.Ed.2d 260 (1993).

27. Coleman v. Thompson, 111 S. Ct. 2546 (1991).

28. See McCleskey v. Zant, 111 S. Ct. 1454 (1991).

29. See *Clemency: Fail-safe System or Political Football?,* The Oakland Tribune, June 27, 1993 (41 additional clemencies have been granted for judicial expediency, to save time and expense after court rulings requiring a new sentencing).

30. See, e.g., J. Berry, *Governors Shy Away from Death Row Pardons,* The Dallas Morning News, Aug. 15, 1993, at 1J.

31. See *New Turns in Case of a Texan Scheduled to Die,* The New York Times, Aug. 13, 1993 (stay was ordered pending appeal of judge's order).

32. Herrera v. Collins, slip op. No. 91-7328-Dissent (Jan. 25, 1993) (emphasis in original), at 11.

26

An Appeal for Clemency: The Case of Harold Lamont Otey

LARRY MYERS

In 1978 in Omaha, Nebraska, Harold Lamont "Wili" Otey, a twenty-seven-year-old black male, was convicted by a jury of the rape and murder of Jane McManus. Ms. McManus, a single white woman in her early twenties, was alone in her home the night she was raped and stabbed. Harold Otey was a transient racetrack worker living in Omaha for only a few months during the horse racing season.

After a separate sentencing hearing to weigh the aggravating and mitigating evidence, a three-judge panel sentenced Otey to die in the electric chair. Otey spent the next thirteen years on death row at the Nebraska State Penitentiary in Lincoln as his case was appealed through the state and federal court systems.

The legal appeals raised questions about the fairness of the trial and particularly the effectiveness of his counsel. During the trial, Otey was represented by a young court-appointed public defender only two years out of law school who was busy trying other jury cases and had only three weeks to prepare for Otey's trial. There also were questions about the fairness of the sentence. Otey had no prior criminal convictions. Even though it was required by state statute, the three-judge panel that sentenced Otey never conducted a proportionality review comparing Otey's case with prior homicide cases. The issue of race also cast a general cloud of doubt over the fairness of Otey's sentence. Otey was not only black but also an "outsider" and a "drifter." The victim was white. The jury consisted of eleven whites and one black. As Otey sat on Nebraska's death row, studies from several other states conclusively demonstrated that black offenders who murder white victims are more likely to receive more severe sentences than either black or white offenders who murder black victims.

By October 1990, after twelve years of legal battles in the state and federal courts, Harold Otey had exhausted his judicial remedies. The Nebraska Supreme Court set December 5, 1990, as his execution date, and the prospects for Harold Otey were dimming. His legal options were running out.

The author wishes to thank Shawn Renner and Scott Wesley for their assistance in drafting this paper.

Precedent and Preparations for Otey's Clemency Hearing

The legal system provided one other option for Otey—he could petition the State Board of Pardons to commute his sentence to life imprisonment. While a pardon is the best-known form of clemency, clemency actually consists of a menu of powers, each of which either postpones or cancels all or part of a criminal conviction or sentence. The most relevant form of clemency for a person sentenced to death is commutation, in which the clemency authority reduces a death sentence to some lesser penalty, most commonly life in prison.

In the majority of states the clemency power is exercised by the governor. In a few states the governor is required to consult with some form of board composed of executive department employees, but even then the final decision is nearly always left by law to the governor alone. Nebraska is an exception. Since a revision of the Nebraska Constitution in 1920, Nebraska's clemency power has been vested in a three-person Board of Pardons consisting of the governor, secretary of state, and attorney general. Nebraska clemency law also differs from the norm because it imposes an automatic stay of execution upon the filing of a clemency application by a death-sentenced individual that prohibits execution of the sentence until the application has been considered.

Nebraska is a conservative and relatively peaceful state. Historically, a majority of Nebraska citizens favored the death penalty in theory, but as a practical matter executions have rarely been carried out. In 1990, as Otey's clemency request was being prepared, Nebraska had not executed anyone since the infamous multiple murderer Charles Starkweather in 1959. Only four men had been executed since 1930; after the Nebraska Board of Pardons was created in 1920, nearly half of all condemned prisoners who applied to the board had been granted commutations to life imprisonment. In 1979 the Nebraska legislature voted to repeal the death penalty, but the governor vetoed the bill.

In the fall of 1990 the imminence of Harold Otey's execution date coupled with the apparent exhaustion of realistic legal remedies caused quite a stir in the press. Candidates for the offices of governor and attorney general (1990 was an election year) had proclaimed their support for the death penalty in debates and in advertisements designed to demonstrate that they were "tough on crime." The *Omaha World-Herald*, the state's largest newspaper, had always been vociferously pro–death penalty and had been particularly vehement in its editorials urging Otey's execution. On the other hand, the state's second-largest newspaper, the *Lincoln Journal Star*, opposed capital punishment in its editorials.

There is no authority for appointment of counsel by the Board of Pardons for inmates seeking executive clemency. Thus, any lawyer representing Otey in the clemency process would have to do so without pay, and with the prospect of bearing substantial out-of-pocket expenses. In the fall of 1990 two attorneys—Shawn Renner and Victor Covalt—volunteered to represent Otey for free. Renner practiced commercial litigation at a large law firm in Lincoln. He had also done volunteer work on some death penalty cases and was on the Steering Committee of Nebraskans Against the Death Penalty (NADP). Vic Covalt, who practiced bankruptcy law at another large firm in Lincoln, was one of Renner's friends. Covalt initially declined Renner's request that he serve as Otey's official attorney at the clemency hearing, pointing out that he knew very little about criminal law or the clemency process in particular. But by mid-November, with the execution date just three weeks away, Covalt agreed to represent Otey before the Board of Pardons.

Substantial precedent existed to support Otey's request for mercy. Seventy death penalty commutations in ten different states had been granted in the prior two decades, with the reasons for these decisions falling under nine general headings: (1) The offender's innocence had been established, (2) the offender's guilt was in serious doubt, (3) equity in punishment among equally guilty codefendants required clemency, (4) the public had shown conclusively, albeit indirectly, that it did not want any death sentences to be carried out, (5) a divided vote by the appellate court upholding the trial court left disturbing doubts about the lawfulness of the death sentence, (6) the statutes under which the defendant was sentenced to death were unconstitutional, (7) mitigating circumstances affecting the death row prisoner's status warranted commutation to a lesser sentence, (8) while on death row the defendant had been rehabilitated, or (9) the governor believed the death penalty was morally unjustified.

Harold Otey was a strong candidate for commutation under several of these criteria. Although he had originally confessed to the murder under intense police interrogation, he later recanted the confession and had since steadfastly maintained his innocence. Since four of the ten Eighth Circuit judges had found that Otey had received ineffective representation at trial, Renner and Covalt could raise at least some questions about his guilt, the unfairness of his trial, and the disparity of his sentence.

In addition, there was substantial evidence showing rehabilitation. By all accounts, including his own, Otey had arrived on death row angry and arrogant. But over the years he had embarked on a disciplined, self-directed educational program. He had converted to Islam; he had read widely, studing literature and philosophy (especially logic) with several university professors. Otey had also written poetry, publishing three books of poems with assistance from several foundation grants. With this intellectual growth had come a level of social maturation as well. Through his studies, poetry, and letter writing, Harold Otey had earned a wide circle of friends who wanted to testify about the beneficial impact he had had upon their lives and to ask the Board of Pardons to spare his life.

The clemency decision would be made by three high-ranking elected officials, elected in November 1990, and the political implications of their decision could not be ignored. All three were white, middle-aged males, attorneys by profession, and raised in small Nebraska towns. All three were married and had children.

Allen Beermann (age fifty), a Republican, was secretary of state, a lifelong Nebraskan, and a Creighton University Law School graduate. Although he had been secretary of state for twenty years, his position concerning capital punishment was not known.

Ben Nelson, (age forty-nine), the new governor, had won the election by a narrow margin. A conservative Democrat, born and raised in McCook, a small town in western Nebraska, Nelson had graduated from the University of Nebraska and Nebraska College of Law, becoming state insurance commissioner and later the president of a large Nebraska insurance company. Although this was Nelson's first elective office, he was no political novice: For two decades he had been actively involved in fund-raising and in managing political campaigns for other candidates. Nelson had run as a "law and order" candidate and a supporter of the death penalty, but in public statements prior to Otey's clemency hearing he pledged to listen to all the evidence and to keep an open mind. He was not interested, he said, in "dancing around the electric chair."

Don Stenberg (age forty-three) was the newly elected attorney general. A Republican from Tekamah, a small town in northeastern Nebraska, he had graduated from the University of Nebraska and Harvard Law School. Stenberg also was no newcomer to politics: He had run four years earlier for attorney general but was defeated in the primary; earlier, he had run and lost twice in campaigns for lower political offices. The major emphasis of Stenberg's campaign was on capital punishment; he vowed repeatedly to make Nebraska's death penalty a reality. Following his election he continued to support his campaign pledge. During the spring of 1991 Stenberg gave luncheon speeches to civic groups across Nebraska and expressly stated that he favored Otey's execution because he was "sickened" by the details of the crime.

Just two weeks before Otey's scheduled December 5, 1990, execution date, the Nebraska Supreme Court unexpectedly and without explanation entered an order that stayed the execution and did not set a new date. But four months later, on March 19, 1991, that court set a new execution date for June 10. Stenberg opposed Otey's request for the U.S. Supreme Court to hear his case and filed a brief with the Nebraska Supreme Court opposing Otey's motion for a stay of execution. In early May Stenberg wrote to Governor Nelson, noting that he and his office would "strongly oppose" any further legal actions on behalf of Otey, and that "there is a reasonable likelihood that the execution can be carried out on June 10, 1991 as scheduled." Stenberg's letter asked Nelson to schedule a meeting of the Board of Pardons in early June and to instruct the board staff to assemble background information so that the board could act on any clemency request prior to the execution date.

On June 7 Otey's attorney Vic Covalt filed Otey's application for clemency, automatically staying the execution. When the Board of Pardons met to establish its procedures for consideration of Otey's clemency application, it set the hearing date for June 28 and 29, 1991; it also broke precedent in significant ways. All previous boards had met the condemned man face-to-face at the penitentiary, but this board voted to allow Otey to submit a personal videotape rather than let him talk with the board in person. The board also decided to limit witnesses to five minutes in their presentations, except for the attorneys representing Otey and the victim's family. Although it did not seem terribly significant at the time, Stenberg amended the motion to include "counsel for the State" among those who could speak without time limitation. It later turned out that this was part of Stenberg's plan to ensure that Otey's commutation request would be rejected.

Covalt's applications attempted to present a comprehensive picture of Harold Otey as a person. It contained background information about his youth in New Jersey, when he had been shuttled from relative to relative, ultimately dropping out of school and living on the streets, as well as testimonials from a dozen or so individuals who had had regular contact with Otey over the previous ten years. These witnesses, mostly university professors and religious leaders, told of Otey's desire to improve himself in prison, his self-imposed educational regime, his struggle to control his anger, and the social maturation reflected in his poetry and friendships. So that it could not fairly be accused of presenting a sugarcoated view of the applicant, the application also contained every reported court decision involving Otey's appeals.

In the weeks before the hearing, Otey's attorneys tried to assess his chances of receiving a commutation. One fact was clear: Attorney General Stenberg had already made up his mind to vote against clemency. Indeed, he had publicly said that he supported Otey's execution. It thus became necessary to win the votes of the governor and secretary of state, who at least had not publicly stated their positions on the issue of clemency for Harold Otey.

For two reasons, Otey's attorneys decided to forgo any argument that he was innocent. First, at its June 6 meeting, the board had made it clear that it did not intend to "retry the case." Second and more importantly, the attorneys concluded that any attempt to prove their client's innocence would have to be extremely persuasive in order to succeed. While Otey had recanted his confession, and there was some evidence suggesting that the crime could have been committed by someone else, this evidence had already been rejected by several courts. Vic Covalt chose instead to focus the major portion of his presentation on three issues: Harold Otey's rehabilitation; the unfairness of his trial; and the unfairness or disparity of his sentence.

In the ten days before the hearing, press coverage became increasingly widespread and intense. Local newspapers and television retold the details of the crime. Several television stations went to the prison, where they were allowed to film the electric chair and were shown how it operated by prison officials. Otey also began to receive national press attention. CBS contacted him and explained that *48 Hours* wanted an interview as part of a one-hour television program to be aired later during prime time concerning the hearing and its outcome. Otey agreed to cooperate with CBS.

A few days before the hearing, another unexpected event occurred. Vic Covalt received a copy of a report to the Board of Pardons from the Nebraska Board of Parole. The parole board is a separate administrative agency created by the Nebraska Constitution, and its primary job is to evaluate parole-eligible prisoners for release. The state constitution provides that the parole board "may advise [the Board of Pardons] on the merits of any application for commutation." (A statute also requires the pardons board to "consult" with the parole board before deciding a commutation request.)

The parole board report was definitely favorable to Otey. It noted that his early years were "marked by deprivation"; it recognized his educational efforts and found "evidence of personal growth and rehabilitation." It stated that Otey would not "constitute a long-term management problem" within the prison if his sentence were commuted, and it reported that literary critics had judged Otey's poetry publications to be "significant literary contributions." Most important was this conclusion in the report: "Mr. Otey's disciplined and growth oriented daily routine, which differs significantly from that of most prisoners, constitutes additional evidence of maturing, and may serve as a positive role model for other prisoners."

Given these positive comments and the parole board's constitutionally granted authority to advise the pardons board on the merits of the application, the fact that the parole board's report did not contain an express recommendation of clemency for Otey initially seemed strange to Otey's attorneys. But the reason for the omission was explained in the report itself: "The charge given us by the Pardon Board specifically excluded making a recommendation on the larger issue of commutation, and limited our role to that of gathering and organizing information." Attorney General Stenberg had expressly instructed Board of Parole officials *not* to include its recommendation regarding the issue of commutation, even though he had no legal authority to issue such an order.

The Clemency Hearing and the Pardons Board Decision

The hearing on Otey's commutation request began at 1:30 P.M. on Friday, June 28, 1991, at the state capitol in Lincoln in a large legislative hearing room packed with cameras, news media representatives, witnesses, and spectators. CBS's *48 Hours* sent a full camera crew and several reporters, and all of the local newspapers and television and radio stations were present. Since even this large room could not accommodate the audience, the proceedings were broadcast by closed-circuit television to other rooms in the capitol. Whatever the outcome of the hearing, it was sure to generate widespread local and national publicity. The only person conspicuously absent was the subject of the hearing, Harold Otey, who had been prohibited from attending by the board that would judge him.

There was unmistakable tension in the hearing room, and tight security measures had been arranged. Uniformed and plainclothes state patrol officers were spread throughout the room and at all entrances and exits. Governor Nelson convened the hearing by announcing ground rules:

> Just a few words about what this hearing is about and what it isn't. This is an informal hearing; it is not a trial. No rules of evidence will be in place. We do not intend to retry the case against Mr. Otey. This is an Executive Board of clemency, and it is not our task to determine legal guilt or innocence nor to determine the merits or demerits of . . . the death penalty as a sentencing alternative available to the courts. . . . We are most interested in, today, focusing on those aspects of this particular applicant's situation which militate for or against commutation of his sentence.

Nelson then set out the procedures to be used. Otey's attorney would give his opening statement, followed by opening statements from counsel for the victim's family and "counsel for the State." Witnesses in favor of commutation would speak next, followed by a "presentation of the case by counsel for the State and/ or counsel for the victim's family." Final arguments would be heard in reverse order. For an informal hearing in which guilt or innocence was not to be at issue, this procedure seemed very formal and resembled trial procedures used in a courtroom.

Vic Covalt's opening statement told the board that he would not contest Otey's guilt but would instead focus on Otey's rehabilitative efforts while incarcerated. Covalt previewed the testimony the board would hear from over sixty witnesses, all of whom would tell the board that Otey was a positive role model for other inmates and for citizens outside the prison walls. Covalt also made it clear that he was asking for a reduction in Otey's sentence to life in prison *without possibility of parole*—no one was even suggesting that Otey should eventually be released from prison,[1] but only that he should be allowed to continue his social and moral development and to continue to enrich the lives of other people while spending the rest of his life in prison.

When Covalt's opening statement concluded, Governor Nelson asked, "Is there someone here on behalf of the State of Nebraska?" Assistant Attorney General Sharon Lindgren announced that she would represent the state. Lindgren was the prosecutor on the staff of Attorney General Stenberg who had been responsible for upholding Otey's death sentence in the courts for ten years.

This was the pardons board's second unprecedented break with its own traditions. Since the board's creation, no attorney general or assistant attorney general had ever stood before it to argue against clemency; such arguments had been left to the victim's family, the local county prosecutor, or others. On its face there appeared to be a conflict of interest for the attorney general to sit as a judge while his assistant argued the case against clemency. Once again, Harold Otey was being treated differently from previous applicants for clemency.

Covalt objected to the assistant attorney general's arguing the case against Otey, and the following exchange occurred:

> *Covalt:* I challenge the appearance of counsel of Nebraska Attorney General's Assistants Lindgren and Brown. The State should not be allowed to appear on behalf of the State.
>
> *Lindgren:* Yes, the situation is unique. But we have not discussed our presentation with Attorney General Stenberg. We have attempted to insure that Mr. Stenberg is not tainted.
>
> *Stenberg:* The Board of Pardons should have a full picture and hear from both sides.
>
> *Governor Nelson:* I will allow the testimony by the Assistant Attorney General. In a sense, this hearing is adversarial, but it's not like a Court, and it's more of a fact gathering hearing.

Before Ms. Lindgren could begin, however, Attorney General Stenberg asked permission to make a statement. He acknowledged that Lindgren was appearing at his direction because he felt the board should hear "both sides of the case." Stenberg stated:

> Right, let me offer a little note there. It was obviously necessary for me to make an initial decision that we should, that the State should be represented and the general direction needed to be given to the staff which is what I have done. The presentation they have put together I have not heard. I have some idea of some of what will be in it, necessarily, but I have not, the presentation they have made will be making is what they have prepared and designed to give the whole Board a full picture and a picture which we will not see if the State is not represented at these proceedings.

Thus, it quickly became apparent that the board would be hearing a retrial of the case by the prosecution, despite the governor's statement that "we do not intend to retry the case against Mr. Otey." Such a retrying of the case was also unnecessary because Otey's attorney had intentionally presented "both sides" by supplying the board with all of the judicial opinions in the case; the board also had available the presentence investigation, which included all police reports as well as much other factual information about the crime. Stenberg presented himself as unbiased, and he insisted that any "presentation" by his assistants would not necessarily reflect his own views and that he had "not instructed them in what opinions they should or should not offer." As would later become clear, however, the attorney general's involvement in opposing the clemency request, while simultaneously sitting as a judge deciding the request, was far greater than his denial of involvement implied.

Lindgren then spoke on behalf of "the State" and urged the pardons board to reject Otey's application for clemency. She likened the pardons board to a capital sentencing panel and said she would be presenting "aggravating circumstances." She also told the board that she would speak for the victim, Jane McManus. When Lindgren sat down, an attorney representing the McManus family also gave a brief statement, asking the board on behalf of the family to carry out the execution.

After these opening statements, more than sixty witnesses came forward during a twelve-hour period to testify on Otey's behalf. The Board of Pardons first watched a forty-five-minute videotape of Covalt interviewing Otey, presented because Otey was not allowed to personally testify at the hearing. On the tape Harold Otey described his youth. One of thirteen siblings, he was shipped off to an uncle's house early in life because his mother could not care for all her children. While living with his uncle, Otey was kept from socializing with other children; he was regularly beaten and locked naked overnight in a basement room. When he was fourteen, his uncle sent him back to his mother. Thus Otey went from a severely restricted, loveless life to a life on the streets with no supervision. By age fifteen he had left home and joined the racetrack circuit working as a groom. In essence, Otey had lived the life of a drifter until he wound up on death row.

During the balance of the videotape Otey told of his efforts to improve himself while in prison: his conversion to Islam, his philosophy studies, the comprehensive reading program he had set for himself, the three poetry books he had published in prison. He explained that he used poetry as a means of self-discovery and finished by asking the board to commute his sentence. He had, he said, found some meaning for his life in his studies and friendships, and he wanted to continue to grow.

The balance of the day (until 10:00 that night) and the first five hours of the following day saw a parade of witnesses attesting to Otey's rehabilitation and urging the board to spare his life. Many of the witnesses were academicians who had tutored Otey at the prison. They described their admiration for his ability to learn and to keep a positive attitude while living in the stressful environment of death row. They also told the board that they would lose a valued and trusted friend if Otey were executed. A number of religious leaders, including the local Muslim Imam and several ministers from Protestant churches, spoke about Otey's spiritual growth and about the friendships they had forged with him over the years.

Regarding the issue of the unfairness of Otey's trial in 1978, the public defender who had represented Otey at the trial told the Board of Pardons that he had been unprepared for the sentencing hearing, in part because of work overload and in part because of the relative newness of Nebraska's capital sentencing statute at the time. He told the board that he had not presented some mitigating evidence to support a life sentence because the statute did not allow it. (After Otey's trial the U.S. Supreme Court, in *Lockett v. Ohio,* allowed capital defendants a constitutional right to offer any mitigating evidence they wished, whether or not it was specified by statute.) He talked about the requirement of a proportionality review enacted by the legislature during Otey's trial, requiring a sentencing court in a capital case to compare the case before it with prior homicide cases to determine whether death or life is the appropriate sentence. However, because the statute was new, the public defender offered no cases for comparison, and the sentencing panel of judges never conducted any real proportionality review.

Evidence was also introduced concerning the unfairness of Otey's death sentence when compared with others who had committed worse crimes but received life sentences. Covalt explained in detail the facts of at least six other murders that were "uglier" or "more heinous" but for which the murderer received a life sentence. Covalt drew the board's attention to one particularly glaring example of disparity, the case of Erwin Charles Simants, a white male who had murdered six people and was currently enjoying weekend furloughs in Lincoln.

Expert testimony further addressed Covalt's claim of disproportional sentencing. Marj Marlette, a former Nebraska Board of Parole member and then the editor of *Corrections Compendium Magazine,* had known Otey since 1978, when she was a reporter covering the prison for the *Lincoln Journal.* Ms. Marlette stated: "Right now there are 150 'lifers' in our penal complex, and about 100 of them were convicted of first degree murder. Many of these 'lifers' committed crimes worse than Otey's. Life in prison is not leniency. The Pardons Board is the conscience of the State, and we need equal justice in the State of Nebraska."

Interestingly, the state had actually already conceded the issue of disparity of sentence. In a letter sent earlier to the Board of Pardons, Otey's original prosecutor, Sam Cooper, admitted there were some cases of "greater crimes and lesser sentences" when compared with Otey's.

Regarding the issues of rehabilitation and nondangerousness, two prison employees voluntarily came forward and testified in favor of commutation for Otey. Both Brad Exstrom, an official on death row, and Russ Schuester, a personal case manager, had known Otey for many years; both said that Otey used his time productively and that he got along well with other inmates and was not a disciplinary problem. These prison employees testified that Otey would function well in the prison's general population if his sentence were reduced to life imprisonment. Schuester stated: "Five years ago Wili could be argumentative, but he's changed. He is more patient and easier to work with. He would not be a disciplinary problem in the general prison population." One of the few times that any pardons board member asked a question of any witness occurred when Governor Nelson interrupted Russ Schuester with two questions:

Governor: Is he [Otey] manipulative and trying to beat the system?
Schuester: No.
Governor: Do you think that he has sincerely changed?
Schuester: Yes.

Schuester, it later emerged, had received a visit prior to the hearing from Attorney General Stenberg's assistant, Ms. Lindgren, who had instructed him not to offer any of his personal opinions at the hearing. Exstrom ignored this warning and testified about the Harold Otey he had learned to know over many years of working inside the prison.

Also addressing the issue of Otey's potential danger was the parole board's own report, which had earlier been sent to the pardons board and thus was already in the record. That report clearly stated that Otey would not be dangerous within the prison if his sentence were commuted to life imprisonment.

On the issue of Otey's intellectual growth, several professors verified his work ethic and desire to improve. Nelson Potter, a University of Nebraska professor of philosophy, described Otey's disciplined study of logic and said that Otey's course exercises had risen to the level of a college sophomore. Nebraska's official poet laureate, William Kloefkorn, critiqued Otey's poetry for the board:

> I think Wili's writing today is very uneven; he has poems in his new books that I'm not sure I understand. He has sections of poems that I think I understand in their totality, but certain sections of the poems confuse me. He has other poems that I think are very lucid, he has some poems that propagandize, he has some poems that I think are very mellow, and very, very effective, but that is characteristic of almost any poet. He has his high moments, and he has his low moments, and some low moments, as a matter of fact, get into print.

Kloefkorn explained to the board that the quality of Otey's poetry was not as important as Otey's personal growth and progress, that what counts for any poet or any writer is growth and the ability to learn and change. In that regard Otey's poetry was successful. Kloefkorn asked the board to spare his life.

Some of the most powerful witnesses on Harold Otey's behalf were people who had met him through religious organizations or prison outreach groups; others had simply exchanged letters with him, some for as long as ten years. All these witnesses testified that knowing Otey had enriched their lives, and they told the board of the pain they would feel if he were electrocuted. Some were articulate and impassioned, while others were obviously nervous at voicing such personal thoughts in a public forum.[2]

When the hearing reconvened on Saturday morning, Otey's mother and several of his siblings closed the testimony in favor of commutation by begging for Otey's life. Julia Wheeler, his mother, looked the three politicians in the eyes and said: "I feel sorry for the McManus girl, I don't know her just like I don't know you but I've been here all these years. If I had all the tears that I've shed through the last 13 years, I'd have my own ocean. I'm asking that you let my son live."

When attorney Covalt indicated he had finished with Otey's witnesses, Governor Nelson called for the presentation by "counsel for the State and/or counsel for the victim's family," and Assistant Attorney General Sharon Lindgren stood to address the board. Covalt again objected to an assistant attorney general's arguing against clemency on behalf of the state while her boss, Don Stenberg, sat as a member of the board making the final decision. Lindgren again defended her appearance, explaining that the attorney general was unaware of the content of the presentation, which she alleged would "ensure Mr. Otey's rights of due process." Governor Nelson agreed that Lindgren should proceed, and he assured Otey's attorney that the board "will not be unduly prejudiced by argument that might be considered at least in the general judgment adversarial."

Lindgren's first witness on behalf of the state was another assistant attorney general, J. Kirk Brown, who told the board that he had witnessed more than twenty executions while employed by the Texas Department of Corrections. He said that although executions were never pleasurable, he was able to go home from those executions, look in on his sleeping daughter, and sleep well himself. He talked about feeling safer as a child when he heard that Charles Starkweather had been electrocuted. What Brown did not do was talk much about Harold Otey, except to say that no personal or intellectual growth on Otey's part could "excuse" his crime. Brown told the story of Jack Henry Abbott, a felon who had been befriended by Norman Mailer. With Mailer's help Abbott was paroled—and promptly committed another violent felony and was returned to prison. Brown warned the board: "To excuse Harold Otey from responsibility for his killing of Jane McManus or to moderate his punishment in any manner because someone has seen fit to publish his verse would make Nebraska the state where poets have a license to kill." No one on the board noted that Otey was not asking to be "excused" of the crime—he was asking for a lifetime prison term.

Lindgren's next witness was Charlie Parker, the detective who had arrested Otey in 1977. Notwithstanding Covalt's statement to the board that Otey did not contest his guilt for purposes of the hearing, Parker wanted to review the evidence that he believed supported Otey's guilt. Parker recounted Otey's confession and told the board of other crimes he believed Otey had committed.

For the next forty-five minutes, Assistant Attorney General Lindgren testified for the state. She accused Otey's witnesses of "depersonalizing" Jane McManus by asking the board to spare his life. Lindgren noted that she and Jane McManus were born the same year, and that Otey had deprived McManus of her ability to grow and add value to society. She gave the board the crime scene photos introduced at the trial in 1978, warning them that the pictures were "gruesome." She described in detail every wound inflicted on Jane McManus and quoted from the autopsy report. Lindgren described how the police investigation had pointed to Otey as a suspect. Then she played an audiotape with excerpts of Otey's confession which the police had obtained after eight hours of interrogation and which Otey later recanted.

The McManus family, who had been present throughout the hearing, left in tears when the confession tape was played. They later returned to testify. Laura McManus, Jane's sister, urged the board not to "excuse" Otey simply because he seemed to have changed: "I can't bring Jane's friends that she's made in the last fourteen years here today to tell you what a changed woman she is, or how she's grown. Harold Otey took that away from her." Another sister spoke only briefly, noting, "I believe Mr. Brown and Ms. Lindgren, both from the Attorney General's office, have said whatever we could say to you."

Jane McManus's mother also asked the board to deny Otey's application: "We're only asking that the original sentence of the court in 1978 be carried out. We as a family are not being vindictive nor are we the executioners. On the contrary, we're asking that the original intent of the court not be interrupted."

After a short break the board heard closing arguments from Lindgren and Covalt. Lindgren's summary emphasized her earlier themes: the details of the crime, the need not to forget the victim, and the desirability of following the decision and sentence of the courts.

Covalt's summary took about one hour. He emphasized that Harold Otey was poor, a minority, and an "outsider" who had made excellent progress in prison; that more than sixty witnesses had testified concerning Otey's rehabilitation and the fact that he had made a positive contribution to their lives. He spoke of Otey's potential contributions to society as a teacher of other inmates through his poetry and writings. Covalt reminded the board that at least six persons in Nebraska convicted of more heinous murders had eventually been given the lesser sentence of life imprisonment. He also reviewed, once more, the basic facts about the unfairness of the original trial: the inexperience of Otey's counsel and of his lack of time to prepare an adequate defense, thanks to the trial court's "rush to judgment."

In summary, Covalt argued that Otey's trial was unfair, that his sentence was unfair and disproportionate, and that Otey had changed for the better; he was not dangerous, and in 1991 he was a totally different and better human being from the person who had been convicted thirteen years earlier. Covalt reminded the Board of Pardons that Nebraskans historically have been "a peaceful people" and how relatively few death sentences had actually been carried out (none in more than thirty years). Covalt asked the Board of Pardons to reward Harold Otey for his progress by sparing his life.

At the end of final arguments, the board announced there would be approximately an hour's recess; each of the three members retired to his own private office to contemplate his decision. At about 4:00 P.M. the board reconvened to announce its decision. Governor Nelson spoke first and announced that he was voting to deny the application for clemency. He did not attempt to address the arguments presented by Otey's attorney but rather spoke generally about "the rule of law" and the fact that the courts had decided the matter. He concluded by stating that it was "a time for tears."

Attorney General Stenberg spoke next; to no one's surprise he said that he, too, was voting against clemency. He gave few details to support his decision, stating simply that "it is hard to tell whether or not Otey had been rehabilitated."

Third and last, Secretary of State Beermann announced that he dissented and voted in favor of clemency for Otey. In contrast to the governor and attorney general, Beermann gave several specific reasons supporting his decision and referred to the evidence introduced during the hearing:

> I have some lingering doubts about this case. I have lingering doubts about whether Otey got a fair trial. His defense counsel was inexperienced and had only three weeks to prepare. . . . I have lingering doubts about the fairness of his sentence, because of the three charts showing comparative sentences for other murderers. . . . Due process of law gives the executive branch the right to grant clemency. Clemency is the conscience of the people. Execution in this case is not best, and I vote "no."

Thus, as in the federal courts, Harold Otey lost by a split decision, two to one. At 6:00 P.M. on Saturday evening, June 29, the Board of Pardons, upon motion by Attorney General Stenberg, voted to set the time for Otey's execution just thirty hours away, at 12:01 A.M. on Monday morning, July 1, 1991. Attorney Vic Covalt immediately left the capitol and went to the law office of his colleague, Vince Powers, who was already preparing a petition for habeas corpus relief in the federal court.

The Judicial Appeals Based Upon Alleged Flaws in the Clemency Proceedings

From the conclusion of the clemency hearing in late June 1991, Harold Otey's interests were represented in various ways by a group of attorneys and citizens who collectively became known in public and legal circles as the Otey Defense Team. From 1991 to 1994 Otey's attorneys attacked the clemency proceedings in the courts on three basic legal grounds, all of which revolved around the conduct of Attorney General Stenberg and his assistants at the time of the clemency hearing:

1. Otey was denied due process of law because the attorney general acted both as Otey's prosecutor and as a decision maker on Otey's clemency application. At issue here were the age-old prohibitions against biased judges and against any appearance of conflicts of interest by a judge or decision maker.
2. Otey was denied equal protection of the laws because he was treated differently from all other clemency seekers in capital cases throughout Nebraska's modern legal history.
3. The Board of Pardons violated Otey's rights when it prevented the Nebraska

> Board of Parole from presenting its own independent recommendation in favor of commutation to the pardons board.

On June 29, 1991, the most immediate challenge to Otey's attorneys was stopping the execution scheduled just thirty hours away. Vince Powers and Vic Covalt worked throughout the night on a petition for federal habeas corpus (unrelated to issues arising from the clemency hearing), which they presented the next morning to District Court Judge Warren Urbom in Lincoln. Judge Urbom decided against Otey, and his decision was immediately appealed to the Eighth Circuit Court of Appeals sitting in St. Louis; that court stayed the execution just six hours prior to the scheduled execution.

A separate legal action attacking the clemency hearing was filed in July 1991 in the state trial court. Nebraska District Court Judge Bernard McGinn decided in Otey's favor, declaring the clemency hearing void and enjoining the state from setting a new execution date. Judge McGinn's decision was eventually overruled by the Nebraska Supreme Court in May 1992, and a new execution date was set for August 6, 1992. The same claims related to the pardons board hearing were then brought in federal court on a habeas corpus action, and federal District Court Judge Urbom issued an order staying the execution. His decision was upheld in July 1992 by the Eighth Circuit Court of Appeals, and the stay was further extended when the U.S. Supreme Court sustained the ruling of the Eighth Circuit. Upon learning of these further delays, Attorney General Stenberg called a press conference; he became emotional and publicly criticized the ruling by the court. When the television press began to ask questions, Stenberg stuck his hand in front of the camera's lens and called an end to his own press conference.

Attorneys Shawn Renner and Vic Covalt then pursued further actions in the federal courts to void the 1991 pardons board hearing. In late 1993 Otey lost a two-to-one decision in the Eighth Circuit Court of Appeals when it ruled that the court had no jurisdiction to review the matter. Federal Court of Appeals Judge John Gibson dissented with these conclusions:

> Substantive due process protects individuals from government conduct that ''shocks the conscience.'' . . . The idea of a prisoner pleading for his life before a board that includes the very official responsible for his prosecution and conviction is shocking to the judicial conscience. . . . The participation of the Nebraska Attorney General as a voting member of the Board of Pardons renders the Nebraska clemency procedure fundamentally unfair. Attorney General Stenberg's statements of personal objectivity at the hearing do not cure this defect.

The Supreme Court later denied certiorari to Otey's appeal, and in early July 1994 the Nebraska Supreme Court set a new execution date for September 2, 1994.

Otey's attorneys attempted to cure the jurisdictional defect found by the Eighth Circuit Court by raising their legal issues under federal civil rights statutes. On August 24, 1994, District Court Judge Warren Urbom ruled that Otey did not have a valid claim, but the judge took the unusual step of adding a ''personal note'' to his written opinion: ''Writing an opinion such as this is painful for me, more painful than words can tell. I do not like the prosecutor being judge of his own cause. I do not like the death penalty. I would abolish it if I could.''

An appeal was immediately filed with the Eighth Circuit Court of Appeals; on August 30, two days before the scheduled execution, Shawn Renner argued the case to a three-judge panel of federal appeal court judges sitting in Kansas City, Missouri. During oral argument, Renner argued that Otey's substantive due process rights had been violated by Stenberg's conduct before and during the clemency hearing. The assistant attorney general, Kirk Brown, argued that Attorney General Stenberg had uncontrolled discretion at clemency hearings. Judge John Gibson interrupted and asked Brown this question:

Judge: Are you saying that during a hearing to determine a man's life or death that the Attorney General of Nebraska can play with a stacked deck?

Brown: Yes, that's right.

The next day, the federal court issued its opinion; Otey had again lost on a two-to-one split decision. An appeal was immediately filed with the Supreme Court, but certiorari was denied six-to-two just four hours prior to the time set for execution.

Thus, over three years of litigation and appeals through the state and federal courts had produced one basic legal conclusion: The chances were very slim that any court would claim jurisdiction over the clemency function of the executive branch of government. Harold Otey had exhausted his judicial appeals. His only hope was that Governor Nelson, the swing vote on the Board of Pardons, would change his mind and vote in favor of clemency.

The First Meeting with the Governor

Following the 1991 clemency hearing, the Otey Defense Team made two strategic decisions: There was no point in communicating with Attorney General Stenberg because he had clearly made an irrevocable decision against clemency; there might be a chance of persuading Governor Nelson to change his mind if new evidence could be found in areas of concern to him.

On a Sunday evening in early August 1991, Nelson agreed to a three-hour private meeting, which was held around the dining room table at the governor's mansion. Meeting with the governor were attorneys John Miller and me; Professor Hugo Adam Bedau of Tufts University, author of several books and many articles on all aspects of capital punishment; and Professor Michael L. Radelet, a sociologist at the University of Florida and also an author of books and articles on capital punishment. Prior to meeting with Nelson, Bedau and Radelet spent many hours studying the case and talking with Otey at the prison.

Governor Nelson explained to the non-Nebraskans that in his opinion there were some differences between agrarian eastern Nebraska, which he compared to Iowa and Illinois, and the high plains at the other end of the state ''where the West begins.'' Nelson explained that where he grew up in western Nebraska, the general philosophy of the citizens was strong for law and order, and that a "hang 'em high" attitude toward criminal offenders was widespread.

A candid discussion then occurred over the next three hours, with the attorneys and professors reviewing more than a dozen reasons for commutation and the weight of the evidence, which they contended justified a vote for mercy. As the evening grew late, Governor Nelson seemed interested in what was presented, and he invited his guests to return for a second meeting over breakfast the next morning.

Another discussion ensued over breakfast; Governor Nelson was asked to reconsider his position, to change his vote, and to grant clemency to Harold Otey. Nelson said he "would keep an open mind" and that he "welcomed" receiving new evidence in five areas of concern to him: (1) Would Otey agree to stop talking to the press? (2) Was Otey genuinely remorseful about the crime? (3) Were there precedents? Had other governors used similar criteria to support their decisions for clemency? (4) Was Otey dangerous? (5) Was Otey truly rehabilitated?

Governor Nelson was told that the inquiry and research would begin immediately on these issues. Over the next eight months substantial evidence was delivered to the governor in each of the five areas.

Evaluations of Otey's Personal Conduct During the Years Following the Clemency Hearing

Governor Nelson's first concern was quickly satisfied. Otey agreed to cease talking to the press; he made no further statements to the media during the next three years.

Nelson's second concern was more difficult to satisfy. At the clemency hearing, there was evidence from the testimony that Otey's poetry and his statements to friends had indirectly shown that he was sorry the crime had been committed. But Otey had not made a direct expression of sorrow to the victim's family. When Professors Bedau and Radelet interviewed Otey, they discovered that he was confused over the difference between sorrow and remorse. Otey continued to maintain his innocence, and he thought that any expression by him of sorrow over the murder of Jane McManus would be an admission of his guilt in the crime. When he realized this was not so, Otey felt free to express his sorrow. In October 1991 Otey wrote a letter to the victim's mother, Joan McManus, in which he expressed his sorrow about the crime and about the unhappiness it had brought to the McManus family. The McManus family acknowledged receiving the letter but rejected its message as insincere. Later psychological evaluations verified that Otey's sorrow was genuine and deep.

The governor's third concern asked for precedent for clemency, and in response Bedau and Radelet sent him several law review articles, other reports, and excerpts from books exploring the criteria used by other governors in the ten states where seventy commutations had been granted to condemned inmates between the years 1973 and 1992. Attention was drawn to one case in particular, that of William Neal Moore in Georgia. Moore had pled guilty to breaking into a home, killing its seventy-seven-year-old female owner, and stealing more than five thousand dollars. The day before his scheduled execution in 1990, the Georgia Board of Pardons had commuted his sentence to life imprisonment; the reasons for clemency were very similar to those presented in Otey's case: an exemplary prison record; an expression of remorse; a religious conversion; and various pleas for clemency from a wide range of citizens who personally knew the defendant.

The final two concerns—whether Otey was dangerous and whether he was genuinely rehabilitated—were addressed over the next seven months through the detailed psychological evaluations and reports from three nationally recognized experts in various aspects of mental health and criminology—Kent Miller, Wesley Profit, and Michael L. Radelet. Kent Miller, a clinical psychologist and professor emeritus in the Department of Psychology of Florida State University, spent more than thirty hours in October 1991 evaluating Otey and studying his life history and prison record. His report to Governor Nelson summarized his conclusions as follows: "In my experience, I am not aware of a death row inmate who has made more dramatic progress in rehabilitation with respect to self-education, control of emotions and aggressive behavior, continuing meaningful contacts with groups and individuals outside the prison, and a disciplined use of his day within the prison." Miller further stated that Otey would not be dangerous inside the prison if his sentence were commuted to life imprisonment.

In early November 1991, Wesley Profit, a psychologist and a professor in the Department of Psychiatry at Harvard Medical School, spent four days testing and evaluating Harold Otey. Dr. Profit had immense practical experience because he was also the head of mental health services for the entire Massachusetts correctional system and in that capacity had studied and evaluated more than a thousand persons convicted of murder. During the next several months Dr. Profit spent the equivalent of ten days interviewing, testing, and studying Otey's behavior and psychological profile, and writing his analysis. His twenty-three-page report was delivered to the governor's office in March 1992, with an evaluation that concluded as follows: "To the extent that consideration of a petition for mercy is to be based upon concepts of rehabilitation, reduced likelihood of future dangerousness, and the presence of prosocial adaptation, it is my opinion that Harold Otey presents one of the strongest cases for commutation which I have seen."

Both Miller and Profit had worked in previous cases with prosecutors as well as defense attorneys, and thus they were well qualified to detect manipulation by prison inmates. The state never produced any evidence from any mental health professional to contradict their findings.

The third and final expert was Michael L. Radelet. Professor Radelet, who had postdoctoral training in psychiatry, had studied in detail the case histories of over two hundred death row inmates around the nation. After spending more than thirty hours interviewing and evaluating Harold Otey over a period of three years, his report to Governor Nelson concluded:

> Of the 200 death row inmates I have met, Mr. Otey's adjustment to the prison life, rehabilitation, and potential to contribute are second to none, and are matched by only

> a small handful. I have also studied the issue of clemency in capital cases and the reasons for it. I know of no death row inmate in America who is more deserving of commutation than Mr. Harold Lamont Otey. . . . I also know that some in Nebraska are claiming otherwise. However, few of those who paint Mr. Otey as manipulative or dangerous have ever met him, and fewer still can claim any special expertise in conducting psychological evaluations or in the study of prisoner manipulation. For my own part, I spent two years in the Department of Psychiatry, University of Wisconsin Medical School, studying prisoner manipulation and impression management. For most of the 1980's I also taught the required course in Medical Ethics at the University of Florida Medical School. Every ounce of that training leads me to believe that Mr. Otey's rehabilitation is genuine and sincere.

That Governor Nelson was even concerned that Otey might be dangerous if commuted to life imprisonment was somewhat baffling to Otey's attorneys. During sixteen years in prison, the record showed that Otey had been involved in no violent incidents and had threatened violence toward no one.

It should be noted that the testimony of all three mental health experts supported the evidence from the state's own prison professionals, which expressly attested that Otey was not dangerous, and the state parole board's 1991 report, which was very favorable regarding Otey's prison conduct explicitly stated that he was not dangerous.

By March 1992 the evaluations and reports from all of the experts had been personally delivered to the governor's office. Otey's attorneys believed that each of the governor's five concerns had been satisfied by the overwhelming weight of the evidence, and that there was no valid reason not to commute Otey's sentence to life in prison.

Governor Nelson never responded to any of the reports, evaluations, or letters.

The Final Meeting with the Governor

On July 8, 1994, the Nebraska Supreme Court set a September 2 execution date for Harold Otey.

On Monday, August 22, I called the scheduling secretary in Governor Nelson's office and said that Professor Radelet was coming to Lincoln later in the week and would like to schedule a meeting with the governor to discuss the Otey case. The next day, the governor's secretary returned the call and said that the governor "would be happy to meet with you and Dr. Radelet to discuss any subject *except* the Otey case." Thus, no meeting was scheduled.

Radelet did return to Lincoln, and he and I held a press conference on the steps of the capitol on Saturday, August 27, to release to the public the details about the 1991 private meetings with Governor Nelson, the governor's stated concerns, and how we believed those concerns had been satisfied, thus providing the governor with a moral imperative to reverse his vote and commute Otey's sentence. It was also revealed to the press that prior to the clemency hearing in 1991, the governor's staff had called various officials and citizens around the state to poll them about capital punishment and the Otey case, thus raising questions about the political character of Nelson's decision against clemency.

During this period Governor Nelson was in New York attending fund-raising events for his reelection campaign. On August 29 Governor Nelson's secretary called me and announced: "The governor would like to meet with you to talk about the Otey case." The meeting was scheduled at the governor's office for 2:00 P.M. on Wednesday, August 31, thirty-four hours before the scheduled execution.

Attorney Alan Peterson and I met with the governor and one of his assistants at his office in the capitol for about half an hour on August 31. We thanked the governor for meeting with us and gave him a six-page outline organizing the evidence that justified clemency under seven categories:

1. Lingering doubts about the fairness of the trial
2. Uncontested proof of the disparity of the death sentence, which the state conceded was disproportionate relative to prior cases
3. Otey's genuine expression of sorrow in his letter to the victim's mother
4. Uncontested evidence that Otey was not dangerous
5. Abundant evidence that Otey was genuinely rehabilitated
6. Written opinions from distinguished jurists stating that the 1991 Otey clemency hearing offended them
7. Precedent from other states where other governors had commuted similar crimes and sentences to life in prison

After Governor Nelson perused the outline, a courteous conversation followed. Nelson reaffirmed his earlier statement at the clemency hearing that his decision in the Otey case would be "the most important decision" he would make as governor. The dialogue continued:

Myers: Governor, over the past three years have you received the letters, articles, reports and evaluations from Drs. Bedau, Radelet, Miller, and Profit?

Governor: Yes, I did, and I'm sorry that I did not respond to them.

Peterson: Well, it's not too late. We have their telephone numbers, and if you have any remaining questions, they would be happy to talk with you. Do you also remember when you met with Dr. Bedau and Dr. Radelet over three years ago, and at the end of the meeting you said you would keep an open mind and that you had five areas of concern where you would welcome new evidence?

Governor: Yes, I do.

The attorneys and the governor then briefly reviewed the evidence that was organized under each concern in the written outline. The attorneys stated their position that the evidence was sufficient to satisfy each concern and they asked the governor if he had any remaining concerns

Governor: It bothers me that Otey recanted his confession and still does not admit that he committed the crime.

Myers: Even if we assume that Harold Otey committed the crime, in his own mind-he could sincerely believe that he is innocent. Your concern was addressed back in 1991 when you received a letter from Dr. Frank Menolascino, the head of the Department of Psychiatry at Nebraska Medical School. Dr. Menolascino explained the syndrome known as "post traumatic stress disorder"—even if a person did commit a violent crime, he psychologically blocks it out and cannot admit even to himself that he could commit such an act. As you will recall, Dr. Radelet also explained such psychological blocking mechanisms three years ago.

Governor: Well, I'm still worried that Otey could be dangerous.

Peterson: All of the evidence shows that he is not dangerous. Otey has been a model inmate with no violent incidents. The evaluations by the national experts, Drs. Radelet, Profit and Miller, confirm that he would not be dangerous if you commute his sentence. Even the two officials at the prison testified that Otey would not be dangerous within the general prison population, and the report of the State Parole Board agrees. You know, you have never met Harold Otey face to face. Perhaps it would be helpful if you would visit with him at the prison and personally chat about your concerns.

Governor: Oh, I can't go to the prison. It's too dangerous. Prison officials have advised me that it's too dangerous for me to go out there.

Myers: Well, we're going to leave this outline with you, and we hope you will review it and think about it. It's not too late to reconvene the Pardons Board and change your vote. We submit that all of the evidence shows that Harold Otey is one of the greatest examples of rehabilitation in American penal history. Killing him would send the wrong message to other prisoners. Rather than killing him, the Nebraska penal system should be proud of what its educational system has achieved.

Governor: I assure you that I will review and think about this material.

Peterson: Thank you for meeting with us. (end of meeting)

There was no further communication between the governor and Otey's attorneys.

In the end, Governor Nelson never changed his original vote denying clemency. He knew that he was the swing vote and therefore held Otey's life in his hands, but he never explained his reasoning in choosing to deny clemency. It was clear that he was under tremendous political pressure from the *Omaha World-Herald,* from friends of the victim's family, and from supporters of Attorney General Stenberg.

In late August 1991 Professor Nelson Potter met with Governor Nelson at the capitol to discuss the case. Potter later reported that the governor seemed to have little understanding of the life of prison inmates in general, or of how, over a long period of acquaintance, one could correctly assess the character of a prisoner. Potter had spent hundreds of hours inside Nebraska's prison teaching logic to inmates, including Otey. Potter understood what an effort it took and what an achievement Otey had made in rehabilitating himself, but the governor was not interested in hearing about this aspect of the case. Though Governor Nelson had never met Otey or even talked with him over the telephone, he nonetheless told Potter that he thought Otey was "a survivor" and "a manipulator."

One final incident in 1991 indicates that the governor had been less than candid when he earlier said that he "welcomed" new evidence and would "keep an open mind'' about clemency for Otey. On a Saturday evening in October 1991, Governor Nelson attended a dinner party at the home of some friends in west Omaha. During conversation before dinner a friend and supporter of Nelson asked him: ''What is happening in the Otey case?'' Governor Nelson answered: ''I feel sorry for the lawyers in the Otey case. Some of them are my friends, and they are working so hard to try to get Otey clemency, but *it's just not going to happen*'' (emphasis added).

The Political Atmosphere Surrounding the Execution

The attitude of most members of the press toward the Otey case was also crystal clear. Television stations' capsule reports on the progress of the Otey case always featured quotes from Attorney General Stenberg or from the victim's family. As the execution date approached, more and more media attention was devoted to the death penalty. Stories about the legal battle were overshadowed by stories about the nature of the death penalty itself. Front-page articles and photographs of the victim and Otey greeted the readers of Nebraska's two largest newspapers. The *Omaha World-Herald* carried a large diagram of the electric chair with each component labeled. Articles appeared with the minute-by-minute schedule for Otey during the last week before his execution. Opinions were solicited from witnesses to other states' executions and to the most recent execution in Nebraska. The *Lincoln Journal Star* carried features about issues surrounding the death penalty, including deterrence, costs, race, and poverty, and the paper conducted a nonscientific phone-in poll of public opinion, which favored the death penalty two to one.

During the three-year hiatus between the pardons board hearing and Otey's latest execution date, Attorney General Stenberg had held frequent press conferences to criticize the delays and to restate his support for Otey's execution. To add to the drama, Stenberg occasionally used the victim's family members standing behind him as a backdrop for his television press conferences.

Public advocacy for Otey's clemency also came from two former Nebraska governors, Frank Morrison and Robert Crosby. They coauthored an editorial, which was published in many newspapers across Nebraska, opposing the death penalty. They also spoke in Otey's favor at a campus church in Lincoln.

On Monday, August 29, clerical leaders and church members carried the thousand-plus petition signatures and more than three dozen letters to the capitol and presented them to Lieutenant Governor Kim Robak, who represented the governor. Rev. Lauren Ekdahl called upon the governor as a fellow Methodist to follow the moral directive of their church and to stop the execution.

Thursday, September 1, was Harold Otey's last day. During the prior week Otey had been housed in the infirmary above the execution chamber. From the infirmary window, he could see the crowd control fences segmenting the parking lot.

In front of the governor's mansion, those holding vigil stood from noon to midnight. There, a final press conference was held to release a letter signed by major national celebrities and human rights advocates on Otey's behalf. That afternoon, Governor Nelson held his own press conference, saying that he saw "no reason" to change his vote and that he would have no further comment.

By 8:00 P.M. the U.S. Supreme Court had issued its ruling denying Otey certiorari. The judicial appeals were exhausted, and only a change in the governor's vote could stay the executioner's hand.

As darkness fell, several thousand people gathered outside the prison. The pro–death penalty and anti–death penalty crowds were separated by a double fence, and state patrol officers were positioned in the neutral area to maintain order. The Plainsmen, a pro–death penalty group, were greeted with cheers as they marched into the crowded pro–death penalty side of the penitentiary lot, bearing signs and frying pans and waving swastikas and explicit racist signs. Their signs read "Nebraska State 1st BBQ", "Otey Today—O.J. Tomorrow," "Execution Is A-Otey." The spotlight of dozens of television cameras lit their signs, and the yells of "Go Big Red!" and "USA!" could be heard for blocks as the midnight hour approached.

In contrast, the antiexecution side sang hymns and quietly held candles and a few banners and signs. They could see Harold Otey through the window of the infirmary, and he could see them. Just before he was taken from that room, he spent a few minutes waving to the crowd. His supporters waved back, grateful for this last good-bye.

At 12:20 A.B. on September 2, 1994, Harold Otey was executed. His body was returned to his family in New Jersey for burial. He had made no final statement to the press or to prison officials. The official witnesses reported that Otey had died with composure and dignity, mouthing to his three chosen witnesses the words "I love you" just before the hood was placed over his head.

Conclusion

The day following the execution brought various televised comments by public officials and legal commentators. Judge John Grant, who originally sentenced Otey in 1978, stated: "I was shocked by the carnival atmosphere at the prison." Governor Nelson commented that he was "surprised" and "disgusted" by the "circus atmosphere."[3] Tom Riley, an Omaha public defender, commented: "This is disturbing to society. The crowd's screaming and yelling is not civilized. The whole thing has been so politicized that it's outrageous. Stenberg ran on a platform to execute Otey. The whole process is so wrong in that people cannot do what is right, but only what is expedient." A well-known political analyst and commentator on Nebraska politics, Creighton University law professor Richard Shugrue, aptly summarized the situation: "Some say that executions desensitize society. The role of Stenberg as both prosecutor and judge at the Pardons Board hearing was fundamentally unfair. Then the entire Otey issue became politicized."

No one had understood the political situation better than Harold Otey, an avid reader who read both the Lincoln and Omaha newspapers every day. Otey never gave up hope, but he was also realistic and he knew that the odds were against him. One week before the execution date, Otey commented to a close friend: ''If I die, it will be a political killing.''[4]

Notes

1. It should be noted that Otey was content to remain in prison for the rest of his life. He was willing to sign an official agreement with the State of Nebraska guaranteeing he would never be released. It would have terminated a commutation of his sentence to life in prison if he ever requested a further commutation of the life sentence to a term of years.

2. There was also testimony at Otey's clemency hearing regarding the racial issue. Fred Conley, a black attorney and city council member from Omaha, testified as follows: ''Historical data in America unquestionably shows that a grossly disproportionate percentage of poor and black defendants have been executed, and especially when the victim was white or rich or both. This is not equal treatment under the law.'' Alan Peterson, a trial attorney in Lincoln, stated to the board: ''This case fits into the ugly, problematical trend when there is a white victim and a black offender. The national pattern is clear. Our nation is not a fair society in dealing equally with all citizens.''

3. Robert Kerrey, one of Nebraska's U.S. senators, saw fit to call a public press conference the day after the execution. Kerrey was a former Nebraska governor (1983–87) and had previously not made any public statements about the Otey case. He was also involved in his own campaign for reelection, which was scheduled for nine weeks after the execution, in early November 1994. Senator Kerrey stood outside the Nebraska prison and stated: ''I don't support capital punishment. It's not a deterrent, and I'm against it. But it may be the right punishment in some cases. In this case, it gave relief to the McManus family.''

4. The following Nebraska citizens (known as ''The Otey Defense Team'') assisted either in the research and preparation for the clemency hearing or in the subsequent judicial trials and appeals: professors Nelson Potter, William Roundey, Garnet Larsen; attorneys James Mowbray, Dorothy Walker, Vincent Powers, Victor Covalt, Shawn Renner, Alan Peterson, Paula Hutchinson, John P. Miller, J. Patrick Green, Larry Myers, Mike Gooch, and Scott Helvey. Also assisting on appeal briefs was Seattle attorney Tim Ford.

27

To See or Not to See: Televising Executions

Why KQED Should Win

HENRY SCHWARZSCHILD

I don't want to see it on TV. I don't particularly want other people to see it. It is bound to be depressing and disgusting. It will inure the public to violence and barbarism and will further coarsen the sensibilities of the society.

I am talking about the [Gulf] war. Now, would anyone other than the Defense Department think those reasons sufficient for banning television coverage of the war? I suspect not. And the same commitment to a free press ought to prompt us to favor KQED in its lawsuit against the warden of San Quentin.

The prospect of television transmitting executions to me "in live color" while I am at the dinner table is revolting. The spectacle may entertain some, gratify some, appall others. It may redound to the advantage of supporters of the death penalty or to that of abolitionists; none of us can be sure. But KQED should have the right to videotape and air the execution.

In this lawsuit (whose negative ruling by the trial court may well be appealed), the claim to the right to televise is properly made contingent on the consent of the prisoner. That safeguards his/her privacy concerns. What else is left to consider? The First Amendment's guarantee of a free press, nothing more. In a decent society, the press must be free to cover public events in whatever way it chooses, and abolitionists (who believe that a decent society also does not kill human beings) should not be heard to want to muzzle the press for some speculative gain on our agenda or for the prevention of speculative harm.

Both the print and electronic media every day report scores of matters that I think have a deleterious effect on public morality and politics. I would not be a censor of the media, nor do I want the warden of San Quentin to be the censor. I won't here dwell on the irony of some of my friends and colleagues siding with the Corrections Department of California on this matter—the same agency that will

Reprinted by permission of the National Coalition to Abolish Capital Punishment from *Lifelines,* no. 53, July/August/September 1991, pp. 2, 7.

do the execution. But I say in all seriousness that the important problem is whether executions are *done,* not whether they are *seen to be done.* The notion that executions are too revolting to be seen by the general public is to misapply squeamishness to the wrong part of the problem. The fear that the public will become so used to the spectacle that executions will lose their taboo quality or the horror of the imagined is no more likely than that the public will be horrified and begin to turn away from the death penalty. Whichever predictions turn out to be true, the resolution of this uncertainty cannot be a test of our commitment to a free press. I do not doubt that other death-row inmates will be profoundly angered, that the family of the prisoner to be executed will be anguished, and I take no pleasure from these thoughts. But a free press is uncomfortable sometimes and yet essential to our society and an essential medium of public education for abolitionists.

KQED should win its lawsuit against San Quentin.

Why KQED Should Lose

ROBERT R. BRYAN

My worst nightmare is an execution scene. I am led into a death chamber and placed in a strange chair. I sit there, frightened. They are about to kill me and there is nothing I can do. I gaze at the good men of the law going about the task of strapping my legs, arms and chest. Ironically, they are careful not to cause pain by tightening the leather too much. That dreaded of all moments is rapidly approaching. My heart is pounding. There are spectators, peering at me as if I were a caged animal in a zoo. It seems silly, but I am embarrassed. Why do they all stare so? This is a very private moment, but I have no privacy. I am the focus of their entertainment. I awake, in a cold sweat. It was just a terrible dream.

For many, my illusion is their reality. Now, rather than just a select few watching the ritual of death, there is a move to broadcast that final agonizing moment into virtually every home in the country through the medium of television. If the proponents of televising executions are successful, we will be able to watch in the comfort of our living rooms while government officials ceremoniously engage in the barbaric practice of killing fellow human beings.

In defending those facing the death penalty, I have frequent contact with death row prisoners across the country. As the debate on televising executions became a hot topic, clients began to express their feelings about becoming a source of public entertainment. Many were strongly against such a notion, while others felt it might help the struggle to end capital punishment. One appeared to be preoccupied with the thought of gaining a few minutes of notoriety. Their comments caused me to reevaluate the issue in a much more personal context. I still appreciate the more global arguments for televising executions, but now feel they are wrong: I do not want those whom I represent to be the subject of America's seemingly unquenchable appetite for violent and tasteless amusement.

Executions bring out the worst in people. The history of public killings is a pathetic commentary on a species that prides itself on being civilized. Regardless of the country, the effect has been the same. The death scene lures crowds as if it were a featured sporting event.

One of the last public executions in this country involved a hanging in Owensboro, Kentucky, on August 14, 1936. Rainey Bethea, African-American, had been convicted of rape. A photograph was taken of the scene just seconds after the trap doors sprung the man into eternity. He was dangling in the presence of more than 20,000 spectators. People can be seen gawking from utility poles, leaning out of windows, and even crammed on the execution platform. Many of the good, God-fearing citizens were in their Sunday finest. If it were not for the man at the end of the rope, one would think it was a festive occasion like the fourth of July.

Many of my colleagues in the abolitionist community feel that by televising executions, a significant segment of the public will be appalled by the reality of seeing a person killed. But television tends to depersonalize. It is not three dimensional. If anything, I fear that televising executions will make them even more palatable to the public.

Governments have been publicly inflicting the ultimate penalty upon their subjects since the dawn of mankind. The cruelty involved has often defied even the most active imagination. People have been stoned, crucified, impaled, garroted, burned at the stake, drawn and quartered, hung, and shot. The killing goes on. Society has yet to respond by demanding abolition of capital punishment. And there has always been the macabre fascination with death, which continues to attract so many.

Regardless of where one stands on the debate over televising executions, the most compelling arguments reflect the inescapable conclusion that capital punishment is wrong. The real issue is whether governments should be in the business of killing. The answer is clear. No.

28

Witness to Another Execution

SUSAN BLAUSTEIN

The road from Austin to Huntsville, Texas, runs past oil rigs and tin-roofed homes whose ramshackle porches sag under the weight of old refrigerators and trailer parts, past red barns and white fences and hand-painted signs advertising Brahman Bulls and Suzie's Bar-B-Q, and on a quiet evening last August, following the road by a succession of tiny Baptist graveyards and watching the swifts dive and glide in the deepening blue, I noticed an antilittering sign (DON'T MESS WITH TEXAS!) and remembered why I was driving northeast. After that night, at least one man wouldn't be messing with Texas any time soon, and I was going to witness his execution.

Outwardly a sleepy little Southern town, Huntsville is surrounded by seven prisons that house 11,800 inmates, 376 of them locked in five-by-nine-foot cells awaiting their carefully premeditated, supposedly painless, government-administered deaths. The Texas Department of Criminal Justice, known as the TDC, is Huntsville's principal industry, and during the busier seasons the state executes as many as two men a week, making the town the nation's capital of capital punishment. As a member of the press pool, I planned to attend the execution later that night of Carl Eugene "Bo" Kelly of Waco, Texas, who had spent twelve years under sentence of death for his part in the brutal murder of two young men. The series of efforts by Kelly's lawyers to get his execution stayed—on the grounds that he had suffered brain damage as a result of severe childhood abuse; that he had been high on barbiturates, Valium, marijuana, and alcohol at the time of his crime; that he was improperly compelled by police to confess and sentenced more harshly than his accomplice; that he had been heartwarmingly rehabilitated—had all failed. That morning, in Austin, the governor's office had informed Kelly's lead attorney, Rob Owen, that his client's chances of executive clemency were slim.

The town square was deserted, but beyond its one-block stretch of quaintly renovated shops I found a glowing white Dairy Queen in which two female prison guards, both of them in gray uniforms, were sharing gossip and ice-cream sundaes.

The DQ is just a block from the Walls Unit, which houses the death chamber where, by state law, all executions in Texas must be carried out, but neither guard knew that another convict was scheduled to die later that night, "at any time," in the language of the statute, "before the hour of sunrise." Nor did the crowd at Zach's, a college hangout ten blocks away, where students from Sam Houston State University (known locally as Sam) were eating nachos and shooting pool. The university (the second largest business in town) is known nationally for its fine criminal justice center, which graduates hundreds of "CJ" majors and where active-duty TDC officials are trained. Like the prison guards, the students at Zach's didn't much care that a man was going to be executed in Huntsville that night, but a freshman dance major volunteered that an escaped convict had taken a female student hostage a few weeks back. One bright-eyed CJ major named Kevin Pooler said that because two of his buddies had been murdered recently in Houston he had no qualms about capital punishment.

"Burn 'em, fry 'em!" shrugged Pooler, who said he hoped to become a prosecutor and then a Supreme Court justice. "So what if a few innocent people slip through. That's better than having a lot of guilty people on the street! If criminals start seeing people getting popped off after six months, I'm sorry, but that's going to change some minds."

The state of Texas apparently has taken its cue from citizens like Pooler. A poll conducted in 1992 by a group of Texas newspapers found that 79 percent of the state's citizens favor the death penalty. Since 1976, when the Supreme Court ruled the death penalty constitutional (thereby resurrecting execution in the United States after a four-year hiatus), seventy-two men have been executed in Huntsville—more than twice as many as in Florida, the next most productive state in the execution market, and more than three times as many as in Virginia and Louisiana, which rank third and fourth. In the last two years, the rate of Texas executions has more than tripled, and the seventeen men executed in 1993 alone constitute nearly a fourth of those put to death since executions resumed in Texas in 1982.

At 8:00 P.M. I called Kelly's lawyers, who told me that his petition had been denied by the U.S. Court of Appeals for the Fifth Circuit and that a new appeal had just been faxed to the Supreme Court. This, I knew, meant that Kelly's chances for a stay of execution had all but vanished, but, as it so happened, I didn't see him die. The wire services and the Texas press had filled the five available places in the media pool—that pale reminder of the once madding crowd that for centuries has reveled in witnessing the grim administration of justice. Prison officials assured me, however, that I wouldn't have to wait long for my turn, what with twenty-four more executions scheduled in the next eight weeks. When the death penalty was reactivated here, the first executions were mobbed. Now they have become so commonplace that few turn out for them. Nonetheless, I decided to post myself outside the Walls Unit, which was cordoned off to keep out possible rabble-rousers, to see who might show up to mark Carl Kelly's death.

Built in 1849 and by the turn of the century decked out with tropical atrium gardens, turrets, porticoes, and a clock tower that the whole town told time by,

Texas's aptly named oldest prison is now a faceless brick bunker flanked by forty-foot walls topped by razor wire. A lone guard manned the corner tower, beneath which a dozen anti-death-penalty demonstrators, known locally as Amnesty people because of the affiliation some of them have with Amnesty International, had gathered for their sober candlelight vigil. By 11:20 prison officials learned that the Supreme Court had unanimously denied Kelly a stay. Shortly before midnight the official witnesses filed inside the Walls to the polite din of the protesters' pots, pans, and wooden flutes. Suddenly, two pickups roared into the parking lot, spewing out drunken college students who launched into raucous, inebriated choruses of "You're on the highway to hell" and "So long, farewell, auf wiedersehen, fuck you."

"Get a life!" a young woman hollered at the Amnesty people as she drove by. "We're trying to save one!" one demonstrator responded meekly. When one of the students asked who was being killed and why, and how the protesters would feel had the inmate's victim been their mother, he was quickly regaled with anti-death-penalty statistics; Carl Kelly's case never came up.

At 12:27 A.M. the witnesses emerged from the Walls, reporting that Kelly had been pronounced dead at 12:22; that he had requested wild game for his last meal but instead was given hamburgers, water, and fries (which he didn't eat); and that his last words were, "I'm an African warrior, born to bleed, born to die." (The mother of one of Kelly's victims was not impressed when I read his final words to her over the phone. "Oh yeah, right," she said. "What about the rest of us? When I heard he said that, any feelings I might have had for him just kinda snapped and I said, 'Okay, justice has been served.' ")

Ask anyone in Huntsville and he or she will tell you that the rapid clip of executions has absolutely nothing to do with life there. "It's just not our issue," explained City Manager Gene Pipes. "This is the state carrying out a legal mandate that has nothing to do with the local community. It happens to be DATELINE, HUNTSVILLE, but it's just not what's being talked about on the square."

Indeed, the morning after Kelly's execution there was no sign anywhere near the square that anything unusual had happened. The yellow tape outside the Walls was gone; across the street, in their telltale white prison suits, trusties were mowing the lawn and hosing down the family car at the TDC director's vast, neo-Georgian mansion. At the Cafe Texan, the regular 9:30 coffee crowd of retired white ranchers and constables joshed with a sassy veteran waitress and rehashed old cowboy yarns, while black workers shouldered trays of steaming, clean dishware and ate in the kitchen. At the Masonic Lodge coffee klatch, a group of mostly older men (a TDC guard, a cook, a retired chaplain, an engineer, the county judge, the founder of the local John Birch Society, and a retired crime-scene photographer) took it upon themselves to explain that Huntsville had been called the Rome of Texas, built as it was on seven hills and seven creeks, as well as the Athens of Texas, because the state's first law school and teachers college were founded here. Huntsville's founders donated the land for the state penitentiary, confident that legislators would then also locate the state capital there, but the Texas legislature, by one vote, chose Austin, and the disappointed Huntsville citizenry had to content itself with the eleven horse thieves who were the Walls' first reluctant guests.

Over the course of the next few weeks, while waiting my turn to witness an execution, I discovered that most of the people in town preferred to know as little as possible about Huntsville's main industry. "This is a marvelous place to raise a family," said Jane Monday, a former mayor and historian. "It's a university town, a town that cares a great deal about its young; it's warm, it's cozy, it's a very caring community. I wouldn't take a million dollars to live anywhere else." When I asked about the effect all of Huntsville's prisons and executions had on its young, Monday shook her head firmly. "It might sound funny to you, but I don't think it affects the children or the community at all."

City Councilman Jimmy Carter at first agreed. "That's the prison system," he said automatically when I asked why no one in Huntsville seemed to bother about executions. "The town is very distinct from that. Or maybe that's just part of our defense mechanism. We don't want to identify with executions or acknowledge that we are involved with that in any way."

Tommy Cole, a physician whose great-grandfather headed the TDC and whose family home has abutted the Walls for more than a century, admitted that he too is unaware of the executions. Dr. Cole likened himself to those living in small towns outside Nazi death camps. "We just visited Weimar, a few miles outside of Buchenwald, and no one there had any idea what went on, just like we have no idea what goes on behind those walls over there," he volunteered over a scotch in his fuchsia-damasked living room, in which much of the elegantly carved antique furniture was made by prison labor.

The obliviousness of townspeople to the executions was notable, but more striking was the way in which career TDC employees involved in the work managed to keep it from impinging on their consciousness. "It's real simple: I either do my job or I don't eat," the assistant director for public information, Charles L. Brown, told me when I asked how he felt about witnessing every execution. "My position is purely defensible: if I'm going to have to answer questions about it, I ought to be there. It's got nothing to do with my feelings about the death penalty; I'm just doing my job professionally and to the best of my ability. It works perfect, in that regard. And nobody would know whether I'm for or against capital punishment. You'd be surprised," Brown added, "how many people here are opposed to capital punishment."

I asked the same question of Brother Cecil McKee, a retired Walls Unit chaplain whose job it was to walk condemned men to the electric chair until the U.S. Supreme Court effectively placed a moratorium on executions in 1972. "It was hard to be there, but I didn't have to see it," he told me. "I closed my eyes. . . . You know, the flesh burns—it leaves a terrible odor. I'd go home and take my clothes off, leave 'em out, we'd go to sleep. Next day, I had to send my clothes to the cleaners. It was just part of the job."

I asked Brother McKee how he felt about assisting the state in taking lives. He looked at me with watery blue eyes. "I've never said this before: I do not believe in capital punishment of any kind. My philosophy is this: we have no right to demean, diminish, or destroy a life. If they can't be rehabilitated, they should be incarcerated. But I was working in a system that says we're going to do it. It's not right for me to say how a man should die."

Chaplain McKee's successor, the Reverend Carroll L. Pickett, said that because the death penalty was in abeyance when he started to work at the Walls, he had no idea that walking men to their death would be among his responsibilities; his first walk into the death chamber was "extremely traumatic," he said, not least because the technique of killing by lethal injection had never been tried before. Over the years, Reverend Pickett has tried to make the process as humane as possible by devoting himself to comforting the condemned men and their families, honoring their final requests, and shortening the time each must lie strapped to the gurney before receiving his deadly dose.

I asked Reverend Pickett how he would feel if any of the men he escorted turned out to be innocent. He shook his head impatiently. "I can't deal in 'ifs,' " he said. "I don't look back at what the man did twelve years ago. I can't get involved in the legal stuff; I'm not a lawyer. My concern has to be that human being and what he needs that day."

The reverend may well be at peace about his role in the prison system, but physicians and rehabilitation specialists told me that TDC employees work under tremendously stressful and abusive conditions. Not only do many workers suffer from severe headaches, depression, and alcoholism; they also commonly inflict their pent-up aggression on their subordinates and spouses—many of whom suffer serious physical and emotional damage from this battering—and on their children, who in turn wreak havoc at school and are often rough with their peers. "It's pretty stressful," admitted Huntsville police detective Dave Collins, who quit his TDC job after four years spent guarding one of the toughest units at Ferguson, the prison for youthful offenders. "You see all kinds of garbage in there. A lot of [guards] let themselves get run over by the inmates; a lot can't take it and quit. Some of my family members noticed a change in me, said I'd become more cynical."

Sharon, a prison guard in her late forties who declined to give her last name, works the morning shift on death row. "It's not just tough, it's very depressing," she said. "There are not too many people who can do this—who can walk in and see someone who you know has killed somebody or raped a child, who's not been out in the free world for ten or fifteen years. You have to get very callous, feeding a guy that spits in your face and says, 'Yeah, and I'd kill *your* mother too.' "

Because Texas has no public-defender system, most death-row inmates are forced to rely on woefully incompetent, court-appointed counsel, and the churning of court-imposed execution dates and inmates' frantic appeals has meant that a number of inmates without any legal representation have come within minutes of being executed. Four death-row inmates in the last four years were found to be innocent and were released; at least four more have presented to the courts compelling claims of innocence. But their pleadings have been dismissed repeatedly because Texas law requires an inmate to produce new evidence of his innocence within thirty days of his conviction—an impossibly short time for a newly condemned person to procure trial transcripts (just preparing these often takes the court as long as thirty days), hire a new lawyer to reinvestigate the case, and file a motion for a new trial.

The thirty-day rule was upheld last year by the U.S. Supreme Court, much to the horror of Justice Harry A. Blackmun, who in his dissent warned his colleagues that "the execution of a person who can show that he is innocent comes perilously close to simple murder."[1] The Court majority countered that those with technically inadmissible evidence can always fall back on executive clemency, "the 'fail-safe' in our criminal justice system." However, since 1976 not one appeal for clemency on the grounds of innocence has succeeded in Texas, where decisions are meted out by the governor and a parole board consisting of political appointees who follow no fixed set of procedures, are reluctant to second-guess the courts, and are accountable to no one.

As in many other death-penalty states, the dispensation of capital punishment in Texas is also tinged with racism. The disproportionate number of blacks on death row suggests that discriminatory practices continue to infect the state's police work, jury trials, and capital sentencing. Civil-rights groups have grown increasingly vocal on this issue. Meanwhile, violent crime continues, and frustrated white citizens, politicians, and law-enforcement officials have organized a slew of victims' rights groups that furiously condemn defense attorneys' "frivolous delaying tactics" and call for "justice now."

The debate and the high-stakes legal gambits for inmates' lives take place mostly in Austin, where a politically ambitious attorney general and a conservative legislature seem intent on maintaining and even expanding the death penalty; in Houston, which has the fourth-highest homicide rate of the nation's largest cities and thus has had seven times as many men executed as any other Texas jurisdiction; and as far away as Washington, where national anti-crime sentiment has inspired President Clinton to dream up fifty ways to expand the death penalty and the Supreme Court to progressively narrow death-row inmates' access to the federal courts.

But the eye of this storm is Huntsville, where the convicted killers wait. Life on "the row" has little to recommend it. Prisoners can choose to lift weights, work in the death-row garment factory, or pursue their appeals. Visitation rights are limited; the inmates are separated from all "free world" beings by bars and a narrow panel of thick glass laced with wire mesh. Those deemed security risks are chained inside metal cages when entertaining guests.

"Death row is the loneliest place in the world," said Lester Leroy Bower, a white, forty-six-year-old inmate who edits one of the row's two newspapers, attends Bible classes, and studies Hebrew and Greek. "You have people around you all the time, but you have very few friends. There is too much dying on the row, so you don't build really true bonds. And the hardest," added this husband and father of two teenage girls, his voice suddenly subdued, "is separation from family—never being able to touch 'em, hold 'em."

Death-penalty proponents have little pity for such talk from convicted murderers. Bower, however, insists he is innocent of the four murders for which he was sentenced to death in 1984 and says he has strong evidence pointing to four other suspects. Because of the thirty-day rule, however, no Texas court has agreed to hear his story.

Bower believes he was framed by corrupt law-enforcement officials allegedly involved in drug transactions with at least one of the murder victims. All of the evidence gathered against Bower was circumstantial; potentially exculpatory evidence mysteriously disappeared before the trial. Although within days of his conviction witnesses began coming forward with new evidence supporting Bower's innocence, his lawyer, off on a Mexican vacation, failed to meet the thirty-day deadline. Bower's harrowing trial experience, followed by a decade spent studying the cases of his neighbors on the row, has persuaded him that inside Texas's sometimes Kafkaesque criminal-justice system, one's innocence can have astonishingly little bearing on one's fate.

"You can convict almost anybody in Texas," he told me. "I'm white, fairly well educated, moderately articulate, have taken paralegal courses, and now I even have a good lawyer. That puts me a step up on a lot of people—and that has nothing to do with my innocence! Say I'm black, poor, uneducated, inarticulate, have no lawyer, have been put through the mill: I haven't got a chance."

Yet most Huntsville residents are sure that those executed in their town are guilty. "If they were innocent, it would've been found out way back then," insisted Diamond Kornegay, a retiree who, like many of Huntsville's relative newcomers, fled crime-ridden Houston for a peaceful life in the country. "Just look at all these lawyers, all these witnesses and everything!" Diamond, a chatty lady whose "daddy" was a cotton farmer and who grew up close to Huntsville, said the executions never bothered her.

"It's not a big deal to me. When I was a little bitty girl, they used to open up the Walls and take the schoolchildren through there. I saw the electric chair, but I never did think about it; I just put that out of my mind. If anyone ended up getting killed, well, they just did a bad thing, and that's the law."

It wasn't hard to see how such attitudes have been forged. Each morning, shrill whistles at 6:00 A.M., 7:00 A.M., and noon (denoting times for head-counting, work detail, and more head-counting) make it impossible for those within earshot to forget that their neighbor is a bureaucracy run on involuntary labor. The reminders continue all day long: trusties in their prison whites performing menial tasks, the changing of the guards in gray, prison vans trucking manacled inmates from unit to unit, and the startling profusion of wisecracking sheriffs and wardens who gather from all over Texas for seminars at Sam's prestigious Criminal Justice Institute and who stroll through town resplendent in starched jeans, smart cowboy hats, boots, and huge silver belt buckles.

Each weekday between 11:00 A.M. and 3:00 P.M., convicts from all over Texas are released at the Walls. For years their first stop was usually Bustin' Loose, a clothing store one block from the prison, where they could cash their release checks and pick up new clothes. But the state recently cut the stipend from $200 to $100, and since most new ex-cons are less willing to blow their few bucks, last fall the owners of Bustin' Loose were forced to close shop. But before they did, I met a burglar and a dope dealer there; both were in their twenties and both had trained to be bricklayers while inside (though neither seemed particularly interested in laying bricks now that he was free). By early afternoon both men, sporting new T-shirts and shorts, were stumbling down Twelfth Street, stone drunk.

Most ex-cons hightail it out of Huntsville within hours of being released, using the Greyhound vouchers the prison provides in their release packets. During my weeks in Huntsville I would occasionally stop by the Greyhound station to chat with the men as they waited for their buses to Houston or Dallas, Lubbock, Beaumont, or Port Arthur. Most releases I met were repeat offenders; almost all were Hispanic and black. An immensely unlikable murderer with a gold necklace and twisted grimace who had served only four years practically spat at me as he assured me that he had paid his debt to society. One, a large, drunken, white-haired black man, became quite chummy. He told me his name was Mr. Bum, or Mr. Wannabe, that he was "a bona fide Christian," that "prison is hell, emotionally, physically, intellectually, and don't let anybody tell you anything different," and that I was his kind of woman, baby. When he shook my hand good-bye, he tried to steal my ring.

On November 9, I learned that my turn had come and that I had been assigned to the media pool for the execution that night of Anthony Cook, a white thirty-two-year-old construction worker from nearby Crockett who had abducted and murdered a University of Texas law student in 1988. Cook was what is known in the trade as "a volunteer," meaning that he had waived his right to appeal and was ready to submit to his sentence, and it was a pretty sure bet that his execution would proceed on schedule. Until the last minute, attorney Elizabeth Cohen from the federally funded Texas Resource Center tried to persuade Cook to change his mind, but he was not to be swayed. Cook believed that he'd been saved by the Lord Jesus back in 1991 and that he was headed straight for the right hand of God.

Cook spent his last day with his family, who Cohen said were "not happy" about his decision and were "having a really hard time." At 4:00 P.M. he was moved to the Walls' holding cell, and after his double-meat-and-bacon cheeseburger, strawberry shake, and shower, he and Cohen sat within yards of the death chamber and talked about God.

"He's doing great, he can't wait," Cohen reported to me afterward. "He has no interest in changing his mind; he has more interest in bringing me to Christianity. He keeps praying for me, and he looks at me with tears in his eyes because I'm not saved." After Cohen left, Cook visited with his closest spiritual advisers, Baptist volunteer chaplains Jack and Irene Wilcox, who later told me Cook begged them to "follow up on" Cohen's conversion after his death.

Jack Wilcox had nothing but enthusiasm for the force of Cook's conversion. "We walk into the death house, and he says to me, 'Hey, Jack, I'm excited!' Two hours before he's going to die and he's excited? I say, 'Fantastic! That's great!' . . . This man saw prison five times, he committed a horrible kidnapping and murder . . . a sure loser!" exclaimed Jack, who himself had found the Lord after a life on the streets. "And then three years later, you be lookin' at a person prayin' to God."

"We would have liked to have seen him continue with his appeals, because he was a great witness," Irene interrupted, "but he believed in the death penalty."

Jack jumped back in, impatient. "It's not for us to say. A lot of the men [on the row] are upset because he gave up his appeals. I say, 'Look, the man's been prayin' to God for two years—you don't get between a man and his prayers.' We wanna let God drive the car," he explained, and then asked whether I had yet let the Lord Jesus into my heart.

The evening of Cook's execution I attended a City Council meeting where neither the mayor, city manager, city councilmen, student body president, nor student-newspaper editor had any idea that Tony Cook had accepted with pleasure the state's invitation to be put to death later that night. Everyone came in talking about the day's big news: the Huntsville Hornets' star football coach was retiring after nineteen years. The main item on the City Council's agenda that evening was a hotly contested bid by Sam students and five bar owners to get drinking hours extended from midnight until 1:00 A.M. on weekdays and from 1:00 to 2:00 A.M. on Saturdays. The initiative lost by a wide margin—and not surprisingly: Huntsville is heavily Baptist and was dry until 1971. The students were up in arms at the outcome, and they stormed out of the meeting after threatening to unseat the councilmen in the upcoming January election (though only a few hundred Sam students ever bother to vote in local elections).

But I was thinking about that evening's execution. I'd never even seen anyone die, and here I was, about to witness a man's death, to observe it without objection. Already I felt sullied, voyeuristic. Yet this is the law, I told myself. What's more, this one should be easy: this man *wants* to die. And he did pump four bullets into that poor law student's head. I kept up this interior debate until it was time to report in at the TDC "Admin" building, just across from the Walls. I parked near the Dairy Queen and hurried through the foggy chill to the triple set of doors.

Several reporters had already gathered in the tiny Public Information Office. Two were chatting with assistant information director Brown about other executions they had attended; another, like me a first-time witness, was earnestly jotting down facts from his "Execution Information" briefing packet. Cook had requested no personal witnesses at his death, Brown told us; the family would not claim the body, which meant that Cook would be buried at state expense in the Colonel Joe Byrd Cemetery, named for the late assistant warden who not only supervised every execution from 1949 until his death in 1964 but also took it upon himself to tend the dead men's graves.

The phone rang at 11:56. Brown answered. "That's quick; they're ready to go," he said, getting up from his desk. We walked across the street to the Walls, some of us chatting, barely aware of a couple of protesters almost invisible in the fog. The Walls' handsome old clock face read 10:02. I wondered how many men had died inside the Walls since its clock last told the correct time.

Once we were inside the gates, an assistant warden led us across the interior courtyard with locked chain-link fences, down white corridors with white-tile floors, through one thick gray door after another, each opened with an enormous brass key. Brown was amazed by the different style of the new warden, Morris Jones, who was presiding tonight over his first execution. ''I tell ya, this Jones, he's a new kind: quick, quick,'' he said. ''No point in waiting, I guess.''

We then were marched single file to the death house. The other woman reporter must have seen the fearful look in my eyes. She told me that she couldn't sleep for three nights after her first execution. ''Just attend to the business at hand,'' she advised. As we sat waiting to be admitted into the witness room, Reverend Pickett walked Cook the dozen-odd steps from his tiny holding cell with its bright orange bars, past a shower and toilet, and into the antiseptic death chamber, where he would be strapped down onto the chrome gurney while the warden and reverend stood by. I asked public-information officer David Nunnelee whether it made any difference to him when the men whose death he witnessed were volunteers.

''I appreciate that they accept what they did and want to pay the penalty,'' he said, without hesitation. ''You gotta respect that.''

Defense attorney Owen subsequently disparaged this view. ''Actually, Cook was the perfectly rehabilitated prisoner,'' Owen said, then mused about the fine theological line between the insanity plea of an inmate who claims to hear voices, and is therefore not competent to be executed, and a volunteer such as Cook, whose execution was expedited because he had heard the voice of Jesus promising him a heavenly escape from death row.

We got our signal and were abruptly herded into the carpeted witness room, along with two large wardens in khaki jackets and a small dark man in an even darker suit, who, I was told, was the one assistant attorney general who never talked to the press. We stood behind bars and a pane of thick glass, which separated us from the actual death chamber.

The view was stunning. Cook lay spread-eagled on the gurney, ready, bound by six thick leather straps. Although the press briefing listed his height as only five foot six, he looked enormous. His eyes were only partly open; his strong chin pointed upward. He was balding, and his longish auburn hair looked blond beneath the chilling fluorescent light. Ace bandages covered both hands and IVs were inserted into both forearms, his thin, short-sleeved prison shirt revealing a blurry tattoo. He wore blue, standard-issue prison garb and his own Etonic sneakers, purchased, I later learned, in the prison commissary for $21.75.

Near Cook's head stood Warden Jones; near Cook's feet stood Reverend Pickett, his hands folded. Suddenly I saw movement in front of me and realized that on Cook's far side was a one-way mirror in which we all were reflected. It was our own movement, not that of the symmetrical threesome in the death chamber itself, that had been captured in the glass. The effect was eerie; not only would I witness an execution but I would witness myself witnessing it. Behind the mirror, in an adjacent room, stood the executioner (whether man or woman, or more than one, no one would tell me), who would, upon a signal from the warden, activate the death device and introduce into Cook's veins the $71.50 fix consisting of what prison officials term ''those substances necessary to cause death'': sodium thiopental, which is the lethal component, pancuronium bromide, to relax and anesthetize, and potassium chloride, to stop the heartbeat.

"Do you have anything to say?" the warden muttered at 12:08. Cook opened his eyes.

"Yessir," he said, speaking into a big black microphone hung just over his head. "I just want to tell my family that I love them and I thank the Lord Jesus for giving me another chance and for saving me."

With that, Cook shut his eyes. The warden gave a small, sharp nod toward the person or persons behind the mirror. We all stood rigid, frozen. The silence was absolute, a perfect vacuum. Within seconds Cook took a sudden deep breath, gagged once, and stiffened his chin upward, all in one gesture. His chest expanded tremendously when he breathed, as if he had eagerly inhaled his own death. His arms were still outstretched and bound; his mouth and eyes were slightly open; nothing else moved.

My eyes slowly traced the contours of his body—the ninety degrees from his shiny bald crown to the end of his outstretched left arm, down the length of his pants leg, across the white sneakers, and up the near side—searching for signs of life, a cough, a twitch, a moan, a second thought. None came. I waited for him to exhale. But the air he had so urgently seized a moment before remained trapped in Cook's chest. The show was over; the passage from life to death was horrifyingly invisible, a silent and efficient erasure.

We waited. Finally, the warden called in Dr. Darrell Wells, a bearded emergency-room physician who attends most of the prison's executions. Wells checked Cook's eyes with a flashlight and his heart with a stethoscope. The play had ended. At 12:15, within five minutes of Anthony Cook's last gasp, the doctor pronounced him dead.

We filed out the way we came, more quickly this time, with little conversation. When I reached the Public Information Office, one of the reporters was already calling his bureau.

"Hi, Harry. He's history," he greeted his editor. Another reporter filed his story by modem while press officer Brown invited us all to the opening of a new 2,250-bed prison later that morning.

"Cold, ain't it?" a thin young guard greeted me as I walked back to my car. The clock at the Walls still read 10:02. A yellow traffic light flashed in front of the closed, eternally lit Dairy Queen. Cook's death made the 1:00 A.M. news on CNN, flickering in the nation's consciousness but an instant.

By 7:30 that morning at the Huntsville Funeral Home (which handles the bodies of all executed men), Tony Cook's mother, stepfather, brother, sister, assorted in-laws, cousins, and the Wilcoxes were paying their last respects to his open casket. Cook looked smaller than he had on the gurney; he had pretty, long eyelashes and delicate hands, a slightly cleft chin, and the shadow of a beard. He was dressed now in a blue oxford shirt with white stripes, and his mother stood over him, gently caressing his thin hair, his cheek, his ear. "He feels like you could just squeeze him back to life," she said. He had called her two hours before his death to tell her how excited he was about dying. "He certainly was at peace with hisself," she said.

"No more cages," sighed his sister as she touched her brother's chest, arms, face. "He's free, free, free!" She clutched his hand again and again, then finally kissed his forehead good-bye. I tried to fathom what it must feel like, after five years of no physical contact, to be allowed to touch a son or brother only after he is dead.

We followed the hearse through town to the muddy cemetery, where the six inmates who had prepared the grave were warming themselves over an ashcan fire. The seventeen family members clustered together, held one another, and cried, while Reverend Pickett read some prayers. Chaplain Jack Wilcox, in a hot-pink tie with a bright paisley print, said he'd never heard Tony say a bad word about anybody and read us a statement that Cook had written for the occasion: "Someday you will read in the papers that I have died—don't you believe a word of it . . ."

After the service Chaplain Wilcox pointed to one of the hundreds of crosses in the cemetery. "That's one of Tony's best friends, right there," he said. Since the markers have only prison numbers and no names, I asked how he knew. "I buried him," he said. "Last June." I later asked Reverend Pickett why the crosses have no names.

"It makes it more accurate," he told me. "We have many at the prison with the same name. There'll be another Tony Cook, but there'll never be another number like that number."

The air was dank and cold as I drove out of town, and I hoped the day's sharp rawness would clear my numbed senses. I headed north out to farm route 980, past sallow fields, unkempt trailer clusters, and the occasional satellite dish. Suddenly I saw, strung from a ragged barbed-wire fence, what looked like a wild dog or wolf, hanging upside down by its right rear foot. Its tail was splayed in a lazy S; its other legs were beautifully poised as if the animal had been caught in mid-leap by a photographer's lens.

I sped by, stopped, then backed up to make sure I wasn't hallucinating. The animal had been shot in the right shoulder, and bloody organs were dribbling out. So far only a single fly had discovered the catch; long-tailed, white-bellied birds took no notice as they hopped along the fence and pecked at the unmowed field.

Like somebody's trophy, the animal hung there, far more dignified than its surroundings. It was a coyote, I was later told, a predator. Nothing to feel sorry for, in other words: all crossbreeds were coyotes out here, and they ate the calves and young deer. It was hung there "as a warning to other coyotes," said one veteran hunter; another suggested it was hung "to let other farmers know they're doin' their part" in keeping the coyote population down. "That's just kinda the old way here in Texas," a former state game warden told me. Another old-timer, a man who'd mounted the rear end of a deer on the wall of his tiny living room, gave one more reason: "Somebody wants to show off that he killed somethin'," he said, then broke into a toothless grin.

All these explanations somehow made sense. But I wondered why I was so transfixed by this roadside display of a predator's comeuppance. Something about the crude, fresh death jarred me in a way that Cook's execution had not. That meticulous choreography had anesthetized me to the reality that a man was being killed before my eyes. But the flesh and blood of this handsome, dripping creature made both its death and its outlaw status immediately palpable.

From what I'd read about the stench of electrocution and the vividness of public hangings, I imagined that witnessing deaths by these means would have an immediacy that would preclude numbness. The lethal-injection method, first used in Texas in 1982 and now adopted by most death-penalty states as more humane, has turned dying into a still life, thereby enabling the state to kill without anyone involved feeling anything at all.

I wondered how viewing such a non-event could satisfy the desire for retribution so often expressed by death-penalty advocates and the families of victims. I wondered whether Huntsville's sterile, bloodless executions of the last twelve years might partly account for residents' wholesale disinterest and denial that what went on deep inside the Walls might have anything to do with them.

But it's not just here in Huntsville; we are all inured to such smooth exterminations. Any remaining glimmers of doubt—about whether the man received due process, about his guilt, about our right to take a life—cause us to rationalize these deaths with such catchwords as "heinous," "deserved," "deterrent," "justice," and "painless." We have perfected the art of institutional killing to the degree that it has deadened our natural, quintessentially human response to death.

When I returned to town, a student activist was waiting at my hotel to let me know how upset he and his colleagues were by the City Council's refusal to extend legal drinking hours. Outside my window, Sam cheerleaders feverishly waved their pink banners in practice for Saturday's game. A TDC official phoned to tell me not to bother to show up the following night for Dorsie Johnson's execution: he'd just gotten stayed until January.

Feeling hungry, I decided to check out Mr. Hamburger, Huntsville's original fast-food shack, which since it went up in the Fifties has stood a block west of the Walls. A now-faded sandwich board out front reads, TRY OUR KILLER BURGERS.

So I tried one: "Double meat, double cheese, lettuce, tomato, mustard, mayonnaise, pickle, and jalapeños," explained Willie Mae Jenkins, a pretty short-order cook with a monogrammed gold tooth who has been serving up Killer and Jr. Killer Burgers for eighteen years.

"So why's it called a Killer Burger?" I asked.

Willie Mae smiled, apparently surprised by the question and a little embarrassed at not having a ready answer. "I really don't know," she said. "I think it has something to do with the jalapeños."

Note

1. After a career of affirming the death penalty, Justice Blackmun recently concluded that capital punishment is not constitutional as it is currently applied in Texas and other states, in large measure because he now firmly believes that innocent men have in fact been executed. In February he dissented from an unsigned Supreme Court order denying review

of yet another Texas death-penalty case. Blackmun concluded that ''the death penalty experiment has failed.'' ''Perhaps,'' he wrote, ''one day this Court will develop procedural rules or verbal formulas that actually will provide consistency, fairness, and reliability in a capital-sentencing scheme. I am not optimistic that such a day will come. I am more optimistic, though, that this Court eventually will conclude that the effort to eliminate arbitrariness while preserving fairness 'in the affliction of (death) is so plainly doomed to failure that it and the death penalty must be abandoned altogether.' (Godfrey v. Georgia, 1980 . . .) I may not live to see that day, but I have faith that eventually it will arrive. The path the Court has chosen lessens us all. I dissent.''

29

Millions Misspent: What Politicians Don't Say About the High Costs of the Death Penalty

RICHARD C. DIETER

Introduction

Over two-thirds of the states and the federal government have installed an exorbitantly expensive system of capital punishment which has been a failure by any measure of effectiveness. Literally hundreds of millions of dollars have already been spent on a response to crime which is calculated to be carried out on a few people each year and which has done nothing to stem the rise in violent crime. . . .

Local governments often bear the brunt of capital punishment costs and are particularly burdened. A single death penalty trial can exhaust a county's resources. Politicians singing the praises of the death penalty rarely address the question of whether a government's resources might be more effectively put to use in other methods of fighting crime. A million dollars spent pursuing the execution of one defendant could provide far more effective long-term crime reduction: many additional police officers; speedier trials; or drug rehabilitation programs. Instead, in today's political atmosphere, politicians worry about appearing soft on crime, even if soft means espousing proven methods of crime reduction. Thus, there is little debate about whether the death penalty accomplishes any good at all. . . .

In the 1990 elections, politicians were particularly blatant in their promotion of the death penalty. It was advanced at all levels of the political process as an answer to crime and was used by liberals and conservatives alike. This year, the death penalty rhetoric, while not as blatant, continues the charade: vital crime fighting programs are being cut while the high-priced death penalty goes unchecked. . . .

This report will focus first on the role the death penalty plays in the economic crisis facing states and local governments. As budgets everywhere are being tight-

Reprinted by permission of the author from a report of the Death Penalty Information Center, Washington, D.C., revised edition, fall 1994. Some footnotes and text have been deleted and the remaining footnotes renumbered. Amanda Smith assisted in the preparation of the epilogue.

ened, the death penalty looms as an exorbitant and superfluous "luxury item." Some counties have been pushed to the brink of bankruptcy and have had to enact repeated tax increases to fund these extremely expensive cases. As money is spent on the death penalty, it is thereby less available for the very programs which are the backbone of the effort to reduce crime in this country. Secondly, the report will illustrate how politicians have manipulated the death penalty issue and avoided debate on the real causes of crime. Their approach has been typically marked by a simplistic rhetoric of revenge which ignores the ineffectiveness and costs of capital punishment. This superficial treatment comes precisely at a time when the economic crisis in criminal justice and crime prevention demands that the death penalty be given a harder look.

The Financial Costs of the Death Penalty

Death penalty cases are much more expensive than other criminal cases and cost more than imprisonment for life with no possibility of parole. In California, capital trials are six times more costly than other murder trials.[1] A study in Kansas indicated that a capital trial costs $116,700 more than an ordinary murder trial.[2] Complex pre-trial motions, lengthy jury selections, and expenses for expert witnesses are all likely to add to the costs in death penalty cases. The irreversibility of the death sentence requires courts to follow heightened due process in the preparation and course of the trial. The separate sentencing phase of the trial can take even longer than the guilt or innocence phase of the trial. And defendants are much more likely to insist on a trial when they are facing a possible death sentence. After conviction, there are constitutionally mandated appeals which involve both prosecution and defense costs.

Most of these costs occur in every case for which capital punishment is sought, regardless of the outcome. Thus, the true cost of the death penalty includes all the added expenses of the "unsuccessful" trials in which the death penalty is sought but not achieved. Moreover, if a defendant is convicted but not given the death sentence, the state will still incur the costs of life imprisonment, in addition to the increased trial expenses. For the states which employ the death penalty, this luxury comes at a high price. In Texas, a death penalty case costs taxpayers an average of $2.3 million, about three times the cost of imprisoning someone in a single cell at the highest security level for 40 years.[3] In Florida, each execution is costing the state $3.2 million.[4] In financially strapped California, one report estimated that the state could save $90 million each year by abolishing capital punishment.[5] The New York Department of Correctional Services estimated that implementing the death penalty would cost the state about $118 million *annually.*[6]

The Recession and the Death Penalty

The effects of the present financial crisis on the criminal justice system vary widely, but the common thread has been cutbacks in critical areas.... New Jersey, for example, laid off more than 500 police officers in 1991. At the same time, it was implementing a death penalty which would cost an estimated $16 million per year,[7] more than enough to hire the same number of officers at a salary of $30,000 per year. In Florida, a mid-year budget cut of $45 million for the Department of Corrections forced the early release of 3,000 inmates. Yet, by 1988 Florida had spent $57.2 million to accomplish the execution of 18 people.[8] It costs six times more to execute a person in Florida than to incarcerate a prisoner for life with no parole.[9] In contrast, Professors Richard Moran and Joseph Ellis estimated that the money it would take to implement the death penalty in New York for just five years would be enough to fund 250 additional police officers and build prisons for 6,000 inmates.[10] . . .

Illinois built new prisons but does not have the funds to open them. It does, however, have the fourth largest death row in the country. Georgia's Department of Corrections lost over 900 positions in the past year while local counties have had to raise taxes to pay for death penalty trials.

Police officers on the beat, imprisonment of offenders, and a functioning criminal justice and correctional system form the heart of the nation's response to crime. Yet, in state after state, these programs are suffering drastic cuts while the death penalty absorbs time, money and political attention.

The Cost to Local Governments

An increasingly significant consequence of the death penalty in the United States is the crushing financial burden it places on local governments. The current economic recession has made it clear that there is no unlimited source of government largesse. Counties, which bear the brunt of the costs of death penalty trials, are also the primary deliverers of local health and human services in the public sector.[11] Hard choices have to be made among the demands of providing essential services, creative crime reduction programs such as community policing, and the vigorous pursuit of a few death penalty cases.

As Scott Harshbarger, Attorney General of Massachusetts, put it: "Virtually every major program designed to address the underlying causes of violence and to support the poor, vulnerable, powerless victims of crime is being cut even further to the bone. . . . In this context, the proposition that the death penalty is a needed addition to our arsenal of weapons lacks credibility and is, as a sheer matter of equity, morally irresponsible. If this is really the best we can do, then our public value system is bankrupt and we have truly lost our way."[12]

While state and national politicians promote the death penalty, the county government is typically responsible for the costs of prosecution and the costs of the criminal trial. In some cases, the county is also responsible for the costs of defending the indigent. Georgia, Alabama and Arkansas, for example, provide little or no funding for indigent defense from the state treasury.[13] In Lincoln County, Georgia, citizens have had to face repeated tax increases just to fund one capital case. Even where the state provides some of the money for the counties to pursue the death penalty, the burden on the county can be crushing. California, for example, was spending $10 million a year reimbursing counties for expert witnesses, investigators and other death penalty defense costs, plus $2 million more to help pay for the overall cost of murder trials in smaller counties. (Now, even that reimbursement is being cut.) But many financially strapped smaller counties still could not afford to prosecute the complicated death penalty cases. Some small counties have only one prosecutor with little or no experience in death penalty cases, no investigators, and only a single Superior Court judge.[14] . . .

In Meriwether County, Georgia, a county of 21,000 residents and a $4 million annual budget, the prosecutor sought the death penalty three times for Eddie Lee Spraggins, a mentally retarded man. The case cost the county $84,000, not including the defense attorney's bill for appealing, and the third conviction was again overturned by the Georgia Supreme Court.[15] Spraggins was finally granted a plea and received a life sentence. In Mississippi, Kemper and Lauderdale Counties recently conducted a border survey battle to avoid responsibility for a capital murder trial. Faced with a case that could cost the county $100,000, Kemper County wanted to show that the scene of the murder was outside their border and conducted two surveys of the site. County Supervisor Mike Luke explained, "As much as we were talking about the taxpayers of Kemper County having to pay out, we believed we needed to be sure." Luke said that the decision to seek the death penalty was not his—he only had to come up with the money. Lauderdale County, where the trial was originally scheduled, has now sent a bill to Kemper County for expenses incurred while holding the defendant in jail for 19 months. Kemper County is considering how much it will have to raise taxes just to pay the initial costs of the prosecution. . . . [16]

With more death row inmates and more executions than any other state, Texas is also experiencing the high costs of executions. Norman Kinne, Dallas County District Attorney, expressed his frustration at the expense: "[E]ven though I'm a firm believer in the death penalty, I also understand what the cost is. If you can be satisfied with putting a person in the penitentiary for the rest of his life . . . I think maybe we have to be satisfied with that as opposed to spending $1 million to try and get them executed. . . . I think we could use (the money) better for additional penitentiary space, rehabilitation efforts, drug rehabilitation, education, (and) especially devote a lot of attention to juveniles."[17]

Vincent Perini, of the Texas Bar Association, calls the death penalty a "luxury": "There's some things that a modern American city and state have got to have. You have to have police and fire and public safety protection. You have to have a criminal justice system. You do not have to have a death penalty. The death penalty in criminal justice is kind of a luxury item. It's an add-on; it's an optional item when you buy your criminal justice vehicle."[18] Chief Criminal Judge, James Ellis, came to a similar conclusion in Oregon: "Whether you're for it or against it, I think the fact is that Oregon simply can't afford it."[19] James Exum, Chief Justice of the North Carolina Supreme Court, agrees: "I think those of us involved in prosecuting these (death penalty) cases have this uneasy notion that . . . these cases are very time-consuming and very troublesome and take a lot of resources that might be better spent on other kinds of crimes. . . .''

Efforts are under way in both Congress and the Supreme Court to reduce the avenues of appeal available to death row inmates. But most of the costs associated with the death penalty occur at the trial level.[20] Whatever effect cutting back on the writ of habeas corpus may have on the time from trial to execution, it is not clear that the changes will make the death penalty any less expensive, and they may result in the execution of innocent people. With the number of people on death row growing each year, the overall costs of the death penalty are likely to increase.

Some state appeals courts are overwhelmed with death penalty cases. The California Supreme Court, for example, spends more than half its time reviewing death cases.[21] The Florida Supreme Court also spends about half its time on death penalty cases.[22] Many governors spend a significant percentage of their time reviewing clemency petitions and more will face this task as executions spread. As John Dixon, Chief Justice (Retired) of the Louisiana Supreme Court, said: ''The people have a constitutional right to the death penalty and we'll do our best to make it work rationally. But you can see what it's doing. Capital punishment is destroying the system.''[23] . . .

Epilogue—Fall 1994

Since the publication of *Millions Misspent* in the fall of 1992, more judges, prosecutors and other state officials have joined those questioning the death penalty in light of its exorbitant costs. At a time when crime is the nation's primary concern, new data confirms the Report's earlier conclusion that the death penalty is draining state treasuries of funds which could be spent on effective crime prevention measures.

The financial burden is particularly acute in counties where administrators are being forced to choose between raising taxes and bankruptcy in order to prosecute death penalty cases. While many politicians continue to ignore these costs in using the death penalty to sound tough, some prosecutors are now deciding not to seek executions because the cases are simply too expensive.

The Duke University Study

In May 1993, a federally funded study brought a new perspective to the cost debate.[24] This model study was prompted by an American Bar Association proposal and was conducted at Duke University's Terry Sanford Institute of Public Policy. It is one of the most comprehensive and thorough analyses on this topic.

Authors Philip Cook and Donna Slawson spent two years comparing the costs of adjudicating capital and noncapital cases in North Carolina and concluded that capital cases *cost at least an extra $2.16 million per execution,* compared to what taxpayers would have spent if defendants were tried without the death penalty and sentenced to life in prison.[25] Moreover, the bulk of those costs occur at the trial level. Applying their figures on a national level implies that $82 million was spent just for U.S. executions in 1993, and that the national bill for the death penalty has been over $500 million since the death penalty was reinstated.[26] Yet, the national concern about crime indicates that few feel safer for all this expense.

Time Is Money

Death penalty cases are so expensive because they take longer at every stage and require vast resources for both the prosecution and the defense. The authors of the North Carolina study identified 24 principal areas in which a death penalty case would likely be more expensive than if the case were tried non-capitally.[27] These areas included:

- More investigative work by both law enforcement officials and the defense team
- More pre-trial motions
- More questioning concerning individual jurors' views on capital punishment and more peremptory challenges to jurors at jury selection
- The appointment of two defense attorneys
- A longer and more complex trial
- A separate penalty phase conducted in front of a jury
- A more thorough review of the case on direct appeal
- More post-trial motions
- Greater likelihood that counsel will be appointed for a federal habeas corpus petition
- Greater likelihood that there will be full briefing and argument on federal review
- More preparation for, and a longer clemency proceeding.

The North Carolina study estimated that a death penalty trial takes about four times longer than a non-capital murder trial. And, of course, not every death penalty trial results in a death sentence. Based on the experience in North Carolina, the authors found that less than a third of capital trials resulted in a death sentence.[28] Nevertheless, each of the these trials had the extra expense associated with death penalty proceedings. The trial costs alone were about $200,000 *more for each death penalty imposed* than if no death penalty was involved.[29]

The authors computed the costs of appealing a death penalty case and subtracted the savings which accrue to the state when an execution finally occurs. The "savings," which are due to the inmate no longer being kept at state expense, only occur when an execution is actually carried out. As with the trial level, there is a "failure" rate resulting from the fact that many inmates who are sentenced to death will never be executed. Many cases will be overturned on appeal, some inmates will commit suicide, others will die of natural causes. Again, based on the experience in North Carolina, the authors estimated that only one inmate would likely be executed for every ten who are sentenced to death.[30] This is actually higher than the national rate where only about one in every eleven cases which have been resolved has resulted in an execution.[31]

Bulk of Costs at Trial Level

The importance of accounting for this failure rate is critical for two reasons. First, it represents a truer picture of what it is actually costing the state to achieve an execution. It is not just the cost of a single person's trial and appeals. That would be comparable to saying that the cost of landing a man on the moon was the cost of fuel for the one rocket which brought him there. The state has to pay more for all the trials and appeals which start out as death penalty cases but for which there will never be the "saving" associated with an execution.

Second, the per execution costs reveal that the bulk of death penalty costs occur at the *trial* level. Often those who acknowledge the high costs of the death penalty believe that the expense is due to "endless appeals." By taking into account the capital cases which will never result in an execution, the North Carolina study makes clear that the *trials* produce the largest share of death penalty costs and these costs will not be substantially lessened by tinkering with the opportunities that death row inmates have to appeal. A significant financial corollary of this finding is that taxpayers must pay death penalty expenses up front, whereas the costs of a life sentence are meted out gradually over many years, making that alternative even less expensive.

Evidence from Other States

There have been numerous indications from other areas of the country that the death penalty is straining the budgets of state and local governments and that the financial drain is getting worse. Some countries have been brought to the brink of bankruptcy because of death penalty cases. More county commissioners have risked going to jail for balking at paying for capital prosecutions,[32] while others reluctantly raise taxes to pay the costs of even one capital case.

- In San Diego, California, the prosecution costs alone (not counting defense costs or appeals) for three capital cases averaged over half a million dollars each.[33] One estimate puts the total California death penalty expense bill at $1 billion since 1977.[34] California has executed two people during that time, one of whom refused to appeal his case.
- In Jasper County, Mississippi, the Circuit Judge and the District Attorney had to address the county supervisors to get more money for death penalty prosecutions. The only solution was to raise county taxes. "It's going to be a fairly substantial increase," said the board president, John Sims. "I hope the taxpayers understand. . . ."[35]

- In South Carolina, *The Sun News* reported that the bills for death penalty cases are "skyrocketing" because of a state supreme court ruling that attorneys in death penalty cases deserve reasonable fees. Before the decision, attorneys received no more than $2,500 for each death penalty case.[36]
- In Harris County, Texas, there are 135 pending death penalty cases. State Judge Miron Love estimated that if the death penalty is assessed in just 20 percent of these cases, it will cost the taxpayers a minimum of $60 million. Judge Love, who oversees the county's courts, remarked: "We're running the county out of money."[37]

Reactions to the High Costs

There have been many similar reactions from state and local officials who wonder about the wisdom of spending such exorbitant sums on such unpredictable and isolated cases. In Tennessee, the number of people sentenced to death has dropped because prosecutors say death penalty cases cost too much.[38]

In Texas, Judge Doug Shaver from Houston was also concerned about the high costs of so many capital cases: "I can't figure out why our county is prosecuting so many more [death] cases than comparably large counties around Texas. When the law changed so defendants can be sentenced to 40 years flat time [as an alternative to death], and when you start taking into account what the taxpayers are getting for their money, it seems like some defendants should be tried . . . without the death penalty."[39] Former Texas Attorney General Jim Mattox agrees: "Life without parole could save millions of dollars." "In other words," he wrote, "it's cheaper to lock 'em up and throw away the key. . . . As violent crime continues to escalate, it's something to consider."[40]

California has been hit particularly hard by natural disasters and the economic recession. Many social programs have had to be cut. Yet the state continues to spend hundreds of millions of dollars on the death penalty which has resulted in two executions in seventeen years. Even supporters of the death penalty recognize that it is a financial loser. In financially strapped Orange County, Vanda Bresnan, who manages the criminal courts, remarked: "Even though I do believe in the death penalty, I wonder how long the state or county can afford it,"[41] Defense attorney Gary Proctor, who practices in the same county, believes that the solution will be found by cutting other services: "What I see happening is that other services provided to the taxpayer—such as libraries and parks—will be cut back. Certain people are not aware of the tradeoffs." He added: "Strong beliefs are easy enough to hold if you don't think they're coming out of your pocket."[42]

In rural Kentucky, tax bases are small and budgets are already stretched. When an expensive capital case is about to be heard in court, the state and county often argue for weeks about who will pay. As Michael Mager, executive director of the Kentucky County Judge-Executives Association, points out, "A little rural county in Kentucky just can't deal with bills like that."[43] . . .

Conclusion

Recent studies of death penalty costs reinforce the existing evidence that the death penalty is becoming unmanageably expensive. Like a black hole, it absorbs vast quantities of resources but emits no light. Nevertheless, politicians and much of the public are drawn to it in the hope of finding a quick fix to the crime problem. But as the actual costs of capital punishment become clearer, the public should be in a better position to judge the death penalty as they would other programs. If a program is highly cost intensive, given to years of litigious expense, focused on only a few individuals, and produces no measurable results, then it should be replaced by better alternatives.

Notes

1. S. Magagnini, *Closing Death Row Would Save State $90 Million a Year,* The Sacramento Bee, March 28, 1988, at 1.

2. Kansas Legislative Research Department study, cited in D. Von Drehle, *Bottom Line: Life in Prison One-sixth as Expensive,* The Miami Herald, July 10, 1988, at 12A.

3. C. Hoppe, *Executions Cost Texas Millions,* The Dallas Morning News, March 8, 1992, at 1A.

4. D. Von Drehle, *Bottom Line: Life in Prison One-sixth as Expensive,* The Miami Herald, July 10, 1988, at 12A.

5. Magagnini, see note 1.

6. The New York Department of Correctional Services study cited in Moran & Ellis, *Death Penalty: Luxury Item,* New York Newsday, June 14, 1989, at 60; see also the Massachusetts Bar Association Section News, *The Dollar and Human Costs of the Death Penalty,* April 1992, at 5.

7. M. Garey, *The Cost of Taking A Life: Dollars and Sense of the Death Penalty,* 18 University of California Davis Law Review 1221, 1261 (1985).

8. Von Drehle, see note 4.

9. Id.

10. Moran & Ellis, see note 6, at 62

11. Testimony of Carole Carpenter on behalf of the National Association of Counties before the U.S. Senate Subcommittee on Juvenile Justice, April 29, 1992, at 7.

12. Harshbarger, *Statement on Reinstating the Death Penalty in the Commonwealth,* Massachusetts Bar Association, see note 6, at 3.

13. Tabak & Lane, *Judicial Activism and Legislative "Reform" of Federal Habeas Corpus: A Critical Analysis of Recent Developments and Current Proposals,* 55 Albany Law Review 1, 31 (1991).

14. Magagnini, see note 1.

15. K. Wood, *Can State Afford Fourth Prosecution of Spraggins?,* Fulton County Daily Report, March 3, 1988, at 1.

16. *Maxwell Murder Trial May Up Kemper Taxes,* The Meridian Star (Mississippi), July 21, 1992; phone conversation with Michael Luke, September 11, 1992.

17. Hoppe, The Dallas Morning News, see note 3.

18. Id.

19. J. Painter, *Death Penalty Seen as Too Costly for Oregon's Pocketbook,* The Oregonian (Portland), July 27, 1987.

20. Kansas, for example, estimated that the annual cost for implementing the death penalty would be $11.4 million, of which $9.2 million would be for trial costs. Kansas Legislative Research Dept. Memorandum, Feb. 11, 1987. New York estimated a cost of $1.8 million per case, through the first level of appeals, of which $1.5 million would be trial costs. *Capital Losses: The Price of the Death Penalty for New York State,* NY State Defenders Association, Albany, 1982.

21. Magagnini, see note 1.

22. M. Hansen, *Politics and the Death Penalty,* The Palm Beach Review's Florida Supreme Court Report, Feb. 25, 1991, at 10B, 26B.

23. D. Kaplan, *Death Mill, USA,* The National Law Journal, May 9, 1989, at 40.

24. P. Cook and D. Slawson, *The Costs of Processing Murder Cases in North Carolina* (May, 1993).

25. Id. at 98.

26. There were 38 executions in the U.S. in 1993 and there have been 252 executions since 1976 as of Sept. 20, 1994. See NAACP Legal Defense & Educational Fund, Inc., Death Row, U.S.A. 5 (Summer 1994) (7 additional executions occurred since that publication).

27. P. Cook, note 24, at 22–23.

28. Id. at 68.

29. Id. at 70.

30. Id. at 98.

31. Bureau of Justice Statistics, *Capital Punishment 1992,* at 10, Appendix table 1 (1993) (of 4,704 people sentenced to death, 2,129 were removed from death row, including 188 executions).

32. See J. Gerth, *Counties Balk at Paying Experts to Testify for Indigents,* Louisville Courier-Journal, April 4, 1994, at 1.

33. See B. Callahan, *Lawyers No Longer Get Millions in Capital Cases,* San Diego Tribune, June 26, 1994, at A-1, A-18 (prosecutions of David Lucas, Ronaldo Ayala, and Billy Ray Waldon).

34. C. Linder, *Capital Cases Are Crippling State Courts,* The Sacramento Bee, Sept. 5, 1993, at Forum 1.

35. M. Hatcher, *Judge and D.A. Warn Supervisors About High Cost of Capital Murder Trials,* Jasper County News, Mar. 9, 1994.

36. B. Kudelka, *The High Cost of Pursuing the Death Penalty,* The Sun News (Myrtle Beach, SC), May 1, 1994, at 1A.

37. J. Makeig, *Capital Justice Takes a Lot of County Capital,* The Houston Chronicle, Aug. 15, 1994.

38. *Death Sentences Fall in Tenn.; Costs Cited,* The Commercial Appeal (Memphis), Sept. 6, 1994 (Associated Press).

39. J. Makeig, note 37.

40. J. Mattox, *Texas' Death Penalty Dilemma,* The Dallas Morning News, Aug. 25, 1993.

41. A. Tugend, *Death Penalty's High Cost,* The Orange County Register, Aug. 9, 1993, at 1.

42. Id. at 2.

43. J. Gerth, *Counties Balk at Paying Experts to Testify for Indigents,* Louisville Courier-Journal, April 4, 1994, at 1.

PART VII

The Death Penalty: For and Against

Who supports the death penalty in America? Who opposes it? How do its supporters and opponents weave together the facts, their interpretation, and various alternative hypotheses into coherent arguments? Because this part is devoted exclusively to reprinting selected arguments for and against, it may be helpful to look first at the nature and organization of the disputants.

There is not now and there never has been any national organization devoted to the single issue of defending and expanding the use of the death penalty in this country—unless one counts the Association of Government Attorneys in Capital Litigation, mordantly known as the Fryers Club—the prosecutors who seek capital convictions and then fight in the appellate courts not to lose them.[1] Such organized support as there is for the death penalty is confined at present to a handful of multi-issue organizations in law enforcement, politics, and religion. Since the 1970s, the National District Attorneys Association,[2] the National Association of Attorneys General,[3] and the Washington Legal Foundation[4] have endorsed the death penalty. So have the National Sheriffs' Association,[5] the International Association of Chiefs of Police,[6] and the International Conference of Police Associations.[7] Testimony from these organizations has often been presented in state legislatures and Congress when hearings have been held on the death penalty in recent years. Fundamentalist and Pentecostal churches as well as the Church of Jesus Christ of Latter-day Saints (Mormons) typically support the death penalty on Old Testament biblical grounds.[8] In the 1970s the National Association of Evangelicals (NAE)—representing more than ten million conservative Christians and 47 different denominations[9]—and the Moral Majority were among the Christian groups supporting the death penalty.[10] So does its successor, the Christian Coalition; according to executive director Robert E. Reed Jr., "The Christian Coalition does support the death penalty in capital murder cases as well as other cases involving gross brutality."[11] For two decades or more, leading Republican Party spokesmen have endorsed the death penalty.[12]

Opposition to the death penalty, on the other hand, has been nationally organized, beginning with the American Society for the Abolition of Capital Punishment, founded in Philadelphia in 1845, and succeeded by the American League to Abolish Capital Punishment, founded in New York in 1926.[13] Neither organization exists today. However, in July 1976, immediately after the Supreme Court's decision in

Gregg, the NCADP was organized in New York under the initiative of Henry Schwarzschild, then director of the Capital Punishment Project of the ACLU. With its headquarters in Washington, D.C., the NCADP consists of several dozen state and national affiliates. Chief among these are the ACLU, AI-USA, and the LDF. Most of the mainstream Protestant churches are affiliated (Baptists, Episcopalians, Lutherans, Methodists, Presbyterians, United Church of Christ). So are several Catholic organizations (U.S. Catholic Conference, Catholic Peace Fellowship) and Jewish groups (Jewish Peace Fellowship, Union of American Hebrew Congregations). Many nonreligious organizations are members as well, including (to name but a few) the American Orthopsychiatric Association, the Martin Luther King Center for Nonviolent Social Change, the National Bar Association, the National Conference of Black Lawyers, the National Council on Crime and Delinquency, the National Lawyers Guild, and the National Legal Aid and Defender Association.[14]

Opposition to the death penalty by many of America's organized religious groups precedes the founding of the NCADP by several years.[15] But the broad public approval of the death penalty today suggests that the leaders of these churches are preaching to the unconverted among their own parishioners when they criticize the death penalty. Worth special attention during the years ahead is the question whether the opposition to the death penalty in the recent papal encyclical, *Evangelium Vitae* (1995), will galvanize the Catholic hierarchy in America into taking a more vigorous teaching and preaching role on this subject.[16]

The two pairs of essays in this part give a selective but not, I hope, an unrepresentative view of the range of arguments for and against the death penalty as they appear in current public debate. The first two essays (chapters 30 and 31), by H. Wayne House and John Howard Yoder, are excerpted from their book, *The Death Penalty Debate* (1991). This volume is without rival in presenting in some detail both sides of the argument on capital punishment as seen from diverging Christian points of view. The House-Yoder debate in effect amounts to trying to decide which is the key insight: Genesis 9:6 ("Whosoever sheddeth man's blood by man shall his blood be shed") or John 8:7 ("He that is without sin among you, let him first cast a stone at her"). House is a theologian on the faculty of Western Baptist College in Salem, Oregon; he explains and defends the death penalty in a manner that most thoughtful American fundamentalists should find congenial.[17] Yoder, a Mennonite, is a theologian on the faculty of Notre Dame; he argues for an interpretation of the biblical message that opposes the death penalty but without diluting that message into a thinly disguised secular argument.

The second pair of essays is by Ernest van den Haag and me. He is a retired professor of jurisprudence at Fordham Law School in New York, and is well known for his conservative views on many issues. Over the past twenty years he has been second to none in the public advocacy for the death penalty.[18] In 1983 he coauthored *The Death Penalty: A Debate,* with John P. Conrad, a whole volume devoted to arguing all aspects of the capital punishment controversy.[19] In the essay reprinted here as chapter 32, van den Haag assembles a range of arguments—constitutional, empirical, and moral—in support of retaining and expanding the death penalty.

Over the past two decades van den Haag has publicly debated the death penalty dozens of times, on radio, television, and before live audiences large and small. Many years ago I took to print to disagree with him over the death penalty,[20] and it seemed a fitting way to close this volume by doing so once again.[21]

Notes

1. See Kaplan 1990.

2. See the capital punishment issue of *NDAA,* the *Journal of the National District Attorneys Association,* for July–August 1965, and the testimony in the Senate hearings on S. 1382 of E. J. Salcines, state attorney, on behalf of the NDAA, 18 May 1977.

3. New York Times, 7 Dec. 1972, p. 30.

4. See the testimony in the House hearings on H.R. 2837 and H.R. 343 of George C. Smith, director, WLF, on 16 April 1986, and the testimony in the Senate hearings on S. 22 and related bills by Paul D. Kamenar, executive legal director, WLF, on 27 September 1989.

5. See the testimony in the Senate hearings on S. 114 by Lucas Ferris, executive director, National Sheriffs' Association, 10 April 1981.

6. See the testimony in the Senate hearings on S. 114 of Norman Darwick, executive director, International Association of Chiefs of Police (IACP), 27 April 1981, and the testimony of C. Roland Vaughn III on behalf of the IACP in the Senate hearings on S. 32 and related bills, 19 September 1989.

7. See the testimony in the Senate hearings on S. 1 and related bills by Edward J. Kiernan, president, International Conference of Police Associations, 13 June 1973.

8. See Gardner 1979a, 1979b.

9. An undated memorandum from the NAE office of Public Affairs reports that as of 1972, the organization "believes that the ultimate penalty of capital punishment should be retained for premeditated murder."

10. I once wrote Rev. Jerry Falwell, founder of the Moral Majority (Lynchburg, Virginia), inquiring about the reasons he and his organization relied on for their support of the death penalty. By way of answer I received my own letter back; scribbled in pencil at the bottom was this reply: "See Genesis 9:6."

11. Letter to the author, 26 September 1995. In its *Contract with the American Family* (1995), the Christian Coalition strongly supports punishment for crimes (pp. 121–30) but makes no mention of the death penalty.

12. In 1972, prior to the Supreme Court's decision in *Furman,* Assistant Attorney General Henry Peterson testified before the House Judiciary Committee supporting the death penalty (10 March 1972, p. 16); Richard Kleindienst endorsed the death penalty during his Senate confirmation hearing (New York Times, 29 February 1972, p. 8); and California's Governor Ronald Reagan demanded reinstatement of the death penalty following a declaration by the state supreme court that it was unconstitutional (New York Times, 1 March 1972, p. 46).

13. See Mackey ed. 1976.

14. A complete list of the national, regional, and state organizations belonging to the NCADP is available from the Coalition's Washington, D.C., office.

15. See the pamphlet *Capital Punishment: What the Religious Community Says* (1978), reprinted in House Hearings 1978:32–69. For more recent position statements by American churches, see the pamphlet *The Death Penalty: The Religious Community Calls for Abolition* (1988), published by the NCADP.

16. The argument of the encyclical is inspired by the biblical story of Cain and Abel; God spares Cain, murderer of his brother Abel, but stigmatizes and banishes him (Genesis 4:15). Using this story to guide formulation of a proper penology, the encyclical asserts that there is no moral foundation for the death penalty "except in cases of absolute necessity." Quoting from the new *Catechism of the Catholic Church,* the encyclical concludes: "If bloodless means are sufficient to defend human lives against an aggressor and to protect public order and the safety of persons, public authority must limit itself to such means, because they better correspond to the concrete conditions of the common good and are more in conformity to the dignity of the human person." See Pope John Paul II 1995:100.

For a recent pre-encyclical discussion of the Catholic position, see Drinan 1994. For the fullest historical account of Christian thinking on the death penalty, see Megivern 1996. For a collection of statements against the death penalty by U. S. Catholic bishops, see Catholics Against Capital Punishment 1994.

17. For other conservative Christian defenses of the death penalty, see Vellenga 1959 (reprinted in Bedau ed. 1964) and Gow 1985. An interesting study guide for Christians opposing the death penalty will be found in Gross 1991.

18. See also van den Haag 1969, 1978a, 1978b, 1983, 1985a, 1985b, 1985c, 1986, and 1990.

19. Recent books devoted to defending the death penalty include Berger 1982; Berns 1979; Otterbein 1986; and Sorell 1988. Among the recent books opposing the death penalty, the following deserve mention: Dicks 1991; Endres 1985; Gorecki 1983; Gray and Stanley eds. 1989; Haas and Inciardi 1988; Nathanson 1987; Paternoster 1991; Prejean 1993; von Drehle 1995; White 1991; and Zimring and Hawkins 1986.

20. See Bedau 1970; this essay, like van den Haag's to which it was a reply, had the oddity of being published in two scholarly journals a few months apart

21. Elsewhere I have given arguments against the death penalty that have a broader scope; see especially Bedau 1992a, 1993. Other philosophers who have recently written on the death penalty controversy include Hurka 1982; Leiser 1986; Murphy 1979; Narveson 1993; Perlmutter 1996; Pojman 1992; Primorac 1982; Reiman 1985, 1988, 1990; Satre 1991–92; Sorell 1987; Wasserstrom 1982; Waters 1982; Wellman 1988; and especially Nathanson 1987.

30

The New Testament and Moral Arguments for Capital Punishment

H. WAYNE HOUSE

The New Testament and Capital Punishment

The teachings of Jesus Christ and the apostle Paul provide the theological foundation for New Testament Christianity. Those of us who call ourselves Christians must evaluate our lives from this perspective. There is no question that God commanded capital punishment as part of the Noachian Covenant, nor should there be any debate that the death penalty was part of the Mosaic Covenant. Things, however, were changed after the death, burial, and resurrection of Jesus Christ. If his redemptive work on the Cross changed the application of other aspects of the Old Testament, such as sacrifices, then perhaps he also set aside capital punishment as a legitimate form of punishment. Many think that Jesus and Paul have done exactly this. If true, then the debate is settled. We, however, are convinced that neither Jesus nor Paul abrogated capital punishment. This chapter will examine the Gospels and the Epistles to ascertain the position each held on the death penalty.

The Teachings of Jesus Christ

Clearly the cross-work of Jesus Christ brought about major changes in the relationship of man and God, and none so dramatic as the place of the Mosaic Law in the life of the New Testament believer. Christ ended the sacrificial system (Heb. 10:1–18), unified believing Jew and Gentile into one body (Eph. 2:11–22), and freed believers from the judicial authority of the Law (Rom. 7:1–6, Col. 2:16–23). Not only this, but during his early ministry he challenged the very foundation of Jewish traditionalism, ridiculing the Jewish authorities for their neglect of justice, mercy, and faithfulness:

> Woe to you, teachers of the law and Pharisees, you hypocrites! You give a tenth of your spices—mint, dill and cummin. But you have neglected the more important

Reprinted by permission of the author, from *The Death Penalty Debate: H. Wayne House and John Howard Yoder* (Dallas: Word Publications, 1991), pp. 59–80.

> matters of the law—justice, mercy and faithfulness. You should have practiced the latter, without neglecting the former. You blind guides! You strain out a gnat but swallow a camel. (Matt. 23:23–24 NIV)

In light of this, what changes did Jesus make in the rules of capital punishment? Did he set aside the Mosaic Law or the Noachian Covenant with their emphasis upon retributive punishment, including the death penalty for murder, and replace them with another concept, one based on love and forgiveness? Or did he acknowledge the legitimacy of capital punishment and permit its practice? Although Jesus gave no direct statement on the subject, it is possible to gain an understanding of his position by analyzing three key passages: the Sermon on the Mount, the story of the woman taken in adultery, and his own response to his trials and execution.

Some, however, object to using specific passages to determine Jesus' mind on a given topic. They would rather seek the general tenor of his thinking by looking at the overall content of the Gospels. "It is not what the Bible says in a specific verse, but what it says to us through its total message, interpreted in terms of our own conditions, that is relevant."[1]

The concept sounds valid, but we wonder how to obtain the total message of Christ without studying specific passages which describe what he said and did? Moreover, how is one to guard against the natural tendency to identify the reader's own mind with that of Jesus? Sometimes those who seek the mind of Jesus ignore passages which seem to contradict their preconceived view of the subject. Certain texts are likely to be ruled out of court, since they do not fit the image of a patient, loving, forgiving Lord:

> Physically beating those with whom he disagreed (John 2:13–15); berating those religious leaders who disagreed with him by calling them children "of hell" (Matt. 23:15) who deserve to be sentenced to that place (Matt. 23:29–33); designated the Jews (of which he was a part) carte blanche as children of "the devil" (John 8:44); announced that any place which will not receive his disciples will fare worse than Sodom and Gomorrah (Matt. 10:14–15); responding to a mother's plea for her sick child by telling her that "it is not right to take the children's bread and throw it to the dogs" (i.e., to foreigners, Mark 7:24–27); constantly berating his disciples (e.g., Mark 8:17–18), and even those in need of his help (Mark 9:19); etc.[2]

Our study of capital punishment in the mind of Christ will of necessity center on specific passages in which we find him interacting with the death penalty in his culture. These sections will be the basis for our conclusions.

When we open the New Testament we find a world radically changed from that of the Old. Though the Jewish nation had religious freedom, Palestine was ruled by the Roman Empire. Rome, a Gentile power, was the dominant political and military authority. Judaism had become encrusted with a traditionalism so thick that little of its original light shined forth. Into this context came the Messiah, proclaiming his radical message of repentance and renewal to the Jewish people. He did not come to prophetically hold Rome accountable to God through the Mosaic Covenant. In fact, he commanded his disciples to avoid both the Samaritans and the Gentiles in their preaching (Matt. 10:5). Consequently Jesus said little about the political authority of Rome and its exercise of capital punishment. He acknowledged Caesar's general authority, but did not elaborate on its specific exercise (cf. Matthew 22:21). Consequently we must analyze his personal teachings to his people for insights into his view of capital punishment. Here we also find that he said nothing specific about the death penalty, but it is possible to draw some conclusions about it from his other teachings.

The Sermon on the Mount

In the Sermon on the Mount (Matt. 5–7), Jesus attacked the traditionalism which prevented an accurate understanding of the Mosaic Law and hindered its correct application to the lives of his audience. In this context, he gave the teaching which is most frequently quoted in the capital punishment debate:

> You have heard that it was said, "Love your neighbor and hate your enemy." But I tell you: Love your enemies and pray for those who persecute you, that you may be sons of your Father in heaven. . . . Be perfect, therefore, as your heavenly Father is perfect. (Matt. 5:43–44, 48 NIV).

The first phrase he cites, "love your neighbor," comes from Leviticus 19:18, "Do not seek revenge or bear a grudge against one of your people, but love your neighbor as yourself. I am the Lord." The second phrase does not come from the Old Testament but reflects the traditionalism of his day and the general tendency of sinful humanity. Jesus is not rejecting the Mosaic teaching, but showing his listeners that the life lived in obedience to the Law goes beyond normal expectations. This is in perfect agreement with Leviticus 19:17, "Do not hate your brother in your heart" (also cited in Matthew 5:22). Jesus' call, therefore, is for "mature action in the day-to-day events of ordinary life: to be without prejudice and devoid of self-interested motives."[3]

The entire passage as well as its context centers on personal responses to difficult situations. Jesus' concern is the attitude more than the act: hate more than murder (5:21–24), sexual desire more than adultery (5:27–30), love of enemies rather than hate for them (5:43–48). None of this contradicts any part of the Mosaic Law. Jesus refocuses the Law on the personal lives of his listeners rather than rejects or replaces it with new teaching (5:17–20).

None of his teaching is directed to the governmental authorities of his day. In fact, Jesus acknowledged the existence of courts and councils without rejecting their validity (5:25–26). His commands only "limit the believer's response in these situations to what love and Scriptures impose."[4] There is nothing in the Sermon on the Mount that challenges capital punishment as a part of existing governmental practices, Jewish or Roman. If, as some claim, we had to be perfect to exercise punishment (cf. 5:48), then all punishment for any sin would be eliminated and anarchy would reign supreme. Matthew 5:43–48 does not eliminate the validity of capital punishment.

Matthew 5:21–22, on the other hand, shows that Jesus recognized that murder merits judgment. Certainly he knew that Exodus 20:13 prohibited murder, and that

Exodus 21:12 commanded the death penalty for the crime. Yet, Jesus said nothing against such a judgment. In fact, he built upon its severity to warn against the attitude of hatred in the strongest of terms. If the Sermon on the Mount shows us anything about Jesus' attitude toward capital punishment, it shows us that he accepted it as a valid exercise of governmental authority and a proper part of the Mosaic Code.

The Woman Taken in Adultery

Adultery was a capital offense according to the Mosaic Law, so when the Pharisees brought a woman to Jesus who had been caught in that very act, he looked capital punishment right in the face (John 8:1–11).[5] Those who oppose the death penalty argue that his refusal to condemn the woman shows that Jesus rejected capital punishment in favor of a higher ideal.

> With sovereign authority Jesus transcended the law and demonstrated the grace of God in the forgiveness of sins. His practice like his teaching was based on his conception of God. He had not come to carry out punishment according to legal requirements or exact proper revenge, but to seek the lost, to redeem the ungodly and to reconcile sinners to God.[6]

The argument sounds impressive, especially in light of the radical nature of Jesus' ministry, but it is open to serious, indeed, fatal objections.

The real issue placed before Jesus was not a guilty woman but a baited trap (8:6). Both Pharisees and Messiah knew that Leviticus 20:10 and Deuteronomy 22:22–24 required that the woman guilty of adultery be executed, whether she was married or not. Both Pharisees and Messiah knew that the Law required the testimony of two or three witnesses before conviction. And both Pharisee and Messiah knew that Roman law reserved the right of capital punishment for itself. If Jesus had agreed to her execution, then he would have been guilty of rebellion against Rome.[7] If, however, he waffled on the death penalty, then he would be rebelling against the Mosaic Code. His unexpected response disarmed the accusers and his mercy freed the woman: "If any one of you is without sin, let him be the first to throw a stone at her," and, "Neither do I condemn you . . . go now and leave your life of sin" (8:11). Does Jesus also disarm the death penalty and free humanity from its curse?

If Jesus is both rebuking the Pharisees and rejecting capital punishment, then it is clear that he is dealing only with a specific situation: adultery. The passage cannot be extended to include murder, since that crime is covered by the Mosaic and the Noachian Covenants. It is also clear that Jesus is not demanding complete sinlessness of every witness, jury member, and judge, for then the criminal justice system would not be possible at all. This is inconsistent with the New Testament's general affirmation of judicial sanctions as a demonstration of divine justice (cf. Rom. 13:1–7). What, then, did Jesus do that so effectively silenced his opponents?

The Pharisees were half-right: Leviticus 20:10 and Deuteronomy 22:22–24 demanded the execution of a woman taken in adultery. But the Law also required the execution of the man as well, and the woman's partner was notably absent. Presumably the witnesses saw his sin as well as that of the woman since she was, after all, taken in the very act (8:4). The witnesses, then, were equally guilty of breaking the Law and, according to Deuteronomy 19:16–21, were also guilty of a capital crime.

> The sense . . . is that the scribes and Pharisees were not *without fault* as witnesses in such a judicial proceeding, because they themselves were guilty of violating the provisions of Deuteronomy 22:22–24. Stricken in conscience, the hypocritical witnesses left the scene, and Jesus dismissed the case when no one remained to press charges. Far from abrogating the provisions of the Mosaic law, Jesus demonstrated that he took their procedural guidelines for the protection of accused persons very seriously. This understanding of Jesus' action in this periscope is consistent with his statement in Matthew 5:17 that he did not come to abolish the law of Moses, but to fulfill it.[8]

Capital punishment never became an issue for Jesus. As for the woman, who else could forgive sins except the Lawgiver himself (cf. Luke 5:20–25)? Consequently, this passage does not prove that Jesus intended to abolish the death penalty either in general or for the specific crime of adultery. Arguments against capital punishment must appeal to texts other than this one.

Other Passages

When Pilate warned him that he had "the power either to free you or to crucify you" (John 19:10), Jesus acknowledged the reality of Pilate's authority, but pointed him toward its true source: "You would have no power over me if it were not given to you from above" (John 19:11). Jesus recognized that Pilate's authority as the governing official came from God and that it was being manipulated by others for an unjust end ("The one who handed me over to you is guilty of a greater sin"). However, the validity of Pilate's authority to execute Jesus was never questioned by either.

Jesus also appealed to pre-Mosaic decrees to settle arguments, decrees that were given to the whole of humanity, not just Israel. The basis for marriage is not the Mosaic Law, but the decree of Genesis (cf. Matt. 19:3–9). Jesus did not specifically speak of the Noachian Covenant, but neither did he reject it. The fact that he recognized that pre-Mosaic decrees were still valid even under the Mosaic Law, however, supports our previous contention that the Noachian Covenant was still operative during the theocracy, and is still in effect today.

Summary

Throughout his life Jesus obeyed the Mosaic Code and, as Messiah to Israel, demanded obedience to its precepts. He refocused its demands upon the attitudes of its adherents, not just their acts. When confronted by hypocritical, false witnesses he exposed them for what they were and extended mercy to the guilty. We conclude, therefore, that Jesus accepted the Mosaic Code, complete with capital punishment, and did nothing, by word or deed, to abrogate the death penalty.

The Teachings of the Apostles

Most of the apostolic writings in the New Testament deal with ecclesiastical concerns and touch on the world only when the church is directly involved. Consequently, we do not find the apostles giving any direct statements concerning capital punishment. As with Jesus, we must find their answer to our question by drawing it out of what they said and did.

The New Testament records the detailed response of only one apostle when confronted with execution—Paul. When Festus offered him a chance to go to Jerusalem for trial, a trip on which he would probably have been ambushed, Paul appealed to Caesar, claiming,

> I have not done any wrong to the Jews, as you yourself know very well. If, however, I am guilty of doing anything deserving death, I do not refuse to die. (Acts 25:10–11 NIV)

Two things stand out in this affirmation. First, Paul presumably considered some crimes worthy of death. These are not specified, of course, but his recognition of capital crime runs counter to those who try to employ his teachings to argue against capital punishment. The second point is that Paul did not question Rome's authority to execute him. He claimed the protection afforded him by Roman law, and he also accepted its authority to execute him if a capital crime were involved. This evidence, though circumstantial, argues that Paul accepted the validity of capital punishment.

Only two passages from the Epistles speak to the issue of governmental authority: 1 Peter 2:13–14 and Romans 13:1–7. The Petrine passage, the more general of the two, simply admonishes believers to

> submit yourselves for the Lord's sake to every authority instituted among men: whether to the king, as the supreme authority, or to governors, who are sent by him to punish those who do wrong and to commend those who do right. (NIV)

Peter says nothing about capital punishment, but if other passages show that God has placed the death penalty within governmental authority, then the believer has no option but to accept it. We must look to Paul to see whether capital punishment is still part of governmental authority.

The second passage, Romans 13:1–7, is the determinative one insofar as capital punishment is concerned, and therefore will be examined in detail. Paul discussed many theological points in Romans other than the role of human government. Throughout this epistle and many of his others, Paul affirmed that the Mosaic Code had ended as the judicial measuring stick for the believer's life. The Law had been fulfilled on the Cross, and a new way was open for the believers to approach God. Romans 7, Galatians 3–4, Ephesians 2, and Colossians 2 are major sections in which Paul discusses the believers' new relationship to God and to each other as the result of the sacrifice of Jesus Christ.

It would seem reasonable, then, to infer that the capital punishment provisions of the Mosaic Code had also been set aside. No longer would someone be executed for breaking the Sabbath, adultery, cursing parents, etc. The Law was over, and with it went the commands that outlined capital crimes and the death penalty. Paul knew this, but nowhere does he affirm that the death penalty is invalid. Nowhere does he state that capital punishment has been abrogated in the New Testament economy. It is also true that he nowhere directly affirms the validity of capital punishment, either, although his response to Festus points in that direction.

With the end of the Mosaic Code before him, Paul commanded submission to human government because that institution was established by God and carries out essential functions on behalf of God in this world.

Ryrie identifies four principles affirmed by Paul in Romans 13:1–7:

> (1) Human government is ordained by God (v. 1), yet it is a sphere of authority that is distinct from others like that of the home or the church; (2) human government is to be obeyed by the Christian because it is of God, because it opposes evil (v. 4), and because our consciences tell us to obey (v. 5); (3) the government has the right of taxation (vv. 6–7); and (4) the government has the right to use force (v. 4).[9]

The context of this passage is instructive in appreciating the importance of the principles Ryrie has identified. In Romans 12:17–21, Paul commands believers not to repay evil with evil, to give up personal revenge, to make room for God's wrath, and to overcome evil with good. God, according to Paul, will take care of justice. The personal responsibility of the Christian is to exercise patience, act in love, and get out of God's way so that he can exercise his wrath in vengeance (cf. Lev. 19:18). But how will God accomplish this if the individual believer does nothing to obtain vengeance on his own? The answer, of course, is human government.

This is why Paul identifies governmental authorities as agents of "God's wrath," for they are authorized by God to do what individual believers are prohibited from doing: exercising God's wrath on sin through judicial actions. Romans 13:1–7 answers the "how" of Romans 12:17–21. God's judicial wrath is exercised through human government. We are not implying that all governments are perfect, that all governments properly punish evil and reward good, nor that all governments should be obeyed. We are affirming that God has established human governments as his agents to punish sin on this earth, regardless of whether they properly carry out this mandate.

The establishment of human government obviously antedated the Mosaic Code and when the Law ended at the Cross, human government continued with God's blessing. As we have seen, the first reference to human government, that is, judicial authority, is Genesis 9:6. Here God gives mankind judicial authority to exercise his wrath for the sin of murder, and he establishes the death penalty as punishment for that crime. The obvious question, then, is whether contemporary governments still have God's authorization to exercise capital punishment.

Paul speaks of a governmental "sword" (*machaira*), and his statement has been given widely differing interpretations. Some affirm that it is a clear reference to the instrument of decapitation and thus affirmation of capital punishment.[10] Others look at it as a symbolic reference to the use of force, much like the policeman's club and pistol today.[11] The sword, however, appears to be a significant item in the magistrate's arsenal. Therefore, the reference seems to go beyond the merely symbolic to the actual use of the instrument. This does not prove, however, that Paul is affirming the death penalty, but his terminology is far closer to an affirmation than a denial.

To exclude the right of the death penalty when the nature of the crime calls for such is totally contrary to that which the sword signifies and executes. The usage of the sword in the New Testament connotes death (Matt. 26:52; Luke 21:21; Acts 12:2, 16:27; Heb. 11:34, 37; Rev. 13:10).[12] Therefore, we conclude that Romans 13:1–7 endorses capital punishment as a valid option for contemporary governments in their exercise of divine wrath against sin.

Conclusion

The biblical evidence for capital punishment may be summarized with these observations. In Genesis 9 God establishes a covenant with all humanity in which, among other things, he gives mankind permission to exercise judicial authority among themselves to exercise his wrath against the crime of murder. The established penalty for this act is death. The Mosaic Covenant established, among other things, the rules and regulations by which the descendants of Abraham would live as those under the Abrahamic Covenant. Those rules mandated capital punishment for a number of crimes, including murder. While the laws of the Mosaic Covenant, including those of capital punishment, are no longer binding in the New Testament economy, the provisions of the Noachian Covenant are still in force. This covenant provides capital punishment for the crime of murder today. Nothing in the teachings of Jesus or the apostles contradicts this sanctioning. Capital punishment is a proper course of action for governments today in the exercise of their divine mandate to punish evil.

The Moral Arguments for Capital Punishment

Despite the fact that the Bible clearly teaches the validity of capital punishment, many today oppose it on moral grounds. They argue that the death penalty in any form is immoral, in that it violates basic standards of both private and public morality. No person or organization has any right to take the life of a human being, regardless of his or her actions. Our modern sense of justice, some argue, has advanced beyond the crude, revenge-oriented mentality of past centuries, and we no longer need to continue the cycle of violence through executions. For example, former United States Deputy Attorney General Ramsey Clark stated that

> this nation is so great in its resources and too good in its purposes to engage in the light of recent understanding in the deliberate taking of human life as either a punishment or a deterrent to domestic crime.[13]

United States Supreme Court Justice William Brennan claims that the death penalty is inconsistent with human dignity because it treats "members of the human race as nonhumans, as objects to be toyed with and discarded."[14] These arguments seem to eliminate the death penalty, especially in light of God's standards of morality. However, there are sound answers to them which will be explored in this chapter. We will show that capital punishment as a retributive punishment is not only moral, but is a moral imperative according to God's established order.

The Moral Case for Capital Punishment

A person's ethics depends upon one's philosophical presuppositions and, for the Christian, one's view of biblical authority. There can be no true light on any subject from the Christian viewpoint without considering the teachings of Scripture on the subject. This is especially true when questions of morality are involved. Consequently, we will construct this part of our defense of capital punishment from a biblical perspective.

Capital Punishment Respects the Imago Dei

The Bible, as we have seen, teaches that mankind sustains a unique relationship to God because he bears the *imago Dei.* The importance of this concept cannot be overemphasized. Carl F. H. Henry has perceptibly described the significance of the phrase, "the image of God":

> The importance of a proper understanding of the *imago Dei* can hardly be overstated. The answer given to the *imago* inquiry soon becomes determinative for the entire gamut of doctrinal affirmation. The ramifications are not only theological, but affect every phase of the problem of revelation and reason, including natural and international law, and the cultural enterprise as a whole. Any improper view has consequences the more drastic as its implications are applied to regenerate and to unregenerate man, from primal origin to final destiny.[15]

The capital punishment debate is no exception to this observation. Criminal or not, each individual bears God's image and must be treated accordingly, that is, with dignity and worth. Any penalty that degrades humans by treating them as if they had no worth is immoral. So we ask: Does capital punishment per se do this?

First of all, does capital punishment treat individuals as objects to be used for society's benefit without regard to the interests or rights of the criminal? On the contrary, those who would seek to "cure" and "heal" people without receiving their consent treat them as less than human.[16] On the other hand, to punish criminals because they "deserve" it is to respect them as morally responsible persons created in God's image who knew better and therefore have earned this punishment.

Second, while we acknowledge that some types of executions did (and do) treat people as less than human, the concept of capital punishment is not in conflict with mankind bearing the *imago Dei.* God himself ordained capital punishment in the Old Testament.

Capital punishment was established by the image-Giver to protect the dignity of the image-bearers. Willful elimination of the expression of God's image from one individual by another (premeditated murder) merited the penalty of execution, i.e., the elimination of the expression of God's image from the murderer. There was no conflict between capital punishment and the *imago Dei.* Indeed, the former depends upon the latter.

Bailey discusses the divine rationale behind this principle:

> Life originated by a special act of the Deity (by the power of the divine breath, as the ancient story in Gen. 2:7 put it). Consequently, humans were not free to terminate it, save under conditions specified by God. Even food animals must be brought to the sanctuary and slaughtered in a prescribed ritual whereby the blood is removed. Failure to do so results in "bloodguilt" (Lev. 17:4), a term which is elsewhere used for the murder of a human being (Exod. 22:2). How much more the offense, therefore, if human life ("created in the image of God," Gen. 1:26) is taken without proper sanction! One has acted arrogantly against a life-force that is an extension of God's own life-giving power. It is, to put it boldly, "an attack upon God." Even an animal that kills a human is to be destroyed (Exod. 21:28). A human who does so all the more forfeits any right to life (Gen. 9:1–7).[17]

The death penalty, at least for premeditated murder, does not operate in opposition to human dignity. Rather, it was established in respect of human dignity derived from the *imago Dei* within each human being. Capital punishment, then, is the ultimate compliment to the human dignity of both victim and murderer; it implies the most pro-human stance possible. There are, of course, forms of capital punishment which violate human dignity and worth, but the concept is entirely compatible with God's standards of human worth. On the other hand, a penalty of ten years in prison for premeditated murder devalues human life by saying that the victim's life was worth only ten years of penalty. Equity and justice demand a punishment that matches the crime. Capital punishment for premeditated murder provides equity and justice as well as values human life.

Capital Punishment and the Sixth Commandment

When Moses descended from Mount Sinai, he gave Israel ten summary commandments which were to guide their personal lives as God's covenant people. The Sixth Commandment seems to rule out any form of capital punishment: "Thou shalt not kill" (Exod. 20:13).[18] Since capital punishment involves killing, it seems to be a "*prima facie* violation of this fundamental moral principle." Yet, one chapter later God ordered the death penalty for intentional murder.

Has God become a transgressor of his law, or is there another concept at work? Obviously, the latter is the case, and we find that God has established two arenas of moral activity: private and public morality. What seems inconsistent at first glance becomes comprehensible when these two aspects of God's established order are taken into account. What is immoral in one arena—for example, killing a person—may be completely moral in another, e.g., the death penalty. This answers the problem raised by God's orders to Israel to engage in total warfare against the Canaanite tribes. Israel's armies were God's tools of judgment against the sinful rebellion of these people. It also answers the problem raised by the eschatological judgments in which the returning Christ will destroy his enemies in a fierce, destructive battle. Individuals acting as proper agents of governments can do things that are prohibited to them as private citizens. Scripture affirms both public and private moralities as distinct realms of activity.

We find that both Old and New Testaments recognize the existence of human governments. Romans 13:1–7 is the most general statement regarding government in the New Testament.

My neighbor would think it strange if I demanded that he pay me money so that I would personally police our neighborhood. But few people think it strange to pay taxes to governmental bodies to provide police service. Were my neighbor to refuse my demands and I were to lock him in my cellar for a year or two, I would be adjudged a public menace. Government, however, may imprison tax dodgers and in some cases risk public clamor if it refuses to do so. Clearly, governments can do things that individuals cannot, and this has been ordained by God.

When a person argues against capital punishment based on the Sixth Commandment he or she is ignoring the division between individual and governmental morality, between murder and prescribed killing. No person is permitted to murder or kill another. But God has established governmental authority and given it the responsibility for punishing crime—applying, if necessary, the death penalty. Personal vengeance, however, is not permitted:

> Do not take revenge, my friends, but leave room for God's wrath, for it is written: "It is mine to avenge; I will repay," says the Lord. (Rom. 12:19, citing Deuteronomy 32:35 NIV)

Vengeance is God's, and government is one method whereby he exercises this vengeance. Punishment is the responsibility of government, not individuals. Capital punishment is not a violation of God's moral code. Perhaps no biblical reference illustrates the difference between personal and public morality in the realm of capital punishment better than Deuteronomy 21:18–21:

> If a man has a stubborn and rebellious son who does not obey his father and mother and will not listen to them when they discipline him, his father and mother shall take hold of him and bring him to the elders at the gate of his town. They shall say to the elders, "This son of ours is stubborn and rebellious. He will not obey us. He is a profligate and a drunkard." Then all the men of his town shall stone him to death. You must purge the evil from among you. All Israel will hear of it and be afraid.

If the parents had executed their son before they brought him to the government officials (the elders at the gate), they would have been guilty of murder and been punished by those same elders. However, when they present their rebellious son to the elders for official condemnation, the situation changes. Their word becomes the basis of the capital charge and the father becomes one of the executioners (the men of his town). He now acts as an agent of the government and may carry out an act which was forbidden to him as a private citizen. Acts of personal vengeance are condemned as murder, but acts of capital punishment, being sanctioned by the government, are proper. We do not argue that juvenile delinquents should be executed, but we use this reference to establish once and for all that a distinction exists between private and public morality.

Capital Punishment and Inequitable Application

We acknowledge that major inequities exist in the application of capital punishment today. Many have pointed to these as justification for the abolition of the death penalty lest it be applied unfairly. All these arguments, however, raise the same issue: problems in the *application* of capital punishment, not the *concept* of capital punishment. Our discussion concerns the defense of the death penalty as a valid punishment that may be dispensed by government, not necessarily the defense of our current system in its application at every point. However, we will consider these arguments in some detail, for at first glance they do seem persuasive.

Many have recognized the disproportionate number of disadvantaged criminals on death rows. One of these critics, Byron Eshelman, writing in *Death Row Chaplain,* claims that

> as it is now applied, the death penalty is nothing but an arbitrary discrimination against an occasional victim. It cannot even be said that it is reserved as a weapon of retributive justice for the most atrocious criminals. For it is not necessarily the most guilty who suffer it. Almost any criminal with wealth or influence can escape it, but the poor and friendless convict, without means to fight his case from court to court or to exert pressure upon the pardoning executive, is the one singled out as a sacrifice to what is little more than a tradition.[19]

Race is also said to be a factor in discriminatory application of the death penalty. For example, a study by an Iowa law professor found that in Georgia, blacks were 4.3 times as likely to receive the death penalty for killing whites than whites were for killing blacks.[20] Assuming the accuracy of these statistics, capital punishment may be applied unfairly. But this does not justify eliminating the death penalty as a morally proper punishment.

The same line of reasoning, we argue, could be employed to eliminate all other legal penalties. Politicians "fix" parking tickets, influential doctors avoid conviction on malpractice suits, and the rich employ skillful lawyers who get convictions overturned on technicalities. Shall we then do away with all forms of punishment because of inequities, or shall we seek to reform our judicial systems to eliminate such practices? The answer is obvious. We must distinguish between the moral question and the problem of discrimination. Ernest van den Haag speaks to the issue when he writes:

> Discrimination is irrelevant to this moral question. If the death penalty were distributed equally and uncapriciously and with super-human perfection to all the guilty, but were morally unjust, it would be unjust in each case. Contrariwise, if the death

penalty is morally just, however discriminatorily applied to only some of the guilty, it remains just in each case in which it is applied.[21]

Capital Punishment and the Execution of the Innocent

A practical problem more serious than discrimination is the execution of innocent people. This is not a new problem. Indeed, it was anticipated in the Old Testament theocracy in which God established a detailed procedure for carrying out the death penalty:

1. The standard of proof required for conviction amounted to certainty,
2. conviction required the testimony of at least two witnesses,
3. the penalty for perjury in a capital case was execution; thus the witnesses were motivated to speak the truth,
4. in difficult cases the verdict was deferred to experts, reducing the problem of local prejudice, and
5. once the verdict was returned, it was unchangeable, thus motivating the courts to be accurate.

Our present criminal justice system would do well to model itself after these standards, for its deficiencies are obvious to all who take the time to look. However, failure to properly apply capital punishment does not make it immoral. Again, we note that the same argument could be made against most other forms of punishment. The courts can release an individual who has been imprisoned for a crime he or she did not commit, but it cannot return the lost time. Money can be returned, but lost time, reputations, careers, etc., cannot be restored. This should motivate us to ensure that only the guilty are punished, not to eliminate penalties for all crimes.

Summary

It is our conclusion that capital punishment is not contradictory to God's moral standards as revealed in either the Old or New Testaments. Humans bear the image of the eternal God and are to be accorded all the dignity and respect that the *imago Dei* requires. Applying the death penalty as retributive punishment, especially for premeditated murder, respects the dignity of both victim and murderer. The criminal has deliberately eliminated a personal expression of God's image and therefore is required to pay a suitable penalty: the elimination of the embodiment of God's image in and through him. Neither does the death penalty violate God's moral standard as expressed in the Decalogue. Personal vengeance is prohibited and capital punishment is given to governments to apply after proper investigations. Inequities in the application of the death penalty exist, but they are reasons for revamping our criminal justice system, not eliminating capital punishment. If the death penalty is eliminated because of such inequities, then all punishments should have to be eliminated because few, if any, are fairly applied. We find nothing in the commonly advanced moral arguments that requires the elimination of the death penalty as a proper, morally acceptable retribution for capital crimes.

Notes

1. Charles S. Milligan, "A Protestant's View of the Death Penalty," in *The Death Penalty in America,* 175–82, A. Bedau, ed. New York: Anchor, 1964).

2. Lloyd R. Bailey, *Capital Punishment: What the Bible Says* (Nashville: Abingdon Press, 1987), 82.

3. Bailey, 74.

4. D. A. Carson, "Matthew," in *The Expositor's Bible Commentary,* vol. 8, ed. Frank Gaebelein (Grand Rapids, Mich.: Zondervan Publishing House, 1984), 156–57.

5. Many leading textual critics reject this pericope as being a part of the New Testament canon, as the marginal note in the New International Version demonstrates. For purposes of this discussion, we will treat the passage as part of the New Testament.

6. J. Arthur Hoyles, *Punishment in the Bible* (London: Epworth Press, 1986), 56.

7. On occasion Roman authorities looked the other way when the Jews independently executed people, as in the case of Stephen.

8. John Jefferson Davis, *Evangelical Ethics: Issues Facing the Church Today* (Philipsburg, N.J.: Presbyterian and Reformed Publishing Co., 1985), 200.

9. Charles C. Ryrie, "The Doctrine of Capital Punishment," *Bibliotheca Sacra* (July 1972): 216.

10. William G. T. Shedd, *A Critical and Doctrinal Commentary upon the Epistle of St. Paul to the Romans* (New York: Charles Scribner's Sons, 1879), 328.

11. C. E. B. Cranfield, *The Epistle of Romans,* in the *International Critical Commentary Series,* vol. 2 (Edinburgh: T & T Clark, 1979), 667.

12. John Murray, *The Epistle to the Romans* (Grand Rapids, Mich.: Wm. B. Eerdmans Publishing Co., 1968), 152–53.

13. Ramsey Clark, cited by Gerald H. Gottlieb, "Capital Punishment," *Crime and Delinquency* 15 (January 1970): 2–11.

14. *Furman v. Georgia,* 408 U.W. 238 (1972), cited by Walter Berns, *For Capital Punishment* (New York: Basic Books, 1979), p. 27.

15. Carl F. H. Henry, "Image of God," *Evangelical Dictionary of Theology* (Grand Rapids, Mich.: Baker Book House, 1984), 546.

16. C. S. Lewis, *God in the Dock: Essays on Theology and Ethics* (Grand Rapids, Mich.: Eerdmans, 1970) 292.

17. Lloyd R. Bailey, *Capital Punishment: What the Bible Says,* 34–35.

18. The verb translated "kill" in the KJV occurs almost fifty times in the Old Testament as in every relevant use means "to murder," especially with premeditation involved. The LXX translates it with the Greek word for "murder." Consequently the NIV's translation is the more accurate: "You shall not murder."

19. Byron E. Eshelman, *Death Row Chaplain* (Englewood Cliffs, N.J.: Prentice Hall, 1962), 223.

20. Anthony Parker, "Death Penalty Opponents Weigh Change in Strategy," *Sojourners* (June 1988): 12.

21. Ernest van den Haag, "In Defense of the Death Penalty: A Practical and Moral Analysis," *The Death Penalty: A Debate* (New York: Plenum Press, 1983).

31

Noah's Covenant, the New Testament, and Christian Social Order

JOHN HOWARD YODER

Noah's Covenant and the Purpose of Punishment

The case for the death penalty as an institution in modern societies has several quite different roots. Different advocates appeal to quite different reasons in its favor. We have already noted in our beginning pages the need to look at them one by one, each in its own terms. The first reason, as most people read it, is the notion of prevention by threat, or "deterrence," which we have already looked at and seen to be deceptive.

The first religiously based argument, on the other hand, for most Christians, comes from the story of Noah. As we range around the argument, seeking the most solid ground, this is one obviously right place to begin. It appears literally to be a direct divine command:

> Whosoever sheds the blood of Man
> In Man shall his blood be shed
> For in the image of God
> He made Man.[1] (Gen. 9:6)

Does This Text Prove What It Has Been Assumed To?

The first task of the biblical interpreter, as I already said, is not to read a text as if "from scratch," or as if its meanings were self-evident to every well-intentioned reader, but rather to protect the text from misuse, even to "liberate" its original meaning from the deposit of interpretations which have already been laid over it by centuries of readers. To say this is not to suggest that earlier readers were dishonest or insincere. It is merely to take seriously the fact that they were prisoners of their cultures, as we are of ours, even as the text we are seeking to read was the product of its own culture.

Reprinted by permission of the author, from *The Death Penalty Debate: H. Wayne House and John Howard Yoder* (Dallas: Word Publications, 1991), pp. 119–32, 139–48.

We need to make a self-conscious effort to understand the focus of the world-view implicit in the culture from which any ancient text comes to us. Some tend to read a text like this as if it were legislation, providing, prehistorically, at no particular time but with validity for all times, that there should be a particular institution, equivalent to what we call the state, the basis for civil law, to protect threatened social values.

God's covenant with Noah was not that. We need to step back from such modernizing assumptions if we are to have any hope of understanding how the sanctity of life was really understood in the ancient Israelite setting where these words were first recited.

"Recited" is the right description of how this ancient text was originally used. This rhythmic quatrain (further rhythmic in that in Hebrew the words "blood" and "man" rhyme) is not part of a code of laws, though such codes did exist at that time in the ancient Near East. It was formulated as oral lore, recited by sages and priests, repeated by the old, and remembered by the young. It is part of the deep symmetry of things, fitting in with the seasonal, rhythmic reliability of nature:

> As long as earth lasts
> sowing and reaping
> cold and heat,
> summer and winter
> day and night
> shall cease no more. (Gen. 8:22 JB)

This is not legislation for a government to apply. It is wisdom, a prediction, a description, of how things are in fact, in primitive and ancient societies. The nature of things did not come to be this way only because God said these words, as if without the words, or before God spoke them, matters would have been different. That is true of some kinds of human laws, nonexistent before, which come into being only when voted by a legislature or promulgated by a king or other authority.

We also err when we tend to read this text as if the defense of life through the threat to life were a new arrangement, established only after the Flood. It hardly can be taken that way, as the text of Genesis now stands.[2] Things were already that way before the covenant with Noah; in fact, that was the way it was as soon as the first murder was reported. That arrangement is already presupposed in the account of Cain, in Genesis 4. There the first murderer, called to account for the life of the brother he had killed, said:

> My punishment is greater than I can bear;
> behold: you drive me from this ground.[3]
> I must hide from you and be a fugitive and wanderer over the earth.
> Whoever comes across me will kill me. (Gen. 4:13f. JB)

What Cain feared was, as it were, a defensive reflex of society as a whole, of "everyone who sees me." There is no account of there having been a previous divine command demanding blood for blood. The response of Yahweh to the jeopardy under which Cain saw himself was to intervene, to protect his life by a "mark"[4] and to announce the threat of retaliation. Thus, the first intervention of God in Genesis, counter to the ordinary reading, is not to demand that murder be sanctioned by sacrificial killing, but to protect the life of the first murderer. Far from demanding the death penalty for murder, Yahweh saved Cain from it. That is the first and the most characteristic action of the God of the Bible with regard to our subject.[5]

Yet, the pattern of violence continued and escalated out of all proportion. Cain's descendant, Lamech, boasted:

> I have slain a man for wounding me,
> a young man for striking me.
> If Cain is avenged sevenfold,[6]
> truly Lamech seventy-seven-fold! (Gen. 4:23f.)

This is the normal pattern; fallen humanity responds to evil with *escalating* vengeance. Primitive peoples show the same pattern as Lamech, from the intertribal wars of Borneo through the bloody gang justice of the Sicilian hills and the American underworld, to the proverbial "feudin' hillbillies" of the Appalachians. Each *particular* act of vengeance is thought of as "setting things right" or as "defending the peace," but in fact the spiral escalation of vengeance and countervengeance raises the toll of suffering brought about by any one offense, far beyond any proportion to the original damage done.

Having opened our minds to the awareness that the reason for primitive revenge was not the same as our modern arguments, we can and should move on to note what is different about the agents of the action.

The ancient quatrain does not say who the "man" is who shall shed the killer's blood. Certainly, it was not a constitutional government by means of a trial by judge or jury. Historians tell us that it was the next of kin, called "the avenger" (*goel,* the same Hebrew word as "redeemer") who executed family-based vengeance. The mechanism of retaliation, once unleashed, had to run its course. Later laws spell this out. If a corpse was found with no way to know whom to punish, very special ceremonies were needed on the part of the elders of the nearest town to "cover" them against the blood-vengeance which was due (Deut. 21:1–8). A person who killed accidentally could be protected only by taking refuge in one of six designated "cities of refuge" and staying there for the entire life of the high priest (Num. 35:11–28; cf. Deut. 4:42f., 19:1–10). No ransom was possible for blood guilt, even when the death was accidental (Num. 35:32f.). Nor was bloodshed the only occasion for such sanctions. Death was the penalty as well for dozens of other offenses.

There are others who read the Noah story as if it belonged in Exodus or Leviticus, as part of a body of rules set out to govern the particular nation of Israel, to be established much later in the land of Canaan, in the light of the sovereignty of Yahweh, in whose name Moses was to make of his mixed multitude (Exod. 12:38) a nation. It was not that. When that civil legislation did arise later, it too was to have provision for the death penalty, as we shall see, but not for the same reasons, and for many other kinds of offenses.

The context of Genesis 9 is that of ritual sacrifice. The anthropologist will call it "cultic" or "sacred." These four rhyming lines about human killing do not stand alone. In the same breath, the text had just been describing animal sacrifice. As contrasted with the vegetarian arrangement implied before the Deluge, animal flesh may now be eaten, but only subject to a ceremonial sense of the holiness of animate life as such, which is represented by the blood:

> Every living and crawling thing shall provide food for you no less than the foliage of plants
> I give you everything, with the exception that you must not eat flesh with the life—that is, the blood—in it
> I will demand an account of your life blood
> I will demand an account from every beast and from man
> I will demand an account of every man's life from his fellow man
> he who sheds man's blood. . . . (Gen. 9:3–6 JB)

The setting of our text is thus the account, after the Flood, of God's authorizing the killing of animals for human consumption. In the context, it is evident that the subject of the passage is sacrifice. The sacredness of human life is described in the same breath with God's exclusive claim on the blood of the sacrificially slaughtered beasts, and as an extension of the same. To kill animals for food is not like picking fruit from a tree, pulling turnips from a garden, or cutting wheat in a field. It is an interference with the dynamics of animate life, represented by the flow of blood through the body, which humans share with the animal world. Every killing is a sacrifice, for the life of the animal, represented by its blood, belongs to God. To kill an animal is a ritual act; the blood belongs not to the killer but to God. There is no "secular" slaughtering of animals in ancient Israel. The blood of the animal is given to God by being sprinkled on the altar or poured out on the ground. The act of eating that meat is an act of communion with God. The provision for shedding the blood of a human killer is part of the same sacrificial worldview.

The closest approximation in the later Mosaic laws to the sense of the sacred which sanctions killing in Genesis 9 is the prohibition of serving another god (Deut. 13:1–16). This text emphasizes the responsibility of any individual to be the agent of retaliation, even against one's closest kin. A whole town could need to be slaughtered and even the property destroyed.

Other ancient societies, primitive or highly developed, used human sacrifice for many other purposes. The God who renews with Noah his life-saving covenant with humanity permits human sacrifice—for that is what is prescribed here—*only* on one specific grounds, namely, to correct for a previous wrongful taking of human life.

Thus, it is not at all the case that in addressing Noah God intervenes to make blood vengeance a duty, when it had not been so before. The pattern was already old. It is then a mistake to read the word to Noah as if it were a command, ordering its hearers to do something which they would otherwise not have done. It is not that: it is a simple description of the way things already are, an accurate prediction of what does happen, what will happen, as surely as summer is followed by winter, seedtime by harvest. That killers are killed is the way fallen society works; it is not a new measure which God introduced after the Deluge to solve a problem that had not been there before, or for which God had not yet found a solution. It rather restates, as a fact and as a prediction, in the framework of the authorization now being granted to sacrifice and eat animals, that the sacredness of human life, already stated when God had saved the life of the murderer Cain, still stands. Spoken just at the place in the story where the killing of animals is for the first time authorized, the point of God's word in Genesis 9 is to reiterate the prohibition of the killing of humans.[7]

Motives and Meanings for Primitive Revenge

The careful cultural historian will have to ask at this point which of several descriptions or explanations best fits the primitive fact of blood revenge. We cannot yet review fully the several answers to this question as they are operative in modern debate, but we must at least recognize the wrongness of leaping past it to too simple an answer. What were the possible meanings for Cain's contemporaries or Noah's descendants of shedding a killer's blood?

1. It might be more precisely described as eradication, getting rid of the source of trouble. The Old Testament speaks of "purging" evil from the Israelite people.[8] This would be the social equivalent of what white blood cells do to microbes or what exterminators do to vermin. The organism defends itself against a threat by removing whatever threatens. The threatening organism has no rights of its own. It is removed because it is bad, not because of a particular bad behavior.

2. It might be described as imitation, *mimesis.* I do to you what you did to my friend, not out of some general theory of social hygiene but rather, primitively, reflexively, because it does not occur to me do anything else. You "have it coming."

3. It might be understood as intimidation. If as a general pattern it is known that those who harm others are harmed in return, this may keep them from doing it. This interpretation has several levels of meaning. One is the more narrow, mental, and therefore more modern sense. The thought is that an individual, premeditating an evil deed, will "think twice" about the cost, and will therefore renounce the evil deed on cost/benefit grounds. "Deterrence" is another modern term for this. Intimidation also has a less mental, more primitive, more "educational" sense. The generalized practice of avenging certain offenses, it is held, tends to be one way a society has of trying to teach people what deeds are offensive, not to be considered, therefore hoping to make it less likely that they will occur.

4. Both of the above concepts, "imitation" and "intimidation," can be understood to be founded in "retaliation." The root—*tal*—means "such" or "like." One may believe that God or the gods or "the moral order" should be understood in terms of a kind of balancing exercise, whereby each harmful act needs to be "paid back" or "set right" by another harmful act of the same kind and dimensions. When the "moral order" is thought of in analogy to a courtroom, we may

also speak of the *talion* as "vindication," but in the old Semitic setting the courtroom is not the best symbol for that.

5. None of the above is quite what we mean when we use the word *revenge.* Usually the term *revenge* connotes an element of passion.[9] To do something "with a vengeance" suggests disregard for proportion, or for limits or barriers. It reaches beyond "eye for eye." A vengeful society, or the individual avenger, demands retaliation, claims moral legitimacy for the vindictive act, and may draw emotional satisfaction from carrying it out. Some would avow "anger" as a valid description of the motivation that is at work in so punishing the offender, and some would disavow it. Others would say that there is no anger in justice.

6. None of the above is quite what we mean by "expiation." This term points past the harm done to the social order, to the offense against the will of God or the gods. The divine anger must be placated, or the cosmic moral order must be set back in balance, the offender must "pay." In some religious and cultural settings the divine wrath is understood very anthropomorphically: God gets "mad." In others, the claim is that the "balance" needing to be restored by punishment is quite dispassionate, objective like a court's judgment, and holy.

Certainly, these several possible characterizations of why killers are killed are not all the same. The differences are significant. We shall come back later to try to disentangle them more abstractly, as part of our review of the modern debate. But now we want merely to understand the Noah story. Which of them most adequately describes the facts? Which of them is morally most or least acceptable?

On the above scale, most of those who today hold the death penalty to be morally justified would hold to a somewhat sanitized, modernized version of "legislation" combined with "intimidation." This is what we previously referred to under the broader heading of "deterrence." It has the least basis in the ancient text.

On the other hand, most historians studying where the legal killing of humans actually came from in ancient society, including ancient Israel, would point to one of the more angry versions of "vengeance" combined with "imitation." Journalists watching in our own times the public outcry after some particularly brutal killing would agree with the historians.

Our debate to this day is skewed by the difference between these two interpretations. Is killing a killer a vengeful action against the evildoer himself? Or is it the restoration of divine moral balance through sacrifice?

For now, this first overview of the spectrum of reasons is intended only to provoke the reader's vigilance. We need to be warned against the assumption that we know easily just which of those meanings the Genesis text originally had for its first hearers and against the assumption that the ancient meaning has any direct connection with the reasons for the modern death penalty.

The provision of Genesis 9:3–6 is thus not a moral demand, saying that for every pain inflicted there must be another pain inflicted to balance the scales of justice. It is not an educational demand, teaching the offender (or destroying the offender in order to teach others) a lesson to the effect that crime does not pay. It is not a political order describing how to administer a healthy city.

The order underlying the words in question is ritual; human life, human blood is sacred—whoever sheds it forfeits his own. The demand for that "forfeiting" is not vengeance on the part of the victim's family, although it easily degenerates into that; it is the organic society living in immediate awareness of the divine quality of human life. The death which sanctions death is ceremonial, celebrative, ritual.

The killing of a killer is not a civil, nonreligious matter. It is a sacrificial act. The blood—i.e., the life—of every man and beast belongs to God. To respect this divine ownership means, in the case of animals, that the blood of a sacrificed victim is not to be consumed. For humans, it means that there shall be no killing. If there is killing, the offense is a cosmic, ritual, religious evil, demanding ceremonial compensation. It is not a moral matter; in morality a second wrong does not make a right. It is not a civil, legislative matter: it is originally stated in a setting where there is no government.

Ritual Worldview and Cultic Change

One way that the ritual worldview differs from our own is that there is no concern for personal accountability. The death penalty applied to an ox which gored a man. It applied to unintended or accidental killing. If the ritual worldview of Genesis 9: 3–6 were to be applied to our culture literally, there would be no provision for exculpating minors or the mentally ill, no separating of degrees of homicide according to intention. We would execute the contractor whose bridge collapses, the engineer whose train is wrecked, the auto driver whose brakes malfunction, if death results. For every death, blood must flow.

Christians in recent centuries, in order to attempt to understand and describe how the laws of the Old Testament ought to be respected since Christ, have proposed to divide them into civil, ceremonial, and moral laws. They then explain that the "moral" laws continue to apply in all times, but that the ceremonial ones are abrogated when the sacrificial order is fulfilled in Christ as the final sacrifice and the final high priest. Some of the civil laws, it is held, should apply to modern states, and others were intended only for the government of ancient Israel. This threefold (really fourfold) distinction may help to organize our thought, but careful study of the death penalty provisions of the books of Moses makes it clear that the distinction is alien to that world.

The covenant given to Noah involved no such distinction either, but the elements we call "moral" and "civil" were not stated, not separated. We saw that Genesis 9 speaks of the blood of animals and of fellow humans as belonging to God—certainly a sacrificial concept. The covenant given through Moses was no less holistic. Just as the Christ who was to come would be prophet, priest, and king all at once, so the covenant established through Moses was moral, ceremonial, and civil all at once, not one of them in distinction from the others. For centuries after Moses there was in Israel no king, nothing specific to call "civil."

The distinction between different types of law has served, although in an indirect, illogical way, to make room for a valid point. The valid point, which these distinctions alluded to, is that there was going to have to be change over time in how the laws would apply, and that in those changes the sacrifice of Christ was to make the biggest difference.

It is the clear testimony of the New Testament, especially of the Epistle to the Hebrews, that the ceremonial requirements of the Old Covenant find their end—both in the sense of fulfillment and in the sense of termination—in the high-priestly sacrifice of Christ. "Once for all" is the good news. Not only is the sacrifice of bulls and goats, turtledoves and wheatcakes at an end; the fact that Christ died for our sins, once for all, the righteous one for the godless (Heb. 9:26–28; 1 Pet. 3: 18), puts an end to the entire expiatory system, whether it be enforced by priests in Jerusalem or by executioners anywhere else.[10]

Thus, by asking where killing began, and finding in the stories of both Cain and Noah what is said and what is not said there, we have been led to the most precise statement of the specifically Christian reason for the death penalty's being set aside. There are other reasons as well, more widely effective in our world, in which Anglo-Saxon democracy has spelled out the implications of the Hebrew and Christian heritage, but this is the reason closest to the heart of the gospel.

That shedding blood exposes the killer to killing is expiation in the name of the cosmic order. The death of Christ is the end of expiation.

The Ritual Nature of Social Behavior

To kill a killer is a ritual act, we have begun to see, not primordially or only in a political sense. When people gather for the funeral of a public figure, when they build a wall around their house or buy an assault gun, when they fly a flag or take off their hats, the event is not adequately interpreted by asking about a specified moral imperative, or about a pragmatic social goal. We have just attempted briefly to explain something of this sense of the sacred as it shows in the Noah story; now let us note that it is still the case today.

When society takes a life, the action is, obviously, not being undertaken for the well-being of that person. Counter to the general moral rule, most simply stated in modern times by Immanuel Kant, that a person is always to be treated as an end and not as a mere means, when a person is killed, that cannot be an action in that person's interest. It is a public ritual, celebrated in the interest of others, in the interest of the society's controlling elite and those who support them, and their vision of the society's well-being.

When a parent or a teacher spanks a child, when an offender is put in prison or fined, it can be *claimed* that it is done in order to "teach" that guilty person something. Even then, the careful psychologist or social scientist will warn us that the real "learning" resulting from that event is probably something else. A child trained by spanking may grow up to become a teenage gangster or an abusive parent. What beating a child teaches most effectively may well be less "don't get into the cookie jar" than "might makes right," or "if you cannot reason, use force." The same may be true of other punishments as well. The petty pilferer sent to prison may learn there the skills of the professional burglar.

So the claim to "teach him a lesson" is often factually wrong. Nevertheless, it may be sincerely so intended. The sincere intention may be that the offender himself should learn that "crime does not pay," so that he does not repeat the offense. The time behind bars may lead him to think differently.

Rationales for Rehabilitation

This notion of changing the offender, ordinarily called "rehabilitation," *can* be given as a serious reason for depriving the offender of his liberty. He is shown how wrong his actions were. He may become convinced that he is under society's control. He may be led to promise (sincerely or not) that he will not repeat the offense. He may be given time to show by his actions that his promise to behave is credible, and he may even be taught a trade or helped to finish school. This is why prisons were once called "penitentiaries," places to repent. Some persons, after a prison term, do not return to crime. As long as the prospect of a future life in freedom is real, there is *some* chance that this may succeed. Yet even in these cases it is not clear that the time in prison or other kind of punishment is what made the most difference in a person's readiness to become a good member of society.

But when the line of life is crossed, the entire "teach-a-lesson" rationale becomes a lie. The only persons who can "learn" from a lethal public ritual are the others.

- The victims of the past crime (if they are alive) or their relatives can take comfort from the fact that the person who hurt them has been hurt in return: "vengeance" is the ordinary word for this. Vengefulness, taking comfort in the pain of others, is not a good moral quality in an individual, but some feel that it becomes right when the killing is done by the authorities.
- Those who stand to lose by a crime are reassured that it may be less likely to happen to them—although this confidence in the "deterrent" effect is as we have seen often mistaken.
- Persons who have not committed a crime should be warned that they should not think of doing so, out of the fear that they may be caught and punished. Yet, in fact, the limitations of our enforcement system do not make that threat very real in the minds of most potential offenders.
- The civil authorities celebrate and reinforce their posture of social control. In the Aryan feudal roots of our common law, the authority to dispose of the life of one's subjects was what defined a lord's sovereignty. The killer claims to be the instrument of God; he celebrates that his authority to rule is legitimate, by having the right to destroy some of his subjects.

The purpose thus far of our itemizing a few of the diverse modes of motivation has not been to be complete, but only to be broad enough to open for the reader a sense of the complexity of things, and of the inadequacy of simple explanations.

Jesus and the Civil Order

The only clear reference to be found in the New Testament to the infliction of death as a penalty is in John's Gospel (8:1–11). A woman was brought to Jesus with the report that she was known to be guilty of adultery.[11] "Moses has ordered us in the Law to condemn women like this to death by stoning. What have you to say?" The intention of the "scribes and pharisees," we are told, was to put Jesus to a test; i.e., they were not really looking for help with defining or doing God's will. Their primary motivation was not to wipe out adultery. They were, rather, challenging Jesus to continue to exercise the authority he had been claiming while teaching in the Temple (chap. 7). Jesus did not evade the challenge. We may, therefore, rightly take his response as bearing on our study.

Jesus could well have pointed out that "Moses" (i.e., the Law, in Leviticus 20 and Deuteronomy 22) does not say that a woman should be condemned without the man with whom she was caught in the act. Why did they bring him the woman without the man? Jesus could have made an important point about male sexism and the victimizing of women. But he chose not to.

Jesus could well have challenged the factual accuracy of their report about the offense, as the law requires, and as a judge would have done. He did not. Nor did he deny that the provision for death was in the Law. Nor did he cite in the woman's defense, as a rabbinic court would have, the longstanding hesitancy of Jewish local authorities, for several centuries already, to inflict the death penalty. He did not (explicitly) make the point which according to the same Gospel "the Jews" later argued before Pontius Pilate (18:31), namely, that under the Roman rules currently in effect Jewish authorities did not have the right to put anyone to death. All of these responses would have been fitting. In a full account, we should need to consider them all. Jesus, however, preferred to make two other points, to which we should also give priority.

"Let him that is without sin cast the first stone."[12] If the death penalty is understood as an act of God (as it certainly was in ancient Israel), then the judge and executioner must be morally above reproach. "When they heard this they went away one by one, beginning with the eldest. . . ." Why was it the eldest who first disqualified themselves? The Christian challenge to the death penalty properly begins where Jesus does, by challenging the self-ascribed righteousness of those who claim the authority to kill others.

Secondly, Jesus applied to this woman's offense his authority to forgive. He did not deny her guilt, but he absolved it as far as punishment was concerned, and liberated her from its power over her: "Sin no more." He recognized no differentiation between the religious and the civil, according to which the sin could be forgiven, yet punitive justice should still have to be done.

John's concern in telling this story was, of course, not to provide his readers with new information about the legality of capital punishment.[13] His testimony was about the authority of Jesus as the One uniquely sent by the Father. That is just our point. We are not studying law for its own sake; we are learning that the saviorhood of Jesus applies to law, and to social punishment for sin, no less than to prayer. Jesus as the forgiver of sin not only removes sin's power over the sinner's behavior but also its power to dictate guiltiness and demand punishment.

Jesus' Good News Condones the Lesser Moral Level of the Civil Order

Like the divorce which Deuteronomy 24 condoned, like the distortions of the law which Jesus corrected in Matthew 5, like the institution of slavery, and the oppressive presence in Judea and Galilee of the Roman Empire which neither Jesus nor Paul rose up against, capital punishment is one of those infringements on the holy will of God in society, which can claim a certain formal legitimacy. The gospel does not immediately eliminate such from secular society, since, being non-coercive, the gospel cannot "rule the world" in that way. Yet, to condone the way things stand is not approval: "from the beginning it was not so" (Matt. 19:8). Jesus said that literally about the Mosaic provision for divorce; but the Christians of the apostolic generation thought in the same way about the other points as well where the world was ruled by pagan powers.

The new level of mutual love and forgiveness on which the redeemed community is called (and enabled by the Spirit) to live cannot be directly enforced on the larger society; but since it is the gospel, i.e., since it represents authentically good news for the real world, it will necessarily work as salt and light. This should be true anywhere; even more evidently should it be the case in the Anglo-Saxon world, where a large number of citizens claim some kind of Christian sanction for society's values. If Christ is not only prophet and priest but also King, the border between the church and the world cannot be impermeable to moral truth. Something of the cross-bearing, forgiving love, and dignity which Jesus' life, death, and resurrection revealed to be the normative way to be human, must be the norm for all humans, whether they know it or not. We cannot *expect* of anyone, not even of believers, that that norm be lived out perfectly. Yet, is the calling of the followers of Jesus to testify that there is no other norm. The one strategy which will not serve that calling, which could not be done in the first century, and cannot be done in our century, is to claim to possess, and to impose on society, a body of civil rules independent of the faith of the persons called to respect them. The alternative is to work within the acceptance of the others' unbelief, which is what I call "condoning" the lesser moral level of the civil order.

Some will claim that to challenge the death penalty in the name of Christ is to advocate anarchy. If sinners should be forgiven, if only the innocent may "throw the first stone," they ask, where will we stop? Does this not destroy all government?[14]

The question is not always meant sincerely. Most who ask it do not themselves propose to follow the Mosaic law by advocating capital punishment for adultery today. They do not really believe that society will collapse if rebellious sons are not executed by stoning. Nonetheless, the question does merit attention. It illustrates a real problem in relating Christian ethics to non-Christian society.

The first mistake that question makes is to assume that in interpreting a Christian social critique, the right question to ask is how to "carry things to their logical conclusion." That assumption distorts everything. Christian social criticism addresses a fallen world. Since that critique derives its ultimate standards from the kingdom of God—for there are no other *ultimate* standards—to "carry them to their logical conclusion" would mean the presence of that kingdom. Yet, that consistent application would demand faith. It lies beyond the capacities and the intentions of the rebellious world as it is in fact.

The Christian cannot expect that of fallen society. Thus to undercut Christ's call by asking "where would this lead?" is to distort the whole problem. By the fact of its rebellion, the "world" has guaranteed that Christian social critique will not lead "too far." Yet, the resurrection and ascension of Christ guarantee that there is no situation in which nothing can be done. The world can be challenged, one point at a time, to take one step in the right direction, to move up one modest notch in approximation of the righteousness of love.[15] To challenge capital punishment no more undermines government than does the rejection of the oath (Matt. 5:33–37; James 5:12) undermine truth-telling; no more than does the concept of the consent of the governed destroy the authority of the state.

The civil order is a fact. That it might be done away with by pushing the critique of love "too far" is inconceivable. We saw above that Genesis 9, like every primitive government, does not *demand* vengeance, since it is already present, but rather works to restrain it. Thus the Christian (and any believer in democracy) will be concerned to restrain the violent, vengeful potential of the state. That potential for violence does not need our advocacy; it is already there.

"Anarchy," the scare concept quoted above, is a grammatical abstraction, an intellectual construct, an imaginary entity. There is no such reality. There are varying forms of government, from tyranny to constitutional democracy; there are varying degrees of centralization of power, from the independent tribe through the "nation" to world empire. Where the criminal underground is highly organized, or in case of civil war, there may be two powers claiming authority over the same territory. There may be great variation in how effectively a power controls its subjects. Authority may be delegated or seized. It may be exercised wisely or wantonly, overtly or undercover, with or without a constitution, with or without the consent of the governed. But despite all these possible variations there *is* always authority.[16] In the (very rare) cases where it may seem that authority is functioning too little for the welfare and stability of society, the reason is never that the critique coming from the direction of Christian love has been too effective.

The scare concept of "anarchy" does not arise from the study of societies. It is the creature of the mental urge to carry things to their "logical conclusions"; an urge which is out of place in a fallen world.

The second error in the "where will we stop?" argument is the notion that there exists some clear and univocal concept of justice, having the same meaning in all times and places, consisting in an exact logical or mathematical equivalence of offense and retribution, and that such "justice" must (or can) be either wholly respected or fundamentally rejected. In real life—and in clear logic—there is no one sure yardstick by which to measure the "justness" of a penalty. Every culture and every age has different conceptions of what is fair retribution. Opinions have changed enormously from culture to culture as to how much it matters whether the offender was human, adult, free and of a sound mind, and whether he was aware of the law he broke. They vary enormously as well in judging what "equivalent" means. "Eye for eye" is measurable if there has been bodily injury, and "ox for ox" will work in case of material loss; but what are the equivalent penalties for adultery? for covetousness? We noted before that there is no command to lie to a liar or to rape a rapist.

Justice is a direction, not an achievement. It is a relative, not an absolute concept. Moral acts may be more just or less just, but we know of no ideal justice, distinct from love, which "too much emphasis on love" would jeopardize. Justice may well be undermined by lack of wisdom. It may be undermined by idealistic schemes for reformation, by social criticism which does not propose relevant alternatives, by a sentimental misunderstanding of the nature of love, or by failing to recognize to how great an extent order and mutual respect have already been achieved by the society one criticizes; but justice is not endangered by too much love.

Despite Concessions, No Other Lord

The classical Christian confession referred to earlier states that Jesus is not only prophet, priest, and rabbi, but also Lord and King. Those are political names. Even the name "Christ" (the Anointed One) was originally a royal designation. Christians begin to deny their Lord when they admit that there are certain realms of life in which it would be inappropriate to bring Christ's rule to bear. Of course, non-Christians will insist that we should keep our *religion* out of the way of their *politics.* But the reason for that is not that Jesus has nothing to do with the public realm; it is that they want nothing to do with Jesus as Lord.

If we confess that it is the Lamb that was slain who is "worthy . . . to receive power and wealth and wisdom and might and honor and glory and blessing" (Rev. 5:12), we are relating the Cross to politics. If we ask who crucified Jesus and why, the Cross is political at the outset. What we believe about Christ must apply to all our behavior, no matter how many of our neighbors remain unconvinced. Of course, the unbelief and the contrasting beliefs of our neighbors, added to our own disobedience, will mean that no society will fully keep the law of God. When a society falls short of his law, God knows how to use even that disobedience for his glory. "Providence" is the traditional Christian word for the fact that God's being in charge of history includes his power sovereignly and savingly to take into account what the fallen world does against his will. This is not a reason for Christians to justify or to defend the lower level of behavior which results from unbelief, whether it be in the political realm or elsewhere.

The words of Paul in Romans 13:1–7, which affirm that the "powers that be" are subject to God, mean what I have just been saying. They have often been further interpreted to say that, since the powers are under God, therefore Christians have no grounds for criticizing what any given state does, or no standards to guide such a criticism. Paul does not say that. He says that government is "for our benefit'' (v. 4); that it is God's servant when (or insofar as) it ''perseveres toward this very end'' (v. 6).[17]

These expressions, as well as the parallel ones in 1 Peter 2:13ff., indicate that there are standards of good and right order, not dependent on the arbitrary judgment of individual rulers, by which government is to be judged. The state is not a law unto itself. This does not authorize us to rebel against an unjust state by using against it the same weapons it uses oppressively. It does, however, give us standards for identifying oppression and grounds for denouncing it. No standard is more simply applicable to what governments do than ''Thou shalt not kill.''[18]

The Romans passage is but one application of a New Testament truth which is stated more frequently and more clearly in other texts. The broader claim is that ''Christ is Lord'' (Phil. 2:11; 1 Cor. 12:3). His status as ''Lord'' does not apply only to the church; Christ is exalted ''far above every principality and power, and might, and dominion, and every name that is named . . .'' (Eph. 1:21; Phil. 2:10; 1 Cor. 15:27; Matt. 28:18). Protestant tradition as we saw has used the term *providence* to say the same thing.

The world does not acknowledge Christ as Lord; but his being Lord is not dependent on the world's acknowledgement, any more than George Bush's being President in 1989 was dependent on whether all U.S. citizens and resident aliens liked him, or on whether they were all informed that he had been elected and inaugurated. A government, like any rebellious power, can attempt to be independent, can claim to be its own master, but Christians know that the claim is false and the attempt doomed to fail.

It is not our theme here to discuss the Christian view of government in general.[19] The mere confession of Christ's dominion generates conclusions sufficient for our present purpose. If it is as the apostles said, that Jesus Christ and not some other lord rules at the right hand of God over the powers of this world, then the purpose, goals, and standards of that rule can be no other than this same Jesus revealed to us, when in the flesh; he came not to destroy but to save. On the grounds of his rule, it can then not be the duty of governments to destroy life.

The Sword in Apostolic Thought

The New Testament Epistles are silent about capital punishment. The apostles do instruct their readers that they are to be subject to their rulers. Rulers are supposed to rule ''for your benefit'' (Rom. 13:4). Those who chose to break the law called down punishment upon themselves; but there is no reference in the epistles to specific penalties. Rulers should enable us to ''lead religious and reverent lives in peace and quiet'' (1 Tim. 2:2). Governors should ''punish criminals and encourage good citizenship'' (1 Pet. 2:14), but there is no specification of the content either of the citizenship or the ''punishment.''

The ''sword'' (*machaira*), of which Paul writes to the Romans that rulers do not ''bear it in vain,'' is the symbol of judicial authority, not the weapon of either war or the death penalty. In imperial Rome the *machaira* was not the arm either of the soldier in combat or of the executioner. The civil order as such is the theme of the passage. The state's taking of life is not.

There is in the Epistles no allusion to the provision for animal sacrifice or for killing killers in the covenant with Noah, and none of the apostles—Jews that they all were—would have thought of the Roman courts as applying the Mosaic penal provisions.

The Epistles say even less than do the Gospels about urging society to move toward the Kingdom; that should be no surprise. The Epistles are addressed to believers who constitute an infinitesimal minority within Roman/Mediterranean culture; there was no place for them to contemplate immediately effective social critique. The Gospels, on the other hand, recount Jesus' impact in a setting where Hebraic notions of divine justice were less alien. Jesus' gracious demands (or rather, offers) were not accepted by all who heard him, but they were not inconceivable for his Jewish hearers. The notions of a personal, caring, intervening, righteous, demanding, chastising God which underlay Jesus' message, and his forgiving practice, had been understandable to Jesus' Jewish hearers, but they would not have been to the polytheistic Romans.

It is thus formally wrong to look in the New Testament for specific guidelines for a good civil society. If such prescriptions had been given, they would embarrass us, as they would have had to be written to fit first-century Mediterranean conditions. We should rather look there for a general orientation toward ultimate human values and the nature of redemption, and then ask for our time what *those meanings* have to say. This is what happens when we remember that the foundational level of the Hebraic vision with which we began was not about civil penalties but about ritual expiation.

Notes

1. The noun translated "man" (Hebrew *adam*) here is generic; it means humankind. The Hebrew reader's mind is thrown back to the beginning of chapter 2, where *adam* meant the human race, without gender division or individuation. That Creation narrative was the only place where God's "image" had previously been referred to.

2. Expert Scripture scholarship has projected diverse hypotheses as to the original dates and original authorship of the several strands of the Mosaic literature. That speculation would call into question some simple arguments based on the assumption that a text like that of Genesis was originally a literary unity. There is, however, no serious scholarly claim according to which Genesis 9 would be older than Genesis 4.

3. The ground is personified. "The voice of your brother's blood cries to me from the ground" (4:10); the metaphor of "blood" for life is the same as in chapter 9. Yet the "cry" of the blood is not to be satisfied. God intervenes to save the murderer.

4. Patristic symbolic theology speculated that the "sign" given to Cain to protect him was *tau* or the cross. Biblical scholars hypothesize that it may have been the trace of a tattoo worn by metalworkers; in the ancient world smelting was thought of as a secret stolen from the gods of the underworld. Lloyd R. Bailey, *Capital Punishment: What the Bible Says* (Nashville: Abingdon Press, 1987), 40.

5. JHWH (usually pronounced "Yahweh") is the proper name of God. "Lord" in the

AV and in Jewish piety is a reverent substitution. Jehovah and Yahweh are hypothetical reconstructions of the name. Bailey (39 and 107) suggests that Yahweh made a mistake; that if vengeance against Cain had been permitted, then "violence in the earth" would not have escalated so as to necessitate the Deluge. This would take more argument than either Bailey or Genesis provides. Genesis 6:6 says that what God regretted was having created mankind, not having protected Cain. Bailey also makes much of the claim (40, 70) that narrative texts should not be taken as bearing moral instruction. This is an assertion without an argument. Of course each genre of literature should be read in its own terms. Bailey would have done well to distinguish more than he does between Genesis 9 and the Mosaic civil code, or between "moral" and "civil" texts. But narrative can be the vehicle of moral instruction, especially in settings called *etiological,* i.e., texts which deal with why and how things came to be, or in texts exhibiting God's or Jesus' character.

6. Lamech's reference to Cain should not mislead us to think that he was escalating what had been said before by Yahweh. (a) The vengeance threatened in Genesis 4:15 was to be inflicted by Yahweh, but Lamech avenged himself; (b) the threat of 4:15 was successful in deterring harm to Cain, and was not carried out.

7. Some have argued that "by man shall his blood be shed" is a simple future rather than an imperative; a prediction but not an authorization. That is too little. God avows that the retributive process is under his rule: "I will require a reckoning." Yet, what God thus owns is an extant practice; he does not create a new institution nor decree a new duty.

8. Bailey, 32.

9. Under "retribution" we shall return later to the question of emotion.

10. Cf. Karl Barth Church Dogmatics (Edinburgh: Clark, 1961), Vol. III/4, p. 442f.: "Which category of particularly great sinners is exempted from the pardon effected on the basis of the death penalty carried out at Calvary? Now that Jesus Christ has been nailed to the cross for the sins of the world, how can we still use the thought of expiation to establish the death penalty?"

11. The first narrative in chapter 8 is missing in some of the ancient manuscripts, and some doubt that it was originally part of the Gospel; but even those scholars who doubt that these verses were originally in John's Gospel tend to grant that it nonetheless represents an authentic tradition.

12. That the persons bearing the incriminating witness should cast the first stone is part of the provision of Deuteronomy 17:7.

13. Cf., note 5, the reference to Bailey's exaggerated dislike for seeing moral meaning in narrative texts.

14. ". . . the opponents of capital punishment offer no theory of civil government . . ."; Gordon H. Clark, "Capital Punishment and the Bible," *Christianity Today,* February 1, 1960, p. 10. As a rationalistic philosopher, Clark felt that to have the right to say anything about human justice you must have a theory covering everything in the field.

15. Cf. my *Christian Witness to the State* (Newton, Kans.: Faith and Life Press, 1964), 60ff.

16. The above argument has to do with authority in the sense of the state. Sober social science will add that there are also always other kinds of nonstate authority holding societies together; the orders of the clan, the marketplace, the school, religion, entertainment. . . .

17. Cf. my *Politics of Jesus* (Grand Rapids: Eerdmans, 1972), pp. 207ff.

18. Jean Lasserre, "The 'Good' in Romans 13" in Donald Durnbaugh, ed., *On Earth Peace* (Elgin, Ill.: Brethren Press, 1978), 130–35.

19. I do offer some of this in my *Christian Witness to the State,* (note 15 above), and in my *Priestly Kingdom* (Notre Dame, Ind.: Notre Dame University Press, 1985), 151–71.

32

The Death Penalty Once More

ERNEST VAN DEN HAAG

People concerned with capital punishment disagree on essentially three questions: (1) Is it constitutional? (2) Does the death penalty deter crime more than life imprisonment? (3) Is the death penalty morally justifiable?

I. Is The Death Penalty Constitutional?

The fifth amendment, passed in 1791, states that "no person shall be deprived of life, liberty, or property, without due process of law." Thus, with "due process of law," the Constitution authorizes depriving persons "of life, liberty or property." The fourteenth amendment, passed in 1868, applies an identical provision to the states. The Constitution, then, authorizes the death penalty. It is left to elected bodies to decide whether or not to retain it.

The eighth amendment, reproducing almost verbatim a passage from the English Bill of Rights of 1689, prohibits "cruel and unusual punishments." This prohibition was not meant to repeal the fifth amendment since the amendments were passed simultaneously. "Cruel" punishment is not prohibited unless "unusual" as well, that is, new, rare, not legislated, or disproportionate to the crime punished. Neither the English Bill of Rights, nor the eighth amendment, hitherto has been found inconsistent with capital punishment.

A. Evolving Standards

Some commentators argue that, in *Trop v. Dulles,* the Supreme Court indicated that "evolving standards of decency that mark the progress of a maturing society" allow courts to declare "cruel and unusual," punishments authorized by the Constitution. However, *Trop* was concerned with expatriation, a punishment that is not specifically authorized by the Constitution. The death penalty is. *Trop* did not suggest that "evolving standards" could de-authorize what the Constitution re-

Reprinted by permission of the publisher, from *University of California–Davis Law Review,* 18, no. 4 (summer 1985): 957–72.

peatedly authorizes. Indeed, Chief Justice Warren, writing for the majority in *Trop,* declared that "the death penalty . . . cannot be said to violate the constitutional concept of cruelty."[1] Furthermore, the argument based on "evolving standards" is paradoxical: the Constitution would be redundant if current views, enacted by judicial fiat, could supersede what it plainly says. If "standards of decency" currently invented or evolved could, without formal amendment, replace or repeal the standards authorized by the Constitution, the Constitution would be superfluous.

It must be remembered that the Constitution does not force capital punishment on the population but merely authorizes it. Elected bodies are left to decide whether to use the authorization. As for "evolving standards," how could courts detect them without popular consensus as a guide? Moral revelations accepted by judges, religious leaders, sociologists, or academic elites, but not by the majority of voters, cannot suffice. The opinions of the most organized, most articulate, or most vocal might receive unjustified deference. Surely the eighth amendment was meant to limit, but was not meant to replace, decisions by the legislative branch, or to enable the judiciary do what the voters won't do.[2] The general consensus on which the courts would have to rely could be registered only by elected bodies. They favor capital punishment. Indeed, at present, more than seventy percent of the voters approve of the death penalty. The state legislatures reflect as much. Wherefore, the Supreme Court, albeit reluctantly, rejected abolition of the death penalty by judicial fiat. This decision was subsequently qualified by a finding that the death penalty for rape is disproportionate to the crime,[3] and by rejecting all mandatory capital punishment.[4]

B. Caprice

Laws that allowed courts too much latitude to decide, perhaps capriciously, whether to actually impose the death penalty in capital cases also were found unconstitutional. In response, more than two-thirds of the states have modified their death penalty statutes, listing aggravating and mitigating factors, and imposing capital punishment only when the former outweigh the latter. The Supreme Court is satisfied that this procedure meets the constitutional requirements of non-capriciousness. However, abolitionists are not.

In *Capital Punishment: The Inevitability of Caprice and Mistake,* Professor Charles Black contends that the death penalty is necessarily imposed capriciously, for irremediable reasons. If he is right, he has proved too much, unless capital punishment is imposed more capriciously now than it was in 1791 or 1868, when the fifth and fourteenth amendments were enacted. He does not contend that it is. Professor Black also stresses that the elements of chance, unavoidable in all penalizations, are least tolerable when capital punishment is involved. But the irreducible chanciness inherent in human efforts does not constitutionally require the abolition of capital punishment, unless the framers were less aware of chance and human frailty than Professor Black is. (I shall turn to the moral as distinguished from the legal bearing of chanciness anon.)

C. Discrimination

Sociologists have demonstrated that the death penalty has been distributed in a discriminatory pattern in the past: black or poor defendants were more likely to be executed than equally guilty others. This argues for correction of the distributive process, but not for abolition of the penalty it distributes, unless constitutionally excessive maldistribution ineluctably inheres in the penalty. There is no evidence to that effect. Actually, although we cannot be sure that it has disappeared altogether, discrimination has greatly decreased compared to the past.[5]

However, recently the debate on discrimination has taken a new turn. Statistical studies have found that, *ceteris paribus,* a black man who murders a white has a much greater chance to be executed than he would have had, had his victim been black.[6] This discriminates against black *victims* of murder: they are not as fully, or as often, vindicated as are white victims. However, although unjustified per se, discrimination against a class of victims need not, and here does not, amount to discrimination against their victimizers. The pattern discriminates *against* black murderers of whites and *for* black murderers of blacks. One may describe it as discrimination for, or discrimination against, just as one may describe a glass of water as half full or half empty. Discrimination against one group (here, blacks who kill whites) is necessarily discrimination in favor of another (here, blacks who kill blacks).

Most black victims are killed by black murderers, and a disproportionate number of murder victims is black. Wherefore the discrimination in favor of murderers of black victims more than offsets, numerically, any remaining discrimination against other black murderers.[7]

D. Comparative Excessiveness

Recently lawyers have argued that the death penalty is unconstitutionally disproportionate if defendants, elsewhere in the state, received lesser sentences for comparable crimes. But the Constitution only requires that penalties be appropriate to the gravity of the crime, not that they cannot exceed penalties imposed elsewhere. Although some states have adopted "comparative excessiveness" reviews, there is no constitutional requirement to do so.

Unavoidably, different courts, prosecutors, defense lawyers, judges and juries produce different penalties even when crimes seem comparable. Chance plays a great role in human affairs. Some offenders are never caught or convicted, while others are executed; some are punished more than others guilty of worse crimes. Thus, a guilty person, or group of persons, may get away with no punishment, or with a light punishment, while others receive the punishment they deserve. Should we let these others go too, or punish them less severely? Should we abolish the penalty applied unequally or discriminatorily?[8]

The late Justice Douglas suggested an answer to these questions:

> A law that . . . said that blacks, those who never went beyond the fifth grade in school, those who made less than $3,000 a year, or those who were unpopular or unstable

> should be the only people executed [would be wrong]. A law which in the overall view reaches that result in practice has no more sanctity than a law which in terms provides the same.[9]

Justice Douglas' answer here conflates an imagined discriminatory law with the discriminatory application of a non-discriminatory law. His imagined law would be inconsistent with the "equal protection of the laws" demanded by the fourteenth amendment, and the Court would have to invalidate it ipso facto. But discrimination caused by uneven application of non-discriminatory death penalty laws may be remedied by means other than abolition, as long as the discrimination is not intrinsic to the laws.

Consider now, albeit fleetingly, the moral as distinguished from the constitutional bearing of discrimination. Suppose guilty defendants are justly executed, but only if poor, or black and not otherwise. This unequal justice would be morally offensive for what may be called tautological reasons:[10] if any punishment for a given crime is just, then a greater or lesser punishment is not. Only one punishment can be just for all persons equally guilty of the same crime.[11] Therefore, different punishments for equally guilty persons or group members are unjust: some offenders are punished more than they deserve, or others less.

Still, equality and justice are not the same. "Equal justice" is not a redundant phrase. Rather, we strive for two distinct ideals, justice and equality. Neither can replace the other. We want to have justice and, having it, we want to extend it equally to all. We would not want equal injustice. Yet, sometimes, we must choose between equal injustice and unequal justice. What should we prefer? Unequal justice is justice still, even if only for some, whereas equal injustice is injustice for all. If not every equally guilty person is punished equally, we have unequal justice. It seems preferable to equal injustice—having no guilty person punished as deserved.[12] Since it is never possible to punish equally all equally guilty murderers, we should punish, as they deserve, as many of those we apprehend and convict as possible. Thus, even if the death penalty were inherently discriminatory—which is not the case—but deserved by those who receive it, it would be morally just to impose it on them. If, as I contend, capital punishment is just and not inherently discriminatory, it remains desirable to eliminate inequality in distribution, to apply the penalty to all who deserve it, sparing no racial or economic class. But if a guilty person or group escaped the penalty through our porous system, wherein is this an argument for sparing others?

If one does not believe capital punishment can be just, discrimination becomes a subordinate argument, since one would object to capital punishment even if it were distributed equally to all the guilty. If one does believe that capital punishment for murderers is deserved, discrimination against guilty black murderers and in favor of equally guilty white murderers is wrong, not because blacks receive the deserved punishment, but because whites escape it.

Consider a less emotionally charged analogy. Suppose traffic police ticketed all drivers who violated the rules, except drivers of luxury cars. Should we abolish tickets? Should we decide that the ticketed drivers of nonluxury cars were unjustly punished and ought not to pay their fines? Would they become innocent of the violation they are guilty of because others have not been ticketed? Surely the drivers of luxury cars should not be exempted. But the fact that they were is no reason to exempt drivers of nonluxury cars as well. Laws could never be applied if the escape of one person, or group, were accepted as ground for not punishing another. To do justice is primarily to punish as deserved, and only secondarily to punish equally.

Guilt is personal. No one becomes less guilty or less deserving of punishment because another was punished leniently or not at all. That justice does not catch up with all guilty persons understandably is resented by those caught. But it does not affect their guilt. If some, or all, white and rich murderers escape the death penalty, how does that reduce the guilt of black or poor murderers, or make them less deserving of punishment, or deserving of a lesser punishment?

Some lawyers have insisted that the death penalty is distributed among those guilty of murder as though by a lottery and that the worst may escape it.[13] They exaggerate, but suppose one grants the point. How do those among the guilty selected for execution by lottery become less deserving of punishment because others escaped it? What is wrong is that these others escaped, not that those among the guilty who were selected by the lottery did not.

Those among the guilty actually punished by a criminal justice system unavoidably are selected by chance, not because we want to so select them, but because the outcome of our efforts largely depends on chance. No murderer is punished unless he is unlucky enough both to be caught and to have convinced a court of his guilt. And courts consider evidence not truth. They find truth only when the evidence establishes it. Thus they may have reasonable doubts about the guilt of an actually guilty person. Although we may strive to make justice as equal as possible, unequal justice will remain our lot in this world. We should not give up justice, or the death penalty, because we cannot extend it as equally to all the guilty as we wish. If we were not to punish one offender because another got away because of caprice or discrimination, we would give up justice for the sake of equality. We would reverse the proper order of priorities.

II. Is the Death Penalty More Deterrent Than Other Punishments?

Whether or not the death penalty deters the crimes it punishes more than alternative penalties—in this case life imprisonment with or without parole—has been widely debated since Isaac Ehrlich broke the abolitionist ranks by finding that from 1933–65 "an additional execution per year . . . may have resulted on the average in seven or eight fewer murders."[14] Since his article appeared, a whole cottage industry devoted to refuting his findings has arisen. Ehrlich, no slouch, has been refuting those who refuted him.[15] The result seems inconclusive.[16] Statistics have not proved conclusively that the death penalty does or does not deter murder more than other penalties. Still, Ehrlich has the merit of being the first to use a sophisticated statistical analysis to tackle the problem, and of defending his analysis, although it showed deterrence. (Ehrlich started as an abolitionist.) His predecessors cannot be accused of mathematical sophistication. Yet the academic community uncritically accepted their abolitionist results. I myself have no contribution to make to the mathematical analyses of deterrent effects. Perhaps this is why I have come to believe that they may becloud the issue, leading us to rely on demonstrable deterrence as though decisive.

Most abolitionists believe that the death penalty does not deter more than other penalties. But most abolitionists would abolish it, even if it did.[17] I have discussed this matter with prominent abolitionists such as Charles Black, Henry Schwarzschild, Hugo Adam Bedau, Ramsey Clark, and many others. Each told me that, even if every execution were to deter a hundred murders, he would oppose it. I infer that, to these abolitionist leaders, the life of every murderer is more valuable than the lives of a hundred prospective victims, for these abolitionists would spare the murderer, even if doing so would cost a hundred future victims their lives.

Obviously, deterrence cannot be the decisive issue for these abolitionists. It is not necessarily for me either, since I would be for capital punishment on grounds of justice alone. On the other hand, I should favor the death penalty for murderers, if probably deterrent, or even just possibly deterrent. To me, the life of any innocent victim who might be spared has great value; the life of a convicted murderer does not. This is why I would not take the risk of sacrificing innocents by not executing murderers.

Even though statistical demonstrations are not conclusive, and perhaps cannot be, I believe that capital punishment is likely to deter more than other punishments because people fear death more than anything else. They fear most death deliberately inflicted by law and scheduled by the courts. Whatever people fear most is likely to deter most. Hence, I believe that the threat of the death penalty may deter some murderers who otherwise might not have been deterred. And surely the death penalty is the only penalty that could deter prisoners already serving a life sentence and tempted to kill a guard, or offenders about to be arrested and facing a life sentence. Perhaps they will not be deterred. But they would certainly not be deterred by anything else. We owe all the protection we can give to law enforcers exposed to special risks.

Many murders are "crimes of passion" that, perhaps, cannot be deterred by any threat. Whether or not they can be would depend on the degree of passion; it is unlikely to be always so extreme as to make the person seized by it totally undeterrable. At any rate, offenders sentenced to death ordinarily are guilty of premeditated murder, felony murder, or multiple murders. Some are rape murderers, or hit men, but, to my knowledge, no one convicted of a "crime of passion" is on death row. Whatever the motive, some prospective offenders are not deterrable at all, others are easily deterred, and most are in between. Even if only some murders were, or could be, deterred by capital punishment, it would be worthwhile.

Sometimes an anecdote, invented in the 19th Century, is told to suggest that the threat of the death penalty does not deter. Some pickpockets are said to have gone eagerly about their business in a crowd assembled to see one of them hang. We are not told what the level of their activity was, compared to the level in crowds of similar size assembled for different purposes. Thus, the anecdote merely shows that the death penalty does not deter some criminals. This never was contested.

Almost all convicted murderers try to avoid the death penalty by appeals for commutation to life imprisonment. However, a minuscule proportion of convicted murderers prefer execution. It is sometimes argued that they murdered for the sake of being executed, of committing suicide via execution. More likely, they prefer execution to life imprisonment. Although shared by few, this preference is not irrational per se. It is also possible that these convicts accept the verdict of the court, and feel that they deserve the death penalty for the crimes they committed, although the modern mind finds it hard to imagine such feelings. But not all murderers are ACLU humanists.

Because those sentenced to death tend to sedulously appeal the verdict of the trial courts, executions are correctly said to be costly. It is doubtful, however, that they are more costly than life imprisonment. Contrary to widely shared assumptions, life prisoners spend much of their time preparing habeas corpus appeals (not to speak of other lawsuits) just as prisoners condemned to death do.[18] But even if execution were more costly than life imprisonment, it should not be abandoned if it is just. If unjust, execution should not occur, even if it were cheap and imprisonment costly. But execution probably is less costly than life imprisonment.

III. Is the Death Penalty Moral?

A. Miscarriages

Miscarriages of justice are rare, but do occur. Over a long enough time they lead to the execution of some innocents.[19] Does this make irrevocable punishments morally wrong? Hardly. Our government employs trucks. They run over innocent bystanders more frequently than courts sentence innocents to death. We do not give up trucks because the benefits they produce outweigh the harm, including the death of innocents. Many human activities, even quite trivial ones, foreseeably cause wrongful deaths. Courts may cause fewer wrongful deaths than golf. Whether one sees the benefit of doing justice by imposing capital punishment as moral, or as material, or both, it outweighs the loss of innocent lives through miscarriages, which are as unintended as traffic accidents.

B. Vengeance

Some abolitionists feel that the motive for the death penalty is an un-Christian and unacceptable desire for vengeance. But though vengeance be the motive, it is not the purpose of the death penalty. Doing justice and deterring crime are the purposes, whatever the motive. Purpose (let alone effect) and motive are not the same.

The Lord is often quoted as saying "Vengeance is mine." He did not condemn vengeance. He merely reserved it to Himself—and to the government. For, in the same epistle He is also quoted as saying that the ruler is "the minister of God, a revenger, to execute wrath upon him that doeth evil." The religious notion of hell indicates that the biblical God favored harsh and everlasting punishment for some. However, particularly in a secular society, we cannot wait for the day of judgment to see murderers consigned to hell. Our courts must "execute wrath upon him that doeth evil" here and now.

C. Charity and Justice

Today many religious leaders oppose capital punishment. This is surprising, because there is no biblical warrant for their opposition. The Roman Catholic Church and most Protestant denominations traditionally have supported capital punishment. Why have their moral views changed? When sharing secular power, the churches clearly distinguished between justice, including penalization as deserved, a function of the secular power, and charity, which, according to religious doctrine, we should feel for all those who suffer for whatever reasons. Currently, religious leaders seem to conflate justice and charity, to conclude that the death penalty and, perhaps, all punishment, is wrong because uncharitable. Churches no longer share secular power. Perhaps bystanders are more ready to replace justice with charity than are those responsible for governing.

D. Human Dignity

Let me return to the morality of execution. Many abolitionists believe that capital punishment is "degrading to human dignity" and inconsistent with the "sanctity of life." Justice Brennan, concurring in *Furman,* stressed these phrases repeatedly. He did not explain what he meant.

Why would execution degrade human dignity more than life imprisonment? One may prefer the latter; but it seems at least as degrading as execution. Philosophers, such as Immanuel Kant and G. F. W. Hegel, thought capital punishment indispensable to redeem, or restore, the human dignity of the executed. Perhaps they were wrong. But they argued their case, whereas no one has explained why capital punishment degrades. Apparently those who argue that it does degrade dignity simply define the death penalty as degrading. If so, degradation (or dehumanization) merely is a disguised synonym for their disapproval. Assertion, reassertion, or definition do not constitute evidence or argument, nor do they otherwise justify, or even explain, disapproval of capital punishment.

Writers, such as Albert Camus, have suggested that murderers have a miserable time waiting for execution and anticipating it.[20] I do not doubt that. But punishments are not meant to be pleasant. Other people suffer greatly waiting for the end, in hospitals, under circumstances that, I am afraid, are at least as degrading to their dignity as execution. These sufferers have not deserved their suffering by committing crimes, whereas murderers have. Yet, murderers suffer less on death row, unless their consciences bother them.

E. Lex Talionis

Some writers insist that the suffering the death penalty imposes on murderers exceeds the suffering of their victims. This is hard to determine, but probably true in some cases and not in other cases. However, the comparison is irrelevant. Murderers are punished, as are all offenders, not just for the suffering they caused their victims, but for the harm they do to society by making life insecure, by threatening everyone, and by requiring protective measures. Punishment, ultimately, is a vindication of the moral and legal order of society and not limited by the *Lex Talionis,* meant to limit private retaliation for harms originally regarded as private.

F. Sanctity of Life

We are enjoined by the Declaration of Independence to secure life. How can this best be achieved? The Constitution authorizes us to secure innocent life by taking the life of murderers, so that any one who deliberately wants to take an innocent life will know that he risks forfeiting his own. The framers did not think that taking the life of a murderer is inconsistent with the "sanctity of life" which Justice Brennan champions. He has not indicated why they were wrong.[21]

G. Legalized Murder?

Ever since Cesare Bonesana, Marchese di Beccaria, wrote *Dei Delitti e Delle Pene,* abolitionists have contended that executing murderers legitimizes murder by doing to the murderer what he did to his victim. Indeed, capital punishment retributes, or pays back the offender. Occasionally we do punish offenders by doing to them what they did to their victims. We may lock away a kidnapper who wrongfully locked away his victim, and we may kill the murderer who wrongfully killed his victim. To lawfully do to the offender what he unlawfully did to his victim in no way legitimizes his crime. It legitimizes (some) killing, and not murder. An act does not become a crime because of its physical character, which, indeed, it may share with the legal punishment, but because of its social, or, better, antisocial, character—because it is an unlawful act.

H. Severity

Is the death penalty too severe? It stands in a class by itself. But so does murder. Execution is irreparable. So is murder. In contrast, all other crimes and punishments are, at least partly or potentially, reparable. The death penalty thus is congruous with the moral and material gravity of the crime it punishes.[22]

Still, is it repulsive? Torture, however well deserved, now is repulsive to us. But torture is an artifact. Death is not, since nature has placed us all under sentence of death. Capital punishment, in John Stuart Mill's phrase, only "hastens death"—which is what the murderer did to his victim. I find nothing repulsive in hastening the murderer's death, provided it be done in a nontorturous manner. Had he wished to be secure in his life, he could have avoided murder.

To believe that capital punishment is too severe for any act, one must believe that there can be no act horrible enough to deserve death.[23] I find this belief difficult to understand. I should readily impose the death penalty on a Hitler or a Stalin, or on anyone who does what they did, albeit on a smaller scale.

Conclusion

The death penalty has become a major issue in public debate. This is somewhat puzzling, because quantitatively it is insignificant. Still, capital punishment has separated the voters as a whole from a small, but influential, abolitionist elite. There are, I believe, two reasons that explain the prominence of the issue.

First, I think, there is a genuine ethical issue. Some philosophers believe that the right to life is equally imprescriptible for all, that the murderer has as much right to live as his victim. Others do not push egalitarianism that far. They believe that there is a vital difference, that one's right to live is lost when one intentionally takes an innocent life, that everyone has just the right to one life, his own. If he unlawfully takes that of an other he, *eo ipso,* loses his own right to life.

Second, and perhaps as important, the death penalty has symbolic significance. Those who favor it believe that the major remedy for crime is punishment. Those who do not, in the main, believe that the remedy is anything but punishment. They look at the causes of crime and conflate them with compulsions, or with excuses, and refuse to blame. The majority of the people are less sophisticated, but perhaps they have better judgment. They believe that everyone who can understand the nature and effects of his acts is responsible for them, and should be blamed and punished, if he could know that what he did was wrong. Human beings are human because they can be held responsible, as animals cannot be. In that Kantian sense the death penalty is a symbolic affirmation of the humanity of both victim and murderer.

Notes

1. 356 U.S. 86 (1958) at 99.

2. The courts have sometimes confirmed the obsolescence of non-repealed laws or punishments. But here they are asked to invent it.

3. In Coker v. Georgia, 433 U.S. 584, 592 (1977), the Court concluded that the eighth amendment prohibits punishments that are " 'excessive' in relation to the crime committed." I am not sure about this disproportion. However, threatening execution would tempt rapists to murder their victims who, after all, are potential witnesses. By murdering their victims, rapists would increase their chances of escaping execution without adding to their risk. Therefore, I agree with the court's conclusion, though not with its argument.

4. See Woodson v. North Carolina, 428 U.S. 280 (1976); Roberts v. Louisiana, 428

U.S. 325 (1976). Once more I disagree with the reasoning, at least in part, but welcome the conclusion, since mandatory capital punishment risks jury cancellations.

5. Most discrimination occurred in rape cases and was eliminated when the death penalty for rape was declared unconstitutional.

6. For a survey of the statistical literature, see, e.g., Bowers, *The Pervasiveness of Arbitrariness and Discrimination Under Post-*Furman *Capital Statutes,* 74 J. CRIM. L. & CRIMINOLOGY 1067 (1983). His article is part of a "Symposium on Current Death Penalty Issues" compiled by death penalty opponents.

7. Those who demonstrated the pattern seem to have been under the impression that they had shown discrimination against black murderers. They were wrong. However, the discrimination against black victims is invidious and should be corrected.

8. The capriciousness argument is undermined when capriciousness is conceded to be unavoidable. But even when capriciousness is thought reducible, one wonders whether releasing or retrying one guilty defendant, because another equally guilty defendant was not punished as much, would help reduce capriciousness. It does not seem a logical remedy.

9. Furman v. Georgia, 408 U.S. 238, 256 (1972) (Douglas, J., concurring).

10. I shall not consider here the actual psychological motives that power our unending thirst for equality.

11. If courts impose different punishments on different persons, we may not be able to establish in all cases whether the punishment is just, or (it amounts to the same) whether the different persons were equally guilty of the same crime, or whether their crimes were identical in all relevant respects. Thus, we may not be able to tell which of two unequal punishments is just. Both may be, or neither may be. Inequality may not entail more injustice than equality, and equality would entail justice only if we were sure that the punishment meted out was the just punishment.

12. Similarly, it is better that only some innocents suffer undeserved punishment than that all suffer it equally.

13. It would be desirable that all of the worst murderers be sentenced to death. However, since murderers are tried in different courts, this is unlikely. Further, sometimes the testimony of one murderer is needed to convict another, and cannot be obtained except by leniency. Morally, and legally it is enough that those sentenced to death deserve the penalty for their crimes, even if others, who may deserve it as much, or more, were not sentenced to death.

14. Ehrlich, *The Deterrent Effect of Capital Punishment: A Question of Life or Death,* 65 AM. ECON. REV. 397, 414 (1975).

15. Ehrlich, *Fear of Deterrence,* 6 J. LEGAL STUD. 293 (1977); Ehrlich & Gibbons, *On the Measurement of the Deterrent Effect of Capital Punishment and the Theory of Deterrence,* 6 J. LEGAL STUD. 35 (1977).

16. At present there is no agreement even on whether the short run effects of executions delay or accelerate homicides. See Phillips, *The Deterrent Effect of Capital Punishment: New Evidence on an Old Controversy,* 86 AM. J. SOC. 139 (1980).

17. Jeffrey Reiman is an honorable exception. See Reiman, *Justice, Civilization, and the Death Penalty: Answering van den Haag,* 14 PHIL. & PUB. AFF. 115 (1985).

18. Often the marginal cost of appeals is erroneously compared to the average cost of imprisonment. See, e.g., Kaplan, *The Problem of Capital Punishment,* 1983 U. ILL. L. REV. 555.

19. Life imprisonment avoids the problem of executing innocent persons to some extent. It can be revoked. But the convict also may die in prison before his innocence is discovered.

20. In *Reflections on the Guillotine,* Camus stated that "[t]he parcel [the condemned person] is no longer subject to the laws of chance that hang over the living creature but to mechanical laws that allow him to foresee accurately the day of his beheading. . . . The Greeks, after all, were more humane with their hemlock." A. Camus, RESISTANCE, REBELLION AND DEATH 175, 202 (1960).

21. "Sanctity of life" may mean that we should not take, and should punish taking innocent life: *"homo homini res sacra."* In the past this meant that we should take the life of a murderer to secure innocent life, and stress its sacredness. Justice Brennan seems to mean that the life of the murderer should be sacred too—but no argument is given for this premise.

22. Capital punishment is not inconsistent with Weems v. United States, 217 U.S. 349 (1910), which merely held that punishment cannot be excessive, that is, out of proportion to the gravity of the crime. Indeed, if life imprisonment suffices for anything else, it cannot be appropriate for murder.

23. The notion of deserving is strictly moral, depending exclusively on our sense of justice, unlike the notion of deterrence, which depends on the expected factual consequences of punishment. Whilst deterrence alone would justify most of the punishments we should impose, it may not suffice to justify all those punishments that our sense of justice demands. Wherefore criminal justice must rest on desert as well as deterrence, to be seen as morally justified.

33

A Reply to van den Haag

H. A. BEDAU

Ernest van den Haag divides his defense of the death penalty into three sections: its constitutionality, its preventive effects, and its moral status. It will be convenient to address his criticisms in the order in which he presents them, even though that may make for somewhat tedious reading. For readers of this book, he devotes disproportionate space to constitutional questions; they have already received substantial discussion in part IV. Conversely, he underdevelops the moral issues; they seem not to weigh very heavily in his thinking. I propose to remedy this to the extent limits of space permit.

I

Van den Haag argues five different issues on the constitutionality of the death penalty, the first of which rests on the text of the Fifth Amendment in the Bill of Rights (1791). Since "due process of law" is mentioned there in connection with lawful deprivation of "life, limb, or liberty," he concludes that "the Constitution . . . authorizes the death penalty." But this is triply wrong.

First, the text in question does not *authorize* the death penalty; instead, it presents us with a conditional proposition: *If* life is to be taken as a punishment, then it *must* be done with due process of law. In effect, this text presents the government with a choice: Either repeal the death penalty or carry it out according to the requirements of due process. As for any "authorization" of the death penalty, or any other punishment, that depends on the exercise of legislative power within the constraints of the Constitution. As for this mention of the death penalty in the Fifth Amendment, I agree that it shows that the Framers did not consider the possibility that there might be an inconsistency between permitting this mode of punishment under the constraint of due process and any of the other provisions of the Bill of Rights. In any case, it is essential to realize that this conditional proposition is consistent with the rejection of the death penalty (in standard logic, the truth of a conditional neither depends upon nor implies accepting the antecedent).

Second, van den Haag passes over the crucial question whether our current procedures for imposing the death penalty really do satisfy the requirements of due process. I take his silence on the point to imply that he has no qualms here. Well, I do, and I invited him and others who would agree with him to read carefully the essay by Stephen Bright reprinted earlier in this book (chapter 22), as well as other evidence in the same vein.[1] To be sure, due process of law is a complex and contested concept, and reasonable people can disagree over its requirements. Former Supreme Court Justice Harry Blackmun (see pp. 242–43) is not the only erstwhile supporter of the death penalty in America who has abandoned hope that ''the machinery of death'' can be operated according to the requirements of due process of law.[2]

Finally, by parity of reasoning to van den Haag's own argument, if a state legislature were to enact corporal punishments of extreme cruelty, say cutting off the hand of a thief after his third felony conviction, the legislature could count on the reference to deprivation of ''limb'' in this clause of the Fifth Amendment to enable such a punishment to pass the Supreme Court's scrutiny—so long as the maiming were done with ''due process of law.'' Are we seriously to believe that the Court would endorse such reasoning? I cannot; nothing in the Fifth Amendment precludes the Court from relying on the Eighth Amendment, prohibiting ''cruel and unusual punishments,'' to rule out as unconstitutional any punishments that maim. The same is true of punishments that kill.

Van den Haag next attacks the argument that the Eighth Amendment prohibition against ''cruel and unusual punishments'' undermines the legitimacy of the death penalty in our day, even if it did not do so when the amendment was passed, because the clause must be interpreted (in the language of the Court's ruling in *Trop v. Dulles* [1958]) according to ''evolving standards of decency.'' He dismisses this judicial language as ''paradoxical'' if used to interpret the Constitution in order to repeal punishments having statutory authority, since it would make the Constitution as written ''superfluous.'' Van den Haag seems to think *Trop* was nonetheless correctly decided because the punishment ruled out by the Court in that case was ''expatriation, a punishment not specifically authorized by the Constitution.'' But the Eighth Amendment nowhere mentions (and certainly doesn't ''authorize'') capital punishment, either.

The issue here is twofold: how to interpret the ''cruel and unusual punishment'' clause of that amendment, and how to apply that interpretation to the death penalty in light of the relevant facts. As the ratification discussions in 1789 show,[3] it was even then anticipated that at some future date this language might plausibly be used to strike down the death penalty. Nothing in either the Fifth or the Eighth Amendments prohibits the Supreme Court from concluding that two hundred years of experience with capital punishment reveals that it is, after all, cruel and unusual, that its administration makes a mockery of due process of law, and that it also violates ''the equal protection of the law'' (Fourteenth Amendment).

In this regard it is important to notice that van den Haag mentions in passing (though without implying his approval) that the Supreme Court has declared the death penalty for rape (in *Coker v. Georgia* [1977]) and the mandatory death penalty for murder (in *Woodson v. North Carolina* [1976]) to be in violation of the Eighth Amendment. Consistent with his prior argument here, he must reject the legitimacy of these rulings. On his view, any legislature that wants to have the death penalty for rape is constitutionally ''authorized'' to do so, whether or not it is ''disproportionate'' to the crime. And the same is true of any other crime—armed robbery, kidnapping, treason, espionage, arson, train robbery, desecration of a grave—each of them punishable by death earlier in this century in one or another American jurisdiction. But by van den Haag's reasoning, since disproportionality is nowhere mentioned in the Eighth Amendment (having been invented by the Supreme Court in *Weems v. United States* [1910] as an appropriate interpretive principle to explain what a ''cruel and unusual punishment'' is), he must infer that courts have no authority to invoke disproportionality as a ground for declaring *any* penalties unconstitutional. Thus, he implicitly rejects the Supreme Court's authority to nullify the death penalty for murder by means of an argument that prevents the Court from applying the Eighth Amendment to invalidate *any* penalty, so long as that penalty is carried out by ''due process of law'' and was tolerated by the Framers.

Van den Haag next addresses the objection that the death penalty as administered is too capricious to be tolerated on constitutional grounds. (As his essay preceded the Court's decision in *McCleskey v. Kemp* by two years, he had no opportunity to mention that this decision supports his own views.) He replies in two steps: First, he endorses the Supreme Court's decision in *Gregg* that the post-*Furman* statutory reforms have eliminated whatever caprice infected the administration of pre-*Furman* death penalties. This judgment simply will not withstand scrutiny. The good-faith hopes of the *Gregg* majority in 1976 (especially evident in the concurring opinion by Justice White) have simply not been borne out in practice in the two decades since then. No serious and informed student of the administration of the death penalty believes these statutes have so far accomplished more than cosmetic reforms, however well-intentioned they may have been when enacted.[4]

The next objection van den Haag raises is that unless we are to believe the administration of the death penalty today is *more* capricious than it was in the previous century, its capriciousness today fails to show any constitutionally relevant defect. This is a bad argument because it ignores the holding in *Furman,* which (as I pointed out in the preface to Part IV) was based above all on the capricious, arbitrary, and discriminatory administration of the death penalty of that day. Unless there is *less*—indeed, little or no—caprice in the death penalty as administered today, in contrast to what there was when *Furman* was decided, the post-*Furman* statutes ought to be invalidated by the reasoning that prevailed in *Furman.* One way around this, of course, is to argue that *Furman* was wrongly decided in the first place and ought to be overruled—an argument I am sure van den Haag would want to make. The fact that the Supreme Court has so far failed to reverse its ruling in *Gregg,* or to hold the states on a short tether where the death penalty is concerned, tells us more about the ideology and politics of the majority of the Court since 1975 than it does about the constitutionality of the death penalty.

Van den Haag devotes two paragraphs to attacking the claim that racial discrimination in administering the death penalty establishes that penalty's unconstitutionality. (Subsequent to his essay, David Baldus and his two coauthors published

Equal Justice and the Death Penalty: A Legal and Empirical Analysis [1990], amply establishing just such discrimination.) Van den Haag concedes that there is some racial discrimination in the way this penalty is administered. The importance of this concession is not to be underestimated; few defenders of the death penalty today are willing to concede as much. Van den Haag probably attaches little weight to it because he probably would also concede that the whole criminal justice system is tilted slightly against nonwhites, thus reducing to relative insignificance whatever racial discrimination the death penalty involves. He insists that the remedy is not to abolish the death penalty but to abolish the discrimination (which, he adds, favor murderers of blacks and therefore favors blacks over whites, since most black murder victims are killed by blacks). When this is taken as an abstract proposition, one must agree with van den Haag: Since capital statutes as they are written do not discriminate on racial grounds, they ought not to be repealed just because they are administered with discriminatory results.

But this remedy of nondiscrimination, which van den Haag so easily proposes, simply flies in the face of everything we know about the history of the death penalty in this nation, and especially in the South. Are we seriously to think that in Texas or Alabama or South Carolina (or even outside the South, in California, Illinois, or New York) prosecutors and trial juries will remedy their history of racial discrimination by meting out death penalties regardless of the race of the victim or the offender? No, we are not. (See the sobering story told at length by James W. Marquart and his two coauthors in their book, *The Rope, The Chair, and the Needle: Capital Punishment in Texas, 1923–1990* [1994].)[5] Van den Haag's argument is simply beside the point; it is a frivolous appeal to an abstract possibility that two centuries of experience tell us will not be put into practice, not in our lifetimes and not in those of our children or their children. If we really want to improve on the rough justice of our current practices involving the death penalty, the only way to do so is to abolish it and sentence *all* convicted murderers to prison, whatever their race and the race of their victim(s). No doubt inequities will remain, but their magnitude will have been dramatically reduced.

Van den Haag's final and lengthiest constitutional consideration takes up proportionality review. A year after his essay was published, the Supreme Court ruled in *Pulley v. Harris* (1984) as he would have wished, rejecting the argument to make proportionality review a constitutional requirement in capital cases. However, nowhere in his discussion does he address the equal protection clause of the Fourteenth Amendment and what relevance it may have, although that ought to be his chief, if not his sole, concern here. Instead, he invites us to consider which is worse—giving some murderers their just deserts (a death penalty) even when we do not give it to all murderers, or giving it to none because we cannot give it to all. Van den Haag favors, he says, justice over equality if we cannot have both. Again, taken abstractly, his position here is plausible.

But, also once again, why take the matter so abstractly? We have ample empirical evidence, based on actual research (some of it presented earlier in this book, especially in parts V and VI) on prosecutorial decision making, the deliberations of capital juries, and the conduct of clemency hearings in capital cases, to believe that the disproportionality in sentencing is *not* the result of a random "lottery" or of mere "chance" (van den Haag's favorite explanatory factors). Rather, it is due to illegitimate factors of race, class, and social policy. (Stephen Nathanson has discussed this point with some care; see Nathanson 1987.) This is why the decision to execute a given capital offender is vulnerable to criticism on equal protection grounds.

In another place, van den Haag and I debated the question, Can any legal punishments of the guilty be unjust to them? As might be expected, he argued the negative and I argued the affirmative (see van den Haag 1987 and Bedau 1987c). Since part of what I said there is relevant to the present issue, I will quote from that essay:

> Once it is known that the jurisdiction's sentencing practices are producing disparities, and these disparities are based on irrelevant factors such as gender or race, then it is known that a social practice (i.e., discretionary sentencing) is producing inequities owing to impermissible causes—factors that sentencers are not entitled to consider in justifying the disparate exercise of their sentencing discretion. Whatever the mechanisms through which these causes (e.g., unconscious racism) affect social practices, the result is not unlike the paradigm of injustice in which guilty parties are victimized by punishments determined by factors irrelevant either to their culpability or to the unlawful harm they have caused. In the case of unconscious racism, as in the previous cases, the offender has a right that irrelevant factors not determine his sentence. But, the sentencing practice that imposes the heavier sentence on Smith demonstrably violates this right, quite apart from whether there is any evidence that the sentencer intentionally discriminated against Smith. Such sentencing practices do not violate Smith's right to the lesser sentence, for he has no such right. Instead, these practices violate Smith's right not to be sentenced one way rather than another owing to adventitious factors that bear no relation to his guilt. This is why the heavier sentence is an injustice *to* him.
>
> The point underlying this conclusion is simple. Injustice in punishment, which for our purposes is injustice in sentencing, is an injustice to the guilty offender only when the sentencing disparities are explained by factors that have nothing to do with the desert of the offender. Clearly, sentence disparities based on the gender, race, color, or nationality of the offender, as well as the arbitrary outcomes of a fair lottery, are irrelevant to the offender's desert. Every guilty offender has a right that his sentence not be determined by factors irrelevant to his desert. The fact that some sentences are based on such criteria is merely another variation of the general theme that arbitrary or unfair procedures, which produce irrelevant grounds for exercising sentencing discretion, yield an unjust result, quite apart from whatever may be said about the justice of the result from some other perspective. (Bedau 1987c: 1429–30)

II

With constitutional issues disposed of, van den Haag addresses deterrence and the empirical research on which judgments of deterrence are and ought to be made. Oddly, he says nothing explicit about incapacitation, although the special incapacitative effects of the death penalty are usually touted by those of its defenders who attach importance to deterrence. (Perhaps, following the bad practice of many criminologists, he thinks of executions as "special deterrence"; see my objections on p. 128.) He concludes that the results of all the empirical research are "inconclusive," and so he is inclined to advise partisans on each side of the death penalty debate to distrust reliance on research of this sort. This is a minimalist interpretation of the evidence if ever there was one, since it wrongly encourages the inexperienced student of this subject to think that the empirical pros and cons about the special deterrent effects of the death penalty are at a standoff. Van den Haag and others who support the death penalty on deterrent grounds need to ponder the essay in this book by William C. Bailey and Ruth D. Peterson (chapter 9) to see just how completely without foundation is any belief in the deterrent efficacy of the death penalty in the United States during the past half century.

Van den Haag then insists that despite the lack of empirical evidence he still believes the death penalty is a better deterrent. Why? "[B]ecause people fear death more than anything else." Perhaps they would say they do, if they were asked to answer the question, Which do you fear more, a death penalty or life in prison? But armed robbers, gangland hit men, kids in cars hell-bent on drive-by shootings, and other persons really interested in murdering someone are not thinking about that question. They are thinking instead about this question: "What's the best way for me to commit the crime and not get caught?" Van den Haag also argues that the death penalty must be a better deterrent because death row convicts would rather have their sentences commuted to life in prison. This preference tends to show that life imprisonment is believed to be a less *severe* punishment than death. It does not show that death is a better *deterrent*—unless you accept as an axiom that the more severe a punishment is thought to be, the better a deterrent it is. The truth of that belief matters not at all if rational people will be deterred from murder as well by a long prison sentence as by a death sentence.

Van den Haag concedes that many murderers are undeterrable but adds: "Even if only some murders were, or could be, deterred by capital punishment, it would be worthwhile." Many agree with him (though they might not, if there were to read the critique by David Conway; see Conway 1974). But one must ask, What cost are you prepared to pay to gain this elusive extra deterrence? The dollar costs, as Richard Dieter has shown (see chapter 29), are mounting rapidly, with no end in sight. Quite apart from these costs are the moral costs, chief of which is the great risk of executing the innocent (I will return to this later).

Before turning to his third category of issues, van den Haag addresses the relative costs of execution versus imprisonment. He argues that imprisonment is the more costly of the two and that, even if it weren't we should pay the extra cost of justice—which involves putting to death all who are sentenced to death, preferably with more dispatch than we currently do. We all should agree with him about paying what justice costs, but it remains to be shown that executing prisoners *is* what justice requires (an issue to which I will return in the following). And on the empirical question of the relative costs, the best current information and research, summarized by Dieter, suggest van den Haag is simply wrong—just as he is wrong in claiming that it is primarily the postconviction appeals that run up the economic costs of capital punishment.

Throughout his discussion of deterrence, van den Haag fails to address a crucial question: If the death penalty is to be defended on grounds of its superior deterrence (or incapacitation), what stops us from defending even more savage penalties if they prove (or seem likely to prove) to be an even better deterrent than the death penalty as currently used? Later in his essay, he dismisses torture on the subjective ground that it is "repulsive to us." Well, it is not repulsive to torturers, and to them van den Haag evidently has nothing to say except to express his personal disapproval. It's of no use to his argument that everyone agrees the Constitution prohibits such "cruel and unusual punishments" as boiling in oil or crucifixion or burning at the stake. He has to explain, consistent with his endorsement of the importance of extra deterrence, how and why he respects the moral basis of the constitutional prohibition. He fails to do that; his ethical subjectivism prevents him from doing so. Like every other defender of the death penalty on deterrent grounds, van den Haag has nursed an asp to his bosom that will destroy whatever limits he thinks might be morally appropriate on cruel punishments—limits that in any case he can treat as nothing more than collective subjective preferences.

I complete my criticism of van den Haag's view on deterrence by responding to his claim that I and other abolitionists who oppose the death penalty on principle would evidently tolerate the murder of hundreds rather than execute any convicted murderers even if we knew that by doing so we could have prevented those murders by the extra deterrence the death penalty provides. I cannot speak for the others whom van den Haag mentions in this connection (Charles Black Jr., Ramsey Clark, and Henry Schwarzschild), though I am delighted to be in their company, here or anywhere. But speaking only for myself, I would point out two things.

First, my unwillingness to execute (or to have the state hire someone to execute) a convicted murderer is not the same as someone else's decision to commit murder. Neither is it in any sense the cause of such a decision. My refusal to authorize killing the guilty is not equivalent to my authorizing the death of the innocent. So my refusal to authorize executions does not make me responsible for murder, even if those executions would have deterred murderers that imprisonment would not.

Second, as is evident from contemporary philosophical discussion, it is extremely difficult to resist the lure of torture, murder, and other dark deeds when it can be argued that without such acts thousands, or millions, of innocents will surely die.[6] Where the death penalty today is concerned, however, any version of this dilemma is so conjectural that worrying about it is as implausible as worrying about sharks on dry land. Van den Haag is right that I oppose the death penalty in principle and without exceptions; he is wrong in implying that I would tolerate with equanimity the deaths of innocents simply to avoid lawful execution of one who is guilty. I favor abolition, not least because I am confident that zero deterrence would be lost.

III

In the final and most important (but briefest and least coherent) part of his argument, van den Haag raises eight scattered issues collected under the heading of the morality of the death penalty. On the first of these, miscarriages of justice, he concedes that in the long run the death penalty "lead[s] to the execution of some innocents." This is another important concession, and he repeated it a few years later (1986:1664). But these losses are rare and worth it, he argues, because of the offsetting advantages that *only* the death penalty provides—at which point he recycles his belief in the deterrent superiority of the death penalty. As for his analogy (we tolerate high-speed highways despite our knowledge that they increase traffic deaths), all one can say is that there is *no* analogy between a morally defensible practice in which lethal accidents do occur that take statistical lives and a morally dubious practice in which lethal events are designed for particular individuals in the mistaken belief that they deserve it.

Van den Haag turns next to the role of "vengeance." Insofar as his interest in this concept arises from its role in Judeo-Christian religious morality, I direct the interested reader to the earlier debate between H. Wayne House and John Howard Yoder (as well as to their book, *The Death Penalty Debate* [1991], where vengeance is a major theme; see also the scholarly monograph by Marvin Henberg, *Retribution: Evil for Evil in Ethics, Law, and Literature* [1990]). I am troubled by van den Haag's endorsement of vengeance as a legitimate "motive" for the death penalty, even if not its real "purpose." Insofar as vengeance is the motive, does he want us to believe that only supporters of the death penalty *can* act from this motive? Or that only they are *entitled* to act from it? Neither is plausible. That to one side, vengeance is too eruptive and violent an emotion to encourage in ourselves and others. It cannot be confined and channeled to tolerate, much less support, due process of law in punishment, and is likely to spill over into private violence. However, as van den Haag rightly notes, subjective "motives" such as vengeance are not what is at issue in evaluating punitive policy; it is the objective "purposes" that govern the discussion. So, asking us to tolerate vengeance as a legitimate motive for the death penalty is really a red herring, and a dangerous one.

Van den Haag rebukes Christian religious leaders who oppose the death penalty, reminding them that "there is no biblical warrant for their opposition." (Again, I invite the interested reader to review the debate between House and Yoder.) However, even if van den Haag is right about how to read and interpret the Bible, all he has done is put in question the legitimacy of professing Christians opposing the death penalty on narrowly biblical (constructing "biblical" to mean "literally textual") grounds. This does nothing to undermine any nonreligious moral arguments against the death penalty, which Jews and Christians are as entitled to advance as well as anyone else.

Van den Haag next tackles the concept and role of "human dignity" and denies that there is any mileage for abolitionists to be gained by invoking this value. He adds that "no one has explained why capital punishment degrades" human dignity, and he implies that no one can. In an essay published some years after his and designed to explain the idea of the death penalty as a violation of human dignity, I began by using the four principles Justice Brennan introduced in his concurring opinion in *Furman* (recall chapter 12) in order to explain why the death penalty was an affront to human dignity and thus in violation of the Eighth Amendment's prohibition of "cruel and unusual punishments." The essential part of my argument, taken out of the context of a rather long discussion, was this:

> Let us reformulate Brennan's four principles in a more uniform manner that emphasizes their connection to human dignity. Taking them in the order in which he mentions them, this is what we get: First, it is an affront to the dignity of a person to be forced to undergo catastrophic harm at the hands of another when, before the harm is imposed, the former is entirely at the mercy of the latter, as is always the case with legal punishment. Second, it offends the dignity of a person who is punished according to the will of a punisher free to pick and choose arbitrarily among offenders so that only a few are punished very severely when all deserve the same severe punishment if any do. Third, it offends the dignity of a person to be subjected to a severe punishment when society shows by its actual conduct in sentencing that it no longer regards this severe punishment as appropriate. Finally, it is an affront to human dignity to impose a very severe punishment on an offender when it is known that a less severe punishment will achieve all the purposes it is appropriate to try to achieve by punishing anyone in any manner whatsoever.
>
> These reformulations link the concept of human dignity explicitly with the concept of "cruel and unusual punishments" via the notion of appropriate limits to the permissible severity of punishments. This is easily seen if we recall several of the constitutive elements of human dignity discussed earlier: Respect for the autonomy of rational creatures forbids its needless curtailment in the course of deserved punishment. Respect for the equal worth of persons forbids inequitable punishments of convicted offenders equally guilty. The fundamental equal rights of persons, including convicted offenders, precludes treating some offenders as if they had ceased to be persons. (Bedau 1992a:160–61)

Van den Haag turns to the law of retaliation, *lex talionis,* only to reject its authority. This is another important concession because it deprives him of arguing from this general principle of retaliatory punishments to the special case of the death penalty for murder, in which we take "a life for a life." (Of course, his disavowal of *lex talionis* also spares him the embarrassment of trying to cope with the inapplicability and absurdity of this law for a wide range of crimes, just as it frees him to defend the death penalty, should he wish to, for crimes that include no murder.) Instead, he argues that "[p]unishment, ultimately, is a vindication of the moral and legal order of society." No doubt it ought to be, although it behooves those who would defend punishment in these terms to convince us that the current moral and legal order is sufficiently just to warrant our punitive practices (Jeffrey Reiman's retributive argument against the death penalty rests primarily on the structural injustices in our society; see Reiman 1985 and 1988). But of course one can grant van den Haag's claim about the nature or ultimate purpose of state punishment without for one moment suggesting that law and moral order can be vindicated *only* or *best* by the use of death penalties or any other unnecessary punishment. This is precisely what I would deny and what van den Haag apparently believes and ought to defend. But he doesn't. (Others, such as Walter Berns, have tried to do so at some length; see his book *For Capital Punishment: Crime and the Morality of the Death Penalty* [1979].)

Before turning to the next of van den Haag's moral considerations, we should notice how the fundamental principle of much of his overall argument is badly neglected. He makes it clear in passing that murderers *deserve* to die, and that the principal justification of the death penalty is *justice.* He seems to believe that *desert* tells us *whom* to punish (guilty criminals), *what* they deserve as their punishment (murderers deserve death), and *why* this is what they deserve (justice). Yet his position on these issues is incomplete and unsatisfactory, for at least two reasons. First, he does not defend a mandatory death penalty; in principle that ought to prevent the arbitrariness, which he concedes, of our current discretionary death penalty, just as it ought to increase deterrence and retribution. So why doesn't he support it? Because (as he says in a footnote) a mandatory death penalty "risks jury cancellations." Historically, there is evidence to support this worry, but it is a silly reason for him to endorse, unless he believes that the future death penalties likely to be canceled by this route are so many that they vastly exceed in number the future death penalties not meted out under the current discretionary system, with the result that a return to mandatory death penalties would achieve less deterrence and retribution than the current system. Why van den Haag would believe this, when he believes the public overwhelmingly favors the death penalty and when he knows that opponents of the death penalty are routinely excluded from capital trial juries, beats me. And how our current arbitrary and discretionary death penalty system "vindicates the moral and legal order" in a manner of which we can be proud remains a mystery.

Second, what are we to make of his fundamental proposition that *murderers deserve the death penalty?* Is it supposed to be a necessary moral truth that anyone can see to be true simply by understanding the concepts used to express it, an analytic a priori proposition? I hope van den Haag would not take this route to defend this proposition because it will be difficult to prevent turning it into a mere prejudice. To avoid that, this proposition must be somehow established by derivation from more fundamental norms. What are they? Since he has rejected *lex talionis*—the obvious if unsatisfactory answer—and supplied no alternative, we are left to guess. It is interesting to note that in the face of a resurgent approval among philosophers during the past two decades for a retributive justification of punishment, only a few have gone on to endorse a purely or primarily retributive defense of capital punishment.[7]

The next target of his critique is the ideal of "the sanctity of life," which some abolitionists (notably, Justice Brennan) insist the death penalty violates. He does not try to explain this ideal or why one might think it is inconsistent with the death penalty. Instead, he recycles constitutional considerations, purporting to show that the Framers, who accepted this ideal, did so in a manner that did not rule out capital punishment. But none of this really speaks to the moral issues involved. For my part, I would put this ideal to one side in the present discussion because the *sanctity* of life (all life? only human life? only innocent human life?) is not a secular concept but a religious one—unlike the *right* to life, which is a secular concept. For some reason, van den Haag has virtually nothing to say about this idea (but see my penultimate paragraph below). Whatever role the sanctity of life properly plays in a religiously based morality, it really cannot be used as a building block for a secular morality. Nor can it be properly used to evaluate from a secular perspective such controversial issues as suicide, euthanasia, abortion, war—or the death penalty. Since van den Haag does not discuss the bearing of our right to life on the morality of the death penalty, I will excuse myself from doing so here.[8]

Van den Haag's penultimate barb is directed at those abolitionists who think that executing murderers "legitimizes murder by doing to the murderer what he did to his victim." He rejects this objection because it confuses the legitimate killing of convicted murderers with the illegitimate killing by murderers. This strikes me as completely begging the question. The point of the objection he wishes to refute is that where the legitimacy of killing lies in the eye of the killer, we must be very careful what killings we are prepared to permit.

Consider by contrast for a moment the idea of killing in self-defense. Opponents of the death penalty do not condemn such killings, arguing that killing in self-defense legitimates murder. (Notice, by the way, that van den Haag nowhere claims that when society uses the death penalty, it does so in self-defense. Perhaps he would grant that this is an implausible claim for defenders of the death penalty to advance, because nowhere in Europe today, or in Michigan for a century and a half, to cite but one local example, has social defense required reliance on the death penalty.) The reason abolitionists believe the death penalty legitimates murder in the eyes of some is that the grounds on which the government acts in deciding whom to prosecute for a death sentence, whom to convict of capital murder, whom to sentence to death, whom to refuse clemency, looks suspiciously vindictive, arbitrary, and illegitimate. This invites some to reason as follows: "If the government is permitted to kill for its reasons, then I should be permitted to kill for mine." Van den Haag's argument is not with abolitionists, who do not endorse this reasoning, but with whoever does reason in this manner. Simply declaring that murder is wrong and the death penalty legitimate is hardly sufficient.

Finally, van den Haag turns to the question whether the death penalty is "too severe" and concludes that it is not. Yes, it is "irreparable"—but so is murder. No, it is not "repulsive"—since we all must die someday. And he ends by informing us how readily he would put to death a Hitler, a Stalin, or "anyone who does what they did, albeit on a smaller scale." But whether the death penalty is too severe depends on what one thinks the purpose and rationale of its severity is. Whatever that purpose or rationale, I think it is unnecessary for deterrence or incapacitation, arbitrary and discriminatory in the retribution it inflicts, and therefore an affront to our civilized sensibilities.

As to whether the death penalty is repulsive, I suggest that van den Haag inform himself more vividly about what happens during a typical electrocution—a pretty ugly affair at best, as Deborah Denno has shown in considerable detail (Denno 1994a, 1996) and as demonstrated by the repulsive 1990 electrocution of Jesse

Tafero in Florida (von Drehle 1995:409). I would grant, on the strength of Susan Blaustein's witness (chapter 28), that the physical act of execution by lethal injection is not repulsive typically or necessarily—no doubt, a widely shared belief and a significant factor in explaining the popularity of lethal injection with American legislatures during the past twenty years. But this emphasis on the details of particular executions or on techniques for carrying out the death penalty obscures what is arguably repulsive about executions as such: It is not only that the prisoner dies, or dies in agony, or dies with ugly disfigurement, but that the lethal act itself is the result of calculated planning by the impersonal state in which the state's overwhelming power is on display against the helplessness of the prisoner (a point I stressed earlier in chapter 17).

When van den Haag reminds us that death is inevitable in the nature of things, he does not make a very persuasive point. Human disappointment, pain, loneliness, bereavement, and other forms of misery and suffering are part of the human condition and virtually inevitable for each of us. Yet is that a good reason for complacency in their face if it is within our power to remedy or mitigate, even if only briefly or slightly, these inevitabilities? Van den Haag does not address this question.

As for Hitler and Stalin, they are often the trump card used by modern defenders of the death penalty who cannot believe that anyone really would oppose *all* executions. The trouble is that appealing to Hitler and Stalin sheds no light on whether to execute all or some or none of the more than three thousand prisoners on American death rows today. For myself, I would be glad to make an exception to my absolute rejection of the death penalty by permitting van den Haag to destroy tyrants such as these if he would give me the lives of those actually under sentence of death today, whose crimes are pathetically insignificant if measured against genocide, aggressive warfare, and the other crimes against humanity of which these dictators and their henchmen were guilty.

Van den Haag ends his essay by making two points with which abolitionists ought to agree—in part. First, he insists that the national debate over the death penalty is important because it involves "a genuine ethical issue." He is right, but what is this issue as he sees it? It is whether "the right to life" extends to all humans and cannot ever be forfeited. He thinks it can be; I think it cannot, and elsewhere I have tried to explain why (Bedau 1987b:55–59). Even if I am right, I suggest that this is not the important ethical issue in the debate. The paramount ethical issue posed by the death penalty is this: Whether or not everyone has an unforfeitable right to life, do *we* do the right thing in authorizing killing some criminals when we know there is an adequate alternative punishment (imprisonment), or do we do the right thing when we refuse to kill any, no matter how guilty they are? The issue, in short, is not the right to life; it is the right to *kill.*

Second, van den Haag insists that we are rightly concerned about the death penalty because it has important "symbolic significance," a significance far beyond its practical import. Again, this is correct. For him, however, this symbolic significance lies in its "affirmation of the humanity of both victim and murderer." Van den Haag here has the support of no less a philosopher than Immanuel Kant, though he does not mention this. I, on the other hand, think the whole idea is bizarre. The very thought that I affirm the humanity of a murderer by treating him more or less as he treated his innocent and undeserving victim would be funny were it not so momentous. For me, the death penalty symbolizes *unlimited impersonal power* over the individual, with dramatically final and irreversible results whenever it is expressed. As long as we choose to hang this moral albatross around our necks, I see no way for us to enjoy, much less help the rest of the world to enjoy, the benefits of a truly human community.

Notes

1. See, e.g., Greenberg 1982, 1986; Weisberg 1983; Radelet and Pierce 1985; Goodpaster 1983; Brennan 1986; Marshall 1986; Tabak and Lane 1989; Burt 1987; Amsterdam 1988; V. Berger 1988.

2. This was the chief point of Charles Black's objection to the death penalty; see Black, 1981.

3. See R. Berger 1982:45–46 and my review of his book, Bedau 1983:1159–60.

4. Justice White supported the decision in *Gregg v. Georgia* by arguing that the Georgia legislature "has made an effort" to identify appropriate aggravating and mitigating circumstances relevant to the choice of sentence in capital cases (pp. 221, 222); he added that "[t]here is reason to expect that Georgia's current system would escape the infirmities which invalidated its previous system" (p. 222); and so on regarding prosecutorial discretion in indictments (pp. 224–25) and proportionality review by the Georgia Supreme Court (pp. 223–24). What Justice White has not done since he wrote these words in 1976 is to revisit in appropriate detail the administration of the death penalty in Georgia and elsewhere, to see how the promise of compliance with the mandate of *Furman*—which he supported—has not been kept.

5. See also my review of this book, Bedau 1997.

6. See, e.g., Glover 1977; Taurek 1977; Parfit 1978; Saunders 1988.

7. See Sorell 1987; Primoratz 1989; and the as yet unpublished volume by Michael Davis, *Justice in the Shadow of Death* (1996). Retributivists who oppose the death penalty include von Hirsch 1976; Murphy 1979; Pugsley 1981; and Reiman 1985, 1988.

8. As I mentioned previously p. 234 note 6, the contemporary philosophical discussion of the right to life leaves much to be desired. My own discussions, beginning with Bedau 1967, are at best a starting point.

BIBLIOGRAPHY

Bibliographies

Subsequent to the bibliographies provided in earlier editions of *The Death Penalty in America* (1st ed. 1964, 3d ed. 1982), Michael L. Radelet and Margaret Vandiver published *Capital Punishment in America: An Annotated Bibliography* (New York: Garland, 1988). They list a thousand items, 90 percent of them published since *Furman v. Georgia* (1972). Their book also contains a subject index and thus is an indispensable research tool. An updated successor to the Radelet-Vandiver volume is in the course of publication by Garland under the editorship of Rebecca Trammel.

A "Topical Bibliography: Capital Punishment," listing more than two hundred items, was published by the National Institute of Justice, Department of Justice. Each item listed is abstracted, but no items subsequent to 1981 are cited. Bibliographical information is also available at irregular intervals from the Washington, D.C., office of the National Coalition to Abolish the Death Penalty. Especially valuable are the newspaper and magazine items cited in these NCADP bibliographies.

Collections

Most of the best articles, essays, reports, and other documents on the death penalty in America have been reprinted in various books, where they are more easily obtained than in their original place of publication. From among such volumes cited in the general bibliography, below, the following deserve special mention: Bedau ed. 1964, Bedau ed. 1982, Bedau and Pierce eds. 1976, Coyne and Entzeroh 1994, Koosed ed. 1996a, 1996b, 1996c, Mackey ed. 1976, Streib ed. 1993, and Vila and Morris eds. 1997.

Government Documents

Department of Justice. Bureau of Justice Statistics.
Capital Punishment, annually under various titles and by different agencies since 1950.

Department of Justice. Bureau of Justice Statistics.
Sourcebook of Criminal Justice Statistics, annually since 1973.

Department of Justice. Federal Bureau of Investigation.
Crime in the United States—Uniform Crime Reports, annually since 1930.

Congress. General Accounting Office. Report to the Senate and House Committees on the Judiciary.
1990 *Death Penalty Sentencing: Research Indicates Pattern of Racial Disparities.*

House of Representatives. Committee on the Judiciary, Subcommittee on Criminal Justice.
99th Cong., 1st and 2d Sess.

1986 "Capital Punishment," *Hearings on H.R. 2837 and H.R. 343,* November 1985 and April–June 1986.

House of Representatives. Committee on the Judiciary, Subcommittee on Civil and Constitutional Rights.

1990a "Death Penalty Legislation and the Racial Justice Act," *Hearings on H.R. 4618,* May.

House of Representatives. Committee on the Judiciary, Subcommittee on Crime.

1990b "Federal Death Penalty Legislation," *Hearings on H.R. 2102, etc.* March.

House of Representatives. Committee on the Judiciary, Subcommittee on Civil and Constitutional Rights.

1991a "Death Sentencing Issues," *Hearings,* July.

House of Representatives. Committee on the Judiciary, Subcommittee on Crime and Criminal Justice.

1991b "Selected Crime Issues: Prevention and Punishment," *Hearings.* May–June.

House of Representatives. Committee on the Judiciary, Subcommittee on Civil and Constitutional Rights. Staff Report.

1993 *Innocence and the Death Penalty: Assessing the Danger of Mistaken Executions.*

National Governors' Association.

1988 *Guide to Executive Clemency Among the American States.* Washington, D.C., National Institute of Corrections.

Senate. Committee on the Judiciary. 98th Cong., 1st Sess. Report of the Committee on S. 1765.

1983a "Establishing Constitutional Procedures for the Imposition of Capital Punishment." September.

Senate. Subcommittee on Criminal Law, Committee of the Judiciary.

1983b "Prison Violence and Capital Punishment," *Hearing to Examine Capital Offenses by Federal Prisoners.* November.

Senate. Committee on the Judiciary, 99th Cong., 1st Sess.

1985 "Death Penalty Legislation," *Hearing. . . . on S. 239.* September.

Senate. Committee on the Judiciary. Report of the Committee on S. 239.

1986 "Establishing Constitutional Procedures for the Imposition of Capital Punishment."

Senate. Committee on the Judiciary, 101st Cong., 1st Sess.

1989a "Death Penalty," *Hearings. . . . on S. 32, S. 1225, and S. 1696.* September–October.

Senate. Committee on the Judiciary, 101st Cong., 1st Sess. Report of the Committee [on S. 32].

1989b "The Federal Death Penalty Act of 1989."

Senate. Committee on the Judiciary, 103d Cong., 1st Sess.

1993 "Innocence and the Death Penalty," *Hearing on S. 221.* April.

General

Abu-Jamal, Mumia

1996 *Live from Death Row.* Reading, Mass.: Addison–Wesley.

Acker, James R.

1985 "Mandatory Capital Punishment for the Life Term Inmate Who Commits Murder: Judgments of Fact and Value in Law and the Social Sciences." *New England Journal on Criminal and Civil Confinement* 11(summer): 267–327.

1993 "A Different Agenda: The Supreme Court, Empirical Research Evidence, and Capital Punishment Decisions, 1986–1989." *Law and Society Review* 27:65–88.

Acker, James R., and Charles S. Lanier

1993a "Capital Murder from Benefit of Clergy to Bifurcated Trials: Narrowing the Class of Offenses Punishable by Death." *Criminal Law Bulletin* 29(July–August): 291–316.

1993b "The Dimensions of Capital Murder." *Criminal Law Bulletin* 29(September–October): 379–417.

1996 "Law, Discretion, and the Capital Jury: Death Penalty Statutes and Proposals for Reform." *Criminal Law Bulletin* 32:134–80.

Acosta, Sandra R.

1990 "Imposing the Death Penalty upon Drug Kingpins." *Harvard Journal of Legislation* 27:596–79.

Acton, Richard

1991 "The Magic of Undiscouraged Effort: The Death Penalty in Early Iowa, 1838–1878." *Annals of Iowa* 50(winter): 721–50.

American Bar Association (see Robbins 1990)

1990 "Toward a More Just and Effective System of Review in State Death Penalty Cases."

American College of Physicians et al.

1994 *Breach of Trust: Physician Participation in Executions in the United States.* Philadelphia: American College of Physicians.

Amnesty International (AI; see also Gray and Stanley 1989, and Harlow, Matas, and Rocamora 1995)

1987 *United States of America: The Death Penalty.* London: Amnesty International.

1989 *Report 1989.* London: Amnesty International.

1992 "United States of America: Developments on the Death Penalty During 1991." February. memorandum.

1993 "United States of America: Death Penalty Developments in 1992." April. memorandum.

1994 "United States of America: Developments on the Death Penalty During 1993." March. memorandum.

1995a *Report 1995.* London: Amnesty International.

1995b "United States of America: Developments on the Death Penalty During 1994." January. memorandum.

1996a "United States of America: Developments on the Death Penalty Since 1995." February. memorandum.

1996b "USA: The Death Penalty in Georgia: Racist, Arbitrary and Unfair." June. memorandum.

Amnesty International USA

1995 *The Machinery of Death: A Shocking Indictment of Capital Punishment in the United States.* New York: AIUSA.

Amsterdam, Anthony

1988 "Race and the Death Penalty." *Criminal Justice Ethics* 7(winter/spring): 2, 84, 86.

Bailey, William C., and Ruth D. Peterson

1994 "Murder, Capital Punishment, and Deterrence: A Review of the Evidence and an Examination of Police Killings." *Journal of Social Issues* 50(summer): 53–74.

Baldus, David

1995 "Keynote Address: The Death Penalty—Dialogue Between Law and Social Science." *Indiana Law Journal* 70(Fall): 1033–1042.

Baldus, David, Charles Pulaski Jr., and George G. Woodworth

1990 *Equal Justice and the Death Penalty: A Legal and Empirical Analysis.* Boston: Northeastern University Press.

1994a "False Attacks on the Racial Justice Act." *Des Moines Register,* 7 June, 9A.

1994b "Reflections on the 'Inevitability' of Racial Discrimination in Capital Sentencing and the 'Impossibility' of Its Prevention." *Washington & Lee Law Review* 51(spring): 359–430.

Beccaria, Cesare

1764 *On Crimes and Punishments,* tr. Richard Davies. In Richard Bellamy, ed., *On Crimes and Punishments and Other Writings,* Cambridge: Cambridge University Press, pp. 1–113.

Bedau, H. A.

1968 "The Right to Life." *The Monist* 52(October): 550–72.

1970 "Deterrence and the Death Penalty: A Reconsideration." *Journal of Criminal Law, Criminology, and Police Science* 61:539–48.

1976 "Felony Murder Rape and the Mandatory Death Penalty: A Study in Discretionary Justice." *Suffolk University Law Review* 10(spring): 493–520

1977 *The Courts, the Constitution, and Capital Punishment.* Lexington, Mass.: Lexington Books.

1980 "The 1964 Death Penalty Referendum in Oregon: Notes from a Participant–Observer." *Crime & Delinquency* 26(October): 528–36. Reprinted in Bedau 1987a.

1983 "Berger's Defense of the Death Penalty: How Not to Read the Constitution." *Michigan Law Review* 81(March): 1152–65.

1985a "*Gregg v. Georgia* and the 'New' Death Penalty." *Criminal Justice Ethics* 4(summer/fall): 3–17. Reprinted in Bedau 1987a.

1985b "Thinking of the Death Penalty as a Cruel and Unnusual Punishment." *University of California Davis Law Review* 18(summer): 873–925. Reprinted in Bedau 1987a.

1987a *Death Is Different: Studies in the Morality, Law, and Politics of Capital Punishment.* Boston: Northeastern University Press.

1987b "Objections to the Death Penalty from the Moral Point of View." *Revue internationale de droit penal* 58(3e et 4e trimstres): 557–65.

1987c "Justice in Punishment and Assumption of Risks: Some Comments in Response to van den Haag." *Wayne State Law Review* 33(summer): 1423–34.
1990a "Cruel and Unusual Punishment." *Christian Social Action,* November, pp. 7–9.
1990b "Imprisonment vs. Death: Does Avoiding Schwarzschild's Paradox Lead to Sheleff's Dilemma?" *Albany Law Review* 54:481–95.
1990–91 "The Decline of Executive Clemency in Capital Cases." *New York University Review of Law & Social Change* 18:255–72.
1991 "The Death Penalty in America: Yesterday and Today." *Dickenson Law Review* 95(summer): 759–72.
1992a *The Case Against the Death Penalty.* 4th ed. New York: American Civil Liberties Union.
1992b "The Eighth Amendment, Human Dignity, and the Death Penalty." In Michael J. Meyer and William A. Parent, eds., *The Constitution of Rights: Human Dignity and American Values.* Ithaca, N.Y.: Cornell University Press, pp. 145–77.
1992c "Reflections on Psychiatry and the Death Penalty." In Anthony Kales, Chester M. Pierce, and Milton Greenblatt, eds., *The Mosaic of Contemporary Psychiatry in Perspective,* New York: Springer, pp. 44–52.
1993 "Capital Punishment." In Tom Regan, ed., *Matters of Life and Death: New Introductory Essays in Moral Philosophy,* 3d ed. New York: McGraw Hill, pp. 160–91.
1994a "American Populism and the Death Penalty: Witnesses to an Execution." *Howard Journal of Criminal Justice* 33(November): 289–303.
1994b "The Gravest Errors in Capital Cases: Convicting the Innocent." In Jarmila Bednarikova and Frank C. Chapman II, eds., *Essays in Honour of Jan Stepan,* Zurich: Schulthess Polygraphischer Verlag, pp. 275–83.
1995 "Dangerous Liaisons," *Index on Censorship* 24(March/April): 108–16.
1996a "Interpreting the Eighth Amendment: Principled vs. Populist Strategies." *Cooley Law Review,* forthcoming.
1996b "The United States of America." In Hodgkinson and Rutherford 1996:45–76.
1997 "Book review [of Marquart, Ekland-Olson, and Sorenson 1994]." In Schabas ed. 1997, forthcoming

Bedau, H. A., ed.
1964 *The Death Penalty in America: An Anthology.* New York: Doubleday Anchor.
1982 *The Death Penalty in America,* 3d ed. New York: Oxford University Press.

Bedau, H. A., and Chester M. Pierce, eds.
1976 *Capital Punishment in the United States.* New York: AMS Press.

Bedau, H. A., and Michael L. Radelet
1987 "Miscarriages of Justice in Potentially Capital Cases," *Stanford Law Review* 40(November): 21–179.
1988 "The Myth of Infallibility: A Reply to Markman and Cassell." *Stanford Law Review* 41(November): 161–70.

Bedau, H. A., and Constance E. Putnam
1996 "False Confessions and Other Follies." In Connery 1996: 69–83.

Bennett, James V.
1958 "A Historic Move: Delaware Abolishes Capital Punishment." *American Bar Association Journal* 44(November): 1053–54.

Bentele, Ursula
1985 ''The Death Penalty in Georgia: Still Arbitrary.'' *Washington University Law Quarterly* 62:573–646.

Berger, Raoul
1982 *Death Penalties: The Supreme Court's Obstacle Course.* Cambridge: Harvard University Press.

Berger, Vada, et al.
1989 ''Too Much Justice: A Legislative Response to *McCleskey v. Kemp.*'' *Harvard Civil Rights-Civil Liberties Law Review* 24:437–528.

Berger, Vivian
1988 ''Rolling the Dice to Decide Who Dies.'' *New York State Bar Journal* (October): 32–37.
1990 ''Justice Delayed or Justice Denied?—A Comment on Recent Proposals to Reform Death Penalty Habeas Corpus.'' *Columbia Law Review* 90:1665–714.
1992 ''*Payne* and Suffering—A Personal Reflection and a Victim-Centered Critique.'' *Florida State University Law Review* 28(summer): 21–66.
1994 ''*Herrera v. Collins:* The Gateway of Innocence for Death-Sentenced Prisoners Leads Nowhere.'' *William & Mary Law Review* 35(spring): 943–1023.

Berk, Richard A., Robert Wise, and Jack Boger
1993a ''Chance and the Death Penalty.'' *Law & Society Review* 27:89–110.
1993b ''Rejoinder.'' *Law & Society Review* 27:125–27.

Berkman, Harvey
1995 ''Costs Mount for Indigent Defense.'' *The National Law Journal,* 7 August, p. A18.

Berkson, Larry Charles
1975 *The Concept of Cruel and Unusual Punishment.* Lexington, Mass.: D. C. Heath.

Berns, Walter
1979 *For Capital Punishment: Crime and the Morality of the Death Penalty.* New York: Basic Books.

Biddle, Frederic M.
1994 ''TV's Role Part of Debate on Capital Punishment.'' *Boston Globe,* 10 May, pp. 1, 12.

Bienen, Leigh B., et al.
1988 ''The Reimposition of Capital Punishment in New Jersey: The Role of Prosecutorial Discretion.'' *Rutgers Law Review* 41(fall): 27–372.

Bigel, Alan I.
1991 ''William H. Rehnquist on Capital Punishment.'' *Ohio Northern Law Review* 17:729–69.
1994 ''Justices William J. Brennan Jr. and Thurgood Marshall on Capital Punishment: Its Constitutionality, Morality, Deterrent Effect, and Interpretation by the Court.'' *Notre Dame Journal of Law, Ethics, & Public Policy* 8:11–164.

Bilionis, Louis D.

1991 ''Moral Appropriateness, Capital Punishment, and the *Lockett* Doctrine.'' *Journal of Criminal Law and Criminology* 82(summer): 283–333.

1993 ''Legitimating Death.'' *Michigan Law Review* 91(June): 1643–1702.

Black, Charles L. Jr.

1981 *Capital Punishment: The Inevitability of Caprice and Mistake.* 2d ed. (1st ed., 1974) New York: W.W. Norton.

Blaine, Quentin

1986 '' 'Shall Surely Be Put To Death:' Capital Punishment in New Hampshire, 1623–1985.'' *New Hampshire Bar Journal* 27(spring): 132–54.

Blaustein, Susan

1994 ''Witness to Another Execution.'' *Harper's,* May:53–62.

Blum, Stephen A.

1992 ''Public Executions: Understanding the 'Cruel and Unusual Punishment' Clause.'' *Hastings Constitutional Law Quarterly* 19(winter): 413–55.

Blume, John, and William Pratt

1990–91 ''Understanding *Teague v. Lane.*'' *New York University Review of Law and Social Change* 18:325–56.

Boaz, Julia E.

1985 ''Summary Process and the Rule of Law: Expediting Death Penalty Cases in the Federal Courts.'' *Yale Law Journal* 95:349–70.

Bohm, Robert M.

1991a ''American Death Penalty Opinion, 1936–1986: A Critical Examination of Gallup Polls.'' In Bohm ed. 1991b:113–42.

———, ed.

1991b *The Death Penalty in America: Current Research.* Cincinnati, OH: Anderson Publishing Co.

Bork, Robert H.

1992 ''An Outbreak of Judicial Disobedience.'' *Wall Street Journal,* 29 April, p. A19.

Bowers, William J.

1990 ''The Death Penalty's Shaky Support.'' *New York Times,* 28 May, p. 21.

1993 ''Capital Punishment and Contemporary Values: People's Misgivings and the Court's Misperceptions.'' *Law & Society Review* 27:157–75.

1995 ''The Capital Jury Project: Rationale, Design, and Early Findings.'' *Indiana Law Journal* 70(fall): 1043–1102.

1996 ''The Capital Jury: Is it Tilted Toward Death?'' *Judicature* 79(March/April): 220–24.

Bowers, William J., and Patricia H. Dugan

1993a ''In Their Own Words: How Capital Jurors Explain Their Life or Death Sentencing Decisions.'' College of Criminal Justice, Northeastern University. May.

1993b ''Critical Issues in Capital Jury Decision Making—Preliminary Findings.'' College of Criminal Justice, Northeastern University. October, p. 11.

Bowers, William J., and Heather S. MacAskill

1992 "Jurors Response to the Defendant's Testimony, or Lack Thereof." College of Criminal Justice, Northeastern University. Unpublished memorandum. November.

Bowers, William J., and Benjamin D. Steiner

1996 "The Pernicious Myth of Early Release From Prison for Convicted First Degree Murderers Not Sentenced to Death." Paper presented in July to the annual meeting of the Law and Society Association.

Bowers, William J., and Margaret Vandiver

1991 "The Capital Juror Project: Background and Research Design." Justice Research Center, Northeastern University. Unpublished memorandum. July.

1992 "In Their Own Words: How Capital Jurors Explain Their Life or Death Sentencing Decisions." Justice Research Center, Northeastern University. Unpublished memorandum. May.

Bowers, William J., Margaret Vandiver, and Patricia H. Dugan.

1992 "In Their Own Words: How Capital Jurors Explain Their Life or Death Sentencing Decisions." College of Criminal Justice, Northeastern University. Unpublished memorandum. November.

1994 "A New Look at Public Opinion on Capital Punishment: What Citizens and Legislators Prefer." *American Journal of Criminal Law* 22(fall): 77–150.

Bowers, William J., and Andrea Waldo

1992 " 'Proof Beyond a Reasonable Doubt': A Review of Jurors Thoughts." College of Criminal Justice, Northeastern University. Unpublished memorandum. November.

Brennan, William J., Jr.

1986 "Constitutional Adjudication and the Death Penalty: A View from the Court." *Harvard Law Review* 100(December): 313–31.

1987 "Color-Blind, Creed-Blind, Status-Blind, Sex-Blind." *Human Rights,* 14(winter): 30–37.

1994 "Forword: Neither Victims Nor Executioners." *Notre Dame Journal of Law, Ethics, & Public Policy* 8:1–10.

Bright, Stephen B.

1990 "Death By Lottery—Procedural Bar of Constitutional Claims in Capital Cases Due to Inadequate Representation of Indigent Defendants." *West Virginia Law Review* 92(spring): 679–725.

1992 "In Defense of Life: Enforcing the Bill of Rights on Behalf of Poor, Minority and Disadvantaged Persons Facing the Death Penalty." *Missouri Law Review* 57:849–70.

1993 Testimony on Habeas Corpus. House of Representatives, Committee on Judiciary, Subcommittee on Civil and Criminal Rights. May.

1994 "Counsel for the Poor: The Death Sentence Not for the Worst Crime but for the Worst Lawyer." *Yale Law Journal* 103(May): 1835–83.

1995a "Discrimination, Death and Denial: The Tolerance of Racial Discrimination in Infliction of the Death Penalty." *Santa Clara Law Review* 35:433–83.

1995b "The Politics of Crime and the Death Penalty: Not 'Soft on Crime,' but Hard on the Bill of Rights." *Saint Louis University Law Journal* 39(winter): 479–503.

Bright, Stephen B., and Patrick J. Keenan

1995 "Judges and the Politics of Death: Deciding Between the Bill of Rights and the Next Election in Capital Cases." *Boston University Law Review* 75(May): 759–835.

Brooke, James

1996 "Utah Debates Firing Squads In Clash of Past and Present." *New York Times,* 14 January, p. 16.

Brown, David

1995 "A Man is Executed in Carolina; 2d of a White Who Killed a Black." *Boston Globe,* 25 January, p. 3.

Brown, Edmund (Pat)

1989 *Public Justice, Private Mercy: A Governor's Education on Death Row.* New York: Wiedenfeld and Nicholson.

Bruck, David.

1983 "Decisions of Death," *The New Republic,* 12 December, pp. 18–25.

1985 "The Death Penalty: An Exchange." *The New Republic,* 20 May, pp. 20–21.

Bruck, David, and Kevin McNally

1996 "Federal Death Penalty Prosecutions, 1988–96." April. Unpublished memorandum.

Brundage, W. Fitzhugh

1993 *Lynching in the New South: Georgia and Virginia, 1880–1930.* Urbana: University of Illinois Press.

Bye, Raymond T.

1919 *Capital Punishment in the United States.* Philadelphia: Committee on Philanthropic Labor of Philadelphia Yearly Meeting of Friends.

Cabana, Donald

1996 *Death At Midnight: The Confession of An Executioner.* Boston: Northeastern University Press.

Calabresi, Steven G., and Gary Lawson

1992 "Equity and Hierarchy: Reflections on the Harris Execution." *Yale Law Journal* 102(October): 255–79

Caminker, Evan and Erwin Chemerinsky.

1992 "The Lawless Execution of Robert Alton Harris." *Yale Law Journal* 102(October): 225–54.

Carlson, Norman A.

1983 Testimony. In Senate 1993b:4–9.

Carroll, John L.

1988 "Death Row—Hope for the Future." In Haas and Inciardi 1988:269–88.

Carter, Dan T.

1979 *Scottsboro: A Tragedy of the American South.* (1st ed., 1969) Baton Rouge: Louisiana State University Press.

Cassell, Paul

1993 Testimony and prepared statement. In Senate 1993b:76–93.

Catholics Against Capital Punishment

1994 "What the U.S. Catholic Bishops Have Said About the Death Penalty (1980–1994)." May. Memorandum.

Chartrand, Sabra

1994 "Given a Push, Maryland Alters Its Death Penalty." *New York Times,* 25 March, p. B18.

Chilton, Roland, and Jim Galvin

1985 "Race, Crime, and Criminal Justice." *Crime & Delinquency* 31(January): 3–159.

Citizens and Parliamentarians Campaign for the Abolition of the Death Penalty Worldwide by 2000

1994 *Hands Off Cain.* Rome: Supplemento at N.1 di Notizie Radicali, 1 October, 36 pp.

Clines, Francis X.

1992 "The Grim List of Those Put to Death." *New York Times,* 18 November, p. A16.

Cobin, Herbert

1964 "Abolition and Restoration of the Death Penalty in Delaware." In Bedau, ed. 1964: 359–73.

Colburn, Don

1990 "The Risky Lives of Young Black Men." *Washington Post Health,* 18–25 December, p. 7.

Conference

1995 "The Death Penalty in the Twenty-First Century." *American University Law Review* 45(December): 239–352.

Connery, Donald S., ed.

1996 *Convicting the Innocent: The Story of a Murder, a False Confession, and the Struggle to Free a "Wrong Man."* Cambridge, Mass.: Brookline Books.

Conrad, John, and Ernest van den Haag

1983 *The Death Penalty: A Debate.* New York: Plenum.

Constanzo, Mark

1997 *Just Revenge: Costs and Consequences of the Death Penalty.* New York: St. Martin's Press.

Conway, David A.

1974 "Capital Punishment and Deterrence: Some Considerations in Dialogue Form." *Philosophy & Public Affairs* 3(summer): 431–33.

Cook, Philip J., and Donna B. Slawson

1993 *The Costs of Processing Murder Cases in North Carolina.* Durham, N.C.: Terry Sanford Institute of Public Policy, Duke University.

Cortner, Richard C.

1988 *A Mob Intent on Death: The NAACP and the Arkansas Riot Cases.* Middletown, Conn.: Wesleyan University Press.

Cottrol, Robert J.

1985 "Static History and Brittle Jurisprudence: Raoul Berger and the Problem of Constitutional Methodology." *Boston College Law Review* 26(March): 353–87.

Coyle, Marcia
1995 "Republicans Take Aim At Death Row Lawyers." *National Law Journal,* 18 September, p. A1.
1996 "Death Resource Centers Reborn as Private Groups." *National Law Journal,* 15 January, p. A9.

Coyle, Marcia, Fred Strasser, and Marianne Lavelle
1990 "Fatal Defense." *National Law Journal,* 11 June, pp. 30–38, 40–42, 44.

Coyne, Randall, and Lyn Entzeroth
1994 *Capital Punishment and the Judicial Process.* Durham, N.C.: Carolina Academic Press.
1955 *Capital Punishment and the Judicial Process: 1995 Supplement.* Durham, N.C.: Carolina Academic Press.

Curran, William J., and Ward Casscells
1980 "The Ethics of Medical Participation in Capital Punishment by Intravenous Drug Injection." *New England Journal of Medicine* 302 (21 June): 226–30.

Daly, Martin, and Margo Wilson
1988 *Homicide.* New York: Aldine DeGruyter.

Dann, Robert H.
1952 "Capital Punishment in Oregon." In Sellin ed. 1952:110–14.

Danto, Bruce L., John Bruhns, and Austin K. Kutscher, eds.
1982 *The Human Side of Homicide.* New York: Columbia University Press.

Darrow, Clarence
1991 "The Plea of Clarence Darrow . . . In Defense of Richard Loeb and Nathan Leopole . . ." [1924]. In Darrow, *Clarence Darrow on Capital Punishment.* Chicago: Chicago Historical Bookworks.

Davis, Michael
1981 "Death, Deterrence, and the Method of Common Sense." *Social Theory and Practice* 7(summer): 145–77.
1995 "The State's Dr. Death: What's Unethical About Physicians Helping at Executions?" *Social Theory and Practice* 21(spring): 31–60. Reprinted in Davis 1996.
1996 *Justice in the Shadow of Death: Rethinking Capital and Lesser Punishments* Lanham, Md.: Rowman & Littlefield.

Death Penalty Information Center (DPIC; see also Richard Dieter)
1991 *Chattahoochee Judicial District: The Buckle on the Death Belt—The Death Penalty in Microcosm.* Washington, D.C.: Death Penalty Information Center.

Deets, Lee Emerson
1948 "Changes in Capital Punishment Policy Since 1939." *Journal of Criminal Law, Criminology, and Police Science* 38(March–April): 584–94.

Denno, Deborah
1994a "Is Electrocution an Unconstitutional Method of Execution? The Engineering of Death over the Century." *William and Mary Law Review* 35(winter): 551–692.
1994b "Testing *Penry* and Its Progeny." *American Journal of Criminal Law* 22(fall): 1–75.
1996 "Are Executions Constitutional?" *Iowa Law Review* 82: forthcoming.

Dershowitz, Alan
1982 *The Best Defense.* New York: Random House.

Dicks, Shirley, ed.
1991 *Congregation of the Condemned: Voices Against the Death Penalty.* Buffalo, N.Y.: Prometheus Books.

Dieter, Richard C. (see also DPIC)
1993 *Sentencing For Life: Americans Embrace Alternatives to the Death Penalty.* Washington, D.C.: Death Penalty Information Center.
1995a *On the Front Line: Law Enforcement Views on the Death Penalty.* Washington, D.C.: Death Penalty Information Center.
1995b *With Justice for Few: The Growing Crisis in Death Penalty Representation.* Washington, D.C.: Death Penalty Information Center.

Dingerson, Leigh
1990–91 ''Reclaiming the Gavel: Making Sense out of the Death Penalty Debate in State Legislatures.'' *New York University Review of Law and Social Change* 18:873–86.

Dix, George E.
1981 ''Expert Prediction Testimony in Capital Sentencing: Evidentiary and Constitutional Considerations.'' *American Criminal Law Review* 19(summer): 1–48.

Dorin, Dennis D.
1981 ''Two Different Worlds: Criminologists, Justices and Racial Discrimination.'' *Journal of Criminal Law and Criminology* 72(winter): 1667–98.

Dressner, Richard B., and Glenn C. Altschuler
1975 ''Sentiment and Statistics in the Progressive Era: The Debate on Capital Punishment in New York.'' *New York History* 56(April): 191–209.

Drinan, Robert F.
1994 ''Catholics and the Death Penalty.'' *America* 18(June): 13–14.

Eckholm, Eric
1995 ''Studies Find Death Penalty Tied to Race of the Victims.'' *New York Times*, 24 February, pp. B1, B4.

Edwards, Don, and John Conyers
1995 ''The Racial Justice Act—A Simple Matter of Justice.'' *University of Dayton Law Review* 20:699–723.

Eisenberg, Theodore, and Martin T. Wells
1993 ''Deadly Confusion: Juror Instructions in Capital Cases.'' *Cornell Law Review* 79(November): 1–17.

Eldred, Charles Kenneth
1994 ''The New Federal Death Penalties.'' *American Journal of Criminal Law* 22(fall): 293–306.

Ellsworth, Phoebe C.
1988 ''Unpleasant Facts: The Supreme Court's Response to Empirical Research.'' In Haas and Inciardi 1988:177–212.

Ellsworth, Phoebe C. and Samuel R. Gross
1994 "Hardening of the Attitudes: Americans' Views on the Death Penalty." *Journal of Social Issues* 50(summer): 19–52.

Ellsworth, Phoebe C. and Lee Ross
1983 "Public Opinion and Capital Punishment: A Close Examination of the Views of Abolitionists and Retentionists." *Crime & Delinquency* 29(January): 116–69.

Endres, Michael E.
1985 *The Morality of Capital Punishment: Equal Justice Under the Law?* Mystic, Conn.: Twenty-Third Publications.

Espy, Watt (see Clines 1992)

Evans, Robert
1996 "US Death Sentences Arbitrary, Biased, Jurists Say." *Boston Globe,* 17 July, p. A6.

Fellman, David
1992 "Habeas corpus." In Kermit L. Hall, ed., *The Oxford Companion to the Supreme Court of the United States.* New York: Oxford University Press, pp. 357–58.

Filler, Louis B.
1952 "Movements to Abolish the Death Penalty in the United States." In Sellin ed. 1952:124–36.

Finckenauer, James O.
1988 "Public Support for the Death Penalty: Retribution as Just Deserts or Retribution as Revenge?" *Justice Quarterly* 5(March): 81–100.

Foley, Timothy
1984 "The Ongoing Debate: The Constitutionality of Death." *Harvard Civil Rights-Civil Liberties Law Review* 19:246–60.

Fox, James Alan
1995 "A Disturbing Trend in Youth Crime." *Boston Globe,* 1 June, p. 19.

Fox, James Alan, and Michael L. Radelet
1989 "Persistent Flaws in Econometric Studies of the Deterrent Effect of the Death Penalty." *Loyola of Los Angeles Law Review* 23(November): 29–44.

Fox, James Alan, Michael L. Radelet, and Julie Bonsteel
1990–91 "Death Penalty Opinion in the Post-*Furman* Years." *New York University Review of Law and Social Change* 18:499–528.

Frady, Marshall
1993 "Death in Arkansas." *New Yorker,* 22 February, pp. 105–118, 119–26, 128–33.

Freinkel, Andrew, Cheryl Koopman, and David Spiegel
1994 "Dissociative Symptoms in Media Eyewitnesses of an Execution." *American Journal of Psychiatry* 151(September): 1135–39

Galliher, John F., Gregory Ray, and Brent Cook

1992 ''Abolition and Reinstatement of Capital Punishment During the Early Progressive Era and Early 20th Century.'' *Journal of Criminal Law and Criminology* 83(fall): 538–76.

1995 ''Unsuccessful Death Penalty Abolition Campaigns [in the United States], 1800–1970.'' Unpublished typescript.

Gardner, Martin R.

1979a ''Mormonism and Capital Punishment: A Doctrinal Perspective, Past and Present.'' *Dialogue: A Journal of Mormon Thought* 12(spring): 9–26.

1979b ''Illicit Legislative Motivation as a Sufficient Condition for Unconstitutionality Under the Establishment Clause—A Case for Consideration: The Utah Firing Squad.'' *Washington University Law Review* (spring): 435–99.

Garnett, Richard W.

1994 ''Depravity Thrice Removed: Using the 'Heinous, Cruel, or Depraved' Factor to Aggravate Convictions of Nontriggermen Accomplices in Capital Cases.'' *Yale Law Journal* 103(June): 2471–501.

Gattrell, V. A. C.

1994 *The Hanging Tree: Execution and the English People 1770–1868.* Oxford: Oxford University Press.

Gey, Steven G.

1992 ''Justice Scalia's Death Penalty.'' *Florida State University Law Review* 20(summer): 67–132.

Gillespie, Ed, and Bob Schellhas

1994 *Contract With America: The Bold Plan by Rep. Newt Gingrich, Rep. Dick Armey, and the House Republicans to Change the Nation.* New York: Random House.

Gillers, Stephen

1983 ''Berger Redux.'' *Yale Law Journal* 92:731–48.

Givelber, Dan

1994 ''The New Law of Murder.'' *Indiana Law Journal* 69(spring): 375–423.

Glover, Jonathan

1977 *Causing Death and Saving Lives.* Harmondsworth, Eng.: Penguin Books.

Goldberg, Arthur J.

1978 ''The Death Penalty for Rape.'' *Hastings Constitutional Law Quarterly* 5: 1–13.

1986 ''Memorandum to the Conference *Re:* Capital Punishment, October Term, 1963.'' *South Texas Law Review* 27:493–506.

Goldstein, Steven M.

1990 ''Expanding the Federal Habeas Corpus Review Process in Capital Cases: An Examination of Recent Proposals.'' *Capitol University Law Review* 19(summer): 599–648.

1990–91 ''Chipping Away at the Great Writ: Will Death Sentenced Federal Habeas Corpus Petitioners be Able to Seek and Utilize Changes in the Law?'' *New York University Review of Law and Social Change* 18:357–414.

Goodman, Ellen
1984 "Tuning Out TV Executions." *Boston Globe,* 20 March, p. 15.

Goodman, James
1994 *Stories of Scottsboro: The Rape Case That Shocked 1930's America and Revived the Struggle for Equality.* New York: Pantheon.

Goodpaster, Gary
1983 "The Trial for Life: Effective Assistance of Counsel in Death Penalty Cases." *New York University Law Review* 58(May): 299–362.

Gorecki, Jan
1983 *Capital Punishment: Criminal Law and Social Evolution.* New York: Columbia University Press.

Gottlieb, Gerald
1961 "Testing the Death Penalty." *Southern California Law Review* 34(spring): 268–81.

Gow, Haven Bradford
1985 "Should Religious Support Capital Punishment?" *Human Events,* 12 March.

Gray, Ian, and Moira Stanley, eds.
1989 *A Punishment in Search of a Crime: Americans Speak Out Against the Death Penalty.* New York: Avon.

Greenberg, Jack
1982 "Capital Punishment as a System." *Yale Law Journal* 91(April): 908–36.
1986 "Against the American System of Capital Punishment." *Harvard Law Review* 99(May): 1670–80.

Greenhouse, Linda
1992 "Justices Weigh Limiting U.S. Courts." *New York Times,* 25 March, p. A16.
1994a "Death Penalty is Renounced by Blackmun." *New York Times,* 23 February, p. A1.
1994b "A Capacity to Change as Well as to Challenge." *New York Times,* 27 February, p. E4.

Greene, Norman, et al.
1995 "The O.J. Simpson Case and Capital Punishment." *Howard Law Journal* 38(spring): 247–96.

Gross, Bob
1991 *The Death Penalty: A Guide for Christians.* Elgin, Ill.: faithQuest.

Gross, Samuel R.
1993 "The Romance of Revenge: Capital Punishment in America." *Studies in Law, Politics, and Society* 13:71–104.
1996 "The Risks of Death: Sources of Error in Capital Prosecutions." *Buffalo Law Review,* forthcoming

Guillot, Ellen Elizabeth
1952 "Abolition and Restoration of the Death Penalty in Missouri." In Sellin ed. 1952:105–09.

Haas, Kenneth C. and James A. Inciardi, eds.
1988 *Challenging Capital Punishment: Legal and Social Science Approaches.* Newbury Park, Calif.: Sage.

Haines, Herb
1992 "Flawed Executions, the Anti-Death Penalty Movement, and the Politics of Capital Punishment." *Social Problems* 39(May): 125–38.
1996 *Against Capital Punishment: The Anti-Death Penalty Movement in America, 1972–94.* New York: Oxford University Press.

Haney, Craig
1995 "Taking Capital Jurors Seriously." *Indiana Law Journal* 70(fall): 1223–55.

Haney, Craig, and Deana Dorman Logan
1994 "Broken Promise: The Supreme Court's Response to Social Science Research on Capital Punishment." *Journal of Social Issues* 50(summer): 75–102.

Haney, Craig, Lorelei Sontag, and Sally Costanzo
1994 "Deciding to Take Life: Capital Juries, Sentencing Instructions, and the Jurisprudence of Death." *Journal of Social Issues* 50(summer): 149–76.

Hans, Valerie P.
1995 "How Juries Decide Death: The Contributions of the Capital Jury Project." *Indiana Law Journal* 70(fall): 1233–1240.

Hare, Glenn, publisher
1989– *Death Row.* Carlsbad, Calif.: Glenn Hare Publications, annually.

Harlow, Enid, David Matas, and Jane Rocamora, eds.
1995 *The Machinery of Death: A Shocking Indictment of Capital Punishment in the United States.* New York: Amnesty International USA.

Harris, Philip W.
1986 "Oversimplification and Error in Public Opinion Surveys on Capital Punishment." *Justice Quarterly* 3(December): 429–55.

Hayner, Norman S., and John R. Craynor.
1952 "The Death Penalty in Washington State." In Sellin ed. 1952:101–104.

Henberg, Marvin
1990 *Retribution: Evil for Evil in Ethics, Law, and Literature.* Philadelphia: Temple University Press.

Hentoff, Nat
1991 "Execution in Your Living Room." *The Progressive,* November, pp. 16–17.

Hillman, Harold
1993 "The Possible Pain Experienced During Execution by Different Methods." *Perception* 22:745–53.

Hodgkinson, Peter, and Andrew Rutherford, eds.
1996 *Capital Punishment: Global Issues and Prospects.* London: Waterside Press.

Hodgkinson, Peter, et al.
1996 *Capital Punishment in the United States of America: A Review of the Issues.* London: Parliamentary Human Rights Group.

Hoffman, Jan

1992 "Wanted: A Few Good Lawyers for Tough Cases in 'the Deathbelt.' " *New York Times,* 10 May, p. E7.

Hoffman, Joseph L.

1992 "Starting from Scratch: Rethinking Federal Habeas Review of Death Penalty Cases." *Florida State University Law Review* 20(summer): 133–62.

1995 "Where's the Buck?—Juror Misperception of Sentencing Responsibility in Death Penalty Cases." *Indiana Law Journal* 70(fall): 1137–60.

Holland, Nancy

1985 "Death Row Conditions: Progression Toward Constitutional Protections." *Akron Law Review* 19:293–310.

Holleman, Joe

1995 "Hard Time in Hell." *San Francisco Examiner,* 25 June, p. A13.

Holmes, Ronald M., and Stephen T. Holmes

1994 *Murder in America.* Thousand Oaks, Calif.: Sage.

Hood, Roger

1989 *The Death Penalty: A World-wide Perspective.* Oxford: Clarendon Press. 2d ed, 1996.

House, H. Wayne.

1991 "In Favor of the Death Penalty." In House and Yoder 1991:1–104.

House, H. Wayne, and John Howard Yoder

1991 *The Death Penalty Debate.* Dallas: Word Publishing.

Hurka, Thomas

1982 "Rights and Capital Punishment." Reprinted in David Theo Goldberg, ed., *Ethical Theory and Social Issues: Historical Texts and Contemporary Readings.* Orlando: Harcourt Brace, 1995, pp. 496–504.

Ingle, Joseph B.

1990 *Last Rites: 13 Encounters with the State's Justice.* Nashville: Abingdon.

International Commission of Jurists

1996 Administration of the Death Penalty in the United States: Report of a Mission. Geneva, Switz.: International Commission of Jurists.

Ita, Timothy A.

1983 "Habeas Corpus—Expedited Appellate Review of Habeas Corpus Petitions Brought by Death-Sentenced State Prisoners." *Journal of Criminal Law and Criminology* 74:1404–24.

Jacobs, Sonia

1995 "A Survivor's Tale." In Harlow, Matas, and Rocamora 1995:152–55.

Jeffries, John C. Jr.

1994 *Justice Lewis F. Powell Jr.: A Biography.* New York: Scribners.

Johnson, Robert

1990 *Death Work: A Study of the Modern Execution Process.* Pacific Grove, Calif.: Brooks/Cole.

Johnson, Sheri Lynn

1988 "Unconscious Racism and the Criminal Law." *Cornell Law Review* 73: 1016–37.

Jones, Michael, and James Austin

1983 ''How Much Time Do Prisoners Really Serve?'' San Francisco: National Council on Crime and Delinquency. December, pp. 5–7.

Kalis, Peter J.

1983 ''Book Review [of Berger, *Death Penalties*]: Sense and Censure.'' *University of Pittsburgh Law Review* 44(spring): 635–46.

Kaplan, David A.

1990 ''The Fryers Club Convention.'' *Newsweek,* 27 August, pp. 54–55.

1991 '' 'Live from San Quentin . . . ' '' *Newsweek,* 1 April, p. 61.

Keedy, E. R.

1949 ''History of the Pennsylvania Statute Creating Degrees of Murder.'' *University of Pennsylvania Law Review* 97:749–77.

Kennedy, Randall L.

1988 ''*McCleskey v. Kemp:* Race, Capital Punishment, and the Supreme Court.'' *Harvard Law Review* 101(May): 1388–443.

Klein, Stephen P., and John E. Rolph

1991 ''Relationship of Offender and Victim Race to Death Sentences in California.'' *Jurimetrics* 32(fall): 33–48.

Kluger, Richard

1976 *Simple Justice: The History of Brown v. Board of Education and Black America's Struggle for Equality.* New York: Knopf.

Koch, Edward I.

1985a ''Death and Justice.'' *New Republic,* 15 April, pp. 12–15.

1985b ''The Death Penalty: An Exchange.'' *New Republic,* 20 May, p. 21.

Koch, Larry W., and John F. Galliher

1993 ''Michigan's Continuing Abolition of the Death Penalty and the Conceptual Components of Symbolic Legislation.'' *Social and Legal Studies* 2:323–46.

Koosed, Margery B., ed.

1996a *Capital Punishment, Vol. 1: The Philosophical, Moral, and Penological Debate over Capital Punishment.* New York: Garland.

1996b *Capital Punishment, Vol. 2: Capital Punishment Jurisprudence.* New York: Garland.

1996c *Capital Punishment, Vol. 3: Litigating Capital Cases.* New York: Garland.

Kroll, Michael A.

1990 ''The Final Days of Robert Alton Harris.'' *California Lawyer,* April, pp. 34–37, 86, 88–90, 92–94.

1991 ''I Oppose Existing Executions.'' *San Francisco Examiner,* 22 March, p. A-23.

Labaton, Stephen

1996 ''Bars on Death Row.'' *New York Times,* 19 April, p. B9.

Layson, Stephen K.

1985 ''Homicide and Deterrence: A Reexamination of the United States Time-Series Evidence.'' *Southern Economic Journal* 52(July): 68–89.

1986 Testimony and prepared statement. In House 1986:311–23.

Legal Defense Fund (LDF). See NAACP Legal Defense and Educational Fund

Leiser, Burton M.

1986 "Capital Punishment." In Leiser, *Liberty, Justice, and Morals: Contemporary Value Conflicts.* 3d ed. New York: Macmillan.

Lesser, Wendy

1993 *Pictures At an Execution: An Inquiry Into the Subject of Murder.* Cambridge, Mass.: Harvard University Press.

Levine, Murray

1984 "The Adversary Process and Social Science in the Courts: *Barefoot v. Estelle.*" *Journal of Psychiatry and the Law* 12:147–81.

Lewis, Anthony.

1995 "Cruel and Reckless." *New York Times,* 11 August, p. A29.

Liebman, Ellen

1985 "Appellate Review of Death Sentences: A Critique of Proportionality Review." *University of California Davis Law Review* 18:1433–80.

Liebman, James S.

1990–91 "More than 'Slightly Retro': The Rehnquist Court's Rout of Habeas Corpus Jurisdiction in *Teague v. Lane.*" *New York University Review of Law and Social Change* 18:537–636.

1992 "Apocalypse Next Time? The Anachronistic Attack on Habeas Corpus/Direct Review Parity." *Columbia Law Review* 92(December): 1997–2097.

Lincoln, James H.

1987 "The Everlasting Controversy: Michigan and the Death Penalty." *Wayne Law Review* 33:1765–90.

Linebaugh, Peter

1992 *The London Hanged: Crime and Civil Society in the Eighteenth Century.* Cambridge: Cambridge University Press.

Luginbuhl, James, and Julie Howe

1995 "Discretion in Capital Sentencing Instructions: Guided or Misguided?" *Indiana Law Journal* 70(fall): 1161–82.

Lungren, Daniel E., and Mark L. Krotoski

1992 "Public Policy Lessons from the Robert Alton Harris Case." *U. C. L. A. Law Review* 40:295–326.

1995 "The Racial Justice Act of 1994—Undermining Enforcement of the Death Penalty Without Promoting Racial Justice." *University of Dayton Law Review* 20:655–97.

Macartney, Jane

1996 "Chinese Condemn Hundreds Over Drugs." *Boston Globe,* 27 June, p. 2.

Mackey, Philip English

1974 " 'The Result May Be Glorious'—Anti-Gallows Movement in Rhode Island 1838–1852." *Rhode Island History* 33(February): 19–31.

1975 "Edward Livingston and the Origins of the Movement to Abolish Capital Punishment in America." *Louisiana History* 16(spring):145–66.

1982 *Hanging in the Balance: The Anti-Capital Punishment Movement in New York State, 1776–1861.* New York: Garland.

———, ed.
1976 *Voices Against Death: American Opposition to Capital Punishment, 1787–1975.* New York: Burt Franklin.

Margolick, David
1993 "Texas Death Row is Growing, but Fewer Lawyers Will Help." *New York Times,* 31 December, pp. A1, A23.

Markman, Stephen
1994 "Innocents on Death Row?" *National Review,* 12 September. pp. 72, 74, 77–78.

Markman, Stephen, and Paul G. Cassell
1988 "Protecting the Innocent: A Response to the Bedau-Radelet Study." *Stanford Law Review* 41(November): 121–60.

Marquart, James W., Sheldon Ekland-Olson, and Jonathan R. Sorensen
1989a "Gazing into the Crystal Ball: Can Jurors Accurately Predict Dangerousness in Capital Cases?" *Law and Society Review* 23:449–68.
1989b "A National Study of the *Furman*-Commuted Inmates: Assessing the Threat to Society From Capital Offenders." *Loyola of Los Angeles Law Review* 23(November): 5–28
1994 *The Rope, the Chair, and the Needle: Capital Punishment in Texas, 1923–1990.* Austin: University of Texas Press.

Marsel, Robert S.
1986 "Mr. Justice Arthur J. Goldberg and the Death Penalty: A Memorandum to the Conference." *South Texas Law Review* 27:467–92.

Marshall, Lawrence C.
1994 "Book Review: In Spite of Meese." *Journal of Criminal Law and Criminology* 85(summer): 261–80.

Marshall, Thurgood.
1986 "Remarks on the Death Penalty Made at the Judicial Conference of the Second Circuit." *Columbia Law Review* 86(January): 1–8.

Masur, Louis P.
1989 *Rites of Execution: Capital Punishment and the Transformation of American Culture, 1776–1865.* New York: Oxford University Press.

Mayell, Marvin S.
1984 "Eighth Amendment—Proportionality Review of Death Sentences Not Required." *Journal of Criminal Law and Criminology* 75:839–54.

McDowell, Gary
1983 "Book Review [R. Berger, *Death Penalties*]" *George Washington Law Review,* 51(May): 624–30.

McGovern, James R.
1982 *Anatomy of a Lynching: The Killing of Claude Neal.* Baton Rouge: Louisiana State University Press.

Megivern, James J.
1997 *The Death Penalty Appraised: A Chronology of Christian Loss and Retrieval.* Mahwah, N.J.: Paulist Press.

Mello, Michael

1991 "The Jurisdiction to Do Justice: Florida's Jury Override and the State Constitution." *Florida State University Law Review* 18(summer): 923–70.

1996 *Against the Death Penalty: The Relentless Dissents of Justices Brennan and Marshall.* Boston: Northeastern University Press.

Mello, Michael, and Ruthann Robson

1985 "Judge Over Jury: Florida's Practice of Imposing Death Over Life in Capital Cases." *Florida State University Law Review* 13(spring): 31–75.

Meltsner, Michael

1973 *Cruel and Unusual: The Supreme Court and Capital Punishment.* New York: Random House.

Merlo, Joan M. Riedy

1995 "Juvenile Violence and the Death Penalty." In Leonore Loeb Adler and Florence L. Denmark, eds., *Violence and the Prevention of Violence.* Westport, Conn.: Prager, pp. 110–17.

Miller, Arthur.

1992 "Get it Right. Privatize Executions." *New York Times,* 8 May, p. A31.

Miller, Kent S., and Michael L. Radelet

1993 *Executing the Mentally Ill: The Criminal Justice System and the Case of Alvin Ford.* Newbury Park, Calif.: Sage.

Moran, Richard

1985 "Invitation to an Execution—Death by Needle Isn't Easy." *Los Angeles Times,* 24 March, Pt. 4, p. 5.

Morgenthau, Robert M.

1995 "What Prosecutors Won't Tell You." *New York Times,* 7 February, p. A25.

Morris, Norval, and Gorden Hawkins

1977 *Letter to the President on Crime Control.* Chicago: University of Chicago Press.

Murphy, Jeffrie G.

1979 "Cruel and Unusual Punishment." In Murphy, *Retribution, Justice, and Therapy: Essays in the Philosophy of Law.* Dordrecht, Holland: D. Reidel, pp. 223–49.

Mydans, Seth

1990 "Homicide Rate Up for Young Black Men." *New York Times,* 7 December, p. A26.

Myrdal, Gunnar

1944 *An American Dilemma.* New York: Harper and Brothers.

NAACP Legal Defense and Educational Fund, Inc. (LDF)

1996 "Death Row, U.S.A." Spring. Memorandum, 43 pp. (Released quarterly).

Nakell, Barry, and Kenneth A. Hardy

1987 *The Arbitrariness of the Death Penalty.* Philadelphia: Temple University Press.

Narveson, Jan

1993 "Punishment, Capital and Otherwise." In Narveson, *Moral Matters,* Peterborough, Ontario: Broadview Press, pp. 80–107.

Nathanson, Stephen
1987 *An Eye for an Eye? The Morality of Punishing by Death.* Boston: Northeastern University Press.

National Coalition to Abolish the Death Penalty (NCADP)
1981– *Lifelines: Newsletter of the National Coalition Against the Death Penalty.* Released irregularly.

Newell, Gordon.
1965 "The Return of the Gallows." *Perspective* [Olympia, Washington] 9, no. 1: 6–8.

Newton, Brent E.
1994 "A Case Study in System Unfairness: The Texas Death Penalty, 1973–1994." *Texas Forum on Civil Liberties & Civil Rights* 1:1–37.

Noonan, John T.
1992 "Should State Executions Run on Schedule?" *New York Times,* 27 April, p. A17.

Nossiter, Adam
1995 "Balking Prosecutors: A Door Opens to Death Row Challenges." *New York Times,* 11 March, p. 27.

Nozick, Robert
1981 *Philosophical Explanations.* Cambridge, Mass.: Harvard University Press.

Otterbein, Keith F.
1986 *The Ultimate Coercive Sanction: A Cross-Cultural Study of Capital Punishment.* New Haven, Conn.: HRAF Press.

Panel Discussion
1996 "Is There Any Habeas Left in This Corpus?" *Loyola University Chicago Law Journal* 27(spring): 523–614.

Parfit, Derek
1984 *Reasons and Persons.* Oxford: Clarendon.

Paternoster, Raymond
1991 *Capital Punishment in America.* New York: Lexington Books/Macmillan.
1993 "Assessing Capriciousness in Capital Cases." *Law & Society Review* 27: 111–23.

Perlmutter, Martin
1996 "Desert and Capital Punishment." In John Arthur, ed., *Morality and Moral Controversies,* 4th ed. Upper Saddle River, N.J.: Prentice–Hall, pp. 390–97.

Perske, Robert
1995 *Deadly Innocence?* Nashville, Tenn.: Abingdon.

Pojman, Louis P.
1992 "Yes, the Death Penalty is Morally Permissible." In Pojman, *Philosophy: The Quest for Truth.* Belmont, Calif.: Wadsworth.

Pope John Paul II
1995 *The Gospel of Life (Evangelium Vitae).* New York: Random House.

Post, Albert
1944 "Early Efforts to Abolish Capital Punishment in Pennsylvania." *Pennsylvania Magazine of History & Biography* 68:38–43.

1945 ''The Anti-Gallows Movement in Ohio.'' *Ohio State Archaeological & Historical Quarterly* 54:105–12.

Poulos, John W.

1986 ''The Supreme Court, Capital Punishment, and the Substantive Criminal Law: The Rise and Fall of Mandatory Capital Punishment.'' *Arizona Law Review* 28:143–257.

1990 ''Capital Punishment, the Legal Process, and the Emergence of the Lucas Court in California.'' *University of California Davis Law Review* 23(winter): 157–332.

Prejean, Sister Helen

1993 *Dead Man Walking: An Eyewitness Account of the Death Penalty in the United States.* New York: Random House.

Primorac, Igor

1982 ''On Capital Punishment.'' *Israel Law Review* 17(April): 133–50.

Pugsley, Robert A.

1981 ''A Retributivist Argument Against the Death Penalty.'' *Hofstra Law Review* 9(summer): 1501–23.

Quindlen, Anna

1991 ''Death Watch.'' *New York Times,* 16 May, p. A23.

Radelet, Michael L.

1989a Testimony and prepared statement. In Senate 1989a:172–204.

1989b ''Executions of Whites for Crimes Against Blacks: Exceptions to the Rule?'' *Sociological Quarterly* 30:529–44.

1996 ''Physician Participation [in Capital Punishment].'' In Hodgkinson and Rutherford 1996:243–60.

Radelet, Michael L., Hugo Adam Bedau, and Constance E. Putnam

1992 *In Spite of Innocence: Erroneous Convictions in Capital Cases.* Boston: Northeastern University Press. [revised paperback ed. published in 1994]

Radelet, Michael L., William S. Lofquist, and Hugo Adam Bedau.

1996 ''Prisoners Released from Death Rows Since 1970 Because of Doubts About Their Guilt.'' *Cooley Law Review,* forthcoming.

Radelet, Michael L., and Michael Mello

1986 ''Executing Those Who Kill Blacks: An *Unusual* Case Study.'' *Mercer Law Review* 37(spring): 911–25.

Radelet, Michael L., and Glenn L. Pierce

1985 ''Race and Prosecutorial Discretion in Homicide Cases.'' *Law & Society Review* 19:587–621.

1991 ''Choosing Those Who Will Die: Race and the Death Penalty in Florida.'' *University of Florida Law Review* 43(January): 1–34.

Radelet, Michael L., and Margaret Vandiver

1988 *Capital Punishment in America: An Annotated Bibliography.* New York: Garland.

Radelet, Michael L., and Barbara A. Zsembik.

1993 ''Executive Clemency in Post-*Furman* Capital Cases.'' *University of Richmond Law Review* 27(winter): 289–314.

Radin, Margaret Jane

1980 "Cruel Punishment and Respect for Persons: Super Due Process for Death." *Southern California Law Review* 53(May): 1143–85.

1983 "Book Review [R. Berger, *Death Penalties*]" *Journal of Criminal Law and Criminology* 74(fall): 1115–22.

Rapaport, Elizabeth

1990 "Some Questions About Gender and the Death Penalty." *Golden Gate University Law Review* 20:501–65.

1991 "The Death Penalty and Gender Discrimination." *Law & Society Review* 25:367–83.

Riedel, Marc, Margaret A. Zahn, and Lois Felson Mock

1985 *The Nature and Patterns of American Homicide.* Washington, D.C.: National Institute of Justice.

Reimann, Jeffrey

1985 "Justice, Civilization, and the Death Penalty: Answering van den Haag." *Philosophy & Public Affairs* 14(spring): 115–48.

1988 "The Justice of the Death Penalty in an Unjust World." In Haas and Inciardi 1988:29–48.

1990 "The Death Penalty, Deterrence, and Horribleness: Reply to Michael Davis." *Social Theory and Practice* 16(summer): 261–72.

Reinhardt, Stephen

1992 "The Supreme Court, the Death Penalty, and the *Harris* Case." *Yale Law Journal* 102(October): 205–23.

Reinhold, Robert

1986 "Lawyers Shunning Death Row Cases." *New York Times,* 22 September, p. A15.

Richards, David A. J.

1983 "Constitutional Interpretation, History, and the Death Penalty: A Book Review." *California Law Review* 71(July): 1372–98.

Rise, Eric W.

1995 *The Martinsville Seven: Race, Rape, and Capital Punishment.* Charlottesville: University of Virginia Press.

Robbins, Ira P.

1990 "Toward a More Just and Effective System of Review in State Death Penalty Cases." *American University Law Review* 40(fall): 1–296.

Rodriguez, Joseph H., Michael L. Perlin, and John M. Apicella

1984 "Proportionality Review in New Jersey: An Indispensable Safeguard in the Capital Sentencing Process." *Rutgers Law Journal* 15(winter): 399–442.

Rogers, Alan

1993 " 'Under Sentence of Death': The Movement to Abolish Capital Punishment in Massachusetts, 1835–1849." *New England Quarterly* 66(March): 27–46.

Rosen, Richard A.

1986 "The 'Especially Heinous' Aggravating Circumstance in Capital Cases—The Standardless Standard." *North Carolina Law Review* 64(June): 941–92.

Rosenberg, Tina
1995 "The Deadliest D. A." *New York Times Magazine,* 16 July:20ff.

Rothman, Stanley, and Stephan Powers
1994 "Execution by Quota?" *The Public Interest,* summer: 3–17.

Rush, Benjamin
1787 "Abolish the Absurd and Unchristian Practice." In Mackey ed. 1976:2–13.

Russell, Gregory D.
1993 *The Death Penalty and Racial Bias: Overturning Supreme Court Assumptions.* Westport, Conn.: Greenwood Press.

Samuelson, Glenn W.
1969 "Why Was Capital Punishment Reinstated in Delaware?" *Journal of Criminal Law, Criminology, and Police Science* 60:148–51.

Sandys, Marla
1995 "Cross-Overs—Capital Jurors Who Change Their Minds about the Punishment: A Litmus Test for Sentencing Guidelines." *Indiana Law Journal* 70(fall): 1183–222.

Sarat, Austin.
1995 "Violence, Representation, and Responsibility in Capital Trials: The View From the Jury." *Indiana Law Journal* 70(fall): 1103–136.

Satre, Thomas W.
1991–92 "Human Dignity and Capital Punishment." *Journal of Philosophical Research* 16:229–45.

Saunders, John T.
1988 "Why the Numbers Should Sometimes Count." *Philosophy & Public Affairs* 17(winter): 3–14.

Savitz, Leonard D.
1955 "Capital Crimes as Defined in American Statutory Law." *Journal of Criminal Law, Criminology, and Police Science* 46(September–October): 355–61.
1958 "A Brief History of Capital Punishment in Pennsylvania." *Prison Journal* 38(October): 50–62.

Schabas, William A.
1993 *The Abolition of the Death Penalty in International Law.* Cambridge: Grotius Publications.
1994 "Execution Delayed, Execution Denied." *Criminal Law Forum* 5:180–93.
1995 "Invalid Reservations to the International Covenant on Civil and Political Rights: Is the United States Still a Party?" *Brooklyn Journal of International Law* 21:277–325.

———, ed.
1997 *International Sourcebook on Capital Punishment—1997.* Boston: Northeastern University Press.

Sellin, Thorsten
1959 *The Death Penalty.* Philadelphia: American Law Institute.
1980 *The Penalty of Death.* Beverely Hills, Calif.: Sage.

———, ed.

1952 "Murder and the Penalty of Death." *Annals of the American Academy of Political and Social Science* 284(November): 1–166.

1967 *Capital Punishment.* New York: Harper and Row.

Sharlitt, Joe H.

1989 *Fatal Error: The Miscarriage of Justice that Sealed the Rosenbergs' Fate.* New York: Scribner's.

Sheleff, Leon Shaskolsky

1987 *Ultimate Penalties: Capital Punishment, Life Imprisonment, Physical Torture.* Columbus: Ohio State University Press.

Sherman, Jonathan

1991 "Pictures At an Execution." *New York Times,* 3 May, p. A31.

Sherman, Steven J.

1995 "The Capital Jury Project: The Role of Responsibility and How Psychology can Inform the Law." *Indiana Law Journal* 70(fall): 1241–48.

Simon, James F.

1995 *The Center Holds: The Power Struggle Inside the Rehnquist Court.* New York: Simon & Schuster.

Slobogin, Christopher

1995 "Should Juries and the Death Penalty Mix? A Prediction about the Supreme Court's Answer." *Indiana Law Journal* 70(fall): 1249–70

Smothers, Ronald

1993 "A Shortage of Lawyers to Help the Condemned." *New York Times,* 4 June, p. A21.

1994 "Court-Appointed Defense Offers the Poor a Lawyer, But the Cost May Be High." *New York Times,* 14 February, p. A12.

Sorell, Tom

1987 *Moral Theory and Capital Punishment.* Oxford: Blackwells.

Southern Center for Human Rights

1995 "Significant U.S. Supreme Court Decisions in Capital Cases Since 1970." 14 July. Unpublished memorandum, 19 pp.

Spangenberg Group

1993– "The Spangenberg Report." (quarterly newsletter).

Spector, Arlen

1991 "The Time Has Come for a Terrorist Death Penalty Law." *Dickenson Law Review* 95(summer): 739–58.

Steiker, Carol S. and Jordan M.

1995 "Sober Second Thoughts: Reflections on Two Decades of Constitutional Regulation of Capital Punishment." *Harvard Law Review* 109(December): 355–438.

Steiker, Jordan

1993a "Innocence and Federal Habeas." *U.C.L.A. Law Review* 41(December): 303–89.

1993b "The Long Road Up from Barbarism: Thurgood Marshall and the Death Penalty." *Texas Law Review* 71(May): 1131–62.

Stolz, Barbara Ann
1983 ''Congress and Capital Punishment: An Exercise in Symbolic Politics.'' *Law and Policy Quarterly* 5(April): 157–80.

Stout, David G.
1988 ''The Lawyers of Death Row.'' *New York Times Magazine,* 14 February, pp. 46, 48, 52–54.

Streib, Victor
1987 *Death Penalty for Juveniles.* Bloomington: Indiana University Press.
1988 ''Imposing the Death Penalty on Children.'' In Haas and Inciardi 1988:345–67.
1990 ''Death Penalty for Female Offenders.'' *University of Cincinnati Law Review* 58:845–80.
1992 ''Death Penalty for Battered Women.'' *Florida State University Law Review* 20(summer): 163–94.
1995a ''Capital Punishment of Female Offenders: . . . January 1, 1973, to March 31, 1996.'' Unpublished memorandum.
1995b ''The Juvenile Death Penalty Today: . . . January 1, 1973, to March 31, 1996.'' Unpublished memorandum.

———, ed.
1993 *A Capital Punishment Anthology.* Cincinnati: Anderson Publishing.

Streib, Victor, and Lynn Sametz
1989 ''Executing Female Juveniles.'' *Connecticut Law Review* 22(fall): 3–59.

Sullivan, Joseph F.
1995 ''Death Row Lessons from New Jersey.'' *New York Times,* 12 March, p. 42.

Sweeney, Laura T., and Craig Haney
1992 ''The Influence of Race on Sentencing: A Meta-Analytic Review of Experimental Studies.'' *Behavioral Sciences and the Law,* 10:179–95.

Tabak, Ronald J.
1986 ''The Death of Fairness: The Arbitrary and Capricious Imposition of the Death Penalty in the 1980's.'' *New York University Review of Law and Social Change* 14:797–848.
1990–91 ''Is Racism Irrelevant? Or Should the Fairness in Death Sentencing Act Be Enacted to Substantially Diminish Racial Discrimination in Capital Sentencing?'' *New York University Review of Law and Social Change* 18:777–806.

Tabak, Ronald J., and J. Mark Lane
1991 ''Judicial Activism and Legislative 'Reform' of Federal Habeas Corpus: A Critical Analysis of Recent Developments and Current Proposals.'' *Albany Law Review* 55:1–95.

Tagliabue, John
1996 ''Italian High Court Blocks Extradition, Citing Death Penalty in U.S.'' *New York Times,* 28 June, p. A3.

Taurek, John M.
1977 ''Should the Numbers Count?'' *Philosophy & Public Affairs* 6(summer): 293–316.

Terry, Don

1996 "Clemency Given to Woman Who Wanted Death Sentence Carried Out." *New York Times,* 17 January, p. A10.

Tonry, Michael

1995 *Malign Neglect: Race, Crime, and Punishment in America.* New York: Oxford University Press.

Trombley, Stephen

1992 *The Execution Protocol: Inside America's Capital Punishment Industry.* New York: Crown.

Urofsky, Melvin I.

1984 "A Right to Die: Termination of Appeal for Condemned Prisoners." *Journal of Criminal Law and Criminology* 78(fall): 553–82.

Van den Haag, Ernest

1969 "On Deterrence and the Death Penalty." *Journal of Criminal Law, Criminology, and Police Science* 60(July): 280–88.

1978a "The Collapse of the Case Against Capital Punishment." *National Review,* 31 March, pp. 395–97, 402–7.

1978b "In Defense of the Death Penalty: A Legal–Practical–Moral Analysis." *Criminal Law Bulletin* 14(January): 51–68. Reprinted in part in Bedau ed. 1982.

1983 "For the Death Penalty." *New York Times,* 17 October, p. A21.

1984 "Reply" [to Robert Johnson], *Justice Quarterly* 1(December): 581–84.

1985a "The Death Penalty: The Death Penalty Vindicates the Law." *American Bar Association Journal* 71(April): 38–40, 42.

1985b "The Death Penalty Once More." *University of California Davis Law Review* 18(summer): 957–72.

1985c "New Arguments Against Capital Punishment?" *National Review,* 8 February, pp. 33–35.

1985d "Refuting Reiman and Nathanson." *Philosophy & Public Affairs* 14(spring): 165–76.

1986 "The Ultimate Punishment: A Defense." *Harvard Law Review* 99(May): 1662–69.

1990 "Why Capital Punishment?" *Albany Law Review* 54:501–14.

van den Haag, Ernest, and John P. Conrad

1983 *The Death Penalty: A Debate.* New York: Plenum Press.

Vellenga, Jacob J.

1959 "Is Capital Punishment Wrong?" *Christianity Today,* 4(12 October): 7–9. Reprinted in Bedau ed. 1964.

Verhovek, Sam Howe

1995 "Across the U.S., Executions Are Neither Swift Nor Cheap." *New York Times,* 22 February, pp. A1, B2.

Vidmar, Neil, and Phoebe C. Ellsworth

1974 "Public Opinion and the Death Penalty." *Stanford Law Review* 26(June): 1245–70. Reprinted in Bedau 1982.

Vila, Brian, and Cynthia L. Morris, eds.

1977 *Capital Punishment in the United States: A Documentary History.* Westport, Conn.: Greenwood.

Vitiello, Michael

1994 "*Payne v. Tennessee:* A Stunning *Ipse Dixit.*" *Notre Dame Journal of Law, Ethics & Public Policy* 8:165–238.

von Drehle, David

1994 "Retired Justice Changes Stand on the Death Penalty." *Washington Post,* 10 June, p. A1.

1995 *Among the Lowest of the Dead: The Culture of Death Row.* New York: Random House.

Wasserstrom, Richard

1982 "Capital Punishment as Punishment: Some Theoretical Issues and Objections." *Midwest Studies in Philosophy* 7:473–502.

Waters, Raphael T.

1982 "The Moral Justification of Capital Punishment." *Social Justice Review* (July–August): 99–106.

Weinstein, Bob, and Jim Bessent

1996 *Death Row Confidential.* New York: HarperPaperbacks.

Weisberg, Robert

1984 "Deregulating Death." *Supreme Court Review 1983*: 305–95.

Wellek, Jeffrey Alan

1984 "Eighth Amendment—Trial Court May Impose Death Sentence Despite Jury's Recommendation of Life Imprisonment." *Journal of Criminal Law and Criminology* 75:813–38.

Wellman, Carl

1988 "Capital Punishment." In Wellman, *Morals and Ethics,* 2d ed., Englewood Cliffs, N.J.: Prentice–Hall, pp. 244–66.

White, Welsh S.

1987 "Defendants Who Elect Execution." *University of Pittsburgh Law Review* 48:853–77

1991 *The Death Penalty in the Nineties: An Examination of the Modern System of Capital Punishment.* Ann Arbor: University of Michigan Press.

1993 "Effective Assistance of Counsel in Capital Cases: The Evolving Standard of Care." *University of Illinois Law Review* 323–78.

Wickert, John H.

1983 "Eighth Amendment—The Death Penalty and Vicarious Felony Murder: Nontriggerman May Not be Executed Absent a Finding of Intent to Kill." *Journal of Criminal Law and Criminology* 73(winter): 1553–71.

Wiehl, Lis

1995 "Program for Death-Row Appeals Facing Its Own Demise." *New York Times,* 11 August, p. B16.

Willbanks, William

1986 *The Myth of a Racist Criminal Justice System.* Monterey, Calif.: Brooks/Cole.

1988 "Reactions to *McCleskey v. Kemp.*" *Journal of the National District Attorneys Association* 21(spring): 21–26.

Winn, Billy

1991a ''Balancing the Scales.'' *Columbus [Ga.] Ledger–Enquirer,* 2 June, pp. E–1ff.

1991b ''The Color of Justice.'' *Columbus [Ga.] Ledger–Enquirer,* 19 May, pp. C–1ff.

1991c ''Under Penalty of Death.'' *Columbus [Ga.] Ledger–Enquirer,* 26 May, pp. C–1ff.

Wolfe, Burton H.

1973 *Pileup on Death Row.* Garden City, N.Y.: Doubleday.

Wolfgang, Marvin E.

1974 ''The Social Scientist in Court.'' *Journal of Criminal Law and Criminology* 65:239–47.

Wolfgang, Marvin E., and Marc Riedel

1973 ''Race, Judicial Discretion, and the Death Penalty.'' *Annals of the American Academy of Political and Social Science* 407(May): 119–33.

Wolfson, Wendy

1982 ''The Deterrent Effect of the Death Penalty Upon Prison Murder.'' In Bedau 1982:159–73.

Wright, Julian H. Jr.

1990 ''Life-Without-Parole: An Alternative to Death or Not Much of a Life At All.'' *Vanderbilt Law Review* 43:529–68.

Yoder, John Howard

1979 ''The Death Penalty: A Christian Perspective.'' *The Interpreter,* January, pp. 5–6. Reprinted in Bedau 1982.

1991 ''Against the Death Penalty.'' In House and Yoder 1991:105–79.

Yunker, James A.

1976 ''Is the Death Penalty a Deterrent to Homicide? Some Time Series Evidence.'' *Journal of Behavioral Economics* 5:1–32.

Zeisel, Hans

1968 *Some Data on Juror Attitudes towards Capital Punishment.* Chicago: University of Chicago Law School, Center for Studies in Criminal Justice.

1977 ''The Deterrent Effect of the Death Penalty: Facts v. Faith.'' *Supreme Court Review 1976*: 317–43.

1981 ''Race Bias in the Administration of the Death Penalty: The Florida Experience.'' *Harvard Law Review* 95(December): 456–68.

Zeisel, Hans, and Alec M. Gallup

1989 ''Death Penalty Sentiment in the United States.'' *Journal of Quantitative Criminology* 5(September): 285–96.

Zimring, Franklin E., and Gordon Hawkins

1986 *Capital Punishment and the American Agenda.* Cambridge: Cambridge University Press.

TABLE OF CASES

Aikens v. California, 406 U.S. 813 (1972)
Barefoot v. Estelle, 463 U.S. 880 (1983)
Blystone v. Pennsylvania, 494 U.S. 299 (1990)
Booth v. Maryland, 482 U.S. 496 (1987)
Boyde v. California, 494 U.S. 370 (1990)
Burger v. Kemp, 483 U.S. 776 (1987)
Callins v. Collins, 510 U.S.—(1994)
Clemons v. Mississippi, 494 U.S. 738 (1990)
Coker v. Georgia, 433 U.S. 584 (1977)
Coleman v. Thompson, 501 U.S. 722 (1991)
Crampton v. Ohio, 402 U.S. 183 (1971)
Eberhart v. Georgia, 433 U.S. 917 (1977)
Enmund v. Florida, 458 U.S. 782 (1982)
Felker v. Turpin,—U.S.—(1996)
Fiero v. Gomez, 865 Fed. Sup. 1387 (N.D. Cal. 1994), *affirmed* 9th Cir. 21 February 1996.
Ford v. Wainwright, 477 U.S. 399 (1986)
Furman v. Georgia, 408 U.S. 238 (1972)
Godfrey v. Georgia, 446 U.S. 420 (1980)
Gregg v. Georgia, 428 U.S. 153 (1976)
Herrera v. Collins, 506 U.S.—(1993)
Jurek v. Texas, 428 U.S. 262 (1976)
Lockett v. Ohio, 438 U.S. 586 (1978)
Maxwell v. Bishop, 398 F.2d 138 (8th Cir. 1968), 398 U.S. 262 (1970)
McCleskey v. Kemp, 481 U.S. 279 (1987)
McCleskey v. Zant, 499 U.S. 467 (1991)
McFarland v. Texas,—U.S.—,114 S.Ct. 2568 (1994)
McGautha v. California, 402 U.S. 183 (1971)
Moore v. Dempsey, 261 U.S. 86 (1923)
Murray v. Giarrantano, 492 U.S. 1 (1989)
Payne v. Tennessee, 501 U.S. 808 (1991)
Penry v. Lynaugh, 492 U.S. 302 (1989)
Powell v. Alabama, 287 U.S. 45 (1932)
Pratt et al. v. Attorney General of Jamaica 4 All E.R. 767 (PC).
Presnell v. Georgia, 439 U.S. 14 (1978)
Proffitt v. Florida, 428 U.S. 242 (1976)
Pulley v. Harris, 465 U.S. 37 (1984)

INDEX